Simple Interest $F = P(1 + ni)$

Summary of Compound Interest Formula

Single-Payment Compound-Amount

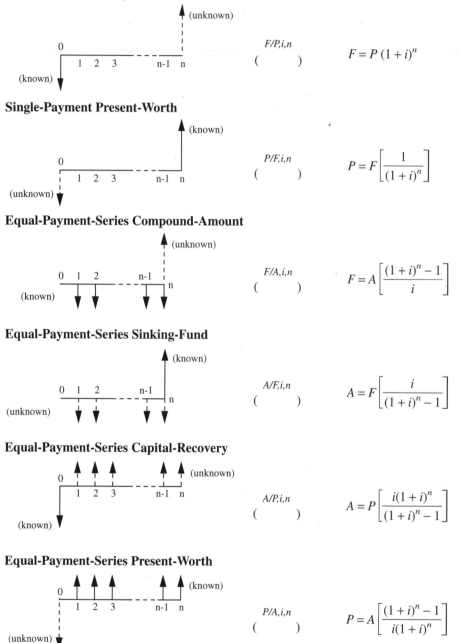

$F/P,i,n$

$(\quad)$

$F = P (1 + i)^n$

Single-Payment Present-Worth

$P/F,i,n$

$(\quad)$

$P = F \left[\dfrac{1}{(1 + i)^n} \right]$

Equal-Payment-Series Compound-Amount

$F/A,i,n$

$(\quad)$

$F = A \left[\dfrac{(1 + i)^n - 1}{i} \right]$

Equal-Payment-Series Sinking-Fund

$A/F,i,n$

$(\quad)$

$A = F \left[\dfrac{i}{(1 + i)^n - 1} \right]$

Equal-Payment-Series Capital-Recovery

$A/P,i,n$

$(\quad)$

$A = P \left[\dfrac{i(1 + i)^n}{(1 + i)^n - 1} \right]$

Equal-Payment-Series Present-Worth

$P/A,i,n$

$(\quad)$

$P = A \left[\dfrac{(1 + i)^n - 1}{i(1 + i)^n} \right]$

PRAISE FOR *RETURN ON SOFTWARE*

"This pioneering book highlights critical, overlooked skills needed by true software professionals."

—Steve McConnell
CEO and Chief Software Engineer
Construx Software

"It's about time someone took this stuff seriously."

—Stephen Mellor
Chief Scientist
Embedded Systems Division
Mentor Graphics Corporation
Co-Author of *Executable UML: A Foundation for Model Driven Architecture* and six other books

"Despite the fact that engineering economics is considered a core area of any engineering field, virtually no books have been written in the area of software engineering economics. Steve Tockey's *Return on Software* nicely fills this gap by providing a comprehensive introduction to software engineering economics accessible both to students and to new software professionals."

—Donald J. Bagert, Ph.D., P.E.
Director of Software Engineering and
Professor of Computer Science & Software Engineering
Rose-Hulman Institute of Technology

"The elements of this book are useful not only in making decisions but also in understanding why and how other people and organizations make decisions."

—Shari Lawrence Pfleeger
Senior Researcher, RAND
Co-Author of *Security in Computing*
and eight other software engineering titles

"This is just what the doctor ordered to help software programs solve the problem of how to introduce engineering economics and business decision-making into their curricula. The economics of software development should not only be part of any computing curriculum they are an essential element of recent accreditation and certification recommendations. This book is an accessible and relevant text for any student of software engineering. The style is clear and straightforward and the software examples will be appealing to students and faculty alike. I can't wait to use it in class!"

—Thomas B. Hilburn, Professor
Department of Computer and Software Engineering
Embry-Riddle Aeronautical University

Return on Software: Maximizing the Return on Your Software Investment

Return on Software: Maximizing the Return on Your Software Investment

Steve Tockey

✦ Addison-Wesley

Boston • San Francisco • New York • Toronto • Montreal
London • Munich • Paris • Madrid
Capetown • Sydney • Tokyo • Singapore • Mexico City

Return on Software

Maximizing the Return on Your Software Investment

The publisher offers discounts on this book when ordered in quantity for bulk purchases and special sales. For more information, please contact:
U.S. Corporate and Government Sales / (800) 382-3419
            corpsales@pearsontechgroup.com

For sales outside of the U.S., please contact:
International Sales / (317) 581-3793
            international@pearsontechgroup.com

Visit Addison-Wesley on the Web: *www.awprofessional.com*

Library of Congress Cataloging-in-Publication Data
2004105898

ISBN 0-321-22875-8
Text printed on recycled paper
1 2 3 4 5 6 7 8 9 10

Publisher: John Wait

Acquisitions editor: Paul Petralia

Editorial assistant: Michelle Vincenti

Marketing manager: Chris Guzikowski

Senior project editor: Kristy Hart

Indexer: Larry Sweazy

Composition: The Scan Group

Proofreader: Debbie Williams

Cover designer: Alan Clements

Manufacturing buyer: Dan Uhrig

Contents

Dedication

To my friends and family

Acknowledgements

They say that imitation is the sincerest form of flattery. I hope that's true because there has been a deliberate attempt to imitate the easy-to-read style of Steve McConnell's classics (*Code Complete* [McConnell04], *Rapid Development* [McConnell96], *Software Project Survival Guide* [McConnell98], and *Professional Software Development* [McConnell03]). I would also like to acknowledge the assistance of the entire team at Construx Software, especially Mark Nygren, Eric Rimbey, and Melissa Feroe. Special thanks go to Dr. Shari Lawrence-Pfleeger, Steve Mellor (Project Technology), and Meilir Page-Jones (Wayland Systems) for their advice and support. Professor Sid Dyjkstra, whose impact on the software industry has been immeasurable, certainly deserves mention as well.

The book benefited greatly from reviews and encouragement from the following people:

- Renate Bahnemann (Micromuse)
- Adam B. Bloom
- Jim Brosseau (Clarrus Consulting Group)
- Daniel Danecki
- Heeral Dedhia
- Michael C. Develle
- Ellen Gottesdiener (EBG Consulting, Inc)
- Karl F. Hoech
- Vsevolod (Simon) Ilyushchenko
- Rob Jasper (Intelligent Results)
- Francesca Johnson
- David Kane (SRA International)
- Xena Kinkaid (Peopleware)
- Cindy McComiskey
- Ken Rose (Genesis Microchip, Inc)
- S. V. Sivzattian, Ph.D. (Imperial College of Science, Technology and Medicine, London)
- James Snell
- Fred Waskiewicz (Object Management Group)

Their feedback, questions, suggestions, and general support were instrumental.

The SWEEP (SoftWare Engineering Economy Project) team at Seattle University—Sheri Brown, Mike Fidler, Craig Kulfan, Steve Rinn, Suneela Vaidyula, and faculty advisor Dr. David Umphress—deserves mention for their work in developing a prototype "engineering economy workbench" that automates many of the calculations described here. I hope SWEEP can be turned into a full-featured product someday.

I would also like to acknowledge H. Thuesen, G. Thuesen and W. Fabrycky, authors of *Engineering Economy* [Thuesen50] [Thuesen93]. The 1950 edition was a textbook in my father's electrical engineering degree at the University of Nebraska in the early 1950s, and my reading that book in the early 1980s led me to recognize the importance of the topic and its relevance to software engineering. The 1993 edition was used as a textbook for a course on software engineering economy at Seattle University. The Seattle University course was well received by the students; the only problem was that the text was not written for software professionals.

Foreword

An Introductory Tale

A few years ago I attended a software project-initiation meeting in which Levesley,* the newly appointed project manager from IT, was making a pitch to various project stakeholders, including business VPs. I happened to know that Levesley had majored in economics and political science, with a minor in information technology. So what came next didn't surprise me, but it caused the eyes of the VP of Finance to pop out like organ stops.

Levesley showed slides about the one-off, short- and medium-term benefits of addressing particular business problems. He then demonstrated multiple solution options whose lifecycle costs differed and which also demanded differing up-front capital investments. He discussed things like interest-rate trends and the potential lost-opportunity costs of the capital investment.

This was the first time that anyone from IT had made a pitch in terms that the Finance VP could identify with. Usually, IT people stood up and spoke of distributed relational databases, object layers, component environments, and such strange things from other dimensions.

Eventually, Levesley did get to "universal-client Web solutions," "application-integrating portals," and so on. But by that time, he had set up such a solid business and—dare I say it—economic context for the project that the VPs of Finance and Marketing were ready to eat from his hands.

As a consultant, I followed the project for the next year. It ran very differently from the way that most other IT projects in that shop had run. First, there was a sound, business-founded charter for the overall undertaking, with buy-in from the top to the bottom of the organization. (In truth, the buy-in didn't come easily. There were many long days of violent argument, but when buy-in eventually was reached, it was solid.)

---

*To protect his anonymity I have not used his real name.

Second, there was tremendous cooperation, even enthusiasm, from the business folk. In part, this came from the top (the VPs) down. But there was also genuine zeal at the grass-roots level. It was all in sharp contrast to the past, when, should an IT person come a'calling, business people would make hurried excuses about dental appointments and would leave for the day.

The project ended well, but not perfectly—I'd say four stars out of five, both technically and managerially. But they were not done yet. Six months after deployment, they tested the effects of the new approach (system and business re-engineering) in an economic way. Yes, they tested their charter, using financial yardsticks.

They looked at increased revenue, reduced costs, and improved customer service that could be attributed to their project. They learned, as you might expect, that some things didn't pan out nearly as well as they'd set forth in the project charter. They used these shortfalls as grist for a Version 2, course-correction project. Conversely, however, some project changes had improved corporate competitiveness far more than they'd hoped for.

And so (cue: harp music and shimmering visual effects), that brings us back to the present and to the book by Steve Tockey that you're holding right now.

What Is Economics and Why Is it Important to Us?

Thomas Carlyle once called Economics "the dismal science." I can't blame him for that assessment (because he'd just finished reading Thomas Malthus' gloomy work on population density and the economics of famine). But I'd prefer to follow Steve in endorsing Leon Levy's view that economics is the science of reasoned choice, at least as it applies to engineering.

So, according to this view, science generates the possibilities, while economics selects among them: science sets 'em up; economics knocks 'em down, until only both the technically feasible and economically viable options remain. This is engineering.

Or, as Steve puts it so succinctly:

Engineering = Science + Economics

Software Engineering = Computer Science + Software Economics

Why should we software folk care about economics, as opposed to just coding—about engineering as opposed to science? The answer lies in our chances of survival in the capitalist environment. And that, in turn, depends on how high our shop sets the bar for its notion of software success.

I've seen many definitions of "success" in shops that I've visited over the years, such as:

1. *Success:* We're still here at the end of the project.

2. *Success:* We're still here at the end of the project and we've written a bunch of code.

3. *Success:* We're still here at the end of the project and we we've written a bunch of code that runs.

4. *Success:* We're still here at the end of the project and we have a bunch of code (from various sources) that does something useful.

5. *Success:* We're still here at the end of the project and we have implemented cost-effective solutions to real business problems and cost-effective exploitations of real business opportunities, involving a combination of manual and automated systems.

Shops in the first three categories are on very thin ice when it comes to survival in a tough economic environment. And the economic environment enveloping software shops is getting tougher all the time.

Among companies whose business is software, competition is fierce. IT shops will not be cocooned indefinitely in a benign enveloping corporation; they too will become more and more subject to economic factors. When software was a minor issue in many companies, even a grossly inefficient IT shop could be kept afloat by cash infusions by the business-at-large. But nowadays, with software a bigger and more important factor in everything, grossly inefficient IT shops are an impediment that can bring down an entire corporation.

Making an economic choice is akin to adaptability. Levesley's shop is a good example of a software outfit that consciously assessed the economic environment before making a move. More and more shops are taking this approach. They have to or they will simply go away: When the Grim Economic Selector stops by for a quick reap, he's far more likely to wipe out a "#1 shop" than a "#5 shop."

What, How, and Why

Much has been written over the decades on the *what* and the *how* of software. This book is about the *why* of software. Clearly knowing the *why* will illuminate decisions on the *what* and the *how*.

This book does not come out in favor of a spiral lifecycle or a waterfall one, a heavyweight methodology or a lightweight one. It does not rule for or against an "agile" or an "extreme" approach. It does not recommend exhaustive testing, rather than "good enough" testing.

No, this book is not about religion; it's about engineering. Assuming that you already know your way around software, it teaches you the tools and techniques for making each of the above decisions in a reasoned way, a way that depends on your shop's circumstances, what you are trying to achieve and the economic factors that apply to your organization. Rather than handing you a fish on a plate, it teaches you how to fish.

Title Inflation

President Lincoln liked to ask: "If I call a tail a leg, how many legs does a dog have?" "Why, Mr. President," would come the inevitable response, "five." "No." Lincoln would retort, "Four. Calling a tail a leg doesn't make it a leg."

During my stretch in the software industry I've seen several generations of title come and go. Once upon a time we were all *coders*. Then *programmers*. Then *programmers/ analysts*. Then *software developers*. Then *software engineers*. (The latest vogue title, I believe, is *software architect*.)

Merely *calling* someone a software engineer certainly doesn't *make* them one. Even today—although computers are faster, memories are larger, screens are gaudier, languages are generally richer, modeling approaches are more complex, and development tools are more sophisticated—most so-called software engineers simply develop software, just as software people always have.

The "software engineer" misnomer was perhaps at its worst in the late 1990s. That's when I saw this bumper sticker in Palo Alto, a real souvenir of 1990s *Zeitgeist*:

> LAST YEAR I COULDN'T SPELL
> SOFTWARE ENGINEER.
> NOW I ARE ONE.

It was indeed a time when almost anyone who learned to spell *HTML* could get a well-paid software position. But to think that someone can join the software industry and become a true software engineer in less than a year is ludicrous.

As the great software luminary Sid Dijkstra (no relation to the late Edsger Dijkstra) once said: "Software is too important to be left to programmers."

In this book, Steve refines that statement: "Yes, and its effects are too bloody *expensive* to be left to programmers too." Instead, software should be the dominion of engineers. Not people with *I Are a Software Engineer* on their business cards, but authentic engineers who know how to meld economics successfully with software science.

Steve Tockey's book, *Return on Software: Maximizing the Return on Your Software Investment*, is probably the most important, comprehensive, germane, and usable work to date on the economic issues in software. Read it and you'll be well on your way to becoming a *bona fide* software engineer.

Meilir Page-Jones
Renton, WA
June 2004

Preface

There shouldn't be any doubt in anybody's mind that there's a lot of software around, with more being developed every day. Some software is being developed just for fun. For some people developing software is a hobby. Some software is being developed for education: People are studying to be professional programmers, analysts, project managers, and so on, and they need to develop software as part of their education. Some even say that their software is artistic. But let's face it, the vast majority of the software on the planet was created for a purpose: a *business* purpose. To put it bluntly, the software is there so that somebody can make money.

And even though making money was the software's intended purpose, you'll see in Chapter 1 that software doesn't always live up to that purpose. A lot of software has been written that probably shouldn't have been written in the first place. And a lot of good technology has been put into building the right software, but building it the wrong way so the software ends up never achieving its business goals. Software projects can easily end up costing more money than the resulting product ever brings back in. Financially, many organizations would have been better off never starting some software projects.

What Is This Book About?

This book is about software economics. Two quotes from Leon Levy [Levy87] summarize the book:

> *Software economics has often been misconceived as the means of estimating the cost of programming projects. But economics is primarily a science of choice, and software economics should provide methods and models for analyzing the choices that software projects must make.*

and

> *In any software project there is always a balance between short-term and long-term concerns . . . economic methods can help us make enlightened choices.*

This book is about making choices: making software choices in a business context.

Software professionals are faced with choices every day. Some choices are obviously important, such as "Should we even do the Alpha project?", "How much testing is enough?", "Should the Omega project use the Rational Unified Process [Kruchten00] or would eXtreme Programming [Beck00] [Jeffries01] or one of the other Agile [Cockburn02] methods be better?", and so on. Other choices may appear to be relatively innocuous, such as "What algorithm should we use in module Gamma?", "Should the Sigma data structure be a linked list or an array?", and so on. However, even apparently innocuous choices can have a noticeable effect on the organization's finances. At a minimum, a poor choice on something as seemingly insignificant as an algorithm or data structure could lead to inadequate performance, low maintainability, or defects and lead to unnecessary downstream maintenance.

If you are a practicing software professional, stop for a moment and think about how choices are usually made today. Does the typical software professional

- Consider more than just a single possible technical solution?
- Ask how much each of those possible solutions will cost?
- Ask how much (or even if) those possible solutions will generate income or reduce the operating expenses for the organization?
- Care what the time frame for the costs and benefits might be?

It's been my experience over more than 25 years in this industry that most software professionals not only don't know how to make financially responsible technical choices, they don't even know that economics should be a factor in their decisions.

Who Is This Book For?

This book is for practicing software professionals and for people on their way to becoming software professionals. By software professional, I don't mean just programmers. I intentionally include software quality assurance/quality control (SQA/QC) professionals as well as project managers, product managers, and program managers. In fact, the book is written for anyone in the software industry who is (or will be) involved in significant technical and managerial decisions. When you get right down to it, eventually that's pretty much everybody in the industry.

Will Reading This Book Make Me a Better Programmer, Designer, Manager, SQA Person . . .?

In one sense, no it won't. This book won't necessarily help a software developer identify new and clever solutions to technical problems. It won't necessarily help a project manager plan or control software projects any better than before. It won't necessarily help a product manager identify new "killer" features to launch into the marketplace. It won't necessarily help a tester come up with more effective test cases nor will it show an SQA person different techniques for finding or preventing software defects in the first place.

On the other hand, this book will help you make better decisions. When you're faced with choosing between some X, Y, or Z, you'll have a much better idea of how to go about making the choice. And later, if someone asks you why you chose the way you did, you'll be able to explain it in specific, business-relevant terms.

> *I could have done X, Y, or Z. I chose Y because it gives us the best*
> *return on our investment. Here, let me show you . . ..*

In addition to helping you become a better professional, these very same concepts and techniques can be used in your own personal finances. How do you decide if it's better to lease a car or buy it? How do you decide between one house loan with higher closing costs and a lower interest rate and another loan with lower closing costs and a higher interest rate? This book gives you the tools to do that and more. For instance, planning a retirement is a self-study question at the end of Chapter 13.

I'm Not the One Who Makes the Big Decisions, Why Does This Apply to Me?

Maybe you don't make the big decisions: which projects to do, what technologies to use, when delivery dates need to be, and so on. Maybe those decisions are made at levels well above your control. But you must at least be making a lot of little decisions. Decisions such as what kind of algorithm to use in this routine, or what kind of data structure to use in that one. Or, which set of test cases is better. Although these may not be the heavy-hitter decisions, they still affect the organization's bottom line. The wrong algorithms, the wrong data structures, the wrong set of test cases—these are all things that can have a noticeable effect over the long haul.

Even though you may not be making the big decisions, chances are that the ultimate decision makers are going to be basing their decision on input from technical people. Knowing the concepts and techniques of business decisions, you'll know exactly what kinds of input to be giving to the ultimate decision makers. Providing a business-relevant argument that supports your technical ideas can help convince the decision makers why your recommendations should be chosen. Being familiar with the methods and techniques in this book may also help you better understand and appreciate the decisions that are made at those higher levels.

Another way to look at it, however, is to rephrase the question. Maybe you don't make the big decisions *today*. But what about a few years down the road? Maybe by then you *will* be in a position to be making substantial decisions. It would be better for you to get practice with the concepts and techniques now and have a few years of experience under your belt rather than be put into the position with no knowledge of how the big decisions should be made. On the other hand, if you don't know how to approach making big decisions—by practicing and showing competence in how you make smaller decisions—what are the chances that you'd be promoted in the first place?

Why Would Anyone Bother When Everybody Knows That Schedule Is King?

This question can be answered by thinking in terms of the "time value" of the software product. How much more income could be generated (or costs could be avoided) if a software solution to some problem were available sooner? The time value of the software is essentially that income or cost difference. If a new online order processing system could save a company $50,000 per month, that's its time value: $50,000 for every month sooner the solution is delivered. Would it be wise to spend $100,000 on some tool or technology that would help deliver a solution six months earlier than otherwise? Sure, the organization would be saving about $200,000 in the deal. But what if that tool or technology were able to help deliver the software only one month earlier. Would it still make sense? Probably not, the organization would be spending $100,000 to save $50,000. Again, this is a book about helping you make business-wise choices on software projects. Schedule may very well be king, but sometimes that king isn't as all-important as people think he is.

Won't Paying Attention to Economics Just Reduce Quality?

This question is similar to the last one. This time, think about the cost of poor quality. What kind of damage could a defective software product cause? Would it cause users to lose work? Would it cause them to lose data? Would it cause them to lose their customers? If it came down to a product liability suit, how much might the jury award to the victims? Software product liability suits have already happened. Suppose, for sake of argument, an organization could be exposed to a $100,000 liability if a certain kind of defect were in their software product. Should they be willing to spend $5000 to have a high degree of confidence that that kind of defect isn't there? Probably. Would they be willing to spend $500,000? Probably not.

In fact, the age-old question of "how much testing is enough?" has traditionally been very difficult to answer. But that's because most organizations have been approaching it from entirely the wrong perspective. It's not a technical question at all; it's a business question. Literally, how much does testing cost and what's the reduction in exposure to liability that comes along with it? Somewhat oversimplified, until the cost of additional testing outweighs the benefit, keep testing. When the cost outweighs the benefit, stop testing because you're wasting money and time that could be put to better use elsewhere.

If I Do My Work More Efficiently, Won't It Make Me Less Valuable to My Employer?

No, in fact exactly the opposite, you become more valuable to your employer. If you're the one who consistently makes business-wise technical or managerial decisions, if you're the one who can justify your decisions in terms that the rest of the business understands, you'll be the one who is respected and valued by the organization.

But I Work for the Government (or Some Other Nonprofit Agency). Does All This Economics Stuff Still Apply to Me?

Not all of it, but most of it. Of course, the government isn't out to make a profit. However, the idea of choosing solutions that are both efficient and cost-effective still applies. Techniques for decision making in government and other nonprofit organizations are explained in Chapter 18.

Why Focus on Economics When It's The New Technologies That Provide All the Big Gains in Software?

Do the new technologies really provide all the big gains? Almost every organization has been burned by at least one "hot new technology" that didn't live up to its promises. Haven't you ever had a hard time selling the rest of the organization on some technology that you thought held promise? Whether you personally have ever been burned or not, your organization probably has experienced the pain of a technology that didn't live up to its promises. That's why it's often so difficult to sell new technology. Simply, people are scared; "once bitten, twice shy."

So what does economics have to do with this? First, by investigating the financial implications of the new technology yourself, you can figure out whether that technology is really as promising as people say it is. Second, after you've determined for yourself that the new technology is a wise path to follow, you can present the same business-relevant explanation to the rest of the organization. This book gives you the tools and techniques for doing both.

Okay, We Know That New Technologies Don't Always Live Up to Their Advertised Benefits. What Happens If I Make My Choice Based on False Claims? How Does This Book Help Me Then?

Nothing can help you if you wait until after the fact. On the other hand, Chapters 24 and 25 explain the techniques for making decisions under risk and uncertainty. If you're not entirely certain that the new technology will pan out as advertised—which should almost always be the case—these techniques allow you to factor in your degree of confidence (or lack thereof) and see how it impacts the decision.

Dr. Barry Boehm Already Has a Well-Known Book Called *Software Engineering Economics.* How Is This Book Different from His?

Without question, Dr. Boehm is one of the pioneers in considering the economic consequences of software. Dr. Boehm's landmark work clearly paved the way for most subsequent software economics research and application. With all due respect to Dr. Boehm, however, compared to its title his book [Boehm81] somewhat missed the mark. First, there's more to engineering economy than what is covered, including income taxes, inflation, and depreciation. Second, much of his book is about the Cocomo estimation model. Cocomo is only one of a whole family of estimation models; many others are available. (Chapters 21 and 22 of this book cover estimation.)

What About the Other Books on This Topic? Why Should I Care About This Book?

The concepts and techniques in this book aren't new or unique (see, for example, [DeGarmo93], [Eschenbach03], [Grant90], or [Thuesen93]). They've been around for a long time—more than 100 years by some accounts, and well over 70 years at a minimum. The subject, engineering economy, is even a required part of the curriculum in most recognized undergraduate engineering degree programs (*recognized* means, for example, civil engineering, mechanical engineering, aeronautical engineering, chemical engineering, structural engineering, etc.).

In the end, a return-on-investment analysis (Chapter 8) is a return-on-investment analysis, whether it's trying to determine the best structure for a bridge span, the best material for the foundation of a building, the best airfoil and wingspan for a commercial jet airliner, or the best catalyst for a certain reaction in a chemical production plant. The problem is that software professionals usually aren't familiar with the different kinds of bridge structures, building materials, airfoil cross-sections, or chemical catalysts. So books about making business-wise decisions for civil, mechanical, aeronautical, chemical, or structural engineers aren't likely to help us software professionals very much.

But a book that explains how to use return-on-investment analysis to figure out whether it was better to keep maintaining an existing software system or throw it out and rebuild it from scratch? Now that would be a useful book for a software professional. Or, a book that helps you decide whether the next release should incorporate that brand-new function or should have fixes for Problem Reports 459, 585, and 661, because you already know that you don't have the money or the people to do both? Wouldn't that be a handy reference? This is that book. This book presents those same concepts and techniques in a way that software professionals can understand.

Who Is the Author and What Is His Background?

Steve Tockey is the principal consultant at Construx Software (http://www.construx.com) in Bellevue, Washington. He started programming in 1975 and had his first professional software job in 1977. Since then he's worked at

- Helgeson Scientific Services (radiation monitoring equipment for the nuclear industry)
- Lawrence Livermore National Laboratory (data acquisition and process control system for laser isotope separation)
- The Boeing Company (software engineering research, a business process reengineering effort involving over 800 software professionals, automated functional test equipment for the Boeing 767 and 777 final assembly lines, corporate employee records, visualization of computational fluid dynamics data, and a host of other smaller projects)
- The Collins Avionics division of Rockwell International (more software engineering research and some participation in the development of a microwave landing system (MLS) receiver for commercial airliners)
- Seattle University (adjunct professor teaching courses including analysis, design, programming methods, object-oriented programming, software project management, and engineering economy for software)
- And finally, Construx (where he consults on software development projects and teaches both public and on-site seminars).

Steve received a Bachelor of Arts degree in Computer Science from the University of California, Berkeley in 1981 and a Masters of Software Engineering from Seattle University in 1993. He is a member of the IEEE Computer Society and is a Certified Software Development Professional (CSDP). Steve is also Construx's representative to the Object Management Group (OMG, http://www.omg.org).

If I Have Any Questions, Can I Contact the Author?

Absolutely. Just e-mail him at stevet@construx.com. Questions, comments, and suggestions for improving the book are all welcome.

Does Construx Offer a Seminar Covering the Material in the Book?

At the time this book was published, Construx did not offer a seminar based on this material. For the current list of seminars, see http://www.construx.com.

PART ONE

INTRODUCTION AND FOUNDATIONS

Part One introduces making software technical decisions in a business context and provides the background needed to understand the rest of the book. The concepts and techniques presented in this part include the fundamentals of business decisions, the time value of money (interest), financial equivalence, along with ways to characterize proposed solutions such as present worth, internal rate of return, and discounted payback period. When you understand these concepts and techniques, you'll be ready to see how to make business decisions in for-profit organizations (Part Two and Part Three) and in nonprofit organizations (Part Four).

1

Return on Software: Maximizing the Return on Your Software Investment

Almost every software organization on the planet is in the unenviable position of having to do the best it can with limited resources. We could always do more, and we could probably do it better, if we just had more people, more time, or more money. How do we get the most out of the resources we do have? How do we maximize our "bang for the buck"? That's what this book is about—helping you, the practicing software professional (or, the software professional-in-training), make purposeful, appropriate, business-conscious technical decisions so that you and your employer can get the most out of the limited resources you do have. This chapter explains why software professionals need the concepts and techniques in this book and gives a survey of the rest of the book.

Software on Purpose

There are hundreds, if not thousands, of books on how to develop software. Books on C, C++, Java, CORBA, XML, databases, and the like abound. However, most software organizations don't have a very good track record with the software they develop. After studying thousands of software projects, the Standish Group observed that about 23% of software projects fail to deliver any working software at all [Standish01a]. Unfortunately, these projects aren't being cancelled until well after their original schedule and budget have been exceeded.

3

The Standish study also showed that for projects that do deliver software, the average one is 45% over budget, 63% over schedule, and delivers only 67% of the originally planned features and functions. Based on our industry's track record, a software project that's estimated to take 12 months and cost $1 million can be reasonably expected to take closer to 20 months and cost about $1.5 million, while meeting only two thirds of its requirements.

Tracy Kidder [Kidder81] reports that about 40% of the commercial applications of computers have proven uneconomical. These applications don't show a positive return on investment in the sense that the job being automated ended up costing more to do after the system was installed than it did before. Return on investment is defined in Chapter 8, but, simply, those organizations paid more to develop the software than the software ever earned back for them.

Assuming the Standish and Kidder data can be combined, the resulting statistics are rather grim. If 23% of all software projects are cancelled without delivering anything, and 40% of the projects that do deliver software are net money losers, then about 54% of all software projects are counterproductive in the business sense. Over half the time, the organizations that paid for software projects would actually have been better off financially had they never even started those projects.

The total amount of money spent on software development in the United States has been estimated to be more than $275 billion annually [Standish01b]. This means a sizeable amount of money is being wasted every year—around $63 billion in cancelled software projects alone. The money wasted annually could be as much as $149 billion if projects not showing a positive return on their investment are included. These numbers may even be conservative when you consider that larger projects are much more likely to fail than smaller projects [Standish01b], [DeMarco99]. Be aware that this cost data is for the United States only; there's a lot of software development going on outside the United States. There's not necessarily any reason to believe that software organizations outside the United States are any more—or any less—successful, so the worldwide annual results could be staggering.

There might be a million and one different reasons for the poor software project performance observed by the Standish Group. Maybe

- The customer's requirements and specifications were incomplete, vague, or ambiguous.
- Those requirements kept changing throughout the project.
- Bad design decisions were made.
- The staff didn't have enough expertise in new technologies used on the project.
- The projects weren't given enough resources to be successful.
- The projects weren't sufficiently planned and managed.
- The project's externally imposed deadlines were unrealistic to begin with.
- . . .

Underlying all of these reasons is the more fundamental reason of bad business decisions being made. Either consciously or unconsciously *someone* decided to

- Not provide the project team with complete, precise requirements
- Allow the requirements to change throughout the project without considering—or maybe even being aware of—the effect of requirements change on project success
- Use an inappropriate design
- Not properly address—or even consider—the risks and uncertainties new technologies impose on software projects
- Not provide enough resources for the project to be successful
- Not sufficiently plan or manage the project
- Impose unrealistic deadlines on the project
- . . .

In spite of there being so many books on how to develop software, there aren't many books on why that software is being developed in the first place. Knowing why the software is being developed will help decision makers make better business decisions. This book doesn't say anything about how to develop software. It's all about why, and why not.

Waste Not, Want Not

Even in the best of financial times, a software organization shouldn't be sloppy or wasteful with its resources: people, money, and time. There will always be more functions that could be added to the existing software if there were just a few more people around to do the work. There will always be more new software that could be developed if we just had a bit more money. There will always be a few more defects in existing systems that could be fixed if we just had a bit more time to fix them.

When financial times get tough, there are even fewer people around to do the work. There is also less money. But getting the work done quickly is even more critical than before. In tough financial times, it's even more important for the organization to use its resources wisely. A wasted person-day, a wasted dollar, or a wasted calendar-day will always be just that: wasted. As resources get scarcer, it becomes that much more important to get the best return out of your software investment.

This book is about getting the most out of your software investment. A lot of time and money has been spent on software since the first programs were written. Some of it was spent wisely, but some of it was not. Regardless of whether it will be spent wisely or not in the future, people will continue to spend time and money on software. So how will you know if *your* organization's time and money are being well spent? How can you find out if you'd get more return from investing your limited resources in some other way? When your boss asks you, "Is this the best way for us to be spending our limited time and money?" how can you answer in a way that gives your boss confidence you really know what you're talking about?

The Primary Message

This book is about engineering economy, it's about aligning software technical decisions with the business goals of the organization. Many software professionals not only don't know how to look at the business aspects of their technical decisions, they don't even know that it's important to do so. Decisions such as "Should we use eXtreme Programming or should we use the Rational Unified Process on this project?" may be easy from a purely technical perspective, but those decisions can have serious implications on the business viability of the software project and the resulting software product. From my own experience teaching object-oriented development, I've asked more than 1,500 students why they were learning object-orientation. Reasons such as "It will help me develop higher quality software, quicker" or "It will be good for the company's bottom line" were extremely rare—fewer than 100 students total ever gave this kind of answer. The vast majority of the students answered, essentially, "It'll look good on my resumé."

In another case I was developing software to monitor radiation at nuclear power plants. Part of that software needed a sorting routine. I wrote a simple insertion sort routine and had that part of the system running in a matter of hours. A coworker insisted on developing a QuickSort routine because "everybody knows that QuickSort is better than insertion sort." At that time (early 1980s) reusable QuickSort routines weren't available; if you wanted one, you had to write it yourself. Unfortunately, QuickSort is a recursive algorithm, and the programming language we were using, Fortran-IV, didn't support recursion. My coworker spent more than a week developing QuickSort in Fortran-IV. Only later did he realize that the list that needed sorting averaged only about 30 entries and was predominantly sorted to begin with. Small lists that are already mostly sorted cause QuickSort to have extremely poor performance, typically worse than simpler algorithms such as insertion sort. Moreover, sorting happened in this system fewer than 50 times a day. Even if QuickSort did perform better than insertion sort, it would take decades for the company to recover its investment. My coworker's effort turned out to be a pretty big waste of the company's money and time.

The object-orientation and QuickSort examples are just two simple examples. Over the years I've seen technical decisions be inconsistent with the organization's business goals far more often than I've seen them be consistent. The software industry is hardly unique, however. This isn't the only time in history when the business impact of technical decisions was questionable. Eugene Grant [Grant90] wrote the following, referring to Arthur Wellington (a pioneer in the field of engineering economy).

> Railway location obviously is a field in which many alternatives are likely to be available. Nevertheless, Wellington observed what seemed to him to be an almost complete disregard by many locating engineers of the influence of their decisions on the prospective costs and revenues of the railways. In his first edition (1877) he said of railway location, "And yet there is no field of professional labor in which a limited amount of modest incompetency at $150 per month can set so many picks and shovels and locomotives at work to no purpose whatsoever."

The average salary of software professionals today is well over $150 per month, but are our decisions really that much better than the railway-locating engineers' of the late 1800s? As software professionals, we had better be concerned with the impacts of our technical decisions on our employer—I'd say that Wellington's "*a limited amount of modest incompetency*" describes the contemporary software industry quite well.

This book bridges the gap between software technical decisions and business goals. The concepts and techniques in this book will allow you—the practicing software professional—to align your technical decisions with the business goals of your organization. This will help you waste less of your employer's limited time and money. The fundamental question that software professionals should always ask is, "Is it in the best interest of the organization to invest its limited resources in this technical endeavor, or would the same investment produce a higher return elsewhere?"

A Secondary Message: Software Engineering Versus Computer Science

Many software professionals like to refer to themselves as "software engineers." Unfortunately, simply wanting our work to be considered engineering and continually saying that it is doesn't make it so. In several U.S. states, including New York and Texas [TBPE98], the term "engineer" is actually a legally reserved word. Those who inappropriately, or even inadvertently, misuse the term—such as calling themselves a software engineer—without meeting legally defined criteria can be subject to civil or criminal penalties. Similarly, under the law in Canada no one can call himself or herself an engineer unless licensed as such by the provincial engineering societies.

Another message in this book is the relationship between software engineering and computer science. There has been a fair amount of debate over the similarities and differences between the two. Instead of endlessly discussing opinions, we can look at "first principles"—what do scientists believe it means to be a scientist and what do engineers believe it means to be an engineer?

Science is defined as [Webster94]

> a department of systematized knowledge as an object of study; knowledge or a system of knowledge covering general truths or the operation of general laws esp. as obtained and tested through scientific method.

The Accreditation Board of Engineering and Technology (ABET) is the recognized authority for accrediting engineering and technology degree programs at colleges and universities in the United States. ABET defines engineering as [ABET00]

> the profession in which a knowledge of the mathematical and natural sciences gained by study, experience, and practice is applied with judgment to develop ways to utilize, economically, the materials and forces of nature for the benefit of mankind.

DeGarmo et al. [DeGarmo93] paraphrase the definition of engineering as

> finding the balance between what is technically feasible and what is economically acceptable.

Arthur Wellington offers a somewhat more lighthearted description [Wellington1887]:

> It would be well if engineering were less generally thought of, and even defined, as the art of constructing. In a certain sense it is rather the art of not constructing; or, to define it rudely but not inaptly, it is the art of doing that well with one dollar which any bungler can do with two.

Comparing and contrasting these definitions shows that science is the pursuit of knowledge and engineering is the application of that knowledge for the benefit of people. As an example, chemistry as a science is concerned with expanding our knowledge of chemical processes so we can better understand and explain phenomena observed in the universe. Chemical engineering, on the other hand, applies the knowledge derived from this "chemical science" to filling human needs. At the core of chemical engineering is an understanding of the body of chemical theory. In addition, chemical engineering calls upon the practical aspects of chemical processes, such as the design of pressure vessels and waste-heat removal mechanisms, together with the use of engineering economy as the basis for decisions.

The science branch and the engineering branch of a technical discipline are related but distinct. The science branch is concerned with expanding the body of theoretical knowledge about that discipline, whereas the engineering branch is concerned with the practical and economical application of that theoretical knowledge. The following equation is a simplified description of the general relationship between science and engineering:

$$\text{Engineering} = \text{Scientific theory} + \text{Practice} + \text{Engineering economy}$$

People who are recognized engineers (for instance, civil, mechanical, chemical, aeronautical) are usually required to take a course in engineering economy as part of their undergraduate education.

Based on the dictionary definition of science, above, computer science can be defined as

> a department of systematized knowledge about computing as an object of study; a system of knowledge covering general truths or the operation of general laws of computing esp. as obtained and tested through scientific method.

Based on the ABET definition of engineering, software engineering can be defined as

> the profession in which a knowledge of the mathematical and computing sciences gained by study, experience, and practice is applied with judgment to develop ways to utilize, economically, computing systems for the benefit of mankind.

So, from the equation above we can derive

Software engineering = Computer science + Practice + Engineering economy

Both computer science and software engineering deal with computers, computing, and software. The science of computing, as a body of knowledge, is at the core of both. Computer science is concerned with computers, computing, and software as a system of knowledge, together with expanding that knowledge. Software engineering, on the other hand, should be concerned with the application of computers, computing, and software to practical purposes, specifically the design, construction, and operation of efficient and economical computing systems.

The software industry as a whole has shown movement, albeit slow, toward becoming a legitimate engineering discipline: true software engineering. For that transition to fully take place, software professionals will need to learn about—and use—engineering economy as the basis for their technical decisions. This book is an engineering economy reference book for software professionals. It covers the same topics as would be found in its typical industrial engineering counterpart. Largely, only the examples have been translated into a software context.

> Lack of engineering economy isn't the only issue preventing software from being generally recognized as a legitimate engineering discipline. For other perspectives on this topic see, for example, [Hooten90], [McConnell03], [Shaw90], and [SWEBOK01].

There will always be a need for qualified computer scientists to continue the advancement of computing theory. To be sure, every recognized engineering discipline has a corresponding science that is populated by dedicated researchers. The computer science curriculum is appropriate for meeting this need. But the software industry also has a distinct need for [Ford91]

> a practitioner who will be able to rapidly assume a position of substantial responsibility in an organization.

Providing those qualified practitioners should be the primary goal of software engineering education.

An Overview of the Book

Here is a quick look at the topics that are covered in this book. The book is divided into eight parts:

- **Part I: Introduction and Foundations**. This part introduces the subject and provides the background needed to understand the rest of the book. Topics include the fundamental concepts of business decisions, the business decision-making process, the time value of money (interest), financial equivalence, and ways to characterize proposed solutions including present worth, internal rate of return, and discounted payback period.

- **Part II: Making For-Profit Business Decisions.** In this part, the basic mechanics of making business decisions in for-profit organizations are presented. Specific topics are for-profit decision analysis, the concept of economic life and its impact on planning horizons, and two special cases in for-profit decision analysis: replacement decisions and asset-retirement decisions.
- **Part III: Advanced For-Profit Decision Techniques.** This part presents additional concepts and techniques that may be included in a for-profit decision analysis. These techniques don't always need to be applied; you would only use them when you need more precision in the decision analysis. The topics in this part are inflation and deflation, depreciation, general accounting, income taxes, and the consequences of income taxes on business decisions.
- **Part IV: Making Decisions in Government and Nonprofit Organizations.** This part explains the concepts and techniques for decision making in government agencies and in not-for-profit organizations. Specific topics are benefit-cost analysis and cost-effectiveness analysis.
- **Part V: Present Economy.** In this part, the concepts and techniques of break-even analysis and optimization analysis are discussed.
- **Part VI: Estimation, Risk, and Uncertainty.** Estimation is an essential part of business decision analysis. This part goes into detail about the concepts and techniques of estimation and explains risk and uncertainty and how they can influence, and be addressed in, decisions.
- **Part VII: Multiple-Attribute Decisions.** Parts I through VI explain how to make decisions when there is one decision criterion, money. Money will usually be the most important decision criterion, but it is often only one of several important decision criteria. This part presents several different techniques for addressing more than just one decision criterion, or attribute, in a decision analysis.
- **Part VIII: Summary.** This part summarizes the book.

Summary

Almost every software organization that has ever existed has had to deal with limited resources. However, these same software organizations have tended to not be very efficient or effective with the resources they do have. About 23% of all software projects are cancelled without delivering any usable software at all. Of the software projects that do deliver, they tend to run about 45% over budget, 63% over schedule, and satisfy only 67% of the original requirements.

There may be many specific reasons for this level of performance, however they almost all boil down to one underlying reality: Inappropriate decisions are being made somewhere in the organization. Maybe the inappropriate decision was to do the project at all. Maybe the inappropriate decision was to provide insufficient funding, inadequate staff, poor requirements, or overconstrain the project schedule (or all of these combined). Maybe the inappropriate decision was about how to plan or manage the project. Maybe the project team members themselves made inappropriate decisions. By being more careful about aligning software technical decisions with business goals, software organizations can better maximize the return on their software investment.

The alignment of technical decisions with business realities is also at the core of the difference between software engineering and computer science. Science is about expanding knowledge, and engineering is about applying that knowledge to build, operate, and maintain efficient and economical systems. Making technical decisions that align with the business realities is at the heart of software engineering.

This book is about getting the most out of your software investment. It's about helping you, the practicing software professional (or, the software professional-in-training), make purposeful, appropriate, business-conscious technical decisions so that you can get the most from the limited resources you do have. After learning the concepts and techniques in this book, if your boss were to ask you, "Is this the best way for us to be spending our limited time and money?" you could answer that question in a way that gives them confidence that you really know what you are talking about.

The next chapter explains why businesses exist and how they "work" in a financial sense.

Self-Study Questions

1. A software project has been estimated to cost $850,000 and take 10 months. Given the project outcomes from the Standish Group report mentioned at the beginning of the chapter, if the project completes at all what will its cost and schedule more likely turn out to be?

2. Name at least one software-intensive company that was in business in the year 2000 that isn't in business today. When did they go out of business? Why did they go out of business?

3. Name at least one software-intensive company that was in business in the year 2000 that is much smaller today (fewer employees, smaller market share, etc.) than they were then. What happened to the company between then and now? Why are they so much smaller now than before?

4. Can you describe a software project that was a net money loser for an organization? Who was that organization? What was the project? When did it happen? How much money do you think was spent on the project? How much, if any, do you think the software project recovered? Justify your answers.

2

Business on Purpose

Reduced to the simplest of terms, a business exists for one purpose: to make money for its owners. This book is about making sure that the activities and decisions in a business's software organization contribute to that purpose. Before you can understand how to align the software activities and decisions with the business's purpose, you need to understand how the business works in a financial sense: where does the money come from and where does it go? Of course, software is also developed in and for not-for-profit organizations: government agencies, universities, charities, and so on. Even though these organizations aren't intending to make a profit, this chapter shows that it's still important to align the software activities and decisions to these organizations' goal.

Why Are Companies in Business, Anyway?

Let's start by asking what might be the single, most fundamental question to a business, "Why are we in business in the first place?" You might want to think a company is in business because it's fun, it's educational, or because it's a way to have a positive impact on society. These are all good secondary reasons, but the primary reason is simple: to make a profit for the owners of the company.

Granted, the idea that profit is the primary reason to be in business may sound crass, but the plain truth is just that. Whether we like it or not, a company that doesn't make a profit for its owners doesn't stay in business very long, regardless of how fun, educational, or socially uplifting it might be. If you don't believe this, then try explaining the "dot-com crash" of 2001. Did those companies go out of business because they stopped being fun? Being educational? Being socially responsible? Or, did they simply not make enough money to stay in business?

Given that the ultimate goal of a company is to make a profit, it should follow that the decisions made inside the company should be guided by that same goal. When faced with two or more possible courses of action, the company should generally choose the one that leads to the higher profit.

Sometimes there may not be any profit in a business decision; it may be a case of minimizing the loss. A company may be forced to make changes to its accounting software because of a change in tax law. Or a company may have to port software off of obsolete hardware. Consider the alternatives: If the company doesn't comply with the new tax laws, they could be liable for serious legal and financial penalties. It's cheaper to comply than not comply. If the software isn't ported to new hardware, then operating and maintenance costs on the old hardware could quickly exceed the cost of the new hardware and the porting effort combined. Even in cases like these, the long-term decision is largely based on maximizing profit. Sometimes the best outcome is simply the least-worst outcome.

The phrase "should generally choose" is important. Of course everyone needs to recognize that profit isn't the only factor in making decisions. This is where the secondary factors—fun, education, social impact, etc.—come in. Issues such as ethics, concern for the customer, concern for the employees, concern for the environment, corporate citizenship, and so on can play a part in the decision-making process. All these other things being equal, however, the ultimate decision criteria will end up being profit.

Let's take a quick tour of the (somewhat simplified) financial view of a company and see how it goes about making money for its owners.

WHERE DOES THE MONEY COME FROM?

For-profit companies bring in money by selling products and services, and sometimes by making investments in other companies. A computer hardware manufacturer brings in money by selling and leasing its products as well as by offering repair services and service contracts. A software company that sells a computer-aided design (CAD) package brings in money by selling the CAD software package along with training and consulting on the use of that package. The CAD software company may also bring in money by performing custom modifications to the software for specific customers, for instance adding a data-transfer interface to a computer-aided manufacturing (CAM) system used by a particular customer. The big automobile makers not only sell and service cars and trucks, they also invest in other companies such as rental car companies.

The sum total of all the income a company brings in is often called its **gross revenue**.

WHERE DOES THE MONEY GO?

Figure 2.1 shows where the gross revenue typically goes in a for-profit company. Each successive step down the figure shows a factor that subtracts from gross revenue and gives an approximation of how much impact that factor typically has on profit.

Cost of Goods Sold

The first, and usually the largest, drain on gross revenue is the cost of producing the goods and services that were sold. In an automobile manufacturing company, this would be all of the expenses required to make cars. In a software company, this would be all of the expenses to package, deliver, and support the software products and services. The components of the cost of goods sold are as follows:

- **Materials**—The cost of the raw material inputs. A furniture company buys wood, cloth, glue, fasteners, and such to build the furniture. In a pure software company, the material costs will probably be a very small percentage of the overall expenses but will still probably not be zero. Costs to buy the distribution media (blank disks, blank CDs), print the manuals, etc. would all be considered material costs. Even a software company that distributes software products over the Internet (Web) pays to connect to the Internet.

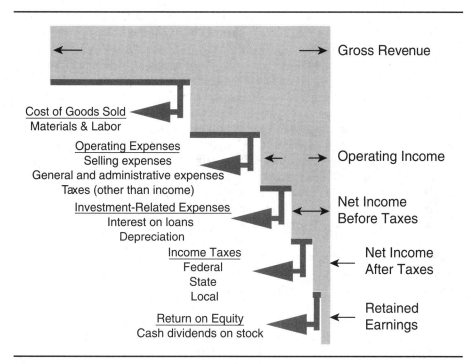

FIGURE 2.1   Where the money goes in a typical corporation

- **Labor**—The money that pays the salaries and wages of the people who create and deliver the products and services. Typically this also includes benefits such as vacation, insurance, retirement, and company-sponsored continuing education together with incentives such as employee profit sharing, bonuses, and stock options.

The cost of goods sold is described in much more detail in Chapter 15.

Operating Expenses

The next drain on gross revenue is operating expenses. Operating expenses are all the additional costs necessary to run the company beyond just producing the products and services. Operating expenses usually include things such as the following:

- **Selling expenses**—All of the expenses related to selling the products and services. These include salaries and wages of the sales and marketing staff, advertising costs, free samples, showrooms, and so on.
- **General and administrative expenses**—Expenses such as equipment rental and lease, facilities rent and lease, maintenance costs, insurance, salaries and wages of administrative and management staff.
- **Research and development expenses**—Expenses related to creating new products and services or finding more efficient ways of producing existing products and services. Software development and maintenance costs in a typical for-profit organization are classified either as research and development or general and administrative expenses.
- **Taxes (other than income)**—This is all of the taxes that the corporation pays, except income taxes (which are addressed later). Examples are property taxes on real estate the corporation owns, business and occupation taxes, excise taxes, etc.

After the operating expenses are taken out of gross revenue, the remainder is called operating income. Keep in mind that there is no guarantee that at this point, or any point beyond this, the remaining income is actually positive. The company might not bring in more money than it spends. One airplane manufacturer stopped selling commercial airplanes when they realized that their airplanes could only be sold for about $1 million but they cost more than $1.2 million to produce. They were losing about $200,000 on every airplane they sold. A company's operating income could be zero, or even negative.

Investment-Related Expenses

The next drain on income derives from expenses related to the company's investments. This includes interest and depreciation:

- **Interest**—The typical corporation is at least partially financed through borrowed money (loans). Part of the payments on those loans goes to paying back the principal (the money that was borrowed) and the rest goes to paying interest. Loans, loan payments, interest, and separating interest from loan payments are covered in detail in Chapters 5 and 6.

- **Depreciation**—Conceptually, depreciation is a way to spread the purchase price of a long-lived capital asset (a building, some expensive piece of equipment, etc.) over the life of that asset. If the company invests $1 million to buy a special high-performance computer, the entire $1 million doesn't leave the company right away. The company will "carry" the asset for several years and write off a portion of the original value year by year. Don't worry about the details of depreciation right now; they are discussed in Chapter 14.

Any expenses related to investments the company makes in other companies (such as buying and selling the other company's stock) are also included in investment-related expenses. After subtracting all of the investment-related expenses from the operating income, the corporation is left with its net income before taxes. Again, net income before taxes isn't guaranteed to be a positive number.

Income Taxes

The next drain is income taxes. Federal, state, and local income taxes can add up to take more than 50% of the net income before taxes. Income taxes are discussed in Chapter 16. The remainder after income taxes are subtracted is called net income after taxes.

RETURN ON EQUITY

Assuming there is any money left, this is the real profit of the corporation. One of the first uses of net income after taxes is to pay cash dividends to the stockholders (the owners of the company). These dividends are one way that stockholders earn money from their investment in the company. (An increase in the stock price is the other.)

What's left after all of the above has been taken out is called retained earnings. This is, along with new loans and equity capital (issuing more stock), the money that the corporation has available to invest in future growth and expansion (i.e., beyond just continuing as is).

WHY ARE INCOME AND EXPENSES IMPORTANT?

One measure of a company's financial health is its **profit margin**. The profit margin is the percentage of gross revenue that ends up as profit.

$$\text{Profit Margin} = \frac{\text{Net Income After Taxes}}{\text{Gross Revenue}}$$

Even in the best of financial times, it's unusual for the profit margin of many companies to be much more than about 10%. The profit margin in a lot of companies can be as low as 2% or even less. With such a slim margin, it should be easy to see how making every investment count is an important goal—money wasted in expenses eats directly into the profit margin, which means less for the owners (which, through stock-ownership plans, are often the employees themselves) and less available for future software projects and the like.

HOW EXPENSIVE IS SOFTWARE?

Labor is usually the dominant cost on a software project. Although there may be capital costs for buying equipment such as new computers, this is almost always a relatively small percentage of the overall software project cost.

The average annual salary of a software professional in the United States in 2001 was approximately $60,000 [Copeland01]. A five-person-year project (five people working for one year, one person working for five years) would seem like it costs $300,000. That's a lot of money, to be sure. But it's not an overly shocking amount. It isn't the whole story either.

Many companies use the term **full-time equivalent** (FTE) to refer to the actual annual cost of an employee. Sometimes called a "fully burdened salary," the FTE includes salary, benefits, plus all of the overhead costs for management, facilities, equipment, and so on. In 2002, the U.S. FTE was at least $125,000 per year and could have been as much as $300,000 per year in high-rent districts such as Manhattan and Silicon Valley. The five-person-year project actually costs at least a half-million dollars and, depending on location, could cost as much as $1.5 million. Paraphrasing a quote often attributed to the late Senator Everett McKinley Dirksen (R., Illinois, 1951 to 1969):

> a few million here, a few million there, and pretty soon you're talking real money.

If you are working as a software professional, think about how much the project(s) you are involved in will cost. What is your company's FTE rate? How many people work on your project? How long has your project been running? Do the math and see how much it has cost so far. How much longer until the project finishes? Do the math and see how much the project is likely to cost when it completes. Is it likely that the company will get more benefit out of the project than it cost? From a stockholder's perspective, has the money been spent wisely? Developing and maintaining software is expensive. You have to be careful to get the most value out of your limited resources.

Business Decisions in For-Profit Organizations

Management's role in the typical for-profit company—from the manager of a software project all they way up to the executive management and board of directors—is to make the operational and strategic (investment-level) business decisions that will maximize profit over the life of the company. Decisions such as: should Feature A be developed before Feature B? Should the company move into some new market? Is it time to retire Product Y? Similarly, the role of the technical staff, and I'm talking here about technical staff in general—electrical, mechanical, structural, chemical, software, etc.—should be to design and improve the company's products and services as well as to design and improve the means of producing and delivering those products and services. The technical staff at a computer chip manufacturing company develops new chips or they develop more efficient ways of producing those chips. The technical staff at your local electric utility develops better ways to convert coal, gas, water, or atomic energy into electricity and distribute it to your home or office.

The essence of getting the biggest bang for your technical buck, at least in for-profit companies, is to align the technical decisions with the goal of maximizing profit: Can the products and services be designed so that they can be produced with a minimum of resources? Can the means of production be designed to generate the most product from the smallest investment?

> All other things being equal, the role of a technical person in a for-profit company should be to choose—from the set of technically possible solutions to some problem—the solution that maximizes the organization's objective: profit.

Business Decisions in Not-for-Profit Organizations

This should all make sense in for-profit companies, but what about not-for-profit organizations? Take the government, for example. The goal of government is discussed in detail in Chapter 18, but we should agree that the goal of government is not to make a profit. Nonetheless, the government does deliver products and services. The products are things such as public roads and bridges, parks, public buildings, etc. The services are things such as education, public libraries, fire and police protection, etc. These are delivered to the residents, but not through a marketplace. People don't buy government products and services in the same way that they buy, say, televisions and microwave ovens. There's one supplier of roads, and you use the roads that are available if you want to go somewhere. There's one supplier of fire protection, and you use that supplier if your house catches fire.

The government gets its income through taxes of various sorts: sales taxes, property taxes, income taxes, etc. Taxation is, to a degree, like putting the brakes on the economy, so taxation should be held to a reasonable minimum. Similarly, an independent charity organization is usually funded through private donations, which it has to work hard to get. The proverbial bottom line is that the government and nonprofit organizations also have to deal with limited resources.

The role of business decisions in not-for-profit organizations is still to maximize the delivery of products and services while keeping resource use to a minimum. So although the measure of success isn't profit in this case, there's still plenty of reason to pay attention to maximizing the benefit while using a minimum of cost.

All other things being equal, the role of a technical person in a not-for-profit organization should be to choose—from the set of technically possible solutions to some problem—the solution that maximizes the organization's objective: providing the greatest benefit at the least cost.

Notice that between for-profit and not-for-profit organizations the goals are not exactly the same, maximizing profit vs. maximizing benefit, but they are very similar. So, although there are some important differences in the business decision-making process between these two environments, most of the concepts and techniques are applicable to both.

Business Decisions in Your Own Personal Finances

If you're like most people, you don't have an unlimited supply of money. You work hard for the income you get, so you want to make the most out of it. Why spend more on that car or that house than you need to? But how would you know that you're getting the most out of your hard-earned income? After reading and understanding this book, you'll know how to answer that question.

Summary

Businesses exist for one primary reason: to make money for the owners. To do that, the business needs to bring in more money than it spends. The money coming into the business is mostly from the sales of products and services, whereas the money going out is for all kinds of different expenses:

- Cost of goods sold
- Operating expenses
- Investment-related expenses
- Income taxes

The amount of money left after all of the expenses have been paid, the profit margin, averages around 10% in a typical business.

Not-for profit organizations exist for a different reason: to maximize the benefit to some relevant population. But not-for-profit organizations also have limited resources.

Software is a lot more expensive than most people think it is. The total cost of employing a software professional in most areas of the United States is at least $125,000 annually and can be as much as $300,000. A five-person-year project will cost anywhere from a half-million dollars to $1.5 million in labor costs alone. This is a big bite out of the income of any organization.

Limited resources combined with high software costs means that whether a software professional is in a for-profit or not-for-profit organization, there is always a need to align the software technical decisions with the goals of that organization. The fundamental question is, then, whether any proposed use of the organization's resources would provide the highest return or whether a higher return could be achieved some other way. The next chapter explains the fundamental concepts of making this kind of business decision.

Self-Study Questions

1. Assume that Zymurgenics, Inc.* had gross revenues of $12,500,000 last year. Various costs for labor, material, operating expenses, etc. totaled $9,750,000. Income taxes amounted to $1,080,200. What was their actual profit for the year? What was their profit margin?

2. If you are currently employed, what are your company's sources of gross revenue (what kinds of products and services does your company sell)? If you are not currently employed, choose a company (or have one assigned to you) and answer the same question.

3. Does the company in Question 2 have any other sources of gross revenue? (For instance, does it invest in other companies?)

4. What was the company in Question 2's gross revenue last year?

5. Using the company in Question 2, give specific examples of each of the categories of cost shown in Figure 2.1. What was the cost category and how much money was spent on it?

    Direct labor

    Direct material

    Indirect expenses

    Operating expenses

    Investment-related costs

    . . .

6. What was the total amount of expenses (excluding income taxes) the company in Question 2 paid last year?

7. How much income tax did the company in Question 2 pay last year?

8. What was the company in Question 2's profit margin last year?

*All references to company names are fictitious references. Any similarity of these companies to real companies is purely coincidental.

9. If you are employed, what's your organization's FTE rate? If unknown, proprietary, or you aren't employed, assume an FTE rate of $200,000 per year. Calculate the labor cost of a six-person-year project using that FTE rate.

10. If you are working on a project, describe that project's staffing level (how many people for how long). Using the FTE rate from the previous question, how expensive is this project (labor costs alone, ignore any hardware or vendor-purchased software)?

11. For the project identified in Question 10, is it reasonable to assume that the company will be able to recover that investment in your project (either through reduced costs or increased sales)? Explain your answer.

12. If you are employed, identify one or more software systems that are critical to the operation of your employer. What might be the consequences of a total failure in one of these systems? Could the company survive if that system failed totally? How? If you are in school, identify one or more software systems that are critical to the operation of that school. What could be the consequences of a total failure of one of these systems? Could the school survive?

13. Name at least one situation, other than what was already identified in this chapter and in the preface, where the concepts and techniques in this book would be useful in helping you make decisions about your own personal finances.

3

The Fundamental Concepts of Business Decisions

There is a set of concepts fundamental to aligning technical decisions with the organization's purpose. These include proposals, cash-flow instances, cash-flow streams, and cash-flow diagrams. You need to understand these concepts to understand the rest of this book. Each of these topics is presented in this chapter.

Proposals

Making a business decision begins with the notion of a **proposal**. A proposal is a single, separate option that is being considered, such as carrying out a particular software development project or not. Another proposal could be to enhance an existing program, and still another might be to redevelop that same software from scratch. Each proposal represents a unit of choice—either you can choose to carry out that proposal or you can choose not to. The whole purpose of business decision making is to figure out, given the current business circumstances, which proposals should be carried out and which ones shouldn't.

Although the focus of this book is on software-specific business decisions, the concepts and techniques in this book are just as useful for other financially significant decisions that happen in a business. Is a proposal to develop and launch Product X better or worse than a proposal to develop and launch Product Y? Is either of those better or

worse than a proposal to invest the corporation's money in a stock buy-back program?
Are any of those proposals better or worse than a proposal that the company make no
new investments at all?

Cash-Flow Instances and Cash-Flow Streams

To make a meaningful business decision about any specific proposal, that proposal must
be evaluated from a business perspective. The concepts of cash-flow instances and cash-
flow streams are used to describe the business perspective of a proposal. A **cash-flow
instance** is a specific amount of money flowing into or out of the organization at a specific time as a direct result of some proposal.

Some examples of cash-flow instances in a software organization include the
following:

- In a proposal to develop and launch Product X, the payment for new development
  computers, if new hardware is needed, could be an example of an outgoing cash-
  flow instance. Money would need to be spent to carry out that proposal.
- The sales income from Product X in the eleventh month after market launch could
  be an example of an incoming cash-flow instance. Money would be coming in
  because of carrying out the proposal.
- In a proposal to buy a new office building and buy-down the loan interest rate by
  paying "points," the actual payment of the points when the loan is closed would
  be an example of an outgoing cash-flow instance.
- Each separate payment on a loan would also be an outgoing cash-flow instance.

The term **cash-flow stream** refers to the set of cash-flow instances, over time, which
would be caused by carrying out some given proposal. The cash-flow stream is, in effect, the complete financial picture of that proposal. How much money goes out? When
does it go out? How much money comes in? When does it come in? Simply, if the cash-
flow stream for Proposal A is more desirable than the cash-flow stream for Proposal B
then—all other things being equal—the organization would be better off carrying out
Proposal A than Proposal B.

CATEGORIES OF CASH FLOW

Cash-flow streams usually contain the following categories of cash flow. These categories are described to help you be sure you include all of the relevant kinds of cash flow
in the cash-flow stream for a proposal.

Initial Investment

The initial investment captures all of the one-time, nonrecurring costs associated with starting up a proposal. The down payment on a new office building is an example of an initial investment. When the initial investment is for things such as computer equipment, it also includes any necessary installation costs, sales taxes, etc. In a software project proposal, the initial investment might include hiring and/or training the development and QA staff, buying and installing new computers or related equipment, obtaining facilities for the project team to work in, and so on.

It's important to include the initial investment in the cash-flow stream for a proposal; sometimes proposals that are otherwise highly profitable turn out to be impossible to start because the organization simply can't afford the initial investment.

Operation and Maintenance Cost

Operation and maintenance costs occur only after the activity is started and continue through to its retirement. Insurance and fuel are examples of operation costs associated with a car. Oil changes and repairs are examples of maintenance costs. In a software project proposal, operation and maintenance costs could include things such as the following:

- Electricity to operate the computers and heat or cool the building
- Support staff to keep the computers and the network running
- Maintenance costs on software licenses
- Paper, disks, and other typical office supplies
- . . .

Sales Income

Sales income refers to the direct income generated by the proposal. Maybe the proposal creates a new product. Or maybe the proposal increases the market share of an existing product. Either way, the proposal could be generating income for the organization. A shrink-wrap software company, for example, wouldn't want to develop a new product (or even upgrade an existing one) if they didn't have some degree of confidence that the product would generate enough sales income to cover the development costs with some amount left over for profit.

Cost Avoidance

A less-obvious, but still very important, source of income is cost avoidance. Cost avoidance is not directly income in the sense of somebody paying for a product or service, but because it reduces the expenses needed to produce those products and services, it leaves more of the gross revenue as profit. Converting a company from a manual payroll system to an automated one probably won't cause the company to sell more products and services; however, if it cuts down on operational expenses because the payroll department can be run by fewer people, there's more money left as profit. A computer-controlled milling machine might make fewer mistakes than a human operator, and the reduction in the number of defective parts produced would also be an example of cost avoidance.

Salvage Value

Salvage value refers to any remaining value in assets (equipment, facilities, etc.) at the end of a proposal. The salvage value of a computer, for instance, is the amount that you expect the computer can be sold for when you are ready to get rid of it. When considering salvage value, be sure to include the cost of removal if appropriate. If a computer is worth $1000 at the end of the proposal but someone would have to pay $100 to remove it, its salvage value is really $900. Salvage value can sometimes be negative; if the computer is in such bad shape that it can only be sold for $50 and it would cost $75 to have it removed, its salvage value is −$25.

Cash-Flow Diagrams

A **cash-flow diagram** is a picture of a cash-flow stream. In the same sense that a picture is worth a thousand words, the cash-flow diagram gives the reader a very quick overview of the financial picture of that subject. Figure 3-1 shows an example cash-flow diagram for a proposal.

A cash-flow diagram shows the cash-flow stream two dimensions: Time runs from left to right, and amounts of money run up and down. Each cash-flow instance is drawn on the diagram at a left-to-right position relative to the timing of that cash flow after the start of the proposal. The horizontal axis is divided into units of time that represent either years, months, weeks, etc. as appropriate for the proposal being studied.

The other dimension, the amount of the cash-flow instance, is shown as an upward or downward arrow. Upward arrows mean that money is coming in (income), and downward arrows mean that money is being spent (expense). The lengths of the arrows are usually drawn proportional to the amount of money; for instance, a cash-flow instance that's twice as much money as another would be drawn with an arrow that's twice as long. The actual amounts of the cash-flow instances are usually written on the diagram next to the arrows because it's hard to get an accurate interpretation of the amount from the length of the arrow alone.

In practice, many cash-flow instances will happen during each time period, especially when the periods represent months or years. The diagram will get cluttered if each individual cash-flow instance is drawn. Instead, all of the cash-flow instances within a time period will be added together and a single "net cash-flow instance" for

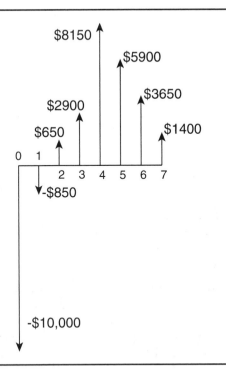

FIGURE 3.1 An example cash-flow diagram

that time period will be drawn on the diagram. That period's net cash-flow instance shows the sum of all the individual cash-flow instances during that time period.

By convention, cash flows are shown at the end of the corresponding period. The initial investment in a proposal is shown "at the end of period zero."

The cash-flow diagram in Figure 3.1 starts with $10,000 being spent at the beginning ("end of period zero") and another $850 being spent at the end of the first period. The end of the second through seventh time periods show incomes of $650, $2900, $8150, $5900, $3650, and $1400, respectively. This kind of pattern is fairly typical of business decisions, an initial investment followed by income at some later time.

A cash-flow stream, and the resulting cash-flow diagram, is always based on the specific perspective of the organization considering the proposal. Changing perspectives will change the cash-flow stream and, therefore, the cash-flow diagram. Figure 3.2 shows a single exchange of money (a series of cash-flow instances) from two different perspectives. The diagram on the left is from the perspective of someone who borrows

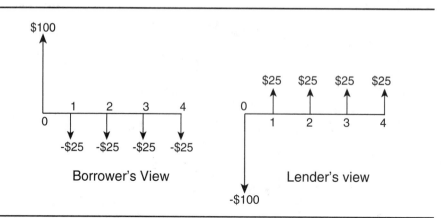

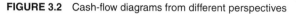

FIGURE 3.2 Cash-flow diagrams from different perspectives

$100 at the beginning and then pays that $100 back in four equally timed payments (such as monthly) of $25. This is the perspective of the borrower. The diagram on the right is from the perspective of someone who is loaning out $100 and is being repaid in four equal payments. This is the perspective of the lender. It's the same actual cash-flow instances in both cases, but one perspective sees it as money coming in while the other perspective sees it as money going out. The cash-flow instances in a proposal need to be from a consistent perspective; don't mix borrower cash-flow instances into the lender's perspective cash-flow stream.

Developing Cash-Flow Streams

One common way to develop the cash-flow stream for a proposal is to create a **work breakdown structure** (WBS). The WBS is a hierarchical decomposition that lists all the work associated with the proposal being studied. A common notation for a WBS is to show levels of decomposition by indenting. Developing a WBS is explained more fully in Appendix A. An example WBS for buying and operating a car might be as follows:

        Own and operate a car for transportation
            Buy the car
                Pay the down payment
                Pay the taxes, licensing, and registration fees
                Get insurance on the car
                Make the monthly car-loan payments
            Operate and maintain the car
                Pay the semiannual insurance payments
                Fill the car with gas when needed

Change the oil every 3000 miles

Other routine maintenance as needed

Sell the car

The typical interpretation of a WBS, say from a software project manager's perspective, is that it represents work—things that cost money. But we're interested in the full financial picture of the proposal, so we'll also need to be sure to include all the things that represent income cash-flow instances (sales income, cost avoidance, and salvage value), not just outgoing ones (initial investment and operating and maintenance costs).

Inherent in the agile development methods (e.g., [Beck00], [Cockburn02], [Schwaber02]) is an assumption that the nature of the software itself is either unknowable or will be unstable over the life of the project. In these situations, the business case of the project changes. Instead of the business case being "it will cost you this much and take that long to achieve that set of known, relatively stable goals," the business case in an agile software project is "as long as you, the customer, are willing to commit resources in stages (i.e., in two- to four-week iterations), the development team will do its best to deliver the most business value it can at the end of each stage. You have the right to change your definition of business value at the end of any iteration. You also have the right to put your resources elsewhere (i.e., cancel this project) at the end of any stage if you decide that the business value delivered was not worth your investment."

The WBS is a means to estimate the cost and schedule needed to achieve a relatively stable set of known goals. Agile development projects, on the other hand, are aligned to returning the most business value given a fixed level of investment over time. The WBS will not be of much use in making the business case for an agile project. The agile project's business case involves estimating how much business value can be returned (and when it is returned) given the level of investment the customer is willing to make.

After you have the complete WBS, the next step is to estimate the dollar amounts(s) and the timing(s) for each of the bottom-level items. We'll see several different estimation techniques in Chapter 22. For now, just assume that we have a way of creating reasonable estimates. For the car example, assume that the amounts and timings over 2 years of ownership are as follows:

Own and operate a car for transportation

Buy the car

Pay the down payment ($2000 on the day you buy it)

Pay the taxes, licensing, and registration fees (another $1500)

Get insurance on the car ($350 on the day you buy the car)

Make the monthly car-loan payments ($500 per month)

Operate and maintain the car

Pay the semiannual insurance payments ($350 every six months)

Fill the car with gas when needed (about $25 every two weeks)

Change the oil every 3000 miles (about $25 every four months)

Other routine maintenance as needed (roughly $200 per year)

Sell the car (assume you will net $1000 after paying off the car loan)

The next step is to add up the estimated bottom-level cash-flow instances. Notice that several of the items happen at different frequencies. You think you'll be filling the car with gas about twice a month, but the insurance payments are only due every six months. You'll need to pick a consistent time period for the overall study. It makes intuitive sense in this case to choose one month as the time period for the car-ownership example. In the end, the time period is rather arbitrary; it should be frequent enough that it gives you something to work with, but not so frequent that there are too many separate cash-flow instances. We could have just as easily chosen quarters or years in this example, if we wanted to.

You could develop separate cash-flow streams for each of the components in the WBS. The car loan, for example, could be diagrammed separately. Or, similarly, the in-surance payments could be on a separate diagram. This certainly isn't necessary, and you should only do it when it will tell you something you want or need to know.

Take the WBS with amount and timing estimates from above and convert, where necessary, the timings and amounts into the chosen time period. Assume we've chosen one month as the time period for the car example:

Own and operate a car for transportation

Buy the car

Pay the down payment ($2000 when you buy the car)

Pay the taxes, licensing, and registration fees (another $1500)

Get insurance on the car ($350 when you buy the car)

Make the monthly car-loan payments ($500 each month)

Operate and maintain the car

Pay the semiannual insurance payments ($350 every sixth months)

Fill the car with gas when needed (about $50 every month)

Change the oil every 3000 miles (about $25 every fourth month)

Other routine maintenance as needed (roughly $17 per month)

Sell the car (assume you net $1000 after paying off the car loan)

The oil change every fourth month can either be represented as a $25 cash-flow instance every fourth month or it can be averaged out to $6.75 per month. It probably makes sense to keep the insurance payments separated to every sixth month, but they could also be averaged out to about $58 each month. Again, this ends up being a judgment call; you can do it either way. Showing the insurance payments when they actually occur might be a bit better because the cash-flow stream would more accurately reflect the actual flow of money. The oil change cash flows are small enough that they are probably fairly insignificant, so they shouldn't need to be represented individually.

Now it's simply a matter of adding up all of the individual cash-flow instances that happen in each period to find the net cash-flow instance for that period.

In the car example

- The initial investment is $2000 down + $1500 license and tax + $350 insurance, which equals $3850 at the end of month zero.
- Most months will be $500 for the monthly loan payment + $50 for gas + $6.75 for oil + $17 for other routine maintenance; this equals $573.75.
- Months 6, 12, and 18 will have the $573.75 monthly from above plus the $350 insurance, for a total of $923.75.
- Selling the car at the end gives a salvage value of $1000.

The cash-flow stream for owning and operating the car is shown in Table 3.1.

Figure 3.3 shows the cash-flow stream in cash-flow diagram format.

In general it will be to your advantage to peer review the WBS and the estimates (either separately or together) to gain confidence that they are complete, consistent, reasonable, etc. References for peer review resources include [Wiegers02], [Gilb93], [Freedman90], and [Wheeler96].

TABLE 3.1   The Cash-Flow Stream

Month	Amount	Month	Amount	Month	Amount
0	−$3850	9	−$573.75	18	−$923.75
1	−$573.75	10	−$573.75	19	−$573.75
2	−$573.75	11	−$573.75	20	−$573.75
3	−$573.75	12	−$923.75	21	−$573.75
4	−$573.75	13	−$573.75	22	−$573.75
5	−$573.75	14	−$573.75	23	−$573.75
6	−$923.75	15	−$573.75	24	−$573.75
7	−$573.75	16	−$573.75	25	$1,000
8	−$573.75	17	−$573.75		

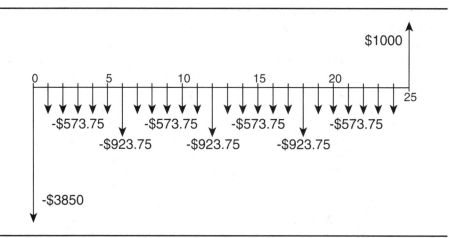

FIGURE 3.3   The cash-flow stream, in cash-flow diagram format

Summary

The concepts presented in this chapter are necessary for aligning software technical decisions with the goals of the organization. Those concepts are as follows:

- A proposal is a unit of choice. It's a single, separate option that is being considered.
- A cash-flow instance is a single occurrence of money flowing into or out of the organization at a specific time as a direct result of a given proposal.
- A cash-flow stream models the financial view of a proposal by presenting the flow of cash into and out of the organization over time due to that proposal.
- One useful strategy for developing the cash-flow stream for a proposal is to use a work breakdown structure (WBS).
- A cash-flow diagram is a picture of a cash-flow stream. Simply, a picture is worth a thousand words.

The next chapter describes the high-level, systematic process for using these concepts to make a business decision.

Self-Study Questions

1. Consider a proposal at a third-party systems development house to build and sell a system that helps overnight-package delivery companies find a delivery location using GPS (Global Positioning System) navigation and a detailed map database. Give one or more examples of the different categories of cash flow that should be included in the cash-flow stream for this proposal.

2. Consider a proposed in-house project at an overnight-package delivery company to create web-based software that enables customers to print shipping labels while at the same time notifying the delivery company of the need for a pickup. Give one or more examples of the different categories of cash flow that could be included in the cash-flow stream for this proposal.

3. Draw the net cash-flow diagram for the following cash-flow stream.

Year	Income	Expenses
0	$0	$7000
1	$0	$1000
2	$1000	$1000
3	$2000	$1000
4	$4000	$2000
5	$5000	$2500
6	$6000	$3000
7	$3000	$1500
8	$2000	$0

4. Identify a software project proposal (possibly the GPS project or shipping-label projects from the earlier questions) and develop a work breakdown structure that breaks the project down into at least three levels of decomposition. Include development activities such as requirements, design, and construction (coding) along with quality assurance and project management activities.

5. Estimate the costs and timings associated with each of the bottom-level activities in the WBS from the previous question.

6. Use the estimated costs from the previous question to develop an estimated cash-flow diagram for that project.

7. If you are currently involved in a software project, develop a WBS and cash-flow diagram for that project.

8. Make a WBS for your own typical (average) monthly income and expenses. Include reasonable sources of income. Include reasonable expenses. Make sure that the WBS is at least three levels deep.

4

The Business Decision-Making Process

For any technical problem, there is almost always more than one technically viable solution. If you want to make the most out of your organization's limited resources, then you, the technical person, should choose the solution that maximizes the return on your organization's software investment. To do this, you should follow a systematic process for making that choice. That systematic process is explained in this chapter. The remainder of this book fills in the details of the process.

Introducing the Business Decision-Making Process

Software professionals should already know how to come up with technical solutions to technical problems. But remember that for a single technical problem, there will almost always be more than one technically viable solution. A distributed system for automating public libraries could be written in C++ or Java or any one of dozens of other languages. It could use any one of a number of off-the-shelf persistent object store products, or the development team could choose to build their own persistence service. The software could be Web-enabled or not. The distribution middleware could be CORBA, Java RMI, SOAP, or some home-grown service. The software might use XML or not. The list of possibilities goes on and on.

If we assume that all of these candidate solutions solve the technical problem equally well, why should the business care which one is chosen? The answer is that there is probably a large difference in the costs and incomes from the different solutions. A commercial off-the-shelf CORBA-compliant object request broker product might cost a few thousand dollars, but the effort to develop a home-grown service that gave the same functionality could easily cost several hundred times that. If the candidate solutions all adequately solve the problem from a technical perspective, the one that maximizes the return on the organization's investment is the one that should be chosen.

Given that money spent in the design and production portion of the corporation (referring to the expenses section of Figure 2.1 in Chapter 2) cuts directly into profit, software professionals should do their best to align their technical decisions with the business realities. We should be creating **business-wise** technical solutions to our technical problems. To do this, you, the technical person, should follow a systematic process for making decisions. That systematic process is shown in Figure 4.1 and described in the rest of this chapter.

Figure 4.1 shows the process as mostly stepwise and serial. The real process is more fluid. Sometimes the steps can be done in different order, and often several of the steps can be done in parallel. The important thing is to be sure that none of the steps are skipped or shortcut. It's also important to understand that this same process applies at all levels of decision making: from a decision as big as should a software project be done at all, down to a decision on an algorithm or data structure to use in a software module. The difference is how financially significant the decision is and, therefore, how much effort should be invested in making that decision. The project-level decision is financially significant and probably warrants a relatively high level of effort to make the decision. Selecting an algorithm is much less financially significant and warrants a much lower level of effort to make the decision, even though the same basic decision-making process is being used. Each of the steps is described below.

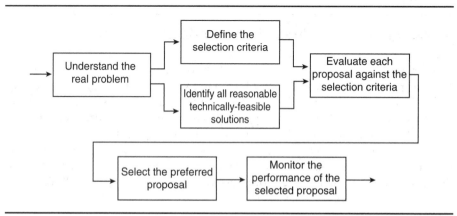

FIGURE 4.1   The business decision-making process

Understand the Real Problem

The first step in solving a technical problem, or any problem for that matter, is to first understand what that problem really is. This may seem rather obvious, but it's surprising how often the technical solutions don't really solve the actual problem. In software, understanding the real problem means eliciting, analyzing, specifying, and validating the requirements. This book isn't a tutorial on software requirements; there are already several good books on that topic (see, for example, [Gause89], [Robertson99], and [Wiegers03]). A few of the most important guidelines are worth mentioning here.

AMBIGUITY IN REQUIREMENTS STATEMENTS

One of the biggest problems with software requirements, especially requirements stated in natural languages, is ambiguity. Different people can usually look at the same natural language requirement statement and interpret it entirely differently. Consider the classic statement "the system shall be fast." What does it mean to be "fast"? How fast is fast enough? The recommendation is that you consider defining "fit criteria," or "abstract test cases," alongside each requirement. The fit criteria "handle at least 500 transactions per second" is a much more precise definition than just "fast." The key question is this: "Does the requirement supply enough information for someone to demonstrate it has been satisfied, through one or more reasonable tests?" Fit criteria are discussed in much more detail in [Robertson99].

Another way to help avoid ambiguous requirements is to minimize to use of natural languages. Languages such as the Unified Modeling Language (UML) [OMG03] can be used to specify requirements much more precisely. Requirements- and design-modeling languages can be thought of as the software industry's equivalent to the blueprints used in the construction world or circuit schematics and circuit-timing diagrams in electrical engineering. For more information on requirements- and design-modeling languages, see, for example, Craig Larman's *Applying UML and Patterns* [Larman01], Fowler and Scott's *UML Distilled* [Fowler03], or Mellor and Balcer's *Executable UML* [Mellor02].

MISTAKING A SOLUTION FOR THE PROBLEM

It's not at all unusual for people to mistake a solution for the problem, but it's important to not be misled by solutions masquerading as problems. This is as true in software as it is anywhere else. One useful technique for focusing on the real problem is known as the "five whys." In this technique, look at each requirement statement and ask the question "why." Why does *that* need to be the requirement? Is it the real requirement, or is it really just one possible solution to an underlying, as-yet unstated requirement.

If the answer to the "why" question is "because that's what it takes to satisfy the business need," you've found the real requirement. Otherwise, the explanation hints at an underlying candidate requirement, which should be brought out and subjected to the same "why" questioning. The name "five whys" comes from the observation that it's unusual to have this process repeat more than three or four cycles for any given candidate requirement. Trying to apply the technique five times virtually guarantees you've uncovered the real requirement.

To illustrate the "five whys" technique, assume that the original stated requirement is as follows:

> Put a 24-character text field in the travel-expense report table in the database and allow that field to be set through a text box on screen 47, displayed through text boxes on screens 65 and 68, as well as be printed on the weekly travel-expense summary report.

Ask why. Suppose the answer comes back, "Because the system needs to track whether travel-expense reports have been routed to the expense report manager in the accounting department." Routing the expense report to the manager in the accounting department is closer to the real requirement than adding the field to the database table, the screens, and the reports. But is that the real requirement or is it a potential solution to an underlying requirement? So we again ask, "Why?" Suppose the answer this time is that the expense report manager needs to approve the meal expenses. Ah, approving expense reports is closer to the real requirement, but is it also a solution? Again, "Why?" Suppose this time the answer is that it's because the corporation limits meal reimbursements to $50 per day, but expense reports with higher claims have been getting through because the approving managers weren't enforcing the policy.

Is that the real requirement? Ask again, "Why?" If the answer this time is that the business is losing too much money in uncontrolled, excessive meal claims on employee travel-expense reports, then we've run into the real business need: limiting excessive meal claims. Is there another way to solve this same problem? Yes, we could also solve it by putting in a range limit on the meal claim input screen. Don't allow meal claims over $50 to be entered into expense reports in the first place. No approval necessary, no routing to the expense report manager, no text field in the database, no inputs through screen 47, nor displays on screens 65 and 68 . . . The real requirement is to limit excessive meal claims on expense reports, and there are a number of different solutions to this one problem. The one that solves it most efficiently and effectively should be chosen. It would probably be much cheaper to put the range limit on the meal claim input screen than modify the database and the screens and reports. Aside from that, keeping the expense report manager in the accounting department from having to manually approve every expense report would be a big cost advantage for this new solution.

As your understanding of the real problem takes shape, especially through using fit criteria and the five whys technique, you should refine the requirements statements.

ANALYZING SEPARATE DECISIONS SEPARATELY

Another important principle in understanding the problem is that if two or more decisions are not necessarily connected, those decisions should be separated and analyzed (decided) independently. A decision to retire Product X might not need to be coupled with a decision to launch Product Y. If these are coupled and treated as one decision, your only options are to retire Product X and launch Product Y versus not retire Product X and not launch Product Y. But it may be that these really are separable decisions. Maybe retiring Product X has nothing to do with launching Product Y. In this case, you should be considering all four possible options:

- Don't retire Product X, don't launch Product Y.
- Retire Product X, don't launch Product Y.
- Retire Product X, do launch Product Y.
- Don't retire Product X, do launch Product Y.

Decisions that have been inappropriately coupled can blind you to possible options that might be better than the ones you are considering. Only when the independent choices are separated can all different combinations be considered. This is explained in more detail in Chapter 9.

Define the Selection Criteria

Decisions are often based on more than just one criterion. The decision to select the vendor for an outsourced software development project is likely to be based on cost, delivery date, and the quality of the vendor's work. Not just cost alone. Typically, the more important the decision, the more criteria that need to be considered. You'll need to be careful to identify all criteria that are relevant and be sure that all of those criteria are properly prioritized and considered. Selecting decision criteria is covered in more detail in Chapter 26.

IRREDUCIBLES

As much as possible, every criterion used in making a business decision should be expressed in objective terms. Ideally, those terms will be money, but this isn't necessarily so. Some decision criteria may still be numeric, but not in terms of money. For instance, "Acceptable solutions must support 60 simultaneous users and still have an average response time of less than 1.5 seconds." However, there may also be important decision criteria that can't be expressed objectively. These criteria are the **irreducibles**, the "unquantifiables."

It's one thing to talk about the financial impact on the company of laying someone off, but it's another thing entirely to look at the impact of that decision on the person who is actually being laid off. It might be a reasonable decision from a purely financial perspective to lay off some number of people, but the company might instead want to look for other less-financially-effective options (salary deferrals or across-the-board salary cuts, for example) because they know the personal impact the layoff will have on the people who get laid off.

Similarly, what's the "worth" of a clean stream? Does it make sense to put a dollar value on the stream by multiplying the cost per pound of the kinds of fish in the stream by an estimate of the number of pounds of fish that are there?

Where necessary, identify all the irreducible decision criteria and be sure to factor them into the decision-making process. Chapter 26 explains how to address irreducible factors in a business decision analysis.

PRIORITIZE THE SELECTION CRITERIA

In addition to just identifying the selection criteria, be sure to prioritize them. Is cost more important than delivery date when considering a vendor's proposal on an out-sourced software project? Should the quality of the vendor's work be considered more important than cost? Unless the priorities are made clear, different people will end up applying their own prioritization. Making sure that the priorities are clear helps everyone agree on the final decision. There's more on this topic in Chapter 26.

After the selection criteria have been defined, peer reviews (see [Wiegers02], [Gilb93], [Freedman90], or [Wheeler96], for example) can help you be sure that the criteria are complete and consistent.

Identify All Reasonable Technically Feasible Solutions (the Proposals)

The ultimate goal of the concepts and techniques in this book is to guide you in finding the best—considering both an economic and technical perspective—choice from a set of proposals that are being considered. It doesn't do much good to go through a systematic decision process when the best proposal isn't even among those being considered.

Unfortunately, there's never any guarantee that the best proposal really is in the set being considered. It's ultimately up to you to consider all appropriate reasonable candidates. The creative-thinking techniques of De Bono [DeBono92] and von Oesch [vonOesch98] can be useful in creating a variety of potential solutions. Another effective way to increase the chances that the best proposal is in the set is to have someone else look at that set and see if that person can think of any others that should also be considered. Design reviews and peer reviews can also be very useful approaches.

Adding more proposals to the set being considered increases the chances that the best one is in that set, but there's an added cost to considering each additional proposal. It takes time (and, therefore, money) to come up with each proposal plus the extra time and money spent in the decision analysis. You'll have to use your best judgment to decide when you have enough alternatives to go ahead with the decision-making process.

Evaluate Each Proposal Against the Selection Criteria

In this step, each of the proposals is evaluated against the selection criteria. This step is fairly self-explanatory, but one useful hint is to build a matrix with the proposals listed on one axis and the selection criteria listed on the other. The matrix helps you be sure you've evaluated every proposal against every selection criterion. Table 4-1 shows an example.

TABLE 4-1   Evaluating the Proposals Against the Selection Criteria Using a Matrix

	Initial Investment (Priority 1)	Present worth (Priority 2)	Quality (Priority 3)	Quoted Delivery Date (Priority 4)	. . .
Vendor 1	$52,250	$174,350	Excellent	October 18	. . .
Vendor 2	$47,000	$139,500	Very good	September 12	. . .
Vendor 3	$61,000	$151,000	Acceptable	August 8	. . .
. . .	. . .	. . .	. . .	. . .	. . .

When a selection criterion involves money, each of the proposals needs to be judged from the same viewpoint. Be sure to use the same time frame and consider the same kinds of costs and incomes across all of the proposals. Suppose, for example, you are trying to decide between buying and adapting an off-the-shelf software product versus building a custom program from scratch. If you consider the inevitable maintenance and support costs and use a longer time frame for one proposal than the other, the one with the shorter time frame and no maintenance or support costs will probably look much better even though it might not be the better choice.

Start by defining the context of the study. Where is the boundary for measuring costs and income? Define the time period of the study (more on this in Chapter 11 on economic life and planning horizons). Be sure to use this consistent context when creating the cash-flow stream for every proposal. You've already seen how to develop the cash-flow stream for a proposal (Chapter 3), but also you may want to refer to Part VI on estimation.

Business decisions will be based on estimates. There are theoretical and practical limits to how certain your estimates can be, and the amount of uncertainty is very dependent on the specifics of the situation. (Have we ever made predictions like this before? Can we look back on actual experience to validate or otherwise gain confidence in the predictions? Do we really understand the full scope of the estimated factor? Could some important issue about the thing being estimated change between now and when the actual value is discovered?)

The degree of uncertainty in an estimate could be big enough that variations of that estimate across its uncertainty range could change the outcome of the decision. Suppose we're trying to decide whether to develop and launch a commercial product. The income side of the cash-flow stream would be based on the estimate for the number of units sold over time. Suppose that the estimate of total sales is between 7,000 and 10,000 units. Running through the computations, we may find that there's a healthy return on our investment if we actually sell 10,000 units. On the other hand, we may find that if only 7,000 units are sold, we stand to lose a substantial chunk of money. Maybe the minimum number of units sold to just recover the development costs is 8,250. Does it make sense to go ahead with this product? Or should we play it safe and not do this product?

As uncertainty increases, your degree of confidence in any decisions based on that estimate should decrease. By explicitly stating the degree of estimate uncertainty, anyone who wants to evaluate the decision analysis will be able to form his or her own opinion on how much confidence to have in the expected outcome. Estimates and uncertainty are explained in much more detail in Part VI.

Select the Preferred Proposal

Comparing proposals from the financial perspective is the main topic in most of this book. Part II and Part III explain how selection is done in for-profit organizations, and Part IV explains how it is done in not-for-profit organizations. Part VI provides a set of techniques for making decisions when there are more than just financial selection criteria to consider.

Monitor the Performance of the Selected Proposal

Estimation is a fundamental part of good decision making. The quality of the decision depends on the quality of the estimates; bad estimates can easily lead to bad decisions. It's very important for you to "close the loop" on your estimation techniques by comparing the original estimates to the actual outcomes. Otherwise you'll never know if your estimates were any good. This will also help you improve your estimation techniques over time. Use the difference between the original estimates and the actual results to refine your estimation techniques so they account for the factors that made up the differences. There are three parts to this:

- **Look at where you've been**—See if the selected alternative is living up to your expectations as the best solution. Is the estimated cash-flow stream matching the actual cash flows? Is the project on schedule? If not, are the estimates still close enough that it warrants continuing down this same path? If the estimates are way out of sync with reality, does it make sense to reconsider the other proposals (after revalidating *their* estimates based on what you now know)? Or, is it too late to switch to one of the other proposals, anyway?

- **Look at where you are**—Use recent history to refine future estimates on this project. A technique known as **earned value** [Fleming00] uses the ratio of estimated effort and schedule for WBS tasks already completed to the actual effort and schedule for those same tasks as a means to assess the accuracy of the remaining estimates. If your project is 10% over cost and 15% behind schedule with only 25% of the work completed, the estimates for the remaining cost and schedule are most likely also low by at least 10% and 15%, respectively. The concept of "velocity" from eXtreme Programming [Beck00] accomplishes this same goal.

- **Look at where you're going in the future**—Plan to use the history from this project (when completed) to refine estimates on future projects. A very common mistake on schedule estimates is to assume that people will be allocated 100% to one project. This rarely happens on real projects. Vacations, sick time, training, getting pulled off for other crash projects, fixing problems in earlier versions, and such are all fairly typical interruptions making 100% allocation to the current project impossible. So the first project estimated at 100% allocation will almost certainly end up being late. At the end of the project, lateness can often be at least partially attributed to less-than-100% allocation to the project. When you know the causes, go back and revise your estimation techniques to account for those new factors. Try to measure the degree of distraction that's inherent in your organization and feed this back into subsequent estimates so that a less-than-100% allocation factor is used next time. This way, rather than projects being chronically underestimated (leading to excessive overtime, frayed nerves, burn-out, etc.), your estimates will become better and better with every project.

Remember the saying:

Does that person have 10 years of experience, or is it really just 1 year of experience 10 times over?

Without monitoring the performance of your selected proposal, you could easily end up with 1 year of experience many times over instead of having many years of experience.

Summary

For any technical problem, there is almost always more than one technically viable solution. To make the most of your organization's limited resources, you, the technical person, should choose the solution that maximizes the return on your organization's software investment. This means you should follow a systematic process for making that choice. This chapter described that systematic process:

1. Understand the real problem. This includes avoiding ambiguity, using the five whys technique to help avoid mistaking a solution for the real problem, and analyzing separable decisions separately.

2. Define and prioritize the selection criteria that are relevant in the decision. Some criteria are "irreducible" and can't be quantified in terms of money.

3. Identify reasonable technically feasible solutions (the proposals).

4. Evaluate each proposal against the selection criteria.

5. Select the preferred solution.

6. Monitor the performance of the selected solution to learn and improve from the experience.

These steps aren't necessarily done in exactly this order, and often some amount of iteration is required.

The next chapter presents one of the most important factors in business decisions, the time value of money.

Self-Study Questions

1. Give at least three examples of where the decision-making techniques described in this chapter could be applied at a number of different levels in a typical software organization.

2. For one of the examples from Question 1, specify which situation you chose and identify at least three relevant selection criteria.

3. What would be a reasonable prioritization of the criteria in Question 2? List your criteria in order of decreasing importance.

4. Which of these selection criteria would be "irreducible" and which ones wouldn't?

5. Given the stated requirement "the system shall be user-friendly," describe at least three possible valid interpretations.

6. Give an example of an ambiguous software requirement statement, and describe at least two possible valid interpretations.

7. Give an example of using the five whys technique to find a real requirement. Use at least three cycles of asking "why" and interpreting the response.

8. Give an example of a technical problem.

   Identify at least three relevant decision criteria. Identify all that are irreducible.

   Prioritize the decision criteria.

   Come up with at least three technically viable proposed solutions.

   Estimate the cash flow for each solution.

   Build the decision matrix and fill in the values.

9. Do the same thing for a choice to be made in your home life.

   Identify at least three relevant decision criteria.

5

Interest: The Time Value of Money

One of the most fundamental concepts in business—and therefore, in business decisions—is that money has time value; its value changes over time. A specific amount of money right now almost always has a different value than having the same amount of money at some other time. This concept has been around since the earliest recorded human history and is commonly known as "interest." Anyone making a business decision needs to understand interest and how it affects that decision. This chapter defines and explains interest and shows how to relate the value of money at one time to the value of money at other times using a series of mathematical formulas. Later chapters show how interest is addressed in a business decision.

Time *Is* Money

The old saying is "time is money." In business, this is true both figuratively and literally; time *is* money. A given amount of money today doesn't have the same value as an identical amount of money later on. Consider this simple experiment: Give someone $10 today and at the same time promise to give someone else $10 a month from today. Which of the two people is better off? Of course, the person who gets the $10 today is better off. That person can use the money right now. The person could either spend it or invest it. The person who has to wait not only can't use the money today but also runs the risk that it won't actually be there next month as promised.

The question is, then, *how much* better off is the person who gets the money today than the person who has to wait? The person who has to wait might be willing to give up a part of his promised money so that he could get it sooner. If so, how much would he be willing to give up? The person who is given the money today might be willing to wait for it instead, but probably only if she knew she would get even more money later on. The difference is significant, and it can be quantified. People are almost always willing to pay more later to use someone else's money now. A bank loan is exactly that; the borrower is agreeing to pay more later on for the use of someone else's money right now. Likewise, someone who has more money than needed right now might be willing to lend it to someone else, but only in return for more money later on. A savings account is exactly that, letting someone else use your money now in return for (at least the promise of) a larger amount of money later.

Banks operate on the difference between what they charge for borrowed money and what they pay on deposited money. The deposited money is, after all, what they have available to lend in the first place. A bank that charges 9% on borrowed money and pays 5% on deposits nets 4% on the money it lends. The real story is actually more complicated than this, but this is the basic idea.

Interest

The difference in the time value of money is quantifiable. It is measured in terms of **interest**—the money that someone pays to use someone else's money. Archeological evidence suggests that interest has been an established part of society as far back as the earliest recorded history (e.g., in Babylon circa 2000 B.C.).

Interest is, in a sense, a fee charged for renting someone else's money. It's exactly like renting a house, a car, or any thing else—the renter takes possession of the thing and later returns that thing plus some amount of money. In this case, the thing being rented just happens to also be money. The renter (borrower) takes possession of some amount of money now, using it to start a business, buy a computer or house or car, take a Caribbean cruise, etc., and pays back a larger amount of money later on.

The amount that the borrower pays to use the borrowed money depends on how much money is being borrowed, how long it's being borrowed, and the "rental fee" for money—the **interest rate**. The interest rate is usually stated as a percentage of the amount borrowed and, by convention, is in per-year terms unless otherwise specified.

As a simple example, suppose someone borrows $1000 at 7.5% (per year) for 1 year. At the end of the year, that person is expected to pay back $1075. Of that, $1000 of it is to return the money originally borrowed, and the remaining $75 is interest—the rental fee for being able to use the $1000. Interest rates in the United States have historically tended to range between about 4% and about 25%.

Technically speaking, the interest rate is the rate of gain received (when lending money) or paid (when borrowing money). The interest rate changes over time and is driven by market forces; it can go up or down. Clearly, the people who have money to lend will try to get the highest interest rate they think they can get, whereas borrowers will try to find the lender with the lowest interest rate. As the supply of money available to lend goes up, the interest rate goes down. Similarly, as the supply of borrowable money goes down, the interest rate goes up.

The makeup of the real interest rate is actually more complex than what is described here, but it can be explained from the lender's perspective as follows:

- What's the probability that the borrower won't repay the loan? If there are $2 in defaulted loans per $100 loaned, then the lender should ask for 2% to cover the defaults.
- What's the cost of setting up and administering the loan? If the average cost is $1 per $100 loaned, then the lender should ask for another 1% to cover these costs.
- While the money is lent out, the lender can't use it. What does the lender think is adequate compensation for not being able to use their own money? Assume that the lender expects 5.5% as compensation.
- What's the probability that the interest rate will change significantly before the loan is fully paid off? Even if the lender thinks that 8.5% is enough today, if the lender expects that interest rates will go up over the life of the loan, they may want to ask for a little extra, say 0.5%, in anticipation of the increase.

All of this suggests that this lender will want to ask for about 9.0% interest.
From the borrower's perspective

- If the money is being borrowed for personal use (to finance a house, car, vacation, etc.), the interest rate is an indicator of how much that person is willing to pay for satisfaction now instead of satisfaction later. If the loan to pay for a Caribbean cruise this year would take 3 years to pay off, the prospective vacationer could certainly save at least an equal amount in 3 years. In fact, it would probably take less than 3 years if the money were put into an interest-bearing investment— meaning that the prospective vacationer becomes a lender. The vacationer would be earning interest rather than paying it. The interest rate is a measure of how much extra the vacationer is willing to pay to take the vacation this year instead of waiting until 3 years from now.
- If the money is being borrowed for business use (for example, to finance new office space, a new machine, or new product development), the expected return from the borrowed money should be much higher than the interest rate. It wouldn't make sense to borrow at an interest rate of 12% if the biggest expected return from the business use of that money was, say, only 3%.

More broadly speaking, interest can be thought of as the return that can be gained from the productive investment of money. This broader point of view is implied throughout the remainder of this book, but it can be helpful to start with the more narrow definition above.

TABLE 5.1 The Names and Meanings of the Common Variables in Interest Formulas

Name	Meaning
P	The principal amount. How much is the money worth right now? This term is also known as the present value or present worth.
F	The final amount. How much will the money be worth at a later time? This term is also known as the future value or future worth.
i	The interest rate per period. What is the rental fee for using someone else's money? (Assumed to be an annual rate unless stated otherwise.)
n	The number of interest periods between the two points in time.
A	The annuity, a stream of recurring, equal payments that would be due at the end of each interest period. More on this below.

Naming Conventions in Interest Formulas

There are six standard formulas for converting money at one time to money at another time. Table 5.1 shows the names and meanings of the variables used in those formulas. These variables and their meanings are used commonly throughout business, finance, and engineering.

Simple Interest

So far, I've explained interest using the logic of "simple interest." Although simple interest usually isn't available in practice, it's much easier to understand than what is usually available. I describe simple interest because it's a convenient starting point for explaining compound interest, which is discussed below. Compound interest is the one most commonly found in practice.

Under simple interest, the entire interest payment is due at the end of the loan. The interest owed can be calculated by multiplying the amount borrowed (P) times the interest rate (i) times the number of interest periods the money is being borrowed for (n).

$$I = P * i * n$$

As an example, suppose that Company A needs to borrow $10k for 3 years. They find a lender who is willing to loan the money and let them pay it back in full after the 3 years provided Company A* pays 11% simple interest. How much will Company A need to

---

*All references to company names are fictitious references. Any similarity of these companies to real companies is purely coincidental.

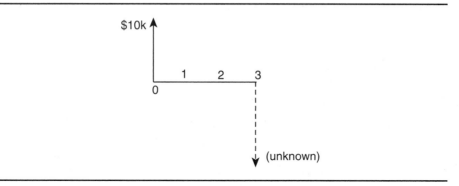

FIGURE 5.1 The cash-flow diagram for Company A's $10k, 3-year loan

pay to the lender at the end of the 3 years? The cash-flow diagram for Company A's loan is shown in Figure 5.1. In this part of the book, I use the dashed-arrow notation in cash-flow diagrams to show which cash-flow instance is unknown.

The total amount that they need to repay, F, is equal to the original amount borrowed, P, plus the interest, I.

$$F = P + I = P + Pni = P(1 + ni)$$

The answer to Company A's question is as follows:

$$F = P(1 + ni) = \$10k(1 + 3 * 0.11) = \$13.3k$$

The $13.3k Company A would repay at the end of the loan includes $10k to repay the principal (the amount originally borrowed) plus $3.3k in interest (the rental fee for being able to use the lender's $10k for those 3 years).

Sometimes the situation is reversed. Instead of wanting to figure F from a known P, F is known and P needs to be found. For example, Bee Co. knows they want to invest enough to end up with $10k at the end of 3 years. They found an investment that pays 11% simple interest. How much do they need to invest? The cash-flow diagram for this situation is shown in Figure 5.2.

In this case, the original F-given-P formula can be rearranged to solve for P:

$$P = \frac{F}{1 + ni}$$

The answer to Bee Co.'s question is as follows:

$$P = \frac{\$10k}{1 + 3 * 0.11} = \$7518.80$$

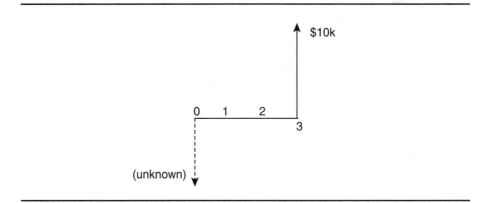

FIGURE 5.2   The cash-flow diagram for Bee Co.'s investment

Bee Co. needs to invest $7518.80 at 11% simple interest to have $10,000 at the end of 3 years. The difference, $2481.20, is the interest paid by the borrower to rent Bee Co.'s $7518.80 for those 3 years.

Discrete Compounding of Interest

Simple interest works in favor of the borrower. Think about Company A's $10k loan, but consider it from the lender's perspective. If it were only a 1-year loan, the interest due at the end of the first year would be this:

$$I = Pni = \$10k * 1 * 0.11 = \$1.1k$$

Company A actually owes $11.1k at the end of the first year. From the lender's perspective, the $1100 interest from the first year should be considered a loan itself during the second and third years. The interest due on the second year of the loan could also be considered a loan in the third year. This introduces the idea of **compound interest**. Literally, it's interest on interest.

The typical loan lasts more than one interest period, and the interest accrued during each period is payable at the end of that period. If the borrower doesn't pay the interest at the end of the period, that interest is added to the principal (the amount owed). The interest due at the end of any period will be the interest on the original principal plus the interest on all previously accrued interest.

Figure 5.3 illustrates the idea of compound interest through a graph. At the beginning of period T_k, the borrower owes some principal amount, P_k. At the end of period T_k, the borrower owes I_k in interest where $I_k = P_k * i$. Assuming the borrower didn't make any payments on the loan during T_k, they would owe $P_k + I_k$ at the end of T_k. This

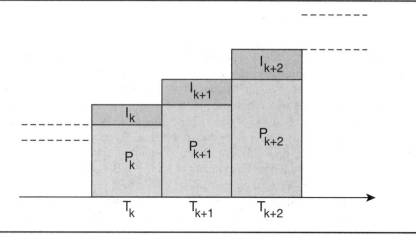

FIGURE 5.3   Compound interest shown through a graph

is exactly the same as owing P_{k+1} at the beginning of T_{k+1} and the cycle repeats. At the end of T_{k+1} the borrower would owe $I_{k+1} = P_{k+1} * i$ in interest, for a total owed of $P_{k+1} + I_{k+1}$. And this is exactly the same as owing P_{k+2} at the beginning of period T_{k+2} and so on until the loan gets paid off.

Notice in Figure 5.3 that because $P_{k+1} = P_k + I_k$, I_{k+1} will always be greater than I_k. This is the effect of compounding of interest; interest is owed on earlier interest.

Notice that if a loan lasts for exactly one interest period, simple interest and compound interest behave exactly the same. The same amount would be owed at the end of that loan.

Six different forms of compound interest formulas are described in this chapter:

- Single-payment compound-amount (F/P)
- Single-payment present-worth (P/F)
- Equal-payment-series compound-amount (F/A)
- Equal-payment-series sinking-fund (A/F)
- Equal-payment-series capital-recovery (A/P)
- Equal-payment-series present-worth (P/A)

Three of these formulas allow you to calculate forward from a known present situation to an unknown future amount, and the other three allow you to calculate backward from a known, desired future to an unknown present situation. The formulas also vary depending on whether the present and future situations are single payments or a series of equal payments spread over time. Each of the six different forms is discussed separately. A chart for helping you decide which form to use in a specific situation is provided in Figure 5.10 at the end of this chapter.

Single-Payment Compound-Amount (*F/P*)

The most straightforward of the six compound interest formulas is known as single-payment compound-amount. The name refers to the idea that a single payment is due at the end of the loan and that payment includes all of the compounded interest. A clear application of this formula is when some amount of money is put into a bank account at a fixed interest rate for some period of time. This formula can be used to calculate how much money will be in the account at the end of that time. Keeping in mind that putting money into a bank account is exactly like loaning that money to the bank, this same formula is used when a borrower gets an amount of money and repays the entire amount plus compound interest as a single payment at the end of the loan.

Because simple interest isn't available under usual circumstances, any time the term *interest* is used from here on, assume that it means compound interest unless otherwise explicitly stated that simple interest is meant.

We'll use a situation similar to the Company A example used above in explaining simple interest. This will allow single-payment compound-amount to be contrasted with simple interest. Figure 5.4 shows the generic cash-flow diagram for single-payment compound-amount situations. In this case, Cee Inc. invests $10k for 3 years at 11% compound interest.

DERIVING THE FORMULA

It isn't really critical that you memorize the details of how or why each interest formula works. This chapter shows you how each one works because you may find it interesting plus it will allow you to understand and "trust" the formula.

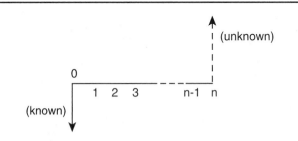

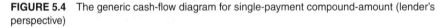

FIGURE 5.4   The generic cash-flow diagram for single-payment compound-amount (lender's perspective)

TABLE 5.2 Deriving the Single-Payment Compound-Amount Formula

Year	Amount Owed at Start of That Year	Interest Payable Year During That Year	Compound Amount Owed at the End of That Year
1	P	Pi	$P + Pi = P(1 + i)^1$
2	$P(1 + i)$	$P(1 + i)i$	$P(1 + i) + P(1 + i)i = P(1 + i)^2$
3	$P(1 + i)^2$	$P(1 + i)^2 i$	$P(1 + i)^2 + P(1 + i)^2 i = P(1 + i)^3$
n	$P(1 + i)^{n-1}$	$P(1 + i)^{n-1} i$	$P(1 + i)^{n-1} + P(1 + i)^{n-1} i = P(1 + i)^n$

TABLE 5.3 Step-by-Step Solution to Cee Inc.'s Problem

Year	Amount Owed Cee Inc. at the Start of That Year	Amount of Interest Cee Inc. Earns That Year	Compound Amount Owed Cee Inc. at End of That Year
1	$1000	$1000 * 0.11 = $110	$1000 + $110 = $1110
2	$1110	$1110 * 0.11 = $122	$1110 + $122 = $1232
3	$1232	$1232 * 0.11 = $136	$1232 + $136 = $1368

This formula is derived step by step using exactly the same logic that was shown in Table 5.2.

The loan starts with P being given to the borrower at the beginning of the first year. The interest due at the end of the first year is Pi so that the total amount owed (to pay off the loan entirely) is $P + Pi = P(1+i)$. The compound amount at the end of the first year becomes the amount owed at the beginning of the second year—the interest owed at the end of the previous year is now part of the principal. Similarly, the interest payable at the end of the second year is $P(1+i)i$ so that the total loan amount at the end of the second year is $P(1 + i)^2$. Generalizing this for n years:

$$F = P(1 + i)^n$$

SOLVING THE SAMPLE PROBLEM

We can now use the formula to answer Cee Inc.'s question:

$$F = P(1 + i)^n = \$10k(1 + 0.11)^3 = \$13.68k$$

Compared to Company A's simple interest case, where only $13.3k was due at the end of the 3 years, the additional $380 ($13.68k – $13.3k) Cee Inc. gets is from the compounding of interest—again, interest due on previously owed interest. Table 5.3 shows the computations for answering Cee Inc.'s question in the same step-by-step form as Table 5.2.

A SHORTHAND NOTATION . . .

When you are serious about maximizing the bang for your buck, you need to pay close attention to interest because it can have a big impact on the final decision. Interest calculations are so common in business decisions that there is a standard shorthand notation to make them easier to write.

The thing to notice is that if you are given some specific interest rate, i, and a number of interest periods, n, then the future value, F, will always be a constant value times the present value, P, where that constant equals $(1 + i)^n$. When i is 11% and n is 3 years, that constant is $(1 + 0.11)^3 = 1.368$. In the standard shorthand notation, that constant factor is abbreviated as follows:

$$\left(\overset{F/P,i,n}{} \right)$$

As in:

$$F = P \left(\overset{F/P,i,n}{} \right)$$

Single-payment compound-amount factors always appear in this form. The F/P part of the notation means that this is the factor that converts present values, Ps, to future values, Fs. The i part identifies the interest rate, and the n gives the number of interest periods. The shorthand

$$\left(\overset{F/P,11\%,3}{} \right)$$

refers to the factor that will convert any present value to its corresponding future value at an interest rate of 11% over three interest periods.

. . . AND A TABLE-BASED SOLUTION

In these days of computers, high-level programming languages, and spreadsheets, table-based solutions to interest problems may be considered quaint and old fashioned. Regardless, it's sometimes easier to pull the conversion factor out of an interest table than to access the same information in the computer (that is, until financial calculators and financial applications become more common).

The tables in Appendix B are intended to help you quickly solve typical interest problems. A spreadsheet for making your own interest tables can be found at http://www.construx.com/returnonsw/. The procedure is as follows:

1. Find the table for the (closest) interest rate, i.

2. Find the row, R, corresponding to the value of n.

3. Locate the column, C, for the interest formula being used.

4. The number at the intersection of row R, column C is the conversion factor you need.

The tables in Appendix B contain precomputed conversion factors for all the various forms of interest equations. Any problem of the general form $(1 + i)^n$ can usually be solved using these same tables.

As an example of using interest tables, consider Derby Industries who invests $10k at 9%. How much will their investment be worth 7 years from now? Again, this is a single-payment compound-amount problem. In the shorthand notation, it looks like this:

$$F = \$10\text{k}(\overset{F/P,9\%,7}{\qquad})$$

Table 5.4 is an excerpt from the 9% interest table in Appendix B.

1. Find the table for the (closest) interest rate, i. In this case, it will be the page for 9% interest, Appendix B-13, or the excerpt in Table 5.4.

2. Find the row, R, for the given value of n. In this case, it will be the seventh row of the table.

3. Locate the column, C, for the formula being used. In this case it will be the single-payment compound-amount column ($F/P,i,n$). This is the second column from the left, just to the right of the n column.

4. The number at the intersection of the F/P column and the seventh row is the factor, in this case, 1.8280. The ($F/P,9\%,7$) factor is boxed in Table 5.4.

Substitute the factor into the equation and do the arithmetic:

$$F = \$10\text{k}(\overset{F/P,9\%,7}{1.8280}) = \$18.28\text{k}$$

TABLE 5.4 Excerpt from the 9% Interest Table in Appendix B

9.00% Interest Factors for Discrete Compounding

	Single Payment		Equal-Payment Series			
	Compound Amount	Present Worth	Compound Amount	Sinking Fund	Present Worth	Capital Recovery
n	Find *F* given *P*	Find P given *F*	Find *F* given *A*	Find *A* given *F*	Find *P* given *A*	Find *A* given *P*
	(*F/P,I,n*)	(*P/F,I,n*)	(*F/A,I,n*)	(*A/F,I,n*)	(*P/A,I,n*)	(*A/P,I,n*)
1	1.0900	0.9174	1.0000	1.0000	0.9174	1.0900
2	1.1881	0.8417	2.0900	0.4785	1.7591	0.5685
3	1.2950	0.7722	3.2781	0.3051	2.5313	0.3951
4	1.4116	0.7084	4.5731	0.2187	3.2397	0.3087
5	1.5386	0.6499	5.9847	0.1671	3.8897	0.2571
6	1.6771	0.5963	7.5233	0.1329	4.4859	0.2229
7	1.8280	0.5470	9.2004	0.1087	5.0330	0.1987
8	1.9926	0.5019	11.0285	0.0907	5.5348	0.1807
9	2.1719	0.4604	13.0210	0.0768	5.9952	0.1668
10	2.3674	0.4224	15.1929	0.0658	6.4177	0.1558

At 9% compound interest, Derby Industries' $10k investment is worth $18.28k after 7 years.

Looking back to Cee Inc.'s situation, the table-based solution using the shorthand notation is as follows:

$$F = \$10k(\overset{F/P,11\%,3}{\qquad})$$

$$= \$10k(1.368) = \$13.68k$$

The shorthand notations and table-based solutions for the other forms are explained in the sections discussing those other formulas.

Single-Payment Present-Worth (*P/F*)

The single-payment compound-amount formula (just discussed) calculates the unknown future value of some known present amount (*F* given *P*). The single-payment present-worth turns this around and calculates the unknown present value needed to return a known future value (*P* given *F*) at the interest rate and term. If you know that a certain interest rate is available and you know how much money you want to end up with over

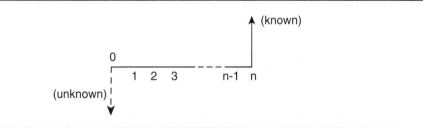

FIGURE 5.5   The generic cash-flow diagram for single-payment present-worth (lender's view)

some period of time, this formula tells you how much to invest now. The generic cash-flow diagram for this situation is shown in Figure 5.5.

We'll use a variation of Bee Co. from above. This time, it's Evans Software who found an investment that pays 11% compound interest. Evans also wants to end up with $10k after 3 years. How much do they need to invest now?

DERIVING THE FORMULA

The formula is easily derived by starting with the single-payment compound-amount (*F/P,i,n*) formula and rearranging it to solve for *P*.

$$P = F\left[\frac{1}{(1 + i)^n}\right]$$

SOLVING THE SAMPLE PROBLEM

Evans' question, answered using the longhand approach, is as follows:

$$P = \$10k\left[\frac{1}{(1 + 0.11)^3}\right] = \$7312.00$$

Evans Software would need to deposit $7312.00 to end up with $10k after 3 years at 11% compound interest. Remember that Bee Co. needed to invest $7518.80 with a simple interest investment. Even though Bee Co. and Evans Software were both investing at 11% for 3 years, Evans can invest $306.80 less because of compounding.

THE SHORTHAND NOTATION AND TABLE-BASED SOLUTION

The shorthand notation for single-payment present-worth factor is as follows:

$P/F,i,n$

(   )

The *P/F* means that the factor converts future values, *F*s, into present values, *P*s, at interest rate *i* over *n* periods (find *P* given *F*).

Evans' question, answered using the shorthand approach, is as follows:

$$F = \$10k(\overset{P/F,11\%,3}{})$$

$$= \$10k(0.7312) = \$7312.00$$

Equal-Payment-Series Compound-Amount (*F/A*)

In some situations, instead of looking at a single payment, we want to know the future value of a series of equal payments. In other words, if we deposit or borrow a series of *n* equal payments at a given interest rate, how much will they be worth immediately after the last payment? This formula is used in situations such as retirement accounts where a series of equal payments are made over time, building up to a single final value.

> It is important to remember that this formula, and all of the equal-payment-series formulas, uses the "end-of-period convention." The end-of-period convention assumes that all equal-payment-series cash-flow instances happen at the end of the interest period and that the first one is at the end of period one.

The generic cash-flow diagram for this situation is shown in Figure 5.6.

As an example, consider Company F, who will start saving to build a new office building in 10 years. Company F's directors found that they will have an extra $10k at the end of each of the next 10 years, and they'd like to invest it to help pay for the new office building. If they can find an investment that pays 11% compound interest, how much will they have when they are ready to build?

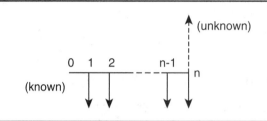

FIGURE 5.6 The generic cash-flow diagram for equal-payment-series compound-amount (lender's view)

DERIVING THE FORMULA

The formula can be derived by recognizing that each individual payment of amount *A* adds to the final total as if it were a separate single-payment compound-amount:

$$F = A(1) + A(1 + i) + \ldots + A(1 + i)^{n-2} + A(1 + i)^{n-1}$$

The term $A(1)$ represents the very last payment, which earns no interest because it's made on the final day. The term $A(1 + i)$ represents the second-to-last payment, which earns interest for one period. The term $A(1 + i)^{n-1}$ represents the first payment, which earns interest for $n - 1$ interest periods.

Multiplying the previous equation by $(1 + i)$ gives the following:

$$F(1 + i) = A(1 + i) + A(1 + i)^2 + \ldots + A(1 + i)^{n-1} + A(1 + i)^n$$

Subtracting the first equation from the second then gives this:

$$F(1 + i) \quad = \quad A(1 + i) + A(1 + i)^2 + \ldots + A(1 + i)^{n-1} + A(1 + i)^n$$

$$-F = -A - A(1 + i) - A(1 + i)^2 - \ldots - A(1 + i)^{n-1}$$

$$F(1 + i) - F \quad = -A \qquad\qquad\qquad\qquad\qquad + A(1 + i)^n$$

Rearranging and solving for *F*

$$F + Fi - F = A(1 + i)^n - A$$

$$Fi = A(1 + i)^n - A$$

$$Fi = A[(1 + i)^n - 1]$$

$$F = A \left[\frac{(1 + i)^n - 1}{i} \right]$$

SOLVING THE SAMPLE PROBLEM

In the longhand form, Company F's question is answered as follows:

$$F = \$10k \left[\frac{(1 + 0.11)^{10} - 1}{0.11} \right] = \$167.22k$$

Company F will have $167,220 for the new building if they invest $10k at the end of each of the next 10 years into an account that pays 11%.

THE SHORTHAND NOTATION AND TABLE-BASED SOLUTION

The shorthand notation for equal-payment-series compound-amount is as follows:

$$\left(\overset{F/A,i,n}{} \right)$$

In this case, the shorthand notation shows the future value, F, being computed from a series of equal payments, A (short for *annuity*), as in "F given A" at an interest rate of i over n interest periods.

The answer to Company F's building-fund question, using the shorthand notation, is as follows:

$$F = \$10k\left(\overset{F/A,11\%,10}{} \right)$$

$$= \$10k(16.722) = \$167.22k$$

Equal-Payment-Series Sinking-Fund (*A/F*)

In the same sense that single-payment compound-amount (F given P) and single-payment present-worth (P given F) are inverses of each other, equal-payment-series compound-amount (F given A) and equal-payment-series sinking-fund (A given F) are inverses of each other. This formula answers the question "what amount would need to be deposited or borrowed in n equal amounts at a given interest rate to be worth a desired amount immediately after the last payment?" The generic cash-flow diagram for this situation is shown in Figure 5.7. In this case, you know how much you want to end up with, and you are trying to find out how much to deposit each time.

Just down the street from Company F is another company who will build a new office building in 10 years, Gee Co. Gee Co.'s directors know that they want to have $500k at the start of building. They'd like to build up to that amount in small steps. They've found an investment that pays 11%. How much should they invest at the end of each year to end up with the $500k immediately after the last payment is made?

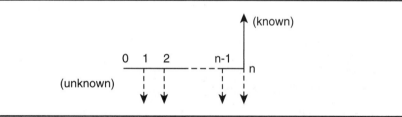

FIGURE 5.7 The generic cash-flow diagram for equal-payment-series sinking-fund (lender's view)

DERIVING THE FORMULA

The derivation simply starts with the equal-payment-series compound-amount (*F* given *A*) formula and rearranges it to solve for *A*.

$$A = F\left[\frac{i}{(1 + i)^n - 1}\right]$$

SOLVING THE SAMPLE PROBLEM

The answer to Gee Co.'s question in longhand is as follows:

$$A = \$500k\left[\frac{0.11}{(1 + 0.11)^{10} - 1}\right] = \$29.9k$$

At 11% interest, Gee Co. would need to deposit only $29.9k at the end of each of 10 years to have the $500k immediately after the last deposit.

THE SHORTHAND NOTATION AND TABLE-BASED SOLUTION

The shorthand notation for equal-payment-series sinking-fund shows the annuity, *A*, being calculated from the future value, *F* (*A* given *F*).

$$\left(\begin{array}{c} A/F,i,n \\ \end{array}\right)$$

The answer to Gee Co.'s question, using the shorthand notation, is as follows:

$$A = \$500k(\overset{A/F,11\%,10}{})$$

$$= \$500k(0.05980) = \$29.9k$$

Equal-Payment-Series Capital-Recovery (*A/P*)

In this situation, we are trying to figure out how much to pay, in a series of equal payments, to recover a given initial amount (*A* given *P*). More precisely, if a known amount is deposited or borrowed today at a given interest rate, how much of an equal payment over the next *n* periods will reduce the amount to zero immediately on the last payment? This is the standard formula for computing payments on a loan.

The generic cash-flow diagram for this situation is shown in Figure 5.8.

As an example problem, Hill Software wants to borrow $100k and pay it back in ten annual payments. They find a lender who will lend the money at 11% compound interest. What are their annual payments going to be?

DERIVING THE FORMULA

From the equal-payment-series sinking-fund (*A* given *F*) formula, we know the following:

$$A = F\left[\frac{i}{(1 + i)^n - 1}\right]$$

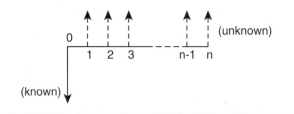

FIGURE 5.8   The generic cash-flow diagram for equal-payment-series capital-recovery (lender's view)

And, from the single-payment compound-amount (*F* given *P*) formula, we know the following:

$$F = P(1 + i)^n$$

Substituting for *F* in the equal-payment-series sinking-fund formula, we get the following:

$$A = P(1 + i)^n \left[\frac{i}{(1 + i)^n - 1} \right]$$

Rearranging

$$A = P \left[\frac{i(1 + i)^n}{(1 + i)^n - 1} \right]$$

The formula can also be written as follows:

$$A = P \left[\frac{i}{1 - (1 + i)^{n-1}} \right]$$

This second form has fewer terms, so it will be easier to compute when using a calculator.

SOLVING THE SAMPLE PROBLEM

Answering Hill Software's question in longhand form,

$$A = \$100k \left[\frac{0.11(1 + 0.11)^{10}}{(1 + 0.11)^{10} - 1} \right] = \$16.98k$$

Hill Software's annual payments on a $100k loan at 11% for 10 years would be $16.98k.

THE SHORTHAND NOTATION AND TABLE-BASED SOLUTION

The shorthand notation for this formula is as follows:

$$\left(\overset{A/P,i,n}{} \right)$$

The answer to Hill Software's question, using the shorthand notation, is as follows:

$$A = \$100k \left(\overset{A/P,11\%,10}{} \right)$$

$$= \$100k(0.16980) = \$16.98k$$

The next chapter shows how to calculate monthly payment amounts, early payoff amounts, and how to separate the interest part and the principal part of loan payments. Separating interest from principal is important when you are dealing with the effects of income taxes on business decisions (Chapter 16).

Equal-Payment-Series Present-Worth (*P/A*)

Equal-payment-series present-worth (*P* given *A*) is the inverse of equal-payment-series capital-recovery (*A* given *P*). In other words, how much money today would be equivalent to a future series of equal payments made over *n* periods at some interest rate? The generic cash-flow diagram for this situation is shown in Figure 5.9.

Irving Industries can afford ten annual payments of up to $100k each. They know they can borrow money from a lender who will take annual payments. If the lender is asking for 11% interest, what's the maximum amount they can borrow?

DERIVING THE FORMULA

Start with the equal-payment-series capital-recovery formula and rearrange it to solve for *P*:

$$P = A \left[\frac{(1 + i)^n - 1}{i(1 + i)^n} \right]$$

SOLVING THE SAMPLE PROBLEM

Answering Irving Industries' question in longhand form

$$P = \$100k \left[\frac{(1 + 0.11)^{10} - 1}{0.11(1 + 0.11)^{10}} \right] = \$588.9k$$

At 11% interest, Irving can only borrow $588.9k if the most they can pay is $100k annually for 10 years.

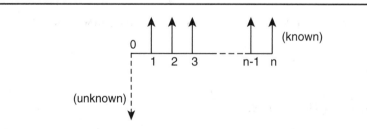

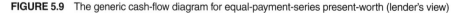

FIGURE 5.9 The generic cash-flow diagram for equal-payment-series present-worth (lender's view)

THE SHORTHAND NOTATION AND TABLE-BASED SOLUTION

The shorthand notation for this formula is as follows:

$$P/A,i,n$$
$$(\qquad)$$

The answer to Irving Industries' question, using the shorthand notation, is as follows:

$$P/A,11\%,10$$
$$A = \$100\text{k}(\qquad)$$

$$= \$100\text{k}(5.889) = \$588.9\text{k}$$

Summarizing the Formulas

Notice again how the formulas vary depending on whether you are calculating forward from a known present into an unknown future or you are calculating backward from a known, desired future into an unknown present situation. The formulas also vary depending on whether the cash-flow stream is a single-payment amount or equal-payment-series amounts. The decision process in Figure 5.10 can help you decide which interest formula to use in any given situation.

If you already have, or can visualize, the cash-flow diagram for the situation, you can also simply match it to the generic cash-flow diagrams in this chapter to find the appropriate interest formula.

Some Other Handy Relationships

The following relationships between the interest formulas may come in useful in some situations. Specifically, Relationship 2 is used in the next chapter on separating interest and principal for loan payments. These are provided for reference only.

$$F/P,i,n \qquad F/A,i,n$$
1. $(\qquad) = i\,(\qquad) + 1$

$$P/F,i,n \qquad P/A,i,n$$
2. $(\qquad) = 1 - (\qquad)\,i$

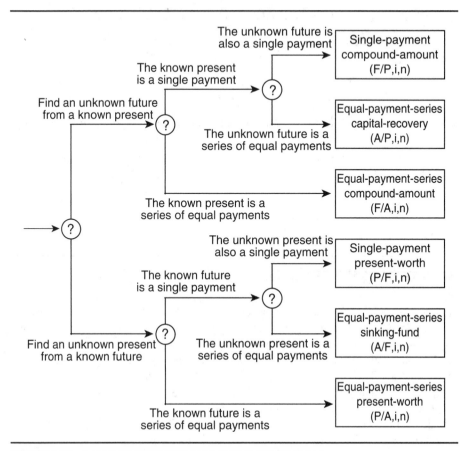

FIGURE 5.10 A guide for determining which interest formula to use

$$\overset{F/A,i,n}{3. \;(\quad)} = 1 + \overset{F/P,i,1}{(\quad)} + \overset{F/P,i,2}{(\quad)} + \ldots + \overset{F/P,i,n-1}{(\quad)}$$

$$\overset{A/F,i,n}{4. \;(\quad)} = \overset{A/P,i,n}{(\quad)} - i$$

$$\overset{P/A,i,n}{5. \;(\quad)} = \overset{P/F,i,1}{(\quad)} + \overset{P/F,i,2}{(\quad)} + \ldots + \overset{P/F,i,n-1}{(\quad)}$$

$$\overset{A/P,i,n}{6. \;(\quad)} = i \,/\, [\, 1 - \overset{P/F,i,n}{(\quad)} \,]$$

Summary

One of the most fundamental concepts in business decisions is that money has time value. A given amount of money at one point in time almost always has a different value than the same amount of money at some other time. Money's time value is quantified in terms of interest, which is literally a rental fee for money.

Under simple interest, the interest charge is directly proportional to the interest rate, the amount borrowed, and the duration of the loan. Simple interest is not available to a typical business.

The typical business loan uses compound interest, where unpaid interest is added to the principal amount of the loan. Literally, interest is paid on interest.

Six different compound interest equations were presented in this chapter:

- **Single-payment compound-amount**—How much is a given amount of money today going to be worth at some future point in time?
- **Single-payment present-worth**—How much is needed today to grow to some known, desired amount at a future point in time?
- **Equal-payment-series compound-amount**—How much will the total amount be worth at the end of a series of equal payments that are made at regular intervals?
- **Equal-payment-series sinking-fund**—If you want to end up with a known, desired amount at some future point, how much do you need to pay at fixed intervals to finish with that amount?
- **Equal-payment-series capital-recovery (the standard formula for a loan)**—If you borrow a known amount today, how much do you have to pay back as a series of equal payments to pay off the loan?
- **Equal-payment-series present-worth**—How much money is needed today to be worth the same as a known series of equal payments in the future?

The formulas in this chapter are appropriate for most typical business decisions. The next chapter explains some less-common situations that you also need to be able to work with.

Self-Study Questions

1. Find a financial institution, such as a bank or credit union, which offers both savings accounts and loans. What interest rate do they pay on a typical savings account? What interest rate do they charge for a typical loan? At those interest rates (assume simple interest for this question), if Company A deposits $10,000 for 1 year and the financial institution immediately loans that money to Company B for 1 year, how much money will the institution net over the year on that $10,000?

2. Queue Co. is lending $2500 to a neighboring business. The loan is for 7 years at 9% *simple* interest. Assuming the neighboring business repays the entire loan in a single payment at the end of the 7 years, how much money should Queue Co. expect to receive at that time?

3. Use the same situation from Question 2 (Queue Co.), but this time use *compound* interest:
    *   Draw the cash-flow diagram for this situation.
    *   Name the proper compound interest formula to apply to this problem.
    *   How much should Queue Co. expect to receive?
    *   Is this amount less than, the same as, or greater than the amount expected with simple interest? Why?
    *   Using the same format as Table 5-3, show the step-by-step calculation of the expected amount.

4. The software department at Clever U received a gift of $20,000 from a former student. They know that they will need to buy a new central computer for the department in 5 years and expect that computer to cost $25,000. Assume that they can find a financial institution that will pay 11% interest on a 5-year investment.
    *   Draw the cash-flow diagram that shows how to figure out how much Clever U's software department will need to invest to yield $25,000 in 5 years.
    *   Name the proper compound interest formula to apply to this problem.
    *   How much should the software department at Clever U deposit now to have $25,000 in 5 years?

5. Mr. and Mrs. S want to set up an account to pay for their child's tuition as the child enters a private school. Tuition will be a constant $2500 per year for 12 years (elementary, middle, and high school). Assume they can find a financial institution that will pay an annual interest rate of 11%. The first tuition payment is due 1 year from now.
    *   Draw the cash-flow diagram for this situation.
    *   Name the proper compound interest formula to apply to this problem.
    *   How much should they deposit now so that they can pay the $2500 tuition from the account, leaving the account exhausted following the last tuition payment?

6. Mr. George is thinking about getting a $20,000 second mortgage on his house to help him finance an after-hours software project so he can make some extra money outside of work. He is looking at a 5-year mortgage with fixed 12% (annual) interest. Assume this loan allows him to make annual payments.
    *   Draw the cash-flow diagram for this situation.
    *   Name the proper compound interest formula to apply to this problem.
    *   What will his annual payment be?

7. Pat is a 10-year-old computer hobbyist. She has a paper route that nets her $135 each month in profit and she wants to start saving to buy a new computer. Assume she can find a bank that pays 0.75% interest monthly, she will deposit the entire $135 at the end of each month, and she wants to buy the new computer at the end of 1 year.
    *   Draw the cash-flow diagram for this situation.
    *   Name the proper compound interest formula to apply to this problem.
    *   How much money will Pat have available to spend on her new computer after 1 year?

8. Repeat the same situation as in the previous question. This time, assume that Pat knows she wants to have exactly $1250 to spend on the computer at the end of the year.
    *   Draw the cash-flow diagram for this situation.
    *   Name the proper compound interest formula to apply to this problem.
    *   How much will Pat need to deposit each month?

9. Write a program, create a spreadsheet, or develop some other automated means of calculating a compound interest factor given one or more interest rates (including noninteger interest rates such as 4.7%) and one or more periods. You need to be able to generate values for each of the formulas in this chapter: single-payment present-worth (P/F), single-payment future-worth (F/P), and so on. One use of your resulting mechanism would be, for example, to calculate the (A/F, 4.7 %, 6) factor. Many of the self-study questions in the rest of the book call for compound interest factors, so make sure your mechanism is easy to use.

6

Other Interest(ing) Calculations

The formulas in Chapter 5 cover most decision-making situations where you need to work with interest, but you still need to be able to work with other situations. Among these are using different interest periods and compounding frequencies, cash-flow instances happening more and less frequently than compounding intervals, continuous compounding, determining actual interest rates, paying off loans early, and separating interest and principal in loan payments. Each of these topics is presented in this chapter. There is also a section describing how interest rates may not be what they seem.

Using Different Interest Periods and Compounding Frequencies

All the formulas in Chapter 5 require that the interest rate, i, be an actual interest rate per interest period, whatever that period happens to be—a day, a week, a month, a year, etc. Unless explicitly stated otherwise, the interest period and compounding frequency are both assumed to be 1 year. But interest rates could be quoted for any period and any compounding frequency: daily, weekly, monthly, quarterly, semiannually, etc. Someone could say, for instance, that the interest rate is 3.5% semiannually compounded weekly.

It might seem that an interest rate of 12% per year is the same as 1% per month, but it's not really that simple. If you deposit $1000 into an account with 12% interest per year, you should expect to end up with $1120 at the end of the year. If you deposited $1000 into an account with an interest rate of 1% per month, however, at the end of 12 months you would have the following:

$$F/P,1\%,12$$
$$F = \$1000\,(1.127) = \$1127$$

The extra $7 is due to monthly compounding: Interest earned each month is added to the principal and earns its own interest for the remainder of the year, and 12% per year compounded monthly is actually equal to 12.7% compounded annually.

A **nominal interest rate** is an annual interest rate that hasn't been adjusted for more or less frequent compounding. A nominal interest rate is calculated by multiplying an actual interest rate per compounding period by the number of compounding periods in 1 year. An actual interest rate of 8% semiannually is a nominal interest rate of 16% compounded semiannually. Similarly, an actual interest rate of 4% quarterly is a nominal interest rate of 16% compounded quarterly.

CONVERTING NOMINAL INTEREST RATES TO EFFECTIVE ANNUAL INTEREST RATES

An **effective annual interest rate** is an annual interest rate that has been adjusted for more or less frequent compounding. The effective annual interest rate is calculated using the following formula:

$$i = (1 + \frac{r}{m})^m - 1$$

Where
   i = effective annual interest rate
   r = nominal annual interest rate
   m = number of compounding periods in 1 year

A nominal interest rate of 16% compounded semiannually is an effective annual interest rate of

$$i = (1 + \frac{0.16}{2})^2 - 1 = 0.1664 = 16.64\%$$

A nominal interest rate of 16% compounded quarterly is an effective annual interest rate of

$$i = (1 + \frac{0.16}{4})^4 - 1 = 0.1669 = 16.99\%$$

Table 6.1 shows the effective annual interest rate for several nominal interest rates and compounding frequencies.

TABLE 6.1   Effective Annual Interest Rates for Various Nominal Interest Rates and Compounding Frequencies

Compounding Frequency	Compounding Periods per Year (m)	4%	5%	8%	10%	15%	20%
Annually	1	4.00	5.00	8.00	10.00	15.00	20.00
Semiannually	2	4.04	5.06	8.16	10.25	15.56	21.00
Quarterly	4	4.06	5.09	8.24	10.38	15.87	21.55
Bimonthly	6	4.07	5.11	8.27	10.43	15.97	21.74
Monthly	12	4.07	5.12	8.30	10.47	16.08	21.94
Weekly	52	4.08	5.12	8.32	10.51	16.16	22.09
Daily	356	4.08	5.13	8.33	10.52	16.18	22.13

CONVERTING EFFECTIVE ANNUAL INTEREST RATES TO NOMINAL INTEREST RATES

The formula for computing effective annual interest rates can be rearranged to solve for a nominal interest rate as follows:

$$r = m(\sqrt[m]{1 + i} - 1)$$

An effective annual interest rate of 6.5% converted to a nominal interest rate compounded quarterly is

$$r = 4(\sqrt[4]{1 + 0.065} - 1) = 0.0635 = 6.35\%$$

An effective annual interest rate of 6.5% converted to a nominal interest rate compounded monthly is

$$r = 12(\sqrt[12]{1 + 0.065} - 1) = 0.0631 = 6.31\%$$

CONVERTING BETWEEN ARBITRARY INTEREST PERIODS

The formula for computing effective annual interest rates can be generalized for converting a nominal interest rate with one compounding period into an effective interest rate over a different compounding period. The formula is

$$i = (1 + \frac{r}{m})^c - 1$$

Where

    i = actual interest rate over i's compounding period

    r = nominal interest rate

    m = number of compounding periods in r's interest period

    c = number of r's compounding periods in i's compounding period

A nominal interest rate of 4% semiannually (26 weeks) compounded weekly can be converted into an actual rate per quarter (13 weeks) as

$$i = (1 + \frac{0.04}{26})^{13} - 1 = 0.0202 = 2.02\%$$

A nominal interest rate of 13% annually (12 months) compounded monthly can be converted to an actual rate for a 2 year (24 month) interest and compounding period as

$$i = (1 + \frac{0.13}{12})^{24} - 1 = 0.2951 = 29.51\%$$

If the nominal interest rate's compounding period is the same as the actual interest rate's compounding period, then $c = 1$, so the formula simplifies to

$$i = \frac{r}{m}$$

A nominal interest rate of 12% annually compounded quarterly can be converted to an actual quarterly interest rate:

$$i = \frac{0.12}{4} = 0.03 = 3\%$$

The formula for converting nominal interest rates to effective interest rates can be rearranged to solve for a nominal interest rate, r, as follows:

$$r = m(\sqrt[c]{1 + i} - 1)$$

An actual interest rate of 4.7% quarterly can be converted to a nominal interest period of 1 year compounded semiannually (every half year):

$$r = 2(\sqrt[0.5]{1 + 0.047} - 1) = 0.1924 = 19.24\%$$

An actual rate of 18% annually can be converted to a nominal interest period of 6 months compounded daily:

$$r = 187.5(\sqrt[365]{1 + 0.18} - 1) = 0.085 = 8.5\%$$

If the actual interest rate's compounding period is the same as the nominal interest rate's compounding period, then $c = 1$, so the formula simplifies to

$r = i * m$

An actual interest rate of 2.5% quarterly can be converted to a nominal annual interest rate compounded quarterly as follows:

$r = 0.025 * 4 = 0.10 = 10\%$

ANNUAL PERCENTAGE RATES (APRs)

A nominal annual interest rate is commonly referred to as an **annual percentage rate**, or APR. In the United States, the Federal Truth in Lending Act of 1969 allows companies offering credit to quote an actual interest rate for any time period and compounding frequency as long as they quote the equivalent APR along with it. Here's a direct quote from a credit card statement:

> The daily periodic rate is .03397% . . . The corresponding annual percentage rate is 12.40%.

$$r = 365(\sqrt[1]{1 + 0.0003397} - 1) = 0.124 = 12.4\%$$

Requiring lenders to quote the APR prevents dishonest lenders from playing certain tricks with interest rates; one of those tricks is described in detail in the section "The 7% Plan" below. It also makes it a bit easier to compare one interest rate to another. As shown above, however, APRs and effective annual interest rates aren't the same. Table 6.1 really shows the effective annual interest rate for selected APRs with various compounding frequencies. APRs can't be properly compared unless they've been converted into effective annual interest rates: An APR of 17% compounded annually may seem higher than 16% compounded monthly, but it isn't: 17% compounded annually is an effective annual rate of 17%, whereas 16% compounded monthly is

$$r = (1 + \frac{0.016}{12})^{12} - 1 = 0.1723 = 17.23\%$$

Compounded monthly, 16% is actually a higher effective interest rate than 17% compounded annually. The decision maker needs to convert APRs and compounding frequencies into effective annual interest rates before making important interest rate decisions.

The Relationship Between Cash-Flow Instances and Compounding Interval

Whether you are talking about repaying a loan, putting money into a savings account, paying on and using a credit card (revolving credit), or moving money into or out of any interest-bearing fund, the relative timing of the cash-flow instances and the compounding period can have an effect on the interest—either paid or earned. For instance, money deposited in the middle of the month into an account with monthly compounding does not receive interest for the remaining half of that month.

Three different cases are discussed:

- Cash flow happens at the same time as compounding.
- Compounding happens more frequently than cash flow.
- Cash flow happens more frequently than compounding.

CASH FLOW HAPPENS AT THE SAME TIME AS COMPOUNDING

There aren't any special considerations in this case. This is the easiest case and uses all of the formulas exactly as already discussed. Consider a savings account with an APR of 7.5% compounded quarterly (7.52% effective annual interest rate). How much would be in the account at the end of the year if $1000 were deposited at the end of each of the next four quarters? With an APR of 7.5% compounded quarterly, the actual interest rate per quarter is

$$i = (1 + \frac{0.075}{4})^1 - 1 = 0.0188 = 1.88\%$$

The ending amount would be

$$\overset{F/A,1.88,4}{F = \$1000\ (4.1142)} = \$4114.20$$

COMPOUNDING HAPPENS MORE FREQUENTLY THAN CASH FLOW

In this case, the interest is being compounded more frequently than the cash-flow instances are happening. Consider a savings account with an APR of 7.5% compounded monthly (7.56% effective annual interest rate). How much would be in the account at the end of the year if $1000 were deposited into the account at the end of each of the next four quarters? The solution is to understand that the first deposit earns compound interest for nine interest periods, whereas the second deposit earns compound interest for six. The third deposit earns interest for three periods, and the final deposit doesn't earn any interest at all.

With an APR of 7.5% compounded monthly, the actual interest rate per month is

$$i = (1 + \frac{0.075}{12})^1 - 1 = 0.0063 = 0.63\%$$

The ending amount would be

$$\overset{F/P,0.63,9}{F = \$1000 \, (1.0582)} + \overset{F/P,0.63,6}{\$1000 \, (1.0384)} + \overset{F/P,0.63,3}{\$1000 \, (1.0190)} + \$1000 = \$4115.60$$

CASH FLOW HAPPENS MORE OFTEN THAN COMPOUNDING

Normally, interest is paid only on money that's been on deposit the full interest period. No interest is paid on money that's deposited or withdrawn during an interest period. In this case, the solution is to accumulate the deposits and withdrawals over each interest period and treat them as a single net deposit or withdrawal at the end of that period, after adding the interest on money in that account for the full interest period. The interest and cash-flow frequencies will now be the same and can be treated as shown above.

Figure 6.1 shows money put into and taken out of an account with an APR of 7.5% compounded quarterly. (Note that this is the same 7.52% effective annual interest rate, or 1.88% actual quarterly rate, as above.)

Figure 6.2 shows how the cash-flow instances have been accumulated over each quarterly compounding period.

The ending amount would be

$$\overset{F/P,1.88,3}{F = \$400 \, (1.0575)} - \overset{F/P,1.88,2}{\$275 \, (1.0380)} + \overset{F/P,1.88,1}{\$25 \, (1.0188)} + \$200 = \$363.02$$

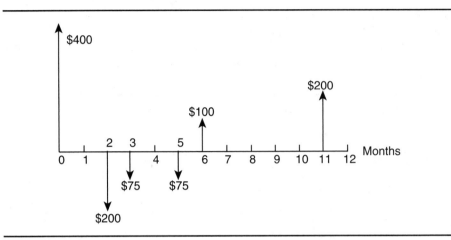

FIGURE 6.1   Cash flows more frequent than the quarterly interest periods

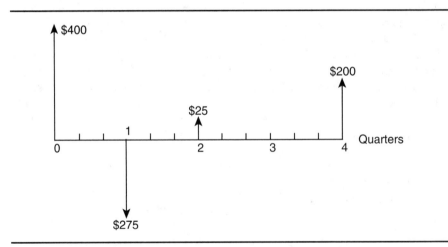

FIGURE 6.2   Cash flows accumulated to match the quarterly interest periods

Continuous Compounding, Discrete Payment

You may need to consider what happens when the compounding period approaches 0; in other words, the compounding occurs continuously (r = nominal interest rate per period, n = number of periods). These situations are relatively rare, so only the formulas are given below, not their derivations. A discussion of the derivations of these formulas can be found in [DeGarmo93], [Grant90], or [Thuesen93] if more information is needed.

SINGLE-PAYMENT COMPOUND-AMOUNT (F/P)

$$F = Pe^{rn}$$

SINGLE-PAYMENT PRESENT-WORTH (P/F)

$$P = F\left[\frac{1}{e^{rn}}\right]$$

EQUAL-PAYMENT-SERIES COMPOUND-AMOUNT (F/A)

$$P = A\left[\frac{e^{rn}-1}{e^{r}-1}\right]$$

EQUAL-PAYMENT-SERIES SINKING-FUND (A/F)

$$A = F\left[\frac{e^{r}-1}{e^{rn}-1}\right]$$

EQUAL-PAYMENT-SERIES CAPITAL-RECOVERY (A/P)

$$A = P\left[\frac{e^{r}-1}{1-e^{-rn}}\right]$$

EQUAL-PAYMENT-SERIES PRESENT-WORTH (P/A)

$$P = A\left[\frac{1-e^{-rn}}{e^{r}-1}\right]$$

To illustrate the difference between discrete and continuous compounding, consider a $1000 deposit at 9% annually for 7 years. Under discrete compounding

$$\overset{F/P,9\%,7}{F = \$1000\ (1.8280) = \$1828}$$

Under continuous compounding

$$F = \$1000 * e^{0.09} * {}^{7} = \$1878$$

The additional $50 is due to continuous compounding.

Determining Actual Interest Rates

So far we've been treating the interest rate, i, as a known amount. Sometimes you know everything else and you need to find i. Imagine, for instance, that SRS Software invested $12,345 in another company. Eight years later SRS Software sold that investment for $49,639. Asking the question, "What was the actual interest rate on their investment?" is the same as asking, "What would the interest rate at a bank need to have been to match this return on that investment?" The two approaches shown here only work for a single payment and a single income at some later time. The more general solution is shown in the next chapter in the section "Internal Rate of Return, IRR."

We know the values for P, F, and for n. Given the single-payment compound-amount formula

$$F = P(1 + i)^{n}$$

Substitute the known values into the following formula:

$$\$49,639 = \$12,345(1 + i)^{8}$$

In this equation, the unknown i is the actual interest rate that SRS Software got on their investment.

There are at least two ways to solve for i. One is to work backward from the interest tables, and the other is to rearrange the single-payment compound-amount (F/P) formula to compute i. Both of these are shown.

WORKING BACKWARD FROM THE INTEREST TABLES

Start by restating the equation as a table-based problem:

$$\$49{,}639 = \$12{,}345\ (\overset{F/P,i,8}{})$$

Solve for the interest factor:

$$(\overset{F/P,i,8}{}) = \frac{\$49{,}639}{\$12{,}345} = 4.021$$

Now, find the interest rate table where (F/P,i,8) is closest to 4.021. This is found in Table B-23, 19% Interest Factors, where the factor is 4.0214. The interest rate SRS Software realized was very close to 19%.

If, as another example, SRS Software ended up with \$47,553, the factor would be

$$(\overset{F/P,i,8}{}) = \frac{\$47{,}553}{\$12{,}345} = 3.852$$

This is between (F/P,18,8) = 3.759 and (F/P,19,8) = 4.021, so the interest rate would be somewhere between 18% and 19%. You can use linear interpolation if you need more accurate results. Linear interpolation is explained in detail in Appendix C. Using linear interpolation, the interest rate is 18.355%

Keep in mind that the interpolated result is really an approximation—the interest equation is nonlinear (curved). However, the equation isn't too far off of linear in these ranges. You'll usually end up with a more accurate result than if you just took the nearest rate from the tables. The real interest rate in this situation is 18.362%, so the interpolated result is only off by 0.007%. And, given that the cash-flow instances in the typical decision analysis will probably be estimates anyway, the inaccuracies introduced by the linear interpolation can usually be ignored safely.

SOLVING THE SINGLE-PAYMENT COMPOUND-AMOUNT FORMULA FOR *I*

Another way to find the interest rate is to rearrange the single-payment compound-amount (F/P,i,n) formula to compute *i*. Start with the original formula:

$$F = P(1 + i)^n$$

Rearrange the formula to solve for i:

$$i = \sqrt[n]{\frac{F}{P}} - 1$$

If you don't have a computer or calculator that gives nth root, but you do have logarithms and exponents, the nth root can be found using the following formula:

$$\sqrt[n]{X} = e^{\frac{\ln(X)}{n}} = \exp(\ln(X)/n)$$

Substitute the known values into the rearranged formula:

$$i = \sqrt[8]{\frac{\$49{,}639}{\$12{,}345}} - 1 = 0.19 = 19\%$$

Similarly, if SRS Software's cash-out was $47,553,

$$i = \sqrt[8]{\frac{\$47{,}553}{\$12{,}345}} - 1 = 0.18362 = 18.362\%$$

Paying off a Loan Through a Single, Lump-Sum Payment

Using the equal-payment-series capital-recovery (A/P,i,n) formula from the last chapter, you can find the payment amount for a loan given the amount borrowed, duration, and interest rate. However, loans don't always run for their full length. The borrower could decide to pay off the loan early if they wanted. The question in this case is, "How much would the borrower need to pay to make an early payoff?" This payoff amount is some-times called the unpaid balance, unrecovered balance, or principal owed.

Assume that SRS Software has a 5-year loan of $25,000 at an APR of 6% com-pounded monthly. According to the formula earlier in this chapter, the 6% APR in monthly terms is i = 6% / 12 = 0.5% per month. For a 5-year loan, there will be 12 * 5 = 60 monthly payments. So SRS Software's monthly loan payment amount is

A = $25,000 ($\overset{A/P,0.5\%,60}{\qquad}$)

= $25,000 (0.0193) = $482.50

Assuming that SRS Software wants to pay off the loan at the beginning of the thirty-seventh interest period, the unpaid balance is simply the equal-payment-series present-worth (P/A) of the remaining 24 payments (payments 37 through 60).

P = $482.50 ($\overset{P/A,0.5\%,24}{\qquad}$)

$$= \$482.50 \ (22.5629) = \$10,886.60$$

SRS Software would need \$10,886.60 to pay off the loan at the beginning of the thirty-seventh interest period. The general formula for the loan payoff amount is as follows:

$$P = A \left(\overset{P/A,i,n-t+1}{} \right)$$

Where

    P = the unpaid balance
    A = the periodic payment amount
    i = the actual interest rate per payment period
    n = the duration of the loan in interest periods
    t = the interest period at the beginning of which the loan is being paid off

Separating Interest and Principal in Loan Payments

When a business decision involves loans and income taxes at the same time, you need to be able to separate the principal part of the loan payments from the interest part because the interest payments are usually deductible but the principal payments aren't. Income taxes are discussed in detail in Chapters 16 and 17.

    Even though each of the loan payments is the same amount of money, early payments are more interest and less principal, whereas later payments are more principal and less interest. Figure 6.3 shows a cash-flow diagram annotated with the interest-to-principal profile for a \$1000, 8%, 10-year loan with annual payments.

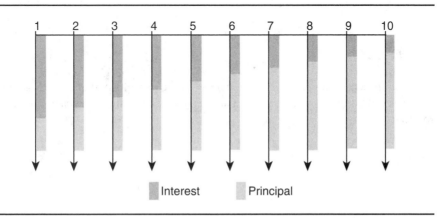

FIGURE 6.3 An interest-to-principal profile on an example loan

The term I_t will represent the part of the tth payment that's interest, and B_t will represent the part of the tth payment that goes to repaying the balance (principal). Each of the loan payments, A_t, will be $A_t = I_t + B_t$. Remember that although all A_t's are the same amount, the I_t's start out big and get smaller, whereas the B_t's start out small and get bigger.

The amount of interest owed at the end of the tth period can be calculated by just multiplying the unpaid balance (as described in the previous section) at the beginning of that period by the interest rate, i. So

$$I_t = A \left(\overset{P/A,i,n-t+1}{} \right) i$$

The rest of the tth payment, A, goes to paying off the principal. So B_t can be calculated as follows:

$$B_t = A - I_t = A - A \left(\overset{P/A,i,n-t+1}{} \right) i$$

$$= A \left[1 - \left(\overset{P/A,i,n-t+1}{} \right) i \right]$$

In the "Some Other Handy Relationships" section at the end of the last chapter, the second relationship is this:

$$\left(\overset{P/F,i,n}{} \right) = 1 - \left(\overset{P/A,i,n}{} \right) i$$

So

$$B_t = A \left(\overset{P/F,i,n-t+1}{} \right)$$

To illustrate separating principal and interest, consider the loan graphed in Figure 6-3, which is $1000 at 8% for 10 years, paid annually. The annual payments will be as follows:

$$A = \$1000 \left(\overset{A/P,8\%,10}{} \right)$$

$$= \$1000 \, (0.1490) = \$149$$

Table 6.2 shows the principal and interest payment profile for this loan. A spreadsheet that automates this calculation can be found at http://www.construx.com/returnonsw/.

TABLE 6.2   Separating Principal and Interest Payments for a Loan

End of Year	Loan Payment A	Principal Payment B_t	Interest Payment I_t
		P/F,8,10	
1	$149	$149 * (0.4632) = $69	$80
		P/F,8,9	
2	149	149 * (0.5002) = 75	74
		P/F,8,8	
3	149	149 * (0.5403) = 81	69
		P/F,8,7	
4	149	149 * (0.5835) = 87	62
		P/F,8,6	
5	149	149 * (0.6302) = 94	55
		P/F,8,5	
6	149	149 * (0.6806) = 101	48
		P/F,8,4	
7	149	149 * (0.7350) = 110	39
		P/F,8,3	
8	149	149 * (0.7938) = 118	31
		P/F,8,2	
9	149	149 * (0.8573) = 128	21
		P/F,8,1	
10	149	149 * (0.9259) = 138	11
Totals	$1490	$1000	$490

Each of the loan payments consists of an interest part and a principal part; the interest part starts out large and decreases over the life of the loan. Using this approach, loan interest payments can be separated so that they can be deducted from income taxes.

Paying Off a Loan Early Through Higher Payments

Instead of paying off a loan in one single lump-sum payoff amount, another alternative is for the borrower to pay more principal with each payment. The question could be phrased as, "If the loan payment were increased by x, how much sooner would the loan be paid off?"

Assuming that the loan is already partially paid off, the solution starts with the formula for calculating the loan-payoff amount described earlier. Because the payoff amount, P, is

$$P = A \left(\overset{P/A,i,n\text{-}t~1~1}{} \right)$$

Then it follows that

$$\frac{P}{A} = (P/A, i, n - t + 1)$$

The increased payment question can be phrased as finding the value of j when E is the amount of the payment increase. The value of j represents the unknown, reduced number of payments remaining on the loan.

$$\frac{P}{A + E} = (P/A, i, j)$$

SRS Software has a 9% APR loan with annual payments of $1423. SRS Software has 17 annual payments left and calculates their current payoff amount to be as follows:

$$P = \$1423 \left(\overset{P/A,9\%,17}{} \right)$$

$$= \$1423 \,(8.5436) = \$12{,}158$$

SRS Software management can afford to pay an extra $775 with each payment and wants to know how much sooner the loan would be paid off if they did:

$$\frac{\$12{,}158}{\$1423 + \$775} = (P/A, 9\%, j)$$

$$5.5314 = \left(\overset{P/A,9\%,j}{} \right)$$

Looking in the 9% Interest Factors table in Appendix B, this is very close to the equal-payment-series present-worth factor for 8 years. By increasing their payment by $775, SRS Software will pay off their loan 9 years sooner.

The value of P/(A + E) will usually be in between factors in the table. If the factor were between, say (P/A,i,14) and (P/A,i,15), the total number of payments remaining is 15. The first 14 of the payments will be the full (A + E) amount, and the final payment would be less than A + E. If it is important to calculate the final payment amount, it will be as follows:

$$Pl = (Pf - Pj) * (\overset{F/P,i,1}{})$$

Where
  Pl = the amount of the final payment
  Pf = the current loan payoff amount
  Pj = the present value of the equal series of full (A + E) payments (using the smaller j):

$$Pj = (A + E) * (\overset{P/A,i,j}{})$$

As a complete example, Bee Co. financed buying their office building with a $125,000 loan at 12% APR compounded monthly for 30 years. Bee Co.'s loan payment (principal and interest only, not including taxes or insurance) is as follows:

$$A = \$125,000 (\overset{A/P,0.5\%,360}{})$$

$$= \$125,000 (0.005995505) = \$749.44$$

Assume that 6 years (72 payments) into the loan, Bee Co. starts thinking about increasing their monthly payment by $200. They want to know how much sooner their loan would be paid off if they increase their payment beginning in the seventy-third interest period.

Bee Co. calculates their current payoff amount as

$$P = \$749.44 (\overset{P/A,0.5\%,289}{})$$

$$= \$749.44 (152.6807) = \$114,425.02$$

So Bee Co.'s question involves finding the j, where

$$\frac{\$114{,}425.02}{\$749.44 + \$200.00} = (P/A, 0.5\%, j)$$

$$120.5184 = (\overset{P/A, 0.5\%, j}{\quad\quad\quad})$$

Using an interest factor calculator—e.g., the interest table spreadsheet available at http://www.construx.com/returnonsw/, Bee Co. finds that

$$120.5107 = (\overset{P/A, 0.5\%, 185}{\quad\quad\quad})$$

$$120.9062 = (\overset{P/A, 0.5\%, 186}{\quad\quad\quad})$$

Bee Co.'s loan would be paid off after 186 payments if they pay an extra $200 each month. This means they would pay off the loan in 15 years and 6 months, which is 7 years and 6 months sooner than if they stay with the original payment schedule. Their next 185 payments would be the full $949.44, but the final payment would be less. Their 185 increased payments would have a present value of

$$P = \$949.44\,(\overset{P/A, 0.5\%, 185}{120.5107}) = \$114{,}417.68$$

So their final payment would be

$$= (\$114{,}425.02 - \$114{,}417.68) * (\overset{F/P, 0.5\%, 1}{\quad\quad\quad})$$

$$= \$7.34 * (1.0050) = \$7.38$$

Interest Rates Might Not Be What They Seem

Two different tricks for hiding the true interest rate are shown in this section. One of the tricks is to hide costs from the borrower. The other trick is having the borrower pay interest on already repaid principal.

HIDDEN COSTS: DIFFERENCES BETWEEN CASH AND CREDIT PRICES

The owner of a midrange computer is trying to sell it for $44,000. The owner is willing to finance the sale for $8800 (20%) down and the remaining $35,200 at an effective annual rate of 8% for 15 years. The owner also requires $1200 in various loan-origination fees.

The monthly payment on the loan (principal and interest only, not including taxes and insurance) can be calculated as follows:

$$i = (1 + \frac{0.08}{1})^{\frac{1}{12}} - 1 = 0.0064 = 0.64\%$$

$$A = \$35,200 \; (\overset{A/P,0.64\%,180}{\qquad\qquad})$$

$$= \$35,200 \, (0.009373) = \$329.93$$

In talking with the seller, a prospective buyer finds that the seller is also willing to take $41,000 cash for the computer.

Notice that a cash buyer pays a flat $41,000 and is done with the transaction, whereas a credit buyer pays $10,000 now (down payment plus loan-origination fees) followed by $329.93 monthly for 15 years. The 180 monthly payments are really the alternative to paying $41,000 now (not $44,000 now), meaning that the avoided immediate payment is actually

$$\$41,000 - \$10,000 = \$31,000$$

To find the real cost of money for the credit buyer, we need to find the interest rate that makes 180 monthly payments of $329.93 equal to the $31,000 the credit buyer is avoiding.

$$\$329.93 \, (P/A,i,180) = \$31,000$$

$$(P/A,i,180) = \frac{\$31,000}{\$329.93} = 93.959$$

Using a loan calculator, for example, we can find that

(P/A,0.80%,180) = 95.2139

(P/A,0.85%,180) = 92.0070

The actual interest rate is between 0.80% and 0.85% per month. By interpolation, it can be calculated to be 0.8196% monthly. Converting the monthly rate back into an effective annual interest rate

$$r = 12(\sqrt[1]{1 + 0.008196} - 1) = 0.0984 = 9.84\%$$

What originally looked like an 8% loan is really at 9.84%. Where did the higher interest come from? The trick here is in two places. One place is the various loan-origination fees; these add to the effective amount that the credit buyer is paying—the cash buyer doesn't pay these at all. The other is that the cash buyer can get the computer at a lower price. The combined effect is that what looks like an 8% loan on $35,200 turns out to really be a 9.84% loan on $31,000.

THE 7% PLAN: PAYING INTEREST ON REPAID PRINCIPAL

Before the Federal Truth in Lending Act of 1969, companies in the United States could quote interest rates in whatever terms they wanted. Some companies took advantage of this by quoting what looked like good interest rates but that actually turned out to be much higher. An example of this is the 7% plan. Under one variation of this plan, the loan company offers to add 7% to the original loan amount on a 1-year loan and have the borrower pay one twelfth of that total each month.

A $5000 loan would have a total payback amount of

$5000 + 7% of $5000 = $5350

This is a monthly payment of

$$\frac{\$5350}{12} = \$445.83 \text{ per month}$$

Given the terms above it might seem like a safe assumption that the actual annual interest rate is 7%, or at least fairly close to that. This turns out not to be true at all. To solve for the actual annual interest rate, start with

P = $5000

n = 12

$A = \$445.83$

The single-payment capital-recovery (A/P,i,n) factor can be calculated as follows:

$$(A/P,i,12) = \frac{A}{P} = \frac{\$445.83}{\$5000} = 0.08917$$

Looking into the interest tables we find that

$$(A/P,1\%,12) = 0.0888$$

$$(A/P,1.5\%,12) = 0.0917$$

So the actual interest rate per month is between 1% and 1.5%. Interpolating (Appendix C) gives an actual interest rate of 1.057% per month. Converting the actual interest rate per month to an annual rate

$$r = 1(\sqrt[12]{1 + 0.01057} - 1) = 0.1268 = 12.68\%$$

The APR is a lot higher than the borrower probably thought. It's much closer to 13% than to 7%. Why? The trick here is that the original interest calculation (7% of the loan amount) is the right calculation if the borrower isn't paying back any of the loan principal until the end of the loan. But, remembering Figure 6-3, each monthly payment is supposed to pay off some of the principal so that the total interest owed should be less than 7% of the principal. Following this plan, the borrower is essentially continuing to pay interest on money already repaid.

If the actual annual interest rate were really 7%, the monthly interest rate would be

$$i = (1 + \frac{0.07}{1})^{\frac{1}{12}} - 1 = 0.0057 = 0.57\%$$

So the actual monthly payment would be

$$A = \$5000 \ (\overset{A/P,0.57\%,12}{\qquad\qquad})$$

$$= \$5000 \ (0.0865) = \$432.50$$

The correct monthly payment is $13.33 less than what the so-called 7% plan asked for.

Summary

The formulas in Chapter 5 are appropriate for most typical business decisions. This chapter explained some less-common situations that you also need to be able to work with. This chapter covered the following major topics:

- Converting between nominal and effective interest rates to address arbitrary interest periods and compounding frequencies.
- Handling cash flows at frequencies longer, equal to, or shorter than the interest-compounding period.
- Formulas for working with continuous compounding of interest.
- Determining actual interest rates when all the other factors are known but the interest rate, i, is not.
- Calculating loan-payoff amounts and computing the effect of increasing the amount paid on each loan payment.
- Separating principal and interest from loan payments to prepare for calculating an after-tax cash-flow stream.
- The interest rate stated by a lender might not always be an accurate statement of the true interest the borrower is paying.

The next chapter extends the ideas from these last two chapters into the concept of equivalence. Equivalence is the starting point for comparing different cash-flow streams to be able to find which one is best for the business.

Self-Study Questions

1. What is the effective annual interest rate when the nominal annual interest rate is 7% compounded monthly?

2. What is the effective annual interest rate when the nominal annual interest rate is 13% compounded quarterly?

3. What is the nominal annual interest rate when the effective annual interest rate is 7% compounded monthly?

4. What is the nominal annual interest rate when the effective annual interest rate is 13% compounded quarterly?

5. What is the actual rate per month when the nominal interest rate is 5% semiannually compounded weekly?

6. What is the actual rate per quarter when the nominal interest rate is 8.5% annually compounded monthly?

7. What is the nominal rate per quarter compounded weekly when the actual interest rate is 2.54% per month?

8. What is the nominal rate over six months compounded monthly when the actual interest rate is 15.4% per year?

9. New Software is buying a new computer and getting a loan to help pay for it. The loan has an APR of 7.8% with monthly payments (i.e., compounded monthly). What is the effective monthly interest rate? If the amount borrowed is $25,000 and the term is 5 years, what is New Software's monthly payment?

10. FunSoft, a startup games-development company, just bought a new office building. Their mortgage has an APR of 9.3% with monthly payments (i.e., compounded monthly). What is their effective monthly interest rate? If the amount borrowed is $147,500 and the term is 15 years, what is FunSoft's monthly payment (principal and interest, not including taxes and insurance)? If FunSoft had gotten a 30-year loan instead, what would their monthly payment have been?

Questions 11 through 14 relate to this situation: TeeSoft opened a savings account at their local bank on February 1. The history of their transactions is shown in the following table. Assume there are exactly four weeks in each month and round all calculations to the nearest penny.

Date	Amount
February 1	$5000
April 1	–$2325
May 1	$1788
July 1	–$457
September 1	$2102
November 1	$506

11. If TeeSoft's savings account has an interest rate of 6.6% APR compounded weekly, how much would be in the account at the close of business on July 1?

12. If TeeSoft's savings account has an interest rate of 7.6% APR compounded weekly, how much would be in the account at the close of business on July 1?

13. Using the same information in Question 12, how much would be in TeeSoft's savings account at the close of business on September 1?

14. If TeeSoft's savings account has an interest rate of 6.6% APR compounded quarterly, how much would be in the account on January 1 of the following year?

15. TeeSoft invests $16,000 in another company. After 12 years they sell their ownership in that company for $64,000. What was the actual interest rate on TeeSoft's investment?

16. Multisoft, Inc. buys an office building in a growing area. They pay $14,250,000 for the building. After using it for 3 years they sell the building for $17,500,000. What was the actual interest rate on Multisoft's investment in the building?

17. In an earlier question, New Software bought a computer by borrowing $25,000 for 5 years at 7.8% APR compounded monthly. If New Software wanted to pay off the loan in a single lump payment after making normal payments for 2 years and 3 months, how much would their payoff amount be?

18. Assuming that New Software didn't pay off their loan early, how much of their second payment would be interest? How much of their last payment would be interest?

19. If New Software decided to pay an additional $100 with every payment beginning with the first, how much earlier would their loan be paid off?

20. If New Software did pay the additional $100 with every payment, how much would their final payment be?

21. In an earlier question, FunSoft bought an office building by borrowing $147,500 for 15 years at 9.3% APR compounded monthly. After using that office building for 6 years and 7 months, FunSoft is looking at buying a different building. What is the payoff amount on their current loan?

22. Construct a loan amortization table, similar to the one shown in Table 6-2, showing the principal and interest separated for the first 6 months of FunSoft's loan.

23. If FunSoft decided to pay an additional $250 with every payment, how much earlier would their loan be paid off?

24. If FunSoft did pay the additional $250 with every payment, how much would their final payment be?

25. Write a program that takes a loan amount, periodic interest rate, and number of payments as input and prints out a loan amortization table similar to the one shown in Table 6-2.

26. If the 7% plan discussed in this chapter were changed to cover a 2-year loan period, what would the total payback amount be? What would the monthly payment be? What would the actual annual interest rate be? Use a $5000 loan as the example in your calculations.

7

Equivalence

As long as the interest rate is not 0%, a given amount of money right now doesn't have the same value as that same amount of money at some other point in time. So it isn't trivial to compare an amount of money at one point in time to an amount of money at some other time. How do we know whether these two amounts of money at these two different times have the same value? How do we find out if they are **equivalent**? The notion of equivalence is key to making business decisions. If one amount of money at one time is the financial view of one proposal and the other amount of money at another time is the financial view of another proposal, how do we choose between them? If they are worth equivalent amounts then, financially, it doesn't make a difference which one we choose. If they aren't worth equivalent amounts, however, we need to know which one is worth more because that's the one that's better for the business.

A Simple Comparison of Two Proposals

The last two chapters showed how interest over time affects the value of money. This means that a cash-flow instance at one point in time doesn't have the same value as an equal-amount cash-flow instance at some other point in time. Because it's hard to compare individual cash-flow instances, it is even harder to compare cash-flow streams. It's not a simple job to compare different cash-flow streams and figure out whether they are equal or not. Or, more importantly, if they aren't equal, then which is better?

TABLE 7.1 The Cash-Flow Stream for Two Different Purchase Proposals

End of year	$7500 today	$1000 over 10 years
0	$7500	$0
1	$0	$1000
2	$0	$1000
3	$0	$1000
4	$0	$1000
5	$0	$1000
6	$0	$1000
7	$0	$1000
8	$0	$1000
9	$0	$1000
10	$0	$1000
Apparent total income	$7500	$10,000

Imagine that Mountain Software receives an offer from one of its customers. That customer offers to buy one of Mountain Software's products at the full price of $7500 today. The customer also offers instead to pay for that same product in $1000 annual payments at the end of each of the next 10 years. As shown in Table 7.1, this looks like a simple choice between $7500 now and $10,000 later. Stated in these terms, it seems like the $1000-each-year proposal is better by $2500.

But this simple analysis incorrectly assumes an interest rate of 0%. The interest rate is rarely ever 0%. If Mountain Software chooses the $7500 today, they could put the money into a savings account or some other interest-earning investment. What would it be worth after those same 10 years? If we use a more realistic interest rate, say 8%, the real story is a lot different and the better proposal becomes obvious.

The $7500 today proposal has a **present worth** of $7500. (The term *present worth* is defined more completely in Chapter 8.) The $1000-for-the-next-10-years proposal can be converted into a present worth using the equal-payment-series present-worth (P/A) factor:

$$P = \$1000 \left(\overset{P/A, 8\%, 10}{} \right)$$

$$= \$1000 \, (6.7101) = \$6710.10$$

The time value of money causes the $7500 today to be a much better choice. Looking at it another way, the $7500 today can be converted into equivalent equal-payments-over-the-next-10-years terms using the equal-payment capital-recovery (A/P) formula:

$$A = \$7500 \ (\overset{A/P,8\%,10}{\qquad})$$

$$= \$7500 \ (0.1490) \ = \$1117.50$$

When these two proposals are compared in consistent terms—using a realistic interest rate and making the comparison in identical time frames—the real difference is obvious. This is the essence of **equivalence**.

> Two or more different cash-flow instances (or cash-flow streams) are equivalent at a given interest rate only when they equal the same amount of money at a common point in time. More specifically, comparing two different cash flows makes sense only when they are expressed in the same time frame.

If two cash flows (instances or streams) are equivalent in one time frame, they are equivalent in all time frames. Two or more cash flows that are equivalent today are also equivalent a year from now or at any other point in time. And they would still be equivalent if they were both spread out as equal payments over some common time period.

Why is equivalence important? Equivalence (or, more appropriately, the lack of equivalence) is at the root of business decision making. If two different proposals turn out to be equivalent, then—purely economically speaking—it doesn't matter which one is chosen. Either one will have the same financial effect on the business. However, finding out that one proposal is better than the other in some common time frame means that the better proposal is always better in every time frame.

This once-better-always-better principle was illustrated in the Mountain Software example. At 8% interest, the $7500 today proposal is better than the $1000-per-year-over-10-years proposal in both present-worth terms ($7500 vs. $6710.10) and in equal-payments-over-10-years terms ($1117.50 vs. $1000).

Simple Equivalence

The interest rate formulas shown in Chapter 5 are actually statements of simple equivalence. The single-payment compound-amount (F/P) formula

$$F = P(1 + i)^n$$

means that at interest rate i, the amount of money P at some point in time is equivalent to the amount of money F at another point in time n interest periods later. If someone thinks that the interest rate, i, was fair, he shouldn't care if he receives P dollars now or F dollars n interest periods from now. If he thinks the interest rate, i, is too low, he would probably rather have the P dollars now. Conversely, if he thinks that the interest rate is too high, he'd probably rather wait and get the F dollars later. The other forms are also expressions of equivalence:

- Single-payment present-worth (P/F)
- Equal-payment-series compound-amount (F/A)
- Equal-payment-series sinking-fund (A/F)
- Equal-payment-series capital-recovery (A/P)
- Equal-payment-series present-worth (P/A)

SIMPLE EQUIVALENCE IN ACTION

In the United States, most state lottery jackpot payoffs come in 20 equal payments adding up to the jackpot amount. A $5 million jackpot is paid as 20 annual payments of $250,000 each. Remember, however, that this analysis is improperly assuming an interest rate of 0%. What happens when we use a more realistic interest rate? Assuming a $5 million payoff with 9% interest, the actual value of the prize in present day terms is as follows:

$$P = \$250K \left(\overset{P/A,9\%,20}{\qquad} \right)$$

$$= \$250K \ (9.1286) = \$2,282,150$$

The state can make the $250k annual payments for 20 years by investing $2,282,150 into an interest-bearing account at 9%. The jackpot is actually worth a lot less than you may have thought.

Equivalence with Varying Cash-Flow Instances

The idea of equivalence at the level of cash-flow instances can be extended to an entire cash-flow stream. Each of the cash-flow instances in the stream can be translated to a common reference time frame where they can be added together and given a single equivalent-to-the-entire-cash-flow-stream amount. Entire cash-flow streams can be translated into equivalent-in-some-other-time-frame terms.

There are two approaches for translating an entire cash-flow stream: an elegant approach and a brute-force approach. The elegant approach works better when the translation is being done by hand, but it tends to be too sophisticated for automation. The brute-force approach is easy to automate but usually takes too many computations if done by hand. The elegant approach is shown first.

THE ELEGANT APPROACH TO EQUIVALENCE

For the elegant approach, follow these steps:

1. Choose the reference time frame. Typically, the reference time frame is the very beginning of the cash-flow stream, but the reference time frame could be the end of the cash-flow stream or even be spread (as equal payments) over some number of interest periods.

2. Break the cash-flow stream into segments that can be handled by the formulas in Chapter 5.

3. For each segment, apply the appropriate formula to translate it into the reference time frame. This may require more than one step using more than one formula.

4. Sum up all the results (adding income, subtracting payments). The final amount represents the net equivalent value of the cash-flow stream in terms of the reference time frame.

Figure 7.1 shows a series of end-of-year net cash-flow instances over a 15-year period along with a picture of the computations that calculate that cash-flow stream's equivalent value. Assume the interest rate is 12%. The steps taken in computing the equivalent value are discussed in order.

For Step 1, arbitrarily choose the beginning of the cash-flow stream (end of period 0) as the reference time frame. We could have chosen any reference time frame, but the beginning of the stream is the most common.

For Step 2, notice that the cash-flow stream breaks nicely into 4 separate segments, a single income at the end of period 3, a series of 5 equal incomes spanning periods 6 through

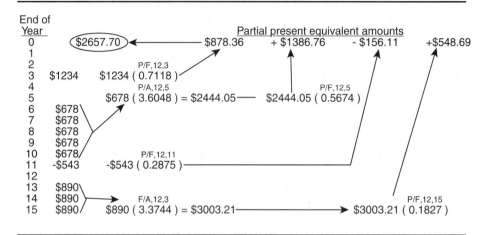

FIGURE 7.1   The elegant approach to finding an equivalent value for a cash-flow stream

10, a single payment at the end of period 11, and another series of 3 equal incomes finishing at the end of period 15.

For Step 3, take each separate segment and translate it into end-of-period-0 terms. The $1234 in period 3 is easily translated by applying the single-payment present-worth factor for 12% and 3 years (P/F,12,3). The series of five $678 incomes takes two calculations to translate. First, the equal-payment-series present-worth factor (P/A,12,5) translates the series into an equivalent value at the end of period 5 and then the (P/F,12,5) factor translates that to the end of period 0. The $543 payment at the end of period 11 is translated simply by using the (P/F,12,11) factor. Finally, the series of three $890 incomes can be translated to end-of-period-15 terms by applying the equal-payment-series sinking-fund (F/A,12,3) factor. This is then translated to end-of-period-0 using the (P/F,12,15) factor.

We could have used the (P/A,12,3) factor to translate the final segment to end-of-period-12 terms and then translate that value to end-of-period-0 terms using the (P/F,12,12) factor. The end result would be the same.

In Step 4, just add up the end-of-year-0 equivalent amounts for each of the original segments, giving a total of $2657.70. When the interest rate is 9%, the cash-flow stream in Figure 7.1 is financially equivalent to a single income of $2657.70 at the end of period 0.

THE BRUTE-FORCE APPROACH TO EQUIVALENCE

The brute-force approach simply translates each individual cash-flow instance directly into the reference time frame using the single-payment compound amount (P/F,i,n) formula. This is shown in Table 7.2.

TABLE 7.2 The Brute-Force Approach for Finding an Equivalent Value for a Cash-Flow Stream

Year, n	Net Cash Flow at End of Year n	Present-Worth Factor, (P/F,12,n)	Equivalent Value at End of Year 0
1	$0	0.8929	$0
2	$0	0.7972	$0
3	$1234	0.7118	$878.36
4	$0	0.6355	$0
5	$0	0.5674	$0
6	$678	0.5066	$343.47
7	$678	0.4523	$306.66
8	$678	0.4039	$273.84
9	$678	0.3606	$244.49
10	$678	0.3220	$218.32
11	−$543	0.2875	−$156.11
12	$0	0.2567	$0
13	$890	0.2292	$203.99
14	$890	0.2046	$182.09
15	$890	0.1827	$162.60
		Total	$2657.71

There's $0.01 difference between this answer and the elegant approach, which is due to rounding errors in the various present-worth factors.

The elegant approach works well for calculations done by hand; it takes fewer math operations. The brute-force version is better for computer-based computations because the algorithms involved in pattern matching to decide how to break up the cash-flow stream would probably take many more calculations than the less-elegant, but straightforward approach.

Equivalence Under Different Interest Rates

The previous section showed how to translate a cash-flow stream under a single interest rate. Usually this will be enough. Although we can be sure that the interest rate will change over time, most business decision analyses just use a single representative "nominal," or average interest rate over the whole study period. On occasion, however, you may need to deal with more than one interest rate over the life of a proposal. This section shows how to handle different interest rates within a time frame.

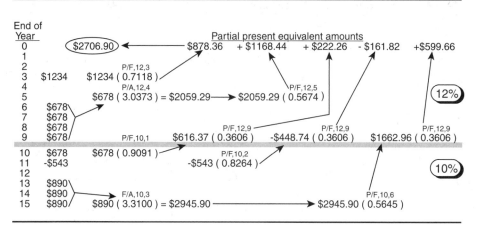

FIGURE 7.2   The elegant approach under multiple interest rates

Simply put, as the cash-flow instances are being translated, you need to remember to use the appropriate interest rate in the computations. Follow the same process as above within each constant interest rate time frame. Just be careful to use that appropriate interest rate. Apply the new interest rate as you cross boundaries from one interest rate time frame to another.

Figure 7.2 shows how this is done for the same cash-flow stream as in Figure 7.1. This time, assume that 12% interest applies through period 9 and 10% interest applies for the rest of the study.

Notice how the interest rate change going into period 10 breaks up the $678 series. The last cash-flow instance in that series needs to be treated separately. All the cash-flow instances in the 12% interest rate region are handled using the same elegant approach shown above. (Note how the first four in the $678 series are translated using the (P/A,12,4) factor.)

The flows in the 10% interest rate region are first translated into end-of-period-9 terms, which is end-of-period-0 from the perspective of the 10% interest rate region. These intermediate values are then translated into end-of-real-year-0 terms using the single-payment present-worth factor at 12% interest over the 9 years (P/F,12,9). The last step is to add up all the end-of-year-0 values. Alternatively, the beginning-of-the-10%-region values could have been added there and that sum could have been translated into end-of-period-0 terms using the (P/F,12,9) factor and added to the rest.

The brute-force approach is similar to what was shown in the single interest rate discussion above. Just start with any given constant interest rate zone and work back to relative end-of-period-0 terms. This is shown in Tables 7.3 and 7.4 for the 12% and 10% interest rate regions, respectively.

TABLE 7.3   The Brute-Force Approach in the 12% Interest Rate Region

Year, n	Net Cash Flow at End of Year n	Present-Worth Factor, (P/F,12,n)	Equivalent Value at End of Year 0
1	$0	0.8929	$0
2	$0	0.7972	$0
3	$1234	0.7118	$878.36
4	$0	0.6355	$0
5	$0	0.5674	$0
6	$678	0.5066	$343.47
7	$678	0.4523	$306.66
8	$678	0.4039	$273.84
9	$678	0.3606	$244.49
		Total	$2046.82

TABLE 7.4   The Brute-Force Approach in the 10% Interest Rate Region

Year, n	Net Cash Flow at End of Year n	Present-Worth Factor, (P/F,10,n)	Equivalent Value at End of Year 0
1 (10)	$678	0.9091	$616.37
2 (11)	−$543	0.8264	−$448.74
3 (12)	$0	0.7513	$0
4 (13)	$890	0.6830	$607.87
5 (14)	$890	0.6209	$552.60
6 (15)	$890	0.5645	$502.41
		Total	$1830.51

The $1830.51 is in the end-of-period-9 time frame for the whole cash-flow stream, so it needs to be translated back to end-of-period-0 using the (P/F,12,9) factor of 0.3606 for a value of $660.08. Now it can be added to the Table 7.3 sum of $2046.82 for a total of $2706.90, the same answer as in Figure 7.2.

If it actually turned out that the end-of-period-0 for the 12% interest rate range was really a part of an even larger cash-flow stream with more interest rate regions, the grand total $2706.90 could be translated appropriately to add it to the totals from any other interest rate region(s) and the entire process shown here could be repeated.

Summary

When the interest rate is not 0%—and it rarely, if ever, is—comparing one cash-flow stream to another is much more difficult than just adding up the cash-flow instances in each stream and comparing the sum.

The interest formulas in Chapter 5 are essentially statements of "simple equivalence": An amount of money in one time frame can be converted into an equivalent amount of money in a different time frame. When there is more than one cash-flow instance in a cash-flow stream, finding equivalence is more complex. Each separate cash-flow instance needs to be converted into a common time frame.

If a cash-flow stream spans different interest rate time periods, the conversion is even more complex because you need to account for the different interest rates in the different time periods.

The next chapter introduces a set of bases for comparison. These are standard ways of characterizing cash-flow streams so that they can be easily compared. The standard bases for comparison include present worth, internal rate of return, and discounted payback period.

Self-Study Questions

1. Given the following cash-flow stream, use equivalence to calculate the value of the cash flow at the end of year 0. Use a constant 6% interest rate over the entire cash-flow stream. Round all results to the nearest whole dollar.

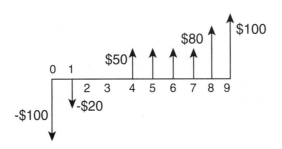

2. Use the same cash-flow stream as in the previous question, but this time the interest rate for years 0 through 2 is 6% and the interest rate for years 3 through 9 is 8%. Use equivalence to calculate the value of the cash flow at the end of year 0. Round all results to the nearest whole dollar.

3. Given the following cash-flow stream, use equivalence to calculate the value of the cash flow at the end of year 0. Assume a constant 7% interest rate over the entire cash flow. Round all results to the nearest whole dollar.

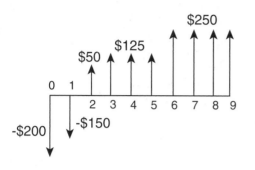

4. Use the same cash-flow stream as in the previous question, but this time the interest rate for years 0 through 3 is 6% and the interest rate for years 4 through 9 is 8%. Use equivalence to calculate the value of the cash-flow stream at the end of year 0. Round all results to the nearest whole dollar.

5. The example in Figure 7.1 showed the cash-flow instances in periods 13, 14, and 15 being equivalenced to the end of period 15 using the (F/A,12,3) factor and then being equivalenced to the end of year 0 using the (P/F,12,15) factor. Show that equivalencing these same three cash-flow instances to the end of year 12 and then equivalencing that to the end of year 0 leads to the same result.

6. A nationwide fast-food restaurant chain offers a $1,000,000 grand prize in a contest. The fine print for the contest says, "The grand prize is payable in $50,000 installments over 20 years." At an interest rate of 8%, what is the equivalent amount the fast-food chain needs to invest to make those payments to the contest winner?

7. A couple wins the mega-prize in a multistate lottery. They are given the choice between 30 annual payments of $3.69 million ($110.75 million total payout) or a one-time lump sum of $60.1 million. Use linear interpolation to find, to the nearest 1/10th of a percent, what interest rate the lottery authority is using.

Questions 8 through 12 relate to the following situation: SaylorSoft has decided to buy a new computer and even decided which model to buy. They just haven't decided whom to buy it from. The computer costs $20,000 including taxes, delivery, installation, etc. They can't afford to pay cash, so they are considering a 5-year loan at 6% APR. In an effort to get SaylorSoft's business, one dealer offers a choice of a 5-year loan at 0% interest or $2500 cash back. Assume the dealer requires a down payment of $1000 in either case.

8. What would SaylorSoft's monthly payments be if they choose the 0% loan option?

9. If SaylorSoft uses a business interest rate of 3%, what is the present-day equivalent of the loan payments in the previous question?

10. Assuming SaylorSoft chooses the cash-back option, uses $1000 of the cash for the down payment, and keeps the remaining amount for other uses, what would their monthly payments be if they choose the 6% loan option?

11. Using their business interest rate of 3% APR, what is the present-day equivalent of the loan payments in the previous question?

12. Taking into account that SaylorSoft has $1500 left over if they choose the cash-back option, which option is better in present-day terms? Why?

8

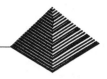

Bases for Comparison

The last chapter showed how cash-flow instances can be added, subtracted, or compared only when they are referenced to the same time frame. That same rule applies to adding, subtracting, or comparing different cash-flow streams. A **basis for comparison** is simply a common frame of reference for comparing two or more cash-flow streams in a consistent way. It's a way of using equivalence to enable you to compare proposals meaningfully. Six different bases are discussed in this chapter:

- Present worth
- Future worth
- Annual equivalent
- Internal rate of return
- Payback period
- Capitalized equivalent amount

These bases for comparison are at the core of the business decision-making process in the next chapter.

TABLE 8.1 Mr. Kinkaid's Estimate of Annual Copies Sold and Resulting Income

Year	Copies sold	Income on Copies Sold
1	0	$0
2	20	$1500
3	50	$3750
4	120	$9000
5	90	$6750
6	60	$4500
7	30	$2250

Comparing Cash-Flow Streams

To compare some set of cash-flow streams, they all need to be converted into the same basis, such as present worth. After all the different proposals are expressed in the same basis for comparison, the best one will be obvious. The mechanics of the actual choice are shown in detail in the next chapter.

Keeping in mind that different proposals need to be compared on a consistent basis, always be sure to use the same interest rate, i, and planning horizon (study period), n, for each of the cash-flow streams. Planning horizons are covered in more detail in Chapter 11.

A Simple Example

A simple example illustrates the different bases for comparison. Suppose that a Mr. Kinkaid is planning to create a new software product that he'll develop and market on his own. He expects this project to last 7 years, and he'll start by investing $10,000 to buy computer hardware and a software-development environment. He estimates that annual operation and maintenance costs for the computer hardware and software will run at about 8.5% of the combined hardware and software costs, or $850 for each of the 7 years.

Mr. Kinkaid is working on this project part-time, so he doesn't expect to sell the first copy until after the beginning of the second year. Income per copy after selling expenses is targeted at $75. Table 8.1 shows his estimated annual sales, in copies, and the resulting annual income.

Table 8.2 shows the estimated net cash-flow stream. Figure 8.1 shows the same net cash-flow stream as a cash-flow diagram.

TABLE 8.2   Mr. Kinkaid's Estimated Net Cash-Flow Stream

Year	Income	Expenses	Net Cash Flow
0	$0	$10,000	−$10,000
1	$0	$850	−$850
2	$1500	$850	$650
3	$3750	$850	$2900
4	$9000	$850	$8150
5	$6750	$850	$5900
6	$4500	$850	$3650
7	$2250	$850	$1400

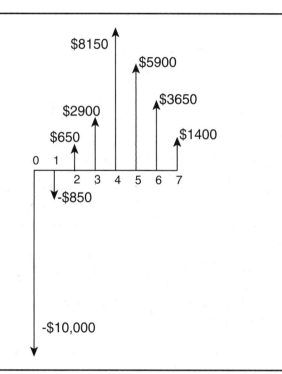

FIGURE 8.1   Mr. Kinkaid's estimated net cash-flow stream shown as a diagram

Present Worth, PW(i)

The present worth, PW(i), of a cash-flow stream shows how much that future stream is worth ("is equivalent to") right now at interest rate, i. The reference time frame for PW(i) is today, or, more precisely, the beginning of the first period (the end of period 0) of the cash-flow stream. Present worth is also called net present value, or NPV. The present worth is the answer to the question, "How much is this cash-flow stream worth today?"

The "present" can be any arbitrary point in time as appropriate for the decision being studied. In 1999, we could have talked about the PW(i) of a cash-flow stream that's planned to begin in 2009 and includes cash-flow instances through 2011.

The formula for calculating the PW(i) of a cash-flow stream is

$$PW(i) = \sum_{t=0}^{n} F_t(1 + i)^{-t}$$

Where F_t is the net cash-flow instance in period t.

The PW(i) formula essentially uses the single-payment present-worth (P/F,i,n) formula to translate each individual net cash-flow instance to its corresponding end-of-year-0 amount and then sums up all of those amounts. This is exactly the same approach as was used in Table 7.2 in the preceding chapter. Table 8.3 shows how PW(i) can be hand-calculated for Mr. Kinkaid's project. A spreadsheet that automates these calculations can be found at http://www.construx.com/returnonsw/. The table shows that Mr. Kinkaid's project is financially equivalent to his receiving a one-time net income of $4557 today.

Notice that except for year 0 the individual present-worth values are always less than their original cash-flow instance. Some people refer to the process of translating cash-flow instances backward in time as "discounting," and also refer to the interest rate used in the calculations as the "discount rate."

Present worth is the second most widely used basis for comparison. Payback period, below, is the most widely used. The main advantages of PW(i) are that it's relatively simple to compute and it's easy to understand the meaning of the result. Any arbitrary cash-flow stream can be converted to a present worth and compared to any other arbitrary cash-flow stream. Expressed in PW(i) form, any two cash-flow streams can be easily compared.

On the other hand, PW(i) hides some possibly important information about the cash-flow stream. The amounts and the timings of the cash flows are hidden; so even though a given cash-flow stream may have a higher PW(i) than another, its initial investment may be more than the organization can afford. That proposal would be impossible to carry out regardless of how profitable it might be.

TABLE 8.3 Manual Calculation of PW(i) for Mr. Kinkaid's Project

Year	Net Cash Flow	Present-Worth Factor	Present Worth
		P/F,9,0	
0	−$10,000	(1.000)	−$10,000
		P/F,9,1	
1	−$850	(0.9174)	−$780
		P/F,9,2	
2	$650	(0.8417)	$547
		P/F,9,3	
3	$2900	(0.7722)	$2239
		P/F,9,4	
4	$8150	(0.7084)	$5774
		P/F,9,5	
5	$5900	(0.6499)	$3835
		P/F,9,6	
6	$3650	(0.5963)	$2176
		P/F,9,7	
7	$1400	(0.5470)	$766

PW(9%) = $4557

SOME ADDITIONAL COMMENTS ON PW(i)

For any given cash-flow stream, there will always be a single value of PW(i) for each unique interest rate. Generally speaking, as the interest rate goes up, the PW(i) of the cash-flow stream goes down. Figure 8.2 shows the PW(i) for Mr. Kinkaid's project over a range of interest rates. Whereas PW(i) calculations are actually meaningful over the range of $-1 < i < \infty$, only the range $0 \leq i < \infty$ is important because negative interest rates are virtually impossible in practice—it's highly unlikely that anyone would ever be willing to pay you to borrow his money.

If Mr. Kinkaid's estimates of all the cash flows are accurate, the graph in Figure 8.2 tells him several important things about his proposal. First, given some interest rate, the graph tells him how much profit (or loss if that interest rate is too high) he would get, in present-day terms, from his project. The graph also tells him what range of interest rates his project would be profitable in and in which ones it wouldn't. Finally, the picture tells him the "critical i" where PW(i) = 0. This critical i is discussed later in this chapter in the section "Internal Rate of Return, IRR."

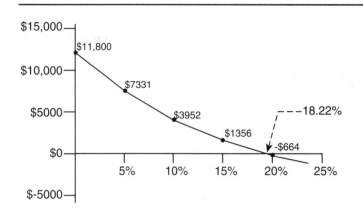

FIGURE 8.2 PW(i) over a range of *i*s for Mr. Kinkaid's project

Future Worth, FW(i)

The future worth, FW(i), is just like the present worth, PW(i), except that it's referenced to a future point in time. Whereas PW(i) is referenced to the beginning of the cash-flow stream, FW(i) is typically referenced to the end. FW(i) is like answering the question, "How much is this proposal worth in the end-of-the-proposal time frame?"

The formula for FW(i) is

$$FW(i) = \sum_{t=0}^{n} F_t(1 + i)^{n-t}$$

Where F_t is the net cash-flow instance in period t.

The FW(i) formula essentially uses the single-payment compound-amount (F/P,i,n) formula to translate each individual net cash-flow instance to its corresponding end-of-cash-flow-stream amount and then sums up all of those amounts.

Table 8.4 shows how FW(i) can be calculated by hand for Mr. Kinkaid's project. His project is financially equivalent to his receiving a one-time net income of $8332 at the end of 7 years.

Because the only difference between FW(i) and PW(i) is the reference time frame, the PW(i) for a cash-flow stream and the FW(i) are mathematically related. Specifically,

$$FW(i) = PW(i) \; (\overset{F/P,i,n}{\quad\quad})$$

TABLE 8.4 Manual Calculation of FW(i) for Mr. Kinkaid's Project

Year	Net Cash Flow	Future-Worth Factor	Future Worth
0	−$10,000	*F/P,9,7* (1.828)	−$18,280
1	−$850	*F/P,9,6* (1.677)	−$1425
2	$650	*F/P,9,5* (1.539)	$1000
3	$2900	*F/P,9,4* (1.412)	$4095
4	$8150	*F/P,9,3* (1.295)	$10,554
5	$5900	*F/P,9,2* (1.188)	$7009
6	$3650	*F/P,9,1* (1.090)	$3979
7	$1400	*F/P,9,0* (1.000)	$1400

FW(9%) = $8332

and

$$PW(i) = FW(i) \left(\overset{P/F,i,n}{\qquad} \right)$$

Using Mr. Kinkaid's project to demonstrate, the single-payment compound-amount factor (F/P,9%,7) can be applied to his PW(i), and the result will equal his FW(i), within the limits of rounding errors on the interest factors.

$$FW(9\%) = PW(9\%) \left(\overset{F/P,9\%,7}{\qquad} \right)$$

$$= \$4557 (1.828) = \$8330$$

For fixed values of i and n, FW(i) always simplifies to PW(i) times a constant, where that constant is the single-payment compound-amount (F/P,i,n) factor. This means that the values of FW(i) and PW(i) will be zero for the same value of "critical i" and that comparing cash-flow streams in terms of FW(i) or PW(i) will always lead to the same conclusion as long as PW(i) or FW(i) is used consistently for all of those cash-flow streams.

Annual Equivalent, AE(i)

PW(i) and FW(i) both represent the cash-flow stream in terms of a one-time net cash-flow instance at a single point in time, either at the beginning or the end of the proposal's cash-flow stream, respectively. With annual equivalent, AE(i), the cash-flow stream is represented as a series of identical cash-flow instances over the life of the study.

AE(i) relates to PW(i) in the same way that A relates to P in the equal-payment-series present-worth (P/A) and the equal-payment-series capital-recovery (A/P) formulas in Chapter 5. The formula for AE(i) can be derived in the same manner that A and P are related. This time, just start with the PW(i) formula and multiply by the appropriate equal-payment-series capital-recovery (A/P,i,n) factor.

Using Mr. Kinkaid's project to illustrate

$$AE(9\%) = PW(9\%) \ (\overset{A/P,9\%,7}{})$$

$$= \$4557 \ (0.1987) = \$905$$

The cash-flow stream in the case study is equivalent to Mr. Kinkaid receiving \$905 at the end of each of the next 7 years.

Because AE(i) is equal to PW(i) times the (A/P,i,n) factor, the AE(i) formula can be derived by substituting in the PW(i) formula from above and the (A/P,i,n) formula from Chapter 5 as shown.

$$AE(i) = PW(i) \ (\overset{A/P,i,n}{})$$

$$= \left[\sum_{t=0}^{n} F_t (1 + i)^{-t} \right] * \left[\frac{i(1 + 1)^n}{(1 + i)^n - 1} \right]$$

Assuming constant values for i and n, AE(i) also simplifies to PW(i) times a constant. The values of AE(i) and PW(i) will also be zero for the same value of "critical i," and that comparison between cash-flow streams in terms of AE(i) or PW(i) will always lead to the same conclusion as long as AE(i) or PW(i) is used consistently for all proposals.

The advantage of the AE(i) form is that repeating cash-flow streams are very easy to represent as annual equivalents. If it were actually possible to repeat Mr. Kinkaid's proposal at the end of the first 7 years and the cash flows were the same in that second 7 year cycle, for instance, the AE(i) for the second 7 years would also be $905, so the AE(i) for the entire 14 year combined period would be $905. A third repetition would mean an identical AE(i) of $905 over a 21-year period, and so on. Whenever a repeatable cash-flow stream, such as a renewable bond, has a known AE(i) over a given *n* year duration, all even multiples of that duration have the same AE(i).

Important Note

PW(i), FW(i), and AE(i) are all equivalent; the only difference is the time frame that they are referenced to.

Internal Rate of Return, IRR

PW(i), FW(i), and AE(i) all express the cash-flow stream as an equivalent dollar amount in some time frame. In contrast, the **internal rate of return**, IRR, expresses the cash-flow stream in terms of an interest rate. Technically, the IRR is the interest rate that causes the present worth of the expenses to equal the present worth of the income. It's exactly the "critical *i*" that brings the PW(i) to zero, as shown above in Figure 8.2. In plain English, this means that if you mimic the proposal's cash-flow stream at a bank (i.e., you deposit exactly those same payments and withdraw exactly those same receipts at exactly those same times), the IRR is the interest rate that the bank has to pay for you to end up with a zero balance at the end of the cash-flow stream. IRR is sometimes called **return on investment**, or, ROI.

The IRR for a cash-flow stream is that critical i^*, where

$$0 = PW(i^*) = \sum_{t=0}^{n} F_t(1 + i)^{-t}$$

To compute the IRR, the cash-flow stream needs to have the following properties:

- The first nonzero net cash-flow instance is an expense.
- That initial expense is followed by 0..*n* further expenses, and there are income net cash flows from then on. (There can be only one sign change in the sequence F_0, $F_1, \ldots, F_n$.)
- The net cash-flow stream is profitable overall—the sum of all income is greater than the sum of all expenses. In other words, PW(0%) > 0.

Cash-flow streams that don't meet these criteria might not have an IRR, or they might have more than one.

> ### Important Note
>
> When a cash-flow stream has more than one IRR, there isn't any rational way to decide which IRR to use. Don't use IRR as a basis for comparison when a cash-flow stream has more than one.

For a more detailed explanation of multiple IRRs, see Appendix B of [Grant90] or Appendix 4.A of [DeGarmo93].

One algorithm for calculating IRR is as follows:

```
Given the cash-flow stream with
    the first nonzero cash flow being negative,
    and only one sign change,
    and PW(0%) > 0
Start with the estimated IRR = 0%
Assume we will move IRR in an increasing (+) direction
Assume an initial step amount (say, 10%)
Calculate PW(i=0%) and save the result
Move the IRR in the current direction by the step amount
Repeat
  recalculate the PW(i=IRR)
  if the PW(i=IRR) is closer to $0.00 than before
    then move the estimated IRR in the same direction
        by the step amount
    else switch direction and cut the step amount in
        half
  until the PW(i=IRR) is within a predetermined range
    of $0.00 (say, 50 cents)
```

This algorithm is suitable for automation but is fairly computationally intensive and will be time-consuming to do by hand. All automated IRR algorithms are based on a similar computationally intensive, iterative approach. The noniterative approach involves analytically finding the root of a potentially large polynomial equation and would be difficult to automate.

Mr. Kinkaid's cash-flow stream meets the three IRR criteria, so we can apply the IRR algorithm to it. The algorithm starts by assuming that the estimated IRR is 0%, moving in an increasing direction, and the step amount is 10%. Calculating PW(0%), it comes out to $11,800. Set the estimated IRR to 10% and go into the "repeat" loop. Each cycle through the "repeat" loop is described here:

1. Calculate PW(10%); it's $3952. That's closer to zero than $11,800, so move the estimated IRR in the same direction (up) by another 10%. It's now estimated to be 20%.

2. Calculate PW(20%); it's –$664. That's closer to zero than $3952, so move the estimated IRR in the same direction by another 10%. It's now estimated to be 30%.

3. Calculate PW(30%); it's –$3527. That's further from zero than –$664, so switch direction and cut the step amount in half, to 5%. The estimated IRR is now 25%.

4. Calculate PW(25%); it's –$2257. That's closer to zero than –$3527, so move the estimated IRR in the same direction (down) by the step amount. It's now 20%.

5. Calculate PW(20%); it's –$664. That's closer to zero than –$2257, so move the estimated IRR in the same direction by another 5%. It's now estimated to be 15%.

6. Calculate PW(15%); it's $1356. That's further from zero than –$664, so switch direction and cut the step amount in half, to 2.5%. The estimated IRR is now 17.5%.

7. Calculate PW(17.5%); it's $284. That's closer to zero than $1356, so move the estimated IRR in the same direction (up) by another 2.5%. It's now estimated to be 20%.

8. Calculate PW(20%); it's –$664. That's further from zero than $284, so switch direction and cut the step amount in half, to 1.25%. The estimated IRR is now 18.75%.

9. Calculate PW(18.75%); it's –$203. That's closer to zero than $664, so move the estimated IRR in the same direction by another 1.25%. It's now estimated to be 17.5%.

10. Calculate PW(17.5%); it's $284. That's further from zero than –$203, so switch direction and cut the step amount in half, to 0.625%. The estimated IRR is now 18.125%.

11. Calculate PW(18.125%); it's $37. That's closer to zero than $284, so move the estimated IRR in the same direction (up) by another 0.625%. It's now estimated to be 18.75%.

12. Calculate PW(18.75%); it's –$203. That's further from zero than $37, so switch direction and cut the step amount in half, to 0.3125%. The estimated IRR is now 18.4285%.

13. . . . and so on while the PW(i) at the estimated IRR converges on $0.00. When the PW(i) is within +/– $0.50 of $0, the loop stops and the estimated IRR of 18.22% is returned.

Payback Period

Whereas PW(i), FW(i), and AE(i) express the cash-flow stream as an equivalent dollar amount and IRR expresses it as an interest rate, payback period expresses it in terms of time. The payback period is simply the time needed to recover the initial investment from the net cash-flow stream. Informally, payback period is just like saying, "This investment will pay for itself in four and a half years."

TABLE 8.5 Manual Calculation of Payback Period for Mr. Kinkaid's Project

End of Year n	Net Cash Flow at End of Year n	Running Sum Through Year n
0	-$10,000	-$10,000
1	-$850	-$10,850
2	$650	-$10,200
3	$2900	-$7300
4	$8150	$850

$$n = 4$$

Unlike PW(i), FW(i), AE(i), and IRR, which are indicators of *profitability*, payback period is an indicator of *liquidity*. Payback period shows the organization's exposure to risk of financial loss. If the proposal is started but gets cancelled before the end of the payback period, the organization will have lost money. A proposal with a payback period of four years exposes the organization to much less risk than a different proposal with a payback period of eight years.

PAYBACK PERIOD WITHOUT INTEREST

Usually people ignore the time value of money when calculating the payback period, PP(i). In this case it is defined as the smallest n, where

$$\sum_{t=0}^{n} F_t \geq 0$$

Table 8.5 shows a manual calculation of payback period for Mr. Kinkaid's case study by computing the running sum of the net cash-flow instances in the stream and watching for that sum to become positive.

Mr. Kinkaid's project recovers its initial investment before the end of the fourth year. If Mr. Kinkaid starts carrying out the proposal but cancels it before then, he'll end up with a net loss. Real profit doesn't start until the fourth year; all the income before that effectively goes to recovering his initial investment.

This is another situation where linear interpolation (Appendix C) can be used for more precise answers. Using linear interpolation, the payback period for Mr. Kinkaid's proposal is 3.90 years.

Payback period (without interest) is probably the single most popular basis for comparison. It's easy to compute and easy to understand the result. Just like all the other bases for comparison, however, payback period hides information about the timings and the amounts of the cash flows. Again, even though one cash-flow stream has a shorter payback period than another, it may be impossible to carry out because its initial investment is too high. Payback period also ignores the duration of the proposal and total profit. This tends to discriminate against proposals with slow payback but higher total profits.

Payback period without interest also makes the mistake of ignoring the time value of money.

TABLE 8.6 Manual Calculation of Discounted Payback Period for Mr. Kinkaid's Project

End of Year n	Net Cash Flow at End of Year n	Compound-Amount Present-Worth (P/F,i,n) Factor	Discounted Cash Flow	Running Sum (with Interest)
0	−$10,000	1.0000	−$10,000	−$10,000
1	−$850	0.9174	−$780	−$10,780
2	$650	0.8417	$547	−$10,233
3	$2900	0.7722	$2239	−$7993
4	$8150	0.7084	$5774	−$2220
5	$5900	0.6499	$3835	$1615

$n = 5$

PAYBACK PERIOD WITH INTEREST, THE DISCOUNTED PAYBACK PERIOD

The discounted payback period, DPP(i), is just like the nondiscounted payback period except that it does include the effect of interest. The discounted payback period is defined as the smallest n, where

$$\sum_{t=0}^{n} F_t(1 + i)^{-t} \geq 0$$

Table 8.6 shows a manual calculation of discounted payback period for Mr. Kinkaid's project by computing the running sum for the discounted cash-flow instances in the stream using a 9% interest rate.

The discounted payback period is before the end of the fifth year. Using the interpolation method described in Appendix C, the more precise discounted payback period is 4.58 years.

Whereas the discounted payback period accounts for interest, just like the payback period, it also hides information about the timings and the amounts of the cash flows. Even though one cash-flow stream has a shorter discounted payback period than another, it may be impossible to carry out because the initial investment is too high. Discounted payback period also ignores the duration of the proposal and total profit; it also tends to discriminate against proposals with slow payback but higher total profits.

Project Balance, PB(i)

Project balance isn't really a basis of comparison, but it's a useful way of looking at a cash-flow stream. It shares several common characteristics with the discounted payback period, so it is relevant to present here.

TABLE 8.7   Project Balance Calculations for Mr. Kinkaid's Project

End of Year n	Net Cash Flow at End of Year n	Partial PW(9%)	PB(9%)$_T$
0	−$10,000	−$10,000	−$10,000
1	−$850	−$780	−$10,780
2	$650	$547	−$10,233
3	$2900	$2239	−$7993
4	$8150	$5774	−$2220
5	$5900	$3835	$1615
6	$3650	$2176	$3791
7	$1400	$766	$4557

The project balance, PB(i), is a profile that shows the equivalent amount of dollars invested in, or earned from, the proposal at the end of each time period over the life of the cash-flow stream. If the proposal is started but cancelled at time t, PB(i)$_t$ shows the equivalent profit or loss at that time. Project balance uses exactly the same computations as the discounted payback period, DPP(i), except that it continues through the entire cash-flow stream. It doesn't stop when the running sum becomes positive.

The formula for PB(i) is

$$PB(i)_T = \sum_{t=0}^{T} F_t(1 + i)^{T-t}$$

Where $PB(i)_T$ is the project balance through time period T. Using Mr. Kinkaid's project, Table 8.7 shows the PB(i) computations at 9% interest.

The graph of PB(9) for Mr. Kinkaid's project is shown in Figure 8.3.

Four important characteristics of a cash-flow stream are shown in the project balance diagram:

- The PW(i) of the cash-flow stream; it's the last PB(i) value (in this case, $4557).
- The DPP(i) of the cash-flow stream; it's the first point when the PB(i) at consecutive times goes from negative to positive (approximately 4.6 years in this example).
- The net equivalent committed dollars exposed to a risk of loss (the zone where PB(i) is negative).
- The net equivalent dollars earned (the zone where PB(i) is positive).

PB(i) isn't widely recognized but is still a useful tool. More information on PB(i) can be found in [Thuesen93].

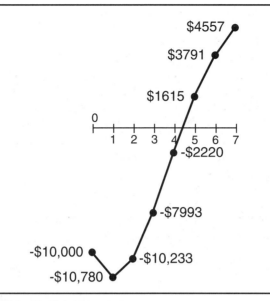

FIGURE 8.3   PB(9) for Mr. Kinkaid's project

Capitalized Equivalent Amount, CE(i)

Technically, the capitalized equivalent amount, CE(i), is a dollar amount now that, at a given interest rate, will be equivalent to the net difference of the income and payments if the cash-flow pattern is repeated indefinitely. Stated more informally, CE(i) is the amount that must be invested at interest rate i to produce an equivalent cash-flow stream on interest alone. CE(i) gives an indication of the equivalent assets that would be frozen in the venture.

CE(i) is defined as follows:

$$CE(i) = \frac{A}{i}$$

Because the AE(9%) for Mr. Kinkaid's project is $905, his CE(9%) is as follows:

$$CE(9\%) = \frac{\$905}{0.09} = \$10,056$$

His project is expected to produce the same amount of income as $10,056 invested at 9% over the life of the project.

A more obvious use of CE(i) is to set up self-supporting endowments. As an example, assume that a software developer who made a fortune in the dot.com craze now feels she can and should share some of her wealth with others. She wants to create an endowment that will pay for computer hardware and teachers' salaries so that an inner-city school can offer computer classes. She estimates that the endowment can be effective with an annual budget of $125,000. How much money would she need to put into an interest-bearing investment at 13.5% so that the program is self-supporting—the program would operate entirely on interest from the investment, and the principal is untouched—indefinitely?

$$CE(13.5\%) = \frac{\$125,000}{0.135} = \$925,926$$

If she put $925,926 into an interest-bearing fund at 13.5%, the annual interest income of $125,000 would provide the funding for the school district and would leave the principal untouched. The program would be self-supporting indefinitely.

Summary

A basis for comparison is just a common frame of reference for consistently comparing two or more cash-flow streams. It's a use of equivalence that helps you meaningfully compare proposals. Six different bases were discussed in this chapter:

- **Present worth**—What is the equivalent value (at a given interest rate) of the cash-flow stream, expressed as a single amount of money at the beginning of the proposal?
- **Future worth**—What is the equivalent value of the cash-flow stream, expressed as a single amount of money at the end of the proposal?
- **Annual equivalent**—What is the equivalent value of the cash-flow stream, expressed as a series of equal amounts at regular intervals over the duration of the proposal?
- **Internal rate of return**—Instead of looking at the proposal in a value-at-a-specific-time perspective, IRR expresses the value of the cash-flow stream as an interest rate.
- **(Discounted) Payback period**—Payback period characterizes the proposal in terms of time: How long does it take for the income generated by the proposal to pay back the amount invested in the proposal? Discounted payback period takes the effect of interest into account.
- **Capitalized equivalent amount**—What amount of money (at the given interest rate) would return the same value over time as interest only, leaving the principal untouched?

Although present worth, internal rate of return, and discounted payback period tend to be the most useful, all of these are at the core of the business decision-making process that's described in later chapters. The next chapter explains how to take a set of proposals, along with their interrelationships, and turn them into a set of mutually exclusive alternatives.

Self-Study Questions

Questions 1 through 10 relate to the following cash-flow diagram.

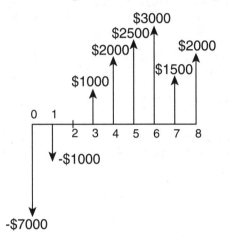

1. What is the PW(7%) of the given cash-flow stream?

2. What is the FW(7%) (at the end of period 8) of the given cash-flow stream?

3. Show that the PW(7%) and the FW(7%) of the given cash-flow stream are equivalent.

4. What is the AE(7%) of the given cash-flow stream?

5. Show that the PW(7%) and the AE(7%) of the given cash-flow stream are equivalent.

6. Calculate the PW(i) of the given cash-flow stream for i = 0%, 2%, 4%, 6%, 8%, and 10%. You may plot the results as a graph similar to Figure 8.2 if you want. What do these PW(i)'s tell you about the IRR for the cash-flow stream?

7. What is the IRR of the given cash-flow stream (to the nearest 0.1%)?

8. What is the payback period (PP) of the given cash-flow stream? Interpolate to the nearest 0.1 year.

9. What is the discounted payback period, DPP(7%), of the given cash-flow stream? Interpolate to the nearest 0.1 year.

10. Draw a graph similar to Figure 8.3 for the PB(7%) of the given cash-flow stream.

11. Write a program, create a spreadsheet, or develop some other automated means to calculate the PW(i), FW(i), and AE(i) given a cash-flow stream and an interest rate, i.

12. Write a program, build a spreadsheet, or develop some other automated means to calculate the IRR of a given cash-flow stream. For the purposes of this question, assume that the cash-flow stream meets the specified criteria. (The first cash-flow instance is negative, PW(0%) is positive, and there is only one sign change.)

13. Write a program, build a spreadsheet, or develop some other automated means to calculate the PP, and given some i, the DPP(i) of a cash-flow stream.

14. Write a program, build a spreadsheet, or develop some other automated way to calculate the PB(i) of a cash-flow stream.

15. Mike wants to create an endowment that will provide his alma mater a perpetual income of $300,000 per year. Assuming he can find an interest-bearing investment that returns 12%, how much does Mike need to invest?

9

Developing Mutually Exclusive Alternatives

The concept of a proposal was introduced in Chapter 3. Proposals, remember, are the basic unit of choice. You can either choose to carry out a specific proposal or you can choose not to. But the real choices confronting an organization typically aren't quite that simple. More often than not, the organization could carry out more than one proposal if it wanted to. And usually there are important relationships between proposals. Maybe you can only carry out Proposal Y if you also carry out Proposal X. Or, maybe you can't carry out Proposal P if you carry out Proposal Q, nor could you carry out Q if you also carried out P. Choices are much easier to make when there are mutually exclusive paths. Either you choose to do A, or B, or C, or whatever. This chapter explains how to turn any given set of proposals, along with their various interrelationships, into a set of mutually exclusive alternatives. The choice can then be made from among these alternatives, as explained in Parts II and III for for-profit organizations and Part IV for nonprofit organizations.

Relationships Between Proposals

There are a number of important potential relationships between different proposals. Each of these relationships is discussed. For now, ignore budget constraints, staffing limits, etc. and just assume that it would be possible to carry out as many of the proposals as we wanted to; these are addressed later in the process.

INDEPENDENT PROPOSALS

The proposals in a set are called **independent proposals** if choosing any proposal from that set has no effect on your ability to choose any other proposal in the set. A proposal to develop financial software that attempts to predict stock prices and another proposal to develop game software that plays chess should probably be considered independent. Choosing to carry out one should have no impact on the other if budget and staffing limitations are ignored.

DEPENDENT PROPOSALS

Two or more proposals in a set are called **dependent proposals** if choosing any one proposal from that set limits your ability to choose any other proposal in that set. There are three different forms of dependence:

- Codependency
- Mutual exclusion
- Contingency

Codependent proposals   A pair of dependent proposals can be called **codependent** if choosing one requires choosing the other and vice versa. In the not too distant past, using the latest operating system often required installing more memory, and accessing the additional memory required the new operating system. The proposal to install the memory was codependent on the proposal to upgrade the operating system. In cases such as this, the two proposals are so dependent on each other that they can't really be considered separately. They should be combined into a single proposal.

Mutually Exclusive Proposals   A pair of dependent proposals is called **mutually exclusive** if choosing either one prevents choosing the other (for other technical or business reasons, not because of financial or staffing limits). This happens, for example, when different proposals are intended to provide the same basic service. Adding functionality to Program S versus replacing S with Program T (where T provides all of the required functionality) would probably be considered mutually exclusive proposals because carrying out either proposal makes the other unnecessary. Another example of mutually exclusive proposals could be the choice between buying a compiler from Vendor A and a similar compiler from Vendor B. As long as both compilers gave you the same features and functionality—such as comparable debugging tools, similar libraries, and so on—then either one would do the job so there would be no need to buy both.

Contingent Proposals   A dependent proposal, P2, is **contingent** if choosing P2 depends on first choosing another proposal, P1, but P1 doesn't depend on choosing P2. Contingency is a one-way dependency; P2 depends on choosing P1, but choosing P1 doesn't mean that you have to also choose P2. As an example of a contingent proposal, consider the situation where using the latest operating system (P2) may be contingent on installing more memory (P1), but use of the additional memory doesn't require upgrading to the new operating system.

Alternatives

The typical business decision involves choosing between more than just two proposals. Five, ten, or even more proposals may be up for consideration. On top of this, it's often possible to choose more than one of the proposals at the same time. Given a set of k proposals, if those proposals are all independent and there aren't any budget (or other resource) constraints, then there would be 2^k different possible unique courses of action. These range from carrying out none of the proposals to carrying out all of the proposals, and includes all of the various combinations in between. Any dependencies among the proposals just make matters more complicated. The decision process is a lot simpler when the choices can be represented entirely in mutually exclusive terms.

Developing Mutually Exclusive Alternatives

Described here is a straightforward, systematic process for turning any set of proposals into a set of mutually exclusive alternatives. An **alternative** is a collection of zero or more proposals that represents a unique, mutually exclusive, potential course of action.

STEP 1: GENERATE ALL THEORETICALLY POSSIBLE COMBINATIONS OF PROPOSALS

The first step in creating mutually exclusive alternatives is to generate the set of all theoretically possible combinations of every proposal. This step intentionally ignores both dependencies between proposals as well as budget and staff (resource) constraints. These limitations are addressed in Step 2.

The easiest way to do this is to make a matrix that has a column for each proposal and a row for each theoretically possible alternative. With a set of k proposals, the matrix will have k columns and 2^k rows. Table 9.1 shows the basic structure of the matrix.

TABLE 9.1 The Structure of the Matrix for Finding All Theoretically Possible Alternatives

	P_1	P_2	$\ldots$	P_k
A_0				
A_1				
A_2				
$\ldots$				
$A_{(2}k-1)$				
$A_{(2}k)$				

TABLE 9.2 An Example of Step 1 for Three Proposals

Alternative	P1	P2	P3	Meaning
A0	0	0	0	Do nothing
A1	1	0	0	P1 only
A2	0	1	0	P2 only
A3	1	1	0	P1 and P2
A4	0	0	1	P3 only
A5	1	0	1	P1 and P3
A6	0	1	1	P2 and P3
A7	1	1	1	All

The cells in the matrix are then filled in as follows:

- Under P_1, alternate 0 and 1 (i.e., 0, 1, 0, 1, . . .) in the cells all the way down the column.
- Under P_2, alternate a pair of 0s then a pair of 1s (0, 0, 1, 1, 0, 0, 1, 1, . . .) all the way down.
- Under P_3, alternate four 0s followed by four 1s (0, 0, 0, 0, 1, 1, 1, 1, 0, 0, 0, 0, 1, 1, 1, 1, . . .).
- Under P_k, alternate 2^{k-1} 0s followed by the same number of 1s.

Table 9.2 shows an example of Step 1 assuming that there are three proposals: P1, P2, and P3. With three proposals, there will be $2^3 = 8$ alternatives. If there were 4 proposals, the table would have 16 rows, with 5 proposals there would be 32 rows, and so on.

Each row in the matrix represents a theoretically possible alternative that's made up of a unique combination of the proposals.

- A 1 in the cell (I,J) means that proposal I is part of alternative J.
- A 0 in the cell (I,J) means that proposal I is not part of alternative J.

As shown in Table 9.2, alternative A3 contains both proposals P1 and P2, whereas alternative A4 contains only proposal P3. Alternative A7 contains all three proposals, P1, P2, and P3. The A0, or "do nothing" alternative is discussed in more detail below.

If you are familiar with binary counting (0, 1, 10, 11, 100, 101, 110, 111, . . .), notice the pattern from row to row. In this format the bits run left to right, not the normal way. You can change the numbering system to have the bits go right to left if you want; that part isn't really important. All that's important is to end up with every possible combination of the proposals included in the table.

In some rare cases it's possible to consider doing a given proposal more than once. In these cases, the alternatives must address the multiple proposals—for example, A1 might be P1 with one instance of P2 while A2 might be P1 with two instances of P2.

The cash-flow stream for any alternative is simply the sum of the cash-flow streams of each proposal it contains.

STEP 2: REMOVE INVALID ALTERNATIVES

The next step in developing mutually exclusive alternatives is to remove all the invalid alternatives. This involves the following:

- Removing any alternative that contains mutually exclusive proposals
- Removing any alternative that contains unsatisfied contingencies (e.g., if P3 is contingent on P2, but P3 is in the alternative without P2, then that alternative is removed)
- Removing any alternatives that exceed budget or other resource constraints

Assume that P1 and P2 are mutually exclusive, P3 is contingent on P2, and that you can't carry out all three because of a budget constraint. Table 9.3 shows the results of removing the invalid alternatives from Table 9.2.

Alternatives A3 and A7 should be dropped because of the mutual exclusivity between P1 and P2. Alternatives A4 and A5 need to be dropped because P3 is contingent on P2 but P2 isn't in either of these alternatives. Alternative A7 needs to be dropped because the budget won't support carrying out all three proposals at the same time as well as the exclusivity between P1 and P2. Now all we need to consider are alternatives A0, A1, A2, and A6, and these alternatives are known to be mutually exclusive.

TABLE 9.3 Removing the Invalid Alternatives

Alternative	P1	P2	P3	Meaning	
A0	0	0	0	Do nothing	
A1	1	0	0	P1 only	
A2	0	1	0	P2 only	
~~A3~~	~~1~~	~~1~~	~~0~~	~~P1 and P2~~	Exclusive
~~A4~~	~~0~~	~~0~~	~~1~~	~~P3 only~~	P3, no P2
~~A5~~	~~1~~	~~0~~	~~1~~	~~P1 and P3~~	P3, no P2
A6	0	1	1	P2 and P3	
~~A7~~	~~1~~	~~1~~	~~1~~	~~All~~	Budget*

*Alternative A7 can also be dropped because P1 and P2 are mutually exclusive.

The "Do Nothing" Alternative

Alternative A0 represents a course of action that, by convention, is called the "do nothing" alternative. This alternative doesn't really mean doing nothing at all, it only means that none of the proposals in the set being considered are carried out. Instead, the money is put into investments that give a predetermined rate of return (bonds, interest bearing accounts, put into a more profitable part of the corporation, etc.).

It's important to consider the do nothing alternative in most business decisions. Sometimes even the best of the stated proposals is worse than what could be achieved by investing somewhere else. When the do nothing alternative comes out the best, it means the organization would be better off not carrying out any of the proposals being considered and should put the money into a more profitable investment elsewhere.

The do nothing alternative is assumed to have the following:

- $PW() = 0$
- $FW() = 0$
- $AE() = 0$

This assumption (justified in Chapter 10) makes it easy to compare the do nothing alternative to the others because the actual detailed cash-flow stream for this alternative doesn't need to be known.

The do nothing alternative should always be considered in a business decision except when there is no choice but to select at least one proposal. An example would be repairing or replacing some necessary, but broken piece of equipment such as a central network router. If the organization can't operate without the router, not replacing it isn't a valid alternative.

The do nothing alternative should also not be considered when the proposals offer identical service and the income side of the cash-flow stream is being ignored. This is known as **service alternatives** and is discussed in more detail in Chapter 11. Different implementations of a compiler for the same language could be considered service alternatives. With service alternatives, the assumption that the PW() of the do nothing alternative equals zero cannot hold. The assumption only holds when both income and expense cash-flow instances are included in the cash-flow stream, but all income is being ignored in a service alternative.

Example Proposals

The following three proposals are used to show how to develop a set of mutually exclusive alternatives:

- Proposal P1 is to buy an XYZZY computer, program it to predict the weather, and then sell weather predictions to the local news media.
- Proposal P2 is to write an additional program for the XYZZY to generate horoscopes, which will be sold at grocery store checkout counters.
- Proposal P3 is to buy a Cray-ola super computer, develop crystallography software, and then lease running time to university physics departments across the country.

The cash-flow streams over a 10-year study period for each of these proposals have been estimated and are shown in Table 9.4. For simplicity's sake, this chapter (and some later chapters) show the cash-flow stream for proposals as an initial investment, equivalent annual income, equivalent annual expenses, and a final salvage value. Clearly, we could use equivalence (Chapter 7) to translate any proposal's actual cash-flow stream into these same terms. The emphasis here is on the decision-making process, regardless of how the proposal's cash-flow stream is being represented. Using a representation that makes the mathematics easier should not be seen as affecting the decision-making process in any way.

TABLE 9.4   Estimated Cash-Flow Streams for the Three Proposals

	P1	P2	P3
Initial investment	$300,000	$550,000	$600,000
Annual income	$350,000	$350,000	$450,000
Annual expenses	$200,000	$200,000	$200,000
Salvage value	$50,000	$50,000	$100,000

TABLE 9.5   The Set of Theoretically Possible Alternatives

Alternative	P1	P2	P3	Meaning
A0	0	0	0	Do nothing
A1	1	0	0	P1 only
A2	0	1	0	P2 only
A3	1	1	0	P1 and P2
A4	0	0	1	P3 only
A5	1	0	1	P1 and P3
A6	0	1	1	P2 and P3
A7	1	1	1	All

TABLE 9.6   Invalid Alternatives Discarded

Alternative	P1	P2	P3	Discard?
A0	0	0	0	No
A1	1	0	0	No
~~A2~~	~~0~~	~~1~~	~~0~~	Contingency
A3	1	1	0	No
A4	0	0	1	No
~~A5~~	~~1~~	~~0~~	~~1~~	Exclusive
~~A6~~	~~0~~	~~1~~	~~1~~	Contingency
~~A7~~	~~1~~	~~1~~	~~1~~	Budget

Assume the following:

- Proposals P1 and P3 are mutually exclusive.
- Proposal P2 is contingent on proposal P1, and there's some other reason why we wouldn't want to buy the XYZZY and just do the horoscope generator.
- The initial investment is limited to $850,000.

TABLE 9.7 Cash-Flow Streams for the Example Alternatives

	A0	A1	A3	A4
Initial investment	$0	$300,000	$850,000	$600,000
Annual income	$0	$350,000	$700,000	$450,000
Annual expenses	$0	$200,000	$400,000	$200,000
Salvage value	$0	$50,000	$100,000	$100,000

First, identify all theoretically possible alternatives. With three proposals there will be a maximum of eight alternatives, as shown in Table 9.5. Second, discard the invalid alternatives. This is shown in Table 9.6.

Alternatives A2 and A6 are discarded because P2 is contingent on P1, but neither A2 nor A6 contain P1. A5 is discarded because P1 and P3 are mutually exclusive. A7 is discarded because the initial investment required to finance all three proposals is more than is available. A7 can also be discarded because P1 and P3 are mutually exclusive.

The alternatives that must be considered in this example are A0, A1, A3, and A4. Alternative A0 is the do nothing alternative and means not carrying out any of the proposals. Alternative A1 means carrying out proposal P1 only. Alternative A3 means carrying out both proposals P1 and P3. Alternative A4 means carrying out proposal P3 only. The cash-flow streams for each of these alternatives are shown in Table 9.7, and the decision analysis is shown in the following chapter.

Summary

Decisions are easiest when the options represent mutually exclusive courses of action. It's common, however, that the proposals in a business decision aren't mutually exclusive courses of action from the start. There are often important interrelationships, such as mutual exclusion or contingency, between the proposals being considered. This chapter described a systematic process for turning a set of proposals, and any important interrelationships, into mutually exclusive alternatives so that the decision making process will be easier. That systematic process is as follows:

1. Generate all theoretically possible combinations of proposals. With k proposals, there will be 2^k theoretically possible candidate alternatives.

2. Remove the invalid alternatives: any candidate alternative that contains mutually exclusive proposals or unsatisfied contingencies needs to be removed from further consideration.

3. The cash-flow stream for an alternative is the sum of the cash-flow streams for the proposals it contains. Candidate alternatives that exceed available resources (e.g., budget limits) are also removed.

The remaining alternatives will be run through the decision processes in Parts II and IV.

Part I presented the basic concepts necessary to make a business decision. Part II presents the process for making business decisions in for-profit organizations, and Part IV presents the process for making business decisions in not-for-profit organizations.

Self-Study Questions

Questions 1 through 3 relate to the following situation: Three different software projects have been proposed. All projects have an identical 8-year lifespan with cash-flow profiles estimated as shown in the following table.

	P1	P2	P3
Investment	$800,000	$600,000	$400,000
Annual revenue	$450,000	$400,000	$300,000
Annual cost	$200,000	$180,000	$150,000
Salvage value	$100,000	$80,000	$60,000

1. Show the matrix of all theoretically possible investment alternatives.

2. Proposal P2 is contingent on P1, and proposals P2 and P3 are mutually exclusive. The budget limit is $1,200,000. Indicate which alternatives are not feasible and explain why they are infeasible.

3. Using the answer to the previous question, calculate the cash-flow profiles for each feasible alternative. Show the cash-flow profiles using the same format (i.e., as a table) as is shown for the original proposals.

Questions 4 through 6 relate to the following situation: Four different software projects have been proposed. All projects have an identical 6-year lifespan with cash-flow profiles estimated as shown in the following table.

	P1	P2	P3	P4
Investment	$200,000	$750,000	$200,000	$450,000
Annual revenue	$250,000	$500,000	$60,000	$200,000
Annual cost	$50,000	$20,000	$10,000	$40,000
Salvage value	$0	$0	$0	$50,000

4. Show the matrix of all theoretically possible investment alternatives.

5. Proposal P1 is to modify an existing system, and P2 is to replace it with a commercial package, so these are mutually exclusive proposals. P3 is an optional add-on to the commercial package, so it is contingent on P2. Indicate which alternatives are not feasible and explain why they are infeasible.

6. Using the answer to the previous question, calculate the cash-flow profiles for each feasible alternative. Show the cash-flow profiles using the same format (i.e., as a table) as is shown for the original proposals.

7. Write a program that takes the names of some set of proposals and any dependencies between them as input that then outputs the list of feasible alternatives to be considered (ignoring budget and resource constraints).

8. Extend the program from the previous question to also address budget constraints.

PART TWO

MAKING FOR-PROFIT BUSINESS DECISIONS

Part Two presents the basic mechanics of making a business decision in a for-profit organization. Specific concepts and techniques in this part include for-profit decision analysis, the concept of economic life and its impact on planning horizons, and two special cases in for-profit decision analysis: replacement decisions and asset-retirement decisions. Using the concepts and techniques in this part, you will be able to make technical decisions in a business context so that you can better align your technical decisions with the goals of the organization. All for-profit business decisions should use the concepts and techniques presented here. Part Three will introduce an optional set of concepts and techniques that can be used when more accuracy is needed in the business decision—including, for example, income taxes and depreciation.

10

For-Profit Decision Analysis

This chapter explains how to take a set of mutually exclusive alternatives, as developed in the previous chapter, and find the best one to carry out in a for-profit organization. A systematic selection process is explained here. Two variations on that process are also explained. One of the variations is to base the decision on total cash-flow streams vs. differential cash-flow streams. The other variation is on the specific bases of comparison (as defined in Chapter 8) to be used. This chapter also introduces and explains the minimum attractive rate of return (MARR), which is a critical factor in for-profit decision analysis.

Minimum Attractive Rate of Return (MARR)

Generally speaking, it wouldn't be smart to invest in an activity with an IRR of 8% when there's another activity that's known to return 16%. An organization's **minimum attractive rate of return** (MARR) is just that, the lowest internal rate of return the organization would consider to be a good investment. The MARR is a statement that an organization is confident it can achieve at least that rate of return.

Another way of looking at the MARR is that it represents the organization's **opportunity cost** for investments. By choosing to invest in some activity, the organization is explicitly deciding to not invest that same money somewhere else. If the organization is already confident it can get some known rate of return, other alternatives should be chosen only if their rate of return is at least that high. A simple way to account for that opportunity cost is to use the MARR as the interest rate in business decisions. An alternative's present worth evaluated at the MARR—its PW(MARR)—shows how much more or less (in present-day cash terms) that alternative is worth than investing at the MARR.

> The assumption that the PW() of the do nothing alternative equals 0 (Chapter 9) is justified by remembering that investments at an IRR equal to the MARR have a PW(MARR) = 0.

The MARR is usually set by a policy decision from the organization's management. An organization needs to think carefully about where it sets the MARR. If it's set too high, alternatives with a good return might not be selected. If it's set too low, you might end up choosing marginally profitable, or even unprofitable, alternatives. The factors typically considered in setting the MARR include the following:

- **What type of organization it is**—For-profit industries are free to set the MARR as they please. Regulated public utilities often have their MARR set by a public utilities commission or other governing entity. Government organizations often use the prevailing bond rate, the investment rate available to citizens, or some other relevant indicator.
- **What the prevailing interest rate for typical investments like savings accounts, bonds, money market, etc. is**—The MARR should be at least as high as the best prevailing interest rate; otherwise the organization could get more profit simply by putting its money in these more typical investments.
- **How much money is available**—When there is less money available for investment, the MARR can go up to focus the organization on activities with the highest profits.
- **Where the money comes from**—If it's borrowed capital, the MARR should probably be set to at least the interest rate on the borrowed money. If it's equity funding, the MARR should be comparable to what the organization is typically able to get through other operations.
- **How many competing proposals there are**—As the number of proposals goes up, the organization might want to be more selective and express this through a higher MARR.
- **Whether the proposals are essential or elective**—The less essential the proposals are, the higher the MARR can be.

- **Whether the analysis is accounting for inflation**—We'll look at how to fully account for inflation in Chapter 13. If the analysis isn't explicitly addressing inflation, the MARR may have to be set even higher to approximate the impact inflation will have.

A discussion of a theoretical basis for setting the MARR can be found in [Eschenbach03].

Before- and After-Tax MARRs

As we will see in Chapter 16, for-profit decision analysis should always account for the effects of income taxes. There are two ways to do this. One is to use a before-tax MARR on the before-tax cash-flow stream. This is really an approximation, but it will probably be accurate enough for most purposes. If more accuracy is needed, the other way is to use an after-tax MARR on the after-tax cash-flow stream. This section shows the relationship between the before- and after-tax MARR. Developing an after-tax cash-flow stream is explained in Chapter 16.

The organization needs to be clear that their MARR is stated in either before-tax or after-tax terms. If the organization has stated the MARR in before-tax terms, the after-tax MARR can be approximated by the following formula. (See Chapter 16 for a detailed explanation of the effective income tax rates and how to calculate them.)

$$\text{After-tax MARR} \approx (\text{Before-tax MARR}) \, (1 - \text{Effective income tax rate})$$

A 30% before-tax MARR in an organization with a 36% effective income tax rate is approximately the same as

$$\text{After-tax MARR} \approx (\,0.30\,) \, (1 - 0.36) = 0.19 \text{ or } 19\%$$

Using a 19% after-tax MARR on the after-tax cash-flow stream will approximate the results of using the 30% before-tax MARR on the before-tax cash-flow stream.

Similarly, if the organization stated the MARR in after-tax terms, the before-tax MARR can be approximated by the following formula:

$$\text{Before-tax MARR} \approx \frac{\text{After-tax MARR}}{(1 - \text{Effective income tax rate})}$$

Assume that an organization has set their after-tax MARR at 18%. If the organization has a 38% effective income tax rate, their before-tax MARR can be approximated by

$$\text{Before-tax MARR} \approx \frac{0.18}{(1 - 0.38)} = 0.29 \text{ or } 29\%$$

Using a 29% before-tax MARR on the before-tax cash-flow stream will approximate the results of using the 18% after-tax MARR on the after-tax cash-flow stream.

The Basic For-Profit Decision Process

Selecting the best alternative uses the same algorithm as a software routine that finds the maximum value in a collection of numbers—successive comparisons against the current best are done on a pair-wise basis. The algorithm is described in terms of a "current best" and a "candidate," where the current best refers to the alternative that's been found to be the best so far, and the candidate refers to the alternative that's being compared with the current best. The selection algorithm is as follows:

```
Assume the first alternative is the current best
for j = 2 to the number of alternatives
    Consider the jth alternative to be the candidate
    Compare the candidate to the current best
    if the candidate is better than the current best
        then make the jth alternative the current best
{* on ending, the current best is the best alternative *}
```

Before using this algorithm, the alternatives should be sorted in order of increasing initial investment. This is especially critical if you're using IRR as the basis of comparison (below), otherwise the differential cash-flow stream may not have a single IRR, as described in Chapter 8. The other reason for sorting the alternatives is that, all other financial consequences being equal, the alternative with the smaller initial investment is better. This leads to a small but important modification to the algorithm:

```
. . .
if the candidate is strictly better than the current best
. . .
```

Figure 10.1 shows a flowchart for the basic for-profit decision process.

Decisions Based on Total Versus Differential Cash-Flow Streams

For some bases of comparison (Chapter 8), it's reasonable to compare the alternatives on a total cash-flow basis. For instance, two alternatives can be compared on total present worth. Simply put, if the present worth (at the MARR) of one alternative is greater than the present worth of the other, the first alternative is the better choice between the two. Comparing total cash-flow streams is reasonable when the basis of comparison is PW(), FW(), or AE().

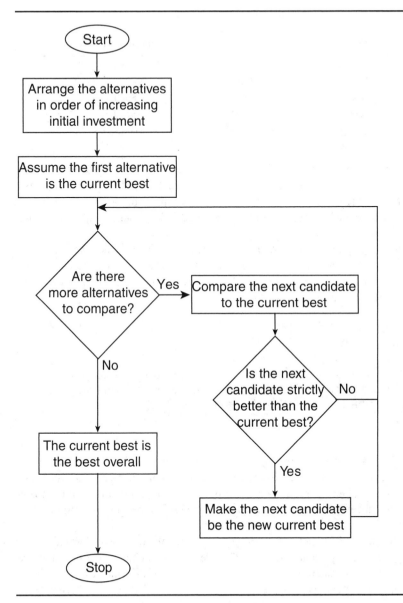

FIGURE 10.1   A flowchart of the basic for-profit decision process

TABLE 10.1   An Example of a Differential Cash-Flow Stream

End of Year	Ax	Ay	Difference (Ay – Ax)
0	–$1000	–$1500	–$500
1	$800	$700	–$100
2	$800	$1300	$500
3	$800	$1300	$500

Comparing with PW(), FW(), and AE() can also be done using the **differential cash-flow stream** (also known as **incremental cash-flow analysis**). The differential cash-flow stream between two alternatives, say Ax and Ay, is simply the cash-flow stream that represents the difference between Ax and Ay. Table 10.1 shows an example of a differential cash-flow stream.

If the differential cash-flow stream, Ay – Ax, is financially desirable (e.g., its PW(MARR) is greater than $0), alternative Ay is better than Ax. If the differential cash-flow stream isn't financially desirable (if its PW(MARR) is less than or equal to $0), alternative Ax is better than Ay.

> ### Important
>
> If you are using IRR as the basis for comparison, you must do the comparison using the differential cash-flow stream. The reason is explained in the section on "IRR on Incremental Investment" later in this chapter.

As a matter of practice, then, it's probably best to get into the habit of comparing on the differential cash-flow stream—it gives the correct answer regardless of the basis of comparison being used. The next sections explain both the differential and total cash flow methods, but the differential cash flow method is shown first because it's preferred for this reason.

To illustrate the decision process, the same set of mutually exclusive alternatives that were developed in the last chapter are used. They're repeated in Table 10.2 for reference.

The alternatives considered in this example are A0, A1, A3, and A4. A0 is the do nothing alternative. Alternative A1 means carry out proposal P1 only. Alternative A3 means carrying out both proposals P1 and P3. Alternative A4 means carrying out proposal P3 only. Remember that:

- Proposal P1 is to buy an XYZZY computer, program it to predict the weather, then sell those predictions to the local news media

TABLE 10.2 Cash-Flow Streams for the Example Alternatives

	A0	A1	A3	A4
Initial investment	$0	$300,000	$850,000	$600,000
Annual income	$0	$350,000	$700,000	$450,000
Annual expenses	$0	$200,000	$400,000	$200,000
Salvage value	$0	$50,000	$100,000	$100,000

- Proposal P2 is to write an additional program for the XYZZY to generate horoscopes, which will be sold at grocery store checkout counters
- Proposal P3 is to buy a Cray-ola super computer, develop crystallography software, and then lease running time to university physics departments across the country

Assume that the organization has set the before-tax MARR at 20% and the cash-flow streams are in before-tax terms.

Present Worth on Incremental Investment

The present worth on incremental investment method is demonstrated first. In a nutshell, a candidate is considered better than the current best if the present worth, evaluated at the MARR, of the differential cash-flow stream is greater than $0.

The step-by-step process is as follows:

1. List the alternatives in order of increasing initial investment.

2. Select the alternative with the smallest initial investment as the current best. (This will usually be the do nothing alternative.)

3. For each of the remaining alternatives, do the following:
   3a. Subtract the current best's cash-flow stream from the candidate's.
   3b. Calculate the present worth at the MARR of this differential cash-flow stream.
   3c. And if the PW(MARR) of the differential cash-flow stream is strictly greater than $0, make the candidate the new current best.

4. After all alternatives have been considered, the final current best is the best choice.

AE(MARR) and FW(MARR) can be used in place of PW(MARR), and will lead to the same choice.

The steps taken in the analysis for the alternatives shown above are, in order, as follows:

1. The alternatives are ordered A0, A1, A4, A3 based on increasing initial investment.

2. Start with alternative A0 as the current best because it has the smallest initial investment.

3. Choose A1 as the first candidate.

4. Compute the differential cash-flow stream, A1 − A0. Because A0 is the do nothing alternative, the differential cash-flow stream is the same as the cash-flow stream for A1.

	A1 − A0
Initial investment	$300,000
Annual income	$350,000
Annual expenses	$200,000
Salvage value	$50,000

5. Compute the PW(MARR) for the differential cash-flow stream:

$$\text{PW(MARR)} = -\$300k + \$150k \overset{P/A,20,10}{(4.1925)} + \$50k \overset{P/F,20,10}{(0.1615)} = \$337k$$

6. Because the PW(MARR) of the differential cash-flow stream is greater than $0, A1 becomes the current best.

7. Choose A4 as the next candidate.

8. Compute the differential cash-flow stream, A4 − A1.

	A4 − A1
Initial investment	$300,000
Annual income	$100,000
Annual expenses	$0
Salvage value	$50,000

9. Compute the PW(MARR) for the differential cash-flow stream.

$$\text{PW(MARR)} = -\$300k + \$100k \overset{P/A,20,10}{(4.1925)} + \$50k \overset{P/F,20,10}{(0.1615)} = \$127k$$

10. Because the PW(MARR) of the differential cash-flow stream is greater than $0, A4 becomes the current best.

11. Choose A3 as the candidate.

12. Compute the differential cash-flow stream, A3 – A4.

	A3 – A4
Initial investment	$250,000
Annual income	$250,000
Annual expenses	$200,000
Salvage value	$0

13. Compute the PW(MARR) for the differential cash-flow stream.

$$\text{PW(MARR)} = -\$250k + \$50k \overset{P/A,20,10}{(4.1925)} + \$0 \overset{P/F,20,10}{(0.1615)} = -\$40k$$

14. Because the PW(MARR) of the differential cash-flow stream is less than or equal to 0, A4 remains the current best.

15. There are no more alternatives. Alternative A4 is the current best at the end, so it's selected as the best alternative.

Alternative A4 means doing Proposal P3 only: buying the Cray-ola super computer, developing crystallography software, and then leasing running time to university physics departments across the country.

IRR on Incremental Investment

If you are making the decision using incremental comparisons, you can also use the Internal Rate of Return (IRR) as the basis for comparison. The incremental investment to carry out the candidate is considered desirable if the IRR of the differential cash-flow stream is greater than the MARR.

> If the incremental cash-flow stream doesn't pass the tests outlined for IRR in the Chapter 8, don't use this process. Use a different basis of comparison instead, such as present worth.

The step-by-step process is as follows:

1. List the alternatives in order of increasing initial investment.

2. Select the alternative with the smallest initial investment as the current best. (This will usually be the do nothing alternative.)

3. For each of the remaining alternatives do the following:
   3a. Subtract the current best's cash-flow stream from the candidate's.
   3b. Calculate the IRR of this differential cash-flow stream.
   3c. And if the IRR of the differential cash-flow stream is strictly greater than MARR, make the candidate the current best.

4. After all alternatives have been considered, the final current best is the best choice.

The steps taken in the analysis for the alternatives shown above are, in order, as follows:

1. The alternatives should be ordered A0, A1, A4, A3 based on initial investment.

2. Select A0 as the current best.

3. Choose A1 as the first candidate.

4. Compute the differential decision cash-flow stream, A1 – A0. Because A0 is the do nothing alternative, the differential cash-flow stream is the same as the cash-flow stream for A1.

	A1 – A0
Initial investment	$300,000
Annual income	$350,000
Annual expenses	$200,000
Salvage value	$50,000

5. Compute the IRR for the differential cash-flow stream; it's 49.2%.

6. Because the IRR of the differential cash-flow stream is greater than MARR, A1 becomes the current best.

7. Choose A4 as the next candidate.

8. Compute the differential cash-flow stream, A4 – A1.

	A4 – A1
Initial investment	$300,000
Annual income	$100,000
Annual expenses	$0
Salvage value	$50,000

9. Compute the IRR for the differential cash-flow stream; it's 31.6%.

10. Because the IRR of the differential cash-flow stream is greater than the MARR, A4 becomes the current best.

11. Choose A3 as the candidate.

12. Compute the differential cash-flow stream, A3 – A4.

	A3 – A4
Initial investment	$250,000
Annual income	$250,000
Annual expenses	$200,000
Salvage value	$0

13. Compute the PW(MARR) for the differential cash-flow stream; it's 15.1%.

14. Because the IRR of the differential cash-flow stream is less than or equal to the MARR, A4 remains the current best.

15. There are no more alternatives and A4 is the final current best, so it is selected as the best alternative.

Again, the proposal to buy the Cray-ola super computer, develop crystallography software, and then lease running time to university physics departments across the country is chosen as the best.

Comparisons Based on Total Cash-Flow Streams

The preferred approach is to always do the comparisons based on incremental investment. The incremental form of comparison always works. But the incremental approach isn't the only approach. Done carefully, the total investment approach works just as well. The trick is to just remember when it can be used and when it can't. Don't use IRR as the basis with total cash-flow streams. The total investment approach can only be used when the basis for comparison is present worth (PW), future worth (FW), or annual equivalent (AE).

The total investment approach is different from the incremental approach in a computational sense, but you will end up with exactly the same decision. The present worth on total investment approach will be shown below. Future worth and annual equivalent on total investment are identical in process except that they use a different basis of comparison.

The investment to carry out the candidate is considered desirable if the present worth, evaluated at the MARR, of the candidate is greater than the present worth (at the MARR) of the current best.

The step-by-step process is as follows:

1. List the alternatives in order of increasing initial investment.

2. Select the alternative with the smallest initial investment as the current best. This will usually be the do nothing alternative.
   2a. Calculate the present worth at the MARR of this alternative

3. For each of the remaining alternatives do the following:
   3a. Calculate the present worth at the MARR of the candidate.
   3b. And if the PW(MARR) of the candidate is strictly greater than PW(MARR) of the current best, make the candidate the new current best.

4. After all alternatives have been considered, the final current best is the best choice.

The steps taken in this analysis are, in order, as follows:

1. The alternatives should be ordered A0, A1, A4, A3 based on initial investment.

2. Select A0 as the current best.

3. Compute PW(MARR) of the current best. Because it is the do nothing alternative, PW(MARR) = 0.

4. Choose A1 as the first candidate.

5. Compute PW(MARR) of A1. It is $337k.

6. Because the PW(MARR) of A1 is greater than PW(MARR) of A0, A1 becomes the current best.

7. Choose A4 as the next candidate.

8. Compute PW(MARR) of A4. It is $464k.

9. Because the PW(MARR) of A4 is greater than PW(MARR) of A1, A4 becomes the current best.

10. Choose A3 as the next candidate.

11. Compute PW(MARR) of A3. It is $424k.

TABLE 10.3 Cash-Flow Streams for Four Example Alternatives

End of Year	A0	A1	A2	A3
0	$0	−$5000	−$8000	−$10,000
1 through 10	$0	$1400	$1900	$2500

12. Because the PW(MARR) of A3 is less than PW(MARR) of A4, A4 remains the current best.

13. There are no more alternatives and A4 is the final current best, so it is selected as the best alternative.

Rank on Rate of Return

In the rank on rate of return approach, the IRR is calculated for each individual proposal. The proposals are then ranked in order of decreasing IRR. All proposals with an IRR greater than the MARR are selected. This is a fairly well-known approach, but it has two important weaknesses. First, ranking on the IRR will be guaranteed only to select the set of proposals that maximize the total present worth if all the proposals are independent and there are no resource limitations (e.g., budget constraints). Second, even when you are comparing mutually exclusive alternatives, the alternative with the highest rate of return on its total cash flow may not be the alternative that will maximize the total present worth at the MARR.

If you are using IRR as the basis for comparison, the incremental investment approach described earlier in this chapter *must* be used. This is the only way to be sure that the best alternative is selected. In simplest terms, each avoidable increment of investment must earn at least the MARR to be sure the best alternative is chosen. As a specific example of this second problem, consider the alternatives in Table 10.3 when the MARR is 15%.

First, we'll find the best alternative by using present worth on incremental investment. Start with A0 as current best, A1 as candidate:

$$\overset{P/A,15,10}{\text{PW(MARR)}_{\text{A1} - \text{A0}} = -\$5000 + \$1400 \, (5.0188) = \$2026}$$

The PW(MARR) is greater than $0, so A1 is the new current best. Compare A1 to A2 as candidate:

$$\overset{P/A,15,10}{\text{PW(MARR)}_{\text{A2} - \text{A1}} = -\$3000 + \$500 \, (5.0188) = -\$490}$$

TABLE 10.4   Total IRRs for the Four Example Alternatives

Alternative	A0	A1	A2	A3
Total IRR	15.0%	25.0%	19.9%	21.4%

TABLE 10.5   Incremental IRRs for the Four Example Alternatives

Alternative	A0	A1 – A0	A2 – A1	A3 – A1
Incremental IRR	15.0%	25.0%	10.5%	17.7%

The PW(MARR) is less than $0, so A1 remains current best. Compare A1 to A3:

$$\overset{P/A,15,10}{PW(MARR)_{A3-A1} = -\$5000 + \$1100 \,(5.0188) = \$521}$$

The PW(MARR) is greater than $0, A3 is the best alternative according to the present worth on incremental investment method.

Now look at those same alternatives using the rank on rate of return method. The IRRs for each alternative are shown in Table 10.4.

Using total IRR as the selection criterion, alternative A1 appears to be the best followed in order by A3, A2, and A0. On the other hand, if we use the incremental internal rate of return method, the incremental IRRs are shown in Table 10.5.

When the comparison is based on incremental IRR, notice that alternative A3 is the best, not alternative A1. This is consistent with the best alternative calculated using present worth on incremental investment.

Summary

This chapter showed how to take a set of mutually exclusive alternatives, as developed in the previous chapter, and find the best one to carry out in a for-profit organization. The systematic selection process described here uses the same algorithm as a software routine that finds the maximum in a collection of numbers: Successive comparisons against the current best are done on a pair-wise basis.

Comparing alternatives on their differential cash-flow stream is preferred because it works with all bases of comparison. If you are using IRR as the basis for comparison, you *must* do the comparison on the differential cash-flow stream. Comparing alternatives on their total cash-flow streams works in many cases but is not preferred because it isn't valid for all bases of comparison. Comparing on total cash-flow streams is only reasonable when the basis of comparison is PW(), FW(), or AE().

This chapter also introduced and explained the minimum attractive rate of return (MARR). The MARR is the lowest rate of return that the organization would consider to be a good investment. It's a statement that an organization is confident it can achieve at least that rate of return on the average investment. The MARR is used as the interest rate in the selection process.

A commonly used selection process, rank on rate of return, was shown in this chapter to not always lead to the best decision for the organization.

The next chapter builds on the for-profit decision process described here by showing how to choose the planning horizon—which is often based on the concept of economic life—and how to fit proposals with different time spans into that planning horizon.

Self-Study Questions

1. Given a before-tax MARR of 15% and an effective income tax rate of 22%, what is the after-tax MARR?

2. Given a before-tax MARR of 29% and a tax rate of 40%, what is the after-tax MARR?

3. Given an after-tax MARR of 20% and an effective tax rate of 35%, what is the before-tax MARR?

4. Given an after-tax MARR of 15% and an effective tax rate of 42%, what is the before-tax MARR?

Questions 5 through 7 relate to the following table of mutually exclusive alternatives. The planning horizon is 8 years, the cash-flow streams are in after-tax terms, and the after-tax MARR is 15%.

	A0	A1	A2	A6
Investment	$0	$800,000	$600,000	$1,000,000
Annual revenue	$0	$450,000	$400,000	$700,000
Annual cost	$0	$200,000	$180,000	$330,000
Salvage value	$0	$100,000	$80,000	$140,000

5. In what order should these alternatives be compared?

6. Show the present worth on incremental investment calculations and identify the best alternative. Show your work at the same level of detail as was used in this chapter.

7. Show the IRR on incremental investment calculations and identify the best alternative. Show your work at the same level of detail as was used in this chapter.

Questions 8 and 9 relate to the following table of mutually exclusive alternatives. The planning horizon is 6 years, the cash-flow streams are in after-tax terms, and the after-tax MARR is 12%.

	A0	A1	A2	A6	A8	A9	A10	A14
Investment	$0	$200k	$750k	$950k	$450k	$650k	$1200k	$1400k
Annual revenue	$0	$250k	$500k	$560k	$200k	$450k	$700k	$760k
Annual cost	$0	$50k	$20k	$30k	$40k	$90k	$60k	$70k
Salvage value	$0	$0	$0	$0	$50k	$50k	$50k	$50k

8. In what order should these alternatives be compared?

9. Show the present worth on incremental investment calculations and identify the best alternative. Show your work at the same level of detail as was used in this chapter.

10. Write a program that takes in cash-flow streams for various mutually exclusive alternatives and a MARR, then applies the PW on incremental investment method to those alternatives.

11

Planning Horizons and Economic Life

Up to now, we've been requiring that all proposals being compared have the same lifespan. In the real world, however, they won't all have the same lifespan. One proposal might have a 4-year lifespan, and another might have a 7-year lifespan. To compare these proposals consistently, you need to take into account what could happen financially in the 3 years following the 4-year proposal. Or, you need a way to address the financial aspects of the last 3 years if the 7-year proposal is cut short to 4 years. This chapter explains how to find the economic life of an asset and how to use that economic life to help set the planning horizon for a specific decision analysis. The chapter also explains how to place proposals into a planning horizon if their actual time spans are longer or shorter than that horizon.

Planning Horizons

To compare different proposals consistently, they all need to have the same time span. The consistent time span for comparing a set of proposals is called the **planning horizon** (sometimes known as the **study period**, or n^*). The planning horizon can be based on the following:

- Company policy
- How far into the future you can make reasonable estimates
- The economic life of the shortest-lived asset
- The economic life of the longest-lived asset
- The best judgment of the person performing the decision analysis

Whatever the planning horizon ends up being, the economic lives of the assets within a proposal need to be compared with that time period.

Software itself isn't usually considered to be an asset. However, it's not unusual for software professionals to be involved in decisions that do include assets such as computer hardware, so understanding economic life is important.

Capital Recovery with Return, CR(i)

Being able to understand and calculate the economic life of an asset begins with understanding and calculating **capital recovery with return**, CR(i). CR(i) describes the cost of ownership of an asset in terms of an equal-payment-series over some given time span of ownership. CR(i) is a major component in economic-life calculations.

The cost of ownership of an asset is a combination of the drop in value of that asset over time together with the interest on the invested capital. Figure 11.1 illustrates the components of CR(i).

Assume that some special-purpose machine (the asset) was originally bought for $10,000 (its acquisition cost) and sold for $2000 (its salvage value) 7 years later. During those 7 years, the owner incurred two kinds of costs of ownership. One of these was the opportunity cost of the salvage value. Because $2000 was tied up in the machine's salvage value over those 7 years, that money couldn't be used for any other investments. If the money were available for other investments, we can assume that it could be earning the MARR. So you can think of the money frozen in the machine's salvage value as costing the MARR in lost opportunity. That opportunity cost is an annual cost equal to the interest rate (MARR) times the salvage value. In this example, if the MARR is 15%, the opportunity cost is 15% of $2000 for each of the 7 years, or $300 annually.

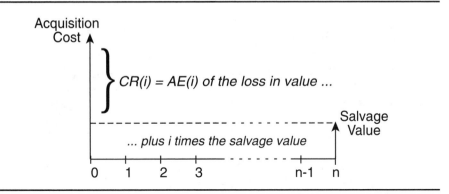

FIGURE 11.1   Cash flow diagram showing the components of CR(i)

The other cost that the owner incurred was the loss in value from its acquisition cost down to its salvage value. In this case, the loss is $8000 over those 7 years. The $8000 loss over 7 years can be converted to annual equivalent, AE(i), terms using the equal-payment-series capital-recovery (A/P,i,n) formula.

$$A = \$8000 \; (\overset{A/P,15\%,7}{\quad\quad})$$

$$= \$8000 \; (0.2404) = \$1923$$

The owner lost the equivalent of $1923 per year because of the drop in value from its acquisition cost down to its salvage value.

The opportunity cost and the loss in value cost, because they are both in AE(i) terms, can be added together.

$$\$1923 + \$300 = \$2223$$

So the equivalent annual cost of owning that special-purpose machine for the 7 years was $2223 per year. Generalizing from this specific example, the capital recovery formula is as follows:

$$CR(i) = (P - F) \; (\overset{A/P,i,n}{\quad\quad}) + Fi$$

Where:

P = the asset's acquisition cost

F = the asset's estimated salvage value

n = the length of time the asset is kept

i = the interest rate (e.g., MARR)

As another example of capital recovery, recall Mr. Kinkaid's computer system from Chapter 8. The purchase price was $10,000 and the salvage value was $1250 after 7 years. Assume that Mr. Kinkaid's MARR is 9%.

$$\overset{A/P,9\%,7}{\text{CR}(9\%) = (\$10,000 - \$1250)\,(0.1987) + \$1250\,(0.09)}$$

$$= \$1739 + \$113 = \$1852$$

Combining the loss in value (acquisition cost minus salvage value) expressed as an annual equivalent amount, together with the annual interest on the frozen salvage value, the computer system will cost Mr. Kinkaid the equivalent of $1852 per year to own for the 7 years he expects to keep it. Keep in mind that CR(i) is only the cost of ownership. Operation and maintenance costs aren't included in CR(i).

Because the salvage value of an asset generally decreases over time, the CR(i) for keeping an asset 1 year is probably going to be different from the CR(i) for keeping that asset for 2 years, for 3 years, and so on. If we assume the salvage values at the end of each year as shown in column (1) of Table 11.1, then column (2) shows the corresponding CR(i) for keeping the special-purpose machine (from above) that many years.

Economic Life

The total lifetime costs of an asset are driven by two components:

- Capital recovery with return, CR(i)
- Operation and maintenance costs

CR(i) will usually start off high and decrease over time, as shown in Table 11.1. On the other hand, the operating and maintenance costs for an asset usually start off low and increase over time. A new car usually costs much less to operate and maintain than an older car.

TABLE 11.1   Example CR(i) Costs for Different Terms of Ownership

End of Year	(1) Salvage Value at End of Year n	(2) CR(i) If Machine Is Kept n Years
1	$8000	$3500
2	$7000	$2895
3	$6000	$2652
4	$5000	$2501
5	$4000	$2390
6	$3000	$2300
7	$2000	$2223
8	$1000	$2156

The operating and maintenance costs over some time period can also be converted to annual equivalent (AE(i)) terms. Simply take the present worth, PW(i), of the operation and maintenance cost cash-flow stream over that time period and multiply it by the equal-payment-series capital-recovery (A/P,i,n) factor. As the operating and maintenance costs are likely to increase over time, the AE(i) of the operation and maintenance cost cash-flow stream is also likely to increase the longer the asset is kept.

Because CR(i) is already in annual equivalent terms, the AE(i) of the operating and maintenance costs can be added to the CR(i), giving the total AE(i) costs of owning, operating, and maintaining the asset for that time period. This is illustrated in Figure 11.2.

As explained earlier, CR(i) tends to start off high, but then goes down over time; whereas the AE(i) of the operating and maintenance costs tend to start off low, but then go up. Adding the two into a total AE(i) cost of ownership, operation, and maintenance will usually follow the U-shaped pattern shown in Figure 11.2. The lowest point on the total cost curve corresponds to the point in time when the total cost of owning, operating, and maintaining the asset is at the minimum. If the asset were sold or scrapped before that time, the AE(i) lifetime costs would be higher than that minimum. Likewise, if the asset wasn't sold or scrapped until after that time the AE(i) costs would also be higher than that minimum.

The point in time when the AE(i) total costs are minimized is known as the **economic life** of the asset. The asset should be held for that length of time only, no longer and no shorter. This same time span is also sometimes called the **minimum-cost life** or the **optimum replacement interval**.

As a real-world example of economic life, consider commercial rental cars. It's common to see advertisements or used car lots where former rental cars are being sold on the used car market. But these cars aren't very old, typically two or three years at most. The

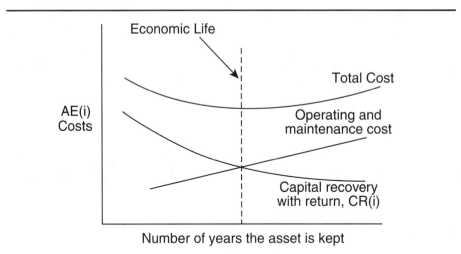

FIGURE 11.2   A graph of the total cost of owning, operating, and maintaining an asset over time

cars clearly have several good years still left in them. Why is the rental car company selling these cars so soon? One answer is that the rental car company has done the economic-
life calculations and found that keeping the car any longer than they have already kept it
actually increases the total cost, which then decreases their profit. They are better off selling the car on the used market and replacing it with a new car, because even though the
CR(i) costs will continue to decrease, the AE(i) of the operating and maintenance costs
are beginning to increase at a rate faster than the CR(i) costs are decreasing.

Finding the Economic Life of an Asset

The procedure for finding the economic life of an asset involves calculating the total
AE(i) costs of holding the asset for various lengths of time. The total AE(i) cost will be
the sum of the CR(i) plus the AE(i) of the operating and maintenance cost cash-flow
stream for that many years. The year with the minimum total AE(i) cost is the economic
life of that asset.

As an example calculation, assume that an organization is planning to buy a new
computer. The relevant estimates are assumed to be as follows:

- The computer has a purchase price of $10,000.
- The salvage value starts at $7000 and decreases by $1000 each year.
- Maintenance and operation costs start at $1000 and increase by $500 each year.
- The MARR is 12%.

Table 11.2 shows how economic-life calculations can be done.

TABLE 11.2   An Example Economic-Life Calculation

End of Year	(1) Salvage Value If Retired at Year n	(2) AE(i) Cost If Retired in Year n [CR(i)]	(3) Operating and Maintenance Costs for Year n	(4) PW(i) of O&M for Year n in Year 0	(5) Sum of Year 0 O&Ms through Year n	(6) AE(i) Cost of Operating for n Years	(7) Total AE(i) If Retired at Year n
1	$7000	$4200	$1000	$893	$893	$1000	$5200
2	$6000	$3087	$1500	$1196	$2089	$1236	$4323
3	$5000	$2682	$2000	$1424	$3513	$1462	$4144
4	$4000	$2455	$2500	$1589	$5102	$1679	$4135 (*)
5	$3000	$2301	$3000	$1702	$6804	$1887	$4189
6	$2000	$2185	$3500	$1773	$8577	$2086	$4272
7	$1000	$2029	$4000	$1810	$10,387	$2276	$4305
8	$0	$2013	$4500	$1818	$12,205	$2457	$4469

(*) The economic life of this computer is 4 years. Assuming that the cash-flow estimates are reasonably correct, the computer should be replaced after 4 years.

Column 1 in the table is the estimated salvage value for the computer if it were sold at the end of that year. This was one of the estimates given in the original problem statement.

Column 2 shows the calculated CR(i) cost—calculated using the formula described earlier—of owning the computer that many years. The number here is the result of feeding the original purchase price and the estimated salvage value from Column 1 into the CR(i) formula with $i = $ MARR.

Column 3 is the estimated operating and maintenance costs for each year in the asset's life. This is also an estimate given in the original problem statement.

Column 4 is the PW(i) of the operating and maintenance costs cash-flow instance for that year equivalenced back to the beginning of year 1 (end of year 0). This is calculated by multiplying the Column 3 value by the appropriate single-payment present-worth (P/F,i,n) factor using the MARR. Note that, for instance, the operation and maintenance costs for year 1 are $1000, but the PW(i) for this year is $893. The operation and maintenance costs are expressed in end-of-year terms, whereas the PW(i) is expressed in beginning-of-year-1 (end-of-year-0) terms. The (P/F,12%,1) factor is 0.893 so $1000 at the end of year 1 is equivalent to $893 at the beginning of year 1.

Column 5 is simply the running sum of Column 4 values through row n. In other words, it's the PW(i) of the operating and maintenance cost cash-flow stream through year n. The value in row 3 of Column 5, $3513, is the sum of the first three values in Column 4, $893+$1196+$1424.

Column 6 is the cost of operating and maintaining the asset for each of the n years, expressed in AE(i) terms. The value is calculated by applying the equal-payment-series capital-recovery (A/P,i,n) factor to the value in the corresponding row of Column 5.

Column 7 is the total AE(i) costs of owning, operating, and maintaining the asset for that many years. It's the sum of the CR(i) value in Column 2 and the corresponding AE(i) operating and maintenance costs in Column 6. A spreadsheet that automates economic life calculations can be found at http://www.construx.com/returnonsw/.

Special Cases in Economic Life

There are two special cases to consider in economic-life calculations. The first special case is when the asset's annual operating and maintenance costs stay constant over its life and the salvage value also stays constant. This is common with purchased software where the salvage value is usually nearly zero (it's hard to sell used software to someone else) and the operating and maintenance costs will be relatively steady. In this case, the longer the asset stays in service, the lower its total AE(i) costs will be, so the economic life will be the same as its physical **service life**. For hardware, the physical service life ends when it just can't be repaired any longer (e.g., it's worn out beyond repair or the replacement parts simply aren't available any more). For software, the physical service life ends when, for example, operating system software upgrades make the software inoperable (e.g., the system runtime libraries no longer support the specific API calls used by that application). In many cases, assets have a constant salvage value of zero. If one of those assets also has constant operating and maintenance costs over its life, the appropriate strategy may be to keep it in service as long as possible.

The second special case is when the acquisition cost and the salvage value are constant and the operating and maintenance costs are always increasing. In this case, the economic life is the shortest possible life (e.g., one year).

Economic Lives and Planning Horizons

If the economic life of a given asset is the same as the planning horizon, no more work needs to be done for that asset. However, it's not that uncommon for the economic life of some assets to be longer or shorter than the chosen planning horizon. To fit these assets into the planning horizon, you need to do some more work depending on whether the economic life is shorter or longer than the planning horizon.

ASSETS WITH ECONOMIC LIVES LONGER THAN THE PLANNING HORIZON

When the economic life of an asset is longer than the study period, there will still be some residual value in the asset that needs to be considered. An asset that has an 8-year economic life has 2 years of residual value to consider if the planning horizon was set at 6 years.

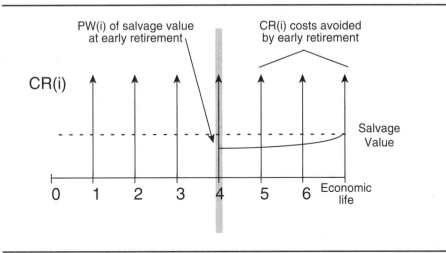

FIGURE 11.3   An explanation of implied salvage value

Implied Salvage Value   The **implied salvage value** of an asset is an estimate of that residual value at some point before the end of its economic life. There are two components in the implied salvage value, unspent CR(i) and earlier availability of the salvage value. Figure 11.3 shows the components of the implied salvage value at 4 years for an asset with a 7-year economic life.

First, as shown in Figure 11.3, the capital recovery, CR(i), of the asset over its life gives the equivalent annual total costs of ownership, operation, and maintenance. If the special-purpose machine shown in Table 11.1 really did have an economic life of 7 years, its CR(i) for each of those 7 years is $2223. If the planning horizon was set, for example, to the end of the fourth year, however, the owner shouldn't actually be considering the annual costs for the asset beyond that fourth year. In effect, there are 3 years of ownership, operation, and maintenance costs that don't have to be paid. These can be "backed up" to the end of the 4-year planning horizon using the equal-payment-series present-worth (P/A) formula as shown below. This represents the PW(i) of the avoided total ownership costs at the end of the study period.

$$\text{Avoided total ownership costs} = \text{CR(i)} \left(\overset{P/A,i,n\text{-}n*}{} \right)$$

$$= \$2223 \, \overset{P/A,15,3}{(2.2832)} = \$5076$$

The PW(i), in end-of-year-4 terms, of the avoided total ownership costs for the last 3 years of the machine's economic life is $5076.

At the end of the economic life of the asset, it also has its estimated "real" salvage value, F. That value can also be backed up from the end of the economic life to the end of the study period. The special-purpose machine had an end-of-year-seven salvage value of $2000. That salvage value can be backed up to end-of-year-four terms using the single-payment present-worth (P/F) formula.

$$\text{Backed-up salvage value} = \text{End-of-economic-life salvage value} \;(\overset{P/F,i,n-n^*}{\quad})$$

$$= \$2000 \;(\overset{P/F,15,3}{0.6575}) = \$1315$$

The combined value at the end of the fourth year is as follows:

$$\$5076 + \$1315 = \$6391$$

The special-purpose machine has an implied salvage value of $6391 at the end of the fourth year.

Generalizing this analysis, the formula for the implied salvage value is as follows:

$$F_n^* = CR(i) \;(\overset{P/A,i,n-n^*}{\quad}) + F\;(\overset{P/F,i,n-n^*}{\quad})$$

As another example, remember that the CR(i) for Mr. Kinkaid's computer system (above) is $1852 per year over the 7 years of the study. Also remember that his salvage value after 7 years is $1250. If the study period were set to 5 years, the implied salvage value at the end of year 5 would be

$$F_n^* = CR(i) \;(\overset{P/A,i,n-n^*}{\quad}) + F\;(\overset{P/F,i,n-n^*}{\quad})$$

$$= \$1852\;(\overset{P/A,9,7-5}{\quad}) + \$1250\;(\overset{P/F,9,7-5}{\quad})$$

$$= \$1852\;(\overset{P/A,9,2}{1.759}) + \$1250\;(\overset{P/F,9,2}{0.8417})$$

$$= \$3258 + \$1052 = \$4310$$

The ownership costs that Mr. Kinkaid would avoid by retiring his computer system at the end of the fifth year are equivalent to $4310 at the end of the fifth year.

For assets with an economic life longer than the study period, you can add the implied salvage value of the asset as an income cash-flow instance at the end of the planning horizon. Mr. Kinkaid would show a one-time income cash-flow instance of $4310 at the end of the fifth year if he wanted to properly account for shortening his 7-year proposal into a 5-year planning horizon.

ASSETS WITH ECONOMIC LIVES SHORTER THAN THE PLANNING HORIZON

The situation is more complex when an asset's economic life is shorter than the planning horizon. Three different methods can be used in this situation. Each method is valid given its assumptions, but the assumptions are different, so different final results can come out of the analysis.

Method 1: Use a Replacement Service to Fill the Gap   This method assumes that there is a replacement service that can be used in place of the original asset and that the cash-flow stream for that replacement service can be estimated.

The approach is to estimate the cash-flow stream needed to provide the replacement service to carry through to the end of the planning horizon. For example, given a computer with a 7-year economic life in a 10-year planning horizon, the remaining 3 years might be provided for by leasing time on a timeshare system or renting appropriate hardware. The cash-flow stream for those 3 remaining years would be based on using the replacement service.

Method 2: Use Multiple Iterations of the Same Asset   This method assumes that at the end of its economic life the asset will be replaced by an identical asset.

The approach is to remember that the AE(i) for a cash-flow stream is identical to the AE(i) for all integer multiples of that cash-flow stream. If the AE(i) for a 3-year period is, say, $1234, the AE(i) for 6 years, 9 years, 12 years, etc. is also $1234.

Simply calculate the AE(i) of the asset's cash-flow stream (include the income cash flows and operating and maintenance costs as necessary, not just the CR(i) costs) and use that cash-flow stream for all intermediate time periods. If an asset has a 5-year economic life and the planning horizon is 10 years, calculate the AE(i) of the cash-flow stream for the first 5 years and duplicate it for the second 5 years.

If the planning horizon isn't an exact integer multiple of the asset's economic life, either use a replacement service to fill the final gap (method 1) or use enough cycles to go beyond the planning horizon and adjust for the implied salvage value on the last cycle. As an example of this, assume that the asset being considered has a 3-year economic life and the planning horizon is 10 years. You could use three cycles of the asset repeated (covering the first 9 years of the planning horizon), and then fill the last year using some replacement service as in method 1. Alternatively, you could use four cycles of the asset repeated (technically covering 12 years), but back the last cycle off by 2 years by adding the implied salvage value as shown.

Method 3: Invest the Profits Somewhere Else   The first two methods are valid for both **revenue alternatives** and **service alternatives**; this third method is appropriate only for revenue alternatives.

- A **revenue alternative** is an alternative that is being described in terms of its complete cash-flow stream; the cash-flow stream has both expense and income cash flows. If Mr. Kinkaid were choosing between building and selling a software project versus becoming a part-time taxi driver, the decision would need to be made on total cash-flow streams. These would be revenue alternatives.
- A **service alternative** is one that's assumed to provide equivalent service to another alternative over their lives; so all of the revenue cash flows are being ignored to simplify the comparison. Only the expense cash flows are shown for a service alternative. Two different compilers for the same programming language could be considered service alternatives because the alternatives should offer effectively identical service over their lives. All of the revenue cash flows can be safely ignored when making comparisons between these two compilers.

This method assumes that the FW(i) of a revenue alternative at the end of its economic life can and will be reinvested at an interest rate, i, through to the end of the study period.

The approach is to calculate the FW(i) of the revenue alternative at the end of its economic life. This number represents the profit from that alternative through its life and corresponds to money that's now available for further investment. The cash-flow stream for the remainder of the planning horizon is set up to represent that investment.

Assume that Mr. Kinkaid was trying to fit his 7-year project into a 10-year planning horizon. If his MARR is 9%, the FW(i) of this alternative is $11,464 (see Chapter 8) at the end of the seventh year. At 9%, the $11,464 will bring in $1032 per year, so Mr. Kinkaid would show income cash-flow instances of $1032 for years 8, 9, and 10.

Summary

Up to now all proposals being compared were required to have the same time span. In practice, all proposals won't have the same time span. This chapter explains how to find the economic life of assets and use that to set the planning horizon for a given decision analysis. This chapter covered the following main points:

- The planning horizon is a consistent study period used for all proposals in a decision analysis.
- Capital recovery, CR(i), is the cost—expressed as an equal-payment-series—of owning (but not operating or maintaining) an asset.

- As the length of ownership of an asset increases, CR(i) tends to decrease. Conversely, the cost of operating and maintaining that same asset increases. An asset's economic life is the optimum time of ownership. Planning horizons can be based on the economic life of the assets in the proposals.
- The implied salvage value of an asset is an estimate of its residual value at some point before the end of its economic life. Implied salvage value is used when an asset's economic life is shorter than the chosen planning horizon.

The chapter also explained how to place proposals into a planning horizon if their actual time spans are shorter or longer than that horizon.

The next chapter deals with two special cases in business decision analysis: replacement and (asset) retirement.

Self-Study Questions

Questions 1 through 3 relate to the following situation: Mountain Systems buys a laser printer for $1200. The end-of-year-1 salvage value is expected to be $1000 and will decrease at a rate of $150 per year for each year after that. The operating and maintenance costs will start at $100 per year and increase at a rate of $25 per year for each year after that. The MARR is 12%.

1. Complete the following table for computing the economic life of the laser printer.

End of Year	(1) Salvage Value if Retired at Year n	(2) AE(i) Cost If Retired in Year n [CR(i)]	(3) Operating & Maintenance Costs for Year n	(4) PW(i) of O&M for Year n in Year 0	(5) Sum of Years 0 O&Ms through Year n	(6) AE(i) Cost of Operating for n Years	(7) Total AE(i) If Retired at Year n
1							
2							
3							
4							
5							
6							
7							

2. What is the economic life of the laser printer and what is the total AE(i) of retiring it at its economic life?

3. Using the economic life calculated in the previous question, what is the implied salvage value of the laser printer at the end of year 2?

Questions 4 through 6 relate to the following situation: InterConnect, Inc. is an Internet service provider (ISP) and is considering buying a network server for $25,000. The end-of-year-1 salvage value is expected to be $20,000 and to decrease at a rate of $2000 per year for each year after that. The operating and maintenance costs will start at $2000 per year and increase at a rate of $500 per year for each year after that. InterConnect's MARR is 12%.

4. Complete the following table for computing the economic life of the network server.

End of Year	(1) Salvage Value if Retired at Year n	(2) AE(i) cost if retired in Year n [CR(i)]	(3) Operating & Maintenance Costs for Year n	(4) PW(i) of O&M for Year n in Year 0	(5) Sum of Years 0 O&Ms through Year n	(6) AE(i) Cost of Operating for n Years	(7) Total AE(i) If Retired at Year n
1							
2							
3							
4							
5							
6							
7							
8							
9							
10							
11							

5. What is the economic life of the network server and what is the total AE(i) of retiring it at its economic life?

6. Using the economic life calculated in the previous question, what is the implied salvage value of the network server at the end of year 3?

7. Mega Industries is considering buying a high-end computer system to support its research group. The system's acquisition cost is $600,000, and at the end of its 10-year economic life it will have a salvage value of $30,000. Mega Industries may retire the system after 7 years and needs to know its implied salvage value at that time. Use an MARR of 14%.

8. InterConnect, Inc. is considering upgrading some of its network switching equipment. The upgrade will cost $250,000 to install and will have a salvage value of $15,000 at the end of its 12-year economic life. InterConnect may decide to replace the entire switch after 8 years and needs to know the implied salvage value of the upgrade at that time. InterConnect's MARR for this study is 16%.

9. Write a program, create a spreadsheet, or develop some other automated means to calculate the economic life of an asset.

12

Replacement and Retirement Decisions

A replacement decision is a special case of the for-profit decision analysis technique presented in Chapter 10. Replacement decisions happen when an organization already has a particular asset and they are considering replacing it with something else, such as deciding between keeping a legacy software system and redeveloping it from the ground up. Replacement decisions use the same decision process as was presented, but there are additional challenges that complicate the decision analysis: sunk cost and salvage value. Retirement decisions are about getting out of an activity altogether, such as when a software company considers not selling a software product any more, or a hardware manufacturer thinks about not building and selling a particular model of computer any longer. This chapter explains why replacement and retirement decisions happen in the first place, explains what's unique about them, and shows how to address that uniqueness in the decision analysis.

Replacement Decisions

As long as an organization is involved in an activity that depends on one or more assets, and the lifetime of those assets is shorter than the duration of the activity, that organization will eventually be faced with a replacement decision. A software development organization will probably continue to be involved in software development well beyond the lifetime of their existing development computers. That organization will be faced with a replacement decision when they consider getting later, more powerful computers for the software development staff.

REASONS FOR REPLACEMENT: DETERIORATION AND OBSOLESCENCE

One reason for replacement is deterioration. As machines and equipment are used, they simply wear out. Cars wear out, and computers wear out. Because of deterioration, the asset is less valuable than before because the process of wearing out usually makes it less capable. An older car won't be as powerful or as fuel efficient as a newer version of the very same car.

The other reason for replacement is suggested by Moore's law [Moore65]:

Processor capacity doubles every 18 to 24 months.

Moore's law is an example of a more general issue that replacements often address, obsolescence. Obsolescence means that there have been changes in the environment of the asset that make it worth less than before. Either more capable assets are available now (newer, more powerful processors in Moore's case) or the demand on the asset has changed significantly. The demand may have gone up, meaning that the asset isn't capable of providing the service it needs to. Alternatively, the demand may have gone down to where a less-capable, but less-costly asset could replace the existing one. The load on a Web server is an example of changing demand. Maybe a Web site is becoming so popular that the existing server can't handle the hits. Or maybe a competitor's site is more popular now and the load on this site has dropped dramatically.

These two causes for replacement, deterioration and obsolescence, may happen separately or together. An office building will probably deteriorate (leaky roof, etc.) long before it becomes obsolete. Software becomes obsolete but it never really "wears out" in the traditional sense. A computer will deteriorate and become more obsolete at the same time.

Sunk Cost and Salvage Value, Special Issues in Replacement Decisions

Replacement decisions use the same for-profit decision analysis technique described in Chapter 10, but two additional factors, sunk cost and salvage value, need to be understood and properly addressed. The sunk cost of an asset is simply the difference between what was paid for it when it was bought and its salvage value—how much it's worth now.

Sunk cost = Acquisition cost − Salvage value

Maybe someone paid $3000 for a laptop computer 3 years ago, and the computer has a salvage value of $700 today. That computer's sunk cost is $2300. Maybe a corporation paid $2.5 million for an inventory control system, but they couldn't sell the system today even if they had to. The sunk cost on the inventory control system is its entire acquisition cost, $2.5 million, and its salvage value is zero.

The problem with sunk costs is mostly psychological. People have a natural tendency to protect their investment; the corporation may mistakenly hold on to the inventory control system even though a more economical system is available. The corporation may be trying to squeeze every penny out of the system and in fact be spending more money than it needs to.

Sunk costs are past history and decision analyses are all about future actions. A sunk cost is just that, sunk. By definition, nothing can be done to recover the money. As much as one might hate to admit it, sunk costs are irrelevant in replacement decision analysis.

Another psychological factor about replacement analyses is that a decision to replace is usually considered more significant than a decision to stay with the existing asset. If someone decides to carry out a replacement and it later turns out to be the wrong decision, that person is likely to be given a harder time than another person who decided to not replace, yet the not-to-replace decision turned out to be wrong. There is a natural psychological bias against deciding to replace.

In addition to the psychological factors, there is a financial factor to consider. Remember from the discussion of capital recovery, CR(i), that the salvage value of an asset has an opportunity cost (see Chapter 11). The fact that the money is tied up in the asset means that it can't be used for something else. That opportunity cost needs to be allocated to the existing asset in the analysis.

The Outsider's Viewpoint: Addressing Sunk Cost and Salvage Value

The outsider's viewpoint is a simple but effective way to be sure the sunk cost and the opportunity cost of the salvage value are properly addressed in the decision analysis. The outsider's viewpoint assumes that you are someone who needs the service provided by either the existing asset or the proposed replacement(s) but you don't own either. As an outsider, you have the choice of either buying the existing asset at its salvage value or buying (any one of) the replacement candidate(s).

Because the outsider only pays the salvage value to buy the existing asset, its original acquisition cost is ignored, exactly as it should be. Whatever was originally paid for the asset is not a part of the replacement decision. Having the outsider pay the salvage value also properly allocates the opportunity cost to the existing asset.

An Example of Replacement Analysis

Replacement analysis is identical to the process described in Chapter 10, but two additional terms need to be defined:

- The **defender** is the existing asset that you are thinking about replacing.
- A **challenger** is an asset being considered as a replacement for the defender.

As mentioned in Chapter 11, defenders will tend to have low capital costs but relatively high operation and maintenance costs. The investment in the defender was probably made a long time ago, and relatively little additional investment, if any, is needed to keep it. However, the operation and maintenance costs are usually relatively high. If you bought a car several years ago, it could already be paid off—you're not making loan payments on it anymore. On the other hand, the older the car is, the less fuel efficient it tends to be, plus it tends to require more (and more substantial) repairs than a newer car.

Challengers typically have high acquisition costs but low operating and maintenance costs. A decision to switch to the challenger will usually require a large capital investment; after the investment has been made, however, the system should have lower operating and maintenance costs. If you decide to buy a new car, the purchase price will be more than if you just kept your existing car, but the operation and maintenance costs will usually be much less.

Software can often be considered in this same light. Existing "legacy" software systems are probably already bought and paid for, but the older they are, the more maintenance they tend to require. Redeveloping an existing legacy system will require a relatively large investment, but (if done right) the operation and maintenance costs should drop significantly.

THE DEFENDER

The example situation is a company that does transaction processing. The defender, a home-grown C program running on a midrange processor, is running close to capacity and can't handle much more load. Marketing research has shown that there is at least two times as much market demand as there is current capacity. The existing equipment has a salvage value of $5k, so the outsider's viewpoint requires using that as the defender's initial investment. The defender's annual income is $130k. The defender requires a full-time operator with a fully burdened salary of $60k on top of operation and maintenance costs of $15k for the equipment itself, so the annual expenses are $75k. The company predicts that the defender has an economic life of 4 years and will still have a salvage value of $5k at that time. The defenders finances are summarized in the following table.

Initial investment	$5000
Annual income	$130,000
Annual expenses	$75,000
Salvage value	$5000

CHALLENGER 1

One possibility that the company is considering is to keep the existing system but also buy another midrange processor and hire another operator. This way they can run the home-grown C program on both processors and split the demand between them. The new processor would cost $30k, but outsider's viewpoint forces adding $5k to cover the cost of the existing processor. The annual income would be double the defender's, as would the annual expenses. The salvage value after the 4-year economic life of this challenger would be $10k. Challenger 1's finances are summarized in the following table.

Initial investment	$35,000
Annual income	$260,000
Annual expenses	$150,000
Salvage value	$10,000

CHALLENGER 2

The other possibility the company is considering is to buy a commercially available application that does everything they need. The net investment for the commercial application is $500k, including scrapping the existing equipment and buying the necessary new equipment. The commercial application has twice the capacity of the defender, so the annual income will be double the existing income. Because the commercial application runs far more automatically than the existing system, the operator would only need to work half time running this application. Assuming that the operator charges the remaining time to other areas of the business, the fully burdened operator costs drop to $30k annually on top of the $15k operating and maintenance costs for the equipment. This system has a 7-year economic life and an estimated $5k salvage value at the end of that time. The second challenger's financial aspects are summarized in the following table.

Initial investment	$500,000
Annual income	$260,000
Annual expenses	$45,000
Salvage value	$5000

THE DECISION ANALYSIS

Start by considering whether the defender and the challenger(s) are mutually exclusive. If they aren't, use the techniques in Chapter 9 to turn them into mutually exclusive alternatives. For this example, treat the defender and challengers as being mutually exclusive.

The company has set the MARR at 16%. They decide to use a 4-year planning horizon because that's the useful life of the defender and challenger 1. They think that the business environment will have changed enough by then that regardless of which alternative they choose today it would need to be revisited after 4 years anyway. To fit the 7-year economic life of challenger 2 into the 4-year planning horizon for the study, the company needs to calculate its implied salvage value. They start by calculating challenger 2's CR(16):

$$\overset{A/P,16\%,7}{CR(16\%) = (\$500,000 - \$5000) \, (0.2476) + \$5000 \, (0.016) = \$122,642}$$

The implied salvage value for challenger 2 is

$$\overset{P/A,16,3 \qquad\qquad P/F,16,3}{F_n{}^* = \$122,642 \, (2.2459) + \$5000 \, (0.6407) = \$278,645}$$

This will be used as the year 4 salvage value for challenger 2.

The company decides to use present worth on incremental investment in making this decision. The steps taken in the analysis are as follows:

1. The alternatives are ordered defender, challenger 1, challenger 2 based on increasing initial investment.

2. Start with the defender as the current best because it has the smallest initial investment.

3. Choose challenger 1 as the first candidate.

4. Compute the differential cash flow stream, Challenger 1 – Defender.

Challenger 1 – Defender

Initial investment	$30,000
Annual income	$130,000
Annual expenses	$75,000
Salvage value	$5,000

5. Compute the PW(MARR) for the differential cash-flow stream.

$$\overset{P/A,16,4}{\quad} \qquad \overset{P/F,16,4}{\quad}$$
$$PW(MARR) = -\$30k + (\$130k - \$75k)\,(2.7982) + \$5k\,(0.5523) = \$127k$$

6. Because the PW(MARR) of the differential cash-flow stream is greater than $0, challenger 1 becomes the current best.

7. Choose challenger 2 as the next candidate.

8. Compute the differential cash-flow stream, Challenger 2 – Challenger 1. Notice that the implied salvage value is being used as the year 4 salvage value for challenger 2.

Challenger 2 – Challenger 1

Initial investment	$465,000
Annual income	$0
Annual expenses	–$105,000
Salvage value	$268,645

9. Compute the PW(MARR) for the differential cash-flow stream.

$$\overset{P/A,16,4}{\quad} \qquad \overset{P/F,16,4}{\quad}$$
$$PW(MARR) = -\$465k + (\$0k - (-\$105k))\,(2.7982) + \$269k\,(0.5523) = -\$13k$$

10. Because the PW(MARR) of the differential cash-flow stream is less than or equal to 0, challenger 1 remains the current best.

11. There are no more alternatives. Challenger 1 is the current best at the end, so it's selected as the best alternative.

The best decision is for the company to buy the additional processor and hire an additional operator.

REPLACEMENT DECISIONS, ECONOMIC LIVES, AND PLANNING HORIZONS

The transaction processing system example used the technique described in Chapter 11, implied salvage value, because its economic life was longer than the planning horizon for the replacement study. If, on the other hand, the economic life of an alternative is shorter than the study period, one of the three techniques in Chapter 11 (using a replacement service, use multiple iterations of the same alternative, invest the profits elsewhere) can be used.

If the planning horizon is long enough, the replacement analysis may need to deal with replacements for the replacements. In a 15-year planning horizon, a challenger with a 5-year economic life would be replaced three times. The replacement analysis will need to make assumptions about how the replacements are themselves replaced over the planning horizon. Options include the following:

- Assume no replacement of current alternatives.
- Assume replacement of each by identical alternatives.
- Assume replacement of each by best challenger.
- Assume replacement of each by dissimilar challenger.

Retirement Decisions

Activities don't continue forever. There are many products and services that were available at one time that aren't available today, at least not in the same form. You can't send a telegram or buy a new rotary-dial telephone today. It would be difficult, if not impossible, to buy a new copy of DOS 3.0 from Microsoft or a new 80286 processor chip from Intel. Eventually a company needs to decide whether to continue an activity or stop it altogether. This is the essence of a retirement (abandonment) decision.

Strictly speaking, retirement decisions only involve the defender: there are no challengers. The mutually exclusive alternatives in a retirement decision analysis are usually as follows:

- Retire immediately.
- Continue the activity for 1 more year then retire.

- Continue for 2 more years then retire.
- Continue for 3 more years then retire.
- . . .

To select the best alternative, find the one that maximizes PW(MARR) of the net cash-flow stream. The PW of retiring immediately is equal to the current salvage value. The PW of retirement in any later year is

PW(MARR) of the salvage value in that year +

PW(MARR) of the revenue cash-flow stream through that year −

PW(MARR) of the operating and maintenance cost cash-flow stream through that year

AN EXAMPLE RETIREMENT PROBLEM

Assume the following estimated cash-flow stream for a given activity. The company has set the MARR at 15%.

End of Year	Revenue	O&M Costs	Salvage Value	
0	—	—	$1200	1391
1	$1000	$300	$900	1138
2	$1000	$900	$600	1538
3	$1000	$500	$800	1550
4	$1000	$550	$500	1519
5	$1000	$800	$300	

The PW of retiring immediately is $1200 because that's the current salvage value.
    The PW of retiring at the end of year 1 is

$$\underset{P/F,15,1}{\$900 * (0.8696)} + \underset{P/F,15,1}{\$1000 * (0.8696)} - \underset{P/F,15,1}{\$300 * (0.8696)} = \$1391$$

The PW of retiring at the end of year 2 is

$$\overset{P/F,15,2}{\$600 * (0.7561)} +$$

$$\overset{P/F,15,1}{[\ \$1000 * (0.8696)} + \overset{P/F,15,2}{\$1000 * (0.7561)\ ]} -$$

$$\overset{P/F,15,1}{[\ \$300 * (0.8696)} + \overset{P/F,15,2}{\$900 * (0.7561)\ ]}$$

$$= \$1138$$

The PW of retiring at the end of year 3 is

$$\overset{P/F,15,3}{\$800 * (0.6575)} +$$

$$\overset{P/F,15,1}{[\ \$1000 * (0.8696)} + \overset{P/F,15,2}{\$1000 * (0.7561)} + \overset{P/F,15,3}{\$1000 * (0.6575)\ ]} -$$

$$\overset{P/F,15,1}{[\ \$300 * (0.8696)} + \overset{P/F,15,2}{\$900 * (0.7561)} + \overset{P/F,15,3}{\$500 * (0.6575)\ ]}$$

$$= \$1538$$

The PW of retiring at the end of year 4 is

$$\ldots$$

$$= \$1556$$

The PW of retiring at the end of year 5 is

$$\ldots$$

$$= \$1519$$

Based on this analysis, the best alternative is to continue the activity for another 4 years and then retire it. The PW of the cash-flow stream is highest at the 4-year point.

In practice, a retirement decision will probably be a bit more complex than shown here. One reason that activities are retired is that they can impact revenue streams for other activities. Boeing stopped selling the 727 because it would have been in competition for the then-new 757. Intel stopped selling the 80286 when it would have cut into the market share of the newer 80386. Microsoft stopped selling DOS when it would damage the revenue stream of the newer Windows family of operating systems. A full-scale retirement study needs to incorporate the revenue and cost impacts on other related products and services if it is relevant to the situation.

A spreadsheet that automates retirement calculations is available at http://www.construx.com/retunonsw/.

Summary

Replacement and retirement decisions are a special case of the for-profit decision analysis techniques presented in Chapter 10. This chapter explained why replacement and retirement decisions happen and what's unique about them. This chapter also showed how to address that uniqueness in the decision analysis. The chapter covered the following major points:

- Replacement decisions happen when an organization already has a particular asset and they are considering replacing it with something else, such as deciding between keeping a legacy software system and redeveloping it from the ground up.
- Replacement decisions use the same decision process as was presented, but there are additional challenges that complicate the decision analysis: sunk cost and salvage value.
- The outsider's viewpoint allows both sunk cost and salvage value to be properly addressed.
- Retirement decisions are about getting out of an activity altogether, such as when a software company considers not selling a software product any more, or a hardware manufacturer thinks about not building and selling a particular model of computer any longer.

The concepts and techniques explained in this part of the book are appropriate for most for-profit decisions, but sometimes more accuracy is needed than can be attained using these techniques. If more accuracy is needed in a particular decision analysis, the concepts and techniques in Part III can also be used.

Self-Study Questions

1. AB-Crystallography, Inc. paid $175k for a processor accelerator for their top-end computer when it was installed 3 years ago. Improvements in technology mean that a new accelerator today would help their system run 22% faster. The manufacturer of the new accelerator offers 30% of the purchase price of the old unit as trade-in on a new unit that would cost $250k installed. The entire present computer system will be replaced in 4 years, and the salvage values of the old and new accelerators are expected to be $30k and $45k, respectively, at that time. AB-C operates the computer 12 hours/day, 21 days per month. Operation and maintenance costs on the existing and the proposed accelerators are considered equivalent. If computer time is valued at $250/hr and the MARR is 15%, should the existing unit be replaced?

2. The central research lab of a major multinational corporation needs to upgrade its computer facilities to increase processing capacity. The computer in use now was bought 2 years ago for $650k. Annual operating and maintenance costs are $80k, and the expected life is 7 years, after which the estimated salvage value is $40k. The existing system has a salvage value of $180k today. One option is to supplement the existing system with a medium-sized computer that would have an initial cost of $100k, operating and maintenance costs of $12k annually, a life of 5 years, and a salvage value of $19k. Another option is to buy a new, larger system that has the needed capacity. The net initial cost, accounting for the trade-in value of the existing system, would be $520k. Operating and maintenance costs would be $50k annually, its service life is 5 years, and its salvage value would be $120k. Still another option is to lease a supplemental computer. The initial cost would be $10k and the annual lease costs—which include operation and maintenance—would run $45k at the beginning of each year. The company's MARR is 12% and study period is 5 years. Which is the lab's best option?

3. AB-Crystallography is also studying options regarding an existing spectrometer whose workload will soon be exceeded. That spectrometer has a salvage value today of $15k. Operating and maintenance costs on it run $2k/year and it has an estimated end-of-life salvage value of $4k. One option is to keep the existing spectrometer for its remaining service life of 4 years and supplement it with a new small spectrometer that cost $10k, has operating and maintenance costs of $3k annually, a service life of 6 years, and a final salvage value of $3k. The second option is to dispose of the current spectrometer and subcontract that work at a cost of $9.5k/yr. Using a study period of 4 years and a MARR of 14%, which option should be selected?

4. Sierra Systems has a CD-ROM labeler that they use to print the labels for their products. By printing the labels in-house, Sierra Systems avoids having to pay an outside printer $5080 annually. The label printer has a remaining useful life of 5 years. The relevant cash-flow instances are listed in the following table.

End of Year	Revenue	O&M Costs	Salvage Value
0	—	—	$3040
1	$5080	$2040	$2640
2	$5080	$3840	$1840
3	$5080	$3640	$1600
4	$5080	$4440	$0
5	$5080	$5240	$0

Given an MARR of 16%, how long should the label printer be kept before retiring it?

5. AB-Crystallography has a special-purpose chemical analysis machine that it uses in one of its laboratories. By using this machine, AB-C avoids having to subcontract the analysis and this saves them $3000 per year. However, the machine has a remaining useful life of 7 years, and maintenance costs are expected to increase. The estimated cash flows for the chemical analyzer are listed in the following table.

End of Year	Revenue	O&M Costs	Salvage Value
0	—	—	$4000
1	$3000	$1600	$3600
2	$3000	$1800	$3200
3	$3000	$2000	$2800
4	$3000	$2200	$2400
5	$3000	$2400	$2000
6	$3000	$2600	$1600
7	$3000	$2800	$1200

Given an MARR of 18%, what is the best retirement option?

6. Another division of Sierra Systems has a CD-ROM duplicating machine that they use to make copies of the product CD for distribution. The duplicator has a remaining useful life of 6 years. The relevant cash flow instances are listed in the following table.

End of Year	Revenue	O&M Costs	Salvage Value
0	—	—	$5000
1	$8000	$4000	$4000
2	$9000	$5000	$3000
3	$10,000	$6000	$2000
4	$10,000	$7000	$1000
5	$10,000	$8000	$500
6	$9000	$9000	$0

Given an MARR of 20%, what is the best retirement option?

PART THREE

ADVANCED FOR-PROFIT DECISION TECHNIQUES

The concepts and techniques in this section are applied on a for-profit business decision when more accuracy is needed than can be achieved using the basic techniques covered in Part Two. The concepts and techniques presented in this part include inflation and deflation, basic accounting, depreciation, income taxes, and the consequences of income taxes on business decisions. Applying these techniques within a business decision will give a more accurate assessment of the true profit in a proposal.

13

Inflation and Deflation

Think about the last time you bought some ordinary thing, such as a movie ticket or a gallon of gasoline. How much did you pay for it? Now think back to the first time you can remember buying that same kind of thing. How much did you pay then? Was it the same price both times? Probably not—the more time that passes between purchases, the less likely it is that the prices would be the same. Simply put, prices change over time. Although there are short-term (on the order of days or weeks) changes in some prices, such as gasoline and groceries, these changes happen too fast and are usually too random to worry about in business decisions. This chapter is concerned with long-term (on the order of months or years) trends in prices. Specific topics addressed in this chapter include the following:

- Price indices, Consumer Price Index, and Producer Price Index
- The inflation rate
- Purchasing power
- Actual dollar analysis and constant dollar analysis
- Planning a retirement

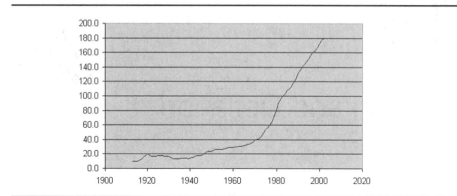

FIGURE 13.1   Average U.S. relative price level (Consumer Price Index), 1913–2002.

Inflation and Deflation

The terms **inflation** and **deflation** describe long-term trends in prices. Inflation means that the same things cost more than they did before. Typical causes for inflation include government price support policies (subsidies) and deficit spending. Higher production costs (caused by wage increases for the workers or tighter environmental protection regulations) or lower availability of resources can have the same effect. Deflation, on the other hand, means that the same things cost less than they did before. Deflation can be caused by more efficient production methods (which lowers production cost) or higher availability of resources.

The terms inflation and deflation usually refer to the overall economy and not to specific products or services. The cumulative effect of price changes over the entire economy means that there are long-term changes in the "purchasing power" of money. Over the last 50 years, purchasing power has tended to decrease (inflation) but significant deflation has happened in the past. Except for wartime inflation in 1812 to 1814 and 1862 to 1865, the general trend in the U.S. economy through the 1800s was deflationary. This deflation was mostly driven by the more efficient production methods of the industrial revolution.

The overall change in prices can be pretty substantial over long periods of time. Figure 13.1 is a graph of relative price levels in the United States from 1913 through 2002. Products and services typically cost about four times as much in 2000 as they did in 1970. If the planning horizon of a business decision is long enough, say a few years or more, or if the inflation rate is over a couple of percent annually, it can cause noticeable changes in the value of a proposal. On the other hand, if the planning horizon is short or inflation is weak, you can safely ignore it. It will be a judgment call on the decision maker's part to decide whether or not to account for inflation in any given decision. Mr. Kinkaid's adventure in Chapter 8, for instance, spans 7 years. It would probably make sense to account for inflation in that decision because of the length of time alone but even more so if the inflation rate is expected to be over 3% to 5%.

Inflation has been far more common over the last 50 or more years, so this chapter shows how to address it. Deflation is handled exactly the same way; the only difference is the actual numbers used to quantify it. Deflation is negative inflation; just use a negative number for the inflation rate.

Price Indices: Measuring Inflation and Deflation

Inflation (or, deflation) is measured using a **price index**. A price index is the ratio (expressed as a percentage) of the historical price of goods or services at some point in time to the price of the same goods or services at another point in time.

$$PriceIndex_{now} = \frac{Price_{now}}{Price_{then}} * 100$$

Several defined price indices are used in the United States today; two of them are described in this chapter. The procedure for making these price indices is the same as for creating your own. This chapter shows how to make your own price index first so that you can better understand what price indices mean and how they work.

To make your own price index, start by defining a benchmark shopping list (known as the "market basket" in technical terms). This shopping list should be representative of the spending patterns of the population you are interested in, both in the kinds of things purchased and the relative quantities. If you were trying to represent the typical American consumer, the shopping list would include housing, utilities, food, transportation, entertainment, and such. Housing would be approximately one third of the total market basket, food would be somewhat less than that, and so on. The market basket for the typical American corporation would be much different. It would include labor, employee benefits, office space, various raw materials, advertising, etc.

The next step is to pick a reference date. The reference date is arbitrary. So long as the reference date is used consistently, it doesn't really matter which particular date is chosen.

Third, find out how much it would have cost to buy everything in the market basket—in the amounts defined—on the reference date. This is the denominator in the price index equation.

Last, find out how much it would cost to buy the same things in the same amounts over time. Each subsequent total price is the numerator in the equation for the price index at that time. The price index is the ratio of the current price to the price on the reference date.

SIMPLE EXAMPLES OF PRICE INDICES

Two simple examples are used, one to show prices going up over time—inflation—and the other showing prices going down.

In 1966, the price of gasoline was about $0.21 per gallon in the United States. In 1996, the price was closer to $1.10 in most of the country.

$$Gasoline\ PriceIndex_{1996} = \frac{\$1.10}{\$0.21} * 100 = 523.8$$

With a price index of 523.8, gasoline cost about 524% in 1996 of what it did in 1966.

Although the nationwide economic trend has been inflationary over the last 50 years, there's been significant deflation in the prices of computer hardware and electronic equipment. This has been driven mostly by decreases in the cost of production of electronics. The smallest, cheapest computer available in the mid-1960s was about the size of a household dishwasher, came with 4K of magnetic core memory (expandable to a then-amazing 32K), was built up out of more than 200 separate circuit boards each about the size of a 3*5 index card, and had a price tag around $10,000. The personal digital assistants (PDAs) of 2004 have vastly more memory (8MB or more), are not much bigger than the 3*5 index card in their entirety, and cost a couple of hundred dollars. And this is without even taking into account that the PDA has many times the computing power of its 1960's ancestor.

In 1986, hard disk storage cost about $10 per on-line megabyte; in 1996, the price was closer to $0.40.

$$HardDisk\ PriceIndex_{1996} = \frac{\$0.40}{\$10.00} * 100 = 4$$

The price index of 4 means that on-line disk memory in 1996 cost about 4% of what it cost in 1986.

When accounting for inflation and deflation in a business decision, be absolutely sure to use a price index that's appropriate for the kind of activity being studied. Don't use a gasoline price index for business decisions involving hard disks, or vice versa. This chapter explains how to account for inflation using any price index—use the price index that's most appropriate.

Popular Price Indices

Two relatively popular price indices are used in the United States today, the Consumer Price Index (CPI) and the Producer Price Index (PPI). These price indices are compiled by the Department of Labor (Bureau of Labor Statistics) and the Department of Commerce (Bureau of Economic Analysis). We'll look at both indices in some detail. More information about the CPI and PPI can be found at http://www.bls.gov/home.htm.

CONSUMER PRICE INDEX

The Consumer Price Index (CPI) measures price change from the retail purchaser's perspective. The CPI is based on the spending habits of the average household consumer; the market basket includes about 400 different goods and services, such as the following:

- Housing
- Food and beverage
- Apparel
- Transportation
- Medical care
- Recreation
- Education
- Utilities and fuels
- ...

A detailed breakdown of the CPI market basket can be found at [BLS2001].

The reference date for the CPI isn't a single point in time; it's the average of three consecutive years, 1982 through 1984. Figure 13.1 is actually a graph of the CPI from 1913 through 2002. Long-term decisions about household or personal finances, if they are accounting for inflation, should use the CPI as the price index. If you are planning your own retirement—which is shown later in this chapter—you should use the CPI. The same goes for personal finance decisions such as buying a house, or buying vs. leasing a car.

PRODUCER PRICE INDEX

The Producer Price Index (PPI) is a family of price indices that measure changes in selling prices for domestic goods and services before they reach the retail consumer. These indices measure price change from the seller's perspective. The sellers' and consumers' prices may be different because of government subsidies, sales and excise taxes, and distribution costs.

The PPI includes over 500 industry-level price indexes along with over 10,000 specific product line and product category subindexes. The PPI tracks price change for practically the entire output of domestic goods-producing sectors:

- Manufacturing
- Agriculture
- Forestry
- Fisheries
- Mining
- Scrap

The PPI also tracks price changes in the service sectors:

- Transportation
- Utilities
- Finance
- Business services
- Health
- Legal
- Professional services

PPI indices are typically used to adjust business-to-business sales contracts for inflation. These contracts specify prices to be paid in the future and often include adjustments for changes in the supplier's input prices. A long-term contract for steel might include an adjustment for changes in iron ore prices by applying the percent change in the PPI for ore to the contracted price for steel. As the price paid for iron ore rises and falls, the price charged for steel follows accordingly. Long-term business decisions, if they need to account for inflation, should use an appropriate price index from the PPI.

The Inflation Rate

The inflation rate measures the rate of increase of the corresponding price index and is usually stated as an annual percentage (for example, 2.3%). Again, the deflation rate is the negative of the inflation rate, 4.5% deflation is the same as –4.5% inflation.

SINGLE-YEAR ANNUAL INFLATION RATE

The inflation rate in any single year can be calculated by dividing the difference between the price index at the end of that year and beginning of that year (which is the price index at the end of the previous year) by the price index at the beginning of that year, as follows:

$$AnnualRate_{year(i)} = \frac{PriceIndex_{year(i)} - PriceIndex_{year(i-1)}}{PriceIndex_{year(i-1)}}$$

Table 13.1 shows the Consumer Price Index (which is graphed in Figure 13.1) and the annual inflation rate derived from the CPI. Based on the CPI data in the table, the inflation rate in 1976 was, for example

$$AnnualRate_{1976} = \frac{PriceIndex_{1976} - PriceIndex_{1975}}{PriceIndex_{1975}} = \frac{56.9 - 53.8}{53.8} = 5.8\%$$

Figure 13.2 is a graph of the annual inflation rate from 1914 through 2002.

TABLE 13.1   Consumer Price Index and Annual Inflation Rates, 1963–2002

Year	CPI	Annual Inflation Rate, %	Year	CPI	Annual Inflation Rate, %
1963	30.6	1.3%	1983	99.6	3.2%
1964	31.0	1.3%	1984	103.9	4.3%
1965	31.5	1.6%	1985	107.6	3.6%
1966	32.4	2.9%	1986	109.6	1.9%
1967	33.4	3.1%	1987	113.6	3.6%
1968	34.8	4.2%	1988	118.3	4.1%
1969	36.7	5.5%	1989	124.0	4.8%
1970	38.8	5.7%	1990	130.7	5.4%
1971	40.5	4.4%	1991	136.2	4.2%
1972	41.8	3.2%	1992	140.3	3.0%
1973	44.4	6.2%	1993	144.5	3.0%
1974	49.3	11.0%	1994	148.2	2.6%
1975	53.8	9.1%	1995	152.4	2.8%
1976	56.9	5.8%	1996	156.9	3.0%
1977	60.6	6.5%	1997	160.5	2.3%
1978	65.2	7.6%	1998	163.0	1.6%
1979	72.6	11.3%	1999	166.6	2.2%
1980	82.4	13.5%	2000	172.2	3.4%
1981	90.9	10.3%	2001	177.1	2.8%
1982	96.5	6.2%	2002	179.9	1.6%

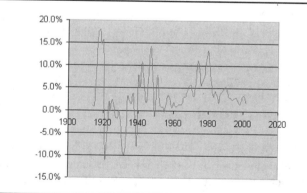

FIGURE 13.2   Annual inflation rate (%), 1914 through 2002

AVERAGE ANNUAL INFLATION RATES

Business decisions that need to address inflation will almost always span more than just one year. And, as shown in Figure 13.2, there can be substantial variations in the annual inflation rate from one year to the next. Accounting for inflation year by year in a business decision would be tedious at best. Instead, the typical business decision assumes an average annual inflation rate and applies this single rate over the entire planning horizon. The average annual inflation rate for multiple years, $\bar{f}$, can be calculated from price indices as follows:

$$CPI_{t+n} = (1 + \bar{f})^n CPI_t$$

Rearranging to solve for $\bar{f}$

$$\bar{f} = \sqrt[n]{\frac{CPI_{t+n}}{CPI_t}} - 1$$

Through the 1970s (from the end of 1969 to the end of 1979)

$$\bar{f} = \sqrt[10]{\frac{CPI_{1979}}{CPI_{1969}}} - 1 = \sqrt[10]{\frac{72.6}{36.7}} - 1 = 7.1\%$$

Notice how inflation over multiple years behaves the same as compound interest—the (F/P,i,n) and (P/F,i,n) formulas can be used, along with the interest tables in Appendix B.

Business decisions spanning a few years or more require estimates of average future annual inflation rates. The actual inflation rates won't be known until those years have passed. Estimates of future inflation rates should be based on the following:

- Recent relevant historical inflation rates
- Predicted economic conditions
- Other economic analysis (such as from financial publications and consultants)
- Judgment

Purchasing Power and Inflation

Inflation means that the purchasing power of money is going down. The inflation rate and the drop in purchasing power are closely related, but aren't exactly the same. Inflation means that the same amount of money later on doesn't buy as much as it did before; the inflation rate measures how much more money is needed to buy the same thing later. Purchasing power is a way of saying, "How much can I buy for a given amount of money?" Around 1970, a candy bar typically cost about 25 cents. Using the Consumer Price Index data in Table 13.1, inflation means the same candy bar would probably cost about $1 in 1997. From the point of view of purchasing power, $1 in 1970 would have bought four candy bars but only one candy bar in early 1997.

TABLE 13.2 Purchasing Power of the Dollar, 1965–1992

Year	Producer Prices	Consumer Prices	Year	Producer Prices	Consumer Prices
1965	$1.045	$1.058	1979	$0.459	$0.461
1966	$1.012	$1.029	1980	$0.405	$0.405
1967	$1.000	$1.000	1981	$0.371	$0.367
1968	$0.972	$0.960	1982	$0.356	$0.346
1969	$0.938	$0.911	1983	$0.351	$0.335
1970	$0.907	$0.860	1984	$0.343	$0.321
1971	$0.880	$0.824	1985	$0.340	$0.310
1972	$0.853	$0.799	1986	$0.345	$0.305
1973	$0.782	$0.752	1987	$0.338	$0.294
1974	$0.678	$0.678	1988	$0.330	$0.282
1975	$0.612	$0.621	1989	$0.313	$0.269
1976	$0.586	$0.587	1990	$0.299	$0.255
1977	$0.550	$0.551	1991	$0.299	$0.248
1978	$0.510	$0.512	1992	$0.293*	$0.241*

*Estimate

The purchasing power for a single year can be calculated from price indices using the following formula:

$$k = PurchasingPower_{year(1)} = \frac{PriceIndex_{year(0)}}{PriceIndex_{year(1)}}$$

For example, in 1976

$$PurchasingPower_{1976} = \frac{PriceIndex_{1975}}{PriceIndex_{1976}} = \frac{53.8}{56.9} = 0.946$$

Meaning that it would take $1 at the end of 1976 to buy the same goods or services that could be bought for 94.6 cents at the end of 1975.

Table 13.2 shows purchasing power between 1965 and 1992 using 1967 as the base year.

The average loss in purchasing power for multiple years can be calculated from price indices as follows:

$$\bar{k} = 1 - \sqrt[n]{\frac{CPI_t}{CPI_{t+n}}}$$

For example, through the 1970s

$$\bar{k} = 1 - \sqrt[10]{\frac{CPI_{1969}}{CPI_{1979}}} = 1 - \sqrt[10]{\frac{36.7}{72.6}} = 0.061 = 6.1\%$$

As stated earlier, the loss in purchasing power and the inflation rate are closely related but are not the same. As shown through the 1970s

$$\bar{f} = \sqrt[10]{\frac{CPI_{1979}}{CPI_{1969}}} - 1 = \sqrt[10]{\frac{72.6}{36.7}} - 1 = 7.1\%$$

The actual relationship between the inflation rate and the drop in purchasing power is as follows:

$$(1 + \bar{f})^n = \frac{1}{(1 - \bar{k})^n}$$

Remember that inflation describes the relative prices of goods and services, whereas purchasing power describes how much a fixed amount of money can buy. If your question is, "How much will <x> cost at <time>?" then use the inflation rate; but if your question is, "How much can I buy for <amount of money> at <time>?" then use the change in purchasing power.

Accounting for Inflation

When accounting for inflation in a business decision, there are two approaches: actual dollar analysis and constant dollar analysis. Under actual dollar analysis, every cash-flow instance represents the actual out-of-pocket dollars received or paid at that point in time. This kind of analysis is also called one of several terms: then-current dollars, current dollars, future dollars, escalated dollars, inflated dollars, and so on. Under constant dollar analysis, every cash-flow instance represents a hypothetical constant purchasing power referenced to a fixed point in time. This kind of analysis is sometimes referred to as real dollars, deflated dollars, today's dollars, zero-date dollars, etc.

A useful analogy to contrast actual dollars and constant dollars is a boat being driven upstream on a large river, as shown in Figure 13.3. Interest over time is like the speed of the boat through the water, and inflation is like the speed of the river in the opposite direction. At some point in time, corresponding to the beginning of the planning horizon, a ball is dropped into the river.

Actual dollars would correspond to the distance between the boat and the ball; as time passes, the dollar amounts increase because of the interest rate. Constant dollars would correspond to the distance between the boat and some fixed point (say a large rock on the shore). The constant dollar values are probably still increasing but at a slower rate than the actual dollars.

Assuming the interest rate is higher than the inflation rate, money will be worth more over time—the boat will be making progress upstream against the river. If the inflation rate is higher than the interest rate, money will be worth less over time—even though the boat is moving through the water, the current is carrying the boat downstream. In either case, the relative distance between the boat and the ball is always increasing.

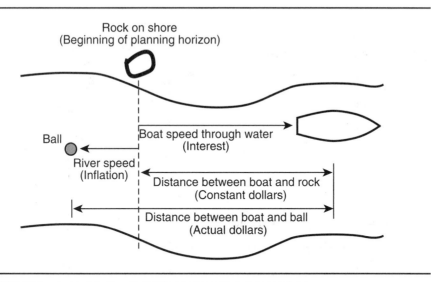

FIGURE 13.3   An analogy for actual dollar and constant dollar analysis

CONVERTING BETWEEN ACTUAL DOLLARS AND CONSTANT DOLLARS

To convert between actual dollars and constant dollars, use the following formulas:

$$ConstantDollars = \frac{1}{(1+f)^n} * ActualDollars$$

And

$$ActualDollars = (1+f)^n * ConstantDollars$$

In the base year (n = 0), constant dollars are equal to actual dollars. Also, notice the similarity again to the (P/F,i,n) and (F/P,i,n) formulas.

As an example, the average inflation rate from 1969 to 1989 was

$$\bar{f} = \sqrt[20]{\frac{CPI_{1989}}{CPI_{1969}}} - 1 = \sqrt[20]{\frac{124.0}{36.7}} - 1 = 6.28\%$$

To convert from 1969 constant dollars to 1989 actual dollars

$$ActualDollars_{1989} = (1 + 0.0628)^{20} * ConstantDollars_{1969} = \$3.38$$

To convert from 1989 actual dollars to 1969 constant dollars

$$ConstantDollars_{1969} = \frac{1}{(1 + 0.0628)^{20}} * ActualDollars_{1989} = \$0.30$$

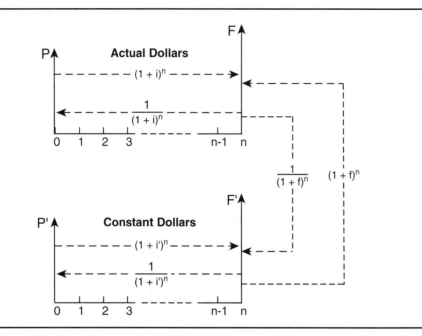

FIGURE 13.4   The relationship between actual dollar analysis and constant dollar analysis

It's important to keep in mind that actual dollar analysis and constant dollar analysis are equivalent. Both lead to the same conclusion as long as you consistently use the right kind of amounts.

Actual Dollar Versus Constant Dollar Analysis

To formalize the relationship between actual dollar and constant dollar analysis, the terms f, i, and i' (*i prime*) need to be defined. f is the inflation rate. It's the average annual percentage of increase in the prices of goods and services (also called the escalation rate or the rate of increase in cost of living). It's like the speed of the river current flowing downstream. i is the market interest rate. It's the actual interest rate in effect at any point in time (also called the combined interest rate, current-dollar interest rate, actual interest rate, or the inflated interest rate). It's like the speed of the boat through the water. i' (*i prime*) is the inflation-free interest rate (i'). It's the apparent interest rate after removing the effects of inflation (the real interest rate, or constant-dollar interest rate). It's like the speed of the boat relative to the fixed point on the shore.

Figure 13.4 shows how actual dollar analysis and constant dollar analysis are related. The top half shows actual dollar analysis. Actual dollar analysis uses the market (actual) interest rate to equivalence dollar amounts over time. Money is brought forward in time using the single-payment compound-amount (F/P,i,n) formula and brought back in time using the single-payment present-worth (P/F,i,n) formula. The bottom half of the picture shows constant dollar analysis. Single-payment compound-amount is still used to equivalence money forward in time, and single-payment present-worth is still used to equivalence back in time. The difference is that constant dollar analysis uses the inflation-free interest rate (i') rather than the market interest rate (i). When converting from constant dollars to actual dollars, the inflation rate, f, is used in the formula $(1 + f)^n$. The reciprocal formula is used to convert from actual dollars to constant dollars.

FINDING THE INFLATION-FREE INTEREST RATE, *I'*

The market (or "actual") interest rate, i, captures the rate of growth of money over time due to interest. The market interest rate is always in terms of actual dollars. The inflation-free interest rate, i', captures the rate of growth of the purchasing power of that same money. Remember that interest causes the *amount* of money to increase but inflation causes the *purchasing power* of that same money to decrease. The inflation-free interest rate takes into account the combined effect of the increasing amount and the decreasing purchasing power.

You must find out what the inflation-free interest rate is if you want to do a constant dollar analysis. You might be able to find it in some kind of financial publication, but it's more likely you will end up calculating it yourself from the market interest rate and the inflation rate (which are more widely available). The inflation-free interest rate can be calculated from the market interest rate and the inflation rate using the following formula:

$$i' = \frac{(1 + i)}{(1 + f)} - 1$$

If the inflation rate is 3%, and the market interest rate is 7%

$$i' = \frac{(1 + 0.07)}{(1 + 0.03)} - 1 = 0.0388 = 3.88\%$$

When the inflation rate is greater than the market interest rate, the inflation-free interest rate will be negative. This is relatively unusual, but it is certainly possible. This only means that the purchasing power of money is falling at a faster rate than the market interest rate is increasing its value. In the boat analogy from above, this means that the current is sweeping the boat downstream faster than it is moving through the water—the boat is moving backward relative to the shore. If the inflation rate is 7%, and the market interest rate is 4%

$$i' = \frac{(1 + 0.04)}{(1 + 0.07)} - 1 = -0.0280 = -2.80\%$$

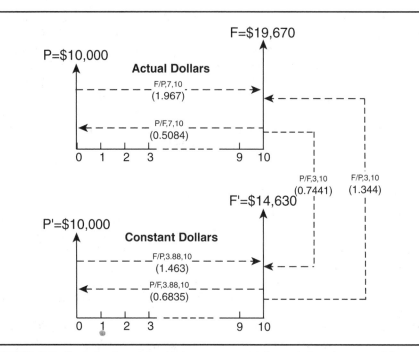

FIGURE 13.5   Illustrating the relationship between actual dollar analysis and constant dollar analysis

A SIMPLE EXAMPLE OF ACTUAL DOLLAR AND CONSTANT DOLLAR ANALYSIS

Assume that you have $10,000 right now, the market interest rate is 7%, and the inflation rate is 3%. What will your money be worth after 10 years in both actual dollar and constant dollar terms? This example, shown in Figure 13.5, will also illustrate the diagram in Figure 13.4 using specific dollar amounts.

To solve, recall that when i is 7% and f is 3%, then i' is 3.88%.

In actual dollar terms (the top of the figure), $10,000 today will grow to $19,670 in 10 years because of the 7% market interest rate. In constant dollar terms, those $19,670 actual dollars will have the same purchasing power as $14,630 dollars today because the 3% inflation rate will reduce the growth of purchasing power to 3.88%.

Mr. Kinkaid's Adventure in Actual and Constant Dollars

Assuming that the net cash-flow stream for Mr. Kinkaid's proposed venture (Table 8.2 in Chapter 8) is in actual dollar terms, it can be used as an example of converting a cash-flow stream from actual dollars to constant dollars. Using 6.5% as the average annual inflation rate for the 7 years of the study, Table 13.3 shows the actual dollar cash-flow stream converted to constant dollars in year 0 (beginning of the planning horizon) terms.

TABLE 13.3 Converting Mr. Kinkaid's Actual Dollar Net Cash-Flow Stream to Constant Dollars

Year	Actual Dollar Net Cash-Flow Stream	Inflation Conversion (P/F,6.5,n)	Constant Dollar Net Cash-Flow Stream
0	$0	0.9390	$0
1	−$3421	0.8817	−$3016
2	−$2671	0.8278	−$2211
3	$329	0.7773	$256
4	$4079	0.7299	$2977
5	$7829	0.6853	$5365
6	$5150	0.6435	$3314
7	$650	0.6042	$393

TABLE 13.4 Comparing Mr. Kinkaid's Actual Dollar and Constant Dollar Cash-Flow Streams

Basis for Comparison	Actual Dollar	Constant Dollar
PW(9)	$6272	$3357
FW(9)	$11,464	$6137
AE(9)	$1246	$667
IRR	35.37%	27.11%
DPP(9)	4.51 years	4.67 years

Table 13.4 shows a comparison of the actual dollar and constant dollar cash-flow streams using the different bases for comparison (Chapter 8).

There's a substantial difference between the actual dollar and the constant dollar perspectives. The constant dollar perspective is a much more realistic view of the true financial performance of a proposal.

Planning a Retirement

One useful application of inflation calculations is in planning one's retirement. This is also a comprehensive, real-world example of how interest and inflation can be applied to a long-term financial analysis. As an example, consider Ms. Johnson. She recently turned 34 and is planning to retire at age 65. Considering her other sources of retirement income, she's confident she can live comfortably on an additional $20,000 per year in present-day dollars. She expects to live 10 years beyond her retirement. She assumes

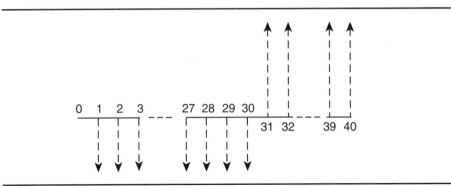

FIGURE 13.6   The cash-flow diagram for Ms. Johnson's retirement

that inflation will average 6% per year between now and retirement and that she can make long-term investments at 11% compounded annually. Her retirement question amounts to this:

> How much should Ms. Johnson save at the end of each year between now and retirement so she can have enough money to allow her to live comfortably for 10 years after her retirement?

She is planning to make deposits at the end of each of the next 29 years with her last deposit when she turns 64. She'll make the first withdrawal on her sixty-fifth birthday and the last when she reaches 74. Figure 13.6 shows a cash-flow diagram for Ms. Johnson's retirement plan.

PLANNING A RETIREMENT USING CONSTANT DOLLARS

Constant dollar retirement planning assumes there is effectively no inflation. Instead, the inflation-free interest rate is used and all dollar amounts are in terms of today's purchasing power. To find Ms. Johnson's inflation-free interest rate

$$i' = \frac{(1.11)}{(1.06)} - 1 = 0.0047 = 4.7\%$$

Now use the inflation-free interest rate to figure out how much she'll need to have in her retirement account after the last deposit on her sixty-fourth birthday. Because she wants 10 years of annual $20,000 withdrawals at a 4.7% interest rate

$$P = \$20,000 \overset{P/A,4.7,10}{(7.8355)} = \$156,710$$

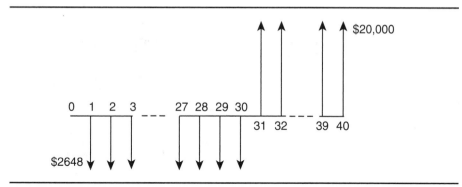

FIGURE 13.7   Constant dollar cash-flow diagram for Ms. Johnson's retirement

TABLE 13.5   Selected actual dollar amounts Ms. Johnson should deposit

End of Year	Ms. Johnson's Age	Inflation Conversion Factor (F/P,6,n)	Actual Dollar Amount to Deposit
1	35	1.0600	$2807
6	40	1.4185	$3756
11	45	1.8983	$5027
16	50	2.5404	$6727
21	55	3.3996	$9002
26	60	4.5494	$12,047
30	64	5.7435	$15,209

She'll need to have $156,710 in her account when she turns 64. To have that much on her sixty-fourth birthday, how much will she need to deposit at the end of each year between now and then?

$$\overset{A/F,4.7,29}{A = \$156,710\ (\ 0.0169\ ) = \$2648}$$

Assuming Ms. Johnson's estimates are correct, she can retire comfortably if she deposits $2648 (in today's dollar terms) at the end of each year between now and retirement. Figure 13.7 shows the constant-dollar cash-flow diagram for Ms. Johnson's retirement.

To make this retirement plan useful to Ms. Johnson, the $2648 constant dollar amounts need to be converted into actual dollar amounts for her to deposit at the end of each year. As an illustration, Table 13.5 shows several representative years.

TABLE 13.6   Actual Dollar Amounts That Ms. Johnson Will Be Withdrawing

End of Year	Her Age (At End)	Convert Present-Day Dollar Amounts to Actual Dollars
31	65	$F/P,6,31$ $20,000 (6.0881) = $121,762
32	66	$F/P,6,32$ $20,000 (6.4534) = $129,068
33	67	$F/P,6,33$ $20,000 (6.8406) = $136,812
34	68	$F/P,6,34$ $20,000 (7.2510) = $145,020
35	69	$F/P,6,35$ $20,000 (7.6861) = $153,722
36	70	$F/P,6,36$ $20,000 (8.1473) = $162,946
37	71	$F/P,6,37$ $20,000 (8.6361) = $172,722
38	72	$F/P,6,38$ $20,000 (9.1543) = $183,086
39	73	$F/P,6,39$ $20,000 (9.7035) = $194,070
40	74	$F/P,6,40$ $20,000 (10.2857) = $205,714

The actual dollar amounts Ms. Johnson needs to deposit each year are constantly increasing. If inflation really does average 6% per year, the actual dollar amount deposited will have the same purchasing power as $2648 today. If her income were to keep pace with inflation exactly, each deposit amount would represent the same percentage of her annual income. The more realistic assumption is that her income will increase faster than inflation, so payments will become easier as the years go by.

PLANNING A RETIREMENT USING ACTUAL DOLLARS

Actual dollar retirement planning uses amounts that represent at-that-moment-in-time dollars. Start by finding the amount, in then-present dollars, required to support her standard of living for the 10 years following her retirement. Her retirement begins 31 years from now, so use the single-payment compound-amount formula to convert her annual

$20,000 current-dollar income into actual dollar amounts using the average inflation rate of 6%. Table 13.6 shows the actual dollar amounts that she will be withdrawing at the end of each of her 10 years of retirement.

Each of these can now be referenced back to her sixty-fourth birthday and added up to calculate how much money she will need to end up with after her final deposit.

$$\overset{P/F,11,1}{} \qquad \overset{P/F,11,2}{} \qquad \overset{P/F,11,3}{} \qquad \overset{P/F,11,4}{}$$
$$P = \$121{,}762\ (0.9009) + \$129{,}068\ (0.8116) + \$136{,}812\ (0.7312) + \$145{,}020\ (0.6587) +$$

$$\overset{P/F,11,5}{} \qquad \overset{P/F,11,6}{} \qquad \overset{P/F,11,7}{} \qquad \overset{P/F,11,8}{}$$
$$\$153{,}722\ (0.5935) + \$162{,}946\ (0.5346) + \$172{,}722\ (0.4817) + \$183{,}086\ (0.4339) +$$

$$\overset{P/F,11,9}{} \qquad \overset{P/F,11,10}{}$$
$$\$194{,}070\ (0.3909) + 205{,}714\ (0.3522)$$

$$= \$899{,}309$$

To double-check, the $156,710 from the constant dollar retirement plan, above, can be converted to actual dollars at 6% inflation:

$$\overset{F/P,6,30}{}$$
$$\$156{,}710\ (5.7435) = \$900{,}063$$

This is within about 0.08% of the $899,309 calculated using actual dollars; the difference is due to rounding errors in the interest factors.

The next step is to find the amount, A, she needs to save each year to end up with $899,309 on her sixty-fourth birthday.

$$\overset{A/F,11\%,30}{}$$
$$A = \$899{,}309\ (\ 0.0050\ ) = \$4497$$

Ms. Johnson needs to deposit $4497 at the end of every year into her retirement account. The cash-flow diagram (in actual dollars) is shown in Figure 13.8.

With actual dollar retirement planning, Ms. Johnson will be depositing the same number of dollars at the end of each year, but the purchasing power of those dollars will decrease as time goes on. Assuming her income exactly keeps pace with inflation, her first deposit of $4497 will be a much greater percentage of her annual income than her last deposit of that same actual dollar amount.

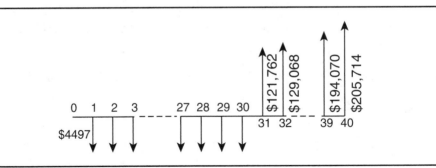

FIGURE 13.8 Actual dollar cash-flow diagram for Ms. Johnson's retirement

Summary

Inflation and deflation describe long-term trends in prices. Inflation means that the same things cost more than they did before, and deflation means they cost less. When a business decision spans several years, or the inflation rate is significant, inflation should be factored into the decision analysis. The chapter covered the following major points:

- A price index measures inflation as the ratio (expressed as a percentage) of the historical price of goods or services at some point in time to the price of those same goods or services at another point in time.
- Two common price indices are used in the United States, the Consumer Price Index (CPI) and the Producer Price Index (PPI).
- The CPI measures price change from the retail purchaser's perspective and is based on the spending habits of the average household consumer.
- The PPI is a family of price indices that measure changes in selling prices for domestic goods and services before they reach the retail consumer. These indices measure price change from the seller's perspective.
- An inflation rate measures the rate of increase of a price index and is usually stated as an annual percentage.
- The inflation rate and the drop in purchasing power are closely related, but aren't quite the same. Inflation measures how much more money is needed to buy the same thing later. Purchasing power measures how much can be bought for a given amount of money.
- Inflation can be accounted for using constant dollar or actual dollar analysis. Constant dollar analysis is based on hypothetical fixed-value dollars and uses an inflation-free interest rate. Actual dollar analysis expresses amounts in actual terms and uses a market interest rate. Formulas are given to convert between actual and constant dollars.

The next chapter explains depreciation, which is how investments in capital assets are charged off against income over several years. Depreciation is an important factor in calculating after-tax cash-flow streams to accurately address income taxes.

Self-Study Questions

1. If you were to develop a price index for owning and operating a home computer, name at least three items that should be included in the market basket.

2. In the year 2000, the cost of a single-ride subway ticket on a metropolitan transit system was $1. That same ticket cost $1.50 in 2003. If 2000 is the reference date, what is the price index for that subway's single-ride tickets in 2003?

3. The metropolitan transit system also sold monthly travel passes that cost $60 in the year 2000. If the price of monthly passes followed the same price index as single-ride tickets (from the previous question), what would the price of a monthly pass be in 2003?

4. In 1996, the monthly cost of a certain cell phone plan was $45. In 2002, that same plan had a monthly cost of $36. If 1996 is the reference date, what is the price index for that cell phone plan in 2002?

5. Using the price index for the cell phone plan from the previous question, assume that the cell phone company has a family plan that cost $68 in 1996. What should we expect that family plan to cost in 2003?

6. Assume that a software development price index had been created and that in 2002 the index was 105.8. If in 2003 the index was 106.6, what was the software development inflation rate between 2002 and 2003?

7. If the cell phone price index was 93 in 2001 and 87 in 2002, what was the inflation rate for cell phone price plans between 2001 and 2002?

8. Assume that a software development price index in 1992 was 88.0. If that same price index was 105.8 in 2002, what was the average annual inflation rate between 1992 and 2002?

9. If the cell phone price index was 103.0 in 1998 and was 87.0 in 2002, what was the cell phone average annual inflation rate between 1998 and 2002?

10. The CPI in 1939 was 13.0 and the CPI in 1949 was 23.8, so the average annual inflation rate for the 1940s was 6.2%. What was the loss of purchasing power over this same time period? Also show, mathematically, how the loss of purchasing power and the inflation rate over this time period are related.

11. The Great Depression ran through the 1930s. The CPI in 1929 was 17.1, and the CPI in 1939 was 13.0, so the average annual inflation rate for the 1930s was –2.7%. What was the loss of purchasing power over this same time period? Also show, mathematically, how the loss of purchasing power and the inflation rate over this time period are related.

12. Mary just invested $7500 into an interest-bearing account that yields 9.0%. Inflation is averaging 4.8% per year.
    a. What will the actual dollar value of Mary's investment be after 15 years?
    b. What is the inflation-free interest rate (rounded to the nearest 0.1 percent)?
    c. What will the constant dollar value of Mary's investment be after 15 years (using today's dollars as the reference dollar)?
    d. Show that the actual dollar value and the constant dollar value of Mary's investment 15 years from now represent the same amount of money.

13. Mario just invested $12,000 into an interest-bearing account that yields 11.0%. Inflation is averaging 6.6% per year.
    a. What will the actual dollar value of Mario's investment be after 9 years?
    b. What is the inflation-free interest rate (rounded to the nearest 0.1 percent)?
    c. What will the constant dollar value of Mario's investment be after 9 years (using today's dollars as the reference dollar)?
    d. Show that the actual dollar value and the constant dollar value of Mario's investment 9 years from now represent the same amount of money.

14. If the net cash-flow stream in Figure 8.1 (also Table 8.2) represented actual dollars, what would the constant dollar cash-flow stream be if inflation averaged 4% annually?

15. What is the PW(9%) of the constant dollar cash-flow stream in the previous question? How does it compare with the PW(9%) of the actual dollar cash-flow stream?

16. If the net cash-flow stream in Figure 8.1 (also Table 8.2) represented constant dollars, what would the actual dollar cash-flow stream be if inflation averaged 6% annually?

17. What is the PW(9%) of the actual dollar cash-flow stream in the previous question? How does it compare with the PW(9%) of the constant dollar cash-flow stream?

18. Assume that Ms. Johnson had just turned 24 instead of 34. (She's starting 10 years earlier.) In constant dollar terms, how much does she need to deposit annually to have the same post-retirement income? How does this compare to the amount she has to deposit if she starts at age 34?

19. Assume that Ms. Johnson had just turned 44 rather than 34. (She's starting 10 years later.) In constant dollar terms, how much does she need to deposit annually to have the same post-retirement income? How does this compare to the amount she has to deposit if she starts at age 34?

Questions 20 and 21 relate to the following situation: Mr. Jones is 28 and is planning to retire at age 65. Based on his family history, he expects to live 20 years beyond retirement. Inflation has averaged 3.2% over the previous 20 years, and he expects it to continue at that rate. He can invest at 9.5%. How much should he deposit on his birthday each year until he retires to meet his post-retirement goal of $33,000 per year in income to supplement his other retirement benefits?

20. Plan Mr. Jones's retirement using constant dollars.

21. Plan Mr. Jones's retirement using actual dollars.

22. Choose a retirement age and assume that you will live 20 years beyond retirement. Considering your existing retirement resources (employee retirement account, IRA, etc.), decide how much additional income you will need to maintain a comfortable standard of living. Use these to plan your own retirement. Use either constant dollars or actual dollars (your choice).

14

Depreciation

Depreciation addresses how investments in capital assets are charged off against income over several years. This is an important part of calculating after-tax cash flows, which is critical to accurately addressing income taxes. Software itself typically isn't depreciated, but if you're working on proposals with a planning horizon longer than one year, the proposals involve capital assets (such as buildings and equipment), and you need to accurately reflect the effects of income taxes in the decision analysis, then depreciation will be an important factor to include in the analysis. Another reason to understand depreciation is that your software project proposals will probably be compared against nonsoftware proposals, so you should understand how the nonsoftware proposals are being evaluated. This chapter presents depreciation as it is defined in the United States. The laws regarding depreciation in other countries will certainly be different, but the same general principles will probably still apply.

As explained in the chapter on the consequences of income taxes (Chapter 17), it would be to a company's advantage to not depreciate assets. Rather, the company is much better off treating them—like software usually is—as expenses and writing off the entire acquisition cost in the year each asset is acquired. A company isn't *allowed* to depreciate its assets; it's *required* to depreciate them.

Introduction to Depreciation

The word *depreciation* has two different meanings in business decisions. First, it refers to how an asset will lose value over time due to effects such as wear and tear. This will be called **actual depreciation**. Second, it refers to how the organization accounts for that loss in value. This will be called **depreciation accounting**. Depreciation accounting is an important factor in decision analyses that need to accurately reflect the effects of income taxes. Income taxes are discussed in more detail in Chapters 16 and 17.

It's important to understand that actual depreciation (the real loss in value) is rarely the same as depreciation accounting (how the loss is accounted for by the organization). Actual depreciation is virtually impossible to determine without selling the asset—the asset is really worth only what someone is willing to pay for it. In practice, the loss in value can only be estimated. That estimation will be done using one of a handful of predefined depreciation methods. Those different methods are explained in this chapter. If, when the asset is sold or scrapped, there is a difference between the actual value and the value estimated by depreciation accounting, that difference would need to be addressed in the organization's taxes.

Actual Depreciation

There are two general causes for actual depreciation, physical depreciation and functional depreciation. Both can happen at the same time or they may happen separately.

PHYSICAL DEPRECIATION

Physical depreciation literally means that the asset is wearing out (for example, wear and tear, corrosion, shock, vibration, abrasion, and such), and it can't do its job as well as it used to. The more it's used, the more it wears out. Physical depreciation also includes natural deterioration such as rust, corrosion, rotting, decomposition, and so on. Deterioration doesn't depend on how much the asset is used; deterioration would happen whether the asset was used or not.

Software isn't a physical thing, so it can't be affected by physical depreciation. On the other hand, software professionals are sometimes responsible for, or have influence on, decisions about computer hardware, peripherals, and computing facilities. These kinds of assets are affected by physical depreciation so software professionals need to be able to address this kind of depreciation in their business decisions.

FUNCTIONAL DEPRECIATION

Functional depreciation means that the environment where the asset is operating has changed, and the asset isn't well matched to that new environment. One kind of functional depreciation is obsolescence. Obsolescence happens when another asset that can do the same job better makes this asset worth less. A newer computer with a faster processor and more memory is a common example of obsolescence in the software industry. Evolving hardware and software standards also lead to obsolescence; assets that don't meet the newer standard may lose value from noncompliance. Another type of functional depreciation is when the demand on the asset increases to the point where the asset can't meet that demand. A Web server designed to serve 10,000 connections but needing to support 20,000 connections because of increased user traffic is an example. Similarly, the demand on the asset might decrease to the point where a smaller, less-capable, and cheaper asset would suffice.

Depreciation Accounting

The key idea in depreciation accounting is that corporations are taxed on profit (net income), not gross income:

Profit = Gross income – Expenses

The expenses charged by the organization in any tax year should be an accurate reflection of the actual expenses incurred during that year. Therefore, those expenses should include at least an approximation of the actual depreciation of the assets the company owns. Through depreciation accounting, the tax authorities are trying to force the accounting and tax recognition of an asset's loss in value to be as close in time as reasonably possible to when that loss actually happens.

Depreciation accounting effectively treats the original cost of an asset as a prepaid expense. Instead of charging the entire cost as an expense when that asset is bought, depreciation accounting spreads the cost over the life of the asset. A $1 million computer wouldn't be counted as a $1 million expense in the year that computer was bought. Instead, the $1 million cost would be spread systematically over the life of the computer. Depreciation accounting tries to approximate the actual depreciation based on assumptions about how the asset loses value over time.

It's important to recognize that the depreciation amounts in depreciation accounting are not actual cash-flow instances. The actual cash-flow instance happens when the company buys the asset. The depreciation amounts are an allocation of the actual expense (the cash-flow instance that happened when the asset was bought) over time. The taxing authorities are forcing the company to spread the recognition of the original expense over the asset's assumed life.

One theoretical alternative to depreciation accounting would be to allow the company to write off the entire expense in the year an asset was bought. This would make the income taxes for that year unrealistically low, whereas the income taxes for the remainder of the asset's life would be unrealistically high. Similarly, if the company could only write off the actual expense (acquisition cost minus salvage value) after an asset had been sold or scrapped, the early years' income taxes would be unrealistically high, whereas the income taxes in the year of disposal would be unrealistically low. Depreciation accounting is the tax authorities' attempt to make each year's income taxes as realistic as possible.

Any asset that

- Is used in a business or trade
- Is used for producing income
- Has a known lifespan that is more than 1 year

is required to be treated with depreciation accounting. However, depreciation accounting only applies when an asset's value decreases over time, either from physical deterioration, functional deterioration, or both. The value of the structure of an office building will be depreciated, but the value of the land that it sits on cannot. The building will eventually wear out, but the land never does.

Any asset with an expected lifespan of less than one year, such as a toner cartridge for a laser printer, printer paper, and so on, is treated as an expense in the year it is bought.

Value-Time Functions

A **value-time function** is a mathematical function that models how an asset loses value over time. The simplest value-time function is known as **straight-line**. The straight-line value-time function assumes that the asset loses value at a constant rate (i.e., as a fixed percentage of the asset's original value) over its lifetime. An asset that originally cost $10,000 and has a 10-year expected life is assumed to have a value of $3,000 7 years after it was bought. The straight-line value-time function is shown in Figure 14.1.

Another value-time function is called **declining-balance**. The declining-balance value-time function assumes that the asset loses value as a fixed percentage of its remaining value over its lifetime (e.g., it's worth 20% less than it was the year before). Using an 80% declining-balance value-time function, a $10,000 asset would be assumed to be worth $8,000 after 1 year, $6,400 after 2, $5,120 after 3, etc. The declining-balance value-time function is shown in Figure 14.2.

Both of these value-time functions, and their corresponding depreciation methods, are described in more detail below.

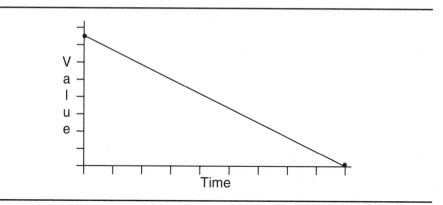

FIGURE 14.1   Straight-line value-time function

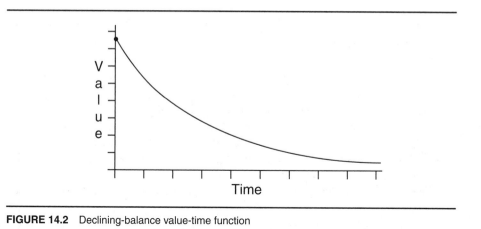

FIGURE 14.2   Declining-balance value-time function

Book Value

The **book value** of an asset is the tax authorities' best estimate, based on depreciation accounting, of that asset's actual value. Another way of looking at book value is that it's the part of the asset's acquisition cost that hasn't been charged off by depreciation accounting. Remember, however, that the book value may not be the asset's actual value. The actual value can't be known for certain unless or until the asset is sold or scrapped. If the company paid $1 million for a high-performance computer and had depreciated it by $100,000 each year for 4 years (using straight-line depreciation), the book value in the fifth year is $600,000. The computer may or may not actually be worth $600,000 at that time, but the organization won't know for certain unless they can sell it for that price.

The book value in any year can be calculated by subtracting the depreciation amount in one year from the book value from the previous year.

$$BookValue_{year(t)} = BookValue_{year(t-1)} - Depreciation_{year(t-1)}$$

Alternatively, the book value can be expressed as the original acquisition cost minus the total depreciation charged so far.

$$BookValue_{year(t)} = AcquisitionCost - \sum_{i=1}^{t} Depreciation_{year(i)}$$

Tables showing the relationship between depreciation amounts and book values are shown in the discussions of each of the depreciation methods below.

Depreciation Methods

Under U.S. tax code, the tax law that's in effect when the asset is bought determines an asset's depreciation method. Even though the tax code can change from one year to the next, bringing with it different depreciation methods, any given asset's depreciation method will stay the same regardless, for as long as the organization owns it. Once the depreciation method is assigned for an asset, that same method is used until it is sold or scrapped. This means that two different instances of the same kind of asset might be depreciated differently if the tax code changed between when each of them was bought.

The U.S. tax code has defined different depreciation methods three times in the recent past:

- Before 1981
- 1981 through 1986
- 1987 and beyond

The rest of this chapter explains each of the depreciation methods prescribed during these times.

There are several reasons for explaining all of these methods even though only one method is prescribed today. First, and most important, looking at each of these methods gives a broad survey of different approaches to depreciation accounting. Second, the earlier depreciation methods are a good foundation for understanding the method used today. Finally, the tax laws could certainly change again in the future, and one of the earlier methods may become prescribed again.

TABLE 14.1   Sample CLADR Lifespans

Asset Description	Lower Limit	ADR Life	Upper Limit
Business aircraft	5	6	7
Automobiles, taxis	2.5	3	3.5
Railroad cars and locomotives	12	15	18
Vessels, barges, tugs	14.5	18	21.5
Agricultural equipment	8	10	12
Computers	5	6	7
Electronic products	6.5	8	9.5
Furniture	8	10	12

Depreciation Methods Before 1981

Before 1981, the organization could choose any one of four different methods for depreciating any asset:

- Straight-line depreciation
- Declining-balance depreciation
- Declining-balance switching to straight-line depreciation
- Sum-of-the-years-digits depreciation

Straight-line and declining-balance time value functions were already introduced earlier in this chapter. Each of these methods is discussed in more detail below.

After first choosing the depreciation method, the next step in pre-1981 depreciation accounting was to estimate the asset's useful life. Intuitively, the useful life of the asset is an estimate of how long it will likely last in business use. Properly cared for, a car can last for 10 years or more, but in typical business use cars tend to be kept for only two or three years at the most. The useful life could either be based on the organization's past experience with similar assets or from the general experience of the industry. Another alternative was to use the class life asset depreciation range (CLADR) system.

The CLADR system gave IRS-approved useful life ranges for different kinds of assets. Sample CLADR ranges are shown in Table 14.1; the complete CLADR tables were listed in Revenue Procedure 83-35. The organization could pick any useful life between the defined lower and upper limits, but government auditors preferred the ADR life value.

TABLE 14.2 An Example of Straight-Line Depreciation

End of Year	Depreciation Amount in Year	Book Value at End of Year
0	—	$7000
1	$1000	$6000
2	$1000	$5000
3	$1000	$4000
4	$1000	$3000
5	$1000	$2000
6	$1000	$1000

STRAIGHT-LINE DEPRECIATION

Straight-line depreciation assumes that the value of the asset decreases at a constant rate over its useful life. The asset loses a fixed percentage of its *original* value each year. ("Original" is emphasized to contrast it with "remaining," as described in declining-balance depreciation, next.) The formula for calculating the straight-line depreciation amount is as follows:

$$Depreciation = \frac{AcquisitionCost - SalvageValue}{LifetimeInYears}$$

Straight-line depreciation is the only method that uses the same depreciation amount each year.

The book value formula for straight-line depreciation simply subtracts t years times the yearly depreciation amount from the original acquisition cost.

$$BookValue_{year(t)} = AcquisitionCost - (t * Depreciation)$$

As an example, consider a computer system with an acquisition cost of $7000, a useful life of 6 years, and an expected salvage value of $1000. The depreciation schedule and the book value at the end of each year are shown in Table 14.2.

The depreciation amount is a constant $1000 over the 6-year useful life. The asset ends its life with a $1000 book value, which is the expected salvage value.

Declining-Balance Depreciation

Declining-balance depreciation assumes that the value of the asset decreases faster earlier in its life and slower later in its life. Under declining-balance depreciation, the asset loses a fixed percentage of its *remaining* value over time. ("Remaining" is emphasized to contrast with straight-line depreciation, which loses a fixed percentage of its original value.) The depreciation amount is a fixed percentage, α, of the book value of the asset at the beginning of that year. As the book value decreases, so does the depreciation amount. The formula for calculating the declining-balance depreciation amount in year t is as follows:

$$Depreciation_{year(t)} = \alpha * BookValue_{year(t-1)}$$

Unlike straight-line depreciation, declining-balance depreciation ignores the salvage value of the asset.

Under current U.S. tax code, the maximum α is double the straight-line rate. An asset with a useful life of n years is limited to

$$\alpha \leq \frac{2}{n}$$

A 6-year asset would have a maximum α of 0.333, and a 20-year asset would have a maximum α of 0.10. Using this maximum depreciation rate is called the **double-declining-balance method** or the **200% declining-balance method**.

Another variation is **150% declining-balance** depreciation. In this case

$$\alpha \leq \frac{1.5}{n}$$

Under 150% declining-balance, a 6-year asset would have $\alpha = 0.25$, and a 20-year asset would have $\alpha = 0.075$.

The book value formula for declining-balance depreciation multiplies the original acquisition cost times the quantity $(1 - \alpha)$ raised to the t power.

$$BookValue_{year(t)} = AcquisitionCost * (1 - \alpha)^t$$

Table 14.3 shows the same computer system as above depreciated using the double-declining-balance method.

$$\alpha = \frac{2}{6} = 0.33$$

Notice how the book value never actually reaches $0, and that the book value falls below the computer's estimated salvage value of $1000 in year 5.

For comparison, the same computer system is shown in Table 14.4 using the 150% declining-balance method.

$$\alpha = \frac{1.5}{6} = 0.25$$

TABLE 14.3 An Example of Double-Declining-Balance Depreciation

End of Year	Depreciation Amount in Year	Book Value at End of Year
0	—	$7000
1	0.33 * 7000 = $2310	$4690
2	0.33 * 4690 = $1548	$3142
3	0.33 * 3142 = $1037	$2105
4	0.33 * 2105 = $695	$1410
5	0.33 * 1410 = $465	$945
6	0.33 * 945 = $312	$633

TABLE 14.4 An Example of 150% Declining-Balance Depreciation

End of Year	Depreciation Amount in Year	Book Value at End of Year
0	—	$7000
1	0.25 * 7000 = $1750	$5250
2	0.25 * 5250 = $1313	$3937
3	0.25 * 3937 = $984	$2953
4	0.25 * 2953 = $738	$2215
5	0.25 * 2215 = $554	$1661
6	0.25 * 1661 = $415	$1246

In this case, the book value is higher each year than with double-declining-balance, and the book value never falls below the $1000 estimated salvage value even after the 6-year useful life.

DECLINING-BALANCE SWITCHING TO STRAIGHT-LINE DEPRECIATION

In this method, the declining-balance formula is used in the early part of the asset's life and the straight-line method is used for the rest. The switch from declining-balance to straight-line happens when the declining-balance depreciation amount becomes less than the straight-line amount. This is shown pictorially in Figure 14.3. Mathematically, the switch to straight line happens when the slope of the declining-balance curve becomes less than the slope of the straight-line method.

The depreciation formula in this method uses the larger of the two depreciation amounts that would be allowed under the declining-balance formula and the straight-line formula.

$$Depreciation_{year(t)} = \max(DecliningBalance_{year(t)}, StraightLine_{year(t)})$$

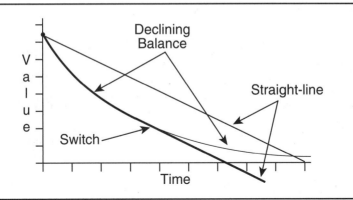

FIGURE 14.3   Declining-Balance Switching to Straight-Line Value-Time Function

TABLE 14.5   An Example of 150% Declining-Balance Switching to Straight-Line Depreciation

End of Year	Depreciation Amount in Year	Book Value at End of Year
0	—	$7000
1	0.25 * 7000 = $1750	$5250
2	0.25 * 5250 = $1313	$3937
3	0.25 * 3937 = $984	
	so switch to $1167	$2770
4	$1167	$1603
5	$1167	$436
6	$436	$0

Like the declining-balance method, the declining-balance switching to straight-line method ignores the asset's salvage value.

The book value formula subtracts the depreciation taken so far from the original acquisition cost:

$$BookValue_{year(t)} = AcquisitionCost - \sum_{i=1}^{t} Depreciation_{year(i)}$$

To illustrate, Table 14.5 shows the same example computer system using 150% declining-balance switching to straight-line depreciation. This can be compared with Table 14.4.

$$\alpha = \frac{1.5}{6} = 0.25$$

$$\text{Straight-line amount} = \frac{\$7000}{6} = \$1167$$

TABLE 14.6 Sum-of-the-Years-Digits Depreciation Formula

Year	Year in Reverse Order	Depreciation Factor
1	k	k/K
2	k-1	$(k-1)/K$
3	k-2	$(k-2)/K$
. . .	. . .	. . .
k-1	2	2/K
k	1	1/K

Sum $\quad K = \sum_{i=1}^{k} i$

TABLE 14.7 Six-Year Sum-of-the-Years-Digits Depreciation Schedule

Year	Year in Reverse Order	Depreciation Factor
1	6	6/21
2	5	5/21
3	4	4/21
4	3	3/21
5	2	2/21
6	1	1/21

Sum K = 21

Note the switch to straight-line depreciation in year 3. This is the year when the declining-balance depreciation amount ($984) falls below the straight-line amount ($1167). Also see how the asset is actually fully depreciated (book value = 0) before its estimated useful life is over.

SUM-OF-THE-YEARS-DIGITS DEPRECIATION

With sum-of-the-years-digits depreciation, the depreciation amount is determined by the rule shown in Table 14.6. The depreciation factor in any given year is determined by a fraction, where the numerator is found by counting down from the useful life, and the denominator is the sum of the numbers from 1 to the useful life.

Sum-of-the-years-digits depreciation allows a nonzero salvage value; the depreciation factors are applied to the difference between the acquisition cost and the salvage value.

We'll again use the same computer system from above. The depreciation schedule for a 6-year asset is shown in Table 14.7.

Using the 6-year depreciation schedule, the depreciation amounts for the example computer and the resulting book value at the end of each year are shown in Table 14.8.

TABLE 14.8 An Example of Sum-of-the-Years-Digits Depreciation

End of Year	Depreciation Amount in Year	Book Value at End of Year
0	—	$7000
1	$6000 * 6/21 = $1714	$5286
2	$6000 * 5/21 = $1429	$3857
3	$6000 * 4/21 = $1143	$2714
4	$6000 * 3/21 = $857	$1857
5	$6000 * 2/21 = $571	$1286
6	$6000 * 1/21 = $286	$1000

Accelerated Cost Recovery System (ACRS), 1981–1986

The accelerated cost recovery system (ACRS) [IRS95] was the defined depreciation method from 1981 through 1986. All depreciable assets put into service during these years used the ACRS method. There are two variants of the ACRS method, the prescribed method and the alternative method. Both are described here.

ACRS PRESCRIBED METHOD

Under the ACRS prescribed method, all depreciable assets are assigned to one of four separate classes of property:

- **3-year property**, which includes cars, light-duty trucks, machinery and equipment used in research, and all other equipment having an asset depreciation range (ADR) life of 4 years or less
- **5-year property**, which includes most production equipment and public utility property with an ADR life between 5 and 18 years. This class also includes all personal property not included in any other class
- **10-year property**, which includes public utility property with an ADR life between 18 and 25 years and depreciable real property (e.g., buildings) with an ADR life less than or equal to 12.5 years
- **15-year property**, which includes depreciable real property with an ADR life greater than 12.5 years and public utility property with an ADR life greater than 25 years

TABLE 14.9 ACRS Prescribed Method Depreciation Schedule

Recovery Year	3-Year	5-Year	10-Year	15-Year
1	0.25	0.15	0.08	0.05
2	0.38	0.22	0.14	0.10
3	0.37	0.21	0.12	0.09
4		0.21	0.10	0.08
5		0.21	0.10	0.07
6			0.10	0.07
7			0.09	0.06
8			0.09	0.06
9			0.09	0.06
10			0.09	0.06
11				0.06
12				0.06
13				0.06
14				0.06
15				0.06

The depreciation schedule, shown in Table 14.9, is prescribed by the IRS and is based on the 150% declining-balance switching to straight-line method. The schedule isn't exactly the same as the 150% declining-balance switching to straight-line method because in this schedule the straight-line part reduces the book value to zero at the end of the depreciation schedule. The straight-line section uses the book value at the point of the switch rather than the original acquisition cost. The value-time function for the ACRS prescribed method is shown in Figure 14.4.

The factors listed in the table, based on the asset's property class and depreciation year, are multiplied by the original acquisition cost of the asset to calculate the depreciation amount in that year. The fourth-year depreciation amount for a 15-year asset would be 0.08 times that asset's acquisition cost.

The ACRS depreciation schedule uses the **half-year convention**. This convention assumes that the asset begins service in midyear (July 1) and ends service midyear (June 30). Two additional rules on the ACRS prescribed method are as follows:

- If the property is sold or scrapped during or before its last recovery year, no depreciation is allowed for that final year.
- If the property is sold or scrapped after the last recovery year, there is no additional depreciation after the last recovery year.

Table 14.10 shows the ACRS prescribed method depreciation for the same computer as above, assuming it is classified as a 5-year asset.

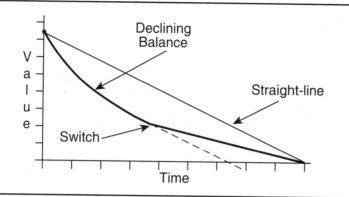

FIGURE 14.4   Value-time function for the ACRS prescribed method

TABLE 14.10   An Example of the ACRS Prescribed Method

End of Year	Depreciation Amount in Year	Book Value at End of Year
0	—	$7000
1	0.15 * 7000 = $1050	$5950
2	0.22 * 7000 = $1540	$4410
3	0.21 * 7000 = $1470	$2940
4	0.21 * 7000 = $1470	$1470
5	0.21 * 7000 = $1470	$0

ACRS ALTERNATIVE METHOD

Under the ACRS alternative method, the organization could choose one of three possible recovery periods based on the type of property.

Type of Property	Optional Recovery Periods Available
3-year property	3, 5, or 12 years
5-year property	5, 12, or 25 years
10-year property	10, 25, or 35 years
15-year property	15, 35, or 45 years

The ACRS alternative method also uses the half-year convention.

Modified Accelerated Cost Recovery System (MACRS), 1987 and Later

The modified accelerated cost recovery system (MACRS) [IRS02] was put in place in 1987 and, as of publication of this book, is still in place. MACRS uses the same basic structure of ACRS but has more property classes and changes the depreciation rates. The "personal property" depreciation schedules still use declining-balance switching to straight-line, and the straight-line section still uses the book value from the point of switch as was shown in Figure 14.4. MACRS also ignores salvage values. The 3-, 5-, 10-, and 15-year classes are still there, but there was some realignment of the class definitions. In addition

- There are two new classes for 7- and 20-year properties.
- The depreciation rates for 3-, 5-, 7-, and 10-year property use 200% declining-balance instead of 150%, the 15- and 20-year property use 150% declining-balance.
- There is no distinction between new and used property. Used property is assumed to be new for the purpose of depreciation; it just has a lower acquisition cost

The MACRS depreciation schedule also uses the half-year convention. In this case, the depreciation schedule is shifted by one half year; it begins on July 1 of the year of service and ends on June 30 n years later. The 10-year depreciation schedule, for example, actually covers 11 calendar years with 6 months of depreciation in the first year and another 6 months in the eleventh year. If the asset is sold or scrapped at or after the end of the depreciation schedule, nothing changes. If the asset is sold or scrapped before the end of the depreciation schedule, only half of the allowable depreciation can be taken.

Table 14.11 shows the MACRS prescribed method depreciation schedules for personal property.

For "real property" (meaning just the buildings—remember that land is not depreciable), the 15-, 18-, and 19-year classes have been increased to 27.5 years for residential and 31.5 years for nonresidential property. All real properties must be depreciated using the straight-line method.

Table 14.12 shows the MACRS prescribed method depreciation for the same computer as above, assuming it is classified as a 5-year asset.

MACRS ALTERNATIVE METHOD

The MACRS system also has a method similar to the ACRS alternative method. For personal property in a defined class, the life to be used is the recovery period for that class. For personal property with no assignable class life, a 12-year recovery period is used. If you choose the alternative method, you must apply it to all property in that same class that was put in service that same year.

TABLE 14.11 MACRS Prescribed Method Depreciation Schedule

Recovery Year	3-Year	5-Year	7-Year	10-Year	15-Year	20-Year
1	0.3333	0.2000	0.1429	0.1000	0.0500	0.0375
2	0.4445	0.3200	0.2449	0.1800	0.0950	0.0722
3	0.1481	0.1920	0.1749	0.1440	0.0855	0.0668
4	0.0741	0.1152	0.1249	0.1152	0.0770	0.0618
5		0.1152	0.0893	0.0922	0.0693	0.0571
6		0.0576	0.0893	0.0737	0.0623	0.0528
7			0.0893	0.0655	0.0590	0.0489
8			0.0446	0.0655	0.0590	0.0452
9				0.0656	0.0591	0.0447
10				0.0655	0.0590	0.0447
11				0.0328	0.0591	0.0446
12					0.0590	0.0446
13					0.0591	0.0446
14					0.0590	0.0446
15					0.0591	0.0446
16					0.0295	0.0446
17						0.0446
18						0.0446
19						0.0446
20						0.0446
21						0.0223

TABLE 14.12 An Example of the MACRS Prescribed Method

End of Year	Depreciation Amount in Year	Book Value at End of Year
0	—	$7000
1	0.2000 * 7000 = $1400	$5600
2	0.3200 * 7000 = $2240	$3360
3	0.1920 * 7000 = $1344	$2016
4	0.1152 * 7000 = $806	$1210
5	0.1152 * 7000 = $806	$404
6	0.0576 * 7000 = $404	$0

TABLE 14.13 An Example of Units of Production Depreciation

End of Year	Pages Printed During Year	Depreciation Amount in Year	Book Value at End of Year
0	—	—	$2000
1	123,000	123,000 * 0.001 = $123	$1877
2	5,000	5,000 * 0.001 = $5	$1872
3	456,000	456,000 * 0.001 = $456	$1416
4	678,000	678,000 * 0.001 = $678	$738
5	100,000	100,000 * 0.001 = $100	$638
6	138,000	138,000 * 0.001 = $138	$500

Units-of-Production Depreciation

Units-of-production depreciation isn't allowed under the current U.S. tax code, but it is worth discussing. It might be allowed someday, and it is a different way of looking at the same basic issue.

All the depreciation methods described previously are based entirely on calendar time and ignore how the asset is actually used during that time. Even if the asset, such as a computer, were stored unopened in its factory shipping crate, it would be depreciated the same way as if it were used in a way that literally destroyed it in as little as two years. In contrast, units-of-production depreciation assumes that depreciation happens based on how much work the asset performs, regardless of its calendar age. The per-unit-of-production depreciation formula is as follows:

$$DepreciationPerUse = \frac{AcquisitionCost - SalvageValue}{LifetimeCapacityForUse}$$

Under units-of-production depreciation, a laser printer might be depreciated on the basis of the number of pages printed. Assume the printer's acquisition cost is $2000 and its salvage value is $500. Also assume that the printer is capable of printing 1.5 million pages over its useful life. The per-page-printed depreciation amount would be as follows:

$$\frac{\$2000 - \$500}{1.5 MillionPages} = \$0.001/Page$$

Table 14.13 shows the yearly depreciation amount and corresponding book values based on the specified number of pages printed during each year of use for this laser printer.

The high-volume use in year 4 gives a high depreciation amount for that year, and the low-volume use in year 2 gives a low depreciation amount.

Relating units-of-production depreciation to the real world, the "blue book" value of a car is largely based on a combination of its age (as if using one of the depreciation methods in the previous sections) and the miles driven (a kind of units of production depreciation).

Depletion

Depletion is similar to depreciation, but it covers intentional piecemeal removal of certain types of natural resource assets, typically the following:

- Mines
- Quarries
- Oilfields
- Timberland
- . . .

Where depreciation is based on time and wear and tear from use, depletion is based on, for example, how much coal has been removed from a coal mine. Depletion is handled in a similar fashion to units of production depreciation. Depletion doesn't apply to software and won't be addressed any further.

Other Aspects of Depreciation Accounting Not Discussed Here

Complete details of depreciation accounting are much more complex than discussed here. One complexity not discussed is the difference between single-asset (or "unit") depreciation and multiple-asset depreciation. Another complexity is the difference between "vintage accounts," where each year's acquisitions of a particular class are kept and depreciated separately, versus "open-ended accounts," where all acquisitions of a particular class are merged into one. Still another complexity is "Section 179 deductions" available to small businesses.

There isn't time nor space for a full description of all the subtle nuances of depreciation accounting, nor are all the details relevant in the typical business decision analysis. If you need a more detailed understanding for a specific decision analysis, you will probably have access to other resources such as a professional accountant (CPA).

Summary

Depreciation addresses how investments in capital assets are charged off against income over several years. This is an important part of calculating after-tax cash flows, which is critical to accurately addressing income taxes. This chapter covered the following major points:

- Actual depreciation refers to how an asset will lose value over time due to effects such as wear and tear.
- Depreciation accounting refers to how the organization accounts for that loss in value.
- Actual depreciation is rarely the same as depreciation accounting. Actual depreciation is virtually impossible to determine without selling the asset—it's really worth only what someone is willing to pay for it.
- Through depreciation accounting, tax authorities are trying to force the accounting and tax recognition of an asset's loss in value to be as close in time as reasonably possible to when that loss actually happens. Depreciation accounting is the tax authorities' attempt to make each year's income taxes as realistic as possible.
- A value-time function is a mathematical function that models how an asset loses value over time (for instance straight-line or declining-balance).
- The book value of an asset is the best estimate, based on depreciation accounting, of that asset's actual value; it's the part of the asset's acquisition cost that hasn't been charged off by depreciation accounting
- Over the years, several different depreciation methods have been used: straight-line, declining-balance, declining-balance switching to straight-line, sum-of-the-years-digits, accelerated cost recovery system (ACRS), and modified accelerated cost recovery system (MACRS)

The next chapter discusses "the language of business," accounting, which involves keeping track of the money coming into, moving around in, and going out of a company.

Self-Study Questions

Questions 1 through 7 use the following situation: XY Computers bought an array processor for doing some high-powered computational fluid dynamics calculations. The array processor has an acquisition cost of $22,500, a 5-year useful life, and an expected salvage value of $500. Use the format shown in Table 14.2 to show depreciation year, depreciation amount, and book value.

1. Show straight-line depreciation.

2. Show 200% declining-balance depreciation.

3. Show 150% declining-balance depreciation.

4. Show 150% declining-balance switching to straight-line depreciation.

5. Show sum-of-the-years-digits depreciation.

6. Show ACRS prescribed method depreciation.

7. Show MACRS depreciation.

Questions 8 through 14 use the following situation: Two years later, XY Computers bought another even higher-powered array processor. This processor has an acquisition cost of $40,000, a 10-year useful life, and an expected salvage value of $2000. Use the format shown in Table 14.2 to show depreciation year, depreciation amount, and book value.

8. Show straight-line depreciation.

9. Show 200% declining-balance depreciation.

10. Show 150% declining-balance depreciation.

11. Show 150% declining-balance switching to straight-line depreciation.

12. Show sum-of-the-years-digits depreciation.

13. Show ACRS prescribed method depreciation.

14. Show MACRS depreciation.

15. Assume that units-of-production depreciation were allowed for equipment such as printers. Also assume that XY bought a printer for $2000, the printer had a salvage value of $0, and a lifetime capacity for 1,000,000 pages. Complete the following depreciation table.

End of Year	Pages Printed During Year	Depreciation Amount in Year	Book Value at End of Year
0	—		$2000
1	140,000		
2	60,000		
3	120,000		
4	192,000		
5	200,000		

16. Again, assume units-of-production depreciation for printers. If a different printer had an acquisition cost of $8000, a salvage value of $1000, and a lifetime capacity for 10,000,000 pages, what could the depreciation schedule be for the following rate of use?

End of Year	Pages Printed During Year	Depreciation Amount in Year	Book Value at End of Year
0	—	—	$8000
1	1,250,000		
2	2,125,000		
3	1,850,000		
4	1,175,000		
5	2,228,000		
6	1,995,000		

17. XY Computers is now looking at constructing a new office building. In studying their options, they've found a plot of appropriately zoned vacant land for sale for $1,750,000. They've also been working with an architect and have preliminary plans for the building itself. The office building is estimated to cost $4,250,000. Under MACRS, what is the annual depreciation amount that XY Computers should use in their studies?

15

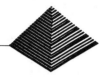

General Accounting and Cost Accounting

Accounting can be informally thought of as keeping track of the money coming into, moving around in, and going out of a company. Accounting is, in effect, "the language of business." Business goals are often defined in accounting terms, so you should become familiar with that language to communicate effectively with managers and financiers. Reading and understanding financial reports will also help you better assess a company's financial health. This is not only useful at a professional level, it can also help you at a personal level because you will be able to evaluate a company before either buying or selling its stock or deciding to work for them. Accounting systems can also be a source of historical data for estimating. (Estimation is covered in Part VI.) This chapter explains general accounting and cost accounting, along with describing how to determine unit cost.

General Accounting

Technically speaking, accounting is the process of recording the financial history of a company. Many people think that accounting is only done to comply with legal requirements. Although it's true that legal compliance is a big reason, there are other important reasons for accounting:

- The people whose money is being used to run the company want to know the results of their investment: Did they get the profit they were expecting or not? The primary role of accounting is to measure the company's actual financial performance.
- Accounting provides data to make operational decisions and allows the results of those decisions to be seen later. Management can decide to cut costs through a corporate initiative, and then make sure the costs actually went down.

A company's financial history is summarized in three financial statements: the balance sheet, the profit and loss statement, and the cash-flow statement.

In the United States, any company whose stock is traded on a public stock exchange is required to publish quarterly and annual financial statements. The investment community refers to the quarterly statement as the 10Q and the annual statement as the 10K. The 10Q and 10K contain these three financial statements along with other important investor information. Publicly traded companies usually make their 10Q and 10K statements available in the "Investor Relations" section of their corporate Web site. 10Q and 10K statements are also available on the Securities and Exchange Commission (SEC) Electronic Data Gathering, Analysis, and Retrieval (EDGAR 1) system (http://www.sec.gov/edgar.shtml). Publishing the 10Q and 10K allows investors to examine the company's financial performance and helps them make decisions on whether to buy or sell that company's stock.

Be aware that accounting is not an exact science. It's very dependent on the laws of the countries, states, and cities involved and often requires interpretation of those laws.

THE BALANCE SHEET

The balance sheet shows the financial position of a company at a particular moment in time. It's a "snapshot" or "freeze-frame" view of the financial strength of the company. It answers the question, "How much is the company worth at this point in time?" Balance sheets are typically generated regularly: monthly, quarterly, and annually. They might also be created as needed, such as to support an independent financial audit.

Gizmo Corporation Balance Sheet for Year Ending December 31, 20x3
(Amounts in thousands)

Assets	20x3	20x2
Cash and cash equivalents	$5623	$4937
Accounts receivable	$1894	$1809
Inventory	$1942	$1989
Property	$6220	$6214
Plant and equipment	$15,339	$15,969
Investments	$105	$108
Total assets	$31,123	$31,026
Liabilities		
Accounts payable	$344	$365
Debt	$11,218	$11,662
Declared dividends	$0	$0
Total liabilities	$11,562	$12,027
Owner's Equity		
Stock	$14,230	$14,230
Retained earnings	$5331	$4769
Total owner's equity	$19,561	$18,999
Total liabilities and owner's equity	$31,123	$31,026

FIGURE 15.1   A sample Balance Sheet

Figure 15.1 shows a simplified balance sheet for Gizmo Corporation, a medium-sized manufacturing company. Financial statements often show comparative data from previous reports to help identify trends. Gizmo's balance sheet shows data from the end of 20x3 along with corresponding data from the end of 20x2.

The balance sheet includes a relatively standard set of accounting categories and is divided into three major sections: Assets, Liabilities, and Owner's Equity. The specific accounting categories in these sections can vary depending on the industry that particular company is in; banks don't have inventory, so this category wouldn't make sense like it does for a manufacturing company. Software and high-technology companies will have accounting categories very similar to those shown in this balance sheet.

Assets   Assets are the things of value that the company owns or is owed by others. Typical assets include the following:

- **Cash and cash equivalents**—Money that the company has available to spend. This is usually money in bank accounts and easily marketable securities such as treasury bonds.

- **Accounts receivable**—Money that the company is owed by others. Typically a company will sell its products and services without requiring immediate payment; the sale will be invoiced for billing later. Accounts receivable is the total sales that have been recorded but not yet paid by the buyer.
- **Inventory**—Raw material, products that are in the process of being built, and finished goods (products that are built and ready to sell) the company owns.
- **Property**—Land owned by the company.
- **Plant and equipment**—Buildings and machines that are used for producing the goods and services. This includes everything from tools, milling machines, automated painting robots, down to the desks and computers the employees use.
- **Investments**—A company can invest in other companies. Most of the major auto manufacturers, for example, are part owners of the major rental car companies.

A software company's assets will be very similar to these; the biggest difference is that the relative value in inventory will probably be lower than in a typical manufacturing company.

Gizmo Corporation shows total assets of $31,123,000 at the end of 20x3.

Liabilities   Liabilities are the opposite of assets; they represent money the company owes to others. Common liabilities include the following:

- **Accounts payable**—The opposite of accounts receivable: When the company buys products and services from other companies but hasn't paid the invoices yet, those unpaid bills are included in accounts payable.
- **Debt**—Loans that the company has. This may be separated into short-term debt, loans that are supposed to be repaid within the next year, and long-term debt (loans that are to be repaid over longer than one year).
- **Declared dividends**—As a reward to the stockholders, the company may pay them a portion of the profit. This shows dividends that have been promised but not yet paid.

A software company's liabilities will be very similar to these.

Gizmo Corporation total liabilities are $11,562,000 at the end of 20x3.

Owner's Equity   The balance sheet is called that because—literally—it needs to "balance"; it needs to conform to the following fundamental accounting equation:

Assets = Liabilities + Owner's equity

Owner's equity is the company's net worth. This same notion applies to the owner of a house, for example. Assume you bought a house for $100k, paying $20k down and borrowing the remaining $80k. Your asset is the house, $100k, your liability is the loan, $80k, and your equity is how much of the house you actually own, $20k. Several years later, suppose your loan balance (the amount you still owe) has been paid down to $65k. If the house value also happens to have appreciated to $115k, then

$115k = $65k + Owner's equity

Owner's equity = $50k

The equity in a company is typically held in capital stock and retained earnings. According to the balance sheet for Gizmo Corporation, the company has an owner's equity of $19,561,000. The owner's equity is a "book value"; you probably couldn't actually buy the company for that amount because the long-term earning potential makes a company worth more than its book value.

Gizmo Corporation's total assets exactly equal the sum of its total liabilities and owner's equity. This is the fundamental accounting equation in action.

THE PROFIT AND LOSS STATEMENT

Whereas the balance sheet is a snapshot at a moment in time, the profit and loss statement (sometimes called an income statement) is an accumulation over a period of time. It answers the question, "How quickly is the company gaining or losing value?" The profit and loss statement summarizes the income and expenses that happened during the reporting period: between one balance sheet and the next. The profit and loss statement explains the difference in the company's value between those two consecutive balance sheets. Figure 15.2 shows a simplified Profit & Loss Statement.

A profit and loss statement has a relatively standard set of accounting categories and is divided into five major sections.

Operating Income   In the course of operating, the company will, or at least should, bring in income.

- **Sales and operating income**—Money the company brought in by selling its products and services. This is sometimes called gross income. This category might be subdivided into the specific products and services so that each one can be monitored separately. This category typically also includes interest income (interest earned from interest-bearing accounts and/or from loans to other entities) along with income from the sale of assets (the "capital gains and losses") and investment income (income from ownership of other companies).

Gizmo Corporation Profit and Loss Statement for Year Ending December 31, 20x3
(Amounts in thousands)

Operating Income	20x3	20x2
Sales and operating income	$9871	$9466
Cost of goods sold	$5298	$5305
Net operating income (loss)	$4573	$4161
Operating Expenses		
Selling expenses	$640	$581
General and administrative expenses	$1722	$1460
Research and development	$66	$75
Investment-Related Expenses		
Interest expense	$563	$560
Investment expense	$11	$16
Depreciation	$649	$610
Net earnings before income taxes (loss)	$922	$859
Income Taxes		
Federal, state, and local income taxes	$360	$332
Net Earnings After Taxes (Loss)	$562	$527

FIGURE 15.2   A sample Profit & Loss Statement

- **Cost of goods sold**—Answers the question, "how much did it cost to produce the goods and services that were sold during this reporting period?" This comes from the cost of goods sold statement and includes raw material costs, labor costs (salaries and wages of production/factory workers), and manufacturing overhead. The cost of goods sold statement is explained in detail below in the section on cost accounting.

Subtracting the cost of goods sold from the sales and operating income leaves the net operating income (or loss). Gizmo Corporation had $9,871,000 in income with a cost of goods sold of $5,298,000, leaving an operating income of $4,573,000. Keep in mind there's no guarantee the operating income will be more than the cost of goods sold.

Operating Expenses   Beyond the cost of producing the products and services, the company needs to spend money to operate. Operating expenses show the different ways the company is spending money beyond the cost of goods sold. The following operating expenses are typical:

- **Selling expense**—Expenses such as advertising, salaries and wages of sales and marketing staff, sales commissions, showroom expenses, etc.

- **General and administrative expense**—Expenses such as salaries and wages of administrative and management staff, insurance, rent. This category typically includes all taxes other than income taxes, which are in a separate category below.
- **Research and development expense**—A company needs to invest in its future. This category is for expenses related to developing new products and services, or for finding new ways of producing and delivering those products and services.

A software company's operating expenses will be similar to these.

> Software development and maintenance costs are usually recorded as research and development or as general and administrative expenses. Software development and maintenance costs do not typically appear under cost of goods sold because it is considered a development (i.e., engineering) cost, not a production cost. Cost of goods sold is focused only on production costs.

Investment-Related Expenses   The company also has to spend money related to its investments. The following investment-related expenses are typical:

- **Interest expense**—If the company is borrowing money through loans, all interest paid on those loans will be counted here.
- **Investment expense**—If the company has other investments, expenses related to those investments would be tracked here.
- **Depreciation**—Spreads lump sum investments in long-lived assets over an appropriate time frame (e.g., 31.5 years for commercial buildings, 10 years for some kinds of machines, and 3 to 5 years for computer hardware). Depreciation is explained in Chapter 14.

A software company's investment-related expenses will be similar.

Subtracting the operating expenses and investment-related expenses from the operating income leaves the net earnings before taxes. Subtracting Gizmo Corporation's operating and investment-related expenses from their operating income leaves $922,000 in net earnings before taxes.

Income Taxes and Net Earnings   Income taxes, and how they are calculated, are explained in Chapter 16. This category shows how much the company paid in federal, state, and local income taxes based on its net earnings before taxes. Subtracting the income taxes from net earnings before taxes gives the net earnings after taxes. This is how much the company actually earned over the stated time period; it's the real after-tax profit. Gizmo Corporation paid $360,000 in income taxes, leaving net after-tax earnings of $562,000.

Gizmo Corporation Cash-Flow Statement for Year Ending December 31, 20x3
(Amounts in thousands)

	20x3	20x2
Cash from Operating Activities		
Net earnings	$562	$527
Depreciation	$649	$654
Changes in accounts receivable	($85)	$145
Changes in accounts payable	($21)	($56)
Changes in inventory	$47	$42
Net cash from operating activities	$1152	$1312
Cash from Investing Activities		
Capital expenditures	($34)	($13)
Acquisitions	$0	($65)
Proceeds from dispositions	$12	$82
Net cash from investing activities (loss)	($22)	$4
Cash from Financing Activities		
New borrowing	$22	$0
Debt repayment	($466)	($425)
Net stock	$0	$0
Dividends paid	$0	($66)
Net cash from financing activities (loss)	($444)	($491)
Net Change in Cash	$686	$825
Cash at beginning	$4937	$4112
Cash at end	$5623	$4937

FIGURE 15.3 A sample Cash-Flow Statement

THE CASH-FLOW STATEMENT

Earnings on the profit and loss statement aren't necessarily the same as cash; a business could have excellent earnings but still have serious cash-flow problems. One reason is that some very real expenses aren't included in the profit and loss statement. A loan payment, for instance, comes from very real cash dollars, but only the interest expense shows up in the profit and loss statement. The other reason is that there are some artificial expenses in the profit and loss statement. One of these is depreciation (Chapter 14). Depreciation is a proper accounting deduction, but it doesn't mean that cash was actually spent. The cash-flow statement shows how the company is paying for its current operations and future growth by detailing the actual flow of cash between the company and the outside. It answers the question, "How much more or less cash does the company have now than it did before?"

Shown in Figure 15.3 is a simplified cash-flow statement. By convention, positive numbers mean cash coming into the company, and negative numbers mean cash going out. Accountants typically show negative numbers in parentheses; for instance, –$1234 would be shown as ($1234). Because the parentheses are easier to see at a glance than minus signs, negative values stand out more clearly.

A cash-flow statement is divided into four standard sections.

Cash from Operating Activities   This section shows how much actual cash was made or lost through the operation of the company.

- **Net earnings**—This is the net income after taxes from the corresponding profit and loss statement.
- **Depreciation**—Depreciation was subtracted from net operating income in the profit and loss statement to calculate net income after taxes. As explained in Chapter 14, depreciation spreads an actual expenditure for an asset over a number of years. Because the money was actually spent in a previous reporting period, the depreciation amount has to be added back into the net earnings to reflect the actual flow of cash.
- **Changes in accounts receivable**—Net earnings on the profit and loss statement counts sales that have been booked but not necessarily paid. The actual flow of cash is driven by how much the total accounts receivable actually changed, so this needs to be reflected as an adjustment to net earnings. The value ($85) in the cash-flow statement above means that $85,000 more cash got tied up in accounts receivable over the reporting period. Notice that the 20x3 value for accounts receivable is $85,000 greater than the 20x2 value for accounts receivable on the balance sheet in Figure 15.1.
- **Changes in accounts payable**—Exactly the same as with changes in accounts receivable.
- **Changes in inventory**—Counts the net amount of cash value added to, or taken out of, the inventory.

Net cash from operating activities is calculated by adding up all the items in this section. This shows how much net actual cash was generated (or spent) through company operations during the time period. Gizmo Corporation generated $1,152,000 though company operations during the reporting period.

Cash from Investing Activities   This section shows how much actual cash was made or spent through investment-related activities.

- **Capital expenditures**—Shows money that was spent buying land, plant and equipment, etc.
- **Acquisitions**—Shows how much was spent or gained through buying or selling other companies
- **Proceeds from dispositions**—Covers income from selling land, plant and equipment, and other capital assets

Net cash from investing activities is the sum of these items. It shows how much net actual cash was gained (or spent) because of the investments the company has. Gizmo Corporation spent a net $22,000 in its investing activities.

Cash from Financing Activities   The company can also raise, or spend, cash through its financing activities.

- **New borrowing**—Money that came in because of new loans that were taken out during this reporting period.
- **Debt repayment**—Shows how much was spent paying down the principal on loans the company has.
- **Net stock**—Shows how much stock was sold, or bought back, by the company.
- **Dividends paid**—Dividends are one way that a company owner (a stockholder) earns money from their investment; an increase in stock price is the other. The company may give a portion of the after-tax earnings to its stockholders. This shows how much, if any, of the after-tax profit was shared with stockholders.

Net cash from financing activities is the sum of these items. It shows how much net actual cash was gained (or spent) because of the financing the company did over the reporting period. Gizmo Corporation spent a total of $444,000 through its financing activities.

Net Change in Cash   The sum of cash from operating activities, cash from investing activities, and cash from financing activities equals the net change in cash over the reporting period. Adding the net change in cash to the cash on hand at the beginning of the period shows how much cash is available at the end of the period. Gizmo Corporation's profit and loss statement showed a total of $562,000 in net earnings during the year, yet the cash-flow statement shows they finished the year with $686,000 more cash than they had at the start. This highlights the difference between profit and loss and cash flow.

RELATING THE BALANCE SHEET, PROFIT AND LOSS STATEMENT, AND CASH-FLOW STATEMENT

The balance sheet, profit and loss statement, and cash-flow statement are closely related. Figure 15.4 describes the relationship pictorially, and this section explains that relationship in more detail.

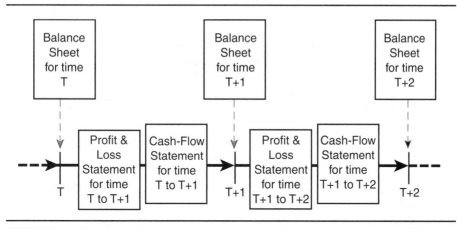

FIGURE 15.4 Relationship between balance sheet, profit and loss statement, and cash-flow statement

The balance sheet shows the company's financial position at a given point in time: How much is the company worth right then? The profit and loss statement covers a period of time and shows how the company's financial position changed over that time: How much did the value of the company go up or down during the reporting period? The overall profit or loss during the reporting period is largely reflected in the change in retained earnings between the beginning and ending balance sheets. Like the profit and loss statement, the cash-flow statement also covers a period of time. Instead of explaining how net worth changed, the cash-flow statement describes how the company's cash position changed: How much more or less cash does the company have than it did at the beginning of the reporting period?

Analyzing what happens when a company makes a capital investment helps highlight the relationship between the financial statements. Suppose, for example, that Gizmo buys a $48,000 computer system—the capital investment—and pays for it with cash (retained earnings):

- There is no impact to the profit and loss statement because there's no change in profit or loss.
- On the cash-flow statement, the $48,000 spent on the computer system shows up in the "capital expenditures" line, which causes the "net change in cash" and "cash at end" lines to decrease by that same amount.
- On the balance sheet, the "cash and cash equivalents" line drops by $48,000—because of the investment recorded in the cash-flow statement—whereas the "plant and equipment" line is increased by that same amount, so the company's total asset value doesn't change.

From a purely financial perspective, the only thing that happened was that one asset, money, was converted into a different asset, the computer system, with exactly the same value. The overall value of the company didn't change.

What would happen if Gizmo buys the same computer system but finances it with a loan?

- There is no impact to the profit and loss statement because there's no change in profit or loss.
- On the cash-flow statement, the $48,000 purchase shows up in the "capital expenditure" line, but there is an equal increase in "new borrowing," so there's no net change in the company's cash position.
- On the balance sheet the "plant and equipment" line is increased by $48,000, but it's offset by an equal increase in "debt," so there is no net change in owner's equity.

Again, from a purely financial perspective, the acquisition was offset by an equal increase in debt, so the company's net value didn't change—at least as far as the acquisition itself is concerned.

Over time, as the $48,000 loan is being paid off, the following occurs:

- On the profit and loss statement, the interest part of each loan payment is added to the "interest expense" line, which causes the "net earnings" line to be reduced by the same amount. This causes a corresponding drop in "retained earnings" on the balance sheet.
- The principal amount of each loan payment is added to the "debt repayment" line on the cash-flow statement. This reflects the cash that was used to repay the loan and causes a corresponding decrease in the "net change in cash" and "cash at end" lines.
- On the balance sheet, the "cash and cash equivalents" line drops by the amount of the principal payments because of the change recorded in the cash-flow statement. The "debt" line is also reduced by the amount of the principal payment. The net decrease in owner's equity is the amount of the interest payment.

The principal part of the loan payment is matched by an equal reduction in debt, so it has no effect on the net worth of the company. The interest part of the payment is an expense that shows up as a reduction in net earnings on the profit and loss statement and causes an equal reduction in the net worth of the company (ignoring income tax effects, which are explained in Chapter 17).

How does the company make money? Assume that the $48,000 computer system was used during a reporting period to produce goods and services that were sold to customers for $150,000.

- That income would be recorded in the "sales and operating income" line of the profit and loss statement. Assume that the cost of goods sold for those same goods and services was $100,000; that cost would show up on the next line of the profit and loss statement. This leads to a net operating income of $50,000. If the total operating and investment-related expenses associated with the sale of those goods and services were $20,000, the net earnings before taxes would be $30,000. Assuming income taxes were $12,000, the net earnings after taxes would be $18,000.
- In terms of cash flow, assume that $5000 of the operating and investment-related expense was for depreciation on the computer system. If there were no other change in accounts receivable, payable, or inventory, and all other investing and financing activities were zero, the net increase in cash would be $23,000.
- Assuming there were no other net changes in the company's assets and liabilities during the reporting period, the increase of $23,000 in cash over the reporting period would show up in the "cash and cash equivalents" line of the balance sheet at the end of the reporting period. The increase in cash, however, would be offset by a $5000 decrease in plant and equipment because of the depreciation on the computer system. The net increase in owner's equity, $18,000, is exactly equal to the net earnings on the profit and loss statement.

Over the course of the reporting period, the company generated $150,000 in sales and operating income while spending $132,000 (all expenses including depreciation), for a net earnings after tax of $18,000. The company actually has $23,000 more in cash, but is only worth $18,000 more than before because of the $5000 decrease in the value of the computer through depreciation.

Cost Accounting

Cost accounting is a specialized branch of general accounting and was developed in about 1919. Companies use cost accounting to find out how much it cost to provide the products and services that were sold during a reporting period. That cost is shown in a cost of goods sold statement and is one of the expenses in the profit and loss statement. Cost accounting is important because the cost of production often has a major influence on profit and should be carefully managed. Cost accounting helps the company maintain cost control on manufacturing expenses.

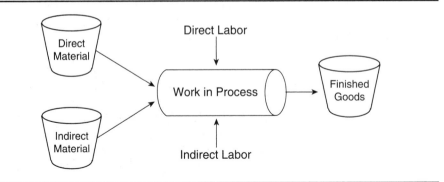

FIGURE 15.5 Cost accounting through the production process

In a typical manufacturing company, costs are accounted as the product flows through the production process. This is diagrammed in Figure 15.5.

Even companies that don't manufacture products in the traditional sense, say, a training company, still have a cost-of-production component. How much does it cost to put on a training seminar? Printing the books, renting the facilities, paying the instructor, etc. are all cost-of-production expenses. Even though there may not be much in the way of physical products, the concept of cost accounting still applies.

> Be aware that even in a "shrink-wrap" software company, the costs to create the product (development and maintenance costs) are typically not considered manufacturing expenses. Manufacturing expenses only include costs associated with producing instances of an already developed product, not costs associated with developing new products.

Figure 15.6 shows a sample cost of goods sold statement.

The cost of goods sold statement breaks down the cost of production into direct costs and manufacturing overhead (also called indirect costs). Direct costs are the costs that can be directly allocated to the units of production. The units of production may be batches rather than individual items, but the direct allocation of cost to production is the key idea. In automobile manufacturing, for instance, the cost of the tires, the radio, and other supplier-produced parts can be directly related to each car that is produced. If the manufacturer paid $175 for the set of tires on the car, those tires clearly contributed $175 to the overall cost of making the car. These assignable costs are the direct costs. Manufacturing overhead are costs that are either impossible or impractical to allocate to specific units of production.

Gizmo Corporation Cost of Goods Sold Statement for Year Ending December 31, 20x3
(Amounts in thousands)

[handwritten: Raw material – things we can touch]

Direct Material		
In process Jan. 1, 20x3	$119	
Applied during the year	$1438	
Total	$1557	*[handwritten: Total cost of Direct Material]*
In process Dec. 31, 20x3	$146	$1411
Direct Labor		
In process Jan. 1, 20x3	$149	
Applied during the year	$1881	
Total	$2030	
In process Dec. 31, 20x3	$198	$1832
Manufacturing Overhead		
In process Jan. 1, 20x3	$205	*[handwritten: stuff not in inventory ex. slipcads CD nuts + bolts]*
Applied during the year	$2213	
Total	$2418	
In process Dec. 31, 20x3	$250	$2168
Cost of Goods Made		$5411
Finished goods Jan. 1, 20x3		$523
Total		$5934
Finished goods Dec. 31, 20x3		$636
Cost of Goods Sold		$5298

FIGURE 15.6   Sample Cost of Goods Sold Statement

Direct Material   Direct material captures the costs of raw material and purchased components that are charged directly to the units of production. Direct material costs tend to include items that are easily measurable, used in the same quantity on identical products, and used in financially significant amounts. The tires, radio, and other components are direct materials for the car manufacturer. The accounting charge for direct material is usually booked when that material is issued from the inventory. The total direct material cost for a unit of production is the sum of the costs of the directly relateable materials used to build it. The total direct material cost for a car is the total of all identifiable costs for the frame, body, engine, transmission, etc.

The company's production process is analogous to a pipeline. To know precisely how much (in this case, money) flowed through the pipeline, you have to know how much was in the pipeline at the beginning, how much came out during the reporting period, and how much was still in the pipeline at the end. Adding how much was in at the beginning to how much came out and then subtracting how much is still left at the end provides a precise measure of how much flowed through during the reporting period. Each of the sections in the cost of goods sold statement follows this pipeline analogy to determine the actual money flow.

In Gizmo Corporation's case, they started the reporting period with $119,000 worth of direct material in the production pipeline. Throughout the year, they put another $1,438,000 into the pipeline, for a total of $1,557,000. At the end of the reporting period, the pipeline held $146,000 in direct material, so the actual dollar amount of direct material that flowed through the production pipeline was $1,411,000.

Even though software is not a physical entity, a company that sells "shrink-wrap" (i.e., retail) software has direct material costs. These direct costs include the blank disks or CD-ROMs, the media duplication costs, printing costs for the documentation, the packaging material, and so on.

Direct Labor Similar to direct material, direct labor covers the employee costs that are directly related to the units of production. The mechanics, painters, welders, and so on who build cars charge their time to the cars they are building. Every hour that a painter spends painting cars is charged directly against the cars produced. Direct labor may include pension, sick leave, vacation, and other fringe benefits, but these are usually included in manufacturing overhead (below). The accounting charge for direct labor is usually logged soon after the time is spent (e.g., on a daily or weekly timecard). Gizmo Corporation had a total of $1,832,000 worth of direct labor flow through the production pipeline during the reporting period.

Again, given that software is not a physical entity, a company that sells shrink-wrap software has direct labor costs, including things such as the labor hours spent packing the product boxes.

Manufacturing Overhead Manufacturing overhead covers all manufacturing expenses that can't be, or would be impractical to, directly charge against the units of production. Manufacturing overhead combines indirect material and indirect labor. Indirect material is the cost of the parts and material that are too inconsequential to directly charge against the units of production. Instead of trying to account for every screw, nut, or bolt used to build a car, the car manufacturer just maintains a supply and replenishes the supply when it drops to a predetermined amount. Any time a new batch of screws is bought, they are charged against manufacturing overhead. It would be impractical to try to track the cost of every individual screw, nut, or bolt to the corresponding car it was used on.

Just like indirect material, indirect labor can't be meaningfully related to the individual units of production. The workers who staff the tool crib, maintain the welding machines, move boxes around the loading dock, and so on are all indispensable people— the company couldn't run without them. However, it's impractical to associate their time directly with the units of production because the tools and machines are typically used for more than just one product line. Indirect labor usually includes pension, sick leave, vacation, and other fringe benefits unless these were included in direct labor. In a typical manufacturing company, the salaries of factory supervisors are also counted as indirect labor and are included in the manufacturing overhead.

Manufacturing overhead is sometimes called factory overhead, shop expense, burden, or indirect costs. Gizmo Corporation had a total of $2,168,000 of manufacturing overhead flow through the pipeline during the reporting period.

Cost of Goods Sold   The cost of producing the products and services made during the reporting period is the sum of the direct material, direct labor, and manufacturing overhead. Gizmo Corporation's cost of goods made was $5,411,000. Adding in the value of the finished goods inventory at the beginning of the reporting period and then subtracting the value of the finished goods inventory at the end of the reporting period shows the amount of money that was spent producing the goods and services that were sold during the reporting period. Gizmo Corporation's cost of good sold was $5,298,000. This cost of goods sold is used in the profit and loss statement to calculate operating income given the sales and operating income.

Determining Unit Cost

The concept of unit cost is quite simple in principle: If Gizmo Corporation sells widgets and fubars, how much does it cost to produce each widget and each fubar? Knowing the unit cost allows the company to determine a minimum price for its products and services. A company almost certainly doesn't want to sell anything for less than it cost to produce; they probably want to allow for some reasonable amount of profit over the unit cost.

Some companies set their prices by adding a fixed profit margin (as a percent) over the unit cost. Suppose the unit cost for widgets is $100. If the company defines an 18% margin, the selling price of widgets is $118. In fact, the selling price should be based on what customers are willing to pay, not how much it cost to produce. If customers are willing to pay $175 for each widget, why sell them for only $118? The real utility of knowing unit cost is in being able to make decisions such as "we can't produce widgets at a unit cost less than what people are willing to pay, so let's get out of that market."

TRADITIONAL UNIT-COSTING METHODS

Computing unit cost is straightforward when the costs are clearly assignable to the products and services—the direct costs. Knowing that the engine cost $1000, the frame cost $250, tires cost $175, the radio cost $75, and the transmission cost $500, the automaker knows that each car costs at least $2000 to produce. It's the overhead costs that cause the complications. Clearly the overhead costs are there and they need to be accounted for; otherwise the calculated unit cost wouldn't accurately reflect the true unit cost. The problem is that, by definition, these costs can't be directly attributed to the individual units produced. Cost accountants have traditionally used one of three different methods for allocating indirect costs:

- Direct-material-cost method
- Direct-labor-hour method
- Direct-labor-cost method

TABLE 15.1   Direct Costs per Unit at Gizmo Corporation

	Direct-Material Dollars per Unit	Direct-Labor Hours per Unit	Direct-Labor Cost per Hour	Direct-Labor Dollars per Unit
Widget	$100	5	$30.00	$150
Fubar	$200	8	$31.25	$250

Each method is based on certain assumptions and works well under those assumptions. Because the assumptions differ, however, the computed unit costs can come out different even though the same factory is producing the same units.

To illustrate the different allocation methods, assume that Gizmo Corporation produces widgets and fubars; the cost data for each are shown in Table 15.1. The direct-labor cost per hour is higher for fubars because they require more highly skilled workers who are paid more.

If Gizmo Corporation produced 2,730 widgets and 5,690 fubars, the total direct material and total direct labor costs would exactly match the cost of goods sold statement in Figure 15.6. Using the overhead costs from Gizmo Corporation's cost of goods sold statement and profit and loss statement (shown in Figure 15.2), the total overhead (in thousands) is as follows:

Manufacturing overhead	$2168
Selling expenses	$640
General and administrative expenses	$1722
Research and development expenses	$66
Interest	$563
Investment	$11
Depreciation	$649
Total overhead	$5819

Direct-Material-Cost Method   The direct-material-cost method assumes that overhead should be allocated in proportion to the cost of the direct material spent on the product. The direct-material-cost formula is as follows:

$$DirectMaterialCostRate = \frac{TotalOverhead}{TotalDirectMaterialCost}$$

The total direct-material cost from Gizmo Corporation's cost of goods sold statement in Figure 15.6 is $1,411,000, so their direct-material-cost-rate would be as follows:

$$\frac{\$5,819k}{\$1,411k} = 4.124 \text{ per direct material dollar}$$

This overhead rate can now be factored in with the direct costs for each product to determine the unit cost. The unit cost for widgets using the direct-material-cost method is as follows:

Direct material	$100
Direct labor	$150
Overhead, 4.124 * $100	$412
	$662

The unit cost for fubars is as follows:

Direct material	$200
Direct labor	$250
Overhead, 4.124 * $200	$824
	$1274

Direct-Labor-Hour Method   The direct-labor-hour method assumes that overhead should be allocated in proportion to the number of direct labor hours spent on the product. The direct-labor-hour formula is as follows:

$$DirectLaborHourRate = \frac{TotalOverhead}{TotalDirectLaborHours}$$

Knowing that Gizmo Corporation produced 2,730 widgets and 5,690 fubars, the total number of direct labor hours is 59,170.

$$\frac{\$5,819k}{59,170} = \$98.34 \text{ per direct labor hour}$$

The unit cost for widgets using the direct-labor-hour method is as follows:

Direct material	$100
Direct labor	$150
Overhead, $98.34 * 5	$492
	$742

The unit cost for fubars is as follows:

Direct material	$200
Direct labor	$250
Overhead, $98.34 * 8	$787
	$1237

TABLE 15.2   Unit Costs Using Different Traditional Overhead Cost-Allocation Methods

	Direct-Material- Cost Method	Direct-Labor-Hour Method	Direct-Labor-Cost Method
Widget	$662	$742	$726
Fubar	$1274	$1237	$1244

Direct-Labor-Cost Method   The direct-labor-cost method assumes that overhead should be allocated in proportion to the cost of the direct labor spent on the product. The formula is as follows:

$$DirectLaborHourRate = \frac{TotalOverhead}{TotalDirectLaborCost}$$

The total direct-labor cost from Gizmo Corporation's cost of goods sold statement is $1,832,000, so their direct-labor-cost-rate is as follows:

$$\frac{\$5,819k}{\$1,832k} = 3.176 \text{ per direct labor dollar}$$

The unit cost for widgets using the direct-labor-cost method is as follows:

Direct material	100
Direct labor	$150
Overhead, 3.176 * $150	$476
	$726

The unit cost for fubars is as follows:

Direct material	$200
Direct labor	$250
Overhead, 3.176 * $250	$974
	$1244

Table 15.2 shows a summary of the unit costs for widgets and fubars under the three traditional overhead cost-allocation methods.

The unit cost for widgets ranges from $662 to $742, and the unit cost for fubars ranges from $1237 to $1274. Notice that the unit costs for widgets are the highest when the unit costs for fubars are lowest (direct-material-cost method) and vice versa (direct-labor-hour method). The traditional cost accountant needs to pick the overhead-allocation method that most accurately reflects how overhead costs drive real unit costs across the company's products and services.

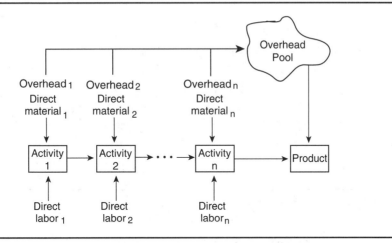

FIGURE 15.7   Allocating overhead using the traditional allocation methods

ACTIVITY-BASED COSTING

The traditional costing methods gather all the overhead costs into a single, rather large pool and then allocate that pool across the company's products and services. This is shown pictorially in Figure 15.7. Naturally, many of the costs in the overhead pool are driven by factors that are completely different from the traditional basis of allocation (direct material cost, direct labor hours, direct labor cost). The computed overhead rate ends up being an average load.

There are bound to be inequities in the traditional allocation. Specifically, products and services with high production rates tend to end up with unnaturally high unit costs, and low-volume products and services tend to come out unnaturally low. Activity-based costing (ABC) was published in 1988 [Cooper88a, Cooper88b] as a unit-costing method that minimizes the distortion caused by arbitrary allocation through average overhead rates.

Using ABC, the entire cost of each activity is averaged out across all occurrences of that activity and is then allocated to individual products based on how much that activity occurs for that product. This is shown in Figure 15.8. It is a finer-grained allocation of overhead, so there is a closer correlation of cost to activity and then from activity to product. Because the allocation of overhead to products is more representative of the true overhead rate, unit costs are more representative of true unit costs.

The following is a slightly simplified description of ABC using a small factory that manufactures pencils and pencil sharpeners as the example. Pencils are produced in lots of 1,000, and sharpeners are produced in batches of 500.

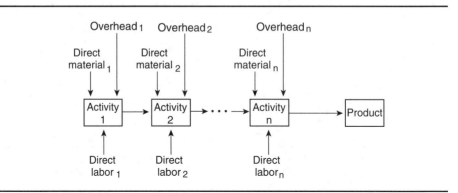

FIGURE 15.8   Allocating overhead using activity-based costing

TABLE 15.3   Activities in the Pencil and Sharpener Factory

Activity

Maintain raw material inventory

Press graphite core

Mill wood shell halves

Bond core and exterior

Paint

Attach eraser

Mold base

Stamp blade

Assemble sharpener

Package product

Ship product

Sales, marketing, and administration

Step 1: Identify the Activities   ABC starts with a list of all the activities (both direct and indirect) associated with all the products and services. Some activities may be specific to a single product or service, and others may apply to all products and services. The important thing is to capture every relevant activity that contributes to unit cost. Table 15.3 shows an example set of activities for the pencil and sharpener factory.

Maintaining the raw material inventory, packaging and shipping products, and the sales, marketing, and administration are examples of non-product-specific activities. Each of the other activities is product-specific; either it applies to pencils or to sharpeners, not both.

TABLE 15.4   Total Costs for the Activities in the Pencil and Sharpener Factory

Activity	Total Cost
Maintain raw material inventory	$45,000
Press graphite core	$18,500
Mill wood shell halves	$17,750
Bond core and exterior	$23,000
Paint	$9125
Attach eraser	$1400
Mold base	$28,500
Stamp blade	$8500
Assemble sharpener	$25,000
Package product	$17,600
Ship product	$360,000
Sales, marketing, and administration	$120,000

Step 2: Determine Total Cost for Each Activity   The next step is to determine the total cost for each activity over some relevant study period. The study period may be a quarter, or a year, or anything, as long as all activities use this same time period. The costs can either be estimated or extracted from the company's accounting system. The total cost needs to include all direct material, direct labor, and overhead associated with that activity. Table 15.4 shows an example of total costs for the activities in the pencil and sharpener factory.

According to Table 15.4, the company spent $18,500 pressing graphite cores for their pencils during the study period. This includes the press operator's salary and benefits, electricity for and maintenance of the press itself, and so on. The company spent $1400 on all material, labor, and overhead associated with attaching erasers to pencils.

Step 3: Define a Measure and Quantity for Each Activity   There needs to be a measure for counting how many times each activity happens over the course of the study period. The measure need not be 100% accurate, but it should represent the primary means of counting how many times that activity takes place over that period of time. Either estimate or count the number of times each activity is performed over the study period. Table 15.5 shows an example set of measurements and quantities for the pencil and sharpener factory.

TABLE 15.5 Measures and Quantities for Activities in the Pencil and Sharpener Factory

Activity	Measure	Quantity
Maintain raw material inventory	Pallet	650
Press graphite core	Lot	2,500
Mill wood shell halves	Lot	5,000
Bond core and exterior	Lot	2,500
Paint	Batch	10,000
Attach eraser	Lot	2,500
Mold base	Run	100
Stamp blade	Cycle	1,000
Assemble sharpener	Cycle	1,000
Package product	Case	3,500
Ship product	Shipment	3,500
Sales, marketing, and administration	Hour	4,500

TABLE 15.6 Average Costs for the Activities in the Pencil and Sharpener Factory

Activity	Average Cost
Maintain raw material inventory	$69.23
Press graphite core	$7.40
Mill wood shell halves	$3.55
Bond core and exterior	$9.20
Paint	$0.91
Attach eraser	$0.56
Mold base	$285.00
Stamp blade	$8.50
Assemble sharpener	$25.00
Package product	$5.03
Ship product	$10.29
Sales marketing, and administration	$26.67

The factory made 100 runs of the sharpener base molding activity and had 4,500 hours of sales, marketing, and administration time over the study period.

Step 4: Calculate Average Cost per Output for Each Activity   The next step is to divide the total cost for each activity by its quantity to calculate the average cost per occurrence. Table 15.6 shows the average cost for each activity in the pencil and sharpener factory.

TABLE 15.7 Activity Quantities for Each Product

Activity	Pencil	Sharpener
Maintain raw material inventory	0.46	0.19
Press graphite core	1	0
Mill wood shell halves	2	0
Bond core and exterior	1	0
Paint	4	0
Attach eraser	1	0
Mold base	0	0.1
Stamp blade	0	1
Assemble sharpener	0	1
Package product	1	1
Ship product	1	1
Sales, marketing, and administration	1	2

Step 5: Specify Activity Quantities for Each Product Next specify the average number of times each activity happens during the course of producing one unit of each product or service. The activity may happen zero times for a product if that activity doesn't have any effect on that product—pressing graphite cores and painting apply to pencils, not sharpeners. Table 15.7 shows the activity quantities at the pencil and sharpener factory.

One lot of pencils uses an average of 0.46 pallets of raw material inventory, and one production cycle of sharpeners uses 0.19 pallets. Each production cycle of sharpeners uses one tenth of the bases molded in a run of the base-molding machine.

Make sure to account for all activity occurrences over the study period—if you know the number of units of each product produced, you can multiply the activity quantities by product quantities and then sum up across all products. This sum needs to equal the total quantity for the activity in Step 3. If 2,500 units of pencils and 1,000 units of sharpeners are produced during the study period, there are 2,500 hours of sales, marketing, and administration for pencils and 2,000 hours for sharpeners and this equals the 4,500 hours of time over the entire study period shown in Step 2.

Step 6: Calculate Unit Costs The final step in ABC is to sum the average activity costs times the activity quantities for a given product. The formula is as follows:

$$UnitCost_i = \sum_{j=1}^{n} CostPerOutput_i * Quantity_jOnProduct_i$$

TABLE 15.8 Activity Costs and Totals for Each Product

Activity	Pencil	Sharpener
Maintain raw material inventory	$32.14	$12.86
Press graphite core	$7.40	
Mill wood shell halves	$7.10	
Bond core and exterior	$9.20	
Paint	$3.65	
Attach eraser	$0.56	
Mold base		$28.50
Stamp blade		$8.50
Assemble sharpener		$25.00
Package product	$5.03	$5.03
Ship product	$10.29	$10.29
Sales, marketing, and administration	$26.67	$53.33
Total	$102.03	$143.5

This gives the total unit cost for that product. Table 15.8 shows the calculated activity costs for pencils and sharpeners, and the total unit cost is shown at the bottom of the table.

ABC is still relatively new in the accounting profession. More companies are switching to it over time, but many companies still use the traditional methods and will for a long time to come.

CAUTIONS ON USING UNIT COSTS

It might seem reasonable to use unit costs to calculate total costs for any arbitrary production rate. If the unit cost for a batch of pencils is $102.03 and 1,000 batches were produced, wouldn't the total cost have to be $102,030? Unfortunately it's not that simple. In addition to direct costs and indirect costs, another categorization of costs are variable costs and fixed costs:

- **Variable costs are costs that are proportional to the rate of production**—If you produce twice as many pencils in one month as the last, the variable costs will be twice as much in the second month. Raw materials are a variable cost because they are proportional to production rate.
- **Fixed costs aren't affected by the rate of production**—Even if the factory didn't produce a single pencil or sharpener, the "capacity for production" has costs. The company still has to pay rent on the factory and office space, interest on loans, property taxes, etc. These are good examples of fixed costs.

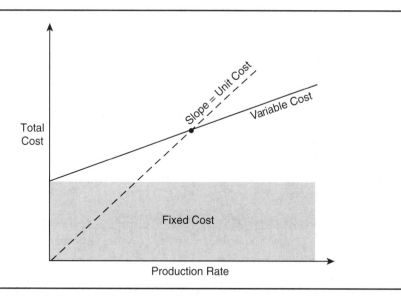

FIGURE 15.9   Relating unit costs to fixed costs and variable costs

Direct costs are clearly variable costs because they are driven by the production rate. Some of the overhead costs will be variable (e.g., the amount of paint or the number of screws), whereas some of the overhead costs are fixed (e.g., loan interest, property taxes, administrative salaries, etc.).

Figure 15.9 shows the relationship between fixed costs, variable costs, and unit costs. Unit cost is essentially the slope of the line through the origin and the point on the total cost curve for a given production rate. If there were no fixed costs, the unit cost would exactly equal the slope of the variable cost line, and the unit cost would be the same at all production rates. However, fixed costs are virtually guaranteed to be nonzero.

Given nonzero fixed costs, as the production rate changes, the slope of the unit cost line will change with it. All other things being equal, if the production rate were halved, unit cost would actually increase because the variable costs would be cut in half but the fixed costs would stay the same. The same fixed overhead would be spread across fewer units. Conversely, if the production rate were doubled (assuming it could be doubled without impacting fixed costs—it didn't require expanding the facility, for instance), the unit cost would go down. The higher the percentage that fixed costs are of the total cost, the more pronounced the change in unit cost will be over different production rates.

Simply multiplying unit cost by production rate to get total cost for any given production rate could be misleading. The actual total cost at that production rate could be quite different from what was calculated.

Summary

Technically speaking, accounting is the process of recording the financial history of a company. Accounting is "the language of business," and business goals are often defined in accounting terms, so software professionals need to be familiar with that language to communicate effectively with the managers and financiers. This chapter covered the following major points:

- The balance sheet shows the financial position of a company at a particular moment in time. It's a "snapshot" or "freeze-frame" view of the financial strength of the company and answers the question, "How much is the company worth at this point in time?"
- The profit and loss statement explains how the company's financial position changed over a period of time. It answers the question, "How quickly is the company gaining or losing value?"
- The cash-flow statement shows how the company is paying for its current operations and future growth by detailing the actual flow of cash between the company and the outside. It answers the question, "How much more or less cash does the company have than before?"
- Cost accounting is a specialized branch of general accounting that finds out how much it cost to provide the products and services that were sold. That cost is shown in a cost of goods sold statement.
- Unit cost shows how much it costs to produce one instance of each of the products and services. Knowing the unit cost allows the company to determine a minimum price for its products and services. Several unit-costing methods are available:
  - Direct-material-cost method
  - Direct-labor-hour method
  - Direct-labor-cost method
  - Activity-based costing (ABC)

The next chapter discusses income taxes and explains how to calculate an after-tax cash-flow stream so that income taxes can be accurately accounted for in business decisions.

Self-Study Questions

1. If you work for a publicly traded company, get your company's most recent 10Q or 10K. (Hint: Use the Investors section of the corporate Web site or use EDGAR. You can also find 10K information in the company's annual report.) If you don't work for a publicly traded company, pick a company that is (or have one assigned) and get their most recent 10Q or 10K. What are the company's total assets? What are its

total liabilities? What is the total owner's equity? Show how their balance sheet conforms to the fundamental accounting equation.

2. MegaStaff Consulting is a software consulting firm. At the end of 20x1 they had assets totaling $3,655,712 and liabilities totaling $2,721,066. What was MegaStaff's owner's equity at that time?

3. At the end of 20x2, MegaStaff Consulting had $1,010,873 in owner's equity and liabilities totaling $3,102,015. What was the total of their assets at that time?

4. Below is a simplified balance sheet (amounts in thousands) for Xenon Game Software, Inc. immediately before they buy new development hardware for an upcoming project.

Assets

Cash and cash equivalents	$90
Accounts receivable	$175
Plant and equipment	$216
Total assets	$481
Liabilities	
Accounts payable	$198
Debt	$122
Declared dividends	$87
Total liabilities	$407
Owner's Equity	
Stock	$58
Retained earnings	$16
Total owner's equity	$74
Total liabilities and owner's equity	$481

Xenon is buying $24,000 of new computer hardware and paying for it with cash. Show the profit and loss statement, cash-flow statement, and ending balance sheet immediately after the purchase. Assume that all other unspecified accounting categories are zero.

5. Using the same starting balance sheet from the previous question, show the profit and loss statement, cash-flow statement, and ending balance sheet assuming that Xenon buys the computer equipment using a loan for the full amount of the purchase.

6. Use the ending balance sheet from Question 4 as the starting balance sheet for this question. Assume that Xenon Software had the following financial results from using the equipment over the reporting period:

Sales and operating income = $240,000

Cost of goods sold = $63,000

Selling expenses = $47,000

General and administrative expenses =$44,000

Research and development = $81,000

Depreciation = $7000

Federal, state, and local income taxes = $29,000

Assume that all other unspecified accounting categories are zero and show the profit and loss statement, cash-flow statement, and ending balance sheet for this situation.

7. Theta Manufacturing had the following starting, during-year, and ending values for cost of goods sold categories. Create a cost of goods sold statement using the format shown in Figure 15-6.

	In Process Jan 1, 20x3	Applied During Year	In Process Dec 31, 20x3
Direct material	$40	$468	$37
Direct labor	$43	$642	$57
Manufacturing overhead	$58	$721	$71
Finished goods	$162	—	$213

Questions 8 through 12 relate to the following situation: TropicalFishTanks.com sells aquariums on the World Wide Web. Their two main products are goldfish bowls and deluxe aquariums. Both products come complete with sand (your choice from a set of available colors), air pump, filter, owner's manual, and a modest supply of fish food. Last year, 18,000 goldfish bowls and 14,000 deluxe aquariums were produced. The following table lists other relevant data.

	Direct-Material Dollars per Unit	Direct-Labor Hours per Unit	Direct-Labor Cost per Hour
Goldfish bowl	$5.67	0.45	$9.75
Deluxe aquarium	$10.47	0.75	$12.25

The total manufacturing overhead was $360,800.

8. What are the unit costs for goldfish bowls and deluxe aquariums under the direct-material-cost method?

9. What are the unit costs for goldfish bowls and deluxe aquariums under the direct-labor-hour method?

10. What are the unit costs for goldfish bowls and deluxe aquariums under the direct-labor-cost method?

11. TropicalFishTanks.com decides to use activity-based costing to calculate unit costs. The following table shows a list of the activities, total costs, measure, and counts.

Activity	Total Cost	Measure	Quantity
Maintain bowl inventory	$106,875	Bowl	18,000
Maintain aquarium glass inventory	$99,550	Sq ft	112,000
Maintain aquarium frame inventory	$63,390	Linear ft	168,000
Maintain air pump inventory	$89,000	Unit	32,000
Maintain sand inventory	$26,200	Pound	74,000
Maintain owner's manual inventory	$32,500	Copy	32,000
Maintain fish food inventory	$37,400	Ounce	106,000
Maintain packing material inventory	$25,900	Pound	32,000
Assemble aquarium	$46,300	Unit	14,000
Pack bowl	$58,900	Unit	18,000
Pack aquarium	$87,025	Unit	14,000
Sales, marketing, and administration	$144,000	Hour	4,000

What are the average costs for each of these activities?

12. The following table shows the activity quantities at TropicalFishTanks.com.

Activity	Goldfish Bowl	Deluxe Aquarium
Maintain bowl inventory	1.00	0.00
Maintain aquarium glass inventory	0.00	8.00
Maintain aquarium frame inventory	0.00	12.00
Maintain air pump inventory	1.00	1.00
Maintain sand inventory	1.00	3.00
Maintain owner's manual inventory	1.00	1.00
Maintain fish food inventory	2.00	4.00
Maintain packing material inventory	1.00	2.00
Assemble aquarium	0.00	1.00
Pack bowl	1.00	0.00
Pack aquarium	0.00	1.00
Sales, marketing, and administration	0.11	0.14

a. Use the average costs for the activities (your answer to the previous question) to calculate the unit cost for TropicalFishTanks.com's fish bowls using activity-based accounting.

b. Use the average costs for the activities (your answer to the previous question) to calculate the unit cost for TropicalFishTanks.com's deluxe aquariums using activity-based accounting.

Questions 13 and 14 refer to Gizmo Corporation's unit costs in Table 15.2. Assume that the actual market prices are $910 for widgets and $1560 for fubars.

13. If Gizmo Corporation has a policy of a minimum 25% profit margin on sales, which traditional overhead cost-allocation methods would probably cause Gizmo Corporation to consider getting out of either the widget market or the fubar market?

14. If Gizmo Corporation has a policy of a minimum 26% profit margin on sales, which traditional overhead cost-allocation methods would probably cause Gizmo Corporation to consider getting out of either the widget or fubar market?

15. Cobalt Lighting, Inc. produces, among other things, a unit called a K-module. Assume that the only thing someone at Cobalt Lighting told you was that the unit cost for each K-module was $115:
   a. What would be your best estimate of the total cost of producing 6,000 K-modules?
   b. What would be your best estimate of the total cost of producing 12,000 K-modules?
   c. What would be your best estimate of the total cost of producing 18,000 K-modules?

16. Following on the previous question, suppose someone told you that the fixed cost for producing K-modules was $225,000 and the variable cost per unit was $96.25:
   a. What would be your estimate of the total cost of producing 6,000 K-modules?
   b. What would be your estimate of the total cost of producing 12,000 K-modules?
   c. What would be your estimate of the total cost of producing 18,000 K-modules?

17. Following on the previous question, suppose someone else told you that the fixed cost for producing K-modules was $450,000 and the variable cost per unit was $77.50:
   a. What would be your estimate of the total cost of producing 6,000 K-modules?
   b. What would be your estimate of the total cost of producing 12,000 K-modules?
   c. What would be your estimate of the total cost of producing 18,000 K-modules?

18. What do the answers to 15b, 16b, and 17b tell you about the $115 unit price quoted in Question 15? What do the other answers (15a and c, 16a and c, 17a and c) tell you in general about the use of unit cost data to predict total production costs?

16

Income Taxes and After-Tax Cash-Flow Streams

The popular saying is that "nothing in life is certain except death and taxes." This may very well be true, so we best learn to deal with taxes in a business-decision analysis because they can have a dramatic effect on profitability. The amounts and timing for most taxes are known ahead of time, so they can be handled by simply including them as expense cash-flow instances in a proposal's cash-flow stream. However, income taxes are another matter because you can't know how much income tax needs to be paid until you know how much profit there is. This chapter introduces income taxes and explains how to calculate an after-tax cash-flow stream so that income taxes can be accurately accounted for in business decisions. This chapter presents income taxes as defined in the United States. Income taxes in other countries will certainly be different, but the same general principles will probably still apply. Chapter 17 then shows how the effects of income taxes can influence business decisions.

Tax laws can change every year. The information here should be accurate as of the date of publication, but changes in tax law may make some of the information out of date. If accurate accounting of taxes is critical to the decision at hand, consult a tax professional who is familiar with the current tax laws.

What Are Taxes?

According to the dictionary, a tax is [Websters86]

> A charge, usually of money, imposed by authority on persons or property for public purposes, or a sum levied on members of an organization to defray expenses.

There are many different kinds of taxes: sales taxes, property taxes, excise taxes, and so on. The amounts and timings of these taxes are either known in advance or can be easily estimated from other information known about the proposal. These taxes can simply be included as expense cash-flow instances along with all of the other cash-flow instances in the proposal.

Income taxes are an entirely different matter. Even the term *income tax* is misleading because it's not really a tax on income. Referring back to Figure 2.1 in Chapter 2, it's really a tax only on the *net* income (revenue minus expenses, or gross "pretax" profit). In the United States, the federal government and most states charge income taxes, which combined can take between 20% and 40% of a corporation's net profit. In some areas, federal, state, and local income taxes can add up to more than 50%. This should make it obvious that a decision analysis that doesn't account for income taxes can lead to the wrong choice. A proposal with a high pretax IRR won't look nearly as profitable in post-tax IRR terms. Not accounting for income taxes can also lead to unrealistically high expectations about how profitable a proposal is.

Income taxes are more complex than other taxes because the amount of tax owed can't be known without first knowing both gross income and the expenses of the proposal. Loan interest payments (Chapter 6) and depreciation accounting (Chapter 14) add an extra complication because they both affect the expenses: Remember that depreciation accounting spreads the acquisition cost of a capital asset over several years.

This chapter only describes U.S. federal income taxes (for both corporations and individuals). We won't talk about state income taxes in any great depth. This is partly because state income tax laws vary widely. And although the state income tax rates tend to be lower than the federal tax rates, the concepts and techniques for addressing them in a business decision are exactly the same as for federal income taxes.

Federal Income Taxes for Corporations

In the United States, federal income taxes as we know them today didn't exist until March 13, 1913, when they were enacted by Congress in the sixteenth amendment to the constitution. Since then, according to the U.S. tax code, any person or organization that acts in a way intended to make a profit is required to pay part of that profit as taxes. Even nonprofit organizations are required to pay income taxes if they end up taking in more money than they spend.

TABLE 16.1   U.S. Federal Income Tax Rates for Corporations

Corporation's Taxable Income	Marginal Tax Rate
$0 to $50,000	15%
$50,001 to $75,000	25%
$75,001 to $100,000	34%
$100,001 to $335,000	39%
$335,001 to $10,000,000	34%
$10,000,001 to $15,000,000	35%
$15,000,001 to $18,333,333	38%
Over $18,333,334	35%

TABLE 16.2 Computing Income Tax Using the Marginal Income Tax Rates

Part of Taxable Income	Marginal Tax Rate	Tax Owed
First $50,000	15%	$7500
Next $25,000	25%	$6250
Next $25,000	34%	$8500
Last $175,000	39%	$68,250
	Total	$90,500

Income taxes are charged against an organization's net income. Net income is, for our purposes, whatever money is left over after all expenses have been subtracted from the income earned by a business activity. This was shown in Figure 2.1 in Chapter 2, a corporation that brings in $1 million in gross revenue in a year but spends $800,000 to make that million only pays income tax on the $200,000 net income—its "taxable income" or "net income before taxes."

The U.S. federal tax rates are shown in Table 16.1.

Notice that the tax rates (the so-called tax brackets) are shown as marginal rates. This means that regardless of the total taxable income, the organization pays 15% tax on all taxable income up to the first $50,000 it earns, 25% income tax on the next $25,000 (if any), 34% on the next $25,000 (if any), and so on. Any taxable income beyond $18,333,334 is taxed at a flat 35%.

Table 16.2 shows how to compute a corporation's tax liability using the marginal tax rates. A company that ended a tax year with $275,000 of taxable income would owe $7500 in income taxes on the first $50,000 earned (0.15 * $50,000 = $7500). They would owe $6250 on the next $25,000 of taxable income, and so on. The total income tax owed on $275,000 taxable income would be $90,500.

Notice that $90,500 in income taxes is actually 32.9% of the $275,000 taxable income. Even though $275,000 is in the 39% tax bracket, the actual tax as a percentage of income is less than 39%. Figure 16.1 shows how the marginal tax rates relate to a flat 34% income tax rate up to $335,000.

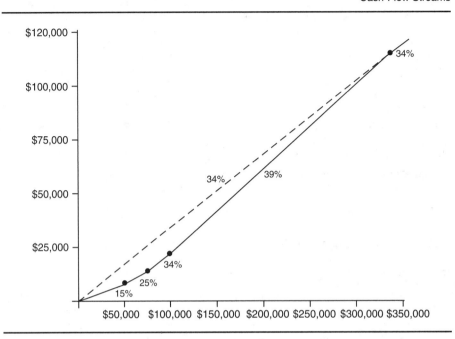

FIGURE 16.1   Actual marginal tax rates compared to a flat 34% tax rate

The marginal rates are set up this way to give a substantial tax break to companies with taxable incomes of $100,000 or less. Even though taxable income in the range of $100,000 to $335,000 is taxed at the highest marginal rate, 39%, the actual income tax owed across this range of taxable income is still less than it would be under a flat 34% rate. The 39% tax rate in that income range makes up the difference between the lower rates on the first $100,000 and the flat 34% rate from $335,000 to $10,000,000.

Federal Income Taxes for Individuals

If you are, or intend to be, a self-employed software professional, the individual income tax rates may be relevant. In the United States, there are several important differences between how corporations and how individuals are taxed. For one, fewer expenses are deductible. (Interest on a house loan is deductible, but credit card interest, food, utilities, and clothes are not.) Second, the tax rates and ranges of income for individuals are different from the corporate rates and ranges. Another difference is that the corporate rates aren't adjusted every year for inflation, but the individual rates are. In theory, an individual won't be pushed into a higher tax rate because of inflation.

TABLE 16.3   Marginal Income Tax Rates for Taxpayers Filing "Single" in 2001

Taxable Income	Marginal Tax Rate
$0 to $27,050	15%
$27,050 to $65,550	27.5%
$65,550 to $136,750	30.5%
$136,750 to $297,350	35.5%
Over $297,350	39.1%

TABLE 16.4   Marginal Income Tax Rates for "Married Filing Jointly or Qualified Widow(er)" in 2001

Taxable Income	Marginal Tax Rate
$0 to $45,200	15%
$45,200 to $109,250	27.5%
$109,250 to $166,500	30.5%
$166,500 to $297,350	35.5%
Over $297,350	39.1%

Table 16.3 shows the marginal tax rates for taxpayers filing "Single" in 2001 [IRS01]. Table 16.4 shows the marginal tax rates for taxpayers filing "Married Filing Jointly or Qualified Widow(er)" in 2001.

Just like corporate income taxes, the income tax rates for individuals are also marginal rates. Amounts over the bottom of each income range are taxed at the rate for that range, up to the maximum income for that range. A married couple filing a joint return with $68,500 taxable income would owe $6780 (15% on the first $45,200 of taxable income) plus $6408 (27.5% on the next $23,300) for a total of $13,188.

Effective Income Tax Rates

An **effective income tax rate** is an average tax rate over a range of incomes. Effective income tax rates make it easier to calculate after-tax cash-flow streams because, by using an effective rate, you don't have to worry about the specific marginal rates talked about above. You would simply use the single effective rate over the entire income range. The effective rate, t, over a given range of taxable income is as follows:

$$t = \frac{Tax_{RangeTop} - Tax_{RangeBottom}}{Income_{RangeTop} - Income_{RangeBottom}}$$

Suppose a small corporation wants to know the effective tax rate over the range of taxable incomes between \$40,000 and \$60,000. The tax payable on \$40,000 is this:

$$15\% * \$40,000 = \$6000$$

The tax payable on \$60,000 is this:

$$\$7500 + 25\% * (\$60,000 - \$50,000) = \$10,000$$

The effective tax rate over this range of taxable income is as follows:

$$t = \frac{\$10,000 - \$6000}{\$60,000 - \$40,000} = 0.20 = 20\%$$

State and local income taxes may make the effective tax rate higher. The effective state tax rate is calculated exactly the same way.

COMBINING EFFECTIVE FEDERAL, STATE, AND LOCAL INCOME TAX RATES

State and local income taxes are deductible as expenses when calculating federal taxes, and this impacts the overall effective income tax rate as follows:

$$t = EffectiveFederalRate * (1 - EffectiveStateAndLocalRate) + EffectiveStateAndLocal\ Rate$$

Given an effective federal rate of 39% and an effective state and local rate of 7%

$$t = 39\% * (1 - 7\%) + 7\% = 43.3\%$$

Calculating After-Tax Cash-Flow Streams

With federal, state, and local income taxes combining to take as much as 50% of the profit in a proposal, these taxes will clearly have a noticeable effect on profitability. One way to address income taxes is just to use a before-tax MARR (see Chapter 10). As discussed, using a before-tax MARR will help account for taxes, but the results may not be accurate enough for a particular decision analysis. If more accuracy is needed, the best way to get it is to do the decision analysis using the after-tax MARR (assuming the organization has stated the MARR in after-tax terms) together with the after-tax cash-flow stream. This section explains how to calculate the after-tax cash-flow stream.

TABLE 16.5   A Form for Calculating After-Tax Cash-Flow Streams

(A) End of Year	(B) Before-Tax Cash-Flow Stream	(C) Loan Principal	(D) Loan Interest	(E) Depreciable Investment	(F) Depreciation Expense	(G) Taxable Income (B + D + F)	(H) IncomeTax Cash-Flow Stream (– Rate * G)	(I) After-Tax Cash-Flow Stream (B + C + D + E + H)
0	. . .	. . .	N/A	. . .	N/A	. . .	. . .	. . .
1	. . .	. . .	. . .	. . .	. . .	. . .	. . .	. . .
2	. . .	. . .	. . .	. . .	. . .	. . .	. . .	. . .
3	. . .	. . .	. . .	. . .	. . .	. . .	. . .	. . .
4	. . .	. . .	. . .	. . .	. . .	. . .	. . .	. . .
5	. . .	. . .	. . .	. . .	. . .	. . .	. . .	. . .

Four pieces of information need to be known about the alternative being studied to calculate the after-tax cash-flow stream:

- The before-tax cash-flow stream
- Loan principal and interest payments (discussed in Chapter 6)
- Depreciation accounting (discussed in Chapter 14)
- The effective income tax rate (above)

The most straightforward approach is to use a form like the one shown in Table 16.5. A spreadsheet automating this table can be found at http://www.construx.com/returnonsw/. By convention, income is shown as positive numbers and expenses are shown as negative numbers.

Column (B) is for the before-tax cash-flow stream. Entries in this column will be the sum of all normal income minus all normal expenses for the corresponding year. The term *normal* means all income and expenses that are not loan related nor depreciation related because those are addressed in other parts of the form.

Column (C) is the cash-flow stream for loan principal amounts. The receipt of the loan amount is shown as a positive number, and loan principal payments are shown as negative numbers. Chapter 5 explained how loan payments can be calculated using the equal-payment-series capital-recovery (A/P,i,n) formula, and the procedure for separating interest and principal in loan payments was described in Chapter 6.

Column (D) is the cash-flow stream for loan interest payments. There shouldn't be any loan interest payments in the initial investment (year 0).

Column (E) shows investments in depreciable assets.

Column (F) is for the depreciation amounts determined through depreciation accounting as explained in Chapter 14. Remember that depreciation amounts are expenses, but they aren't actually cash flows. The original investment (the actual cash flow) happened when the assets were purchased, the corporation just wasn't able to deduct the entire expense at that time. Depreciation accounting spreads the actual expense over several years. The depreciation amounts are needed for calculating the income taxes, which are cash flows. There shouldn't be any depreciation in year 0.

If a depreciable asset will be sold or scrapped before the end of the planning horizon, the difference between its book value when it is sold or scrapped and its estimated salvage value will need to be added to the before-tax cash-flow instance for that year. Also depreciation can't be taken on an asset after it's been sold or scrapped.

If the taxpayer owns only a portion of a depreciable asset, only that portion of the depreciation deduction can be claimed. A company that owns 25% share of a $2 million building can only depreciate the $500,000 share of the building that they own.

Column (G) shows the taxable income that results from subtracting loan interest payments and depreciation amounts (columns (D) and (F)) from the before-tax cash-flow stream (column (B)).

Column (H) shows the taxes owed on (or saved by) the proposal that year. This column is calculated by multiplying the taxable income in column (G) by the effective income tax rate (described earlier in this chapter). Positive numbers in this column mean that the corporation will save that amount on their overall taxes, provided that the rest of the corporation is profitable. As long as the overall corporation is profitable, a loss in one area of the business just reduces the total income taxes owed. If the overall corporation is not profitable, things are much more complicated. Under certain conditions, a loss in one year can be carried backward or forward and deducted from profits in other years. Under other conditions, losses in a year can't be carried. You may need to discuss with a tax accountant how to handle losses in a corporation that isn't profitable overall if it is a significant part of a decision analysis.

Column (I) is the after-tax cash-flow stream. This column is calculated by adding the before-tax cash-flow instance to the loan principal, loan interest, depreciable investment, together with the income tax cash-flow instance.

MR KINKAID'S EXCELLENT ADVENTURE, IN AFTER-TAX TERMS

To demonstrate calculating after-tax cash-flow streams, we'll use Mr. Kinkaid's example from Chapter 8.

The Before-Tax Cash-Flow Stream, Column (B) Mr. Kinkaid's before-tax cash-flow stream is shown in Table 8.2 of Chapter 8. This cash-flow stream is copied into Column (B) of Table 16.7.

Loan Principal and Interest, Columns (C) and (D) Assume that Mr. Kinkaid can finance his project with a $10,000 loan at 9% APR for 5 years, with annual payments. Using the equal-payment-series capital-recovery (A/P) formula, his annual payments will be as follows:

$$A = \$10,000 \underset{A/P,9,5}{(0.2571)} = \$2571$$

TABLE 16.6 Separating Principal and Interest Payments for Mr. Kinkaid's Loan

End of Year	Loan Payment A	Principal Payment B_t	Interest Payment I_t
1	$2571	$P/F,9,5$ $2571 * (0.6499) = $1671	$900
2	$2571	$P/F,9,4$ $2571 * (0.7084) = 1821	$750
3	$2571	$P/F,9,3$ $2571 * (0.7722) = 1985	$586
4	$2571	$P/F,9,2$ $2571 * (0.8417) = 2164	$407
5	$2571	$P/F,9,1$ $2571 * (0.9174) = 2359	$212

TABLE 16.7 Calculating Mr. Kinkaid's After-Tax Cash-Flow Stream

(A) End of Year	(B) Before-Tax Cash-Flow Stream	(C) Loan Principal	(D) Loan Interest	(E) Depreciable Investment	(F) Depreciation Expense	(G) Taxable Income (B + D + F)	(H) IncomeTax Cash-Flow Stream (− Rate * G)	(I) After-Tax Cash-Flow Stream (B + C + D + E + H)
0	−$3000	$10,000	N/A	−$7000	N/A	−$3000	$900	$900
1	−$850	−$1671	−$900		−$1400	−$3150	$945	−$2476
2	$650	−$1821	−$750		−$2240	−$2340	$702	−$1219
3	$2900	−$1985	−$586		−$1344	$970	−$291	$38
4	$8150	−$2164	−$407		−$806	$6937	−$2081	$3498
5	$5900	−$2359	−$212		−$806	$4882	−$1465	$1864
6	$3650				−$404	$3246	−$974	$2676
7	$1400					$1400	−$420	$980

Table 16.6 shows Mr. Kinkaid's interest and principal separated using the method described in Chapter 6.

The principal payments in the third column of Table 16.6 are copied into column (C) of Table 16.7. The interest payments in the right-most column of Table 16.6 go into column (D) of Table 16.7.

Depreciation, Column (E)   Assuming that Mr. Kinkaid's computer system (a depreciable asset) cost $7000 and will be depreciated using the MACRS prescribed method for 5-year property, his depreciation schedule is shown in Table 14.12 in Chapter 14. The depreciation amounts in the middle column of Table 14.12 go into column (E) of Table 16.7.

Completing the Table Table 16.7 shows the calculation of Mr. Kinkaid's after-tax cash-flow stream assuming his effective income tax rate, including state and local income taxes, is 30% and that overall he is profitable (i.e., he has other sources of income that will cover his losses in the early years).

The PW(9) of the before-tax cash-flow stream (column (B) plus column (E)) is $4557, and the after-tax cash-flow stream (Column (I)) is $3452. Clearly there is a significant difference in the before- and after-tax perspectives.

Tax Credits

At the time this book was published, there were no tax credits available for software-related activities (or for most business activities, for that matter). However, tax credits have been available to business and individuals in the past, and they may become available again in the future. This section explains how tax credits would be addressed, should they be available.

For all other things such as expenses, loan interest payments, and depreciation held constant, each additional dollar of before-tax income will result in

$1.00 – (Effective income tax rate as cents)

of additional after-tax income. Each additional dollar of before-tax income with an effective income tax rate of 39% will yield

$1.00 – $0.39 = $0.61

of additional after-tax income. Similarly, if everything else is held constant, each additional dollar of before-tax expenses reduces the after-tax income by the same tax-rate adjusted amount. Adding a dollar of before-tax expense with an effective income tax rate of 39% reduces the after-tax income by $0.61.

In contrast, tax credits are added directly to the after-tax cash-flow stream. Each dollar of tax credit gives the taxpayer $1 of after-tax income. Tax credits are set up to stimulate investment in particular areas of the economy. The U.S. federal government used tax credits for alternative energy sources and energy conservation during the energy crisis of the early- and mid-1970s. Tax credits for individuals are in place to reduce taxes for elderly, disabled, and low-income individuals.

Before 1986, the U.S. federal government offered the "investment credit" to corporations to encourage investment in capital assets. Under the investment credit, the company would receive a 10% credit on the purchase of capital equipment. If a company spent $175,000 on a new computer, for example, they would receive a tax credit of $17,500 the year they acquired that computer. The investment credit didn't affect depreciation accounting; the company was still allowed to depreciate the entire acquisition cost even with the investment credit.

TABLE 16.8   Calculating Mr Kinkaid's After-Tax Cash-Flow Stream with a 10% Investment Credit

(A) End of Year	(B) Before-Tax Cash-Flow Stream	(C) Loan Principal	(D) Loan Interest	(E) Depreciable Investment	(F) Depreciation Expense	(G) Taxable Income (B + D + F)	(H) IncomeTax Cash-Flow Stream (– Rate * G)	(I) After-Tax Cash-Flow Stream (B + C + D + E + H)
0	–$3000	$10,000	N/A	–$7000	N/A	–$3000	$900	$1600
1	–$850	–$1671	–$900		–$1400	–$3150	$945	–$2476
2	$650	–$1821	–$750		–$2240	–$2340	$702	–$1219
3	$2900	–$1985	–$586		–$1344	$970	–$291	$38
4	$8150	–$2164	–$407		–$806	$6937	–$2081	$3498
5	$5900	–$2359	–$212		–$806	$4882	–$1465	$1864
6	$3650				–$404	$3246	–$974	$2676
7	$1400					$1400	–$420	$980

Using Mr. Kinkaid's proposal as an example (refer back to Table 16.7), Table 16.8 shows the calculation of an after-tax cash-flow stream when the investment credit is included. This example assumes a 10% investment credit on Mr. Kinkaid's $7000 equipment purchase. Notice that the depreciation amounts (column (F)) don't change even though Mr. Kinkaid effectively only pays $6300 for the computer system.

The 10% investment credit increases the PW(9) of Mr. Kinkaid's after-tax cash-flow stream to $4152.

The Tax Reform Act of 1986 repealed the regular investment credit for property placed in service after 1986, but investment credits are still available in a few exceptional situations. You may need to consult a tax professional to get information on available investment credits if they are an important factor in a particular decision.

Inflation and After-Tax Cash-Flow Streams

Some of the components in a proposal's before-tax cash-flow stream will be affected by inflation and others will not. Unless you are already explicitly accounting for inflation (Chapter 13), cash flows for revenues, operating and maintenance costs, and future salvage values will probably be expressed in constant dollars. And, even though you may be already accounting for inflation, cash flows for loans and repayment schedules, lease fees, and taxes paid will probably be expressed in actual dollars. Depreciation amounts will also be in actual dollars.

> When calculating after-tax cash flows from before-tax cash flows, use actual dollar
> analysis.

If a decision analysis needs to account for income taxes and inflation in the same study,
start by separating out all the constant dollar components such as revenues, operating
and maintenance costs, salvage values, etc. Then use the techniques in Chapter 13 to
convert these components to actual dollar amounts. Finally, add in the components that
are already in actual dollar terms, except for the loan interest payments and depreciation
amounts. You're now ready to calculate the after-tax cash-flow stream using the technique described above with Table 16.5. The inflation-adjusted before-tax cash-flow
stream is put into column (B) of the table. Interest payments and depreciation amounts,
which are already in actual dollar terms, are put into columns (C) and (D), and the calculations proceed as described above.

Summary

This chapter introduced income taxes and explained how to calculate an after-tax cash-
flow stream so that income taxes can be accurately accounted for in business decisions.
With federal, state, and local income taxes combining to take as much as 50% of the
profit from an activity, these taxes will clearly have a noticeable impact on profitability.
This chapter covered the following major points:

- The amounts and timings for most taxes are known in advance, so they can be
  handled by simply including them as expense cash-flow instances in a proposal's
  cash-flow stream.
- Income taxes are charged against an organization's net income, not its gross
  revenue. You can't know how much income tax needs to be paid until you know
  how much profit there is.
- Loan interest payments are deductible from gross revenue and need to be
  addressed when calculating the after-tax cash-flow stream.
- Depreciation is also deductible from gross revenue and needs to be included when
  calculating the after-tax cash-flow stream.
- An effective income tax rate is an average tax rate over a range of incomes.
  Effective income tax rates make it easier to calculate after-tax cash-flow streams
  because you don't have to use the specific marginal tax rates.
- Unlike deductions, tax credits are added directly to the after-tax cash-flow stream.
  Each dollar of tax credit gives the taxpayer $1 of after-tax income.

The next chapter shows how the effects of income taxes can influence business
decisions.

Self-Study Questions

1. Company A has a taxable income of $37,500. Using the U.S. federal income tax rates for corporations shown in Table 16.1, what is Company A's income tax liability?

2. Company B has a taxable income of $66,000. Using the U.S. federal income tax rates for corporations shown in Table 16.1, what is Company B's income tax liability?

3. Company C has a taxable income of $82,000. Using the U.S. federal income tax rates for corporations shown in Table 16.1, what is Company C's income tax liability?

4. Company D has a taxable income of $216,000. Using the U.S. federal income tax rates for corporations shown in Table 16.1, what is Company D's income tax liability?

5. Company E has a taxable income of $525,000. Using the U.S. federal income tax rates for corporations shown in Table 16.1, what is Company E's income tax liability?

6. What is the effective tax rate between $85,000 and $105,000 taxable income using the U.S. federal income tax rates shown in Table 16.1?

7. Using the effective federal income tax rate from the previous question, if the state and local income tax rate is 8%, what is the effective overall tax rate?

8. What is the effective tax rate between $300,000 and $350,000 taxable income using the U.S. federal income tax rates shown in Table 16.1?

9. Using the effective federal income tax rate from the previous question, if the state and local income tax rate is 12%, what is the effective overall tax rate?

Questions 10 through 14 use the following situation: A company that makes software-based embedded process control systems is thinking about developing a new product. This company's effective tax rate is 44%, and they are profitable overall. The company has established an after-tax MARR of 15%. The following table shows the estimated before-tax cash-flow stream for the project.

End of Year	Before-Tax Cash-Flow Instance
0	–$75,000
1	$28,000
2	$34,000
3	$36,000
4	$34,000
5	$32,000
6	$30,000
7	$28,000

10. What is the after-tax cash-flow stream for the project assuming that no depreciation and no loans are involved? What is the PW(i) of the after-tax cash-flow stream? What's the IRR of the after-tax cash-flow stream?

11. Assume that the company borrowed $50,000 to help finance the project. The interest rate on the 5-year loan is 9%, and payments are made annually. What is the after-tax cash-flow stream for the project assuming that no depreciation is involved? What is the PW(i) of the after-tax cash-flow stream? What's the IRR of the after-tax cash-flow stream?

12. Assume that the $50,000 loan was used to buy a special-purpose machine. Use the MACRS prescribed method with the special-purpose machine classified as 5-year property to depreciate the cost of the special-purpose machine. What is the after-tax cash-flow stream for the project? What is the PW(i) of the after-tax cash-flow stream? What's the IRR of the after-tax cash-flow stream?

13. Using your answer for the previous question, include a 10% investment credit. Now what is the after-tax cash-flow stream for the project? What is the PW(i) of the after-tax cash-flow stream? What's the IRR of the after-tax cash-flow stream?

14. Assume the after-tax cash-flow stream from Question 12 is in actual dollars. Use an average annual inflation rate of 5% over the project and show the constant dollar cash-flow stream (using year 0 as the base year). What is the PW(i) of the after-tax cash-flow stream?

17

The Consequences of Income Taxes on Business Decisions

As explained in Chapter 16, the before- and after-tax cash-flow streams for an alternative can be significantly different and, because of that, the desirability of an alternative will be quite different in before- and after-tax terms. There are some additional issues that may impact, or be impacted by, income taxes, including the following:

- Interest expenses
- Interest income
- Depreciation method
- Depreciation recovery period
- Capital gains and losses for corporations
- Gain or loss when selling or scrapping depreciable assets
- Comparing financing methods in after-tax cash flow terms
- After-tax analysis of replacements

This chapter discusses each of these additional issues and shows how they can affect the desirability of an alternative. This chapter presents the consequences as they relate to businesses in the United States. The consequences in other countries may be different, but the same general principles will probably still apply.

Tax laws are subject to change every year. The information here should be accurate as of the date of publication, but changes in tax law may make some of the information out of date. If accurate accounting of taxes is critical to the decision analysis at hand, consult a tax professional who is familiar with the current tax laws.

TABLE 17.1 ABCSoft's Income Taxes

	ABCSoft
Income before interest deduction	$750,000
Interest expense	$0
Taxable income	$750,000
Taxes (effective rate, 34%)	$255,000

TABLE 17.2 XYZ Software's Income Taxes

	XYZ Software
Income before interest deduction	$750,000
Interest expense	$40,250
Taxable income	$709,750
Taxes (effective rate, 34%)	$241,315

Interest Expenses and Income Taxes

In the United States, corporations (and in some cases, individuals) can deduct interest payments on borrowed money. By allowing taxpayers to deduct interest expenses, the government is effectively reducing the interest rate. To illustrate, consider two nearly identical companies, ABCSoft and XYZ Software. Both have taxable incomes (not including the interest deduction) of $750,000. Assume that ABCSoft doesn't borrow any money. Table 17.1 shows ABCSoft's taxes for the year.

Assume that XYZ Software averages $350,000 in loans at 11.5% interest over the tax year. This means that XYZ will pay about $40,250 in interest expenses. Table 17.2 shows XYZ's taxes for the year.

XYZ Software pays $13,685 less in taxes than ABCSoft. Subtracting that tax savings from XYZ's interest expense means that XYZ effectively paid only $26,565 in interest. This works out to be an effective after-tax interest rate of

$$\frac{\$26,565}{\$350,000} = 0.0759 = 7.59\%$$

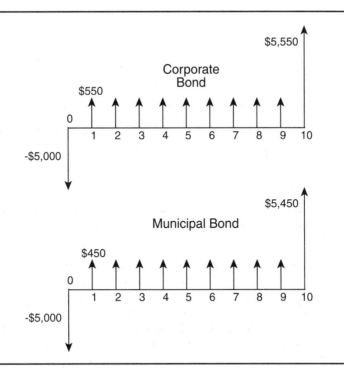

FIGURE 17.1   Before-tax cash-flow diagrams for the corporate and municipal bonds

The effective after-tax interest rate can also be calculated from the loan interest rate and effective income tax rate as follows:

$(1 - EffectiveIncomeTaxRate) * LoanInterestRate = EffectiveAfterTaxInterestRate$

For XYZ Software

$(1 - 34\%) * 11.5\% = 7.59\%$

When interest payments are tax deductible, borrowing money might not be quite as expensive as you thought it was.

Interest Income and Income Taxes

When you loan money to someone else and they pay you interest in return, that interest is usually considered taxable income. Referring back to Figure 2.1 in Chapter 2, that interest income needs to be included in the net income before taxes. There are a few exceptions to this; the most common is when the interest income is from municipal bonds.

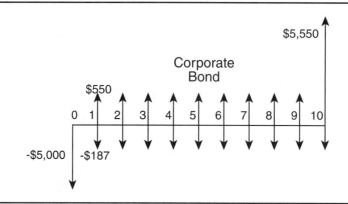

FIGURE 17.2 After-tax cash-flow diagram for the corporate bond

(Bonds are discussed in more detail in Chapter 18.) In the United States, municipal bonds are usually exempt from federal income tax and that exemption can make a difference in the after-tax desirability of different alternatives when bonds are part of the study. Consider two different $5000 bonds, both of which are for 10 years with interest payable annually. Assume that both bonds are selling at face (par) value. One of the bonds is a corporate bond at 11% interest, and the other is a tax-exempt municipal bond at 9%. Figure 17.1 shows the before-tax cash-flow diagrams for both bonds.

The 11% pre-tax IRR on the corporate bond looks a lot better than the municipal bond at 9%. Assume, however, that the investor's effective income tax rate is 34%. The after-tax cash flow for the corporate bond needs to include $187 in income taxes, reducing the real income from $550 per year to $363 per year. The after-tax cash-flow diagram for the corporate bond is shown in Figure 17.2.

The after-tax IRR for the corporate bond is only 7.7%, but the municipal bond's after-tax IRR is still 9%. This is a good example of how income taxes can significantly impact the desirability of alternatives.

Depreciation Method and Income Taxes

When depreciation (Chapter 14) is involved in a decision analysis, the method of depreciation affects the after-tax cash-flow stream, and as a result, the desirability of the alternative. The same before-tax cash-flow stream is compared using two different depreciation methods, straight-line and 150% declining-balance switching to straight-line to highlight the difference.

TABLE 17.3 Blizzard Systems' After-Tax Cash-Flow Stream Using 5-Year Straight-Line Depreciation

(A) End of Year	(B) Before-Tax Cash-Flow Stream	(C) Loan Principal	(D) Loan Interest	(E) Depreciable Investment	(F) Depreciation Expense	(G) Taxable Income (B + D + F)	(H) IncomeTax Cash-Flow Stream (– Rate * G)	(I) After-Tax Cash-Flow Stream (B + C + D + E + H)
0	–$15,000		N/A	–$50,000	N/A	–$15,000	$5700	–$59,300
1	$25,000				–$10,000	$15,000	–$5700	$19,300
2	$30,000				–$10,000	$20,000	–$7600	$22,400
3	$35,000				–$10,000	$25,000	–$9500	$25,500
4	$30,000				–$10,000	$20,000	–$7600	$22,400
5	$25,000				–$10,000	$15,000	–$5700	$19,300

Blizzard Systems makes a $65,000 initial investment in a new computer system for its software developers. Assume that $50,000 of the initial investment is for the depreciable system itself, which has a 5-year useful life. The rest of the initial investment is for nondepreciable expenses such as preparing the facility and doing the actual installation. The before-tax cash-flow stream is shown in Column (B) of Tables 17.3 and 17.5. Blizzard Systems doesn't borrow any money for this activity, is profitable overall, and has an effective overall income tax rate (including federal, state, and local) of 38%. The after-tax MARR has been set at 15%.

Table 17.3 shows the after-tax cash-flow stream when straight-line depreciation is used. Under straight-line depreciation, the annual depreciation amount is $50,000/5 = $10,000. The PW(15) of Table 17.3's after-tax cash-flow stream is $13,590, and the after-tax IRR is 24.2%.

Table 17.4 shows the depreciation schedule for the $50,000 computer system under 150% declining-balance switching to straight-line depreciation.

$$\alpha = \frac{1.5}{5} = 0.3$$

Table 17.5 shows the after-tax cash-flow stream when 150% declining-balance switching to straight-line depreciation is used.

TABLE 17.4 5-Year Depreciation Schedule Using the 150% Declining-Balance Switching to Straight-Line Method

End of Year	Depreciation Amount in Year	Book Value at End of Year
0	—	$50,000
1	0.3 * $50,000 = $15,000	$35,000
2	0.3 * $35,000 = $10,500	$24,500
3	0.3 * $24,500 = $7350 switch to straight-line at $10,000	$14,500
4	$10,000	$4500
5	$4500	$0

TABLE 17.5 Blizzard Systems' After-Tax Cash-Flow Stream Using 150% Switching to Straight-Line Depreciation

(A) End of Year	(B) Before-Tax Cash-Flow Stream	(C) Loan Principal	(D) Loan Interest	(E) Depreciable Investment	(F) Depreciation Expense	(G) Taxable Income (B + D + F)	(H) IncomeTax Cash-Flow Stream (– Rate * G)	(I) After-Tax Cash-Flow Stream (B + C + D + E + H)
0	–$15,000		N/A	–$50,000	N/A	–$15,000	$5700	–$59,300
1	$25,000				–$15,000	$10,000	–$3800	$21,200
2	$30,000				–$10,500	$19,500	–$7410	$22,590
3	$35,000				–$10,000	$25,000	–$9500	$25,500
4	$30,000				–$10,000	$20,000	–$7600	$22,400
5	$25,000				–$4500	$20,500	–$7790	$17,210

In Table 17.5 the PW(15) of the after-tax cash-flow stream is $14,346, and the after-tax IRR is 25%.

In both cases the total depreciation amount is $50,000 (the sum of column (F) of each table) and the total income taxes paid is $30,400 (the sum of column (H) of each table). Table 17.6 shows how the time value of money affects the desirability of the depreciation methods. The 150% declining-balance switching to straight-line depreciation method is better from an after-tax perspective because more tax dollars are avoided earlier when the time value of money makes them worth more. All other things being equal, being able to depreciate a dollar now is better than depreciating the same dollar later. Depreciation methods that allow you to write off more of the value sooner are better from an after-tax perspective.

TABLE 17.6 Comparing the After-Tax Effects of the Different Depreciation Methods

	Straight-Line	150% Declining-Balance Switching to Straight-Line
PW(15) of the depreciation amounts	–$33,522	–$35,513
PW(15) of the income tax payments	–$18,429	–$17,672
PW(15) of the after-tax cash-flow stream	$13,590	$14,346
After-tax IRR	24.2%	25.0%

TABLE 17.7 Blizzard Systems' After-Tax Cash-Flow Stream Using 3-year Straight-Line Depreciation

(A) End of Year	(B) Before-Tax Cash-Flow Stream	(C) Loan Principal	(D) Loan Interest	(E) Depreciable Investment	(F) Depreciation Expense	(G) Taxable Income (B + D + F)	(H) IncomeTax Cash-Flow Stream (– Rate * G)	(I) After-Tax Cash-Flow Stream (B + C + D + E + H)
0	–$15,000		N/A	–$50,000	N/A	–$15,000	$5700	–$59,300
1	$25,000				–$16,667	$8333	–$3167	$21,833
2	$30,000				–$16,667	$13,333	–$5067	$24,933
3	$35,000				–$16,667	$18,333	–$6967	$28,033
4	$30,000					$30,000	–$11,400	$18,600
5	$25,000					$25,000	–$9500	$15,500

Depreciation Recovery Period and Income Taxes

Just as using a depreciation method that writes off more dollars sooner is better from an after-tax perspective, shorter recovery periods are better than longer ones. Even though this leads to higher income taxes being paid in the later years, the present worth of the after-tax tax cash-flow stream will be greater. Again, this is due to the time value of money.

Table 17.7 shows Blizzard Systems' after-tax cash-flow stream using straight-line depreciation with a 3-year recovery period to contrast with the 5-year recovery period in Table 17.3. The straight-line depreciation amount is $50,000/3 = $16,667.

Exactly as with the different depreciation methods, the total depreciation amount in Table 17.7 is $50,000 (sum down column (F)) and the total income taxes paid is $30,400 (sum down column (H)). But the time value of money changes the desirability of these two depreciation recovery periods, as shown in Table 17.8.

TABLE 17.8   Comparing the After-Tax Effects of Different Recovery Periods

	5-Year Straight-Line	3-Year Straight-Line
PW(15) of the depreciation amounts	−$33,522	−$38,055
PW(15) of the income tax payments	−$18,429	−$16,707
PW(15) of the after-tax cash-flow stream	$13,590	$15,311
After-tax IRR	24.2%	26.0%

Again, all other things being equal it will be to the taxpayer's advantage to charge off as much depreciation as soon as possible. This is why—even though software isn't typically depreciable—that it's actually in the company's favor to be this way. Shorter depreciation periods are better, and expensing software in the year it was acquired is the same as being able to depreciate it in one year.

Capital Gains and Losses for Corporations

Ordinary income comes from activity, whereas a **capital gain** is income that comes from an increase in the value of something, without any explicit activity. Nothing special was done to make the value go up; it just did. If a software company buys an office building in a fast-growing area, the building is highly likely to appreciate. The value of the building will go up even though they don't do anything active to increase its value; they just maintain it as expected. When they sell the building, the difference between what it sells for and what they (effectively) originally paid for it is a capital gain. A **capital loss** is the opposite of a capital gain; if the company buys a building and later sells it for less than they originally paid, that difference is considered a capital loss.

Short-term capital gains are capital gains realized from holding the asset less than one year, whereas long-term capital gains are the same kinds of gains realized over a longer time. Someone who buys $2000 of stock and later sells that same stock for $3000 has a capital gain of $1000 regardless of when the stock is actually bought and sold. If the stock were sold less than one year after buying it, the $1000 would be considered a short-term gain; if the sale happens after more than one year, however, the $1000 would be considered a long-term gain. The distinction between short-and long-term capital gains allows the government to apply a higher tax rate to the short-term gains. This gives the taxpayer an incentive to hold on to investments longer to avoid the higher tax rates. In the United States, sometimes the short- and long-term tax rates are the same, and sometimes they are different. You need to know what the current capital gains tax rates are if they are relevant to your decision analysis.

As a recent example, in the United States, both short- and long-term capital gains were taxed as ordinary income, but at a maximum rate of 34%. Capital gains could be taxed at less than 34%, or at 34%, but not more than that. To demonstrate, assume that ABCSoft had $22,000 in capital gains on top of ordinary income of $40,000. The $40,000 ordinary income would be taxed at the 15% marginal rate, meaning they would owe $6,000. The first $10,000 of the capital gain would also be taxed at the 15% marginal rate, so they would owe another $1,500. The last $12,000 of the capital gain would be taxed at the 25% marginal rate, meaning they would owe another $3,000. ABCSoft would owe a total of $10,500 in income taxes in this situation.

Assume that XYZ Software also had $22,000 in capital gains, but its capital gain was on top of an ordinary income of $275,000. The income tax owed on $275,000 ordinary income is $90,500, as shown in Table 16.2. XYZ's ordinary income puts them into the 39% marginal rate bracket, but because capital gains weren't taxed at more than 34%, XYZ would owe $90,500 plus $7,480 (34% of $22,000), or $97,980, in income taxes.

There may also be restrictions on how capital losses are addressed. Sometimes, capital losses can be used only to offset capital gains, not reduce ordinary income. As an example, at one time capital losses for a corporation could be carried back as far as 3 prior tax years, and any remaining capital loss had to be carried forward up to 5 years. A company with $50,000 in capital gains and $30,000 in capital losses would be taxed on the $20,000 net capital gains. If the company had $50,000 in capital gains and $70,000 in capital losses, the $20,000 net capital loss wouldn't reduce the taxable ordinary income this year. Instead, if the company had a $30,000 net capital gain the previous year, they would file an amended return for that previous year and declare only $10,000 in net capital gain. If the company had only $5000 in net capital gains the previous year, they would file an amended return showing no capital gains that year and then attempt to apply the remaining $15,000 loss to the year before that. Any remaining net capital loss would be held in reserve to write off against future net capital gains for up to 5 years later.

Gain or Loss When Selling or Scrapping Depreciable Assets

When a depreciable asset is sold or scrapped, any difference between its book value and the actual amount received needs to be accounted for in the corporation's income taxes. A loss, meaning that the actual amount received is less than the book value, is subtracted from the net ordinary income before taxes. If Blizzard Systems scrapped a computer with a book value of $5000 and their net ordinary income was $165,000, they would be taxed on $160,000 net income.

If the actual value is more than the book value, the difference, called depreciation recapture, is typically taxed as ordinary income. Assuming ABCSoft had a computer with no book value (i.e., it had been completely depreciated) but they were able to sell it to XYZ Software for $5000, ABCSoft would need to add that $5000 to their net ordinary income.

TABLE 17.9 An Example for Comparing Financing Methods in After-Tax Terms

Initial investment	$40,000
Salvage value	None
Annual income	Not shown
Annual operating costs	$8000
Depreciation method	Straight-line, 4 years, half-year convention
Planning horizon	6 years
Effective tax rate	48%
MARR (after-tax)	10%

Comparing Financing Methods in After-Tax Cash-Flow Terms

When a company wants to buy an asset, there are three ways of paying for it, as follows:

- Buy it with money they already have (use retained earnings).
- Buy it using a loan.
- Lease it.

Each of these options has different income tax consequences, which are compared using the example in Table 17.9.

The income cash-flow stream doesn't need to be included because each option will produce the exact same income; these alternatives can be considered service alternatives, as defined in Chapter 11. The asset is the same; the only difference is the financing.

BUY WITH RETAINED EARNINGS

In this alternative, the company is buying the asset with money they earned as profit at some time in the past. The asset will be owned entirely by the company, and all tax benefits from ownership are available to the company. Table 17.10 shows the calculation of the after-tax cash-flow stream. The PW(10) of the after-tax cash-flow stream for buying with retained earnings is –$43,594.

TABLE 17.10 The After-Tax Cash-Flow Stream for Buying with Retained Earnings

(A) End of Year	(B) Before-Tax Cash-Flow Stream	(C) Loan Principal	(D) Loan Interest	(E) Depreciable Investment	(F) Depreciation Expense	(G) Taxable Income (B + D + F)	(H) IncomeTax Cash-Flow Stream (− Rate * G)	(I) After-Tax Cash-Flow Stream (B + C + D + E + H)
0	$0		N/A	−$40,000	N/A	$0	$0	−$40,000
1	−$8000				−$5000	−$13,000	$6240	−$1760
2	−$8000				−$10,000	−$18,000	$8640	$640
3	−$8000				−$10,000	−$18,000	$8640	$640
4	−$8000				−$10,000	−$18,000	$8640	$640
5	−$8000				−$5000	−$13,000	$6240	−$1760
6	−$8000					−$8000	$3840	−$4160

BUY WITH A LOAN

The company could buy the asset by borrowing all or part of the acquisition cost. If a loan can be explicitly identified with buying the asset, then do the calculations with that loan as is. On the other hand, borrowed money might not be directly associated with buying that asset. In this case, look at the corporation's debt load as a percentage of its total capital and consider the purchase to be financed at that percentage. A company that has 35% of its capital coming from loans can consider each asset acquisition as being financed 35% with loans and 65% with retained earnings. That company would run the calculations assuming there is a loan for 35% of the asset's acquisition cost.

Assuming 100% financing for 6 years at 12% APR, Table 17.11 shows the principal and interest payment profile for this loan using the technique described in Chapter 6.

$$A/P,12\%,6$$
$$A = \$40,000 \ (0.2432) = \$9729$$

TABLE 17.11   Separating Principal and Interest Payments for the Loan

End of Year	Loan Payment A	Principal Payment B_t	Interest Payment I_t
1	$9729	P/F,12,6 $9729 * (0.5066) = $4929	$4800
2	$9729	P/F,12,5 $9729 * (0.5674) = $5521	$4209
3	$9729	P/F,12,4 $9729 * (0.6355) = $6183	$3546
4	$9729	P/F,12,3 $9729 * (0.7118) = $6925	$2804
5	$9729	P/F,12,2 $9729 * (0.7972) = $7756	$1973
6	$9729	P/F,12,1 $9729 * (0.8929) = $8687	$1042

TABLE 17.12   The After-Tax Cash-Flow Stream for Buying with a Loan at 12%

(A) End of Year	(B) Before-Tax Cash-Flow Stream	(C) Loan Principal	(D) Loan Interest	(E) Depreciable Investment	(F) Depreciation Expense	(G) Taxable Income (B + D + F)	(H) Income Tax Cash-Flow Stream (– Rate * G)	(I) After-Tax Cash-Flow Stream (B + C + D + E + H)
0	$0	$40,000	N/A	–$40,000	N/A	$0	$0	$0
1	–$8000	–$4929	–$4800		–$5000	–$17,800	$8544	–$9185
2	–$8000	–$5521	–$4209		–$10,000	–$22,209	$10,660	–$7070
3	–$8000	–$6183	–$3546		–$10,000	–$21,546	$10,342	–$7387
4	–$8000	–$6925	–$2408		–$10,000	–$20,804	$9986	–$7743
5	–$8000	–$7756	–$1973		–$5000	–$14,973	$7187	–$10,542
6	–$8000	–$8687	–$1042			–$9042	$4340	–$13,389

Table 17.12 shows the calculation of the after-tax cash-flow stream. The PW(10) of the after-tax cash-flow stream for buying with a 12% loan is –$39,135.

TABLE 17.13   The After-Tax Cash-Flow Stream for Leasing

(A) End of Year	(B) Before-Tax Cash-Flow Stream	(C) Loan Principal	(D) Loan Interest	(E) Depreciable Investment	(F) Depreciation Expense	(G) Taxable Income (B + D + F)	(H) IncomeTax Cash-Flow Stream (– Rate * G)	(I) After-Tax Cash-Flow Stream (B + C + D + E + H)
0	–$9000		N/A		N/A	–$9000	$4320	–$4680
1	–$17,000					–$17,000	$8160	–$8840
2	–$17,000					–$17,000	$8160	–$8840
3	–$17,000					–$17,000	$8160	–$8840
4	–$17,000					–$17,000	$8160	–$8840
5	–$17,000					–$17,000	$8160	–$8840
6	–$8000					–$8000	$3840	–$4160

TABLE 17.14   Comparing the Three Different Financing Options

Buy with retained earnings	–$43,594
Lease	–$40,539
Buy with a loan at 12% interest	–$39,135

LEASE

Lease fees are deductible as an ordinary expense; if the asset is leased, however, the company leasing it can't also depreciate it. Only the actual owner can depreciate it. When leasing there probably isn't a loan involved either, so there probably won't be any interest deduction. Nonetheless, leasing can still be an economical choice. Assume the asset can be leased for an annual fee of $9000 payable at the beginning of each year. The calculation of the after-tax cash flows is shown in Table 17.13. The PW(10) of the after-tax cash-flow stream for leasing is –$40,539.

COMPARING THE FINANCING OPTIONS IN AFTER-TAX TERMS

Table 17.14 compares the PW(10) of the three different financing alternatives. Considering that the income generated by the asset would be identical regardless of financing method, buying with the 12% loan leads to the highest profit because it has the lowest

TABLE 17.15　The After-Tax Cash-Flow Stream for Buying with a Loan at 19.23%

(A) End of Year	(B) Before-Tax Cash-Flow Stream	(C) Loan Principal	(D) Loan Interest	(E) Depreciable Investment	(F) Depreciation Expense	(G) Taxable Income (B + D + F)	(H) IncomeTax Cash-Flow Stream (– Rate * G)	(I) After-Tax Cash-Flow Stream (B + C + D + E + H)
0	$0	$40,000	N/A	–$40,000	N/A	$0	$0	$0
1	–$8000	–$4107	–$7692		–$5000	–$20,692	9932	–$9867
2	–$8000	–$4897	–$6902		–$10,000	–$24,902	11,953	–$7846
3	–$8000	–$5839	–$5961		–$10,000	–$23,961	11,501	–$8299
4	–$8000	–$6961	–$4838		–$10,000	–$22,838	10,962	–$8837
5	–$8000	–$8300	–$3499		–$5000	–$16,499	7,920	–$11,879
6	–$8000	–$9896	–$1903			–$9903	4753	–$15,046

PW(10) after-tax cash-flow stream for the expenses. You probably wouldn't think that borrowing money when the loan interest rate (12%) is higher than the opportunity cost (MARR = 10%) is a good idea. However, remember that the loan interest rate is in before-tax terms, and the MARR in this example is after-tax terms. As shown in the beginning of this chapter, when the effective tax rate is 48%, the actual after-tax cost of borrowing is

$$(1 - 48\%) * 2\% = 6.24\%$$

At an effective income tax rate of 48%, a 10% after-tax loan interest rate is equivalent to a before-tax loan interest rate of

$$\frac{10\%}{(1 - 48\%)} = 0.1923 = 19.23\%$$

Table 17.15 shows the calculation of the after-tax cash-flow stream using a loan at 19.23%. The PW(10) of the after-tax cash-flow stream in this situation is –$43,594. This is the same as the PW(10) for buying with retained earnings.

As long as the after-tax loan interest rate is less than the MARR, buying with a loan is better than buying with retained earnings.

The PW(10) of the lease alternative depends on the lease fee. The higher the lease fee, the more negative the PW(10). This example shows that as long as a lease arrangement is possible, it should be included as one of the alternatives and that the evaluation needs to be carried out in after-tax terms.

After-Tax Analysis of Replacements

Income taxes have some special effects on replacement decisions (Chapter 12). Specifically, keeping an already-owned asset incurs the opportunity cost (remember the discussion about the "outsider's viewpoint"), and it also defers possible depreciation recapture. The replacement alternatives (the challengers) might lead to tax credits in some cases. As well, the depreciation schedule needs to be determined so that tax effects of eventual scrapping or salvage can be identified. Replacement analysis needs to be done in after-tax terms or the wrong decision could be made.

Summary

The before- and after-tax cash-flow streams for an alternative can be significantly different and, because of that, the desirability of the alternative will be quite different in before- and after-tax terms. This chapter showed different ways that business decisions are influenced by income taxes. The chapter covered the following major points:

- By allowing taxpayers to deduct interest expenses, the government is effectively reducing the interest rate. Borrowing money might not be quite as expensive as you thought it was.
- Interest income is usually considered taxable income. One common exception is municipal bonds. The tax-free status of these bonds makes them more attractive than a taxable bond at the same interest rate.
- Depreciation methods that allow you to write off more of the value sooner are better from an after-tax perspective.
- Shorter depreciation recovery periods are also better.
- Capital gain is income that comes from an increase in the value of something, without any explicit activity. Capital gains and losses can affect the taxes an organization, or an individual, pays.
- When a depreciable asset is sold or scrapped, any difference between its book value and the actual amount received needs to be accounted for in the corporation's income taxes. If the actual value is more than the book value, the difference, called depreciation recapture, is taxed as ordinary income.
- Whether an item is bought using retained earnings, using a loan, or is leased instead, it will affect the after-tax cash-flow stream differently. Buying with a loan may actually be the least expensive.

- If you are doing a replacement analysis and you are trying to accurately account
  for income taxes, you need to be careful to address depreciation recapture for the
  existing assets, depreciation accounting for any new assets, and any potential tax
  credits that might be involved.

This part of the book showed how to get more accuracy out of a business decision when
the concepts and techniques in Part II weren't accurate enough. The next part explains
how to make decisions in not-for-profit organizations.

Self-Study Questions

1. FunSoft has a loan with an interest rate of 7% and an effective income tax rate of
   30%. What is the effective after-tax interest rate on their loan?

2. Blizzard Systems has an effective income tax rate of 35.5%. They also have a loan
   with an interest rate of 6.75%. What is the effective after-tax interest rate on their
   loan?

3. Ms. D has $10,000 available to invest. She can buy a $10,000 6-year municipal
   bond at face value that has an interest rate of 7%. Another possibility is for her to
   buy a 6-year corporate bond with an interest rate of 9%. Ms. D has an effective income tax rate of 24%. Which of these bonds would be better for her from an after-
   tax perspective?

4. Mr. S has $5000 to invest. He can buy a 5-year municipal bond at face value that
   has a 7.25% interest rate. He can also buy a 5-year corporate bond with an interest
   rate of 9%. His effective income tax rate is 18%. Which of these investments would
   be better from an after-tax perspective?

Questions 5 through 8 relate to the following situation: Zymurgenics, Inc. is buying a
special high-performance computer system for use on a project. The computer costs
$60,000 and has an expected life of 5 years with no salvage value. The annual income
generated by this project will be $20,000 before depreciation and income taxes. Their
effective income tax rate is 40%, and their after-tax MARR is 12%. Assume that the rest
of the corporation's activities are profitable.

5. What is the present worth of the after-tax cash-flow stream if straight-line depreciation is used?

6. What is the present worth of the after-tax cash-flow stream if double-declining-
   balance depreciation is used?

7. What is the present worth of the after-tax cash-flow stream if the ACRS prescribed method for 5-year property is used?

8. Which of the depreciation method leads to the highest present worth for the after-tax cash-flow stream? Why?

Questions 9 through 12 relate to the following situation: XYZ Co. wants to get a special instrument to control a critical step in their production line. The instrument has an acquisition cost of $25,000 and will lead to a savings of $10,000 per year for 5 years. They want to evaluate different methods of financing the acquisition. Assume that if they buy it they will use MACRS depreciation for 3-year property. Their effective income tax rate is 44%, and their after-tax MARR is 16%. The rest of the corporation is profitable.

9. What's the present worth of the after-tax cash-flow stream if they buy it with retained earnings?

10. What's the present worth of the after-tax cash-flow stream if they buy it using a loan for the full amount at 8% interest (assume annual payments)?

11. What's the present worth of the after-tax cash-flow stream if they lease it for the 5 years with annual payments of $5000? The lease payments will be due at the beginning of the year.

12. What is XYZ Co.'s effective after-tax loan interest rate? Reevaluate the buy-with-a-loan alternative using that interest rate. Compare the resulting present worth with the pay-with-retained-earnings alternative. How does the present worth of these two alternatives compare?

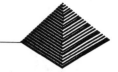

PART FOUR

MAKING DECISIONS IN GOVERNMENT AND NONPROFIT ORGANIZATIONS

The for-profit decision techniques covered in Part Two and Part Three don't apply when the organization's goal isn't profit—and this is the case in government and in nonprofit organizations. In these situations, the organization has a different goal, which means that a different set of decision techniques is needed. The specific techniques used in government and nonprofit business decisions are benefit-cost analysis and cost-effectiveness analysis.

18

Making Not-for-Profit Business Decisions

As shown in Part II of this book, business decisions in for-profit organizations are based on profit. The higher the profit, the more desirable any given proposal is. A government, on the other hand, isn't driven by profit. Instead, governments are driven primarily by "the promotion of general welfare." Similarly, as their name implies, nonprofit organizations also have a different purpose than for-profit organizations. In fact, nonprofit organizations have a role very similar to governments; namely, promoting the general welfare of some relevant population. Because the goals of government agencies and nonprofit organizations are different from for-profit organizations, it should make sense that their decision criteria also differ. This chapter is about decision analysis in not-for-profit organizations, specifically benefit-cost analysis and cost-effectiveness analysis.

Software and Governments

A natural first reaction might be, "But a government doesn't do software." In fact, the U.S. Department of Defense (DoD) is probably the single largest customer of software development in the United States. The U.S. Internal Revenue Service (IRS) has been processing Form 1040 income tax returns by computer since the early 1980s. Many state and local agencies have been moving toward computer-based support of 911 emergency call centers, welfare administration, public schools, etc. Some states, counties, and larger cities are already using enterprise resource planning (ERP) packages for payroll, inventory management, and so on. With each passing year, more and more software is being put to use in the public sector.

THE AIM OF GOVERNMENT

It should be obvious that a government isn't out to make a profit. What, then, does drive a government? According to the U.S. Constitution, there are two primary drivers of the U.S. federal government: national defense and the general welfare of the population. In a similar sense, smaller governmental units such as states, counties, and cities should also follow this same general objective. Specifically, maximizing the general welfare of the constituents in that governmental unit.

THE NATURE OF PUBLIC ACTIVITIES

Public activities tend to be inherently inefficient. There are several reasons, a few of which are discussed here.

First, how do you put a value on most government services? What is the value of a fire department, a jail, an elementary school, or a library? Because these services are hard to set a value for, it's virtually impossible to look at them or manage them in return-on-investment terms.

Second, many government projects serve more than one purpose. A dam may not be just a new power and water source, it may also create a new recreational facility. How much is the power source worth? How much is the water source worth? How much is the recreational facility worth? There will probably even be a conflict of interest between the purposes; the dam would probably upset the people who, understandably, want the valley left in its natural state. Again, it's difficult to manage multipurpose projects in return-on-investment terms.

Third, taxes should be seen as payment for government services: police, fire, public roads, parks, libraries, schools, and so forth. However, the time when people use those services is almost always separated from when the services are paid for. Because you aren't paying for the service when you receive it, it's hard to associate the value of the money spent with the value of the services you get in return. On top of this, the fact that there are many different government services makes it even harder to correlate the spending with the receiving. How much of a property tax payment goes to paying for schools? How much goes to public roads? How much goes to fire protection? Police protection? Libraries?

Next, two basic philosophies in the United States also influence the behavior of the government. Taxation is based on the idea of ability to pay. People who earn more are expected to be more capable of paying more. Taxes are usually based on a percentage of something's value (sales tax as percentage of purchase price, property tax as percentage of assessed property value, income tax as a percentage of taxable income). On the other hand, government spending is often based on the idea of equalizing opportunity: People who have more needs should be given more services. Examples of opportunity equalization include welfare, rent and utilities subsidies for low-income families, and so on. This means that there is little correlation between the benefits any one person gets and how much he or she pays for them.

The last reason discussed here is that the government is the sole provider of many services. You don't really have a choice of who to call if your house is on fire. The lack of competition from alternative providers means that there may be no need for the service providers to worry about efficient use of taxpayer funds. It's not as if they will go out of business if someone else can do a better job, which is the case in the for-profit arena.

FINANCING GOVERNMENT ACTIVITIES

Government finances its activities in three ways. The first, and most obvious, is through taxes. There are many different kinds of taxes, including corporate income, individual income, property, excise, estate, import duties, etc. The second way to finance government activities is through fee-for-use. Examples of fee-for-use are the post office, public utilities such as power and water, government-run parks and museums, etc. The third way to finance government activities is for a governmental unit to borrow the money by issuing **bonds**. Bonds are like an interest-only loan. The borrower decides how much they want to borrow, how long they want to borrow it, and what the interest rate will be. Each "share" of the bond has a face value (its par value). Imagine that a county government needs to borrow $10 million for 10 years and decides to issue $5000 bonds at 8%. There will be 2000 shares issued.

Someone invests in the bond by paying the par value ($5000) to the issuer. The issuer can now use this money for the public activity. At the end of each year, the issuer pays the interest-only amount of $400 (8% of $5000) to the bondholder. At the end of the final year, the issuer pays both the interest and the par value to finish the loan. The cash-flow diagram for this bond is shown in Figure 18.1.

In reality there's no guarantee that the bond will ever be paid back. Just as important, however, investors wouldn't invest unless they had some confidence that they will get their money back. There are two ways for the governmental unit to secure (increase the likelihood of repayment) the bond and, because of this, two different categories of

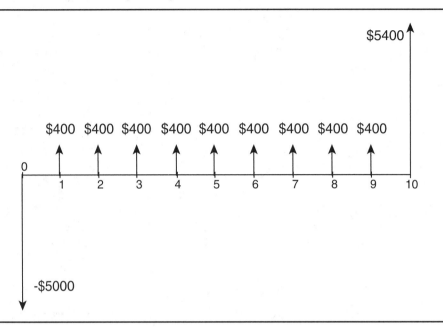

FIGURE 18.1   Cash-flow diagram for a bond

bonds. **General obligation bonds** are secured by the power of the issuing entity to tax. If worse comes to worse, and the public activity fails, the governmental unit can still repay the bonds simply by raising taxes. **Revenue bonds**, on the other hand, are backed by the anticipated income from the project (a toll road, bridge, etc.). Part of the money brought in from user fees goes to repaying the bonds.

Software and Nonprofit Organizations

Just like governments, more and more nonprofit organizations are either using externally developed software or are developing their own software. And, just like the government, the goal of a nonprofit organization is to increase the general welfare of a given population. The Object Management Group (OMG), for instance, exists to develop "technically excellent, commercially viable and vendor independent specifications for the software industry" [OMG04]. Other computer hardware- and software-related nonprofit organizations include the Institute for Electrical and Electronics Engineers (IEEE), the Association for Computing Machinery (ACM), the Internet Engineering Task Force (IETF), and the Software Productivity Consortium (SPC), along with many, many others. These nonprofit organizations are typically financed through membership fees, fee-for-use, donations, and (in some cases) government grants.

Decision Analysis in Government and Nonprofit Organizations

Suppose a city needs to choose between computerizing its property tax department and computerizing its public libraries. It has enough money to do one of these, but not both. The city can't base the decision on profit because neither the property tax automation nor the library automation will generate any directly measurable income for the city. Instead, the choice needs to be based on which of these alternatives would contribute more to the general welfare of the citizens. If the city can consider the benefits brought on by either proposal in relation to each proposal's costs, they can establish a basis for choice. This is the foundation behind the **benefit-cost analysis** technique.

We'll look at benefit-cost analysis from the perspective of analyzing a single proposal and analyzing a set of proposals. We'll also look later at cost-effectiveness analysis, a less-commonly used technique that was derived from benefit-cost analysis.

Benefit-Cost Analysis for a Single Proposal

Benefit-cost analysis is one of the most widely used methods for evaluating nonprofit proposals. The U.S. Flood Control Act of 1936 is generally acknowledged as the first description of this technique:

> It is hereby recognized that destructive floods upon the rivers of the United States, upsetting orderly processes and causing loss of life and property, including the erosion of lands, and impairing and obstructing navigation, highways, railroads, and other channels of commerce between the States, constitute a menace to national welfare; that it is the sense of Congress that flood control on navigable waters or their tributaries is a proper activity of the Federal Government in cooperation with the States, their political subdivisions, and localities thereof; that investigations and improvements of rivers and other waterways, including watersheds thereof, for flood-control purposes are in the interest of the general welfare; that the Federal Government should improve or participate in the improvement of navigable waters or their tributaries, including watersheds thereof, for flood control purposes *if the benefits to whomsoever they may accrue are in excess of the estimated costs*, and if the lives and social security of people are otherwise adversely affected.

The "benefits to whomsoever they may accrue" are the measurable advantages to the population that would be caused by the proposal, minus any measurable "dis-benefits." The benefits in the property tax computerization project would be more timely and accurate tax processing for property owners. Dis-benefits are negative impacts to the population. If property owners needed access to a computer to complete certain property tax transactions, the cost of that computer access would be a burden to the property owners and would be considered a dis-benefit. Benefits and dis-benefits are always in the context of the relevant population.

The costs are defined as all expenses, minus all savings, incurred by the sponsor. This includes any initial investment expenses plus any ongoing operating and maintenance expenses. In the property tax automation example, the expenses include acquisition, operation, and maintenance of the computer hardware and software. The savings will most likely be a reduction in headcount in the property tax department. Costs and savings are always in the context of the sponsor. Note that savings are not benefits to the population; they are reductions in expenses to the sponsor. This is important because adding an amount to the numerator does not have the same effect as subtracting the same amount from the denominator. Incorrect accounting of the savings to the sponsor can result in a misleading benefit-cost ratio.

The benefits, dis-benefits, costs, and savings can be expressed in terms of any of the bases for comparison described in Chapter 8: PW(i), AE(i), FW(i), and so on. Make sure that the net benefits and the net costs for a given proposal are both expressed in the same basis of comparison because comparing benefits in PW(i) terms to costs in AE(i) terms would be extremely misleading.

A proposal will be desirable only when its net benefits are greater than its net costs. For every dollar of cost, there needs to be more than one dollar in net benefit:

$$Benefits > Costs$$

Said another way, the ratio of the benefits to the costs needs to be greater than 1:

$$\frac{Benefits}{Costs} > 1$$

This leads to the idea of a benefit-cost ratio:

$$BC(i) = \left(\frac{BenefitsToThePublic}{CostsToTheGoverment} \right)$$

Some agencies refer to the benefit-cost ratio as the **savings-investment ratio** (SIR).

Any proposal with a benefit-cost ratio of less than one can usually be rejected without any further analysis because it would cost more than it would benefit. The only reason to continue analysis would be when there are overriding irreducible benefits or the investment is mandated for some other reason. Proposals should also be rejected if the initial investment can't be afforded. Even though a proposal may have huge benefit relative its cost, if the initial investment is financially out of reach from the organization then that benefit is irrelevant.

PROPER POINT OF VIEW

To end up with a meaningful BC(i) result, proposals need to be analyzed from a proper point of view. Otherwise the analysis might not capture all the significant effects of that proposal. Generally speaking, the proper point of view includes all the important consequences of the proposal. Points of view are typically based on the following:

- **Geography**—Everyone who lives or works in some particular area
- **Social groups**—Everyone who is interested in some particular issue
- **Organizations**—Everyone who is a member of some particular organization
- **Products or markets**—Such as agricultural markets, fisheries markets, etc.
- . . .

You can get a handle on the proper point of view by identifying all of the different people who would

- Benefit from the proposal.
- Be adversely impacted by the proposal.
- Pay for the proposal.

In the property tax computerization proposal, the beneficiaries could be

- **Property tax assessors, collectors, clerks in the property tax department**— They can get more work done in the same amount of time.
- **Property owners**—Their tax bills will be more accurate and timely. They are also less likely to have their payment lost or forgotten.
- **The city**—Payments would be received in a more timely manner; fewer payments would get lost, forgotten, or intentionally unpaid, meaning that the city would get more complete payment earlier.

People adversely affected by the proposal might be any assessors, collectors, or clerks who could lose their jobs because the computerization makes them no longer necessary.

We've already said that the city government would pay for the proposal, but part of the costs might also be paid through state or federal grants or other sources of funding.

IDENTIFYING BENEFITS, DIS-BENEFITS, AND COSTS

It's easy to fall into the trap of analyzing benefits, dis-benefits, and costs by thinking about the situation *before* and *after* the proposal. However, this could lead to inappropriate conclusions because there may or may not have been changes independent of the proposal. As an example, the number of developed lots in the city may have been increasing consistently for many years and would probably continue to increase with or without the property tax computerization project. The benefits and costs need to be evaluated on the basis of the situation *with* and *without* the proposal. Only the changes caused by the proposal itself are important in benefit-cost analysis.

Some of the benefits and dis-benefits can be stated in economic terms, others can't. All benefits that have a market value need to be represented in terms of money, but those that don't have a market value should also be included in the analysis. These are the "irreducibles" referred to in Chapter 4.

There are two types of benefits (and dis-benefits). **Primary benefits** represent the value to the public of the direct products or services resulting from the proposal. The U.S. Federal Aviation Administration's (FAA) Air Traffic Modernization program is intended to support more airplanes in the air and allow the airplanes to fly more fuel-efficient routes. **Secondary benefits** are all of the additional products and services gained from the activities of, or stimulated by, the project. Commercial handheld Global Positioning System (GPS) receivers are a secondary benefit stimulated by military investments in improved navigation equipment. The National Aeronautics and Space Administration (NASA) space program has led to numerous secondary benefits, including the following:

- Worldwide communication
- Satellite imagery and resource mapping
- Climate research and long-range weather forecasting
- High-density batteries and solar cells
- Advanced materials and structural designs
- Advanced food processing and waste purification systems
- And many more

A benefit-cost analysis always needs to include the primary benefits and, whenever appropriate, should consider the secondary benefits. The decision of whether to include specific secondary benefits should be based on how significant they are in relation to the primary benefits along with how much effort is needed to determine their values.

ASSIGNING A VALUE TO BENEFITS, DIS-BENEFITS, COSTS, AND SAVINGS

When assigning values to benefits, dis-benefits, costs, and savings, start by finding out whether that component has a market price. If it does, that market price might be an appropriate way to value the component. In computerizing a library, one of the benefits could be that fewer books will get lost and need to be replaced. This component could be valued by multiplying the expected reduction in book losses by the average cost of a book.

The market price isn't always accurate because of subsidies, price supports, or restraints. The market price for farm and dairy products, for example, may be misleading because of government subsidies. In the United States, it actually costs more to produce a pound of butter than consumers pay for it in the grocery store; the government gives direct subsidy payments to farmers to help them stay in business.

Another way to value a component is to figure the least expensive way to provide that same service. Still another is to estimate what a user is willing to pay for a service by seeing how much he/she spends to take advantage of it. This is a common method for finding the "value" of recreational facilities such as parks. Multiplying the expected number of visitors by the anticipated entrance fee can approximate the value of the facility.

It could be impossible to assign values to some of the benefits, dis-benefits, costs, or savings. It wouldn't be appropriate to put a value on the fish in a river by just multiplying the estimated number of pounds of fish in that river by the per-pound market price of that kind of fish. Be sure to include the important irreducibles as part of the decision analysis by describing them in whatever terms are appropriate.

In the city property tax computerization proposal, assume that the city has chosen a 10-year planning horizon; any system that is put in place now will need to be replaced after 10 years. In assigning values to the benefits, the city estimates that property owners are spending hundreds of hours each year straightening out bills and assessments. Considering an estimated average hourly income for property owners along with the annual growth rate in taxed parcels, this city estimates this is worth $29,000 in AE(i) terms. The city has also determined that there are no dis-benefits, so the AE(i) of the net benefits are $29,000.

The hardware and software costs for both acquisition and support, in AE(i) terms, have been estimated by the city to be $47,000. The city also knows that the tax department is already overworked. Combining the department's current annual overtime bill with the annual growth rate in taxed parcels, the city estimates the savings to be $14,000 in AE(i) terms. The city also estimates that the reduction in missing and late payments each year, in light of the annual growth rate, will be worth $9,000 in AE(i) terms. The AE(i) net cost to the city is estimated to be $24,000 so the benefit-cost ratio is as follows:

$$BC(i) = \left(\frac{\$29,000}{\$24,000} \right) = 1.21$$

This project has a benefit-cost ratio greater than 1.00, so it is worth considering further.

CHOOSING AN INTEREST RATE

The benefits, dis-benefits, and costs all need to be expressed in a common form, such as PW(i), FW(i), AE(i), or something similar. The interest rate used needs to reflect the organization's actual cost of borrowed money. For a governmental agency, this could be the interest rate on bonds issued to finance the project. Another way to set the interest rate is to look at what rate could have been earned by the citizens if the money hadn't been removed from the private sector. Use whichever is more appropriate in any particular situation.

TABLE 18.1 BC(i) Ratios for Four Mutually Exclusive Alternatives

Alternative	PW(i) Benefits	PW(i) Costs	Overall BC(i) Ratio
A1	$136,500	$68,600	1.99
A2	$125,200	$59,600	2.10
A3	$71,200	$37,500	1.89
A4	$86,300	$58,900	1.47

SUMMARIZING THE BENEFIT-COST RATIO FOR A SINGLE PROPOSAL

Clearly, unless there is some other overriding reason, a proposal with a BC(i) less than 1.00 should be dropped from further consideration. Again, keep in mind that the benefit is unattainable if the organization can't afford the proposal's initial investment. Proposals should be dropped under these conditions, too. Assuming that the city can afford the initial investment in the property tax computerization proposal, with a BC(i) of 1.21 it makes sense to consider this project as being worth further investigation.

Benefit-Cost Analysis for Multiple Proposals

Just as was described in Chapter 9, there may or may not be dependencies between different BC(i) proposals. It may also be possible to carry out more than one of these proposals at a time. So, exactly as was described in Chapter 9, use all the proposals to build up the set of mutually exclusive alternatives. Dependencies, exclusivities, budget constraints, etc. all need to be factored in. The benefits for any alternative will be the sum of the benefits for all the proposals in that alternative. Each alternative's cost will be the sum of the costs for all proposals in that alternative. Keep in mind that all the benefits and costs need to be in the same terms, such as PW(i), FW(i), AE(i), ...

ANALYZING MULTIPLE BC(I) PROPOSALS REQUIRES INCREMENTAL ANALYSIS

Assume that Table 18.1 shows the total PW(i) benefits and PW(i) costs for a set of four mutually exclusive alternatives. It might appear on the surface that alternative A2 would be the best because it has the highest overall BC(i) ratio of 2.10.

TABLE 18.2   Four BC(i) Alternatives Arranged in Order of Increasing Cost

Alternative	PW(i) Benefits	PW(i) Costs
A3	$71,200	$37,500
A4	$86,300	$58,900
A2	$125,200	$59,600
A1	$136,500	$68,600

Whenever you use the benefit-cost ratio to compare mutually exclusive alternatives, you *must* use incremental analysis. Don't think of it in terms of the highest overall benefit-cost ratio but in terms of an incremental benefit that would be gained from an avoidable incremental cost. This chapter walks you through an analysis that leads to a different conclusion than alternative A2 and then explains why that other alternative was actually selected. The incremental BC(i) analysis goes as follows:

1. The first step is to arrange the alternatives in order of increasing costs. This is shown in Table 18.2.

   The first incremental choice is between alternative A3 and doing nothing. The incremental BC(i) ratio in this case is very simple; it's just the overall BC(i) ratio of the A3 alternative, 1.89. Because all the proposals in A3 should already have a BC(i) > 1.0, the BC(i) for this alternative will also be greater than 1.0. As long as you have already discarded all proposals with BC(i) < 1, you can start with the BC(i) for the lowest-investment alternative as being the initial best candidate and not consider the A0 or "do nothing" alternative.

2. The next increment in this example is between alternative A3 as the current best and A4 as the candidate. The incremental benefit in this case is $15,100, whereas the incremental cost is $21,400. The BC(i) of this increment is 0.71, which is less than 1.0, so alternative A3 stays as current best.

3. The next incremental choice is between alternative A3 as current best and A2 as the candidate. The incremental benefit in this case is $54,000, whereas the incremental cost is $22,100. The BC(i) of this increment is 2.44, so alternative A2 becomes the new current best.

4. Finally, the last incremental choice is between alternative A2 as current best and A1 as the candidate. The incremental benefit in this case is $11,300, whereas the incremental cost is $9000. The BC(i) of this increment is 1.26, so alternative A1 becomes the new current best. We've run through all the alternatives, so the final current best, A1, is the best choice.

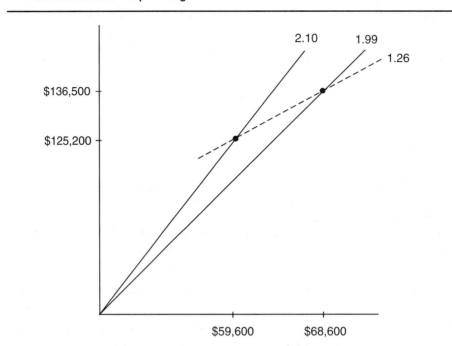

FIGURE 18.2 Explaining the need for incremental BC(i) analysis

It's important to recognize that this is a different choice than you may have first assumed in Table 18.1. In overall BC(i) terms, alternative A2 looks like the best choice, but the real best choice is actually A1. Why isn't the alternative with the highest overall BC(i) also the best under incremental analysis? The reason, as illustrated in Figure 18.2, is that the overall BC(i) ratio for an alternative is mathematically the same as the slope of a line drawn from the graph's origin through the point whose X coordinate is the cost and whose Y coordinate is the benefit. Any point along that line corresponds to the same BC(i) ratio. The lines for BC(i) = 2.10 and BC(i) = 1.99 are shown in the graph.

The incremental BC(i) corresponds to the slope of the line between the two points, A2 and A1. This is shown by the dashed line in Figure 18.2. The slope of the dashed line is 1.26. Because the alternatives were sorted in order of increasing cost, any point along the overall BC(i)=1.99 line whose cost is greater than (or equal to, actually) the cost for alternative A2 would satisfy the constraints that a) it has a higher cost than A2, and b) it has a BC(i) = 1.99. If we were to draw a new line with a slope of exactly 1.0 through the A2 point, this new line would intersect the BC(i) = 1.99 line. Any point on the BC(i) = 1.99 line that's to the right of this intersection point corresponds to a potential situation where its overall BC(i) = 1.99 *and* it has an incremental BC(i) > 1.0 from alternative A2. Any point to the left of the intersection point corresponds to a potential solution where the overall BC(i) is still 1.99 but it has an incremental BC(i) <= 1.0 from alternative A2.

Having already determined that some alternative (call it Ax) is desirable, the real question is whether or not the incremental investment to get to the next-higher-investment alternative (call it Ay) is also desirable. That incremental investment will be desirable as long as *its* BC(i) > 1, in spite of the fact that the overall BC(i) for Ay may be less than the overall BC(i) for Ax. Any point on the overall BC(i) line for Ay that's to the right of the incremental BC(i) = 1 intersection point from alternative Ax would be desirable over Ax. The organization would still be getting more benefit than cost by making that incremental investment.

Cost-Effectiveness Analysis

Cost-effectiveness analysis originated in the defense and space community where it is informally known as "getting the biggest bang for the buck." Cost-effectiveness analysis shares a lot of the same philosophy and methodology with benefit-cost analysis. There are many similarities in the techniques; cost-effectiveness analysis was derived from benefit-cost analysis.

The three requirements for cost-effectiveness analysis to be used in a decision are as follows:

- The problem must be bounded.
- There needs to be more than one possible solution to that problem.
- The proposals being considered are all valid solutions to that problem.

There are two versions of cost-effectiveness analysis. In the **fixed-cost** version, you are trying to maximize the benefit given some upper bound on cost. As an example, many software projects have a fixed software quality assurance (SQA) budget. The fixed-cost approach would mean planning and executing the SQA within the given budget so that it has the highest probability of uncovering software defects. This is, literally, the biggest-bang-for-the-buck approach. Projects involving safety-critical or mission-critical software are more likely to take the **fixed-effectiveness** version. This means that the end goal is fixed and you should minimize the cost needed to achieve that goal. The fixed effectiveness approach in SQA would mean planning and executing the SQA so that it resulted in the required level of reliability but did so for the least cost.

The measure of effectiveness need not be dollars; in fact, it probably won't be. If effectiveness could be measured in dollars, the decision could be done with benefit-cost analysis. An SQA group may define effectiveness as defects found before the software is released to the customer. The number of controlled files handled by a revision control system might be a good measure of effectiveness. The measure of effectiveness needs to be something relevant to the organization.

TABLE 18.3 Costs and Effectiveness for Six Commercial Revision Control Systems

Product	PW(i) Cost	Effectiveness
A	$8750	34,000
B	$6498	16,100
C	$12,492	45,400
D	$7011	28,800
E	$4390	7800
F	$9353	35,800

The standard step-by-step process for cost-effectiveness analysis is as follows:

1. Define the goal(s).

2. Develop alternative solutions that achieve the goal(s). Where appropriate, be sure to use optimum configurations for each alternative (see Chapter 20).

3. Establish evaluation criteria for both cost and effectiveness. How will cost be measured? What's included in the cost measure and what is not? How will effectiveness be measured? What's included and what isn't? Note that cost and effectiveness need not be expressed in monetary terms. There may also be other evaluation criteria in addition to cost and effectiveness. All the evaluation criteria should be ranked, as appropriate for the situation.

4. Decide whether you are using the fixed-cost or fixed-effectiveness approach.

5. Analyze each of the alternatives against the ranked evaluation criteria. Candidate solutions that exceed the fixed-cost or fall short of the fixed-effectiveness can be dropped from further consideration.

6. Analyze the remaining candidates in more detail and make the choice. For example, compare them on an effectiveness-per-cost basis. Also consider each of the other evaluation criteria, how important are they and how well does each alternative measure up. There are several rigorous approaches to this step, which are explained in Chapter 26.

We'll walk through examples of both fixed-cost and fixed-effectiveness analysis to illustrate the techniques. Imagine that two nearly identical software organizations both need to purchase and install a new software revision control system. The costs for each product were determined by the number of licenses required together with the annual maintenance costs over a 7-year planning horizon expressed in PW(i) terms. The critical measure of effectiveness for both organizations is the number of separate files that the revision control systems can handle. In surveying the market, both organizations find six commercial products, which are listed in Table 18.3.

AN EXAMPLE OF FIXED-COST ANALYSIS

The first organization has a maximum budget (in PW(i) terms) of $7500.

1. Define the goal(s). Find the revision control system with the maximum effectiveness given the budget constraint.

2. Develop alternative solutions. These are listed in Table 18.3.

3. Establish evaluation criteria. PW(i) over a 7-year planning horizon for cost and number of files for effectiveness.

4. Decide on fixed-cost or fixed-effectiveness. The budget is capped so this is a fixed-cost analysis.

5. Analyze each of the alternatives against the evaluation criteria. Products A, C, and F exceed the maximum budget, so they are eliminated from further consideration. Products B, D, and E will be investigated further.

6. Analyze the remaining candidates in more detail and make the choice. Product D has the maximum effectiveness of the remaining candidates; it is selected.

AN EXAMPLE OF FIXED-EFFECTIVENESS ANALYSIS

The second organization has a requirement for a minimum effectiveness of 30,000 files.

1. Define the goal(s). Find the revision control system with the minimum cost given the effectiveness requirement.

2. Develop alternative solutions. These are listed in Table 18.3.

3. Establish evaluation criteria. PW(i) over a 7-year planning horizon for cost and number of files for effectiveness.

4. Decide on fixed-cost or fixed-effectiveness. The effectiveness is required to be at least 30,000 files, so this is a fixed-effectiveness analysis.

5. Analyze each of the alternatives against the evaluation criteria. Products B, D, and E are all less than the minimum effectiveness, so they are eliminated from further consideration. Products A, C, and F will be investigated further.

6. Analyze the remaining candidates in more detail and make the choice. Product A has the lowest cost among the remaining candidates; it is selected.

Summary

The government isn't driven by profit, neither are nonprofit organizations. The goal in these organizations is to promote the general welfare of their respective populations. Because the goals are different from for-profit companies, the decision techniques also differ. This chapter explained decision analysis in those not-for-profit organizations.

Benefit-cost analysis is one of the most widely used methods for evaluating non-profit proposals. A proposal will be desirable only when the net benefits are greater than the net costs. Benefit-cost analysis of multiple proposals must be done incrementally.

A more recent technique for analyzing not-for-profit decisions is cost-effectiveness analysis. There are two versions of cost-effectiveness analysis: fixed-cost and fixed-effectiveness. In fixed-cost analysis, the intent is to maximize the benefit given some upper bound on cost. This is, literally, the biggest-bang-for-the-buck approach. In fixed-effectiveness analysis, the goal is fixed and the intent is to minimize the cost needed to achieve that goal.

This part of the book explained how to make business decisions in not-for-profit organizations. The next part of the book introduces present economy, decision techniques that don't involve the time value of money (i.e., future economy).

Self-Study Questions

Questions 1 through 3 relate to the following situation: A local electric utility company is considering installing a system that would allow customers to access their account through a World Wide Web (WWW) interface. Customers could use the interface to find out how much they currently owe, compare current electricity usage to similar periods in the past, and access a Web-based help system to answer common questions about bills, the utility company, and electricity.

1. In preparing to perform a benefit-cost analysis, identify at least two beneficiaries of this system. What would their benefits be?

2. Who would be negatively impacted by this system? What would their dis-benefits be?

3. Who would pay for this system? What would the costs be? Would there be any savings?

Questions 4 through 8 relate to the following situation: A county government is considering three mutually exclusive software project proposals and is not required to select any of them. Project A1 requires an initial investment of $115,000 with net savings estimated to be $34,500 per year. The initial investment for project A2 is $182,900, and net savings have been estimated at $56,000 per year. The initial investment for project A3 is $148,000, and net savings have been estimated at $41,000 per year. Each project has an expected life of 5 years and no salvage value. The interest rate used by this county government is 13%.

4. What is the benefit-cost ratio for Project A1?

5. What is the benefit-cost ratio for Project A2?

6. What is the benefit-cost ratio for Project A3?

7. Should any of the proposed projects be dropped from further consideration? Why or why not?

8. Use benefit-cost analysis for multiple alternatives to demonstrate which of the proposals should be selected.

Questions 9 through 11 relate to the following situation: The Postal Service is considering a number of mutually exclusive software proposals for improving the speed of mail handling in large urban post offices. The measure of effectiveness in evaluating these mail-handling systems is the volume of mail processed per day. The cost of purchasing and installing these various systems, their resulting savings, and their effectiveness are listed in the following table.

System	Initial Cost in $Millions	Annual Savings in $Millions	Effectiveness in Millions of Letters Processed per Day
A	$1200	$100	5
B	$2000	$140	8
C	$2600	$230	12
D	$4000	$340	13
E	$5100	$500	14

The interest rate is 12% and the life of each system is estimated to be 10 years.

9. Make a table showing the PW(i) of the net investment, the effectiveness, and the effectiveness per million dollars of net investment for each of the proposed systems.

10. Based on the information in your table from the previous question, which proposal(s) can be dropped from further consideration? Why?

11. Identify at least three additional criteria (possibly irreducible) that could help you decide between the remaining alternatives.

PART FIVE

PRESENT ECONOMY

This part introduces break-even and optimization analysis. These two forms of decision analysis are referred to as "present economy" because they don't involve the time value of money (i.e., future economy). In break-even and optimization analyses, the choice being made is represented in terms of one or more decision variables and one or more objective functions. Break-even analysis finds values of the decision variable where performance is identical between alternatives and is explained in Chapter 19. Optimization analysis finds the value of the decision variable(s) with the best overall performance and is described in Chapter 20.

19

Break-Even Analysis

Suppose you are trying to choose between two different suppliers to produce copies of a CD for a commercial software product your company is releasing. One of the suppliers offers a lower initial setup charge but costs more per copy, whereas the other supplier offers a higher initial setup charge with a lower per-copy cost. The decision of supplier will probably be based on the number of copies needed. If only a few copies are needed, the first supplier would be cheaper. If many copies are needed, however, the second supplier would be cheaper. Break-even analysis is a way of choosing between two or more alternatives by figuring out which points, if any, would be indifferent between those alternatives. Below the break-even point one supplier is cheaper, and above that point the other supplier is cheaper. This chapter introduces the concepts of decision variables and objective functions, then explains break-even analysis for two alternatives, three alternatives, and then general case break-even analysis.

Decision Variables and Objective Functions

A **decision variable** represents a set of possible values for some choice in a given decision analysis. If you are choosing, for example, among different connection plans offered by Internet service providers (ISPs), the amount of connect time each month could be an important factor in your decision. If you only use a few hours of connect time each month, one plan might be better. If you use lots of hours, however, another plan might be better. The number of hours of connect time each month would be a decision variable: different amounts of connect time per month are possible.

An **objective function** is an equation that relates the values of the decision variable(s) to the performance of an alternative. An objective function that relates values of decision variables to income (e.g., income as a function of units sold) is called an **income function**, whereas a function that relates values to cost is called a **cost function**. If one of the ISP plans charges $10 per month plus $2 per hour of connect time, its cost function is written as follows:

$$C = \$10.00 + \$2.00 * T$$

Where T is the connect time in hours—the decision variable—and C is the resulting cost.

Objective functions aren't always in terms of money. The objective could be expressed in terms of execution time, memory used, or any other important resource. On software projects, objective functions can describe the following:

- The income received as a function of sales volume
- The amount of data processed in some unit of time
- The cost of some quantity of CD copies
- The cost of Internet access through an ISP based on connect time
- How long it takes to sort a list based on the number of entries
- The size of a memory-resident data structure based on the amount of data
- The cost of software development or testing tools based on the number of seats
- . . .

Break-Even Analysis with Two Alternatives

Break-even analysis is simplest when there are only two alternatives. Consider an ISP that offers two different pricing plans for connect time. Suppose that Plan A is the same as given above, a fixed monthly rate of $10 plus $2 per hour of connect time:

$$\text{Cost under Plan A} = \$10.00 + \$2.00 * T$$

Another plan, Plan B, is also available. This plan has a higher fixed monthly rate, say $25, but has a lower per-hour charge, say, $1.

$$\text{Cost under Plan B} = \$25.00 + \$1.00 * T$$

If you didn't plan on using the ISP very much, for example only an hour or two a month, then Plan A is better. At 2 hours per month, Plan A costs $14, whereas Plan B costs $27. If you intend to use much more connect time each month, Plan B is better. At 50 hours per month Plan A costs $110, whereas Plan B costs $75. Somewhere between 2 hours and 50 hours per month of connect time is a point where the costs would be identical for both plans. Where is that point? This is the essence of break-even analysis.

Because we are looking for the value of T where both plans have the same cost, we can set the Plan A cost equal to the Plan B cost and solve for the number of hours of connect time where this happens. Specifically, the same cost under either plan happens for the value of T where

Cost under Plan A = Cost under Plan B

$10.00 + $2.00 * T = $25.00 + $1.00 * T

Solving for T

$2.00 * T − $1.00 * T = $25.00 − $10.00

$1.00 * T = $15.00

T = 15

The break-even point, 15 hours per month, is when the two alternatives have exactly the same cost. Knowing that, you can now choose your plan intelligently. If you expect to use less than 15 hours per month, your monthly bill will be less if you sign up for Plan A. If, on the other hand, you expect to use more than 15 hours per month, your monthly bill will be less if you sign up for Plan B.

Another way to solve break-even problems is to plot the functions on a graph and find the intersection point visually. Figure 19.1 shows the graphical version of the same ISP price plan analysis.

As another example of break-even analysis, consider two preexisting software routines, A1 and A2. Both routines do the same kind of processing on lists of entries; they simply use different algorithms. Either routine will do the job; your task is to figure out which routine to use based on the number of entries you expect to process. In this example, the cost function is in units of time, not money, but the approach is exactly the same.

Suppose, either by experiment or by analysis, you find that the performance (in uSec) of the two different routines are as follows. (The decision variable, e, is the number of entries to be processed.)

$TC_{A1} = 40 * e + 20{,}800$

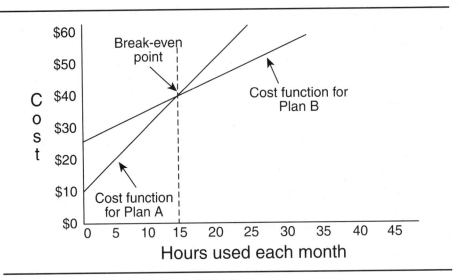

FIGURE 19.1   Solving Break-Even Analysis Graphically

A1 has a relatively low setup cost but a high per-entry cost.

$$TC_{A2} = 9 * e + 58,000$$

A2 has a low per-entry cost but a high setup cost. Obviously, you would use A1 if the list is very small and A2 if the list is very big. But where is the break-even point? It can be found by setting

$$TC_{A1} = TC_{A2}$$

$$40e + 20,800 = 9e + 58,000$$

Solving for e

$$40e - 9e = 58,000 - 20,800$$

$$31e = 37,200$$

$$e = 1,200$$

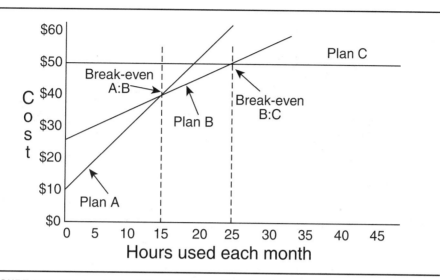

FIGURE 19.2   The graphical solution to the three ISP price plan analysis

The two routines perform identically when the list is 1,200 entries. When the list has fewer than 1,200 entries, algorithm A1 is faster. Algorithm A1 has a lower total cost in spite of its higher per-entry cost. When the list has more than 1200 entries, algorithm A2 is faster. In this range, A2 has a lower total cost in spite of its higher setup cost.

Break-Even Analysis with Three Alternatives

Adding another alternative makes the analysis more complicated, but it's still straight-forward. With three alternatives it's easier to look at the solution graphically than dis-cuss the mathematical method. We'll use the ISP example from above and add in another pricing plan. Suppose that Plan C is a flat rate per month of $50 with unlimited hours.

Cost under Plan C = $50

Figure 19.2 shows the graphical version of the analysis with the three ISP price plans.

There is still a break-even point at 15 hours per month between Plan A and Plan B, but now there is a new break-even point between Plan B and Plan C at 25 hours per month. If you expect to use more than 15 hours per month but less than 25, sign up for Plan B. If you will use more than 25 hours per month, choose Plan C.

There is also a break-even point between Plan A and Plan C at 20 hours per month, but this is an irrelevant break-even point in light of Plan B. If Plan B didn't exist, you would have a legitimate break-even point, but Plan B makes the Plan A:Plan C break-even point irrelevant. Plan B is cheaper than either Plan A or Plan C at 20 hours per month.

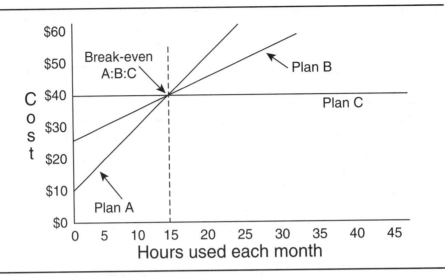

FIGURE 19.3   Case two, a single break-even point

In general, there are three possible situations when analyzing three alternatives. We've already seen one case, where the break-even point between two alternatives is "dominated" by the third alternative. Another case, which is fairly rare in practice, is where all three alternatives share exactly the same break-even point. This would happen if the cost function for Plan C were as follows:

Cost under Plan C = $40

The cost under Plan C at 15 hours per month would be $40, which is the same cost as the break-even point between Plan A and Plan B. This is shown graphically in Figure 19.3.

In this case, Plan B is irrelevant except at the break-even point. Plan A is better than both Plans B and C when use is less than 15 hours per month. Plan C is better than Plans A and B for uses more than 15 hours per month. There are no cases where Plan B is better; it's only equal at exactly 15 hours per month. If you can precisely control connect time to exactly 15 hours per month, any of the plans will give you the same monthly cost. If you can't control connect time to exactly 15 hours per month, Plan A or Plan C would be better depending on if you will be under or over 15 hours per month, respectively.

The third possible situation, shown in Figure 19.4, is where the other two always dominate the third alternative. This would be the case when Plan C had a cost function of

C under Plan C = $20 + $1.50 *

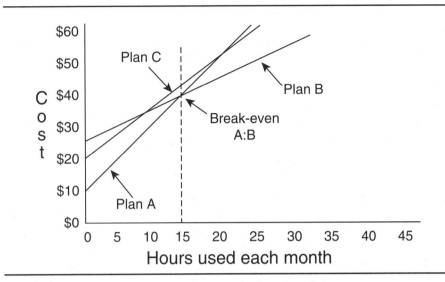

FIGURE 19.4   Case three, one alternative always dominated

The cost function of this Plan C is always worse than the others, even at the other's break-even point. In this case, it is safe to disregard the dominated alternative (after you've figured out which one it is) because the other two alternatives are always better.

A variation in this case is when the cost functions are parallel. Because they never intersect, there will be no break-even point between them. In this case, throw out the higher-cost alternative because it is always dominated by the lower-cost one.

General Case Break-Even Analysis

Looking at the solution graphically, a multi-alternative break-even analysis is simply a matter of plotting each cost function on a graph and visually inspecting for the relevant break-even points. Irrelevant break-even points, such as the break-even point between Plan B and Plan C in Figure 19.4, can be ignored. If the accuracy using the graph isn't good enough, you can use the mathematical approach described above to solve the relevant break-even points.

Looking at the solution algorithmically, it's a matter of first calculating the break-even points between each pair of cost functions. With n cost functions, the number of candidate pairs to consider is

$$\frac{n * (n - 1)}{2}$$

TABLE 19.1   The Break-Even Points Between Each Pair of Cost Functions

Pair	Decision Variable at Break-Even Point	Cost Function at Break-Even Point
C1:C2	75	73uSec
C1:C3	−26	N/A
C1:C4	11	40uSec
C2:C3	9	57uSec
C2:C4	23	61uSec
C3:C4	39	89uSec

For each break-even point, record that pair's name along with the value of the decision variable at that point and the value of the cost functions at that point. Then calculate the value of the other cost functions at each of the break-even points listed above, finding the cost function(s) with the minimum cost. Discard a break-even point if the decision variable's value is outside of the acceptable range or if any other cost function has a lower cost at that value. These break-even points are irrelevant. Finally, arrange the remaining relevant break-even points in order of increasing value of the decision variable. The lowest-cost alternative for each range between the remaining break-even points should now be apparent.

Consider a software organization that has a reusable code library containing implementations of four different algorithms that each performs the same basic function. These algorithms operate on variable size linked lists containing anywhere from 0 to 100 entries. Through experimentation it's determined that the cost function describing the performance of each routine is (where E is the number of entries):

$$C1 = 34uSec + (0.52uSec * E)$$

$$C2 = 55uSec + (0.24uSec * E)$$

$$C3 = 48uSec + (1.06uSec * E)$$

$$C4 = 21uSec + (1.75uSec * E)$$

There will be six pairs (candidate break-even points) to consider.

Table 19.1 shows the decision variable value and the value of the cost function for each pair of cost functions. The break-even point C1:C3 is irrelevant because it happens at −26, an impossible number of entries.

For each break-even point, calculate the value of each of the cost functions at that point. Those are listed in Tables 19.2 through 19.6.

TABLE 19.2   The Cost Functions at Break-Even Point C1:C2

Cost Function	Cost at This Break-Even Point
C1	73uSec
C2	73
C3	128
C4	152

TABLE 19.3   The Cost Functions at Break-Even Point C1:C4

Cost Function	Cost at This Break-Even Point
C1	40uSec
C2	58
C3	60
C4	40

TABLE 19.4   The Cost Functions at Break-Even Point C2:C3

Cost Function	Cost at This Break-Even Point
C1	39uSec
C2	57
C3	57
C4	37

TABLE 19.5   The Cost Functions at Break-Even Point C2:C4

Cost Function	Cost at This Break-Even Point
C1	46uSec
C2	61
C3	72
C4	61

TABLE 19.6 The Cost Functions at Break-Even Point C3:C4

Cost Function	Cost at This Break-Even Point
C1	54uSec
C2	64
C3	89
C4	89

TABLE 19.7 Relevant Break-Even Points Arranged in Increasing Decision Variable Order

Pair	Decision Variable at Break-Even Point	Cost Function at Break-Even Point
C1:C4	11	40uSec
C1:C2	75	73uSec

At the C1:C2 break-even point (75 entries), cost functions C1 and C2 have the lowest cost, meaning that this is a relevant break-even point.

At the C1:C4 break-even point (11 entries), cost functions C1 and C4 have the lowest cost, meaning that this is also a relevant break-even point.

At the C2:C3 break-even point (9 entries), cost function C4 has the lowest cost. This is an irrelevant break-even point, so it is discarded.

At the C2:C4 break-even point (23 entries), cost function C1 has the lowest cost. This is an irrelevant break-even point, so it is also discarded.

At the C3:C4 break-even point (39 entries), cost function C1 has the lowest cost. This is an irrelevant break-even point, so it is discarded too.

Table 19.7 lists the relevant break-even points in order of increasing value of the decision variable.

Because alternative C1 appears in both break-even points, it should be apparent that it is the preferred alternative between those points. From Table 19.7 we can conclude that the appropriate ranges are as follows:

> Routine C4 is best for list sizes up to 11 entries.
> Routine C1 is best when the list size is between 11 and 75 entries.
> Routine C2 is best for list sizes over 75 entries.

Routine C3 is never the lowest cost in the range of 1 to 100 entries.

Summary

Break-even analysis is a method for choosing between two or more alternatives by figuring out which points, if any, would be indifferent between those alternatives. This chapter covered the following major points:

- A decision variable represents a set of possible values for some choice in a given decision analysis.
- An objective function is an equation that relates the values of the decision variable(s) to the performance of an alternative.
- An objective function that relates values of decision variables to income (e.g., income as a function of units sold) is called an income function, whereas a function that relates values to cost is called a cost function.
- To solve a break-even problem for two alternatives, set their objective functions equal to each other and solve for the value of the decision variable where this happens. Another approach is to find the point of intersection on a graph of the objective functions.
- When there are three or more alternatives, the break-even points between each pair need to be considered. Some of those points may be dominated by other alternatives and will need to be discarded if that is the case.

The next chapter, on optimization analysis, studies objective functions over a range of values of the decision variable(s) to find the point where overall performance is most favorable.

Self-Study Questions

1. CDs Plus is one of many companies that offer CD-ROM duplication services. They currently have two different pricing plans. With Plan 1, the customer pays a flat charge of $0.75 per copy with no setup charge. Under Plan 2, the customer pays $0.25 per copy, but there is a setup charge of $600. Write the cost functions for Plan 1 and Plan 2.

2. ABC Software needs to make copies of the CD for the latest release of a software product and CDs Plus is a leading candidate to do the work. What is the break-even point between the two pricing plans?

3. If ABC Software needs 2,500 copies, which plan should they go with and how much would it cost them?

4. Suppose that CDs Plus announces a new pricing plan, Plan 3. With Plan 3, the setup charge is $1000 and the per-copy charge is $0.15. What is the break-even point between Plan 1 and Plan 3, and what is the break-even point between Plan 2 and Plan 3?

5. Given that ABC Software still wants 2,500 copies of their CD, should they switch to Plan 3? Why or why not?

6. In light of Plan 2 still being offered by CDs Plus, is the break-even point between Plan 1 and Plan 3 relevant? Why or why not?

Questions 7 through 9 all use the following situation: A software organization has a reusable code library that contains implementations of four different algorithms that each perform the same basic function. These algorithms operate on variable size linked lists containing anywhere from 0 to 100 entries. Through experimentation it was determined that the performance of each routine is as listed in the following table.

	Initialization Time	Time per Item in Input List
A	34	0.52
B	55	0.24
C	48	1.06
D	21	1.75

7. Identify the break-even points between each pair of routines.

8. Identify the range of input list size over which each routine has superior performance. Caution, one or more of the routines may be poor performers over all ranges of inputs.

9. Which break-even points, if any, are irrelevant?

10. EmbeddedSystems, Inc. is an embedded systems manufacturer. ES is working on a hardware-software tradeoff study for one of their products. The decision is between using a Universal Asynchronous Receiver Transmitter (UART)—the hardware solution—or doing the serial bit-stream control in software. The costs associated with the hardware solution are 5 hours of design time for a hardware engineer at $85/hour plus 25 cents in UART hardware cost per unit produced. The costs associated with the software solution are 20 hours of software development time at $85/hour with no additional cost per unit produced. What is the break-even point between the two proposed solutions?

20

Optimization Analysis

The typical use of optimization is to study an objective function over a range of values of the decision variable(s) to find the point where overall performance is most favorable. Software's classic space-time tradeoff is an example of optimization; an algorithm that runs faster will often use more memory. Optimization balances the value of the faster runtime against the cost of the additional memory. This chapter explains optimization analysis for various combinations of single or multiple alternatives and single or multiple decision variables.

Introducing Optimization

Optimization is useful when the objective function being studied has two or more competing components: One of the components increases as the decision variable increases, whereas the other component decreases. Economic life, discussed in Chapter 11 and repeated in Figure 20.1, is an example of optimization of a cost function.

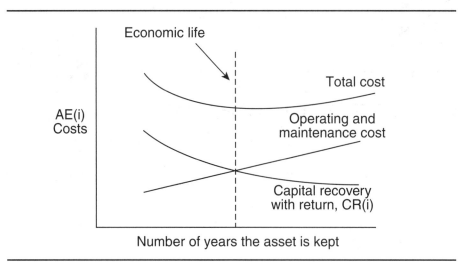

FIGURE 20.1   Economic life of an asset is an optimization problem

The decision variable is the length of time to keep the asset. The $AE(i)$ cost of ownership (the $CR(i)$) decreases the longer the asset is kept, but the $AE(i)$ cost of operation and maintenance increases. Over short ownership times, $CR(i)$ dominates, and with longer times the cost of operation and maintenance dominates. There's a point in the middle where the total cost is minimized. That's the optimum time of ownership.

Optimization can also be applied to maximizing an income function. This involves finding the maximum point on an income function rather than the minimum point on a cost function. The exact same techniques are used, just look for the maximum point rather than the minimum point.

Optimizing a Single Alternative with a Single Decision Variable

The simplest optimization analysis is when there is only one alternative and its value is determined by a single decision variable.

$$Cost = F(DecisionVariable)$$

Suppose that Zymurgenics is in the middle of upgrading software for their inventory management system. One of the modifications to increase performance is to distribute the application and run the parts on separate processors. A network communication link will be needed to connect the parts. One part of the application will generate requests to another part, and the requests are created at a rate where there would be too much network overhead if each request were sent separately. Zymurgenics developers decide to queue the requests into data packets. The developers realize that making the data packets bigger cuts down on the network overhead, but it also increases the average queue time per request. They want to balance the reduced network overhead with the longer average queue time.

After studying the performance of the network and their inventory management software, they've determined that the overall queuing delay is described by the cost function:

$$TD = 20r + \frac{320}{r} + 50$$

Where *TD* is the overall delay in milliseconds, and *r* is the number of requests queued in a data packet. The 20r component is the average cost of waiting for another request before sending; this component increases with *r*. The 320/r component is the network overhead, which decreases as *r* increases. The Zymurgenics developers need to find the value of *r* that minimizes TD.

There are two ways of finding the optimum point. The brute-force approach is to run different sample values for the decision variable through the function and narrow in on the best result. The economic-life calculations shown in Chapter 11 and the asset-retirement calculations at the end of Chapter 12 are both examples of using this brute-force approach. The elegant approach uses differential calculus; the objective function will be at a minimum or maximum whenever its first derivative equals zero. Setting the first derivative function to zero and solving for the value(s) of the decision variable where this happens identifies those minimum or maximum points. Derivatives are explained in more detail in Appendix D.

The first derivative of the queuing delay cost function is

$$\frac{dTD}{dr} = 20 - \frac{320}{r^2}$$

Setting this first derivative to zero and solving for the decision variable

$$\frac{dTD}{dr} = 20 - \frac{320}{r^2} = 0$$

$$r = \sqrt[2]{\frac{320}{20}} = 4$$

The optimum number of requests per data packet is 4, where the overall delay will be 210 milliseconds.

In the general case, there can be several local minimum or maximum points on the objective function. If you identify the minimum or maximum points using differential calculus, you need to run those values back through the objective function to find which one is the overall minimum or maximum. Figure 20-2 shows an example objective function with multiple local minimum and maximum points. The overall minimum is at *P*, and the overall maximum is at *Q*. Points *R* and *S* are local minimums and maximums. When the brute-force approach is used, the overall minimum or maximum points will be obvious from simply looking at the computed values.

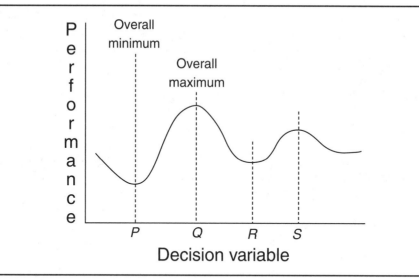

FIGURE 20.2 An objective function with multiple local minimum and maximum points

Also in the general case, some of the maximum or minimum points may be outside the range of reasonableness for the decision variable. For example, a cost function may be a polynomial, and one or more of the minimum points could be at negative values of the decision variable. Any minimum or maximum point that's outside of the reasonable range for the decision variable must be discarded.

Optimizing Multiple Alternatives with a Single Decision Variable

A slightly more complex use of optimization is when there are multiple alternatives and their functions are driven by the same, single decision variable.

$Cost_1 = F_1(DecisionVariable)$

$Cost_2 = F_2(DecisionVariable)$

. . .

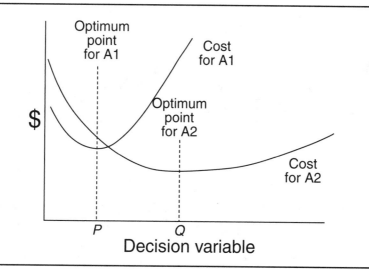

FIGURE 20.3   Optimizing multiple alternatives with a single decision variable

The general approach in this situation is to first find the optimum point for each of the alternatives, using either the brute-force or elegant approach described for a single alternative with a single decision variable. The second step is to compare the value for each alternative at its respective optimum point. Choose the alternative with the best value at its optimum point. Figure 20.3 shows this situation graphically. Alternative A1 has its optimum point at P, whereas A2 has its optimum point at Q. The cost of alternative A2 at Q is lower than the cost of A1 at P, so overall optimum performance is achieved by selecting alternative A2 and setting the decision variable to Q.

In the Zymurgenics network communication example, suppose that two communication technologies are available, CORBA [OMG02] and Java Remote Method Invocation (RMI) [Grosso01]. Assume the delay equation above represents performance of the CORBA solution; optimum performance is at 4 requests per packet where the total delay is 210 milliseconds. Analysis of the Java RMI solution might show that optimum performance happens at 6 requests per packet, but the total delay in this case is 325 milliseconds. The CORBA solution at its optimum point is better than the Java RMI solution at its optimum point, so the CORBA solution is selected and used at 4 requests per packet.

As another example, consider trying to optimize ownership costs in choosing one from three mutually exclusive computer systems, systems SA, SB, and SC. Start by finding the economic life of each system. Suppose the economic lives are as listed in the following table.

Alternative	Economic Life	AE(i) Cost at Economic Life
SA	4 years	$4355
SB	7 years	$5187
SC	5 years	$3994

System SC has the lowest AE(i) cost at its economic life. The most cost-effective computer system is system SC, replacing it after 5 years.

Optimizing a Single Alternative with Multiple Decision Variables

From an analytical perspective, optimizing a single alternative with multiple decision variables is more complex than an alternative with a single decision variable.

$$Cost = F(DecisionVariable_1, DecisionVariable_2, \ldots)$$

Similar to optimizing a single alternative with a single decision variable, there is a brute-force approach and an elegant approach. The brute-force approach involves examining the function at various combinations of decision variable inputs. This may involve a systematic search of the variable ranges. For instance, with two decision variables hold *DecisionVariable1* at a fixed value and run through a range of values for *DecisionVariable2* then go back and repeat this for another value of *DecisionVariable1*, then another, and so on. A simplified algorithm, in this case for three decision variables, is

```
LowestDV1 := some selected value of DecisionVariable1
LowestDV2 := some selected value of DecisionVariable2
LowestDV3 := some selected value of DecisionVariable3
LowestCost = CostFunction ( LowestDV1, LowestDV2, LowestDV3 )
while DV1 runs over the range of DecisionVariable1
   while DV2 runs over the range of DecisionVariable2
      while DV3 runs over the range of DecisionVariable3
         if CostFunction ( DV1, DV2, DV3 ) < LowestCost
            then LowestCost = CostFunction ( DV1, DV2, DV3 )
                 LowestDV1 := DV1
                 LowestDV2 := DV2
                 LowestDV3 := DV3
```

When this systematic search algorithm completes, the optimum point will be (close to) LowestDV1, LowestDV2, LowestDV3 and have a cost of LowestCost. The brute-force systematic search approach is, of course, not much help when the search space is very big. The number of combinations that need to be considered could be enormous.

Instead of a systematic search, Monte Carlo analysis (see Chapter 24) randomly generates different combinations of the decision variables. In both cases, you are looking for the combination of decision variable inputs that has the best overall performance. If necessary, you could use Monte Carlo analysis to identify the most likely areas for the optimum point and then do a more systematic search in just those areas.

The elegant approach is to again use differential calculus, this time using multiple derivatives.

Optimizing Multiple Alternatives with Multiple Decision Variables

The most complex situation, analytically, is when you have multiple alternatives with multiple decision variables.

$$Cost_1 = F_1(DecisionVariable_1, DecisionVariable_2, \ldots)$$

$$Cost_2 = F_2(DecisionVariable_1, DecisionVariable_2, \ldots)$$

$$\ldots$$

This is similar to optimizing multiple alternatives with a single decision variable. The approach is to find the optimum point for each alternative (using whatever means is appropriate), and then choose the alternative with the best value at its respective optimum point.

Summary

Optimization analysis is useful when the objective functions being studied have two or more competing components: One of the components increases as the decision variable increases, whereas the other component decreases. Optimization balances these competing components to find the point where overall performance is most favorable.

There are two ways of finding the optimum point on a single alternative with a single decision variable. The brute-force approach is to run different sample values on the function and narrow in on the best result. The elegant approach uses differential calculus; the objective function will be at a minimum or maximum whenever its first derivative equals zero.

To find the optimum point when there is more than one single-variable performance function, first find the optimum point for each alternative then select the alternative with the most favorable performance at its optimum point.

Optimizing a single alternative with multiple decision variables can either be done using the brute-force method (just like for optimizing with a single decision variable) or by using differential calculus with multiple derivatives.

Optimizing multiple alternatives with multiple decision variables is essentially the same as optimizing multiple alternatives with a single decision variable: Find the optimum point for each alternative and select the alternative with the most favorable overall performance.

This part introduced break-even and optimization analysis. These two forms of decision analysis are referred to as "present economy" because they don't involve the time value of money (i.e., future economy). Part VI explains the concepts and techniques of estimation along with describing how risk and uncertainty can be addressed in a decision analysis.

Self-Study Questions

1. The performance of a particular data reduction routine is described by the following equation:

    $$t = 7.5s^2 - 5625s + 2112$$

    Where t is the execution time and s is the size of the input data set. What is the optimum size, s, for the input data set?

2. The performance of another data reduction routine is described by the following equation:

    $$t = 4s^2 - 3936s + 6621$$

    Where t is the execution time and s is the size of the input data set. What is the optimum size, s, for this routine's input data set?

3. A software organization has a choice between two data processing routines. The number of records in the input stream determines the performance of the two routines. Analysis has shown that the performance of the two routines is

    Routine 1) $t = 2s^2 - 148s + 352$

    Routine 2) $t = 1.5s^2 - 126s + 524$

Where t is the execution time and s is the number of records in the input stream. To get the best overall optimal performance, which routine should be selected, and what should be the size of the input stream?

4. A different software organization has a choice between two data processing routines. Analysis has shown that the performance of these two routines is

Routine 1) $t = 3s^2 - 2442s + 2008$

Routine 2) $t = 3.5s^2 - 3647s + 157$

Where t is the execution time and s is the number of records in the input stream. To get the best overall optimal performance, which routine should be selected, and what should be the size of the input stream?

PART SIX

ESTIMATION, RISK, AND UNCERTAINTY

Business decisions are always about future actions: Should an organization use its limited resources to do this, that, or something else? Because these decisions look into the future, the cash-flow streams for the proposals being considered are necessarily estimates, and the correctness of the business decision will depend on the accuracy of those estimates. The Standish Group's CHAOS study, first mentioned in Chapter 1, showed that the average software project is 45% over budget, 63% over schedule, and delivers only 67% of the required features and functions. One contributing factor in this less-than-stellar performance is probably that the original estimates were not very good. This part explains the concepts and techniques of good estimation, which will lead to making better decisions. This part also explains how a decision analysis can address the inherent inaccuracy in estimates. Risk-based decision techniques are used when the probabilities of the inaccuracies are known. Uncertainty-based decision techniques are used when the probabilities of the inaccuracies are not known.

21

Basic Estimation Concepts

Business decisions depend on estimates, and bad estimates can of course lead to bad decisions. To help you create good estimates, this chapter introduces the basic concepts of estimation. The chapter starts by explaining what an estimate is and why estimates are made in the first place. The chapter then explains estimate uncertainty. It also describes how and why uncertainty changes over time. The chapter closes with a description of different ways to specify estimate uncertainty and how to deal with uncertainty when the schedule is fixed.

What Is an Estimate?

A practical definition of an estimate comes from the Project Management Institute's "Guide to the Project Management Body of Knowledge" [PMI00]. The guide defines an estimate as follows:

> An assessment of the likely quantitative result. Usually applied to project costs and durations and should always include some indication of accuracy (e.g.,+/– x percent).

Literally, an estimate is a prediction. But it's not just any kind of prediction, like a horoscope, tarot card reading, or a fortune-cookie fortune. It's a quantitative prediction, like how much a product will cost to develop, how long that development will take, how many problem reports will come in from customers, how much income will be earned in the sixth month after market availability, and so on.

Why Estimate?

As important as understanding what an estimate is, a key concept to understand is "why do we estimate in the first place?" The answer is that business decisions always look into the future. Decisions are being made based on factors whose values aren't known yet. More often than not, values for those factors *can't* be known for certain at the time the decision needs to be made. How much will it cost to develop some product? You won't know for sure unless you actually develop it and add up all the bills. However, the decision to develop it or not still needs to be made. So you estimate as best you can and try to come as close as possible to what you think the actual outcome is going to be.

What kinds of decisions are made on software projects? They will be all over the map. Some high-level decisions will be about whether a certain project is worth doing at all. As the project progresses, the scope of the decisions gets smaller and smaller but there are more decisions to be made. Should the software be designed like this or like that? Given a particular software design, what's a good data structure for the PQR data? What's a good algorithm for the ABC function? Any time you don't know the value of a key decision criterion (like how much will it cost to develop the product, how long will it take, how many can we sell, how many transactions per second can this design handle, how many can that design handle, how much data will be in the PQR structure, how often does that data need to be accessed, how often will the ABC function be executed, and so forth), you'll need an estimate. In all these cases, you don't know what the actual outcome will be. Although you can't know for certain until well after the decision has been made, you still need to make the decision, so you need an estimate.

Estimates come in all shapes and sizes. And they'll be about all sorts of things. But they are all there to support making decisions based on factors whose values you're not 100% sure of yet. You try your best and hope you weren't too far off in the end. In fact, you'd probably be shocked if you did come out "right on the money" even once, let alone repeatedly. That's okay; estimates don't need to be perfect. They only need to be close enough to allow you to make the right decision.

Estimates and Probabilities

Think about estimating the schedule and cost for a 500-mile car trip. How many hours will it take to get there? How much money will need to be spent along the way? You can't know the exact outcomes unless you actually get into a car and make the trip—or you can ask someone who already made that same trip. Any estimated schedule and cost would have to be predictions. Recognize that there is inherent uncertainty in estimates. The uncertainty in the 500-mile car trip is driven by a number of different causes, including the following:

- What will the weather be like; will you be slowed by rain, snow, fog, or ice?
- What will the traffic be like; will you get caught in any traffic jams?
- How much road construction will there be? Road closures? Detours?
- Will your car break down and need to be repaired?
- Will you take a wrong turn somewhere and get lost? If so, how long will it take to get back on track?
- How many times will you need to stop for food, fuel, or to rest? How long will those rest stops last?

Even if you were to make the trip and measure the actual schedule and cost, if you repeated the trip the second outcome would almost certainly be different than the first for these very same reasons.

No single predicted outcome could always be the right one. There will be lots of possible outcomes, and each one will have an associated probability. Maybe there's a 0.47% chance that it will take you exactly 10 hours and 33 minutes to drive the 500 miles. The probabilities for each possible outcome aren't going to be the same, either. Some outcomes are more likely than others. Your chances of getting there in 11 hours and 12 minutes might be higher or lower than 0.47%.

Just like in long-distance driving, there are a number of different sources of uncertainty in software business decisions:

- **Business environment**—Some kinds of businesses are inherently more uncertain than others. It's much more difficult to predict sales for software in the entertainment industry (video games, for example) than it is for something like tax or inventory management software.
- **Novelty of the activity**—If you've never done anything like this before, there's probably no sound basis for any estimates.
- **Very long planning horizon**—You might simply be looking too far in the future to have any basis for certainty. A 25-year planning horizon will have far more uncertainty than a 5-year planning horizon.

For some estimates, such as cost and schedule, there will be something known informally as "the impossible zone." We know that even the fastest passenger car can't go 250 miles per hour. So there's no way that the 500-mile car trip could ever be completed in 2 hours or less. There's a small chance that if you drove as fast as you possibly could and happened to miss every speed trap along the way that you might be able to get there in, say, 5 hours. However, 6 hours is more likely than 5 hours, and 7 hours is even more likely than that, and so on. Assuming an average sustained speed of 50 miles per hour, to account for rest stops, eating, getting fuel, and allowing moderate times for construction detours, getting

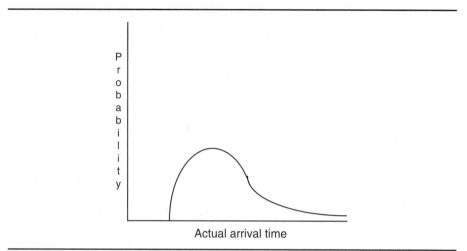

FIGURE 21.1   The shape of a typical probability function for cost and schedule estimates

lost, and so on, the most likely time could be somewhere around 10 hours. It could take 12 hours if you get badly lost somewhere along the way, but that might not be very likely. It might even take 20 hours if the car breaks down and needs repairs. The more pessimistic outcomes, although still possible, are less and less likely to happen.

The set of all outcomes and their associated probabilities is called a probability function. (See Appendix E for a more detailed discussion of probability and statistics.) Figure 21.1 shows a graph of the typical shape of the probability function for cost and schedule estimates.

Notice that the probability function isn't symmetrical. Many software-related estimates are like this; there's a definite lower limit that can't be beat. You just can't do better than that, under any circumstances. However, there isn't any definite upper limit. Although more and more unlikely, you could always take just a little more time and money. One associate quipped that this kind of probability function means that "there's a limit to how good you can be but there really isn't any limit to how bad you can be."

Figure 21.1 illustrates the general shape and nothing more. You'll probably never know the actual probabilities for any given estimate unless you have lots of good historical data. Nonetheless, the key idea is that your estimate, whatever it is, has some probability of being "right"—if right means matching the eventual actual outcome. The probability could even be zero if you mistakenly choose an outcome that's in the impossible zone.

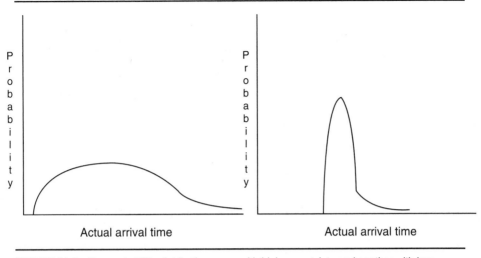

FIGURE 21.2   Two probability distributions, one with high uncertainty and another with low uncertainty

Estimates and Uncertainty

In some situations, the factor being estimated may have a broad range of possible outcomes, and other situations may have a much narrower range. Eleven months into a 12-month software project you should have a much better idea of the finish date than you did at project start. The size of that range is sometimes called **variance** or **uncertainty** (see Appendix E). The more uncertainty in the factor, the less likely you are to hit the actual outcome with your estimate. Figure 21.2 shows examples of probability distributions with different uncertainties compared to Figure 21.1.

EXACT ("ON-THE-MONEY") ESTIMATES VS. AT-OR-LESS ESTIMATES

For most software project decisions, it's not necessary to predict the exact actual outcome. What's important is whether the actual outcome is *at or below* your estimate. Did you finish the project in exactly 10 months? You probably don't care nearly as much as whether you finished in 10 months or less. Finishing at or less is the more relevant issue, especially if you're trying to meet some important market window or be ready for a major trade show. We want to be sure to finish a software project *on or before* some predicted date. We want the project to cost *no more than* some estimated amount.

TABLE 21.1 Example Cumulative Probabilities for Arriving At or Before a Given Time

Arrive At or Before	Cumulative Probability	Arrive At or Before	Cumulative Probability
1	0.000	10	0.500
2	0.000	11	0.683
3	0.000	12	0.899
4	0.000	13	0.964
5	0.001	14	0.976
6	0.002	15	0.979
7	0.009	16	0.982
8	0.113	17	0.996
9	0.375	18	0.999

The probability of an estimate being the exact actual outcome (e.g., finish exactly then, cost exactly that much) isn't terribly useful all by itself. The individual probabilities are usually way too small, for one. The probabilities will be very small fractions in most cases. It's much more useful to consider the probabilities for an actual outcome to be *less than or equal to* the prediction (e.g., finish on or before, cost no more than).

For any predicted outcome, the probability of hitting that outcome or less will be the probability of hitting that exact outcome plus the sum of the probabilities of all the outcomes less than it. Technically speaking, it's the cumulative probability function—the integral of the probability function.

The shape of the cumulative probability function is very different from the shape of the probability distributions, but the impossible zone still applies. Because driving 500 miles in exactly 2 hours has a probability of zero, the probability of getting there in 2 hours or less is also zero. The probability of getting at or less than the smallest outcome with a nonzero probability is the same as the probability of hitting exactly that same outcome. The probability of hitting the second smallest possible outcome or less equals the probability of hitting exactly the smallest plus the probability of hitting exactly the next to smallest. The probability of hitting any given outcome or less is the sum of the probabilities of hitting exactly the outcomes from that one all the way back to the beginning (e.g., add up the probabilities of all the arrive-exactly-on-times from the given time back to the earliest possible arrival time). Figure 21.3 shows the cumulative probability curve overlaid on the original probability distributions from Figures 21.1 and 21.2.

In the 500-mile car trip example, the cumulative probabilities might be as shown in Table 21.1.

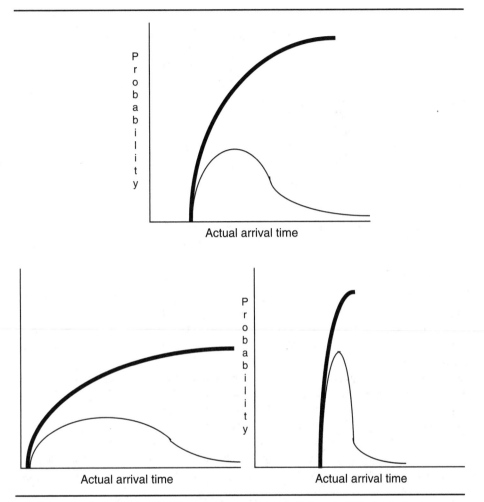

P
r
o
b
a
b
i
l
i
t
y

Actual arrival time

P
r
o
b
a
b
i
l
i
t
y

Actual arrival time

Actual arrival time

FIGURE 21.3   Cumulative probability functions in relation to their probability distributions

THE 50/50 ESTIMATE

Notice in Figure 21.3 and in Table 21.1 that for each cumulative probability function there will be one outcome where the probability of that outcome or less is exactly 0.5. One such point is shown in Figure 21.4. This is an important point; it's the **50/50 estimate**. The actual outcome is just as likely to be higher than that estimate as it is to be lower. From an estimator's perspective, this is a useful way to deal with estimates. You should always target this 50/50 point; you want your estimate to be equally likely to overshoot as to undershoot. One of the best tests of someone's ability to estimate is to see whether the actual outcomes are more than their estimates as often as they are less. Consistently coming out over (or under) the estimate means there is a systemic bias in that estimator's estimates.

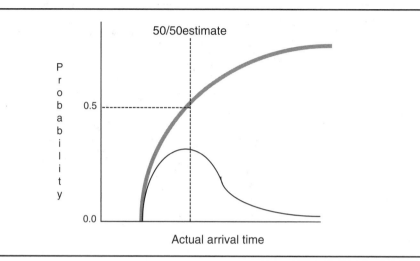

FIGURE 21.4   The 50/50 estimate

The 50/50 estimate might not be the best estimate to share with project stakeholders. The implication is that you will overrun this estimate half the time. But notice how the cumulative probability idea can be extended to a 90/10 estimate (you overrun the estimate only 1 time in 10), the 80/20 estimate (you overrun 2 times in 10), 70/30, etc. From a pure project management and decision-making perspective, the 50/50 estimate is the easiest to work with. It may be appropriate to manage the project to the 50/50 estimate while reporting to the stakeholders at, say, the 80/20 level. The project may be equally likely to cost more than $900,000 as it is to cost less, so you manage the project to a $900,000 budget. But assuming that you don't want to overrun the budget more than 20% of the time, if you're 80% certain the project will cost less than $1,100,000, you can report progress to the stakeholders against this higher number. Project managers need to decide how much risk they are willing to take on in overrunning any estimate.

The Cone of Uncertainty: Uncertainties Change over Time

The degree of uncertainty in any estimate depends on how much is known about the overall situation. You'll have a much better idea of your arrival time for the 500 mile drive when you're halfway there than you will before you even start driving. You'll have an even better idea when you're three fourths of the way there. You'll know exactly when you'll get there just as you arrive, and no sooner.

There are a number of different sources of uncertainty in software projects, including the following:

- Will the customer want feature X or not?
- If they decide to include feature X, how fancy will they want it to be?

- Will they change their mind about feature X or how fancy they want it?
- How will feature X be designed and implemented?
- How much debugging will be necessary to make feature X actually work?

Every mile you drive on a car trip, and every bit of progress you make on a software project, converts uncertainty into certainty. So it should be clear that for many kinds of estimates, especially software project cost and schedule estimates, the uncertainty will change over time. Early estimates will have a much higher degree of uncertainty than later estimates of the same thing.

The **cone of uncertainty** is a way of quantifying uncertainty and showing how it decreases over time. Rather than just jump into it, it's better to show how to build a cone of uncertainty for your organization. You'll get a much better understanding of what it means. You'll also get the instructions for making your own, which you should do since every organization's uncertainties are a consequence of the way they develop software. Your organization's cone of uncertainty is virtually guaranteed to be different from any other organization's.

DEVELOPING A CONE OF UNCERTAINTY FOR YOUR OWN ORGANIZATION

The process is the same for any estimated factor, but assume for now we want to develop the cone of uncertainty for overall project schedule estimates. Start with a single project and assume the project will use a waterfall life cycle. Iterative software life cycles can often be thought of as a series of consecutive waterfalls. (This isn't necessarily true for the agile development life cycles—handling uncertainty in agile software projects is described below in the section on dealing with constrained schedule.) Plan to, and then do, re-estimates of the overall schedule at each major project milestone. Record the different estimates at each milestone so they don't get forgotten. At the end of the project (or iteration), also record the actual outcome. Imagine that Table 21.2 shows the estimates and the actual outcome for the overall schedule estimates for a particular software project.

The next step is to find the relative estimated values by dividing the actual outcome at the end of the project by the estimates at each of the milestones, saving this result for each milestone. An estimate of 6 months at a milestone and an actual outcome of 12 months would equal 2.0 for the relative value at that milestone. The relative value 2.0 means the project actually took twice as long as was estimated at that time. This step normalizes the data so that estimates from a project that took 4 months can be meaningfully combined with the estimates from a project that took 12 months, another that took 18 months, and so on. Table 21.3 shows the calculated relative values for the project shown in Table 21.2.

The relative values for the project can be plotted on a graph but this step isn't necessary. It's only shown here to illustrate the concept. If you do plot the relative values, put the milestones along the horizontal axis and space them according to (approximately) what percent of the project schedule has passed at that milestone. The relative values from the project in Table 21.3 would look like Figure 21.5.

TABLE 21.2 Estimates and the Actual Outcome for the Overall Schedule of One Project

Milestone	Recorded Value
Project scope defined	7 months
Requirements complete	11 months
Design complete	10 months
Code complete	9 months
Testing complete	9.5 months
Actual schedule	10 months

TABLE 21.3 Relative Values for the Overall Schedule Estimates of the Project

Milestone	Relative Value
Project scope defined	1.43
Requirements complete	0.91
Design complete	1.00
Code complete	1.11
Testing complete	1.05
Actual schedule	1.00

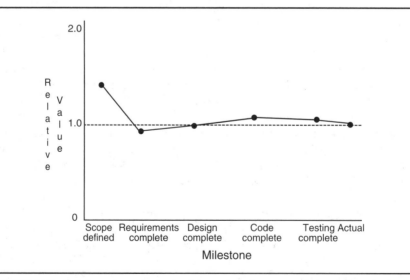

FIGURE 21.5 Relative values of actual outcomes to estimates at milestones in a single project

This same process can now be repeated for several more projects. Table 21.4 shows example schedule estimates and actual outcomes for a number of other projects in an organization.

The next step is to again divide the actual outcomes for each project by the estimate at each milestone. Each individual project can then be plotted on the same kind of graph as was shown in Figure 21.5. The graph for all six projects is shown in Figure 21.6.

TABLE 21.4   Example Schedule Estimates and Actual Outcomes for a Number of Projects

Milestone	Project 2	Project 3	Project 4	Project 5	Project 6
Project scope defined	14	6	1.75	7	24
Requirements complete	10	6	2	10	20
Design complete	11	7	2	9.5	18
Code complete	13	6	2.25	10	16.5
Testing complete	12	6.5	2.25	9.5	15.5
Actual schedule	12 wks	6.5 mos	2.35 yrs	9.5 mos	15 wks

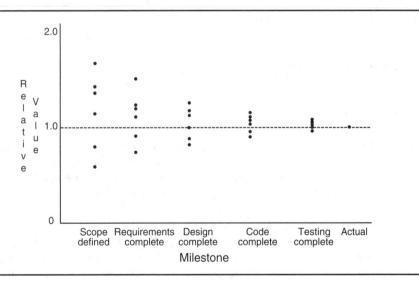

FIGURE 21.6   Relative value of actual outcomes to schedule estimates at different milestones for several projects

TABLE 21.5 Lower, Mean, and Upper Relative Schedule Values over Several Projects

Milestone	Lower Relative Value	Mean Relative Value	Upper Relative Value
Project scope defined	0.40	1.16	1.91
Requirements complete	0.63	1.10	1.56
Design complete	0.73	1.05	1.36
Code complete	0.83	1.00	1.18
Testing complete	0.95	1.01	1.07
Project complete	1.00	1.00	1.0

The specific series of relative values for any one project isn't important, so the dots don't need to be connected as they were in Figure 21.5. What's important is the variance (the "spread") among the relative values at each milestone. You can statistically analyze the set of relative values at each milestone and compute the mean and the n-standard deviation values (where n might be between 1 and 6, depending on how confident your estimates need to be—use a higher n for increased confidence). You can then both subtract the n-standard deviations value from, and add it to, the mean value. This will give you a historically derived confidence range for each milestone. A spreadsheet that automates these calculations is available at http://www.construx.com/returnonsw/. An example table of ranges, at the two-standard deviations level of confidence, is shown in Table 21.5.

Plotted on a graph, the ranges of variation at each milestone should form a cone-shaped figure. This is your organization's cone of uncertainty. The plot for the ranges in Table 21.5 is shown in Figure 21.7.

The probability distributions shown in Figures 21.1 and 21.2 can be thought of as distributions for the same factor at different points in the life of a project. The left-hand distribution in Figure 21.2 could correspond to an estimate early in the project (near the left side of the cone of uncertainty), the distribution in Figure 21.1. could correspond to an estimate in the middle of the project, and the right-hand distribution in Figure 21.2 could correspond to an estimate late in the project (on the right side of the cone).

The shape of any software organization's cone—how wide it starts out and how quickly it narrows—will depend on the specifics of that organization. For uncertainties regarding project schedule and cost, issues such as how precisely the milestones are defined, how quickly projects are able to nail down the requirements, how stable the requirements are over the projects, how quickly the projects tend to resolve risks, and so on will all affect the size and shape of that organization's cone. An organization that develops diverse kinds of software may want to create a cone of uncertainty for each different type of project. The cone for transaction-based systems could be different from the cone for embedded real-time systems even though they are being developed in the same organization.

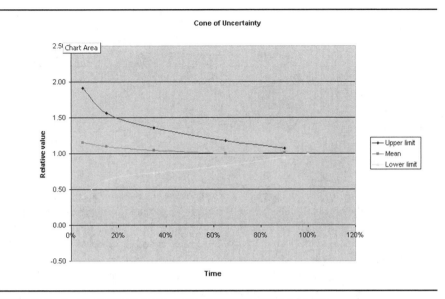

FIGURE 21.7   An organization's "cone of uncertainty" for overall schedule

Each estimated factor could have its own cone of uncertainty. You should think about collecting the data and doing the analysis for each important project estimate, such as schedule and cost. Depending on your organization's needs, you might want to create other cones for, say, cost, functionality delivered (measured in terms of something like source lines of code or function points [Garmus00]), or defects reported.

PUTTING YOUR CONE OF UNCERTAINTY TO WORK

Assuming that you have the uncertainty data for your organization, you are in a position to start using it on projects. Suppose a new project starts up and someone, using the estimation techniques presented in the next chapter, gives their 50/50 estimate that the overall schedule is 22 weeks at the "project scope defined" milestone. Recalling the data in Table 21.5, the mean relative value in this organization at the project scope defined milestone is 1.16. This means that the typical project in this organization is systemically underestimating overall project schedule at this milestone by 16%. Based on the organization's historical track record, you should increase the overall schedule estimate to 26 weeks. This will be a more accurate representation of the true 50/50 point.

Next, the lower relative value at the scope defined milestone in Table 21.5 is 0.40. This means that based on the organization's past performance, it's not impossible for this project to finish in as little as 9 weeks. There's that much uncertainty inherent in this project right now. And, because the upper relative value is 1.91, it's also not impossible for this project to take as long as 42 weeks. Again, there's that much uncertainty right now.

TABLE 21.6   Project Estimates Adjusted Using an Organization's Cone of Uncertainty

Milestone	Original Estimate	Lower Range	50/50 Point	Upper Range
Project scope defined	22	9	26	42
Requirements complete	28	18	31	44
Design complete	31	23	33	42
Code complete	30	25	30	35
Testing complete	32	30	32	34

If the overall schedule for this project is re-estimated at, say, the requirements complete milestone and the new estimate is 28 weeks, the cone of uncertainty data from Table 21.5 would allow the team to say, "Based on what we know now, this project is equally likely to take more than 31 weeks as it is to take less. And, based on our past performance, it's not unreasonable to expect that this project could take as little as 18 weeks or as long as 44 weeks." Table 21.6 shows how the estimates at each milestone in the new project can be adjusted using the organization's cone of uncertainty.

Using the adjusted estimates in Table 21.6, the project team can plot each 50/50 estimate and its uncertainty range. The graph will look something like Figure 21.8. The uncertainties start out very large and decrease over the life of the project as more becomes known.

WHAT IS A GOOD ESTIMATE?

As stated before, an estimate doesn't need to be perfect. It just needs to be "good enough." An informal definition of a good estimate is one that allows the decision maker to make the right decision. More precisely, "good" estimates can be described in terms of Figure 21.8. Given the estimate history for a project, such as the one shown in Figure 21.8, draw a horizontal line back from the actual final outcome. Figure 21.9 shows the actual outcome of 34 weeks drawn back as a dashed line.

The actual outcome is between the upper and lower uncertainty bounds for each milestone estimate. A more precise description of a good estimate is one where the actual outcome is within the uncertainty bounds for that estimate. In contrast, if the actual project schedule was 38 weeks, the "code complete" and "testing complete" milestone estimates shown in Figure 21.10 could be considered bad estimates. The actual outcome was outside of those estimates' uncertainty ranges.

The discussion in this chapter has used schedule estimates as examples. This is appropriate because software projects are more likely to be planned and managed to schedule than to cost. However, everything in this chapter applies to estimates of cost as well.

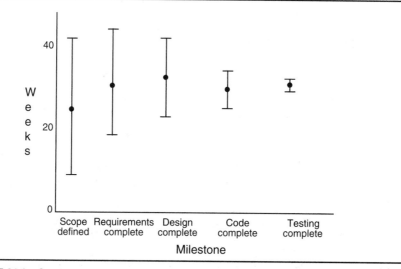

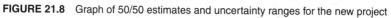

FIGURE 21.8   Graph of 50/50 estimates and uncertainty ranges for the new project

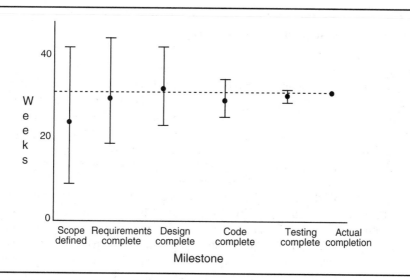

FIGURE 21.9   "Good" estimates, the actual outcome is within the uncertainty range

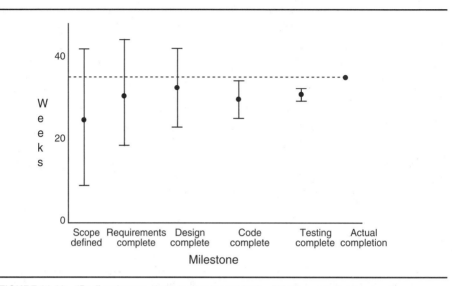

FIGURE 21.10   "Bad" estimates, the actual outcome isn't within the uncertainty range

Expressing Estimate Uncertainty

In the typical software organization it's not at all unusual for a yearlong software project to be scheduled for completion precise to a single day at the very beginning of the project. For instance, "this project will finish on 21 Jan 20xx." Think about the precision of this estimate as a percentage of the total project schedule. If finishing on 20 Jan would be considered "early" and finishing on 22 Jan would be considered "late," the "on-time" window is the 24 hours of 21 Jan 20xx. Given a yearlong project, however, even allowing time off for weekends and holidays (there are typically 260 workdays in a work year) that's a precision of less than half of one percent.

In the 500-mile drive example, an average speed of 50 miles per hour means the trip should be expected to take about 10 hours. One half percent of 10 hours is 6 minutes. Estimating a single, precise completion date on a software project one year in advance is like asking a driver to predict his arrival time to within 6 minutes for a 500-mile journey. Nobody should ever reasonably expect even an experienced long-distance driver to be able to predict that close despite the fact that the driver has significantly more control over the job (smooth roads, maps, the driver can control progress, and so forth) than a project manager has over a software project.

The uncertainties in a software project are orders of magnitude greater than the uncertainties in a 500-mile road trip. A software project might be more analogous to driving a long-distance taxi when the passenger doesn't even have a clear idea of his destination. Even with something as relatively straightforward as driving 500 miles, there's still going to be a fair degree of uncertainty. Why should anyone expect that a software project would have less uncertainty?

Because uncertainty is inherent in every estimate, we need to let others, including the project stakeholders, know what that degree of uncertainty is. Several different techniques are available and we've even already seen one. We saw how the uncertainty could be shown as a range, "the value is expected to be between this and that with a 50/50 point of this other" as in Table 21.5 and Figure 21.7. We'll look at a couple of other options.

One other way of stating uncertainties is to use a +/– ("plus-or-minus") qualifier. You would quote the 50-50 estimate, and then immediately follow it by a "plus or minus this much." The uncertainty range for the project scope complete milestone in Table 21.6 could be stated as "26 weeks plus or minus 16 weeks." The uncertainty range for the code complete milestone could be stated as "30 weeks plus or minus 5 weeks."

Accuracy and Precision in Estimates

Accuracy and precision are two very different concepts in estimation. **Accuracy** means closeness to the truth. How close is an estimate to its actual outcome? If someone estimated it would take 11 hours to drive 500 miles and it actually took 11 hours and 10 minutes, we'd probably say that the estimate was pretty accurate. If someone estimated 11 hours and the actual outcome was, say, 18 hours, then we'd probably say that the estimate wasn't very accurate. **Precision** means how finely the estimate is being expressed. Saying that the 500-mile drive would take "about 11 hours" is a lot less precise than saying it would take "11 hours, 13 minutes, and 42.7693 seconds," regardless of how long the trip actually took.

Everybody wants estimates to be both accurate and precise, but there are never any guarantees. An estimate could be accurate but not precise, such as an estimate of "about 11 hours" with an actual outcome of 11 and one quarter hours. Just as easily—or even more easily—an estimate could be precise but not accurate, such as an estimate of "11 hours, 13 minutes, and 42.7693 seconds," with an actual outcome of 18 hours, 46 minutes, and 38.6173 seconds.

Most people don't understand the difference between accuracy and precision, and using overly precise estimates can imply an unwarranted degree of accuracy. This is illustrated somewhat humorously in the following story:

A tourist was taking a narrated tour of the New York Museum of Natural History. As the group passed each fossil skeleton on display, the tour guide would give a brief description of the dinosaur and would tell how old the fossilized bones were, "Here are the bones of a Tyrannosaurus Rex. T Rex was up to 20 feet tall, 40 feet long, and weighed about 6 tons. The bones you see here are 80 million years old." On one skeleton, the sign was missing and the guide forgot to say how old it was. When the tourist asked how old the bones were the guide replied, "Oh, these are 70 million and six years old." The tourist was puzzled, "How can you know that they are exactly 70 million and six years old?" The guide replied, "Well, when I started here six years ago they told me that this one was 70 million years old."

The degree of precision being used by the tour guide is clearly implying an inappropriate degree of accuracy. The original estimate of 70 million years could easily be off by several million years all by itself.

Another form of expressing uncertainty in estimates is to use units whose implied precision is appropriate for the level of accuracy actually present. Estimating "about a year" implies much less accuracy than estimating "about four quarters," which itself implies less accuracy than "about 12 months." An estimate of "about 52 weeks" implies much less accuracy than an estimate of "about 365 days," even though all of these estimates are approximately the same magnitude. High-uncertainty estimates can be stated using coarse-grained units, and low-uncertainty estimates can be stated using finer-grained units.

It is worth pointing out that the IEEE-CS/ACM Software Engineering Code of Ethics and Professional Practices [IEEEACM99] *requires* software professionals to quote uncertainties along with their estimates:

> 3.09. Ensure realistic quantitative estimates of cost, scheduling, personnel, quality and outcomes on any project on which they work or propose to work *and provide an uncertainty assessment of these estimates*.

The Cone of Uncertainty in Light of a Fixed Schedule

On many projects, completion dates are constrained by external factors. Consumer goods such as video games need to be on store shelves by the end of September to have enough market exposure for the December holiday shopping season. Similarly, tax software in the United States isn't much use after the year's tax season is over on April 15. Agile software development projects use the concept of time-boxes, where iterations are bounded to a fixed duration; an iteration is done when its 2- to 4-week schedule runs out. Does the cone of uncertainty still apply in these projects? Yes, it just looks different. In these situations, what's certain is the completion date. What's uncertain is the specific features (or requirements) that will be included in the product by that date.

On a time-bounded project, an appropriate approach is to first list the desired features in order of highest to lowest priority. Second, create best-case and worst-case estimates for each feature. Next, starting with the highest-priority feature and working down, add up the worst-case estimates until the sum is larger than the time available for the project. These features make up the "definitely in" set. Last, do the same for the best-case estimates. Any feature that's beyond the time available is in the "definitely out" set.

Table 21.7 is the list of prioritized features for a project, along with best-case and worst-case estimates in person weeks. If we know that there are 35 person weeks available, we can confidently say that features F7, F3, and F9 will be included because the sum of their worst-case estimates is 35 person weeks. We can also confidently say that features F4 and F8 won't be included because the sum of the first eight best-case estimates is 35 person weeks. The fate of features F2, F1, F5, F6, and F10 are uncertain for now.

TABLE 21.7 Best- and Worst-Case Estimates for Prioritized Features on a Project

Priority	Feature	Best-Case Estimate	Worst-Case Estimate
1	F7	9	16
2	F3	5	9
3	F9	6	10
4	F2	1	3
5	F1	3	7
6	F5	4	8
7	F6	6	11
8	F10	2	6
9	F4	5	8
10	F8	6	10

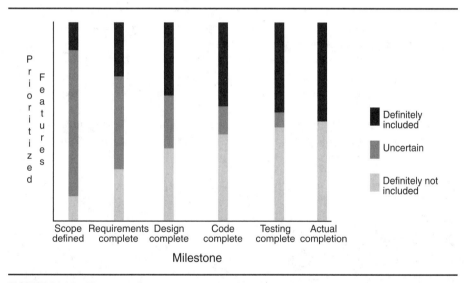

FIGURE 21.11 The cone of uncertainty in light of fixed schedule

Early in the project (or iteration), all you can say is that a few of the highest-priority features will be delivered by the completion date. Just the same, a few of the lowest priority features will definitely not be delivered. The fate of the features in the middle of the prioritized list will be uncertain. Some may make it and some may not; we just don't know which ones. Re-estimates at the subsequent milestones would focus on which of the features that were uncertain before are now certainly in, and which are certainly out. Over a whole project, the number of uncertain features will decrease, as shown in Figure 21.11.

Summary

Business decisions depend on estimates, and bad estimates can lead to bad decisions. To help you create good estimates, this chapter introduced the basic concepts of estimation. This chapter covered the following major points:

- An estimate is "an assessment of the likely quantitative result." Estimates are needed because people need to make decisions based on factors whose values can't be known until after the decision is made.
- An estimate doesn't have to be perfect. A good estimate can be defined as one that allows the decision maker to see the situation clearly enough to make the right decision.
- Estimates are inherently uncertain, and the less that is known about the situation the more uncertainty there is.
- Estimate uncertainty can be expressed using a number of different formats: plus or minus, ranges, coarse (imprecise) quantification, and so on.
- Estimates should target the 50/50 point: The estimated outcome that is equally likely to be over and under the actual outcome.
- Time is a major driver of uncertainty in a software project, and early estimates are far more uncertain than later estimates of the same project. An organization's cone of uncertainty reflects how the uncertainty inherent in a development organization changes over time.
- By collecting and analyzing data from a number of projects, an organization can quantify its cone of uncertainty and use that to objectively provide estimate uncertainties to the decision makers.

The next chapter presents the four general families of estimation techniques.

Self-Study Questions

Questions 1 through 5 relate to the following table of schedule estimates and actual completion data from a set of software projects at Mega Industries.

Milestone	A	B	C	D	E	F
Project scope defined	22	12	36	80	20	5
Requirements complete	17	15	20	68	28	5
Design complete	18	12	23	44	30	6
Code complete	20	16	19	48	28	6
Testing complete	23	16	19	50	33	7
Actual schedule	24 wks	16 mos	18 mos	48 wks	36 mos	8 mos

1. Create a table, similar to Table 21.4, which shows the relative values of the estimates at the point they were made.

2. Using the relative values from the previous question, make a table like Table 21.5 that shows the minimum, mean (average), and maximum relative values at the given milestones for Mega Industries. Note: If you can easily compute the standard deviation of the data at each milestone, use plus and minus two sigma deviations as the minimum and maximum relative values. Otherwise just use the smallest and largest values at each milestone.

3. Draw a graph of Mega Industries cone of uncertainty using the data from your answer to the previous question.

4. Given a schedule estimate of 11 months at the requirements complete milestone on Project G at Mega Industries, use the cone of uncertainty values computed in Question 2 to calculate the minimum, 50/50, and maximum estimates for this project.

5. Given a schedule estimate of 11 months at the code complete milestone on Project G at Mega Industries, use the cone of uncertainty values computed in Question 2 to calculate the minimum, 50/50, and maximum estimates for this project.

Questions 6 through 10 relate to the following table of schedule estimates and actual completion data from a set of software projects at Zymurgenics.

Milestone	P	Q	R	S	T	U
Project scope defined	22	16	22	10	8	32
Requirements complete	23	14	22	14	9	35
Design complete	23	8	20	18	11	37
Code complete	23	9	19	19	14	42
Testing complete	24	10.5	19	21	15	47
Actual schedule	24 wks	10 mos	18 mos	22 wks	14 mos	45 days

6. Create a table, similar to the one shown in Table 21.4, which shows the relative values of the estimates at the point they were made.

7. Using the relative values from the previous question, make a table (like Table 21.5) which shows the minimum, mean (average), and maximum relative values at the given milestones for Zymurgenics. Note: If you can easily compute the standard deviation of the data at each milestone, use plus and minus two sigma deviations as the minimum and maximum relative values.

8. Draw a graph of Zymurgenics' cone of uncertainty using the data from your answer to the previous question.

9. Given a schedule estimate of 36 weeks at the scope defined milestone on Project V at Zymurgenics, use the cone of uncertainty values computed in Question 7 to calculate the minimum, 50/50, and maximum estimates for this project.

10. Given a schedule estimate of 36 weeks at the design complete milestone on Project V at Zymurgenics, use the cone of uncertainty values computed in Question 7 to calculate the minimum, 50/50, and maximum estimates for this project.

11. When the schedule estimate of 10 months was made on the PQR project, the cone of uncertainty values were plus 3 months and minus 2 months. The actual schedule on the project ended up being 12 months. Should that 10-month estimate be considered a "good" estimate? Why or why not?

12. When the schedule estimate of 24 weeks was made on the DEF project, the cone of uncertainty values were plus 6 weeks and minus 3 weeks. The actual schedule on the project ended up being 31 weeks. Should the 24-week estimate be considered a "good" estimate? Why or why not?

13. The following table lists the prioritized features for the Andes project at the South American Division of Mountain Systems. Also given are best-case and worst-case estimates of the effort to develop each feature. The project has a fixed effort budget of 18 person weeks to meet a fixed schedule of 9 calendar weeks. Which of the features should we be confident will make the release, which ones should we be confident will not make the release?

Priority	Feature	Best-Case Estimate	Worst-Case Estimate
1	F6	1	2
2	F3	2	4
3	F5	1	3
4	F1	2	3
5	F8	4	6
6	F10	4	5
7	F2	2	3
8	F4	2	3
9	F9	3	4
10	F7	2	4

14. The following table lists the prioritized features for the Alps project at the European Division of Mountain Systems. Also given are best-case and worst-case estimates of the effort to develop each feature. The project has a fixed effort budget of 40 person months to meet a fixed schedule of 10 calendar months. Which of the features should we be confident will make the release, which ones should we be confident will not make the release?

Priority	Feature	Best-Case Estimate	Worst-Case Estimate
1	F3	12	16
2	F7	3	5
3	F2	4	7
4	F8	2	3
5	F5	6	9
6	F10	5	9
7	F9	3	7
8	F4	2	3
9	F1	4	6
10	F6	1	2

22

General Estimation Techniques

In software development processes, different things can be estimated: size, cost, schedule, execution time, memory usage, network bandwidth utilization, defects, product sales, and so on. This book is not a comprehensive treatise on software estimation; that topic fills an entire book all by itself. Given that this book is about business decisions, the most likely estimates of concern will be of size, cost, income, or schedule. Regardless of what is being estimated, there are four general estimation techniques: expert judgment, analogy, bottom-up, and statistical methods. Every specific estimation technique, software related or not, is based on one or a combination of these four techniques. Each of these basic techniques is described in this chapter. This chapter also explains why you should use more than one estimation technique and why you should make the assumptions behind your estimates explicit.

Expert Judgment Estimation

The simplest, but also the most inaccurate, estimation technique is expert judgment estimation. With this technique, you simply ask one or more "qualified experts" what they think the actual outcome will be. The software professional him/herself (the one carrying out the decision-making study) will probably be that expert in many cases.

As an example of expert judgment estimation, suppose you work at a company that is just getting into the business of building and installing hardware and software that automates public libraries. How do you decide how much to bid when the very first Request For Proposal (RFP) arrives, asking to automate a regional library system with 10 branches and 80,000 books? Maybe the best you can do is making an educated guess that it's as likely to be more than $2.2 million as it is to be less than that. Maybe you've got some confidence that the real outcome will be within $750k of this, but you've got nothing more than your own confidence and reputation to back it up.

Expert judgment estimation has the advantage of being usable even when none of the other techniques are. If you have no previous experience or historical data to base your estimate on, or if you don't have the time to create a bottom-up estimate, expert judgment might be your only option.

Expert judgment estimation is also useful as a "second opinion" to sanity check estimates produced by the other techniques. Suppose you were able to take the time later to develop a bottom-up estimate for the library RFP. If that estimate came out somewhere near $2.2 million, maybe in the range of $2.0 million to $2.4 million, then you'd have a lot more confidence in both the expert judgment and bottom-up estimates because they agree with each other. On the other hand, if the bottom-up estimate came out closer to $1.1 million or, possibly, as high as $4.5 million, we probably shouldn't have much confidence in either estimate because of their divergence. It's often a good idea to make different estimates of the same thing using different estimation techniques, and look for convergence or divergence of those estimates to give a hint on how much confidence you should have.

Expert judgment estimation has the disadvantage of being the most prone to bias and error. People in favor of a project will tend to give favorable estimates and people opposed to that project will tend to give unfavorable estimates. Expert judgment estimation also depends on having qualified "experts" because the credibility of the estimate is limited by the credibility of the person who produced it. If the estimator lacks credibility, any expert judgment estimate made by that estimator will be discounted, regardless of how accurate it might actually turn out to be. Asking a random person who happened to be walking down the street in front of the office would not be seen as very confidence inspiring even though by pure random chance that person may have guessed the actual outcome exactly.

Because expert judgment estimates tend to be the least accurate, it can make sense to review the estimates (as a different kind of sanity check) with one or more other people who should have some amount of expertise in the subject. Independent review is an important confidence-building step for all of the estimation techniques but is most valuable for expert judgment estimates.

If the decisions being made on the expert judgment estimate are important enough to warrant, it can make sense to have several people create independent expert judgment estimates and then meet to converge their individual estimates. Some organizations have a standard practice of choosing a nominal group estimate as two thirds of the way between the lowest and the highest individual estimates.

Nominal group estimate = (Lowest estimate + [Highest estimate – lowest estimate] * .6667)

This approach takes into account the range of estimates provided by the different estimators, and it conservatively biases the final estimate to the high side of that range.

Another approach for building consensus among multiple expert judgement estimators is the Wideband Delphi process [Boehm81].

Estimation by Analogy

A somewhat more sophisticated method that is usually more accurate than expert judgment is estimation by analogy. This method is based on the assumption that if the thing being estimated is a lot like something we already know about, we can base the estimate of the new thing on our experience with the old thing together with allowances for known differences.

Suppose you are still at the library automation company. It's now several months later. The company won the contract on the first library system and has already completed that work. Another RFP shows up for automating a different library system with 15 branch libraries and 60,000 books. Having the experience of the first project, you might now know that it actually cost $1 million in hardware and $1 million in software configuration to automate the first library system. You know that you'll have to adjust the hardware costs up by some amount to account for the new customer's additional branches. You increase it by, say, 50% for an additional half million dollars. You also know that you'll have to adjust the software configuration costs down to address the fact that there are 25% fewer books. So you decrease that part by, say, 25% or $250,000. Based on your experience with the first library system, you now have good reason to expect that the second library system would cost about $2.25 million. That's estimation by analogy.

Of course we're assuming that there aren't any other major differences that would influence the cost. If there were, you'd need to be sure to account for them, too. Notice how the by-analogy estimate will often incorporate expert judgment estimates for the impacts of the individual differences. How do we know that 50% more branches lead to 50% higher hardware costs? How do we know that the software configuration costs are a function of only the number of books? Because you may not have any solid data to back up the lower-level estimates, they may very well end up being expert judgment estimates.

The steps in estimation by analogy are as follows:

1. Understand the new project. Become familiar enough with it that you can find one or more analogous projects. You did that when you decided the first library automation system was a valid basis for estimating the second.

2. Get the detailed results of the analogy project(s). In the library automation example, you got the results from the analogy when you found the actual $1 million hardware and $1 million software configuration costs from the first library project. Be sure to use the *actual* results for the analogy project(s). As little as six months after an analogy project finishes, people will tend to remember the original estimates for that project rather than the actual results. If an analogy project was originally estimated to take six months and cost $100,000 but actually took nine months and cost $150,000, then as little as six months after completing that project people will tend to use six months and $100,000 as the analogy data rather than using the nine months and $150,000 actual result. This would, of course, improperly bias the estimate.

3. Compare the new project to the analogy project(s) at the finest level of detail practical and make a list of the differences. Things that the analogy project had but the new one doesn't will cause the estimate to be adjusted downward, while things the new project has but the old one didn't will cause the estimate to be adjusted upward. You did this in the second library estimate when you decided that the increase in the number of branch offices should drive the hardware cost up, while the decrease in the number of books would drive the software configuration costs down.

4. Estimate the impact of each difference. Use whatever means are appropriate, expert judgement, analogy, etc. to come up with estimates for the impact of each of the differences. You did this for the second library system when you estimated the hardware costs would increase by 50% and the software configuration costs would decrease by 25%.

5. Build up the estimate for the new project based on the *actual results* of the analogy project plus the differences. Add the estimates for the appears-only-in-the-new-project differences and subtract the estimates for the appears-only-in-the-analogy differences. The result is the overall estimate that you were trying to come up with. This was done on the second library system estimate when you added up the total, leading to the $2.25 million estimate.

Because this approach is more complex than expert judgment estimation, let's go through another example:

1. Assume that we're trying to estimate the size, schedule, and cost for a software development project that will build the control software for a factory floor cell controller. In studying this project suppose we find that the cell controller will include drivers for five different automated workstations. Also assume that this same organization has already developed software for a different cell controller that drove three different workstations.

2. The actual results for the earlier project were that it was 18,000 source lines of code, took four people nine months to complete, and cost $600,000.

3. Assuming that there will be no code reuse between the two projects (i.e., both are new development projects, otherwise we'd have to account for the reuse as another difference), the differences are that the analogy had three workstations that aren't in the new project whereas the new project drives five different workstations that weren't in the old project. Assume that the cell controller logic is similar in size, schedule, and cost for both projects. We will have to subtract out the effects of the three original workstation drivers and add back in the effects of the five new workstation drivers.

4. Further investigation of the analogy project shows that the workstation drivers averaged 1,500 source lines of code each and that they were all close to the same size (i.e., 1,500 source lines of code is a reasonable estimate for the new workstation drivers).

5. The size for the new project should be about 21,000 SLOC (18,000 – 4,5000 + 7,500). Based on this, the new project is about 17% bigger than the analogy project. Using the same staffing level as the analogy project (four people), we need to add about 17% to the schedule and the cost making 10.5 months (9 months * 1.17) and $702,000 ($600,000 * 1.17).

The advantage of estimation by analogy is that it tends to produce more accurate results than expert judgment and it is still relatively quick and easy to do. On the disadvantage side, it not only requires past experience with a similar project—the analogy—it also requires good record keeping. If there isn't an analogous project, or good records don't exist, it's much harder to create accurate by-analogy estimates. Remember to use the actual results from the analogy project, not the original estimates.

Bottom-Up Estimation

Bottom-up estimation is a fairly popular approach and is known by many different names including module build-up, by-engineering procedures, top-down, decomposition, and several others. Developing cash-flow streams using a work breakdown structure (WBS), as described in Chapter 3 and Appendix A, is an application of this estimation technique.

Let's step back in time at the library automation company, to when the first RFP was received. Suppose that the CEO didn't quite trust the expert judgment estimate and wanted to have an estimate that she could have more confidence in. In this case, it could be worthwhile to break the proposed system down into the individual components and then sum up estimates of the costs of those components. For instance, if each branch required a central communications server and some number of client computers plus some network hardware, then you could total up the hardware bill by library branch. You might be overestimating the hardware costs at one branch, but you should be just as likely to underestimate the hardware costs in another. Similarly, you may overestimate the costs for software configuration in one branch but underestimate the software configuration costs in another. The inaccuracies in the lowest-level estimates will tend to cancel each other out over the entire bottom-up estimate.

This approach to estimation is based on a statistical property called **the law of large numbers**. The law of large numbers says that the sum of the errors in low-level estimates tends to be less than the error in a single estimate of the whole. Suppose that the person doing the estimates in question may be off by as much as 30% on any one estimate. This means a single estimate of the whole could be off by as much as 30%. When the whole is broken up into parts and each part is estimated, however, any low-level estimate should be as likely to be high by as much as 30% as it is to be low by 30%. In the long run, the overestimates at the lower level will tend to cancel out the underestimates leading to a more accurate estimate of the whole.

By totaling up the hardware and software configuration costs at each branch, we may come up with an overall cost estimate of, say, $2 million.

There aren't any hard-and-fast guidelines on how finely the thing being estimated should be decomposed. Generally speaking, the finer the decomposition, the better the estimate because of the law of large numbers. On the other hand, this needs to be balanced with the effort required to make the breakdown and create the estimates of the smaller pieces. As well, don't decompose beyond your level of knowledge; if you're not sure how an item should be decomposed or the decomposition won't make the higher-level item's estimate more accurate, don't bother decomposing it.

The steps in bottom-up estimation are as follows:

1. Start with a detailed breakdown of the thing being estimated. If you are trying to estimate product size (for example, SLOC), it would be good to start with the design for the system. If you were trying to estimate cost and/or schedule for an entire software project, it would be reasonable to start with the WBS, as described in Appendix A. Either way, you need something that breaks the whole into parts. You did this in the library system estimate when you looked at the overall system on a branch-by-branch basis.

2. Estimate each bottom-level component in the detailed breakdown. Estimate the size of each module in the design or estimate the individual cost and schedule for each task in the WBS. These lower-level estimates can be developed using any method, expert judgement, analogy, or bottom-up (if it can be even further decomposed). This was done when you estimated the branch office-level costs.

3. Build up the overall estimate by summing up through the intermediate levels of the breakdown until the overall total is reached. You did this in the library system when you totaled the costs for all the branches into the overall total.

4. As an optional step, if the bottom level estimates don't include adjustments for system-wide factors, those factors need to be addressed in here. For instance, a project that is trying to estimate cost and schedule by rolling up the cost and schedule estimates for each module in the detailed design needs to include the cost and

schedule impacts for project management, quality assurance activities, documentation, etc. These will need to be addressed, possibly by applying an overall adjustment factor. The library system may have assumed no system-wide costs, but the overall network costs and central, library-wide servers might need to be factored in for that system.

As another example of a bottom-up estimate, consider the following:

1. Consider estimating a project's size and schedule from its object-oriented design if that design has 125 classes.

2. The estimates for the size and schedule to develop each individual class are made by whatever means appropriate: expert judgment, analogy, bottom-up, and so forth.

3. The overall estimate is built up by summing the class-level cost and schedule estimates. Assume that the overall total in this case is 100k SLOC and 18 calendar months with a staff of 30 people (a total of 540 person months of effort).

4. Assuming that the bottom-level estimates don't include project management, quality assurance activities, documentation, etc., these can be factored in by applying an appropriate "overhead rate" of somewhere between 10% and 40%. If we assume this overhead rate to be 20%, the total effort is 648 person months, which could be, for example, a 22-month schedule with a staff of 30 people.

The main advantage of the bottom-up estimation is that the law of large numbers will tend to lead to more accurate estimates than a single overall estimate (such as a single expert judgment or by-analogy estimate of the whole project).

The disadvantages of bottom-up estimation are as follows:

- It can't be used until the detailed breakdown is complete and accurate. If parts of the whole are missing, then obviously the sum of the estimates of those parts will be low. If the breakdown is inaccurate, the lower-level estimates aren't an accurate reflection of the higher-level estimate. This means that bottom-up estimation may not be a practical approach very early in a project.
- Systemic biases in the low-level estimates will be compounded and can lead to large errors in the total estimate. If the estimator(s) consistently underestimates by 10%, for instance, the total estimate will be low by more than 10%. Just the same, if the estimator consistently overestimates by 15%, the total estimate will be high by more than 15%.
- It can be easy to overlook project- or system-wide factors (planning, project management, documentation, testing, rework in a software project). You need to be careful to explicitly account for these; otherwise the estimate will come out on the low side.

- The effort to create and roll up the detailed estimates may make other methods more attractive. It can take a lot of time and effort to create the estimates for each individual piece. With 125 classes in an object-oriented design, you need 125 separate cost and schedule estimates for those classes. This could take a fair amount of time and effort all by itself.

Estimation by Statistical Methods

The last estimation technique, statistical methods, is really a family of estimation techniques. This family is generally the most sophisticated, will usually be the most accurate, and (from an end user perspective, surprisingly enough) the easiest to use. Recalling that estimates are made to support decisions, statistical estimation methods are based on having an equation that relates something that is countable at decision time to the factor that the decision is being based on. Cocomo-II [Boehm00], for instance, takes lines of code to be written as input and outputs project effort and schedule. A specific method's equation is typically derived from historical data, i.e., completed software projects. This family of techniques is sometimes called "parametric estimation."

Statistical estimations are described here from two perspectives: the end user's (the actual estimator) and the formula developer's (those who gather the historical data and derive the equations). Because the end user's view is simpler and far more common, we'll start there.

USING A STATISTICAL METHODS APPROACH

From the end user's perspective a statistical estimation method looks like an equation. The estimator just enters the values for the relevant factors describing the situation at hand and runs through the math. As a simple example, the cost of building a new house (not including the cost of the land or any extras such as landscaping, swimming pool, or spa) can be calculated from the area of the house in square feet. Residential building contractors in a geographic area will have a historically derived factor for relating area to cost. The equation looks like this:

Approximate building cost = Area in square feet * Cost per square foot

In an area where the cost per square foot is $95, a 2,000-square-foot house can be expected to cost close to $190,000. I had a custom house built, and the actual cost was only 2.5% over the statistically estimated cost. Most of that difference was due to a single change order, Corian countertops in the kitchen, which were not included in the original estimate.

Let's jump back to the library automation company, but now imagine it is several years down the road. Suppose that the company has been diligent at tracking and recording actual costs over several projects. Suppose further that equations have been derived from the historical data, as follows:

Approximate hardware cost = $84,000 + (Number of branch offices * $92,000)

Approximate software cost = $121,000 + (Number of books [in thousands] * $10,400)

Approximate total cost = Approximate hardware cost + Approximate software cost

Any time a new RFP shows up, estimating the cost is next to trivial. Just take the number of branch offices and plug that into the first equation. Plug the number of books into the second equation and run the math. A 12-office, 120,000-book library system should cost about $2,557,000.

After the formula has been derived, using it to create estimates is fairly easy. The effort involved in coming up with those equations is a different story, however.

DEVELOPING A STATISTICAL METHODS ESTIMATION MODEL

The steps in developing a statistical method estimation formula are as follows:

1. Identify the observable factor(s) that drive the resulting estimate. In the house construction example, it was the number of square feet in the proposed residence. In the library automation example, two factors were the number of branch libraries and the number of books.

2. Gather as many valid historical data points as possible, being certain that the data is complete and consistent. Each data point needs to have all the quantified factors as well as the actual end result. The building contractors are basing their estimate on a number of actual house construction projects. The library automation company would base its equations on a history of some number of actual library automation projects.

3. Derive a functional relationship between the factor(s) and the observed results. This step can be simple or complex, depending on how straightforward the proposed relationship is. The house example is a simple linear equation; cost goes up as a constant factor times the number of square feet. Based on a history of building houses, the contractor calculates that the conversion rate is $95 per square foot. The library automation example is modeled by the sum of two separate linear equations.

4. Optionally, after the equation is derived, go back and verify that the equation is a good predictor by analyzing its ability to match the historical data. This step can be very complex and involve some heavy-duty statistical analysis. The proposed equation may not, after all, be a very good predictor. It may not have enough factors in it or it may have the wrong factors. If some houses actually cost $45 per square foot, whereas others actually cost $175 per square foot, the simple equation is not really capturing the reality of house construction. By comparing the predictions to the actual results in the historical data, you can see how good a predictor the equation is.

Remaining with the house-price example, consider the following:

1. Start with the observation that the house construction cost is largely driven by the square footage.

2. Get the square footage and construction cost data for as many houses as is reasonable. Be as certain as you can that the data is complete and consistent. The historic house prices shouldn't include land prices or other significant extras such as landscaping, swimming pools, spas, or Corian countertops.

3. Assume that there is a linear relationship (in this case, Cost = K * Area) between square footage and cost. Using the available data points, do the math to solve for that linear relationship (the value of K), ending up with an average of K = $95 per square foot.

4. Optionally, go back and verify that the typical house in the historical data actually fits this equation. Using the equation, how far off might the actual be?

Several statistical estimation models for estimating software projects already exist, including the following

- Cocomo-II [Boehm00]
- Price-S [Price]
- Putnam [Putnam92]
- SEER-SEM [Galorath]
- SLIM [QSM]

The advantages of statistical estimation methods are as follows:

- They can be the most accurate because they're based on historical data.
- They can be quick and easy to use once the functional relationship has been derived.
- They can be as sophisticated as needed.
- They can be self-tuning. The functional relationship can be modified or recalibrated as more data become available, and the predictions can get better and better with each revision of the model.

The disadvantages of statistical method estimations are as follows:

- They require an adequate base of historical data. The more complex the equation (the more input variables it has), the more data is required to derive the relationship. When the functional relationship is based on n input variables, you need at least n historical data points.
- Significant effort along with mathematical and statistical knowledge may be required to derive and verify the functional relationship. This isn't necessarily Ph.D.-level math, but it's not always typical high school math, either.
- The final equation(s) will be sensitive to the quantity, accuracy (consistent accounting practices across all of the historical data), and relevance of the historical data. If you've misidentified the shape of the equation and/or there has been inconsistent accounting in the historical data (say, some of the historical house prices included the cost of the land while others didn't), the final answers won't be as accurate as they could be.
- People may be putting too much faith in a model that hasn't been validated. Just because the estimation model looks like a formal mathematical equation doesn't guarantee that the resulting estimates will be accurate. You should be putting faith only in validated statistical estimation models.

Estimating by Multiple Methods

An organization with good estimation techniques doesn't depend on one single estimation method. The sophisticated organization uses several estimation methods throughout the project. There are two reasons for using different methods. One reason is that the different methods will be used to "sanity check" the others, as described above. The other reason is that the preferred method can change over the life of the project; different methods typically perform better in the different phases of a project. Both of these reasons are described here in more detail.

We already talked earlier about how expert judgment can be used to "sanity check" estimates arrived at by the other methods. This same idea can be generalized: it's a good idea—especially when an estimate is being used for critical decisions—to estimate the same thing using multiple methods. Again, look for convergence or divergence among the different estimates. The more the estimates converge around a small range, the higher degree of confidence you should have in the estimates. The more the estimates diverge, the lower confidence you should have. As a former math teacher of mine used to say, "When you have two different answers to a question that has only one right answer, you can be sure that at least one of those answers is wrong."

TABLE 22.1 Summary of Preferred Estimation Technique by Software Project Phase

	Very Early (Prerequirements)	**Early (To Requirements Complete)**	**Middle (To Design Complete)**	**Late (To Code Complete)**
Expert judgment	Likely to be the only choice	Used at the detailed level	Likely used at the detailed level	Likely used at the detailed level
Analogy	Preferred, if possible	Likely	Likely used at the detailed level	Likely used at the detailed level
Bottom-Up	Unlikely	Maybe, based on WBS	Preferred	Preferred
Statistical	Preferred where possible	Preferred where possible	Likely used at the detailed level	Likely used at the detailed level, plus defect rework estimates or reliability models

The only warning on estimating by multiple methods is that when the same thing is being re-estimated by the same person, be sure that the estimation technique requiring the most judgment is done first. If the same person is producing a by-analogy and a statistical methods estimate for the same project, the by-analogy estimate should be developed first so that it is not unduly biased by the statistical methods estimate.

The preferred technique for estimating overall cost and schedule may very well change throughout the life of the typical plan-based (i.e., nonagile) software project. This is summarized in Table 22.1.

Very early in the typical software project (in the prerequirements phases), not much is known about the work that needs to be done. Maybe there is a list of customer-desired features but probably not much more than that. So it's unlikely that you will have enough information to be able to create a bottom-up estimate. You might not have a usable statistical method, but if you do it would probably be the best choice. A by-analogy estimate is preferred over an expert judgment estimate, but this is possible only when you have a suitable analogy. This early in the typical project, expert judgment may very well be the only reasonable estimation method.

When the requirements effort is underway, you should be rapidly learning much more about the product and the project. Up to the point where the requirements are complete, statistical estimates are preferred but would not be possible if your organization doesn't have an adequate base of relevant historical data. You may be able to do a bottom-up estimate based on the project's work breakdown structure (WBS, see Appendix A) if one is available. If one or more analogy projects are available, use them if you can. Even if expert judgment is not the primary technique, it will probably still be used during these phases to produce the bottom level estimates that feed into both by-analogy and bottom-up estimates.

When the requirements are complete and the design is underway, the preferred method will probably shift to a bottom-up method. Until now, there probably wasn't enough detailed knowledge about what was being built or how it would be built to carry out a bottom-up estimate. By now, you probably do have enough information, so this will become the preferred technique. The other techniques may be used to produce the detailed estimates that feed into the bottom-up estimate.

The situation is pretty much the same through the final stages of software construction; you have enough detail that bottom-up estimates will be preferred, and the other estimation techniques will probably be producing the detailed estimates that feed into the bottom-up estimate. If you have been tracking the effort to repair the defects found on the project so far, you can use this historical data to derive an estimate of defect rework remaining by multiplying the average effort to repair by the number of defects still needing repair. According to Kaner et al [Kaner93, page 89]

> Throughout the last third of the project, the [defect tracking] system provides an independent reality check on the project's status and schedule.

Project planners rarely include the effort and schedule impacts of defect rework in the project plan. However, that rework is present on every software project and can be as much as 30% to 80% of the total project effort [Wheeler96]. If your software project plan doesn't address defect rework and the cost and schedule are already aggressive, having lots of unrepaired defects in the defect tracking system will point out the truth that the project simply cannot finish on time or on budget.

Another possibility during the late stages of a project is to base the decision of when to release the software on "reliability models." Reliability models are statistical estimations of the likely mean time between failure (MTBF) for the product based on its MTBF in the test environment. Several reliability models are described in, for example, Ortiz [Ortiz92], Musa [Musa98]. The Centre for Software Reliability at City University, London (http://www.csr.city.ac.uk/papers/index.html) has an extensive list of publications available on the Internet.

Make Assumptions Explicit

It's almost impossible to make an estimate without making one or more significant assumptions, and those assumptions can have a noticeable effect on the final estimate. All too often, those assumptions aren't made explicit so others who review the estimate or use it to make important decisions aren't aware of the underlying assumptions. Whenever possible, you should make your assumptions explicit and tie them to the estimate itself. It's okay to say, for example, the following:

> I estimate that the Framus project will cost between $0.8 and $1 million and take between 7 and 10 months.

However, it would be much better for you to say this:

> I estimate that the Framus project will cost between $0.8 and $1 million and take between 7 and 10 months, but this assumes that the control algorithms aren't more complex than expected and that the project is staffed according to Ron's projections.

Making your assumptions explicit will allow the consumer of your estimate to assess its validity based on whether they agree with your assumptions.

Summary

This chapter described the four general families of estimation techniques:

- Expert judgment estimation involves having someone—with some level of trust and credibility—give his or her best assessment.
- Estimation by analogy creates an estimate for a new situation by using the actual outcome for one or more known, past situations together with an accounting of the differences.
- Bottom-up estimation divides the thing being estimated into smaller parts and builds up the estimate of that whole from the sum of the estimates of the parts. This technique is based on the law of large numbers; inaccuracies in the bottom-level estimates will tend to cancel each other out and give a more accurate estimate than a single estimate of the whole.
- Statistical estimation uses parametric equations that have been mathematically derived from a number of relevant historical data points.

Convergence or divergence among the estimates of a single thing can indicate how much trust should be put into those estimates: The more convergence there is, the more the estimates can be trusted.

The preferred estimation technique(s) will probably need to change over the life of a software project. Don't count on a single estimation technique being able to give appropriate estimates across the whole project.

Any assumptions that an estimate is based on should be made explicit so that the decision maker(s) can decide whether they agree with those assumptions.

The next chapter shows several techniques for allowing for inaccuracy in estimates.

Self-Study Questions

1. Suppose that the library automation software company described in this chapter receives a new RFP asking about automating a 6-branch, 95,000 book library system. Using the formulas in the section on statistical methods estimation:
   a. What is the approximate hardware cost to automate this library system?
   b. What is the approximate software cost?
   c. What is the approximate total cost?

2. Terry is a software developer on the Mondo project at MegaSoft. Terry has been asked by Pat, the project manager, to estimate how many lines of code will be needed for the user interface. Terry remembers that the user interface for the Giganta project was about 37,500 lines of code. Based on that, Terry thinks that the user interface for the Mondo project will be about 42,000 lines of code because there are more screens and reports to develop. Which general estimation technique is Terry using in this situation?

3. Jack is another software developer on the Mondo project. The project manager asked Jack to estimate how many lines of code will be needed for the business logic. Jack estimates it will take 30,000 lines of code, but he has nothing other than his intuition to base it on. Which general estimation technique is Jack using in this situation?

4. Pat, the project manager on the Mondo project, takes Jack's estimate of the lines of code for the business logic and adds it to Terry's estimate for the user interface as well as line-of-code estimates for several shared-services components from other developers. Pat's estimated size for the Mondo project is 95,000 lines of code. Which general estimation technique is Pat using in this situation?

5. Pat has data from three recent MegaSoft development projects:
   - The Giganta project was 115,000 lines of code and took 27 person years to develop.
   - The Olympic project was 68,000 lines of code and took 14 person years to develop.
   - The Megalith project was 152,000 lines of code and took 34 person years to develop.
   What is the average lines of code per person month at MegaSoft?

6. How many person years should Pat expect for the Mondo project?

7. Which general estimation technique is Pat using in Questions 5 and 6?

23

Allowing for Inaccuracy in Estimates

It's quite likely, and in fact expected, that an estimate and its actual outcome will differ. It's all part of what it means to be an estimate. If the actual outcome will differ, then it could be different enough to change how the decision should have been made. If a decision to develop a new software product was based on estimated sales and the actual sales turned out to be a lot lower than estimated, the actual sales could conceivably be low enough that the product loses a lot of money. If it were known beforehand how low the sales would actually be, the organization would have decided to not develop the product in the first place. So how do you allow for the fact that the estimate and the actual result will differ?

This chapter shows several methods, both ineffective and effective, that allow for inaccuracy in estimates. Two fairly common approaches turn out not to be very effective:

- Increasing the MARR
- Shortening the planning horizon

Three less-common approaches are far more effective:

- Considering ranges of estimates
- Using sensitivity analysis
- Delaying final decisions

Each of these approaches is explained in this chapter. Statistically based approaches—decisions under risk and decisions under uncertainty—are explained in the next two chapters.

Knowledge Drives Estimation Accuracy

The most significant driver of estimation accuracy is, simply, knowledge. The more that's known about the factor being estimated, the more accurate that estimate is likely to be. When an organization has a lot of solid historical data about that factor, fairly accurate estimates can be produced (for example, using estimation by statistical methods as discussed in Chapter 22). Because of this, and the fact that historical data are usually fairly inexpensive to collect, it's a good idea to collect your own historical data for use in future decision analyses. With good historical data, business decisions can be made with a much higher degree of confidence (lower uncertainty).

Most organizations don't have historical data, and don't seem to be in any rush to collect it either. But the business decisions still need to be made, even though those decisions will be based on estimates that might be fairly inaccurate. The actual outcome may, and in fact probably will, be significantly different from the estimate on which the original decision was based. The approaches in this chapter are nonprobabilistic, meaning they aren't based on any statistical techniques. The probabilistic techniques are explained in the next two chapters.

Allowing for Inaccuracy in Estimates

The more knowledge the estimator has, the better the estimate. And the better the estimate, the less allowance needs to be made for inaccuracy. However, allowances for inaccuracy don't make up for a lack of knowledge. The allowances, at best, only reduce the consequences of inaccurate estimates. And these allowances come at a cost.

Miss Jones manages a small shop that sells and services computer hardware for the small businesses in her city. Miss Jones is bidding on a Request For Proposal (RFP) from a local business. The RFP calls for hardware and labor that will cost about $40,000. Miss Jones isn't completely certain that her proposed hardware will meet the customer's requirements and, because the RFP asks for a fixed-price bid, she decides to include a 10% contingency to cover the possibility she may need more hardware than proposed. Her cost base needs to be moved up to $44,000 to cover the contingency. If her store's policy is a 12% profit margin, her final asking price will be $49,280. Miss Jones now runs a higher risk of losing the bid because of the higher asking price and her time and effort to create the bid might be wasted. Her allowance for the uncertainty could conceivably end up costing her this job. You need to consider the cost associated with making allowances for errors.

Allowing for Inaccuracy Using Conservative Decision Criteria

A common—but potentially ineffective—strategy to allow for uncertainties is to use more conservative decision criteria. This includes increasing the MARR for more uncertain alternatives, shortening the study period, or requiring a shorter payback period. People tend to assume that if the alternative is still desirable in spite of the more conservative decision criteria, the alternative should still be desirable at the normal criteria even if one or more of the uncertain estimates turns out less favorable than hoped. The "padding" in the conservative decision criteria is expected to be an allowance for inaccuracy in the estimates. Unfortunately this strategy doesn't always work.

ALLOWING FOR INACCURACY BY INCREASING THE MARR

One common approach is to use a higher value for the MARR. Referring back to Figure 8.2 in Chapter 8, as the interest rate increases, the PW(i) of a cash-flow stream will usually decrease. The idea behind this approach is to penalize a more uncertain project by using a higher-than-typical MARR. The assumption is that if the proposal is acceptable at the higher MARR, it should also still be acceptable at the normal MARR even if one or more of the estimates come out less favorably than expected.

Consider the case of Ninkasa Software, a mythical company that develops and sells inventory management software. Ninkasa has identified two potential projects but only has the resources to carry out one of them. The projects, known simply as Project P1 and Project P2, have the estimated cash-flow streams shown in Table 23.1.

TABLE 23.1 Estimated Cash-Flow Streams for Two Projects

End of Year	Project P1	Project P2
0	–$100,000	–$100,000
1	$75,000	$13,000
2	$37,500	$37,500
3	$0	$75,000
4	$37,500	$37,500

Ninkasa has established a **risk-free** MARR of 10%. The term *risk-free* is somewhat misleading in that it doesn't really mean zero risk. It just means that the risk is not so significant that it needs to be explicitly addressed in the decision analysis. The risk in this case comes from inaccuracy in the estimate(s); the actual outcome may turn out less favorably than anticipated.

Using the risk-free MARR, the PW(i) of Project P1 is as follows:

$$\text{PW}(10) = -\$100,000 + \$75,000 \underset{P/F,10,1}{(0.9091)} + \$37,500 \underset{P/F,10,2}{(0.8265)} +$$

$$\$0 \underset{P/F,10,3}{(0.7513)} + \$37,500 \underset{P/F,10,4}{(0.6830)} = \$24,787$$

For Project P2, the PW(i) is as follows:

$$\text{PW}(10) = -\$100,000 + \$13,017 \underset{P/F,10,1}{(0.9091)} + \$37,500 \underset{P/F,10,2}{(0.8265)} +$$

$$\$75,000 \underset{P/F,10,3}{(0.7513)} + \$37,500 \underset{P/F,10,4}{(0.6830)} = \$24,787$$

At the risk-free MARR, both projects have the same PW(i). From this perspective, neither project is better than the other.

Suppose that both projects are far more uncertain than typical, and Project P1 is thought to be even more uncertain than Project P2. All other things being equal, Project P2 would be the safer choice because of the smaller uncertainties involved.

Ninkasa decides, on the basis of the respective uncertainties, that Project P2 will be held to a risk-adjusted MARR of 17%, whereas Project P1 will be held to a risk-adjusted MARR of 20% because of its higher uncertainty.

The PW(20%) of Project P1 is as follows:

$$PW(20) = -\$100,000 + \$75,000 \,\overset{P/F,20,1}{(0.8333)} + \$37,500 \,\overset{P/F,20,2}{(0.6944)} +$$

$$\$0 \,\overset{P/F,20,3}{(0.5787)} + \$37,500 \,\overset{P/F,20,4}{(0.4822)} = \$6626$$

The PW(17%) of Project P2 is as follows:

$$PW(17) = -\$100,000 + \$13,017 \,\overset{P/F,17,1}{(0.8547)} + \$37,500 \,\overset{P/F,17,2}{(0.7305)} +$$

$$\$75,000 \,\overset{P/F,17,3}{(0.6244)} + \$37,500 \,\overset{P/F,17,4}{(0.5337)} = \$5360$$

Notice the contradiction: At the risk-free MARR, both projects are financially equivalent, so the lower degree of uncertainty of Project P2 makes it the better choice. Even when Project P1 is given a higher risk-adjusted MARR than Project P2, when both projects are evaluated at their respective risk-adjusted MARRs the recommended choice appears to be Project P1. The intent of using a risk-adjusted MARR is to penalize the more uncertain alternative and make it appear less economically attractive, but exactly the opposite happened in this example. Don't count on a risk-adjusted MARR to properly address inaccuracy.

A related issue is that service alternatives (i.e., cost-only projects as described in Chapter 11) are made to seem even more desirable. (They have a less negative PW(i) as the risk-adjusted MARR is increased.) Again, the less-uncertain alternative is being penalized, not the more uncertain one as was actually intended. At extremely high interest rates, the alternative with the smallest initial investment will always end up being favored regardless of the later cash-flow pattern.

ALLOWING FOR INACCURACY BY SHORTENING THE PLANNING HORIZON

Another common but ineffective approach is to shorten the planning horizon (see Chapter 11). The cash-flow diagram for Mr. Kinkaid's adventure (Figure 8.1 in Chapter 8) is fairly typical in business decision analysis: There is an initial investment followed by profit later on. The strategy in this case is that by shortening the study period by, say, 25%, the cash-flow instances that are being ignored typically represent pure profit. If the proposal is profitable without that later profit, it's assumed that the proposal will still be reasonably profitable over its full lifespan even if one or more of the estimates turn out less favorable than anticipated.

Suppose that Ninkasa Software decides to shorten the planning horizon instead of using a risk-adjusted MARR. In this case, they decide to cut the study short by 25%. This will cause them to ignore the cash-flow instances in the last year of both proposals.

Using the risk-free MARR, the PW(i) of the first 75% of Project P1 is as follows:

$$\text{PW}(10) = -\$100,000 + \$75,000 \overset{P/F,10,1}{(0.9091)} +$$

$$\$37,500 \overset{P/F,10,2}{(0.8265)} + \$0 \overset{P/F,10,3}{(0.7513)} = -\$826$$

The PW(i) of the first 75% of Project P2 is as follows:

$$\text{PW}(10) = -\$100,000 + \$13,017 \overset{P/F,10,1}{(0.9091)} +$$

$$\$37,500 \overset{P/F,10,2}{(0.8265)} + \$75,000 \overset{P/F,10,3}{(0.7513)} = -\$826$$

In both cases the PW(i) is negative, so neither project would be selected. Requiring a shorter discounted payback period (Chapter 8) can also be shown to lead to inappropriate decisions.

Using conservative selection criteria increases the chances of a favorable result if the actual outcome is equal to or better than the estimates. However, conservative selection criteria don't guarantee that inaccurate estimates will still lead to profitable results. The assumed margin of safety is not necessarily there.

TABLE 23.2   Estimates for the Main Cost Drivers in the Zymurgenics Project

Initial investment	$100,000
Operating and maintenance (per month)	$1000
Development staff cost (per month)	$10,000
Development project duration	10 months

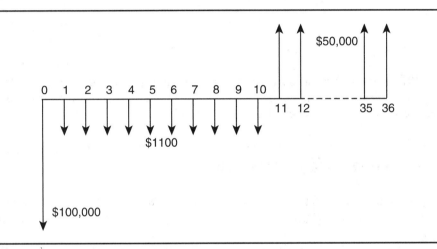

FIGURE 23.1   The cash-flow diagram for the Zymurgenics project

More Effective Strategies

More effective strategies for dealing with uncertainties in estimates include the following:

- Considering ranges of estimates
- Sensitivity analysis
- Delaying final decisions

These strategies are explained using the following case study.

Zymurgenics is a mythical company that makes process control hardware and software for breweries and wineries. Zymurgenics has identified a potential business opportunity; they discovered that a certain government regulation is set to expire in exactly 36 months. Between now and then, if they can develop a special software application they should be able to bring in $50,000 per month in net profit. Zymurgenics expects that the components listed in Table 23.2 are the main drivers of the project's cost. Estimates for each component are also shown.

The cash-flow diagram for the Zymurgenics project is shown in Figure 23.1.
Zymurgenics has established a MARR of 8%. Based on these estimates, the PW(8)
is as follows:

PW(8) = –$100,000 +

expenses

P/A,8,10
((–$1000 + –$10,000) * (6.7101)) +

P/A,8,26   P/F,8,10
($50,000 * (10.8100)) * (0.4632) = $76,545
Income

The IRR of this cash flow stream is 10.35%. It sounds like a worthwhile investment as long
as the estimates are accurate. Suppose, however, Zymurgenics suspects that there could be
significant inaccuracy in these estimates. Does it still make sense to do this project?

Considering Ranges of Estimates

A more rational approach to addressing inaccuracy in estimates is to consider a range of
estimated values. The estimator is asked to create three separate estimates for each factor:

- **A "most-favorable" estimate**—The most-desirable value the estimated factor
  can reasonably be expected to have. It's not the absolute most desirable value;
  it's just the best one that has a reasonable chance of coming true. Estimators
  sometimes assume this to be the value with a 1 in 20 (or 5%) chance of being
  exceeded.
- **A "fair" estimate**—This is the estimate that appears most reasonable given
  careful analysis of the situation. This estimate is assumed to be the 50/50 break-
  even, the actual outcome should be equally likely to be higher than this as it is to
  be lower than this.
- **A "least-favorable" estimate**—The most undesirable value an estimated factor
  can reasonably be expected to have. Again, it's not the very worst that could
  happen. Estimators sometimes assume this to be the value with a 19 in 20 (or
  95%) chance of being exceeded.

TABLE 23.3 Considering Least- and Most-Favorable Estimates

	Least-Favorable Estimate	Fair Estimate	Most-Favorable Estimate
Initial investment	$125,000	$100,000	$90,000
Operating and maintenance	$1500	$1000	$800
Development staff	$14,000	$10,000	$7000
Development project duration	15 months	10 months	7 months
Income	$30,000	$50,000	$70,000
PW(8)	−$162,941	$76,545	$325,148

Zymurgenics expects the monthly operating and maintenance costs to be $1000 per month, but they might also decide that the most-favorable estimate is $800 and the least-favorable estimate is $1500. This means the estimator has a high degree of confidence that the actual outcome will be no worse than the least-favorable estimate, $1500, and no better than the most-favorable estimate, $800.

The most- and least-favorable estimates should not be calculated by just multiplying the fair estimate by some factors, unless those factors are based on reliable historical data such as the organization's cone of uncertainty (see Chapter 21). History has shown, for example, that software projects tend to overrun their schedules by an average of 63% [Standish01a] and up to as much as 400% [Lawlis95]. On the other hand, related research shows that it's virtually impossible for a software project to underrun its nominal schedule by any more than about 30% [Simons91]. Simply choosing 50% and 150% of a project's estimated schedule as the most- and least-favorable estimates, respectively, does not reflect reality.

After considering the ranges, Zymurgenics' estimates are shown in Table 23.3. The table also shows the PW(8) of the project if each of these estimates actually came true.

Using the least- and most-favorable estimates brings out much more information about the situation. Instead of just seeing the single fair-estimate outcome the decision maker can see what amounts to best-case and worst-case scenarios. Keep in mind that the best- and worst-case outcomes might be somewhat misleading because they assume that all the input estimates are at their least- or most-favorable value at the same time. The chances of that happening in practice should be fairly remote.

TABLE 23.4 Sensitivity of i to Uncertainty in F

F	Percent Change in F	i%	Percent Change in i
$1600	−20	8.15	−33.5
$1700	−15	9.25	−24.5
$1800	−10	10.29	−16.0
$1900	−5	11.29	−7.8
$2000	0	12.25	0
$2100	5	13.16	7.4
$2200	10	14.04	14.2
$2300	15	14.89	21.6
$2400	20	15.71	28.2

Sensitivity Analysis

Considering estimate ranges is better than using conservative selection criteria, but there is an even better technique. **Sensitivity analysis** allows the decision maker to understand the full range of possible impacts of inaccuracy. The term *sensitivity* refers to the relationship between the relative change in an estimated factor and the resulting desirability of the alternative. More precisely, if the estimate for a factor is off by some given percentage, does the value of the alternative change a little bit or a lot? Sensitivity analysis shows how much inaccuracies in an estimate would impact the final decision. A moderate change in some factor could have a relatively small impact on desirability, whereas a small change in some other factor could have a large impact. When the various sensitivities are known, the estimator can be careful to get a better estimate for the more sensitive factor(s) and not worry so much about factors with less sensitivity.

SENSITIVITY ANALYSIS FOR A SINGLE ESTIMATE

Assume that an investment of $1000 today is expected to return $2000 after 6 years. The expected rate of return is as follows:

$$i = \sqrt[n]{\frac{F}{P}} - 1 = \sqrt[6]{\frac{\$2000}{\$1000}} - 1 = 12.25\%$$

If the actual return is more or less than $2000, then, clearly, the rate of return will be more or less than 12.25%. Table 23.4 shows how different percent changes between the estimated and actual outcomes for F lead to corresponding percentage changes in the value of i. This is the essence of sensitivity analysis for a single estimate.

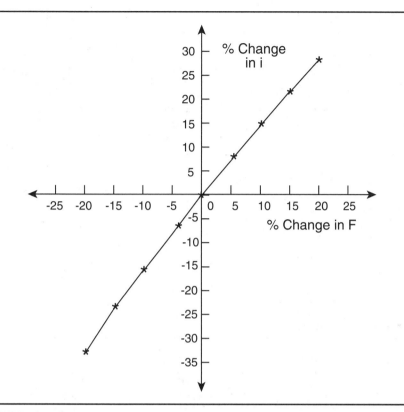

FIGURE 23.2   Sensitivity analysis for a single estimate

If F ends up being $1600 (20% less than $2000), i will be 8.15% (33.5% less than the expected 12.25% IRR). In this example, internal rate of return is very sensitive to changes in F, with slightly more sensitivity to underestimates. Figure 23.2 shows a graph of the sensitivity of i to F given fixed P and n.

SENSITIVITY ANALYSIS FOR A SINGLE ALTERNATIVE WITH MULTIPLE ESTIMATES

To find the sensitivities for multiple estimates in a single alternative, vary just one estimate at a time and hold all the other estimates at their respective most-likely values. Using the Zymurgenics proposal, Table 23.5 shows how the desirability of that proposal changes if everything else is held constant and only the initial investment is varied over its expected least- to most-favorable range.

TABLE 23.5 Sensitivity of the Zymurgenics Proposal to Uncertainty in Initial Investment

Initial Investment	% Change in Initial Investment	PW(8)	% Change in PW(8)
$90,000	−10%	$86,545	13.06%
$95,000	−5%	$81,545	6.53%
$100,000	0%	$76,545	0%
$105,000	5%	$71,545	−6.53%
$110,000	10%	$66,545	−13.06%
$115,000	15%	$61,545	−19.60%
$120,000	20%	$56,545	−26.13%
$125,000	25%	$51,545	−32.66%

TABLE 23.6 Sensitivity of the Zymurgenics Proposal to Uncertainty in Operating and Maintenance Cost

Operation and Maintenance	% Change in Operation and Maintenance	PW(8)	% Change in PW(8)
$800	−20%	$77,551	1.75%
$900	−10%	$77,216	0.88%
$1000	0%	$76,545	0%
$1100	10%	$75,874	−0.88%
$1200	20%	$75,203	−1.75%
$1300	30%	$74,532	−2.63%
$1400	40%	$73,861	−3.51%
$1500	50%	$73,190	−4.38

Table 23.6 shows how the desirability of the proposal changes if everything else is held constant and only the operating and maintenance cost is varied over its expected least- to most-favorable range.

Table 23.7 shows how the desirability of the proposal changes if everything else is held constant and only the development staff cost is varied over its expected least- to most-favorable range.

TABLE 23.7   Sensitivity of the Zymurgenics Proposal to Uncertainty in Development Staff Cost

Development Staff	% Change in Development Staff	PW(8)	% Change in PW(8)
$7000	–30%	$96,675	26.30%
$8000	–20%	$89,965	17.53%
$9000	–10%	$83,255	8.77%
$10,000	0%	$76,545	0%
$11,000	10%	$69,835	–8.77%
$12,000	20%	$63,125	–17.53%
$13,000	30%	$56,414	–26.30%
$14,000	40%	$49,704	–35.06%

TABLE 23.8   Sensitivity of the Zymurgenics Proposal to Uncertainty in Development Duration

Development Duration	% Change in Development Duration	PW(8)	% Change in PW(8)
7 months	–30%	$168,271	119.83%
8 months	–20%	$135,315	76.78%
9 months	–10%	$104,799	36.91%
10 months	0%	$76,545	0%
11 months	10%	$50,383	–34.18%
12 months	20%	$26,159	–65.83%
13 months	30%	$3729	–95.13%
14 months	40%	–$17,039	–122.26%
15 months	50%	–$36,269	–147.38%

Table 23.8 shows how the desirability of the proposal changes if everything else is held constant and only the development duration is varied over its expected least- to most-favorable range.

Table 23.9 shows how the desirability of the proposal changes if everything else is held constant and only the income is varied over its expected least- to most-favorable range.

TABLE 23.9 Sensitivity of the Zymurgenics Proposal to Uncertainty in Income

Income	% Change in Income	PW(8)	% Change in PW(8)
$30,000	−40%	−23,598	−130.83%
$40,000	−20%	26,474	−65.41%
$50,000	0%	76,545	0%
$60,000	20%	126,616	65.41%
$70,000	40%	176,687	130.83%

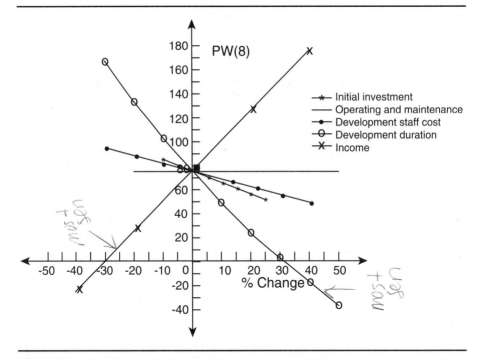

FIGURE 23.3 Sensitivity analysis for multiple estimates in the Zymurgenics proposal

Figure 23.3 shows how the desirability of the Zymurgenics proposal changes as a percentage of change in each of the individual estimates. Each curve represents the sensitivity of one of the estimates. The graph shows how the sensitivities of the individual estimates compare to each other.

Estimates that have relatively flat sensitivity curves, such as operating and maintenance cost in this example, are insensitive to change; the estimator shouldn't worry about these because even if the actual outcome is significantly different from the most-likely value, it won't impact the desirability of the proposal very much. Estimates that

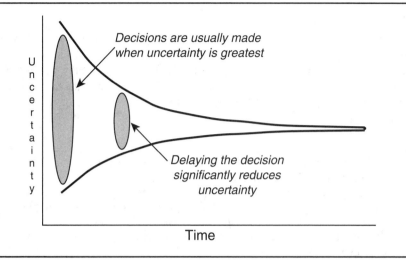

Decisions are usually made
when uncertainty is greatest

U
n
c
e
r
t
a
i
n
t
y

Delaying the decision
significantly reduces
uncertainty

Time

FIGURE 23.4   Delaying the final decision significantly reduces uncertainty

have relatively steep curves are sensitive to change, such as income and development duration. The estimator should be more careful to make sure these estimates are accurate. Based on sensitivity analysis, Zymurgenics may want to consider doing a market survey to more accurately assess income and also study the project in more detail to get a better understanding of development duration. Sensitivity analysis can also, if the proposed activity is carried out, be used to focus management on the more important drivers. The more sensitive the factor, the more it should be actively monitored and controlled.

Delay Final Decisions

The accuracy of estimates is almost always inversely proportional to the amount of time between the estimate and the event. The more time between "How much will the project cost?" and "The project ended up actually costing this much," the more uncertainty there will be in the cost estimate. This is exactly the message of the cone of uncertainty (Chapter 21)—the earlier in the project, the less accurate the estimates will be.

Also remember that estimates are created so that decisions can be made. One very effective way to address uncertainty is to simply delay making the final decision. Wait until more is known about the situation and the uncertainty will go down. This is illustrated in Figure 23.4. Most software organizations make the full commitment to projects at the very beginning: when the uncertainties are the greatest. Just delaying the final project "run-to-completion" decision could significantly reduce the uncertainties in the cost estimate.

A practical way to apply this approach on software projects is called "two-phase acquisition." The organization first commits only to carrying out an investigation phase for the project. The investigation phase typically involves developing the basic product requirements along with investigational prototyping and focused analysis to reduce high-risk aspects of the project. The project plan is also created. At the end of the investigation phase, the organization has a much clearer idea of the product itself and what it's likely going to take to build it. Only then will the organization decide to either continue full development or to cancel it.

> Many people would probably consider a project that got cancelled at the end of the investigation phase to be a "failed" project. In fact, exactly the opposite is true—the project was a resounding success. The project was cancelled as soon as people realized that it wasn't such a good idea after all (which was definitely not apparent at the beginning) and not much time and money were spent figuring that out. More importantly, as little time and money as possible were spent after it was known that the project wasn't a good investment.

Another practical application is "planning checkpoint reviews" [McConnell98]. A planning checkpoint review is a reexamination of a software project's business case (and other project specifics, much like a general feasibility study) at about the 20% progress point. At this point in the project, uncertainties are significantly less and the business case is much more definite.

Other practical applications include prototyping, leasing instead of buying, and agile development life cycles. Prototyping is essentially "buying information"; the value of the information learned from the prototype should be worth more than the investment to develop the prototype. By leasing, the organization isn't committing to owning something for its full useful life—it's much easier to get rid of leased goods than owned goods. Agile development life cycles allow the customer to cancel the project at the end of any iteration yet still have business value from the functionality developed in the iterations completed so far.

This strategy of delaying the final decision is essentially a choice to incur somewhat higher costs in the short term to reserve the right to make a major decision when the situation is clearer. In some cases it really doesn't cost anything to delay the decision, but usually it does. The two-phase acquisition approach comes with all of the investigation phase costs. Certainly, if the decision can be delayed for free, it is in the organization's best interest to do just that. Even if a decision can't be delayed for free, however, the additional expense might be well worth the privilege of deferring the decision. The cost of the flexibility to cancel a project at the end of an investigation phase is probably a lot less than the money that would likely be wasted if a dead-end project were committed to up front. There's more on this topic in the section "The Expected Value of Perfect Information" in Chapter 24.

Summary

This chapter showed several different methods, both ineffective and effective, to allow for inaccuracy in estimates. Two fairly common approaches, increasing the MARR and shortening the planning horizon, are not always effective. Both of these methods assume that safety is achieved by using more conservative decision criteria, thereby penalizing the more uncertain alternative. This chapter showed that, in fact, the assumed margin of safety isn't always there.

Three less common approaches are far more effective:

- A more rational approach to addressing inaccuracy in estimates is to consider a range of estimated values. The estimator is asked to create three separate estimates for each factor: optimistic, most likely, and pessimistic. Instead of just seeing the single fair-estimate outcome, the decision maker can also see what amounts to best-case and worst-case scenarios.
- Sensitivity analysis allows the decision maker to understand the full range of effects of inaccuracy. Sensitivity analysis shows how much inaccuracies in an estimate would impact the final decision. When the various sensitivities are known, the estimator can be careful to get a better estimate for the more sensitive factor(s) and not worry so much about factors with less sensitivity.
- The accuracy of estimates is almost always inversely proportional to the amount of time between the estimate and the event. Just waiting until more is known about the situation causes the uncertainty to go down. Delaying the final decision is a choice to incur possibly higher costs in the short term to reserve the right to make a major decision when the situation is clearer.

The next chapter explains how to address estimate uncertainty using statistical approaches.

Self-Study Questions

Questions 1 through 4 relate to the following pair of proposed projects at Mega Industries.

End of Year	Project P1	Project P2
0	−$100,000	−$100,000
1	$11,000	$72,000
2	$19,000	$42,000
3	$31,000	$6000
4	$42,000	$6000
5	$48,500	$4500

1. Evaluate the PW(i) of both projects using Mega Industries' risk-free MARR of 8%. Does one of the projects appear significantly better than the other?

2. Suppose that Mega Industries knows that Project P1 is somewhat riskier than normal and they also know that Project P2 is significantly riskier than Project P1. In light of their evaluations at the risk-free MARR, does one of the projects seem preferable to the other?

3. Suppose that Mega Industries decides to use a risk-adjusted MARR of 12% for Project P1 and a risk-adjusted MARR of 16% for Project P2. Evaluate both projects at their respective risk-adjusted MARR; does one appear preferable to the other? Compare this answer to your answer to Question 2—does there appear to be a contradiction? Explain.

4. Suppose that Mega Industries decides to shorten the planning horizon from 5 years to 4 years. Evaluate both projects using the shorter planning horizon; does one project appear preferable to the other? Compare this answer to your answer to Question 2—does there appear to be a contradiction? Explain.

Questions 5 through 9 relate to the following situation. A study group at Tropical Pets, Inc. has been investigating the proposed Guppy project. The table below shows the group's least-favorable, fair, and most-favorable estimates for different aspects of the project.

	Least-Favorable Estimate	Fair Estimate	Most-Favorable Estimate
Equipment cost	$13,000	$10,000	$7,000
Development duration	10 months	5 months	4 months
Income	$15,000	$30,000	$45,000

The project has a development cost per month of $40,000 and a 24-month total duration (regardless of the duration of the development phase); if the development phase runs longer than expected it will shorten the income cash-flow stream. Tropical Pets uses a MARR of 8%.

5. Calculate the PW(i) for the least-, fair-, and most-favorable cases.

6. The study group thinks that the equipment cost could vary by as much as plus or minus 30%. Complete the following table to show the sensitivity of the Guppy project to variation in equipment cost.

Equipment Cost	% Change in Equipment Cost	PW(8)	% Change in PW(8)
$7000	−30%		
$8000	−20%		
$9000	−10%		
$10,000	0%		
$11,000	10%		
$12,000	20%		
$13,000	30%		

7. The study group thinks that the development duration could vary by as much as minus 20% to plus 100%. Complete the following table to show the sensitivity of the Guppy project to variation in development duration.

Development Duration (Months)	% Change in Development Duration	PW(8)	% Change in PW(8)
4	−20%		
5	0%		
6	20%		
7	40%		
8	60%		
9	80%		
10	100%		

8. The study group thinks that the income per month could vary by as much as plus or minus 50%. Complete the following table to show the sensitivity of the Guppy project to variation in income.

Income per Month	% Change in Income per Month	PW(8)	% Change in PW(8)
$15,000	–50%		
$20,000	–33%		
$25,000	–17%		
$30,000	0%		
$35,000	17%		
$40,000	33%		
$45,000	50%		

9. Draw a graph of the sensitivities calculated in Questions 6, 7, and 8. Which factor has the highest sensitivity? Which factor has the lowest sensitivity? What should be done about it?

24

Decision Making
Under Risk

Sometimes an organization knows, through past experience or some other means, what the probabilities of different estimates for the same alternative are. This is the case, for instance, when you know that the odds of winning $1 million in a lottery are 1 in 2.5 million, the odds of winning $10,000 are 1 in 52,000, the odds of winning $100 are 1 in 453, and so on. This chapter shows how to incorporate these probabilities into a decision analysis. When probabilities can't (or won't) be assigned to the possible outcomes, use the decision making under uncertainty techniques in Chapter 25. The following topics are covered in this chapter:

- Expected value decision making
- Expectation variance and decision making
- Monte Carlo analysis
- Decision trees
- Expected value of perfect information

TABLE 24.1 The Possible Outcomes and Probabilities for the Sierra Project

	Least-Favorable Outcome	Fair Outcome	Most-Favorable Outcome
AE(MARR)	–$3149	$1436	$5762
Probability of outcome	15%	60%	25%

Expected Value Decision Making

Expected value is a useful technique for addressing risk in business decisions. Expected value is based on the idea that the overall value of an alternative with multiple possible outcomes can be thought of as the average of the random individual outcomes (PW(i), FW(i), or AE(i)) that would occur if that alternative were repeated a large number of times.

To illustrate, suppose that Table 24.1 shows the AE(i), evaluated at the MARR, for the least-favorable, fair, and most-favorable outcomes for the proposed Sierra project at the Western Division of Mountain Systems, Inc. The probabilities of each of those outcomes are also shown.

Imagine being able to set up 1,000 parallel experiments where the Sierra project could be run that many times all at the same time. Given the probabilities, we should expect that the most-favorable outcome would happen in 25% or 250 of those experiments. The fair outcome would happen in 600 of them, and the least-favorable outcome would happen in 150.

The AE(i) income that would be generated from the 250 experiments that ended in the most-favorable outcome would be 250 * $5762, or $1,440,500. The 600 experiments ending in the fair outcome would generate 600 * $1436 or $861,600. The 150 experiments ending in the least-favorable outcome would lose a total of 150 * $3149 or $472,350. The AE(i) total income generated by all 1,000 parallel experiments would be as follows:

$1,440,500
  $861,600
 –$472,350
$1,829,750

The average AE(i) income generated in a single experiment would then be $1,829,750/1,000 or $1829.75.

TABLE 24.2 Mountain Systems Alternative Projects and Their Possible Outcomes

Alternative	Least-Favorable Outcome (15%)	Fair Outcome (60%)	Most-Favorable Outcome (25%)
Sierra	–$3149	$1436	$5762
Cascade	–$276	$1398	$3233
Olympic	–$2605	–$568	$4567

TABLE 24.3 Calculating the Expected Value of Each Alternative Project

Alternative	Calculation	Expected Value
Sierra	0.15* $3149 + 0.60 * $1436 + 0.25 * $5762	$1829.75
Cascade	0.15* –$276 + 0.60 * $1398 + 0.25 * $3233	$1605.65
Olympic	0.15 * –$2605 + 0.60 * –$568 + 0.25 * $4567	$410.20

Notice that $1829.75 is also equal to (0.25 * $5762) + (0.60 * $1436) + (0.15 * –$3149). The expected value from a set of outcomes and probabilities can be calculated by summing the value of each possible outcome times the probability of that outcome. When calculating an expected value, be sure that all possible outcomes are included; the sum of the probabilities needs to equal 1.0. The expected value, in AE(i) terms, of the Sierra project is $1829.75.

$$ExpectedValue = \sum_{i=1}^{n} (Value_i * Probability_i)$$

The expected value technique can be used to help decide between multiple alternatives. What if Mountain Systems Western Division has to choose between three projects knowing that they only have resources for one of them? The proposed projects and their possible outcomes in AE(i) terms are shown in Table 24.2.

The expected value of each of Mountain System's alternatives is calculated in Table 24.3.

All other things being equal, Mountain Systems should choose the Sierra project because it has the highest expected value among all the alternatives under consideration.

Expectation Variance in Decision Making

In the Mountain Systems Western Division example, basing the decision on expected value alone was sufficient because the probabilities for each of the outcomes were the same for each of the alternatives. However, this isn't always the case, and the differing probabilities could themselves influence the decision. Suppose that the Eastern Division of Mountain Systems needs to choose between two of their own alternatives, the Berkshire project and the Pocono project. They know that they don't have the resources to do both.

TABLE 24.4 Outcomes, Probabilities, and Values for the Berkshire Project

Outcome	Probability	PW(i)
Least favorable	45%	−$5,866,000
Nominal	10%	$121,000
Most favorable	45%	$7,698,000

TABLE 24.5 Outcomes, Probabilities, and Values for the Pocono Project

Outcome	Probability	PW(i)
Least favorable	10%	−$320,000
Low nominal	20%	$98,000
High nominal	30%	$314,000
Most favorable	40%	$1,108,000

The details of the Berkshire project are shown in Table 24.4. In PW(i) terms, its expected value is $837,000.

Table 24.5 shows the details of the Pocono project. Its expected value is $525,000.

Considering the expected values alone it would seem that the Berkshire project is the better choice because its expected value is much higher. Notice from the probabilities, however, that it's basically a win-big or lose-big proposition; there's little middle ground. Either the most-favorable or least-favorable outcome will probably happen. The Pocono project, on the other hand, is much more conservative. It doesn't win big, but neither is it likely to lose big.

It might be better for Mountain Systems to go with the Pocono project because it has a much lower probability of losing money (only 10%), or it might be better to go with the Berkshire project because of the higher expected AE(i). The decision maker will have to make a judgement call in assessing the relative importance of the probability of losing money against the higher expected value. Intuitively, when economic times are lean, the Pocono project would probably be preferred because there isn't much money around to be risking. In more favorable economic times, the Berkshire project might be preferred because the possible loss would probably be easier to absorb if it actually happened.

TABLE 24.6   Estimates for the Zymurgenics Project

	Least-Favorable Estimate	Fair Estimate	Most-Favorable Estimate
Initial investment	$125,000	$100,000	$90,000
Operating and maintenance	$1500	$1000	$800
Development staff	$14,000	$10,000	$7000
Development project duration	15 months	10 months	7 months
Income	$30,000	$50,000	$70,000

Monte Carlo Analysis

The name Monte Carlo refers to the famous gambling resort in Monaco. The Monte Carlo analysis technique uses randomly generated combinations of the input variables (estimated factors) and runs them through the cost function to calculate the result under those conditions—much like "rolling the dice" at the casinos in Monte Carlo. This is repeated a large number of times, and then the statistical distribution of the outcomes is analyzed. To do this successfully, the statistical distribution (mean and variance, see Appendix E) of the estimates being input need to be known. Consider the Zymurgenics project from the previous chapter. The estimates are copied in Table 24.6.

Suppose we could establish, either through experiment or analysis, that income has a uniform distribution—any value in the range $30,000 to $70,000 is equally likely. Similarly, suppose that the development project duration has a normal distribution with the mean at 10 months and a standard deviation of 1 month, and so on. Given the probability distributions for each of these five estimates, we can use a tool (or write a program) to generate random sets of the five estimated values, one value from each of the distributions. Assuming the distributions are independent, one potential set might be as follows:

Initial investment = $98,316
Operating and maintenance = $1287
Development staff = $10,993
Duration = 11 months
Income = $56,821

TABLE 24.7 Monte Carlo Simulation Results for the Zymurgenics Project

Income Range	Number of Occurrences
–$75,000 to –$50,001	3
–$50,000 to –$25,001	32
–$25,000 to –$1	76
$0 to $24,999	258
$25,000 to $49,999	655
$50,000 to $74,999	921
$75,000 to $99,999	1,044
$100,000 to $124,999	865
$125,000 to $149,999	586
$150,000 to $174,999	329
$175,000 to $199,999	159
$200,000 to $224,999	53
$225,000 to $249,990	17
$250,000 to $274,999	5

This set of estimates can be run through the alternative's PW(i) function:

PW(8) = –Initial investment +

((–Operating and maintenance + –Development staff) * (P/A,8,duration)) +

(Income * (P/A,8,36 – Duration)) * (P/F,8,duration)

For this set of estimates, the function gives PW(8) = $74,157. If this cycle of generating random sets of estimates and running them through the cost function is repeated, say, 1,000 times or more, the set of resulting PWs can be analyzed. Table 24.7 shows the results of running a Monte Carlo simulation of the Zymurgenics project with 5,000 samples.

In this simulation run, the minimum PW(8) was –$65,382, the maximum PW(8) was $258,783, and the average was $78,001. A graph of the results is shown in Figure 24.1.

Analyzing the distribution of the results can tell us important things about the project. For instance, the number of samples that had negative outcomes (PW(8) < $0) was only 3 + 32 + 76 = 111 out of the total 5,000 samples. According to this simulation, the project has only a 2.2% chance of losing money (PW(8) < $0) and a 97.8% chance of making money for Zymurgenics.

Monte Carlo analysis is also at the heart of the free Construx Estimate tool available at http://www.construx.com. This tool is based on the Putnam statistical estimation model [Putnam92], which estimates effort and schedule for a software project using three input parameters:

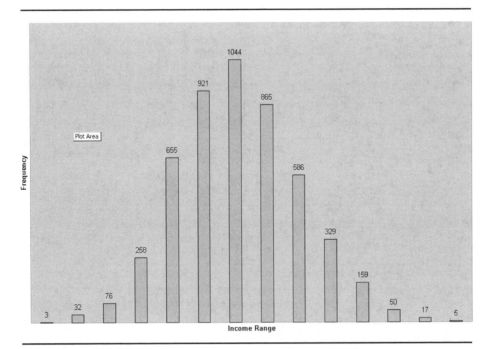

FIGURE 24.1 Monte Carlo simulation results for the Zymurgenics project

- **Size**—The estimated number of source lines of code to be developed.
- **Manpower buildup parameter**—A number describing the rate at which additional people can be brought into a project and become effective contributors. Manpower buildup is constrained by both the local labor pool and how effective the early team members are at partitioning the system into work items that can be passed out to other, later team members.
- **Process productivity parameter**—A number describing the efficiency of the organization's software process.

Size is input by the user while the manpower buildup parameter and process productivity parameter are either determined from the organization's historical data or from industry data. The tool applies predefined distributions around these median values; it has a built-in cone of uncertainty (see Chapter 21) for varying the range of the size input based on the development phase the project is in. Early phases lead to wide ranges for size, and later project phases use much smaller ranges.

The Construx estimate tool runs a Monte Carlo simulation of 500 iterations (user selectable) in which each of the iterations uses a randomly generated value from the distribution of each of the three inputs. The computed effort and schedule outputs for each of the iterations are saved for analysis. Figure 24.2 shows the output for a 20,000-line-of-code Java project that has finished the requirements phase. This example uses industry calibration data for shrink-wrapped/packaged software.

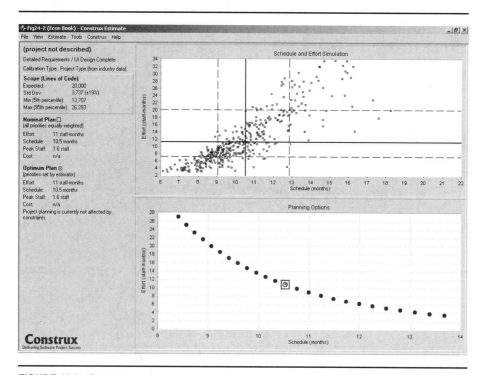

FIGURE 24.2 Distribution of schedule and effort results from a Monte Carlo simulation

Each dot in the Schedule and Effort Simulation graph in the upper-right part of Figure 24.2 corresponds to one iteration: a calculated schedule on the X-axis and a calculated effort on the Y-axis given a trio of randomly generated size, manpower buildup, and process productivity values. The "best-case" iteration corresponds to a calculated schedule of about 6 calendar months and 3.5 staff months of effort. This result was driven from randomly generating a size, manpower buildup, and process productivity from the optimistic sides of their distributions all at the same time. The worst-case iteration for schedule has a calculated schedule of about 18 calendar months with a calculated effort of 19 staff months. The worst-case iteration for effort is about 32 staff months and has a computed schedule of just under 16 calendar months.

The tool calculates the project's 50/50 schedule and 50/50 effort from the median of the data points in the graph and shows this by the dark solid vertical (for schedule) and horizontal (for effort) lines. According to the Monte Carlo simulation, the schedule is as likely to overrun as it is to underrun 10.5 calendar months. Half of the randomly generated scenarios had schedules greater than 10.5, months and the other half had schedules less than 10.5 months. The project appears to be equally likely to overrun and underrun 11 staff months of effort. The estimate tool also calculates twenty-fifth and seventy-fifth percentile results (the dashed lines) for both schedule and effort. This project has an even chance of taking between 9 and 13 calendar months and between 6 and 20 staff months.

In a sense, Monte Carlo analysis is a kind of sensitivity analysis (see Chapter 23) that uses a large number of randomly selected inputs to show the overall effect on the outcomes. Instead of seeing the sensitivity of each individual input, Monte Carlo analysis just shows the composite sensitivity of the entire function across the probability distributions of the inputs.

Decision Trees

A decision tree maps out the possible results when there are sequences of decisions together with a set of future random events that have known probabilities. Decision trees are useful when there are a number of possible future states and decisions can be made in stages. As an example, Mountain Systems Eastern Division can decide to do the Berkshire project first, the Pocono project first, or neither project at all. Based on the outcome of their first choice, they could later decide to do the remaining project or nothing. A decision tree will help them figure out the best first choice.

Decision trees are built from three basic building blocks: decision nodes, chance nodes, and arcs.

- Decision nodes represent points in time where the decision maker makes a decision. Decisions such as whether to carry out a certain project, or which features to include, are examples of decisions that are under the control of the organization. Decision nodes are shown as squares in the decision tree diagram.
- Chance nodes represent points in time where the outcome is outside the control of the decision maker. Either someone outside the organization's control will make that decision or it is a random outcome that isn't under anyone's control. The government passing laws that affect the organization and the market deciding it does or doesn't like the product are examples of chance nodes. Chance nodes are shown as circles.
- The various nodes in the diagram will be time ordered: The marketplace can't decide whether it likes the product until the organization first decides to develop it. Arcs show the time ordering of the various nodes. The diagram is usually drawn from left to right (earlier nodes are to the left of later nodes) but a top-down (earlier nodes are higher than later nodes) layout can also be used. Make sure that all arcs out of a given node are mutually exclusive; only one of them can be taken. Also make sure that all possible outcomes from each node are represented as outgoing arcs; the decision tree needs to cover all known possibilities.

Figure 24.3 shows a sample decision tree. The leftmost (root) node represents an organizational decision: to scrap an existing legacy system and redevelop it, enhance the legacy system, or do nothing with the system. Given that the system is redeveloped, demand on the system will either increase, remain stable, or decrease, and this demand

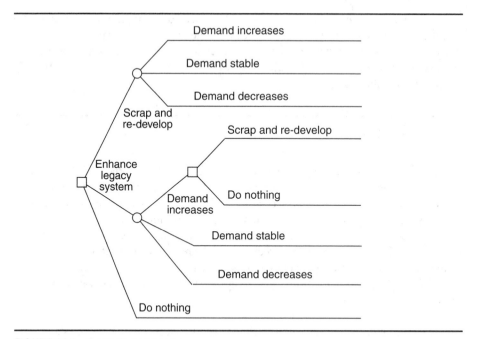

FIGURE 24.3 A sample decision tree

can't be controlled by the organization. If the choice is made to enhance the legacy system instead of redeveloping it, demand will still either increase, stay stable, or decrease beyond control of the organization. Only if demand increases will the organization consider a new choice either to scrap and redevelop the enhanced system or to continue using the as-enhanced system. If they choose to do nothing, it does not matter whether demand changes or stays stable.

Suppose that Mountain Systems Eastern Division wants to analyze its possibilities given that it has resources to do only one project at a time and each project will take a year to complete. They can choose to do either the Berkshire project first or the Pocono project first. Or they could choose to do neither project. They've also decided that they will only do the second project if the first project is highly profitable. If the Berkshire project is done first, the most-favorable outcome needs to occur in order to go on to the Pocono project. If the Pocono project is done first, one of the two most-favorable outcomes needs to occur in order to do the Berkshire project. If they decide to do neither project in the first year, they will not do either project in the second year. The decision tree is shown in Figure 24.4.

Given the decision tree for a situation, the first step in analyzing it is to add in the financial consequences associated with each arc. For each arc, describe its consequences in terms of PW(i), FW(i), or AE(i). Don't use IRR, DPP(i), or benefit/cost because these require incremental analysis (as described in Chapters 10 and 18). Be careful to use consistent expressions of financial consequences: don't mix PW(i) with AE(i) in the same decision tree because the arithmetic will tend to get done wrong.

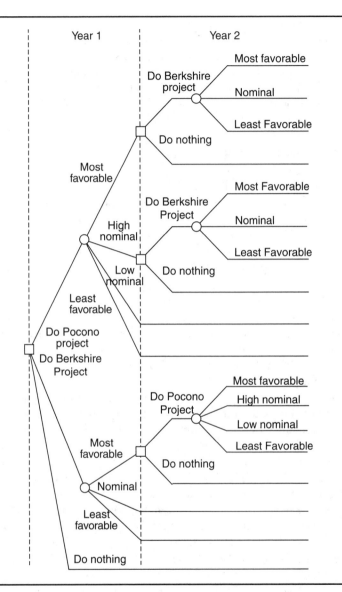

Year 1   Year 2

Most favorable

Do Berkshire
project
Nominal

Least Favorable

Do nothing

Most
favorable

Most Favorable

Do Berkshire
Project
Nominal

High
nominal
Least Favorable

Low
nominal   Do nothing

Least
favorable

Do Pocono
project

Do Berkshire
Project

Most favorable

Do Pocono
Project
High nominal

Low nominal

Least Favorable

Most
favorable
Do nothing

Nominal

Least
favorable

Do nothing

FIGURE 24.4   Decision tree for Mountain Systems Eastern Division

Properly adjust the financial consequences for the time periods as required. In the Mountain Systems example, all second-year values need to be multiplied by the present-worth factor (P/F,8%,1) to put them into beginning-of-year-1 terms. If appropriate, be consistent in the use of real dollars or actual dollars when the analysis needs to address inflation (see Chapter 13). The same holds for pre-tax and post-tax analysis if income taxes are being addressed (see Chapter 16).

The second step in decision tree analysis is to sum the financial consequences from the root node to all leaf nodes. Write the sum of the values on that path at the end of that corresponding path in the decision tree. In the Mountain Systems Eastern Division decision tree, if the Pocono project is done first and has its most-favorable outcome, and then the Berkshire project is done and has its most-favorable outcome, the PW(i) of the final value will be as follows:

$$P/F, 8, 1$$
$$\$1108k + \$7698k * (0.9259) = \$8236k$$

If the Berkshire project is done first and has its most-favorable outcome, and then the Pocono project is done and has its least-favorable outcome, the PW(i) of the final value will be as follows:

$$P/F, 8, 1$$
$$\$7698k - \$320k * (0.9259) = \$7402k$$

The results of these first two steps are shown for the Mountain Systems Eastern Division decision tree in Figure 24.5.

The third step is to write down the probabilities for each arc out of each chance node. Note that the probabilities out of any given chance node must always add up to 1.0. You may need to use the conditional probability formula (Appendix E) to help calculate some of the probabilities.

After the probabilities have been entered for each arc out of each chance node, the fourth step is to roll back the values from the leaf nodes to the root. Starting with the nodes farthest from the root node and working backward, for each node:

- If the node is a chance node, *calculate* the expected value at that node based on the values on all nodes to its right. In the Mountain Systems Eastern Division example the upper-right chance node corresponds to knowing that the Pocono project had the most-favorable outcome and the Berkshire project was selected. The expected value at this chance node is this:

   $$\$8236k * 0.45 + \$1220k * 0.10 - \$4323k * 0.45 = \$1883k$$

- If the node is a decision node, *select* the maximum profit (or minimum cost) from the nodes to its right. In the Mountain Systems example the topmost decision node corresponds to knowing that the Pocono project was selected and the most-favorable outcome occurred. The PW(i) of the chance node for doing the Berkshire project next is $1883k and the PW(i) of the Do Nothing leaf is $1108k, so the $1883k is selected for this node.

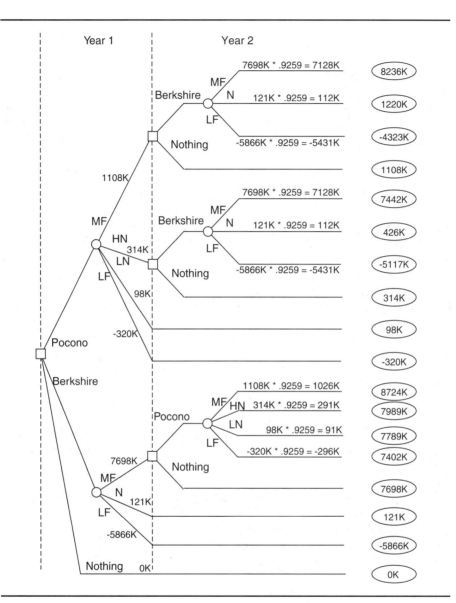

FIGURE 24.5   The decision tree for Mountain Systems with the PW(8) for each leaf node

Repeat these rollback actions until a value is assigned to the root node. The results of the complete rollback for the Mountain Systems Eastern Division are shown in Figure 24.6.

In the Mountain Systems decision tree, the rolled-back value at the root node is $1068k. This corresponds to the path that does the Pocono project first, so this means the best choice under the current circumstances is to do the Pocono project. A year from now, after finding out what the actual outcome of the Pocono project was, all paths made impossible by the previous choices and chance outcomes can be trimmed from the decision tree and the resulting tree can be re-analyzed if there are any remaining choice nodes.

The Expected Value of Perfect Information

The value at the root node is the expected value of the decision tree and is based on current information. The current information is known to be imperfect—the mere fact that there are any chance nodes at all means there is less-than-perfect information about the situation. Given an analyzed decision tree, a reasonable follow-on question is, "Would there be any value in taking actions that would reduce the probability of ending up in an undesirable future state?" If you spent more time or money on research, experimentation, prototyping, or things like that, you might be able to refine the probabilities on one or more of the chance nodes. You might even be able to eliminate one or more paths through the tree because you may discover them to be impossible. The analyzed decision tree provides information that will help you answer that question.

There are two random variables in the Mountain Systems decision tree, the Berkshire outcome and Pocono outcome. If we had a crystal ball and knew ahead of time what the outcomes for these will be, we could figure out which path through the tree would be the best one to take. For instance, if we already knew that both projects would have their most-favorable outcome, the possible paths (and their associated values) are as follows:

- Path A—Do the Pocono project first and the Berkshire project second ($8236k)
- Path B—Do only the Pocono project ($1108k)
- Path C—Do the Berkshire project first and the Pocono project second ($8724k)
- Path D—Do only the Berkshire project ($7698k)
- Path E—Do neither project ($0k)

If we knew ahead of time that both projects would have their most-favorable outcome, we would clearly choose Path C because it has the highest value.

This step of finding the best path through the decision tree can be repeated for all possible combinations of chance node outcomes: Which path has the highest value under those conditions?

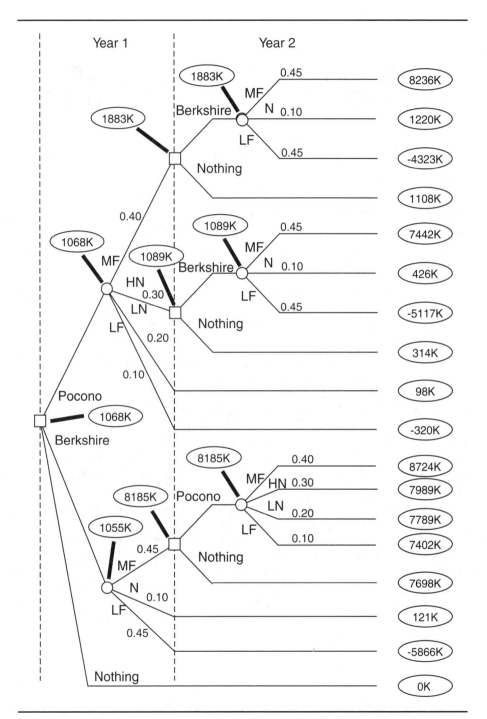

FIGURE 24.6   The rolled-back value for Mountain Systems Eastern Division

TABLE 24.8 The Best Path, Value, and Probability for All Combinations of Random Variable Outcomes

	Berkshire: Least Favorable (45%)	Berkshire: Nominal (10%)	Berkshire: Most Favorable (45%)
Pocono: Least favorable (10%)	Do nothing $0k (4.5%)	Do Berkshire only $121k (1%)	Do Berkshire only $7698k (4.5%)
Pocono: Low nominal (20%)	Do Pocono only $98k (9%)	Do Berkshire only $121k (2%)	Do Berkshire then Pocono $7789k (9%)
Pocono: High nominal (30%)	Do Pocono only $314k (13.5%)	Do Pocono then Berkshire $426k (3%)	Do Berkshire then Pocono $7989k (13.5%)
Pocono: Most favorable (40%)	Do Pocono only $1108k (18%)	Do Pocono then Berkshire $1220k (4%)	Do Berkshire then Pocono $8724k (18%)

We also know the probabilities for the random variables (from Tables 24.4 and 24.5 in the Mountain Systems example), so we can calculate the probability for each combination of outcomes. For instance, P(Berkshire is least favorable) = 0.45 and P(Pocono is most favorable) = 0.40 so P(Berkshire is least favorable and Pocono is most favorable) = 0.45 * 0.40 = 0.18 or 18%. Similarly, P(Berkshire is most favorable and Pocono is least favorable) = 0.45 * 0.10 = 0.045 or 4.5%. Each cell in Table 24.8 shows the best path, the PW(i) of that best path, and the combined probability of that outcome for every possible combination of chance node outcomes in the Mountain Systems Eastern Division example.

Next, for each possible combination expected of random variable outcomes, multiply its value by the probability of that combination. This is shown in Table 24.9.

Finally, add up the results from the value times the probability for all combinations of outcomes (in this case, summing down the columns first then adding across the column totals):

$0k + $9k + $42k + $199k = $250k

$1k + $2k + $13k + $49k = $65k

$346k + $701k + $1079k + $1570k = $3696k

$250k + $65k + $3696k = $4011k

TABLE 24.9 Value Times Probability for All Combinations of Random Outcomes

	Berkshire: Least Favorable	Berkshire: Nominal	Berkshire: Most Favorable
Pocono: Least favorable	$0k * 4.5% = $0k	$121k * 1% = $1k	$7698k * 4.5% = $346k
Pocono: Low nominal	$98k * 9% = $9k	$121k * 2% = $2k	$7789k * 9% = $701k
Pocono: High nominal	$314k * 13.5% = $42k	$426k * 3% = $13k	$7989k * 13.5% = $1079k
Pocono: Most favorable	$1108k * 18% = $199k	$1220k * 4% = $49k	$8724k * 18% = $1570k

This final value, $4011k, is the expected value of all the best outcomes. It's the expected value given perfect information. The difference between this and the expected value given current information (the $1068k from the previous analysis) is the expected value of perfect information. For the Mountain Systems example it's:

$4011k – $1068k = $2943k

Generalizing this approach, the **expected value of perfect information** (EVPI) is as follows:

$$EVPI = \sum_{i=1}^{n} (BestValue_i * Probability_i) - ExpectedValueOfDecisionTree$$

Where:

- BestValue = The value of the path with the best results under that combination of outcomes.
- Probability = The probability of that combination of outcomes happening.
- ExpectedValueOfDecisionTree = The expected value of the decision tree given current information.

Knowing the expected value of perfect information, the decision maker now knows the absolute upper limit for how much to spend on actions to gain further knowledge. Given that it's probably impossible to actually get perfect future information, the organization should plan on spending a lot less than this amount. Mountain Systems should not spend any more than $2943k in an effort to gain that perfect information expected and should probably plan on spending a lot less.

Summary

This chapter showed how to use statistical approaches to incorporate uncertainty probabilities into a decision analysis.

In expected value decision making, the overall value of an alternative with multiple possible outcomes is the average of the random individual outcomes that would occur if that alternative were repeated a large number of times. The alternative with the highest expected value is chosen.

With expectation variance, the differing probabilities could themselves influence the decision. An alternative with lower expected value might be a better choice if it also has a much lower probability of a negative outcome.

Monte Carlo analysis generates random combinations of the input variables (estimated factors) and runs them through the cost function to calculate the result under those conditions. This is repeated a large number of times, and then the statistical distribution of the outcomes is analyzed.

Decision trees map out the possible results when there are sequences of decisions together with a set of future random events that have known probabilities. Decision trees are useful when there are a number of possible future states and decisions can be made in stages.

The expected value of perfect information provides an answer to the question, "Would there be any value in taking actions that would reduce the probability of ending up in an undesirable future state?" That expected value provides an absolute upper limit for how much to spend on actions to gain further knowledge.

The techniques in the next chapter are used when probabilities can't (or won't) be assigned to the possible outcomes.

Self-Study Questions

1. The AE(MARR) of the outcomes and their probabilities for the Uinta project at Mountain Systems Western Division are shown in the following table.

	Least-Favorable Outcome	Fair Outcome	Most-Favorable Outcome
AE(MARR)	−$2166	$2008	$6124
Probability of outcome	20%	55%	25%

What is the expected value of this project?

2. The AE(MARR) of the outcomes and their probabilities for the Wasatch project at Mountain Systems Western Division are shown in the following table.

	Least-Favorable Outcome	Low Nominal Outcome	High Nominal Outcome	Most-Favorable Outcome
AE(MARR)	–$16,455	–$1216	$14,211	$18,578
Probability of outcome	20%	30%	40%	10%

What is the expected value of this project?

3. The proposed Chardonnay project at Bay Laboratories has an initial investment of $50,000. The project is also known to lead to savings of $20,000 annually as long as a certain law is in effect. What's unknown is when the law will be repealed. The probabilities of the law being repealed in any year are shown in the following table.

Number of Years Until Law Is Repealed	Probability of Repeal That Year
1	0.1
2	0.2
3	0.2
4	0.3
5	0.1
6	0.1

Given a MARR of 14%, what is the expected value of the PW(i) of the Chardonnay project? Should the company invest in this project?

4. Zymurgenics has a successful product on the market. Market research reveals that the customer base wants at least an upgraded version, and many want the package to be rewritten because that will allow even more useful features to be added. The market research report contains the following data.

	Initial Investment	AE(i) Income	Probability of Duration of Sales (Years)				
			1	2	3	4	5
Rewrite	$1,000,000	$500,000	0.1	0.2	0.3	0.2	0.2
Update	$400,000	$240,000	0.3	0.3	0.2	0.1	0.1

Given a MARR of 15%, use the expected present worth of each alternative to find which one is preferred.

5. The following table shows the probabilities and payoffs for a state-run lottery. What is the expected value of a $1 lottery ticket given these statistics?

Number of Matches	Gold Ball?	Probability	Payout
0	Yes	1 in 22	$1
1	Yes	1 in 30	$2
2	Yes	1 in 131	$3
3	No	1 in 72	$3
3	Yes	1 in 1575	$15
4	No	1 in 2648	$25
4	Yes	1 in 58,263	$500
5	No	1 in 503,176	$2000
5	Yes	1 in 11,069,877	$3,000,000

Questions 6 through 11 relate to using the free Construx Estimate tool (available at http://www.construx.com) to do a Monte Carlo estimate of the following project:

Size = 50,000 source lines of code
Language = C++
Project phase = High-level design complete
Project type = Telecommunications

6. What is the shortest schedule generated by the tool's Monte Carlo simulation?

7. What is the longest schedule?

8. What is the 50/50 schedule for this project?

9. What is the smallest effort?

10. What is the biggest effort?

11. What is the 50/50 effort for this project?

12. A study group has been investigating the proposed Tetra project at Tropical Pets, Inc. The study shows that project is expected to have an initial investment of somewhere between $80,000 and $120,000. The annual savings from the project is expected to be between $25,000 and $40,000, and the useful life will be between 6 and 10 years. The MARR is expected to be between 9% and 13%. Assuming that all the input factors have uniform distributions (meaning that a typical random number generator can be used), write a program that does a Monte Carlo simulation of the Tetra project using 1,000 samples. What is the smallest PW(i) of the project? What is the largest? What is the average PW(i) across all samples?

13. Starting with the decision tree in Figure 24.3, use the following information to compute the PW(i) for each path through the tree. The PW(i) of scrapping and redeveloping the system are $200k, $40k, and –$220k when the demand increases, stays stable, and decreases, respectively. The PW(i) investment to enhance the legacy system is $40k. The PW(i) income of the enhancements will be $90k, and $0k when the demand stays the same or decreases, respectively. The PW(i) income of the enhancements will be $150k if demand increases but only if they don't scrap and redevelop the system later—in which case the PW(i) of the enhancements will be $0k. If the legacy system is enhanced, the decision to scrap and redevelop if demand increases will be made after one year. The probability of demand increasing is 40%, of staying stable is 40%, and decreasing is 20%. The MARR is 14%.

14. Using the answer from the previous question, roll back the PW(i)s for each path through the decision tree to calculate the expected value at the root node. What is that expected value and what is the best first decision that should be made based on knowing it?

15. What is the expected value of perfect information based on the decision tree from the previous question?

16. Cool Stuff, Inc. has an existing inventory control system that's adequate for their current level of business but will be severely strained if their market share grows. Cool Stuff has been considering either buying or building a new inventory control system. One of the major factors in their decision will be the growth in market share. They don't know exactly what will happen but they are confident that there's a 25% chance of market share growth, a 60% chance it will stay the same, and a 15% chance that it will decrease. The following table shows the PW(i) of their two options for the inventory control system

Market Share	Buy	Build
Increases (+)	$140k	$250k
Same (=)	$120k	$100k
Decreases (–)	–$20k	–$50k

They are also considering developing a data warehouse. The data warehouse is estimated to have a PW(i) of $70k. The decision tree for Cool Stuff's decision is shown here.

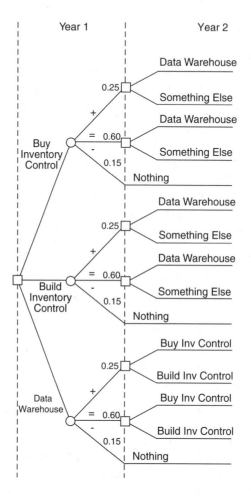

The segments labeled "something else" have a PW(i) = 0. Using Cool Stuff's MARR of 17%, show the PW(i) for each possible path through this decision tree.

17. Roll back the PW(i)s for each path through Cool Stuff's decision tree to calculate the expected value at the root node. What is that expected value and what is the best first decision Cool Stuff should make based on it?

18. What is the expected value of perfect information based on the rolled-back decision tree from the previous question?

25

Decision Making Under Uncertainty

Decision making under uncertainty is used when it's not possible to assign probabilities to the outcomes. A custom software development company might submit a proposal for an outsourced software project but not have any idea whether their proposal will be accepted. These techniques can also be used when you don't want to put probabilities on the outcomes; in a safety-critical software system where a failure could threaten human life, people may not react well to an assigned probability of fatality. If probabilities can be assigned, the decision making under risk techniques in Chapter 24 should be used. Several different techniques for decision making under uncertainty are covered in this chapter:

- Laplace rule
- Maximin rule
- Maximax rule
- Hurwicz rule
- Minimax regret rule

The Payoff Matrix

The techniques for decisions under uncertainty are all based on a **payoff matrix**. The payoff matrix is simply a way of showing all the possible outcomes that need to be considered. One axis of the matrix is a list of the mutually exclusive alternatives. This set of alternatives should be built using the techniques in Chapter 9 and should account for dependencies and mutual exclusivities between the proposals as well as resource constraints.

The other axis of the matrix is a list of all the different **states of nature** that need to be considered. Each state of nature is a future outcome that the decision maker doesn't have any control over. In a custom software contract bid situation, the bidder doesn't have any control over whether their proposal will be accepted.

Table 25.1 shows a sample payoff matrix for Xenon Software, a custom software development company. Assume that they've created a set of mutually exclusive alternatives from the different jobs they are confident they could bid on and win. Xenon expects that, because of the most likely terms of the contracts, outcomes of these alternatives will vary depending on how the national economy shapes up over the next five years. The different states of nature, which Xenon obviously has no control over, are as follows:

- The national economy gets worse than it is now.
- It stays about the same as now.
- It gets better than now.

The cells in the matrix are filled in with the estimated value (in PW(i), FW(i), AE(i), . . . as appropriate) of that alternative under the corresponding state of nature.

In any payoff matrix, it's possible that one of the alternatives is "dominated" by another. An alternative is dominated when there is another alternative that has equal or better payoff under every state of nature. In Table 25.1, alternative A5 is dominated by A1, alternative A1 is at least as good as alternative A5 under every state of nature. This means that alternative A5 is never better than A1, so A5 can be safely dropped from further consideration.

Table 25.2 shows the **reduced payoff matrix** with the dominated alternative, A5, removed. Unless decision analysis is being done with an automated tool, less work is involved if all dominated alternatives are removed. A spreadsheet that automates decision analysis under uncertainty can be found at http://www.construx.com/returnonsw/.

TABLE 25.1 An Example Payoff Matrix (in $1000s)

Alternative	Worse Economy	Same Economy	Better Economy
A1	0	4000	2500
A2	1000	500	4000
A3	−2500	1500	6000
A4	0	1000	5000
A5	−1000	2000	2000

TABLE 25.2 An Example Reduced Payoff Matrix (in $1000s)

Alternative	Worse Economy	Same Economy	Better Economy
A1	0	4000	2500
A2	1000	500	4000
A3	−2500	1500	6000
A4	0	1000	5000

TABLE 25.3 Average Payoffs for the Laplace Rule (in $1000s)

	Average Payoff
A1	(0 + 4000 + 2500) / 3 = 2167
A2	(1000 + 500 + 4000) / 3 = 1833
A3	(−2500 + 1500 + 6000) / 3 = 1667
A4	(0+ 1000 + 5000) / 3 = 2000

The Laplace Rule

The Laplace rule is sometimes called "the principle of insufficient reason"; this rule assumes that each state of nature is equally likely. If you know that the states of nature aren't equally likely and you can assign a probability to each one, you should use expected value analysis as shown in the previous chapter.

Under the Laplace rule, calculate the average payoff for each alternative across all states of nature, as shown in Table 25.3. This is actually the same as using expected value analysis for multiple alternatives; it simply uses equal probabilities for each of the outcomes.

You then choose the alternative with the highest average payoff across all states of nature. In this example, Xenon should choose alternative A1 because it has the highest average payoff, $2,167,000.

TABLE 25.4 Worst Payoffs for the Maximin Rule (in $1000s)

Alternative	Worse Economy	Same Economy	Better Economy	Worst Payoff
A1	0	4000	2500	0
A2	1000	500	4000	500
A3	−2500	1500	6000	−2500
A4	0	1000	5000	0

The Maximin Rule

The Maximin rule is the most pessimistic of the uncertainty techniques. Maximin assumes that the worst state of nature will happen, so you should pick the alternative that has the best payoff from all of the worst payoffs. The formula for the Maximin rule is as follows:

$$\max_{i} \min_{j} [P_{ij}]$$

Under Maximin, find the worst payoff for each alternative. This is shown in Table 25.4.
Choose the alternative with the best of the worst payoffs. In the example, alternative A2 has the best of the worst payoffs at $500,000.

The Maximax Rule

In contrast with Maximin, the Maximax rule is the most optimistic of the techniques. Maximax assumes that the best state of nature will happen, so you should pick the alternative that has the best payoff among all of the best payoffs. The formula for the Maximax rule is as follows:

$$\max_{i} \max_{j} [P_{ij}]$$

Under Maximax, find the best payoff for each alternative. This is shown in Table 25.5.

TABLE 25.5   Best Payoffs for the Maximax Rule (in $1000s)

Alternative	Worse Economy	Same Economy	Better Economy	Best Payoff
A1	0	4000	2500	4000
A2	1000	500	4000	4000
A3	–2500	1500	6000	6000
A4	0	1000	5000	5000

Choose the alternative with the best of the best payoffs. In the example, alternative A3 has the best payoff at $6,000,000.

The Hurwicz Rule

The Hurwicz Rule assumes that without guidance people will tend to focus on the extremes (i.e., Maximin or Maximax). The Hurwicz rule allows a blending of optimism and pessimism using a selected ratio. You will choose an index of optimism, α, between 0 and 1, describing how optimistic you are with the remainder being pessimism. An α of, say, 0.2 means that you are more pessimistic than optimistic. When $\alpha = 0.1$, that means that you are even more pessimistic than at $\alpha = 0.2$. Setting α to 0.85 means that you are very optimistic but a small amount of pessimism (15%) remains.

The formula for the Hurwicz rule is as follows:

$$\max_{i} \left\{ \alpha [\max_{j} P_{ij}] + (1-\alpha)[\min_{j} P_{ij}] \right\}$$

The formula blends $\alpha * 100\%$ of the optimistic payoff with $(1 - \alpha) * 100\%$ of the pessimistic payoff. At $\alpha = 1.0$ (100%), this rule behaves exactly like the Maximax rule; and at $\alpha = 0.0$ (0%), it behaves exactly like the Maximin rule.

Under the Hurwicz rule, calculate the weighted result of blending the most optimistic payoff with the most pessimistic payoff for each alternative using the selected α. Table 25.6 shows the calculations for Xenon Software using $\alpha = 0.25$.

TABLE 25.6   Blended Payoffs for the Hurwicz Rule (in $1000s)

	Best Payoff	Worst Payoff	$\alpha = 0.25$	Blended Payoff
A2	4000	0	0.25 * 4000 + 0.75 * 0	1000
A3	4000	500	0.25 * 4000 + 0.75 * 5000	1375
A4	6000	-2500	0.25 * 6000 + 0.75 * (–2500)	–375
A5	5000	0	0.25 * 5000 + 0.75 * 0	1250

You should choose the alternative with the highest blended payoff given your index of optimism. In this example, Xenon should choose alternative A2 because it has the highest blended payoff when $\alpha = 0.25$. The expected payoff in this situation is approximately $1,375,000.

Figure 25.1 shows a graph of the blended payoffs for each alternative as a function of α. The dashed vertical line is at $\alpha = 0.25$.

Under the Hurwicz rule for Xenon Software's situation, alternative A2 is preferred for all α less than about 0.5. Alternative A4 is preferred when α is between about 0.5 and about 0.7. Alternative A3 is preferred for all α greater than about 0.7. Note that this is an application of break-even analysis as described in Chapter 19.

The Minimax Regret Rule

The Minimax regret rule bases the decision on minimizing the regret that you would have if you chose the wrong alternative under each state of nature. Conceptually, if you had selected an alternative, say A1, and the state of nature happened where A1 had the best payoff (in Xenon's case the economy stayed the same), you would have no regrets for having chosen A1. If, on the other hand, you had selected A1 and the economy got better, you would have regretted having not chosen A3—the best alternative under that state of nature. Your regret can be quantified as the difference between the payoff of the alternative you did choose and the payoff of the best alternative under that same state of nature.

The first step in the Minimax regret is to calculate the **regret matrix** showing the calculated regrets. Table 25.7 shows the regret matrix for Xenon Software. The regret value in each cell is simply the difference between the largest entry in the column and the actual payoff for the given alternative under the given state of nature. The regret value for alternative A4 when the economy stays the same is the maximum value in that column, 4000, minus the payoff for A4 in that column, 1000. The regret value of 3000 means that Xenon would have gotten $3,000,000 more had they chosen A5 instead of A4, knowing that the economy staying the same turned out to be true.

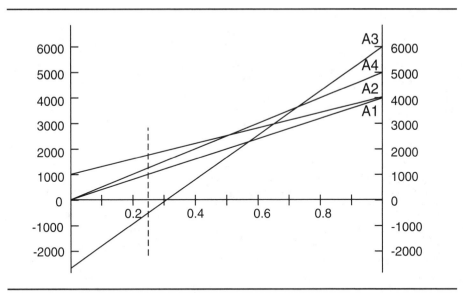

FIGURE 25.1   A graph of blended payoffs for each alternative (in $1000s)

TABLE 25.7   An Example Regret Matrix (in $1000s)

Alternative	Worse Economy	Same Economy	Better Economy
A1	1000	0	3500
A2	0	3500	2000
A3	3500	2500	0
A4	1000	3000	1000

The second step is to find the maximum regret for each alternative. The maximum regret for A2 is 3500, and the maximum regret for A4 is 3000. The maximum regrets for each of Xenon's alternatives are shown in Table 25.8.

TABLE 25.8 Maximum Regrets for Each Alternative (in $1000s)

Alternative	Maximum Regret
A1	3500
A2	3500
A3	3500
A4	3000

TABLE 25.9 Summary of Decision Rule Results and Philosophies

Decision Rule	Alternative Selected	Optimism or Pessimism
Laplace	A1	Neither, equal probabilities
Maximin	A2	Pessimism
Maximax	A3	Optimism
Hurwicz ($\alpha = 0.25$)	A2	Blended optimism and pessimism
Minimax regret	A4	Pessimism

Under the Minimax regret rule, choose the alternative that has the smallest maximum regret. Xenon should choose alternative A4 because the worst they could do is be off by $3,000,000. In all the other cases, Xenon takes a chance of being off by $3,500,000.

Summary of the Decision Rules

Notice that the different decision rules don't give the same results. Each rule has its own merits in assuming a different degree of optimism or pessimism. Table 25.9 shows the alternative that Xenon should select under each decision rule and summarizes the degree of optimism or pessimism underlying that rule.

You'll need to use your judgment in choosing the most appropriate rule for the particular decision being analyzed, based on the degree of optimism or pessimism needed.

Summary

Decision making under uncertainty is used when it's not possible, or practical, to assign probabilities to the outcomes. When probabilities can be assigned, the decision making under risk techniques in the previous chapter should be used. The chapter covered the following major points:

- The payoff matrix shows all of the possible outcomes that need to be considered. One axis of the matrix is a list of the mutually exclusive alternatives. The other axis of the matrix is a list of all the different states of nature. Each cell in the matrix is filled with the PW(), FW(), or AE() of that alternative under the corresponding state of nature.
- The Laplace rule, sometimes called "the principle of insufficient reason," assumes that each state of nature is equally likely. You should pick the alternative with the highest expected value using equal probabilities for all states of nature.
- The Maximin rule is the most pessimistic of these techniques. It assumes that the worst state of nature will happen, so you should pick the alternative that has the best payoff from all of the worst payoffs.
- The Maximax rule is the most optimistic of the techniques. It assumes that the best state of nature will happen, so you should pick the alternative that has the best payoff among all of the best payoffs.
- The Hurwicz rule assumes that without guidance people will tend to focus on the extremes (i.e., Maximin or Maximax). The Hurwicz rule allows a blending of optimism and pessimism using a selected ratio.
- The Minimax regret rule bases the decision on minimizing the regret that you would have if you chose the wrong alternative under each state of nature. Choose the alternative that has the smallest maximum regret.

Parts I through VI of this book discuss a single decision criterion, money. However, decisions can involve more criteria than just money. Part VII presents techniques that can be used when more than one decision criterion, or attribute, is relevant to the decision.

Self-Study Questions

Questions 1 through 6 all relate to the following situation: Xenon Software is bidding on three separate projects, P1, P2, and P3. They know that they will win exactly one of those projects, but they don't know which one. The also have no idea which of the projects is more likely. They need to buy some computer equipment to support the projects. The equipment choices, C1 through C5, are mutually exclusive; Xenon can only buy one of them. Due to lead times in purchasing, they need to buy the equipment before any contract is awarded. Unfortunately, certain choices of equipment are better suited to some projects than others. The following payoff matrix shows the net profit (in thousands) for the various choices of computer equipment under each of the projects.

Equipment	P1	P2	P3
C1	100	90	60
C2	30	30	140
C3	90	90	50
C4	70	80	90
C5	100	20	120

1. If any of the alternatives are dominated, state which one(s) are and show the reduced payoff matrix.

2. What equipment would be purchased based on the Laplace rule?

3. What equipment would be purchased based on the Maximin rule?

4. What equipment would be purchased based on the Maximax rule?

5. What equipment would be purchased based on the Hurwicz rule with $\alpha = 0.3$?

6. What equipment would be purchased based on the Minimax regret rule?

Questions 7 through 12 all relate to the following situation: Mountain Systems is predicting four different potential business futures, F1 through F4, but has no way of knowing which one is more or less likely than another. Based on the possible business futures, Mountain Systems has come up with four mutually exclusive business strategies, S1 through S4. Certain strategies will work better under different futures; unfortunately, the strategy must be chosen now, and the choice is irrevocable. The following payoff matrix shows the net profit (in millions) for the various choices of business strategy under each of the futures.

Strategy	F1	F2	F3	F4
S1	8	8	0	4
S2	0	16	0	0
S3	4	12	0	0
S4	4	4	4	4

7. If any of the alternatives are dominated, state which one(s) are and build the reduced payoff matrix.

8. What strategy would be selected based on the Laplace rule?

9. What strategy would be chosen based on the Maximin rule?

10. What strategy would be chosen based on the Maximax rule?

11. What strategy would be chosen based on the Hurwicz rule with $\alpha = 0.25$?

12. What strategy would be chosen based on the Minimax regret rule?

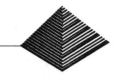

PART SEVEN

MULTIPLE-ATTRIBUTE
DECISIONS

Part One through Part Six present the concepts and techniques used when the decision criterion is money. Aside from technical feasibility, money will almost always be the most important decision criterion. However, decisions can involve more criteria than just money. This part presents techniques that can be used when more than one decision criterion, or attribute, is relevant in the decision.

26

Decisions Based on
Multiple Attributes

Chapters 3 through 25 explain how to make decisions based on a single decision criterion, money. The alternative with the best PW, the best AE, the best incremental IRR, the best incremental benefit-cost ratio, etc. is the one selected. Aside from technical feasibility, money is almost always the most important decision criterion, but it's certainly not always the only one. Quite often there are other criteria, other "attributes," that need to be considered, and those attributes can't be cast in terms of money. If you were responsible for buying a new laptop computer for use on a development project, price would probably be the most important decision criterion. But other attributes such as processor speed, memory capacity, disk capacity, size of the screen, and reliability would probably also be factored into your decision. This chapter presents several techniques for making decisions when there is more than one attribute to consider.

Different Kinds of "Value"

In an abstract sense, the decision-making process—be it a financial decision or not—is about maximizing value. You should always choose, from the set of alternatives available, the one that maximizes total value. When value can be expressed in terms of money (e.g., a cash-flow stream), the decision process may be complex (after all, it took

22 chapters to describe it), but it is still straightforward. However, that's only when value can be expressed as money. Money isn't the only kind of value. Money is, in fact, really only a way to quantify value. Generally speaking, there are two kinds of value:

- **Use-value**—The ability to get things done; the properties of the object that cause it to perform
- **Esteem-value**—The properties that make it desirable

Use-value in a computer comes from its capability to do work. You give it input, and it gives you useful output. A CPU with a higher clock speed can get the work done faster, so it's worth more. A computer with more memory can do more things, so it's worth more. Use-values are convenient for decision making because they can almost always be translated into money. Esteem-values, on the other hand, are far more subtle and difficult, if not downright impossible, to quantify—especially in terms of money. Esteem-values for the laptop computer might be things such as whether it is a brand name or an off-brand, how much noise it makes when it is running, or even what color the case happens to be. Use-values on a car are things such as fuel economy, engine horsepower, reliability, and so on. Esteem-values on the car could be things such as its make, model, and color.

An example multiple-attribute decision situation is used throughout this chapter. Consider the case of UFO Software. UFO needs to buy a new computer to support a project they are starting up. The project is rather unique; in addition to the typical selection criteria of price, speed, and memory, UFO has some peculiar environmental considerations and needs to consider not only the amount of heat generated by the machine, but the noise level that it produces. After surveying the options available on the market and looking at their project's particular needs, UFO decides on the following decision attributes and ways to measure them:

- **AE(i) cost of ownership**—CR(i) plus the AE(i) operation and maintenance costs over a 7-year planning horizon (see Chapter 11).
- **CPU speed in MIPS**—As provided from the manufacturer's specifications.
- **Memory size in gigabytes**—As provided from the manufacturer's specifications.
- **Heat coefficient**—UFO has defined a "heat coefficient" function that considers the volume (in cubic feet per minute) and temperature (in degrees F) of the exhaust air from the computer's cooling fans.
- **Reliability**—A judgment based on experience with that model of computer in the past.
- **Noise level**—UFO doesn't want to buy a decibel meter and doesn't trust the manufacturer's specifications for noise, so they will have employees visit other installations of that type of computer and provide a judgment on the noise level.

All the attributes, with the exception of noise level, are use-value attributes. They all relate to the candidate computer's ability to get work done for UFO. On the assumption that noise level needs to be considered because of "creature comfort" needs of the project team, not on the machine's ability to get its job done, it would be an esteem-value.

Any decision process that's intended to maximize total value will have to deal with the esteem-values in addition to the use-values. But esteem-values often can't be cast in terms of money. So the decision process, by definition, has to be able to deal with multiple decision criteria, some that can be cast in terms of money and some that cannot.

Choosing the Attributes

To make a proper decision, that decision needs to be based on appropriate decision criteria: the decision attributes. A number of guidelines are relevant in choosing the attributes for a decision:

- **Each attribute (each decision criterion) needs to capture a unique dimension of the decision at hand**—The attributes need to be independent and nonredundant; the same characteristic should not be captured in different ways by different attributes. An attribute in the UFO case that captured "general impressions of the candidate computer" would almost certainly implicitly incorporate aspects of speed, reliability, and noise. If a general impressions attribute were to be included, it would need to be defined in a way that excludes those aspects; otherwise there would be a "double accounting" of those characteristics that would bias the decision.
- **The set of attributes needs to be sufficient to cover the important aspects of the decision**—No important factors are being left out of the decision analysis. If there were other important attributes, they would need to be added to the study as other attributes.
- **Differences in attribute values need to be meaningful in distinguishing among the alternatives**—In the UFO example, differences in the AE(i) cost of ownership value are obviously meaningful in distinguishing alternatives; a lower cost of ownership is clearly preferred. An attribute that has no interpretation of preference in its values, such as the color of a computer in the UFO case, does not contribute to deciding which alternative is better and should be ignored.
- **Each attribute needs to distinguish at least two alternatives**—The same attribute value can't apply across all alternatives otherwise that attribute is not a differentiator. If all the alternative computers for UFO were rated "quiet," the noise attribute would not help the decision because all alternatives have the same quietness. That attribute would be irrelevant to the decision and should then be dropped.

In a given decision analysis, the selection of the attributes themselves may be a subjective process. If too many attributes are included, the analysis becomes unwieldy because of the amount of information that needs to be gathered and processed. On the other hand, too few attributes may not give good differentiation between the alternatives and may lead to a less-than-optimal choice. The potential for a better-quality decision will need to be balanced with the extra effort required to gain that quality.

Selecting Measurement Scales

Each alternative must be evaluated, or measured, with respect to each attribute. There are many different ways to measure things—in fact, there are different "classes" of measurements. Further, within a certain class of measurements, some manipulations of those measurements will make sense and others won't. A given multiple-attribute decision, such as the UFO situation, often includes attributes that are in different classes. So it's important for you to know what the different classes of measurements are, how to recognize them, and what can and can't be done with them.

NOMINAL SCALES

The simplest class of measurement is the nominal scale. This kind of scale is used for classification only. Examples of nominal scales include house types (A-frame, craftsman, ranch, colonial, bungalow, Cape Cod, contemporary, and so on), and climate types (desert, tropical, alpine, polar, and so forth). Figure 26.1 shows a conceptual picture of a nominal scale.

The only meaningful comparisons in a nominal scale are same as and different than. It makes sense to say, "Region 1's climate type is the same as Region 2's climate type" and "Region 1's climate type is different than Region 3's climate type."

It is important to understand that there isn't necessarily a meaningful ordering among the values in a nominal scale. Nominal scales don't support better-than or worse-than comparisons, so they can't be used as a basis for comparison between alternatives. It doesn't necessarily make sense to say, "Region 1's climate type is better than Region 2's climate type." The only thing you can meaningfully say is something like "For this decision, the acceptable values of climate type are X, Y, and Z," and throw out (or otherwise penalize) any alternative that doesn't have an acceptable value. If UFO were concerned that certain color schemes on the computer box were acceptable and others weren't, the "color scheme" attribute would be a nominal-scaled attribute.

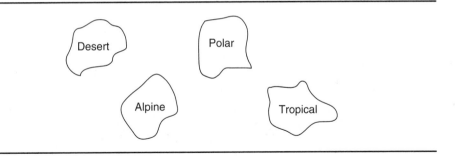

FIGURE 26.1   A nominal scale only shows categories of things

ORDINAL SCALES

The next step up in measurement systems is the ordinal scale. As the name implies, it means there is an order, or ranking, to the values in the measure. Examples of ordinal scales include the finish order in a race (first, second, third, . . .) and temperature categories (very cold, cold, neutral, warm, hot). The Software Engineering Institute's Capability Maturity Model (CMM) [SEI01] rating, a number between 1 and 5, is an ordinal scale. Figure 26.2 shows a conceptual picture of an ordinal scale.

An ordinal scale can be used, just like a nominal scale, for classification; it supports equality and inequality comparisons among alternatives. An ordinal scale is implicitly a nominal scale. We can meaningfully say things such as, "UFO Software's CMM rating is the same as Blizzard Systems' CMM rating."

The ordering of the values also allows greater-than and less-than comparisons that don't make sense in a nominal scale. We can meaningfully say things such as "Today's temperature category, neutral, is warmer than yesterday's temperature category, very cold" and "Zymurgy Systems CMM rating is higher than UFO Software's CMM rating."

If a particular ordinal scale is measuring some aspect of desirability—for instance, food at a restaurant might be rated really bad, bad, okay, good, really good, or gourmet— then you can say that one alternative is better or worse than another. A restaurant with really good food is more desirable than a restaurant with good food. But that's all you can say. You can't necessarily say that the difference between a restaurant with bad food and one with okay food is more, the same, or less than the difference between a restaurant with good food and one with really good food. Similarly, we can say that last year's winner of the Boston marathon finished before the second-place finisher and the second-place finisher finished before the third-place finisher. If we only know the finish order, however, we can't say that the time difference between the first- and second-place finishers has any relationship to the time difference between the second- and third-place finishers, and so on.

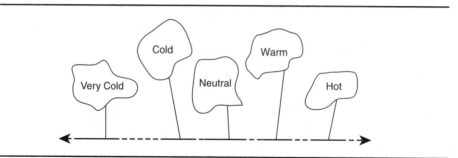

FIGURE 26.2   An ordinal scale puts the categories into a particular order

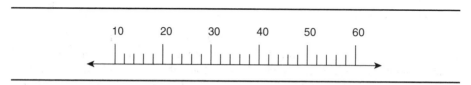

FIGURE 26.3   An interval scale has a constant distance between ordered measurements

INTERVAL SCALES

The interval scale is the next step up in measurement scale sophistication. With an interval scale, not only are the measurements along the scale ordered (an interval scale is implicitly an ordinal scale), the "distances" between the measurements have the same meaning across the scale. Temperatures in degrees Centigrade and in degrees Fahrenheit are good examples of interval scales. Figure 26.3 shows a conceptual picture of an interval scale.

All the operations that are meaningful on an ordinal scale are also meaningful on an interval scale; 29 degrees C is less than 35 degrees C. An interval scale introduces the ability to add and subtract values. It enables you to meaningfully say things such as "The difference between 5 degrees C and 10 degrees C is the same as the difference between 25 degrees C and 30 degrees C." What an interval scale doesn't necessarily allow you to say meaningfully is anything about ratios between different parts of the scale. For instance, 30 degrees C is not necessarily "twice as hot" as 15 degrees C.

RATIO SCALES

Conceptually speaking, what's missing from an interval scale is the notion of a meaningful zero point. An interval scale probably has a zero point, but it might not represent a true zero measurement. Zero degrees C or zero degrees F are measures, but they don't

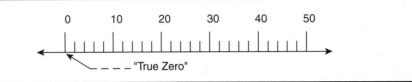

0   10   20   30   40   50

"True Zero"

FIGURE 26.4 A ratio scale has a meaningful zero point

represent the absence of heat. Temperature in degrees Kelvin is a prime example of a ratio scale. The zero point, absolute zero, represents no heat at all—all molecular motion has stopped. When the zero point represents an absence of the characteristic being measured and there is a constant distance between the values, you can now talk about ratios between measurements on different parts of the scale. Figure 26.4 shows a conceptual picture of a ratio scale.

All the operations allowed on an interval scale are also allowed on a ratio scale: The difference between 5 degrees K and 10 degrees K is the same as the difference between 500 degrees K and 505 degrees K. But it also now makes sense to say that 10 degrees K is twice as hot as 5 degrees K, just as it makes sense to say that 500 degrees K is twice as hot as 250 degrees K.

SUMMARIZING MEASUREMENT SCALES

As shown in Table 26.1, ratio scales are the most powerful of the measurement scales. You can do the most meaningful operations with them. All the other scales are limited in one way or another; the more primitive the scale, the more limited your use of that scale. However, the cost of measuring something with a ratio scale may not be worth the investment in either getting the measurement or, worse yet, simply defining the ratio measurement scale itself. Sometimes a lesser scale is either "good enough" or it's as good as you're able to get.

Conveniently, money is a ratio scale:

- The difference between $5 and $10 is the same as the difference between $1005 and $1010.
- $1000 is ten times as much as $100, just as $100 million is ten times as much as $10 million.

This is one of the reasons why money is such a useful measure, especially for decision analysis: The full range of manipulations (adding, subtracting, multiplying, and dividing) is meaningful.

TABLE 26.1 Allowable Operations on Each Scale Type

Scale Type	Allowable Operations
Nominal	=, <>
Ordinal	=, <>, <, <=, =>, >
Interval	=, <>, <, <=, =>, >, +, -
Ratio	=, <>, <, <=, =>, >, +, -, *, /

TABLE 26.2 UFO Software's Alternatives and Their Attribute Ratings

Alternative	AE(i) Cost	Speed	Memory	Heat	Reliable	Noise
A1	$4311	25	4	492	Somewhat unreliable	Average
A2	$7845	60	12	613	Very reliable	Quiet
A3	$6350	36	4	540	Average	Average
A4	$6621	55	8	505	Average	Noisy
A5	$5804	36	6	540	Somewhat reliable	Average

Decisions often have attributes that aren't measured in ratio scales. And for good reason: It's not worth the effort to make every attribute a ratio scale. However, using nonratio scales will necessarily constrain the kinds of manipulations and comparisons that can be done with that attribute. Applying meaningless manipulations and comparisons to "less-than-capable" measurements can lead to inappropriate decisions. We can't, for example, say that "Zymurgy Systems is twice as good at developing software as UFO" just because UFO's CMM rating is level 2 and Zymurgy Systems' rating is level 4.

Table 26.2 shows UFO's alternatives and their attribute ratings on the corresponding scales.

Table 26.3 shows the scale types for the attributes in the UFO Systems case study, based on the measurements shown in Table 26.2.

The heat coefficient attribute, because it is known to be based on air volume in cubic feet per minute (a ratio scale) and temperature in degrees F (an interval scale), will be an interval scale; any scale that is a function of other scales will naturally be no better than the least capable of the scales it is based on. The reliable attribute is ordinal because it has values such as very reliable, somewhat reliable, average, and somewhat unreliable. If UFO were to use mean time between failures (MTBF) as the measure, it would be a ratio scale. Similarly, noise level with values such as quiet, average, noisy is an ordinal scale. Measuring noise in decibels would make it a ratio scale. The interval and ordinal scales are used in the UFO case study to show how these scale types are handled in multiple-attribute decision analyses.

TABLE 26.3 Scale Types for Attributes in the UFO Systems Decision

Attribute	Scale Type
AE(i) cost	Ratio
CPU speed in MIPS	Ratio
Memory capacity in gigabytes	Ratio
Heat coefficient	Interval
Reliable	Ordinal
Noise level	Ordinal

Dimensionality of the Decision Techniques

There are two families of decision techniques that differ in how they use the attributes in the decision. One family is the "compensatory," or single-dimensioned, techniques. This family collapses all the attributes onto a single figure of merit. The family is called compensatory because, for any given alternative, a lower score in one attribute can be compensated by—or traded off against—a higher score in other attributes.

In contrast, the other family is the "noncompensatory," or fully dimensioned, techniques. This family does not allow tradeoffs among the attributes. Each attribute is treated as a separate entity in the decision process.

The different families of techniques are not mutually exclusive. You could, for example, use noncompensatory techniques to reduce the number of alternatives, and then use compensatory techniques to make the final selection.

Techniques in both families are explained, the noncompensatory family first.

Noncompensatory Decision Techniques

In the noncompensatory family of techniques, each decision attribute is treated as a separate entity. Comparison is done on an individual attribute-by-attribute basis. Three specific techniques in this family are described:

- Dominance
- Satisficing
- Lexicography

DOMINANCE

The dominance technique compares each pair of alternatives on an attribute-by-attribute basis, looking for one of the alternatives to be at least as good in every attribute and better in at least one. When that kind of relationship between alternatives is found, there's no problem deciding between the two. One alternative is clearly superior to the other. The inferior alternative can be discarded. Alternative A5 in Table 26.2 dominates A3 because it is at least as good in all attributes and better in cost, memory, and reliability.

The dominance technique is unlikely to select a single alternative, but in some situations it could. If UFO's choice were only between A3 and A5, the dominance technique would be sufficient. At the very least, dominated alternatives can be dropped from further consideration to reduce the amount of work to be done using the other techniques.

SATISFICING

The satisficing technique is sometimes called "the method of feasible ranges" because it's based on establishing acceptable ranges of values. Any alternative that has one or more attributes outside the acceptable range is discarded. If UFO were to define a maximum AE(i) cost at $7000 and a reliability of "average" or better, it would eliminate alternatives A1 and A2.

Just like the dominance technique, the satisficing technique may not lead to selecting a single alternative. However, it's also good for filtering the set of alternatives and reducing the amount of work to be done using other techniques.

The satisficing decision technique can lead to selecting a single alternative when it's used with an iterative propose-then-evaluate process:

```
Repeat
     Propose a new solution
     Evaluate the solution against the decision attributes
Until the solution is within the acceptable range for all
decision attributes
```

As soon as an acceptable solution is found, it is selected. Consider a group of friends choosing a place to meet for lunch. The decision attributes might be things such as not too far away, good food, reasonable price, and prompt service. Friends in the group will start proposing alternatives, "How about Mel's?" and someone might say, "Too far away." Someone else might propose, "Then what about China House on First Street?" and another might say, "Nope, their service is too slow." The cycle continues until one of the friends says something like, "Thai Buffet? It's not too far away, the food is good but reasonably priced, and they've got quick service." Nobody objects because it does satisfy all the criteria. So it's off to Thai Buffet for lunch.

Another restaurant, Dixie's BBQ, might be closer than Thai Buffet, have better food at a more reasonable price, and have quicker service, too. If it wasn't proposed before

Thai Buffet, however, it couldn't have been selected. The iterative version of satisficing stops when the *first* acceptable solution is proposed, not necessarily the *best* solution.

The iterative version of the satisficing technique is appropriate when *satisfactory* performance, rather than *optimal* performance, is good enough for the purposes at hand. If optimal performance is needed, you should always identify several alternatives that all meet the satisficing criteria and then do a further decision analysis using one of the other multiple-attribute decision techniques. A decision that considers several alternatives is almost certain to yield a more optimal choice than a decision that stops at the first minimally acceptable one.

LEXICOGRAPHY

The two previous noncompensatory techniques don't treat any given decision attribute as more important than any other. They assume that all attributes have equal importance. Suppose, however, that one attribute is known to be more important than the others; a final choice could possibly be made on that one criterion alone. The group of friends meeting for lunch might be getting together on a workday, so lunch has to fit within the lunch hour. Prompt service may very well be much more important than the other three attributes: location, food quality, and price. If Thai Buffet has the fastest service in town, it could easily be the best choice.

But what if Thai Buffet and Hamburger Heaven have the same speedy service? When two or more alternatives have identical values for the most important attribute, the lexicography technique uses the next-most-important attribute to try to break the tie. Suppose price is the next most important attribute. If Hamburger Heaven beats Thai Buffet on price, then the friends will be having burgers for lunch. If there are ties at this attribute, lexicography continues comparing at the next most important attribute and so on. The cycle continues until a single alternative is chosen or all alternatives have been evaluated.

What if the process ends without selecting a single alternative? On the assumption that every important attribute has been included in the decision analysis, it doesn't matter which of the remaining alternatives is chosen. Any one of them is, by definition, as good as the other remaining alternatives. In this case, you can choose one at random, go with your gut feeling, etc. Otherwise, you'll need to introduce new attributes into the decision analysis.

Compensatory Decision Techniques

The noncompensatory techniques don't allow for tradeoffs between the attributes. Even though Thai Buffet and Hamburger Heaven have the same speedy service, maybe Thai Buffet has better food than Hamburger Heaven but Hamburger Heaven is less expensive than Thai Buffet. Maybe Hamburger Heaven's prices are so low that it makes up for the difference in food quality. The compensatory family of techniques allows better performance on one attribute to compensate for poorer performance in another, tradeoffs between the attributes will be allowed.

Under the compensatory family of techniques, values for the attributes are converted into a common measurement scale. The units for that common scale will usually be entirely arbitrary, but as long as the common scale is at least an interval scale (the difference between the values have the same significance at all points on that scale), different scores on that scale can be compared in a meaningful way. Three compensatory decision techniques are presented here:

- Nondimensional scaling
- Additive weighting
- Analytic hierarchy process (AHP)

NONDIMENSIONAL SCALING

The nondimensional scaling technique converts the attribute values into a common scale where they can be added together to make a composite score for each alternative. The alternative with the best composite score is selected. In nondimensional scaling, all attributes are defined to have equal importance, so the common scale will need to have the same range, 0.0 to 1.0, 0 to 10, 0 to 100, etc., for all attributes. Assume that UFO chooses 0 to 100 as their common scale.

All attributes need to follow the same trend on desirability; the most-preferred value needs to always be the biggest or always be the smallest common scale value. In UFO's case, more speed is better, so the highest-speed alternative would need to be given, say, the highest common rating for the speed attribute. The speed attribute of alternative A2 would be given 100 as its common scale rating. However, lower cost is better, so the lowest-cost alternative would be given the highest common rating for the cost attribute. The cost attribute of alternative A1 would be given 100 as its common scale rating.

The formula for converting attributes, as long as they are interval- or ratio-scaled, into the common scale is as follows:

$$Rating = Range * \frac{WorstValue - ValueToMakeDimensionless}{WorstValue - BestValue}$$

Table 26.4 shows the results of converting the ratio- and interval-scaled attributes for the UFO Software alternatives in Table 26.2 into the common range of 0 to 100 with 100 being best. The total of the common scores is also shown. The alternative with the highest total common score is best. Based on the total scores in Table 26.4, alternative A4 would be selected.

TABLE 26.4   UFO Software's Alternatives Rated on the Common Scale

Alternative	Cost	Speed	Memory	Heat	Total
A1	100	0	0	100	200
A2	0	100	100	0	200
A3	42	31	0	60	133
A4	35	86	50	89	260
A5	58	31	25	60	174

TABLE 26.5   Combining the Nondimensional Scale with Ordinal-Scaled Attributes for UFO Software

Alternative	Total	Reliable	Noise
A1	200	Somewhat unreliable	Average
A2	200	Very reliable	Quiet
A3	133	Average	Average
A4	260	Average	Noisy
A5	174	Somewhat reliable	Average

When the decision includes attributes that are ordinal scaled, you need to do one of the following:

- Ignore the ordinal-scaled attributes in the decision analysis.
- Refine the ordinal-scaled attributes to use interval or ratio scales and include them in the nondimensional scaling.
- Do the nondimensional scaling for all of the interval- and ratio-scaled attributes, and then finish up the decision using one of the noncompensatory techniques above.

Table 26.5 shows the nondimensional scaling for the UFO decision in the Total column (copied from Table 26.4) along with the two ordinal-scaled attributes, reliability and noise. UFO could apply any of the noncompensatory techniques to the data in Table 26.5 to make a final decision that incorporates the ordinal-scaled attributes.

ADDITIVE WEIGHTING

The additive weighting technique is the most popular compensatory technique. The process is identical to nondimensional scaling with the exception that the attributes can have different "weights" or degrees of influence on the decision. An attribute that's judged to be more important than another will have more influence on the outcome. If UFO decides cost is more important than speed and speed is more important than memory capacity, they will want a way to incorporate those priorities into the decision analysis.

To use the additive weighting technique, start by selecting the common scale for the attributes (0.0 to 1.0, 1 to 100, etc.) and convert all attribute values into that common scale. This is just like the nondimensional scaling technique as shown in Table 26.4 for the UFO case study.

The next step is to assign weights to each attribute based on its relative importance in the decision. There are many different approaches to assigning weights; the one described here has the advantage that it is separates dimensionalizing the attribute values from weighting the attributes themselves, so it reduces decision complexity and allows for more precise analysis. In this step, each of the attributes is given "points" corresponding to importance. An attribute with twice the importance is given twice as many points and so on. The weight for any individual attribute is just its number of points divided by the sum of the points across all attributes.

Suppose that UFO gives the point values shown in Table 26.6 to the ratio- and interval-scaled attributes. This means the heat coefficient is the least important and is half as important as memory capacity. AE(i) cost is most important and is twice as important as speed. The total number of points assigned is $30 + 15 + 10 + 5 = 60$. The weight for AE(i) cost is $30/60 = 0.50$, and the weight for heat is $5/60 = 0.08$.

The final step in additive weighting is to calculate each alternative's total weighted score to identify the best alternative.

$$WeightedScoreForAlternative_i = \sum_{j=1}^{n} (Attribute_j ForAlternative_i \times WeightForAttribute_j)$$

Table 26.7 shows the weighted score calculations for the UFO case study. For example, the weighted score for alternative A4 is $(35 * 0.50 + 86 * 0.25 + 50 * 0.17 + 89 * 0.08) = 55$.

Just like with the nondimensional scaling technique, the decision is made on the total score if there are no relevant ordinal-scaled attributes. Ignoring the ordinal-scaled attributes in the UFO example, alternative A1 is the best under additive weighting. If there are important ordinal-scaled attributes, they will need to be addressed as explained in the nondimensional scaling section.

ANALYTIC HIERARCHY PROCESS

Dr. Thomas Saaty, a pioneer in the field of operations research, developed the analytic hierarchy process (AHP) in the late 1960s [Saaty80] [Saaty94]. AHP is an enhancement of the additive weighting technique and has these features:

- AHP can convert ordinal-scaled values into ratio scales.
- AHP can help derive meaningful weights instead of just arbitrarily assigning them.
- AHP not only allows inconsistency, AHP provides a measure of that inconsistency.

Each of these features is described.

TABLE 26.6   Points and Weights for UFO Software's Ratio and Interval-Scaled Attributes

Attribute	Points	Weight
AE(i) cost	30	0.50
CPU speed in MIPS	15	0.25
Memory capacity in gigabytes	10	0.17
Heat coefficient	5	0.08

TABLE 26.7   Additive Weight Scoring for UFO Software's Alternatives

Alternative	Cost (0.50)	Speed (0.25)	Memory (0.17)	Heat (0.08)	Score
A1	100	0	0	100	58
A2	0	100	100	0	42
A3	42	31	0	60	34
A4	35	86	50	89	55
A5	58	31	25	60	46

TABLE 26.8   Assigning Points to Ordinal Values

Value	Point Score
Very reliable	100
Somewhat reliable	50
Average	20
Somewhat unreliable	0

Using AHP to Convert Ordinal-Scaled Attributes into Ratio-Scaled Attributes

Neither the nondimensional scaling nor additive weighting techniques provides a direct way to incorporate ordinal-scaled attributes into a compensatory decision analysis. Ordinal-scaled attributes need to be ignored, addressed in a follow-on analysis using non-compensatory techniques, or somehow converted into interval- or ratio-scaled measures.

One way to convert ordinal data into a ratio scale is just to assign relative point values to each of the ordinal values. For the noise attribute in the UFO case study, we might assign point values as shown in Table 26.8.

TABLE 26.9 AHP's Comparison Scale

Comparison	Numeric Value
The items have equal importance.	1
One item is weakly more important (experience and judgment slightly favor one over the other).	3
One item is strongly more important (experience and judgment strongly favor one over the other).	5
One item has demonstrated importance over the other (strongly favored as determined by independent authority).	7
One item has absolute importance over the other (the highest order of affirmation compared to the other).	9

If you assign N points to value V1 and M points to value V2, then, by definition, V1 is N/M times as important as V2. If you then assign P points to value V3, then, similarly, V2 is M/P times as important as V3. However, then it also follows that V1 is N/P times as important as V3. Making sure that the point assignments are consistent requires keeping all the values and their points in mind at the same time. This isn't difficult with only four values in the ordinal scale—there are only 12 relationships to manage—but complexity will increase roughly with the square of the number of values in the scale. When there are 10 values in an ordinal scale, there will be about 90 relationships to manage at the same time. One of the difficulties that AHP is designed to address is people's inability to deal with so many comparisons at the same time.

AHP manages that complexity by using a matrix to capture pair-wise comparisons. You never have to deal with more than one pair at a time. AHP also provides a relative comparison scale, shown in Table 26.9. The approach is demonstrated here using the reliable attribute in the UFO case study. Remember that the values in this scale are very reliable, somewhat reliable, average, and somewhat unreliable.

The first step is to build a comparison matrix, CM, like the one shown in Figure 26.5. The number in the ith row and jth column holds the relative importance, based on Table 26.9, of $Value_i$ to $Value_j$:

- The main diagonal (starting in the upper left going straight to the lower right) of the matrix will always contain 1s because any value is always "just as important" as itself.
- When $Value_i$ is more important than $Value_j$, put in the number from Table 26.9.
- When $Value_i$ is less important than $Value_j$, put in the reciprocal (1/N) of the number shown in Table 26.9.
- If the ith row and jth column holds the value N, the jth row and ith column must hold the value 1/N.

Intermediate values (2, 4, 6, 8) can be used to reflect a compromise, but this isn't common in AHP.

$$
CM = \begin{vmatrix} 1 & 5 & 7 & 9 \\ 1/5 & 1 & 3 & 5 \\ 1/7 & 1/3 & 1 & 3 \\ 1/9 & 1/5 & 1/3 & 1 \end{vmatrix} = \begin{vmatrix} 1.000 & 5.000 & 7.000 & 9.000 \\ 0.200 & 1.000 & 3.000 & 5.000 \\ 0.143 & 0.333 & 1.000 & 3.000 \\ 0.111 & 0.200 & 0.333 & 1.000 \end{vmatrix}
$$

FIGURE 26.5   The Value Comparison Matrix for UFO's Reliable Attribute

$$
CM' = \begin{vmatrix} 0.688 & 0.765 & 0.618 & 0.500 \\ 0.138 & 0.153 & 0.265 & 0.278 \\ 0.098 & 0.051 & 0.088 & 0.167 \\ 0.076 & 0.031 & 0.029 & 0.056 \end{vmatrix}
$$

FIGURE 26.6   The Normalized Comparison Matrix for the Reliable Attribute

TABLE 26.10   The Computed AHP Weights for Reliable Attribute Values

Value	Row Values	Weight
Very reliable	(0.688 + 0.765 + 0.618 + 0.500) / 4	0.643
Somewhat reliable	(0.138 + 0.153 + 0.265 + 0.278) / 4	0.208
Average	(0.098 + 0.051 + 0.088 + 0.167) / 4	0.101
Somewhat unreliable	(0.076 + 0.031 + 0.029 + 0.056) / 4	0.048

Assume UFO put the value somewhat unreliable at $i = 1$, average at $i = 2$, somewhat reliable at $i = 3$, and very reliable at $i = 4$. If UFO decides that average is strongly more important than somewhat unreliable, they would put 5 at row 1, column 2 and 1/5 at row 2, column 1. Figure 26.5 shows UFO's completed comparison matrix for the reliable attribute.

The next step is to normalize the comparison matrix. Compute the sum of each column; call it *SumC*. Then divide all the values in that column by that column's *SumC*. The sum of the values in column 1 of Figure 26.5 is 1.000 + 0.200 + 0.143 + 0.111 = 1.454, so divide all of column 1 by 1.454. The normalized matrix, CM', for the reliable attribute is shown in Figure 26.6.

The next step is to compute the weights by taking the average of the values in each row in the normalized comparison table. This is shown in Table 26.10. Note that by construction, the sum of AHP weights will always equal 1.0.

These weights are then converted to the common scale as described for nondimensional scaling. Remember that UFO chose a scale of 0 to 100 with 100 being best. The ratio-scaled values for the reliable attribute are shown in Table 26.11.

TABLE 26.11   The Computed AHP Scores for Reliable Attribute Values

Value	Common Scale Score
Very reliable	(0.048 − 0.643) / (0.048 − 0.643) * 100 = 100
Somewhat reliable	(0.048 − 0.208) / (0.048 − 0.643) * 100 = 27
Average	(0.048 − 0.101) / (0.048 − 0.643) * 100 = 9
Somewhat unreliable	(0.048 − 0.048) / (0.048 − 0.643) * 100 = 0

$$CM = \begin{vmatrix} 1 & 3 & 7 \\ 1/3 & 1 & 3 \\ 1/7 & 1/3 & 1 \end{vmatrix}$$

FIGURE 26.7   The Value Comparison Matrix for UFO's Reliable Attribute

TABLE 26.12   The Computed AHP Scores for Noise Attribute Values

Value	Common Scale Score
Quiet	100
Average	27
Noisy	0

For the noise attribute, assume UFO put the value noisy at $i = 1$, average at $i = 2$, and quiet at $i = 3$. Figure 26.7 shows UFO's value comparison matrix for the reliable attribute, and Table 26.12 shows the computed AHP scores for noise attribute values. (The analysis is a self-study question.)

Using AHP to Develop Attribute Weights   The process for developing attribute weights is virtually identical to the process for converting ordinal-scaled attributes to ratio scales. The only difference is that the comparison is done on an attribute-by-attribute basis rather than a value-by-value basis. The steps taken for the UFO case study are shown. Figure 26.8 shows the attribute comparison matrix for the UFO example with AE(i) cost at $i = 1$ and noise at $i = 6$.

$$
CM = \begin{vmatrix}
1 & 3 & 5 & 9 & 7 & 7 \\
1/3 & 1 & 3 & 7 & 5 & 5 \\
1/5 & 1/3 & 1 & 5 & 3 & 3 \\
1/9 & 1/7 & 1/5 & 1 & 1/3 & 1/3 \\
1/7 & 1/5 & 1/3 & 3 & 1 & 1 \\
1/7 & 1/5 & 1/3 & 3 & 1 & 1
\end{vmatrix}
$$

FIGURE 26.8   The attribute comparison matrix for UFO Software

$$
CM' = \begin{vmatrix}
0.518 & 0.615 & 0.507 & 0.321 & 0.404 & 0.404 \\
0.173 & 0.205 & 0.304 & 0.250 & 0.288 & 0.288 \\
0.104 & 0.068 & 0.101 & 0.179 & 0.173 & 0.173 \\
0.058 & 0.029 & 0.020 & 0.036 & 0.019 & 0.019 \\
0.074 & 0.041 & 0.034 & 0.107 & 0.058 & 0.058 \\
0.074 & 0.041 & 0.034 & 0.107 & 0.058 & 0.058
\end{vmatrix}
$$

FIGURE 26.9   The normalized attribute comparison matrix for UFO Software

TABLE 26.13   The Computed AHP Weights for UFO Software

Attribute	Row Values	Weight
AE(i) cost	(0.518 + 0.615 + 0.507 + 0.321 + 0.404 + 0.404) / 6	0.462
Speed	(0.173 + 0.205 + 0.304 + 0.250 + 0.288 + 0.288) / 6	0.251
Memory	(0.104 + 0.068 + 0.101 + 0.179+ 0.173 + 0.173) / 6	0.133
Heat	(0.058 + 0.029 + 0.020 + 0.036 + 0.019 + 0.019) / 6	0.030
Reliable	(0.074 + 0.041 + 0.034+ 0.107 + 0.058 + 0.058) / 6	0.062
Noise	(0.074 + 0.041 + 0.034+ 0.107 + 0.058 + 0.058) / 6	0.062

The next step is to normalize the weights. The normalized matrix, CM' for the UFO case study is shown in Figure 26.9.

The next step in AHP is to compute the weights by taking the average of the values in each row of the normalized comparison matrix. This is shown in Table 26.13.

Table 26.14 shows the final AHP scoring for the UFO Software decision. The cost, speed, memory, and heat values are copied from Table 26.4 in the discussion of nondimensional scaling. The reliable attribute values are derived from Table 26.11, and the noise values are derived from Table 26.12. The attribute weights are from Table 26.13.

TABLE 26.14 AHP Scoring for UFO Software's Alternatives

Alternative	Cost (0.462)	Speed (0.251)	Memory (0.133)	Heat (0.030)	Reliable (0.062)	Noise (0.062)	Weighted Total
A1	100	0	0	100	0	27	50.9
A2	0	100	100	0	100	100	50.8
A3	42	31	0	60	9	27	31.2
A4	35	86	50	89	9	0	47.6
A5	58	31	25	60	27	27	43.1

According to the AHP technique, and using the weights defined in Table 26.13, UFO Software should choose alternative A1. Notice that alternative A1 is better than A2 by only a very slight margin.

AHP Inconsistency Ratio   AHP provides an "inconsistency ratio" that is based on the eigenvalue of the un-normalized comparison matrix. The description of how to calculate the eigenvalue of a matrix is beyond the scope of this book but can be found in a college-level linear algebra textbook. The inconsistency ratio is computed from the following formula:

$$InconsistencyRatio = \frac{\lambda_{max} - n}{n - 1}$$

Where:

- λ_{max} is the eigenvalue of the un-normalized comparison matrix.
- n is the number of attributes in the comparison matrix.

The eigenvalue for UFO Software's un-normalized comparison matrix for the reliable attribute is 6.255, and the resulting inconsistency ratio is as follows:

$$InconsistencyRatio = \frac{6.255 - 6}{6 - 1} = 0.051 = 5.1\%$$

An inconsistency ratio of 0% means perfect consistency, whereas a ratio of 100% means that the pair-wise comparison values appear to have been assigned at random. An inconsistency ratio of 10% or less is usually considered acceptable, but this needs to be addressed on a case-by-case basis. Sometimes the nature of the decision allows a higher inconsistency or requires a lower inconsistency.

Summary

Aside from technical feasibility, money is almost always the most important decision criterion, but it's certainly not always the only one. Quite often there are other criteria, other "attributes," that need to be considered, and those attributes can't be cast in terms of money. This chapter presented several techniques for making decisions when there is more than one attribute to consider. The chapter covered the following major points:

- Use values are often quantifiable in terms of money. Often, however, one or more esteem-values are relevant in the decision, and esteem-values can't be quantified in terms of money. This means that decisions involving more than one attribute are inevitable.
- Decision attributes need to be chosen so that they cover all the relevant use-values and esteem-values.
- Each alternative needs to be evaluated with respect to each attribute. There are several different classes of measurement: nominal, ordinal, interval, and ratio. Within each class of measurement, some manipulations will make sense and others won't.
- In the noncompensatory family of techniques, each decision attribute is treated as a separate entity. The noncompensatory family includes dominance, satisficing, and lexicography.
- The compensatory family of techniques allows better performance on one attribute to compensate for poorer performance in another; tradeoffs between the attributes are allowed. The compensatory family includes nondimensional scaling, additive weighting, and analytic hierarchy process (AHP).

The final part, next, is a summary of the content in the entire book.

Self-Study Questions

1. Mountain Systems needs to build a new corporate headquarters building. It is still early in the process, so they haven't even decided what city to locate the new building in. Give examples of at least three use-value factors that could be relevant in deciding what kind of building and where to locate it.

2. Give examples of at least three esteem-value factors for the Mountain Systems headquarters building decision.

3. The following are examples of measurement scales; what class of scale are they?
   a. Calendar date
   b. Age
   c. Seasons

4. UFO Software is looking at automating their corporate payroll process. Some of the alternatives include commercially available payroll software packages, subscribing to one of several payroll services, or building their own software system. Give at least four examples of relevant decision attributes. What measurement scales might be appropriate for those attributes?

Questions 5 through 8 relate to the following situation. Carole is shopping for a computer for home use. After researching the market, she's narrowed her search down to the following choices because they seem the closest match to her preferences.

Feature	Store A	Store B	Store C
Price	$1979	$1995	$1999
RAM	512MB	256MB	512MB
Disk	1GB	1GB	1GB
DVD	Yes	No	Yes
Warranty	3 mos	6 mos	3 mos
CPU speed	1.6GHz	1.6GHz	1.8GHz
Monitor size	13"	13"	15"

5. Are any of Carole's choices dominated? If so, which one?

6. Suppose that after further thought Carole decides that the following minimum criteria are necessary:

Price under $2000

At least 512MB RAM

At least 1.6GHz CPU speed

Using the satisficing technique, would any of Carole's choices be eliminated?

7. Assume that the sales people at each store say that they will price-match any competitor's similar offer, and so consider the prices to be identical. Carole decides to prioritize the attributes as follows:

1. Price
2. RAM
3. Disk capacity
4. Has DVD
5. Monitor size

Using the lexicography technique, explain the steps in Carole's decision process. Which choice is best, if any?

8. Assume that the price-match offer is in place as in the previous question but that Carole prioritizes the attributes as follows:

   1. Price
   2. Disk capacity
   3. Duration of warranty period
   4. RAM
   5. Monitor size

   Using the lexicography technique, explain the steps in Carole's decision process. Which choice is best, if any?

Questions 9 through 17 refer to the following situation: Big Software, Inc. has an internally developed customer relationship management (CRM) system. Big Software has grown so much over the years that the existing CRM system isn't going to be capable of meeting the company's needs for much longer. Four technically feasible, mutually exclusive alternative solutions have been identified through a preliminary investigation:

- Modify the existing system, which is implemented in a mixture of Cobol and C
- Redevelop the system from the ground up using Java
- Buy a commercial package from Vendor A
- Buy a commercial package from Vendor B

The decision criteria have been defined as follows:

- Development/acquisition cost and long-term operating and maintenance cost
- Availability date as measured by when the system could be put into production
- How interesting the project would be for the project team
- Reliability of the product
- Adaptability of the product

The following table shows how each of the alternatives measures up on each of the decision attributes.

Alternative	PW(i) Cost	Availability	Interest	Reliability	Adaptability
Modify	$90,000	4 months	Low	Low	Low
Redevelop	$360,000	12 months	High	Medium	High
Package A	$200,000	2 month	Medium	Medium	Medium
Package B	$180,000	1 months	Medium	High	Low

9. Are any of the alternatives dominated? If so, state which one(s).

10. In preparation for using compensatory decision techniques, calculate the common scale values for the cost attribute. Use a range of 0 to 100 with 100 being the best.

11. In preparation for using compensatory decision techniques, calculate the common scale values for the availability attribute. Use a range of 0 to 100 with 100 being the best.

12. Use your answers from the previous two questions to complete the ranking of the alternatives using the nondimensional scaling technique on the cost and availability attributes only. Which alternative would Big Software choose in this situation?

13. Assume that Big Software considers cost to be twice as important as availability. Use the additive weighting technique to show how each alternative compares and identify which alternative (if any) would be preferred.

14. Assume that Big Software considers availability to be 75% more important than cost. Use the additive weighting technique to show how each alternative compares and identify which alternative (if any) would be preferred.

15. Assume that Big Software has decided to use the analytic hierarchy process (AHP) to address the ordinal-scaled attributes (interest, reliability, and adaptability). Because these three attributes use the same low-medium-high scale, Big Software has decided to convert that scale into a ratio scale using AHP. Assume the pair-wise weights have been assigned as shown in the following table. (High is at row and column 1, medium is at row and column 2, low is at row and column 3.)

$$CM = \begin{vmatrix} 1 & 3 & 5 \\ 1/3 & 1 & 3 \\ 1/5 & 1/3 & 1 \end{vmatrix}$$

Calculate the ratio scale values using the AHP process.

16. Using the ratio scaled values for low-medium-high from the previous question, assume that Big Software created the following comparison matrix for the decision attributes. Cost is in row and column 1, availability is in row and column 2, interest is in row and column 3, reliability is in row and column 4, and adaptability is in row and column 5.

$$CM = \begin{vmatrix} 1 & 3 & 9 & 5 & 7 \\ 1/3 & 1 & 9 & 3 & 5 \\ 1/9 & 1/9 & 1 & 1/5 & 1/7 \\ 1/5 & 1/3 & 5 & 1 & 3 \\ 1/7 & 1/5 & 7 & 1/3 & 1 \end{vmatrix}$$

Calculate the attribute weights for this decision using the AHP process.

17. Using the attribute weights calculated in the previous question, complete the calculations to show the relative scores and identify Big Software's best alternative.

18. Show the computations in the conversion of the Noise attribute in the UFO Software example into ratio scale using the AHP process. Start with the comparison data in Figure 26.7 and show how the weights in Table 26.12 were derived. Show your work at the same level of detail as was shown in the computations of the attribute Reliable.

19. If you have a way to compute eigenvalues, use the comparison matrix from question 15 to compute the inconsistency ratio.

20. If you have a way to compute eigenvalues, use the comparison matrix from question 16 to compute the inconsistency ratio.

21. If you have a way to compute eigenvalues, use the comparison matrix from question 18 to compute the inconsistency ratio.

PART EIGHT

SUMMARY

This book is about making choices: software technical choices in a business context. This final part summarizes the book and shows how to apply these concepts and techniques to some important situations commonly encountered on software projects.

27

Closing Remarks

This chapter gives a review of the book and shows several examples of how the concepts and techniques can be applied to some of the important decisions facing a typical software organization. The chapter also revisits the primary and secondary messages in the book.

A Review of the Book

Figure 27.1 shows the business decision-making process introduced in Chapter 4. This process applies at all levels of decision: from a decision as big as should a software project be done at all, down to a decision on an algorithm or data structure to use in a software module. The difference is only how financially significant the decision is and, therefore, how much effort should be invested in making that decision. The project-level decision is usually pretty significant and warrants a relatively high level of effort to make the decision. Selecting an algorithm is much less significant and usually warrants a much lower level of effort to make the decision, even though the same decision-making process is used. In practice the process is more fluid, steps can be done in different orders and some steps can be done in parallel.

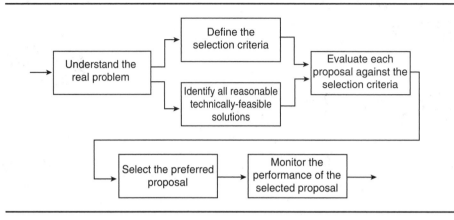

FIGURE 27.1 The business decision-making process

The book is summarized in the context of this process.

UNDERSTAND THE REAL PROBLEM

The process begins with gaining an understanding of the real problem to be solved. The problem may be to decide how to invest the organization's resources, or it may be to design the database for a software system. Without understanding the real problem, the chosen solution would likely not meet the needs of the organization. This step is described in Chapter 4.

DEFINE THE SELECTION CRITERIA

Given a solid understanding of the problem, the decision maker can define the selection criteria. The important part of this step is to capture all of the relevant criteria that will be used in making the decision. This step is detailed in both Chapter 4 and Chapter 26.

IDENTIFY ALL REASONABLE TECHNICALLY FEASIBLE SOLUTIONS

Given a good understanding of the problem, the decision maker is also in a position to start identifying technically feasible solutions to that problem—these are the proposals. As many technically feasible solutions as is practical should be created, to increase the chances that the best overall solution is in the set being considered. This is explained in Chapter 4.

When the organization has resources to carry out more than one solution at the same time—for instance, the problem is to determine how to best invest the organization's limited resources—the proposals need to be converted into mutually exclusive alternatives as described in Chapter 9.

EVALUATE EACH SOLUTION AGAINST THE SELECTION CRITERIA

With the selection criteria and a set of technically feasible solutions in hand, the decision maker can now evaluate each solution against each of the selection criteria. This is described in Chapters 4 and 26. When the decision criteria are financial, it will be necessary to develop the cash-flow stream for each solution described in Chapter 3 (for proposals) and Chapter 9 (for mutually exclusive alternatives).

SELECT THE PREFERRED PROPOSAL

Most of this book described the details of the selection process itself. Part II explained the concepts and techniques for making business decisions in for-profit organizations. Specific topics included the minimum attractive rate of return (MARR), decisions based on differential cash flow vs. total cash flow, economic life and planning horizons, as well as two special cases in for-profit decision analysis: replacement decisions and (asset) retirement decisions.

Part III extended the for-profit process in Part II with concepts and techniques that provide additional accuracy for situations where that accuracy is needed. The topics in this part included inflation and deflation, depreciation, general accounting, cost accounting, income taxes, and the consequences of income taxes on business decisions.

Part IV presented the financial selection process in not-for-profit organizations. The concepts and techniques in this part included benefit-cost analysis and cost-effectiveness analysis.

Part V explained break-even analysis and optimization analysis. These techniques are often called "present economy" because they usually aren't used in a way that addresses the time value of money (interest) (i.e., "future economy").

Estimation is an essential part of making good business decisions. Part VI detailed the concepts and techniques of estimation. It also explained risk and uncertainty and showed how they can influence, and be addressed in, business decisions.

Part VII provided a set of techniques, such as lexicography, additive weighting, and analytic hierarchy process (AHP), that are useful when there are multiple decision attributes.

MONITOR PERFORMANCE OF THE SELECTED SOLUTION

The quality of the decision depends on the quality of the estimates. Simply put, bad estimates can easily lead to bad decisions. It's very important to "close the loop" on estimates by comparing the original estimates to the actual outcomes. Otherwise you would never know whether your estimates were any good. Use the difference between the original estimates and the actual outcomes to refine your estimation techniques to account for the factors that made up the differences. This was explained in Chapter 4.

The Primary Message

Every day, software professionals make decisions that affect the costs and revenues of their employers. Decisions such as "Should we even do the Alpha project?" "How much testing is enough?" "Should the Omega project use the Rational Unified Process [Kruchten00]?" "Or, would eXtreme Programming [Beck00] or one of the other agile [Cockburn02] methods be better?" and so on. These decisions have tended to be made from a purely technical perspective, but they can have serious implications on the business viability of the software project and the resulting software product—maybe on the entire organization.

Having seen the concepts and techniques in this book, let's examine the kinds of important decisions that a typical software organization faces. Instead of looking at them from a strictly technical perspective, however, we'll see how to align those decisions with the goals of the business. The questions examined in this section include the following:

- Which software project(s) should we do?
- Should we add new features or fix known defects?
- Should new technology x be used on this project?
- Which software development life cycle should we use?
- How much software testing is enough?

WHICH SOFTWARE PROJECT(S) SHOULD WE DO?

From a business perspective, answering the question of which software project(s) to do is very straightforward using the concepts and techniques in this book. Simply put, each project is a proposal (Chapter 3):

1. Start by identifying the candidate software projects: the proposals.

2. Develop a cash-flow stream for each proposal (Chapter 3).

3. Use those proposals to identify mutually exclusive alternatives (Chapter 9), paying attention to resource limits and dependencies (e.g., Project Y may not make sense until after Project X has been completed). The best alternative might be some combination of the proposals.

4. Use the decision-making techniques in for-profit (Part II) or not-for-profit (Part IV) organizations as appropriate. In for-profit organizations, if more accuracy is needed in the decision, then also use the advanced for-profit decision techniques (Part III) such as addressing income taxes and inflation.

Because the decision is based on estimates, techniques such as ranges of estimates, sensitivity analysis, or delaying final decisions (Chapter 23) could come in handy. If there are other significant risks or uncertainties in any of the alternatives (e.g., are any of the proposals likely to overrun their cost, schedule, or quality goals? If so, by how much?), the decisions under risk (Chapter 24) or decisions under uncertainty (Chapter 25) techniques can be applied as appropriate.

If other nonfinancial decision criteria are relevant, the multiple attribute decision techniques (Chapter 26) can be used.

SHOULD WE ADD NEW FEATURES OR FIX KNOWN DEFECTS?

Selecting which features to add and what defects to fix is essentially the same as the "which software project(s) should we do?" question. Instead of looking at separate projects as proposals, each new feature—and fixing each known defect—can be treated as proposals.

Often, there are so many candidate features and defect fixes that the number of proposals is unmanageable. The decision can be simplified by grouping sets of related features and/or defect fixes into "packages," where each package is a useful collection of new features and/or defect fixes. Suppose that the packages for a particular software project can be called A, B, and C. Assuming that each package matches the amount of work that can be done with the available resources, the mutually exclusive alternatives correspond to completing the packages in different orders. With the three packages, and assuming there are no dependencies between the packages, the mutually exclusive alternatives would be as follows:

ABC
ACB
BAC
BCA
CAB
CBA

After the mutually exclusive alternatives have been identified and their cash-flow streams have been developed, the remainder of the decision-making process described above can be applied to identify the preferred sequence.

SHOULD NEW TECHNOLOGY X BE USED ON THIS PROJECT?

When deciding whether to use some new technology on a project, there are usually several mutually exclusive alternatives to consider:

1. Use the proposed new technology.

2. Use some existing, already-known technology.

3. Possibly, develop the capability on your own. (This is not always a viable alternative.)

Suppose the proposed new technology is test automation: using a software tool to automatically apply test cases to the software being developed. The mutually exclusive alternatives in this situation would be as follows:

1. Buy an off-the-shelf test automation tool. This could be more than one alternative if different off-the-shelf tools are being considered.

2. Continue to use the organization's existing manual testing method.

3. As part of the project, develop an in-house test automation tool.

The process for making the decision from a business perspective is as follows:

1. Develop cash-flow streams for each of the mutually exclusive alternatives.

2. Use the decision-making techniques in for-profit (Part II) or not-for-profit (Part IV) as appropriate for your organization. In for-profit organizations, if more accuracy is needed, use the advanced for-profit decision techniques (Part III) such as addressing income taxes and inflation

The decision is based on estimates, so you may want to use techniques such as ranges of estimates, sensitivity analysis, or delaying final decisions (Chapter 23). There is likely to be more risk or uncertainty with the new technology alternative(s), so the decisions under risk (Chapter 24) or decisions under uncertainty (Chapter 25) techniques are probably appropriate. If other decision criteria are relevant, the multiple-attribute decision techniques (Chapter 26) can be applied.

WHICH SOFTWARE DEVELOPMENT LIFE CYCLE SHOULD WE USE?

There are dozens of different software development life cycles, and there has always been almost religious debate between the advocates of each. The recent major debate has been between the plan-based life cycle (typified by the Rational Unified Process) advocates and the agile life cycle (e.g., eXtreme Programming, Scrum [Schwaber02], and Crystal [Cockburn02]) advocates. Cutting through the dogma and hype, this decision should be seen as selecting the right tool for the job.

Development life cycles can be seen as a spectrum. A development life cycle on the plan-based end plans the entire project from the start to finish and usually includes a minimum of iteration and feedback. A development life cycle on the agile end does planning but only for the current iteration, which is usually two to four weeks. A middle-of-the-road development life cycle such as the Rational Unified Process would typically include a small number of iterations of two to four months each. A middle-of-the-road life cycle would tend to have detailed planning for the current iteration and only partial planning of the later iterations. The plans for later iterations would be refined as the project progresses—this is known as "rolling wave planning" and is a project management best practice identified in the Guide to the Project Management Body of Knowledge (PM-BOK) [PMI00].

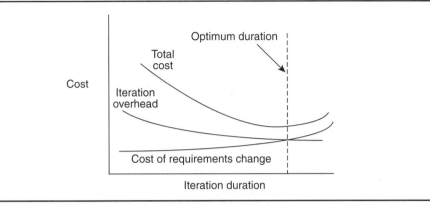

FIGURE 27.2   Optimum iteration duration for a plan-based project

Choosing a development life cycle is essentially an optimization problem (Chapter 20), with the decision variable being the duration of the iterations. The competing components are overhead costs and rework costs due to requirements instability. As iteration duration increases, overhead costs tend to decrease. One decreasing overhead cost is from assumptions made in early iterations about future requirements being invalidated by the real requirement when it is finally discovered later in the project. This leads to re-coding and refactoring that could have been avoided had the complete requirements been known beforehand. Another decreasing overhead cost is QA. Functionality delivered in earlier iterations needs to be regression tested in later iterations; fewer iterations mean less regression testing. On the other hand, as iteration duration increases, the cost from rework due to requirements and design instability tends to increase; the shorter the iteration, the less chance there is for the requirements to change during that iteration.

Figure 27.2 shows the situation for a software project on the plan-based end of the spectrum. Plan-based life cycles tend to minimize overall project cost and schedule in implementing known requirements, but they depend on those requirements staying stable throughout the project. The more stable the requirements are, the more overall cost and schedule can be minimized by using plan-based life cycles with long(er) iterations. In the extreme, perfectly stable requirements can lead to a single iteration; a waterfall life cycle.

Figure 27.3 shows the situation for a software project on the agile end of the spectrum. Agile life cycles do an excellent job of dealing with unstable requirements. The less stable the requirements are, the shorter the iterations need to be to manage that instability; but that flexibility causes a slight increase in overall cost and schedule.

The trick is to choose an iteration length that balances minimizing cost and schedule with the flexibility needed to manage requirements instability. Iterations should be made as long as possible—to minimize overall cost and schedule—but not so long that requirements start to become unstable over that duration. If the requirements are likely to be stable over several months, a plan-based life cycle is more appropriate. If the requirements can't be expected to be stable for more than just a few weeks, the project is a good candidate for an agile life cycle.

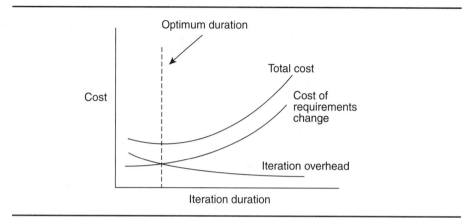

FIGURE 27.3 Optimum iteration duration for an agile project

The full decision is likely to be a multi-attribute decision (Chapter 26). Additional attributes relevant to a software development life cycle decision include the following:

- How soon does the software development life cycle allow the project team to deliver functioning, usable software to the customer? Just as money has time value (Chapter 5), so does functionality delivered to the user; the sooner functionality is delivered, the more valuable it is. Agile life cycles tend to excel at this because they emphasize delivering the most valuable functions to the user as soon as possible.
- How important to the stakeholders is progress visibility and how well does each candidate software development life cycle provide that visibility? Agile life cycles tend to give better visibility because there is more certainty of progress in working functionality than there is in software documentation.
- What life cycles do the project team already know and what would it cost (money, time, and productivity) to learn a different one?

HOW MUCH SOFTWARE TESTING IS ENOUGH?

The question of "how much software testing is enough?" has been a difficult question for many software organizations. However, that's usually because they've been approaching it from the wrong perspective. It's not a technical question at all; it's a business question. Despite what the typical end user license agreement states, shipping software products exposes the software organization to product liability. In the United States, the *Uniform Commercial Code* (UCC) takes precedence over software license agreements for commercial software products (see, for example, http://www.law. cornell.edu/ucc/ucc.table.html). In an internal IS organization, and similarly for nonprofit and government organizations, putting defective software into production (whether that software was internally developed or not) exposes the organization to the risk of lost data, lost production time, and so on.

Essentially this is an optimization question (Chapter 20); the decision variable is how much testing to perform. The more testing that's done, the lower the organization's exposure to risk. On the other hand, the more testing that's done, the higher the testing costs will be. As well, increased testing delays putting the software into productive use for the customer. Simply put, the software should be tested until the cost of additional testing becomes higher than the value of the risk reduction plus the lost business benefit of not having the software in use. Using the concepts and techniques in this book—such as optimization (Chapter20), expected value (Chapter 24) and fixed-cost analysis vs. fixed-effectiveness analysis (Chapter 18)—the question can be answered from a business perspective.

A Secondary Message: Software Engineering Versus Computer Science

Engineering is a well-defined term: It means using relevant theory to generate as many possible solutions as are reasonable and then using business criteria (engineering economy) to select the most cost-effective one. Figure 27.1 is actually a description of the engineering process. According to the engineer's definition of engineering, software is not, today, a legitimate engineering discipline. Wanting our work to be considered engineering and continually saying that it is does not make it so. We, as an industry, need to recognize what is truly required of legitimate engineering disciplines and take positive steps to fill the gaps (see for example, [Hooten90], [McConnell03], [Shaw90], [SWEBOK01]). To accurately call yourself a software engineer, you need a strong foundation in computer science and discrete mathematics. But that's not enough: You also need a strong foundation in engineering economy—the subject of this book—so that your software technical decisions are aligned with the goals of the organization.

Summary

In the end this book is about making choices. Software professionals are faced with choices every day; but even apparently innocuous choices can have a noticeable effect on the organization's finances. As professionals, we need to be making responsible choices: choices that make sense both technically and to the organization. As Leon Levy said [Levy87]

> Software economics has often been misconceived as the means of estimating the cost of programming projects. But economics is primarily a science of choice, and software economics should provide methods and models for analyzing the choices that software projects must make.

Using the methods and models in this book, software technical decisions can be aligned with the goals of the organization.

Self-Study Questions

1. Do you agree that engineering economy is a relevant topic for software engineers? Why or why not?

2. Can software be considered a corporate asset? Should it be? (Remember the implications of depreciating assets vs. writing them off as expenses.)

3. What factor(s) would you consider to be motivators that would push you to use these concepts and techniques on software projects?

4. What factor(s) would you consider to be obstacles that would deter you from using these concepts and techniques on software projects?

Appendix A

Software Project Work Breakdown Structures

A work breakdown structure (WBS) is a decomposition of all the work associated with a proposal (e.g., a candidate software project) being studied. The WBS not only helps you better understand the size and scope of the proposal, it also can be a useful planning and management tool if the proposal is given the go-ahead. The WBS is an important tool in business decisions because it provides a solid foundation for developing a proposal's cash-flow stream. More information about WBSs and how to develop them can be found in [PMI02], [DoD98], and [Fleming00].

A common notation for a WBS is to show the proposal at levels of decomposition using indentation. The highest-level item is the overall proposal itself and is not indented. Under this, the proposal is successively broken down into smaller and smaller units of work, called tasks. As each higher-level task is broken down into smaller tasks, move in one level of indentation on the WBS listing. The decomposition is continued until the bottom-level, primitive tasks represent relatively well-understood units of work. For our purposes, continue breaking each task down into lower level tasks until the lowest-level tasks are small enough that they can be cost- and schedule-estimated with enough accuracy for the decision being studied.

For obvious reasons, the WBS needs to contain *all* the labor, material, etc. relevant to the proposal, but just as important it needs to have *only* the labor, material, etc. associated with that proposal. Tasks that are really part of some other subject shouldn't be included in this proposal's WBS.

Developing a WBS

As an example, we will develop a WBS for owning and operating a car. This example is nontrivial, but it's still straightforward and not too complex. We'll look at a WBS framework for software projects below.

  Start with the overall proposal then break it down as needed. First, there's the highest-level task:

> Own and operate a car

At this high a level, the proposal isn't broken down nearly enough to get good cost, revenue, and schedule estimates. So break it down a level. You'll first have to buy the car, then you can operate it, and finally you will sell it when you're ready to get a new car. It might help to decompose the proposal into one-time-only tasks and recurring tasks, but this isn't necessary. Just make sure that you've included all of the tasks, both one-time and recurring, in the WBS. Buying the car and selling the car are one-time tasks, whereas operating and maintaining the car is a recurring task. The WBS now looks something like this:

> Own and operate a car
> > Buy the car
> > Operate and maintain the car
> > Sell the car

Assuming we can estimate the cash-flow amount and we know the approximate timing of the "Sell the car" task, we won't need to break that task down any further. It's probably fine-grained enough for our purposes. The tasks "Buy the car" and "Operate and maintain the car" are still too coarse-grained to be useful for cost and schedule estimates. So we break them down another level:

> Own and operate a car
> > Buy the car
> > > Pay the down payment
> > > Pay the taxes, licensing, and registration fees
> > > Insure the car
> > > Make the monthly car loan payments
> > Operate and maintain the car
> > > Pay the semi-annual insurance payments
> > > Fill the car with gas when needed
> > > Change the oil every 3,000 miles
> > > Other routine maintenance as needed
> > Sell the car

If we want to, and if we have sufficient knowledge about the situation to do so, we could continue to break the bottom level tasks into even finer-grained items. For example, the task "Change the oil every 3,000 miles" could be broken down like this:

> Change the oil every 3000 miles
>> Take the car to the oil change shop
>> Let them do the work
>> Pay the fees and taxes

This leads to the question, "How far should the WBS be decomposed?" The WBS needs to be broken down finely enough that you can get reasonably accurate estimates for the amounts and timing of the cash-flows instances for each bottom-level task. If you can't make a reasonable estimate at the current level of granularity (for example, "pay for the car when you buy it"), break that task down into its constituent tasks. But don't keep breaking down forever; stop when you have enough detail to make sufficiently accurate estimates given the needs of the decision that is being studied. In this example, the finer level of detail under the oil change item doesn't really add to our knowledge of the situation, so it's not worth breaking it down to that level. If the lower-level breakdown is not knowable, or it is likely to change between now and when the higher-level task is actually carried out (assuming the project is approved), it's better to not break the higher-level task down into subtasks.

Our WBS is being used to help create a cash-flow stream, so it needs to include tasks that represent all costs and income, not just work to be done. If you need to pay for parking at your office or school, for instance, make sure that task is also included under operating and maintaining the car. Similarly, if buying the car includes a rebate, or if the car is going to be used as a taxi, you need to be sure to include those kinds of income as tasks in the WBS.

Now look at a software project. All software projects are very different; they all have different lifecycles, use different programming languages, have different project management techniques, and so forth. So there isn't a complete, detailed, bottom-level WBS that works for every software project. However, you can get a good start at developing the WBS for any individual software project by starting with the high-level software project WBS template that follows. Feel free to drop any tasks that don't apply to your particular project and add in any new tasks that are unique to your project or the way you choose to run it. Feel free to rearrange the items if you think they make more sense organized a different way. Also feel free to adapt and evolve your own WBS template from project to project. The important thing is to have a complete and accurate accounting of all of the cost- and revenue-generating events and activities in the proposal being studied.

Software Project WBS Template

Generic Software Project
  Software development
    Requirements
      Functional requirements
      Nonfunctional requirements
    Design
      External interface design
      High-level architecture
      Detailed design
    Construction
      Coding
      Debugging
    Integration
      Software-to-software
      Software-to-hardware
    Prototyping
  Software quality assurance
    Peer reviews
    Test planning
      Unit test planning
      Integration and component test planning
      System test planning (alpha test, beta test)
      Acceptance test planning
    Test execution
      Unit testing
      Integration and component testing
      System testing (alpha test, beta test)
      Acceptance testing
    Software process improvement
  Software product deployment and support
    Product packaging
    User documentation
    System installation/conversion
      Data installation/conversion
      Software product installation/conversion
    User support/help desk
    Data base administration (DBA)
    System operation
    Ongoing software product maintenance

Software project management
    Project planning
    Project staffing
        Hiring new staff as needed
        Training staff as needed
    Risk management
    Project tracking and control
    Configuration and change management
    Supplier/subcontractor management
    Status meetings and project/program reviews
Administrative support
    Secretarial support
    Other office administration
Computers and other hardware and software
    Acquire and install development environment (purchase/lease) [*]
    Operation, maintenance, and support of development environment
    Acquire and install test environment (purchase/lease) [*]
    Operation, maintenance, and support of test environment
    Connection to external networks (e.g., ISP)
    Disposal/salvage of equipment at end of project [*]
Office space/facilities
    Facility purchase/lease [*]
    Facility provisioning (build-out, furniture, office equipment, etc.) [*]
    Operation, maintenance, and support of facilities
    Utilities (electricity, water, gas, waste, etc.)
    Disposal/salvage of facilities at end of project [*]
Project financing
    Obtain funding (internally, venture capital, loans, etc.)
    Loan repayment (principal and interest) [*]
Project income
    Income through product/service sales and licensing
        New product/service sales and licensing
        Upgrade sales/service and licensing
    Income through product/service support
        Maintenance contracts
        Product/service training
        Product/service consulting services
        Support/help-line subscriptions
    Cost avoidance

NOTES

- There can be debate about where in the WBS any specific task belongs. This is usually a rather meaningless debate. It's much less important *where* things are in the WBS; what's critical is that the right things *are* in the WBS. The WBS needs to be complete (every necessary lower level task is included), concise (every lower level task is really necessary), and detailed enough to support appropriate cost and schedule estimation.
- Under the Software Development section, the next level of decomposition should reflect *your* software development activities (i.e., the phases in your software development life cycle). For example, if your life cycle has an architecture activity/phase, be sure to include it.
- Under the Software Development section, you may choose to break down the subtasks (Requirements, Design, etc.) by subsystem instead of using the activity-based breakdown shown.
- Under the Software Development section, you may choose to represent the breakdown using a project matrix [Shlaer84]. The project matrix represents the technical part of the WBS as a matrix that has a list of the subsystems on one axis and a list of the life cycle phases/activities on the other. Each cell in the project matrix corresponds to the task that applies the named life cycle activity/phase to the named subsystem. This form of WBS tends to be more compact and concise than the traditional hierarchical form found in the typical WBS.
- The tasks marked with [*] may need to be treated special if the decision analysis will be done in terms of the after-tax cash-flow stream because these items may involve loan interest payments or depreciation accounting. Refer to Chapter 6 for separating loan principal and interest payments and Chapter 14 for depreciation accounting. Refer to Chapter 16 for addressing loan interest payments and depreciation accounting in after-tax cash-flow streams.

Checklist

The following checklist can be used to assess a proposed WBS for completeness and consistency:

1. The set of tasks in the WBS are necessary and sufficient for completing the software project: The project will be considered complete if all tasks have been completed and would be considered incomplete it any tasks were not completed.

2. The WBS addresses all relevant perspectives: technical, management, quality, deployment, and, as appropriate, marketing, sales, end-user participation, and so on.

3. Tasks representing all relevant sources of expense (initial expense, operating and maintenance, etc.) appear in the WBS.

4. Tasks representing all relevant sources of revenue (sales income, cost avoidance, and salvage value) appear in the WBS.

5. There aren't any duplicate tasks (i.e., all work appears only once in the WBS).

6. All tasks at a next-lower level in the WBS constitute a necessary and sufficient set of components to make up complete coverage of the task at the higher level. (All lower-level items are necessary, all lower-level items are sufficient.)

7. Bottom-level tasks are finely decomposed enough that reasonable cost and schedule estimates can be made for each.

8. Tasks aren't so finely decomposed that useless extra work is involved in estimating their cost and schedule.

9. Tasks aren't decomposed when their decomposition is uncertain or unstable.

Appendix B

Interest Tables

This appendix contains a set of discrete compounding interest factor tables. Tables are included for each of the following interest rates:

Table	Interest Rate	Table	Interest Rate
B.1	0.25%	B.18	14%
B.2	0.50%	B.19	15%
B.3	0.75%	B.20	16%
B.4	1%	B.21	17%
B.5	1.5%	B.22	18%
B.6	2%	B.23	19%
B.7	3%	B.24	20%
B.8	4%	B.25	25%
B.9	5%	B.26	30%
B.10	6%	B.27	35%
B.11	7%	B.28	40%
B.12	8%	B.29	50%
B.13	9%	B.30	60%
B.14	10%	B.31	70%
B.15	11%	B.32	80%
B.16	12%	B.33	90%
B.17	13%	B.34	100%

To use these interest tables, follow these steps:

1. Find the table corresponding to the (closest) interest rate. If you need the equal-payment-series capital-recovery factor for 15% at 22 years—the (A/P,15%,22) factor—start at Table B.19.

2. Identify the column in that table for the compound interest function you need. Equal-payment-series capital-recovery is the rightmost column.

3. Select the row for the number of periods you need. In this example, the row for $n = 22$.

4. The interest factor needed is at the intersection of the identified column and the selected row. In this case, the factor is 0.1573.

Note: Some of the interest factors—especially those in tables for the higher interest rates—are shown as "##########." This means that the value of the factor is too big to fit in the amount of space available in that table. If you need one of these interest factors, you may either use the spreadsheet tool available at http://www.construx.com/returnonsoftware/ (increasing the column width appropriately) or use the formula in Chapter 5, "Interest: The Time Value of Money."

TABLE B.1 0.25% Interest Factors for Discrete Compounding

	Single-Payment		Equal-Payment-Series			
	Compound- Amount	Present- Worth	Compound- Amount	Sinking- Fund	Present- Worth	Capital- Recovery
n	*Find F Given P* *(F/P,i,n)*	*Find P Given F* *(P/F,i,n)*	*Find F Given A* *(F/A,i,n)*	*Find A Given F* *(A/F,i,n)*	*Find P Given A* *(P/A,i,n)*	*Find A Given P* *(A/P,i,n)*
1	1.0025	0.9975	1.0000	1.0000	0.9975	1.0025
2	1.0050	0.9950	2.0025	0.4994	1.9925	0.5019
3	1.0075	0.9925	3.0075	0.3325	2.9851	0.3350
4	1.0100	0.9901	4.0150	0.2491	3.9751	0.2516
5	1.0126	0.9876	5.0251	0.1990	4.9627	0.2015
6	1.0151	0.9851	6.0376	0.1656	5.9478	0.1681
7	1.0176	0.9827	7.0527	0.1418	6.9305	0.1443
8	1.0202	0.9802	8.0704	0.1239	7.9107	0.1264
9	1.0227	0.9778	9.0905	0.1100	8.8885	0.1125
10	1.0253	0.9753	10.1133	0.0989	9.8639	0.1014
11	1.0278	0.9729	11.1385	0.0898	10.8368	0.0923
12	1.0304	0.9705	12.1664	0.0822	11.8073	0.0847
13	1.0330	0.9681	13.1968	0.0758	12.7753	0.0783
14	1.0356	0.9656	14.2298	0.0703	13.7410	0.0728
15	1.0382	0.9632	15.2654	0.0655	14.7042	0.0680
16	1.0408	0.9608	16.3035	0.0613	15.6650	0.0638
17	1.0434	0.9584	17.3443	0.0577	16.6235	0.0602
18	1.0460	0.9561	18.3876	0.0544	17.5795	0.0569
19	1.0486	0.9537	19.4336	0.0515	18.5332	0.0540
20	1.0512	0.9513	20.4822	0.0488	19.4845	0.0513
21	1.0538	0.9489	21.5334	0.0464	20.4334	0.0489
22	1.0565	0.9466	22.5872	0.0443	21.3800	0.0468
23	1.0591	0.9442	23.6437	0.0423	22.3241	0.0448
24	1.0618	0.9418	24.7028	0.0405	23.2660	0.0430
25	1.0644	0.9395	25.7646	0.0388	24.2055	0.0413
26	1.0671	0.9371	26.8290	0.0373	25.1426	0.0398
27	1.0697	0.9348	27.8961	0.0358	26.0774	0.0383
28	1.0724	0.9325	28.9658	0.0345	27.0099	0.0370
29	1.0751	0.9301	30.0382	0.0333	27.9400	0.0358
30	1.0778	0.9278	31.1133	0.0321	28.8679	0.0346
31	1.0805	0.9255	32.1911	0.0311	29.7934	0.0336
32	1.0832	0.9232	33.2716	0.0301	30.7166	0.0326
33	1.0859	0.9209	34.3547	0.0291	31.6375	0.0316
34	1.0886	0.9186	35.4406	0.0282	32.5561	0.0307
35	1.0913	0.9163	36.5292	0.0274	33.4724	0.0299
36	1.0941	0.9140	37.6206	0.0266	34.3865	0.0291
37	1.0968	0.9118	38.7146	0.0258	35.2982	0.0283
38	1.0995	0.9095	39.8114	0.0251	36.2077	0.0276
39	1.1023	0.9072	40.9109	0.0244	37.1149	0.0269
40	1.1050	0.9050	42.0132	0.0238	38.0199	0.0263
45	1.1189	0.8937	47.5661	0.0210	42.5109	0.0235
50	1.1330	0.8826	53.1887	0.0188	46.9462	0.0213
60	1.1616	0.8609	64.6467	0.0155	55.6524	0.0180
75	1.2059	0.8292	82.3792	0.0121	68.3108	0.0146
100	1.2836	0.7790	113.4500	0.0088	88.3825	0.0113

TABLE B.2 0.50% Interest Factors for Discrete Compounding

	Single-Payment		Equal-Payment-Series			
	Compound-Amount	Present-Worth	Compound-Amount	Sinking-Fund	Present-Worth	Capital-Recovery
n	*Find F Given P* (F/P,i,n)	*Find P Given F* (P/F,i,n)	*Find F Given A* (F/A,i,n)	*Find A Given F* (A/F,i,n)	*Find P Given A* (P/A,i,n)	*Find A Given P* (A/P,i,n)
1	1.0050	0.9950	1.0000	1.0000	0.9950	1.0050
2	1.0100	0.9901	2.0050	0.4988	1.9851	0.5038
3	1.0151	0.9851	3.0150	0.3317	2.9702	0.3367
4	1.0202	0.9802	4.0301	0.2481	3.9505	0.2531
5	1.0253	0.9754	5.0503	0.1980	4.9259	0.2030
6	1.0304	0.9705	6.0755	0.1646	5.8964	0.1696
7	1.0355	0.9657	7.1059	0.1407	6.8621	0.1457
8	1.0407	0.9609	8.1414	0.1228	7.8230	0.1278
9	1.0459	0.9561	9.1821	0.1089	8.7791	0.1139
10	1.0511	0.9513	10.2280	0.0978	9.7304	0.1028
11	1.0564	0.9466	11.2792	0.0887	10.6770	0.0937
12	1.0617	0.9419	12.3356	0.0811	11.6189	0.0861
13	1.0670	0.9372	13.3972	0.0746	12.5562	0.0796
14	1.0723	0.9326	14.4642	0.0691	13.4887	0.0741
15	1.0777	0.9279	15.5365	0.0644	14.4166	0.0694
16	1.0831	0.9233	16.6142	0.0602	15.3399	0.0652
17	1.0885	0.9187	17.6973	0.0565	16.2586	0.0615
18	1.0939	0.9141	18.7858	0.0532	17.1728	0.0582
19	1.0994	0.9096	19.8797	0.0503	18.0824	0.0553
20	1.1049	0.9051	20.9791	0.0477	18.9874	0.0527
21	1.1104	0.9006	22.0840	0.0453	19.8880	0.0503
22	1.1160	0.8961	23.1944	0.0431	20.7841	0.0481
23	1.1216	0.8916	24.3104	0.0411	21.6757	0.0461
24	1.1272	0.8872	25.4320	0.0393	22.5629	0.0443
25	1.1328	0.8828	26.5591	0.0377	23.4456	0.0427
26	1.1385	0.8784	27.6919	0.0361	24.3240	0.0411
27	1.1442	0.8740	28.8304	0.0347	25.1980	0.0397
28	1.1499	0.8697	29.9745	0.0334	26.0677	0.0384
29	1.1556	0.8653	31.1244	0.0321	26.9330	0.0371
30	1.1614	0.8610	32.2800	0.0310	27.7941	0.0360
31	1.1672	0.8567	33.4414	0.0299	28.6508	0.0349
32	1.1730	0.8525	34.6086	0.0289	29.5033	0.0339
33	1.1789	0.8482	35.7817	0.0279	30.3515	0.0329
34	1.1848	0.8440	36.9606	0.0271	31.1955	0.0321
35	1.1907	0.8398	38.1454	0.0262	32.0354	0.0312
36	1.1967	0.8356	39.3361	0.0254	32.8710	0.0304
37	1.2027	0.8315	40.5328	0.0247	33.7025	0.0297
38	1.2087	0.8274	41.7354	0.0240	34.5299	0.0290
39	1.2147	0.8232	42.9441	0.0233	35.3531	0.0283
40	1.2208	0.8191	44.1588	0.0226	36.1722	0.0276
45	1.2516	0.7990	50.3242	0.0199	40.2072	0.0249
50	1.2832	0.7793	56.6452	0.0177	44.1428	0.0227
60	1.3489	0.7414	69.7700	0.0143	51.7256	0.0193
75	1.4536	0.6879	90.7265	0.0110	62.4136	0.0160
100	1.6467	0.6073	129.3337	0.0077	78.5426	0.0127

TABLE B.3 0.75% Interest Factors for Discrete Compounding

	Single-Payment		Equal-Payment-Series			
	Compound-Amount	Present-Worth	Compound-Amount	Sinking-Fund	Present-Worth	Capital-Recovery
n	Find F Given P (F/P,i,n)	Find P Given F (P/F,i,n)	Find F Given A (F/A,i,n)	Find A Given F (A/F,i,n)	Find P Given A (P/A,i,n)	Find A Given P (A/P,i,n)
1	1.0075	0.9926	1.0000	1.0000	0.9926	1.0075
2	1.0151	0.9852	2.0075	0.4981	1.9777	0.5056
3	1.0227	0.9778	3.0226	0.3308	2.9556	0.3383
4	1.0303	0.9706	4.0452	0.2472	3.9261	0.2547
5	1.0381	0.9633	5.0756	0.1970	4.8894	0.2045
6	1.0459	0.9562	6.1136	0.1636	5.8456	0.1711
7	1.0537	0.9490	7.1595	0.1397	6.7946	0.1472
8	1.0616	0.9420	8.2132	0.1218	7.7366	0.1293
9	1.0696	0.9350	9.2748	0.1078	8.6716	0.1153
10	1.0776	0.9280	10.3443	0.0967	9.5996	0.1042
11	1.0857	0.9211	11.4219	0.0876	10.5207	0.0951
12	1.0938	0.9142	12.5076	0.0800	11.4349	0.0875
13	1.1020	0.9074	13.6014	0.0735	12.3423	0.0810
14	1.1103	0.9007	14.7034	0.0680	13.2430	0.0755
15	1.1186	0.8940	15.8137	0.0632	14.1370	0.0707
16	1.1270	0.8873	16.9323	0.0591	15.0243	0.0666
17	1.1354	0.8807	18.0593	0.0554	15.9050	0.0629
18	1.1440	0.8742	19.1947	0.0521	16.7792	0.0596
19	1.1525	0.8676	20.3387	0.0492	17.6468	0.0567
20	1.1612	0.8612	21.4912	0.0465	18.5080	0.0540
21	1.1699	0.8548	22.6524	0.0441	19.3628	0.0516
22	1.1787	0.8484	23.8223	0.0420	20.2112	0.0495
23	1.1875	0.8421	25.0010	0.0400	21.0533	0.0475
24	1.1964	0.8358	26.1885	0.0382	21.8891	0.0457
25	1.2054	0.8296	27.3849	0.0365	22.7188	0.0440
26	1.2144	0.8234	28.5903	0.0350	23.5422	0.0425
27	1.2235	0.8173	29.8047	0.0336	24.3595	0.0411
28	1.2327	0.8112	31.0282	0.0322	25.1707	0.0397
29	1.2420	0.8052	32.2609	0.0310	25.9759	0.0385
30	1.2513	0.7992	33.5029	0.0298	26.7751	0.0373
31	1.2607	0.7932	34.7542	0.0288	27.5683	0.0363
32	1.2701	0.7873	36.0148	0.0278	28.3557	0.0353
33	1.2796	0.7815	37.2849	0.0268	29.1371	0.0343
34	1.2892	0.7757	38.5646	0.0259	29.9128	0.0334
35	1.2989	0.7699	39.8538	0.0251	30.6827	0.0326
36	1.3086	0.7641	41.1527	0.0243	31.4468	0.0318
37	1.3185	0.7585	42.4614	0.0236	32.2053	0.0311
38	1.3283	0.7528	43.7798	0.0228	32.9581	0.0303
39	1.3383	0.7472	45.1082	0.0222	33.7053	0.0297
40	1.3483	0.7416	46.4465	0.0215	34.4469	0.0290
45	1.3997	0.7145	53.2901	0.0188	38.0732	0.0263
50	1.4530	0.6883	60.3943	0.0166	41.5664	0.0241
60	1.5657	0.6387	75.4241	0.0133	48.1734	0.0208
75	1.7514	0.5710	100.1833	0.0100	57.2027	0.0175
100	2.1111	0.4737	148.1445	0.0068	70.1746	0.0143

TABLE B.4 1% Interest Factors for Discrete Compounding

	Single-Payment		Equal-Payment-Series			
	Compound-Amount	Present-Worth	Compound-Amount	Sinking-Fund	Present-Worth	Capital-Recovery
n	*Find F Given P* (F/P,i,n)	*Find P Given F* (P/F,i,n)	*Find F Given A* (F/A,i,n)	*Find A Given F* (A/F,i,n)	*Find P Given A* (P/A,i,n)	*Find A Given P* (A/P,i,n)
1	1.0100	0.9901	1.0000	1.0000	0.9901	1.0100
2	1.0201	0.9803	2.0100	0.4975	1.9704	0.5075
3	1.0303	0.9706	3.0301	0.3300	2.9410	0.3400
4	1.0406	0.9610	4.0604	0.2463	3.9020	0.2563
5	1.0510	0.9515	5.1010	0.1960	4.8534	0.2060
6	1.0615	0.9420	6.1520	0.1625	5.7955	0.1725
7	1.0721	0.9327	7.2135	0.1386	6.7282	0.1486
8	1.0829	0.9235	8.2857	0.1207	7.6517	0.1307
9	1.0937	0.9143	9.3685	0.1067	8.5660	0.1167
10	1.1046	0.9053	10.4622	0.0956	9.4713	0.1056
11	1.1157	0.8963	11.5668	0.0865	10.3676	0.0965
12	1.1268	0.8874	12.6825	0.0788	11.2551	0.0888
13	1.1381	0.8787	13.8093	0.0724	12.1337	0.0824
14	1.1495	0.8700	14.9474	0.0669	13.0037	0.0769
15	1.1610	0.8613	16.0969	0.0621	13.8651	0.0721
16	1.1726	0.8528	17.2579	0.0579	14.7179	0.0679
17	1.1843	0.8444	18.4304	0.0543	15.5623	0.0643
18	1.1961	0.8360	19.6147	0.0510	16.3983	0.0610
19	1.2081	0.8277	20.8109	0.0481	17.2260	0.0581
20	1.2202	0.8195	22.0190	0.0454	18.0456	0.0554
21	1.2324	0.8114	23.2392	0.0430	18.8570	0.0530
22	1.2447	0.8034	24.4716	0.0409	19.6604	0.0509
23	1.2572	0.7954	25.7163	0.0389	20.4558	0.0489
24	1.2697	0.7876	26.9735	0.0371	21.2434	0.0471
25	1.2824	0.7798	28.2432	0.0354	22.0232	0.0454
26	1.2953	0.7720	29.5256	0.0339	22.7952	0.0439
27	1.3082	0.7644	30.8209	0.0324	23.5596	0.0424
28	1.3213	0.7568	32.1291	0.0311	24.3164	0.0411
29	1.3345	0.7493	33.4504	0.0299	25.0658	0.0399
30	1.3478	0.7419	34.7849	0.0287	25.8077	0.0387
31	1.3613	0.7346	36.1327	0.0277	26.5423	0.0377
32	1.3749	0.7273	37.4941	0.0267	27.2696	0.0367
33	1.3887	0.7201	38.8690	0.0257	27.9897	0.0357
34	1.4026	0.7130	40.2577	0.0248	28.7027	0.0348
35	1.4166	0.7059	41.6603	0.0240	29.4086	0.0340
36	1.4308	0.6989	43.0769	0.0232	30.1075	0.0332
37	1.4451	0.6920	44.5076	0.0225	30.7995	0.0325
38	1.4595	0.6852	45.9527	0.0218	31.4847	0.0318
39	1.4741	0.6784	47.4123	0.0211	32.1630	0.0311
40	1.4889	0.6717	48.8864	0.0205	32.8347	0.0305
45	1.5648	0.6391	56.4811	0.0177	36.0945	0.0277
50	1.6446	0.6080	64.4632	0.0155	39.1961	0.0255
60	1.8167	0.5504	81.6697	0.0122	44.9550	0.0222
75	2.1091	0.4741	110.9128	0.0090	52.5871	0.0190
100	2.7048	0.3697	170.4814	0.0059	63.0289	0.0159

TABLE B.5   1.5% Interest Factors for Discrete Compounding

	Single-Payment		Equal-Payment-Series			
	Compound- Amount	Present- Worth	Compound- Amount	Sinking- Fund	Present- Worth	Capital- Recovery
n	Find F Given P (F/P,i,n)	Find P Given F (P/F,i,n)	Find F Given A (F/A,i,n)	Find A Given F (A/F,i,n)	Find P Given A (P/A,i,n)	Find A Given P (A/P,i,n)
1	1.0150	0.9852	1.0000	1.0000	0.9852	1.0150
2	1.0302	0.9707	2.0150	0.4963	1.9559	0.5113
3	1.0457	0.9563	3.0452	0.3284	2.9122	0.3434
4	1.0614	0.9422	4.0909	0.2444	3.8544	0.2594
5	1.0773	0.9283	5.1523	0.1941	4.7826	0.2091
6	1.0934	0.9145	6.2296	0.1605	5.6972	0.1755
7	1.1098	0.9010	7.3230	0.1366	6.5982	0.1516
8	1.1265	0.8877	8.4328	0.1186	7.4859	0.1336
9	1.1434	0.8746	9.5593	0.1046	8.3605	0.1196
10	1.1605	0.8617	10.7027	0.0934	9.2222	0.1084
11	1.1779	0.8489	11.8633	0.0843	10.0711	0.0993
12	1.1956	0.8364	13.0412	0.0767	10.9075	0.0917
13	1.2136	0.8240	14.2368	0.0702	11.7315	0.0852
14	1.2318	0.8118	15.4504	0.0647	12.5434	0.0797
15	1.2502	0.7999	16.6821	0.0599	13.3432	0.0749
16	1.2690	0.7880	17.9324	0.0558	14.1313	0.0708
17	1.2880	0.7764	19.2014	0.0521	14.9076	0.0671
18	1.3073	0.7649	20.4894	0.0488	15.6726	0.0638
19	1.3270	0.7536	21.7967	0.0459	16.4262	0.0609
20	1.3469	0.7425	23.1237	0.0432	17.1686	0.0582
21	1.3671	0.7315	24.4705	0.0409	17.9001	0.0559
22	1.3876	0.7207	25.8376	0.0387	18.6208	0.0537
23	1.4084	0.7100	27.2251	0.0367	19.3309	0.0517
24	1.4295	0.6995	28.6335	0.0349	20.0304	0.0499
25	1.4509	0.6892	30.0630	0.0333	20.7196	0.0483
26	1.4727	0.6790	31.5140	0.0317	21.3986	0.0467
27	1.4948	0.6690	32.9867	0.0303	22.0676	0.0453
28	1.5172	0.6591	34.4815	0.0290	22.7267	0.0440
29	1.5400	0.6494	35.9987	0.0278	23.3761	0.0428
30	1.5631	0.6398	37.5387	0.0266	24.0158	0.0416
31	1.5865	0.6303	39.1018	0.0256	24.6461	0.0406
32	1.6103	0.6210	40.6883	0.0246	25.2671	0.0396
33	1.6345	0.6118	42.2986	0.0236	25.8790	0.0386
34	1.6590	0.6028	43.9331	0.0228	26.4817	0.0378
35	1.6839	0.5939	45.5921	0.0219	27.0756	0.0369
36	1.7091	0.5851	47.2760	0.0212	27.6607	0.0362
37	1.7348	0.5764	48.9851	0.0204	28.2371	0.0354
38	1.7608	0.5679	50.7199	0.0197	28.8051	0.0347
39	1.7872	0.5595	52.4807	0.0191	29.3646	0.0341
40	1.8140	0.5513	54.2679	0.0184	29.9158	0.0334
45	1.9542	0.5117	63.6142	0.0157	32.5523	0.0307
50	2.1052	0.4750	73.6828	0.0136	34.9997	0.0286
60	2.4432	0.4093	96.2147	0.0104	39.3803	0.0254
75	3.0546	0.3274	136.9728	0.0073	44.8416	0.0223
100	4.4320	0.2256	228.8030	0.0044	51.6247	0.0194

TABLE B.6 2% Interest Factors for Discrete Compounding

	Single-Payment		Equal-Payment-Series			
	Compound- Amount	Present- Worth	Compound- Amount	Sinking- Fund	Present- Worth	Capital- Recovery
n	Find F Given P (F/P,i,n)	Find P Given F (P/F,i,n)	Find F Given A (F/A,i,n)	Find A Given F (A/F,i,n)	Find P Given A (P/A,i,n)	Find A Given P (A/P,i,n)
1	1.0200	0.9804	1.0000	1.0000	0.9804	1.0200
2	1.0404	0.9612	2.0200	0.4950	1.9416	0.5150
3	1.0612	0.9423	3.0604	0.3268	2.8839	0.3468
4	1.0824	0.9238	4.1216	0.2426	3.8077	0.2626
5	1.1041	0.9057	5.2040	0.1922	4.7135	0.2122
6	1.1262	0.8880	6.3081	0.1585	5.6014	0.1785
7	1.1487	0.8706	7.4343	0.1345	6.4720	0.1545
8	1.1717	0.8535	8.5830	0.1165	7.3255	0.1365
9	1.1951	0.8368	9.7546	0.1025	8.1622	0.1225
10	1.2190	0.8203	10.9497	0.0913	8.9826	0.1113
11	1.2434	0.8043	12.1687	0.0822	9.7868	0.1022
12	1.2682	0.7885	13.4121	0.0746	10.5753	0.0946
13	1.2936	0.7730	14.6803	0.0681	11.3484	0.0881
14	1.3195	0.7579	15.9739	0.0626	12.1062	0.0826
15	1.3459	0.7430	17.2934	0.0578	12.8493	0.0778
16	1.3728	0.7284	18.6393	0.0537	13.5777	0.0737
17	1.4002	0.7142	20.0121	0.0500	14.2919	0.0700
18	1.4282	0.7002	21.4123	0.0467	14.9920	0.0667
19	1.4568	0.6864	22.8406	0.0438	15.6785	0.0638
20	1.4859	0.6730	24.2974	0.0412	16.3514	0.0612
21	1.5157	0.6598	25.7833	0.0388	17.0112	0.0588
22	1.5460	0.6468	27.2990	0.0366	17.6580	0.0566
23	1.5769	0.6342	28.8450	0.0347	18.2922	0.0547
24	1.6084	0.6217	30.4219	0.0329	18.9139	0.0529
25	1.6406	0.6095	32.0303	0.0312	19.5235	0.0512
26	1.6734	0.5976	33.6709	0.0297	20.1210	0.0497
27	1.7069	0.5859	35.3443	0.0283	20.7069	0.0483
28	1.7410	0.5744	37.0512	0.0270	21.2813	0.0470
29	1.7758	0.5631	38.7922	0.0258	21.8444	0.0458
30	1.8114	0.5521	40.5681	0.0246	22.3965	0.0446
31	1.8476	0.5412	42.3794	0.0236	22.9377	0.0436
32	1.8845	0.5306	44.2270	0.0226	23.4683	0.0426
33	1.9222	0.5202	46.1116	0.0217	23.9886	0.0417
34	1.9607	0.5100	48.0338	0.0208	24.4986	0.0408
35	1.9999	0.5000	49.9945	0.0200	24.9986	0.0400
36	2.0399	0.4902	51.9944	0.0192	25.4888	0.0392
37	2.0807	0.4806	54.0343	0.0185	25.9695	0.0385
38	2.1223	0.4712	56.1149	0.0178	26.4406	0.0378
39	2.1647	0.4619	58.2372	0.0172	26.9026	0.0372
40	2.2080	0.4529	60.4020	0.0166	27.3555	0.0366
45	2.4379	0.4102	71.8927	0.0139	29.4902	0.0339
50	2.6916	0.3715	84.5794	0.0118	31.4236	0.0318
60	3.2810	0.3048	114.0515	0.0088	34.7609	0.0288
75	4.4158	0.2265	170.7918	0.0059	38.6771	0.0259
100	7.2446	0.1380	312.2323	0.0032	43.0984	0.0232

TABLE B.7 3% Interest Factors for Discrete Compounding

	Single-Payment		Equal-Payment-Series			
	Compound-Amount	Present-Worth	Compound-Amount	Sinking-Fund	Present-Worth	Capital-Recovery
n	Find F Given P (F/P,i,n)	Find P Given F (P/F,i,n)	Find F Given A (F/A,i,n)	Find A Given F (A/F,i,n)	Find P Given A (P/A,i,n)	Find A Given P (A/P,i,n)
1	1.0300	0.9709	1.0000	1.0000	0.9709	1.0300
2	1.0609	0.9426	2.0300	0.4926	1.9135	0.5226
3	1.0927	0.9151	3.0909	0.3235	2.8286	0.3535
4	1.1255	0.8885	4.1836	0.2390	3.7171	0.2690
5	1.1593	0.8626	5.3091	0.1884	4.5797	0.2184
6	1.1941	0.8375	6.4684	0.1546	5.4172	0.1846
7	1.2299	0.8131	7.6625	0.1305	6.2303	0.1605
8	1.2668	0.7894	8.8923	0.1125	7.0197	0.1425
9	1.3048	0.7664	10.1591	0.0984	7.7861	0.1284
10	1.3439	0.7441	11.4639	0.0872	8.5302	0.1172
11	1.3842	0.7224	12.8078	0.0781	9.2526	0.1081
12	1.4258	0.7014	14.1920	0.0705	9.9540	0.1005
13	1.4685	0.6810	15.6178	0.0640	10.6350	0.0940
14	1.5126	0.6611	17.0863	0.0585	11.2961	0.0885
15	1.5580	0.6419	18.5989	0.0538	11.9379	0.0838
16	1.6047	0.6232	20.1569	0.0496	12.5611	0.0796
17	1.6528	0.6050	21.7616	0.0460	13.1661	0.0760
18	1.7024	0.5874	23.4144	0.0427	13.7535	0.0727
19	1.7535	0.5703	25.1169	0.0398	14.3238	0.0698
20	1.8061	0.5537	26.8704	0.0372	14.8775	0.0672
21	1.8603	0.5375	28.6765	0.0349	15.4150	0.0649
22	1.9161	0.5219	30.5368	0.0327	15.9369	0.0627
23	1.9736	0.5067	32.4529	0.0308	16.4436	0.0608
24	2.0328	0.4919	34.4265	0.0290	16.9355	0.0590
25	2.0938	0.4776	36.4593	0.0274	17.4131	0.0574
26	2.1566	0.4637	38.5530	0.0259	17.8768	0.0559
27	2.2213	0.4502	40.7096	0.0246	18.3270	0.0546
28	2.2879	0.4371	42.9309	0.0233	18.7641	0.0533
29	2.3566	0.4243	45.2189	0.0221	19.1885	0.0521
30	2.4273	0.4120	47.5754	0.0210	19.6004	0.0510
31	2.5001	0.4000	50.0027	0.0200	20.0004	0.0500
32	2.5751	0.3883	52.5028	0.0190	20.3888	0.0490
33	2.6523	0.3770	55.0778	0.0182	20.7658	0.0482
34	2.7319	0.3660	57.7302	0.0173	21.1318	0.0473
35	2.8139	0.3554	60.4621	0.0165	21.4872	0.0465
36	2.8983	0.3450	63.2759	0.0158	21.8323	0.0458
37	2.9852	0.3350	66.1742	0.0151	22.1672	0.0451
38	3.0748	0.3252	69.1594	0.0145	22.4925	0.0445
39	3.1670	0.3158	72.2342	0.0138	22.8082	0.0438
40	3.2620	0.3066	75.4013	0.0133	23.1148	0.0433
45	3.7816	0.2644	92.7199	0.0108	24.5187	0.0408
50	4.3839	0.2281	112.7969	0.0089	25.7298	0.0389
60	5.8916	0.1697	163.0534	0.0061	27.6756	0.0361
75	9.1789	0.1089	272.6309	0.0037	29.7018	0.0337
100	19.2186	0.0520	607.2877	0.0016	31.5989	0.0316

TABLE B.8   4% Interest Factors for Discrete Compounding

	Single-Payment		Equal-Payment-Series			
	Compound-Amount	Present-Worth	Compound-Amount	Sinking-Fund	Present-Worth	Capital-Recovery
n	Find F Given P (F/P,i,n)	Find P Given F (P/F,i,n)	Find F Given A (F/A,i,n)	Find A Given F (A/F,i,n)	Find P Given A (P/A,i,n)	Find A Given P (A/P,i,n)
1	1.0400	0.9615	1.0000	1.0000	0.9615	1.0400
2	1.0816	0.9246	2.0400	0.4902	1.8861	0.5302
3	1.1249	0.8890	3.1216	0.3203	2.7751	0.3603
4	1.1699	0.8548	4.2465	0.2355	3.6299	0.2755
5	1.2167	0.8219	5.4163	0.1846	4.4518	0.2246
6	1.2653	0.7903	6.6330	0.1508	5.2421	0.1908
7	1.3159	0.7599	7.8983	0.1266	6.0021	0.1666
8	1.3686	0.7307	9.2142	0.1085	6.7327	0.1485
9	1.4233	0.7026	10.5828	0.0945	7.4353	0.1345
10	1.4802	0.6756	12.0061	0.0833	8.1109	0.1233
11	1.5395	0.6496	13.4864	0.0741	8.7605	0.1141
12	1.6010	0.6246	15.0258	0.0666	9.3851	0.1066
13	1.6651	0.6006	16.6268	0.0601	9.9856	0.1001
14	1.7317	0.5775	18.2919	0.0547	10.5631	0.0947
15	1.8009	0.5553	20.0236	0.0499	11.1184	0.0899
16	1.8730	0.5339	21.8245	0.0458	11.6523	0.0858
17	1.9479	0.5134	23.6975	0.0422	12.1657	0.0822
18	2.0258	0.4936	25.6454	0.0390	12.6593	0.0790
19	2.1068	0.4746	27.6712	0.0361	13.1339	0.0761
20	2.1911	0.4564	29.7781	0.0336	13.5903	0.0736
21	2.2788	0.4388	31.9692	0.0313	14.0292	0.0713
22	2.3699	0.4220	34.2480	0.0292	14.4511	0.0692
23	2.4647	0.4057	36.6179	0.0273	14.8568	0.0673
24	2.5633	0.3901	39.0826	0.0256	15.2470	0.0656
25	2.6658	0.3751	41.6459	0.0240	15.6221	0.0640
26	2.7725	0.3607	44.3117	0.0226	15.9828	0.0626
27	2.8834	0.3468	47.0842	0.0212	16.3296	0.0612
28	2.9987	0.3335	49.9676	0.0200	16.6631	0.0600
29	3.1187	0.3207	52.9663	0.0189	16.9837	0.0589
30	3.2434	0.3083	56.0849	0.0178	17.2920	0.0578
31	3.3731	0.2965	59.3283	0.0169	17.5885	0.0569
32	3.5081	0.2851	62.7015	0.0159	17.8736	0.0559
33	3.6484	0.2741	66.2095	0.0151	18.1476	0.0551
34	3.7943	0.2636	69.8579	0.0143	18.4112	0.0543
35	3.9461	0.2534	73.6522	0.0136	18.6646	0.0536
36	4.1039	0.2437	77.5983	0.0129	18.9083	0.0529
37	4.2681	0.2343	81.7022	0.0122	19.1426	0.0522
38	4.4388	0.2253	85.9703	0.0116	19.3679	0.0516
39	4.6164	0.2166	90.4091	0.0111	19.5845	0.0511
40	4.8010	0.2083	95.0255	0.0105	19.7928	0.0505
45	5.8412	0.1712	121.0294	0.0083	20.7200	0.0483
50	7.1067	0.1407	152.6671	0.0066	21.4822	0.0466
60	10.5196	0.0951	237.9907	0.0042	22.6235	0.0442
75	18.9453	0.0528	448.6314	0.0022	23.6804	0.0422
100	50.5049	0.0198	1237.6237	0.0008	24.5050	0.0408

TABLE B.9 5% Interest Factors for Discrete Compounding

	Single-Payment		Equal-Payment-Series			
	Compound-Amount	Present-Worth	Compound-Amount	Sinking-Fund	Present-Worth	Capital-Recovery
n	Find F Given P (F/P,i,n)	Find P Given F (P/F,i,n)	Find F Given A (F/A,i,n)	Find A Given F (A/F,i,n)	Find P Given A (P/A,i,n)	Find A Given P (A/P,i,n)
1	1.0500	0.9524	1.0000	1.0000	0.9524	1.0500
2	1.1025	0.9070	2.0500	0.4878	1.8594	0.5378
3	1.1576	0.8638	3.1525	0.3172	2.7232	0.3672
4	1.2155	0.8227	4.3101	0.2320	3.5460	0.2820
5	1.2763	0.7835	5.5256	0.1810	4.3295	0.2310
6	1.3401	0.7462	6.8019	0.1470	5.0757	0.1970
7	1.4071	0.7107	8.1420	0.1228	5.7864	0.1728
8	1.4775	0.6768	9.5491	0.1047	6.4632	0.1547
9	1.5513	0.6446	11.0266	0.0907	7.1078	0.1407
10	1.6289	0.6139	12.5779	0.0795	7.7217	0.1295
11	1.7103	0.5847	14.2068	0.0704	8.3064	0.1204
12	1.7959	0.5568	15.9171	0.0628	8.8633	0.1128
13	1.8856	0.5303	17.7130	0.0565	9.3936	0.1065
14	1.9799	0.5051	19.5986	0.0510	9.8986	0.1010
15	2.0789	0.4810	21.5786	0.0463	10.3797	0.0963
16	2.1829	0.4581	23.6575	0.0423	10.8378	0.0923
17	2.2920	0.4363	25.8404	0.0387	11.2741	0.0887
18	2.4066	0.4155	28.1324	0.0355	11.6896	0.0855
19	2.5270	0.3957	30.5390	0.0327	12.0853	0.0827
20	2.6533	0.3769	33.0660	0.0302	12.4622	0.0802
21	2.7860	0.3589	35.7193	0.0280	12.8212	0.0780
22	2.9253	0.3418	38.5052	0.0260	13.1630	0.0760
23	3.0715	0.3256	41.4305	0.0241	13.4886	0.0741
24	3.2251	0.3101	44.5020	0.0225	13.7986	0.0725
25	3.3864	0.2953	47.7271	0.0210	14.0939	0.0710
26	3.5557	0.2812	51.1135	0.0196	14.3752	0.0696
27	3.7335	0.2678	54.6691	0.0183	14.6430	0.0683
28	3.9201	0.2551	58.4026	0.0171	14.8981	0.0671
29	4.1161	0.2429	62.3227	0.0160	15.1411	0.0660
30	4.3219	0.2314	66.4388	0.0151	15.3725	0.0651
31	4.5380	0.2204	70.7608	0.0141	15.5928	0.0641
32	4.7649	0.2099	75.2988	0.0133	15.8027	0.0633
33	5.0032	0.1999	80.0638	0.0125	16.0025	0.0625
34	5.2533	0.1904	85.0670	0.0118	16.1929	0.0618
35	5.5160	0.1813	90.3203	0.0111	16.3742	0.0611
36	5.7918	0.1727	95.8363	0.0104	16.5469	0.0604
37	6.0814	0.1644	101.6281	0.0098	16.7113	0.0598
38	6.3855	0.1566	107.7095	0.0093	16.8679	0.0593
39	6.7048	0.1491	114.0950	0.0088	17.0170	0.0588
40	7.0400	0.1420	120.7998	0.0083	17.1591	0.0583
45	8.9850	0.1113	159.7002	0.0063	17.7741	0.0563
50	11.4674	0.0872	209.3480	0.0048	18.2559	0.0548
60	18.6792	0.0535	353.5837	0.0028	18.9293	0.0528
75	38.8327	0.0258	756.6537	0.0013	19.4850	0.0513
100	131.5013	0.0076	2610.0252	0.0004	19.8479	0.0504

TABLE B.10 6% Interest Factors for Discrete Compounding

	Single-Payment		Equal-Payment-Series			
	Compound-Amount	Present-Worth	Compound-Amount	Sinking-Fund	Present-Worth	Capital-Recovery
n	Find F Given P (F/P,i,n)	Find P Given F (P/F,i,n)	Find F Given A (F/A,i,n)	Find A Given F (A/F,i,n)	Find P Given A (P/A,i,n)	Find A Given P (A/P,i,n)
1	1.0600	0.9434	1.0000	1.0000	0.9434	1.0600
2	1.1236	0.8900	2.0600	0.4854	1.8334	0.5454
3	1.1910	0.8396	3.1836	0.3141	2.6730	0.3741
4	1.2625	0.7921	4.3746	0.2286	3.4651	0.2886
5	1.3382	0.7473	5.6371	0.1774	4.2124	0.2374
6	1.4185	0.7050	6.9753	0.1434	4.9173	0.2034
7	1.5036	0.6651	8.3938	0.1191	5.5824	0.1791
8	1.5938	0.6274	9.8975	0.1010	6.2098	0.1610
9	1.6895	0.5919	11.4913	0.0870	6.8017	0.1470
10	1.7908	0.5584	13.1808	0.0759	7.3601	0.1359
11	1.8983	0.5268	14.9716	0.0668	7.8869	0.1268
12	2.0122	0.4970	16.8699	0.0593	8.3838	0.1193
13	2.1329	0.4688	18.8821	0.0530	8.8527	0.1130
14	2.2609	0.4423	21.0151	0.0476	9.2950	0.1076
15	2.3966	0.4173	23.2760	0.0430	9.7122	0.1030
16	2.5404	0.3936	25.6725	0.0390	10.1059	0.0990
17	2.6928	0.3714	28.2129	0.0354	10.4773	0.0954
18	2.8543	0.3503	30.9057	0.0324	10.8276	0.0924
19	3.0256	0.3305	33.7600	0.0296	11.1581	0.0896
20	3.2071	0.3118	36.7856	0.0272	11.4699	0.0872
21	3.3996	0.2942	39.9927	0.0250	11.7641	0.0850
22	3.6035	0.2775	43.3923	0.0230	12.0416	0.0830
23	3.8197	0.2618	46.9958	0.0213	12.3034	0.0813
24	4.0489	0.2470	50.8156	0.0197	12.5504	0.0797
25	4.2919	0.2330	54.8645	0.0182	12.7834	0.0782
26	4.5494	0.2198	59.1564	0.0169	13.0032	0.0769
27	4.8223	0.2074	63.7058	0.0157	13.2105	0.0757
28	5.1117	0.1956	68.5281	0.0146	13.4062	0.0746
29	5.4184	0.1846	73.6398	0.0136	13.5907	0.0736
30	5.7435	0.1741	79.0582	0.0126	13.7648	0.0726
31	6.0881	0.1643	84.8017	0.0118	13.9291	0.0718
32	6.4534	0.1550	90.8898	0.0110	14.0840	0.0710
33	6.8406	0.1462	97.3432	0.0103	14.2302	0.0703
34	7.2510	0.1379	104.1838	0.0096	14.3681	0.0696
35	7.6861	0.1301	111.4348	0.0090	14.4982	0.0690
36	8.1473	0.1227	119.1209	0.0084	14.6210	0.0684
37	8.6361	0.1158	127.2681	0.0079	14.7368	0.0679
38	9.1543	0.1092	135.9042	0.0074	14.8460	0.0674
39	9.7035	0.1031	145.0585	0.0069	14.9491	0.0669
40	10.2857	0.0972	154.7620	0.0065	15.0463	0.0665
45	13.7646	0.0727	212.7435	0.0047	15.4558	0.0647
50	18.4202	0.0543	290.3359	0.0034	15.7619	0.0634
60	32.9877	0.0303	533.1282	0.0019	16.1614	0.0619
75	79.0569	0.0126	1300.9487	0.0008	16.4558	0.0608
100	339.3021	0.0029	5638.3681	0.0002	16.6175	0.0602

TABLE B.11   7% Interest Factors for Discrete Compounding

	Single-Payment		Equal-Payment-Series			
	Compound- Amount	Present- Worth	Compound- Amount	Sinking- Fund	Present- Worth	Capital- Recovery
n	*Find F Given P* *(F/P,i,n)*	*Find P Given F* *(P/F,i,n)*	*Find F Given A* *(F/A,i,n)*	*Find A Given F* *(A/F,i,n)*	*Find P Given A* *(P/A,i,n)*	*Find A Given P* *(A/P,i,n)*
1	1.0700	0.9346	1.0000	1.0000	0.9346	1.0700
2	1.1449	0.8734	2.0700	0.4831	1.8080	0.5531
3	1.2250	0.8163	3.2149	0.3111	2.6243	0.3811
4	1.3108	0.7629	4.4399	0.2252	3.3872	0.2952
5	1.4026	0.7130	5.7507	0.1739	4.1002	0.2439
6	1.5007	0.6663	7.1533	0.1398	4.7665	0.2098
7	1.6058	0.6227	8.6540	0.1156	5.3893	0.1856
8	1.7182	0.5820	10.2598	0.0975	5.9713	0.1675
9	1.8385	0.5439	11.9780	0.0835	6.5152	0.1535
10	1.9672	0.5083	13.8164	0.0724	7.0236	0.1424
11	2.1049	0.4751	15.7836	0.0634	7.4987	0.1334
12	2.2522	0.4440	17.8885	0.0559	7.9427	0.1259
13	2.4098	0.4150	20.1406	0.0497	8.3577	0.1197
14	2.5785	0.3878	22.5505	0.0443	8.7455	0.1143
15	2.7590	0.3624	25.1290	0.0398	9.1079	0.1098
16	2.9522	0.3387	27.8881	0.0359	9.4466	0.1059
17	3.1588	0.3166	30.8402	0.0324	9.7632	0.1024
18	3.3799	0.2959	33.9990	0.0294	10.0591	0.0994
19	3.6165	0.2765	37.3790	0.0268	10.3356	0.0968
20	3.8697	0.2584	40.9955	0.0244	10.5940	0.0944
21	4.1406	0.2415	44.8652	0.0223	10.8355	0.0923
22	4.4304	0.2257	49.0057	0.0204	11.0612	0.0904
23	4.7405	0.2109	53.4361	0.0187	11.2722	0.0887
24	5.0724	0.1971	58.1767	0.0172	11.4693	0.0872
25	5.4274	0.1842	63.2490	0.0158	11.6536	0.0858
26	5.8074	0.1722	68.6765	0.0146	11.8258	0.0846
27	6.2139	0.1609	74.4838	0.0134	11.9867	0.0834
28	6.6488	0.1504	80.6977	0.0124	12.1371	0.0824
29	7.1143	0.1406	87.3465	0.0114	12.2777	0.0814
30	7.6123	0.1314	94.4608	0.0106	12.4090	0.0806
31	8.1451	0.1228	102.0730	0.0098	12.5318	0.0798
32	8.7153	0.1147	110.2182	0.0091	12.6466	0.0791
33	9.3253	0.1072	118.9334	0.0084	12.7538	0.0784
34	9.9781	0.1002	128.2588	0.0078	12.8540	0.0778
35	10.6766	0.0937	138.2369	0.0072	12.9477	0.0772
36	11.4239	0.0875	148.9135	0.0067	13.0352	0.0767
37	12.2236	0.0818	160.3374	0.0062	13.1170	0.0762
38	13.0793	0.0765	172.5610	0.0058	13.1935	0.0758
39	13.9948	0.0715	185.6403	0.0054	13.2649	0.0754
40	14.9745	0.0668	199.6351	0.0050	13.3317	0.0750
45	21.0025	0.0476	285.7493	0.0035	13.6055	0.0735
50	29.4570	0.0339	406.5289	0.0025	13.8007	0.0725
60	57.9464	0.0173	813.5204	0.0012	14.0392	0.0712
75	159.8760	0.0063	2269.6574	0.0004	14.1964	0.0704
100	867.7163	0.0012	12381.6618	0.0001	14.2693	0.0701

TABLE B.12 8% Interest Factors for Discrete Compounding

	Single-Payment		Equal-Payment-Series			
	Compound-Amount	Present-Worth	Compound-Amount	Sinking-Fund	Present-Worth	Capital-Recovery
n	Find F Given P (F/P,i,n)	Find P Given F (P/F,i,n)	Find F Given A (F/A,i,n)	Find A Given F (A/F,i,n)	Find P Given A (P/A,i,n)	Find A Given P (A/P,i,n)
1	1.0800	0.9259	1.0000	1.0000	0.9259	1.0800
2	1.1664	0.8573	2.0800	0.4808	1.7833	0.5608
3	1.2597	0.7938	3.2464	0.3080	2.5771	0.3880
4	1.3605	0.7350	4.5061	0.2219	3.3121	0.3019
5	1.4693	0.6806	5.8666	0.1705	3.9927	0.2505
6	1.5869	0.6302	7.3359	0.1363	4.6229	0.2163
7	1.7138	0.5835	8.9228	0.1121	5.2064	0.1921
8	1.8509	0.5403	10.6366	0.0940	5.7466	0.1740
9	1.9990	0.5002	12.4876	0.0801	6.2469	0.1601
10	2.1589	0.4632	14.4866	0.0690	6.7101	0.1490
11	2.3316	0.4289	16.6455	0.0601	7.1390	0.1401
12	2.5182	0.3971	18.9771	0.0527	7.5361	0.1327
13	2.7196	0.3677	21.4953	0.0465	7.9038	0.1265
14	2.9372	0.3405	24.2149	0.0413	8.2442	0.1213
15	3.1722	0.3152	27.1521	0.0368	8.5595	0.1168
16	3.4259	0.2919	30.3243	0.0330	8.8514	0.1130
17	3.7000	0.2703	33.7502	0.0296	9.1216	0.1096
18	3.9960	0.2502	37.4502	0.0267	9.3719	0.1067
19	4.3157	0.2317	41.4463	0.0241	9.6036	0.1041
20	4.6610	0.2145	45.7620	0.0219	9.8181	0.1019
21	5.0338	0.1987	50.4229	0.0198	10.0168	0.0998
22	5.4365	0.1839	55.4568	0.0180	10.2007	0.0980
23	5.8715	0.1703	60.8933	0.0164	10.3711	0.0964
24	6.3412	0.1577	66.7648	0.0150	10.5288	0.0950
25	6.8485	0.1460	73.1059	0.0137	10.6748	0.0937
26	7.3964	0.1352	79.9544	0.0125	10.8100	0.0925
27	7.9881	0.1252	87.3508	0.0114	10.9352	0.0914
28	8.6271	0.1159	95.3388	0.0105	11.0511	0.0905
29	9.3173	0.1073	103.9659	0.0096	11.1584	0.0896
30	10.0627	0.0994	113.2832	0.0088	11.2578	0.0888
31	10.8677	0.0920	123.3459	0.0081	11.3498	0.0881
32	11.7371	0.0852	134.2135	0.0075	11.4350	0.0875
33	12.6760	0.0789	145.9506	0.0069	11.5139	0.0869
34	13.6901	0.0730	158.6267	0.0063	11.5869	0.0863
35	14.7853	0.0676	172.3168	0.0058	11.6546	0.0858
36	15.9682	0.0626	187.1021	0.0053	11.7172	0.0853
37	17.2456	0.0580	203.0703	0.0049	11.7752	0.0849
38	18.6253	0.0537	220.3159	0.0045	11.8289	0.0845
39	20.1153	0.0497	238.9412	0.0042	11.8786	0.0842
40	21.7245	0.0460	259.0565	0.0039	11.9246	0.0839
45	31.9204	0.0313	386.5056	0.0026	12.1084	0.0826
50	46.9016	0.0213	573.7702	0.0017	12.2335	0.0817
60	101.2571	0.0099	1253.2133	0.0008	12.3766	0.0808
75	321.2045	0.0031	4002.5566	0.0002	12.4611	0.0802
100	2199.7613	0.0005	27484.5157	0.0000	12.4943	0.0800

TABLE B.13 9% Interest Factors for Discrete Compounding

	Single-Payment		Equal-Payment-Series			
	Compound- Amount	Present- Worth	Compound- Amount	Sinking- Fund	Present- Worth	Capital- Recovery
n	Find F Given P (F/P,i,n)	Find P Given F (P/F,i,n)	Find F Given A (F/A,i,n)	Find A Given F (A/F,i,n)	Find P Given A (P/A,i,n)	Find A Given P (A/P,i,n)
1	1.0900	0.9174	1.0000	1.0000	0.9174	1.0900
2	1.1881	0.8417	2.0900	0.4785	1.7591	0.5685
3	1.2950	0.7722	3.2781	0.3051	2.5313	0.3951
4	1.4116	0.7084	4.5731	0.2187	3.2397	0.3087
5	1.5386	0.6499	5.9847	0.1671	3.8897	0.2571
6	1.6771	0.5963	7.5233	0.1329	4.4859	0.2229
7	1.8280	0.5470	9.2004	0.1087	5.0330	0.1987
8	1.9926	0.5019	11.0285	0.0907	5.5348	0.1807
9	2.1719	0.4604	13.0210	0.0768	5.9952	0.1668
10	2.3674	0.4224	15.1929	0.0658	6.4177	0.1558
11	2.5804	0.3875	17.5603	0.0569	6.8052	0.1469
12	2.8127	0.3555	20.1407	0.0497	7.1607	0.1397
13	3.0658	0.3262	22.9534	0.0436	7.4869	0.1336
14	3.3417	0.2992	26.0192	0.0384	7.7862	0.1284
15	3.6425	0.2745	29.3609	0.0341	8.0607	0.1241
16	3.9703	0.2519	33.0034	0.0303	8.3126	0.1203
17	4.3276	0.2311	36.9737	0.0270	8.5436	0.1170
18	4.7171	0.2120	41.3013	0.0242	8.7556	0.1142
19	5.1417	0.1945	46.0185	0.0217	8.9501	0.1117
20	5.6044	0.1784	51.1601	0.0195	9.1285	0.1095
21	6.1088	0.1637	56.7645	0.0176	9.2922	0.1076
22	6.6586	0.1502	62.8733	0.0159	9.4424	0.1059
23	7.2579	0.1378	69.5319	0.0144	9.5802	0.1044
24	7.9111	0.1264	76.7898	0.0130	9.7066	0.1030
25	8.6231	0.1160	84.7009	0.0118	9.8226	0.1018
26	9.3992	0.1064	93.3240	0.0107	9.9290	0.1007
27	10.2451	0.0976	102.7231	0.0097	10.0266	0.0997
28	11.1671	0.0895	112.9682	0.0089	10.1161	0.0989
29	12.1722	0.0822	124.1354	0.0081	10.1983	0.0981
30	13.2677	0.0754	136.3075	0.0073	10.2737	0.0973
31	14.4618	0.0691	149.5752	0.0067	10.3428	0.0967
32	15.7633	0.0634	164.0370	0.0061	10.4062	0.0961
33	17.1820	0.0582	179.8003	0.0056	10.4644	0.0956
34	18.7284	0.0534	196.9823	0.0051	10.5178	0.0951
35	20.4140	0.0490	215.7108	0.0046	10.5668	0.0946
36	22.2512	0.0449	236.1247	0.0042	10.6118	0.0942
37	24.2538	0.0412	258.3759	0.0039	10.6530	0.0939
38	26.4367	0.0378	282.6298	0.0035	10.6908	0.0935
39	28.8160	0.0347	309.0665	0.0032	10.7255	0.0932
40	31.4094	0.0318	337.8824	0.0030	10.7574	0.0930
45	48.3273	0.0207	525.8587	0.0019	10.8812	0.0919
50	74.3575	0.0134	815.0836	0.0012	10.9617	0.0912
60	176.0313	0.0057	1944.7921	0.0005	11.0480	0.0905
75	641.1909	0.0016	7113.2321	0.0001	11.0938	0.0901
100	5529.0408	0.0002	61422.6755	0.0000	11.1091	0.0900

TABLE B.14 10% Interest Factors for Discrete Compounding

	Single-Payment		Equal-Payment-Series			
	Compound-Amount	Present-Worth	Compound-Amount	Sinking-Fund	Present-Worth	Capital-Recovery
n	Find F Given P (F/P,i,n)	Find P Given F (P/F,i,n)	Find F Given A (F/A,i,n)	Find A Given F (A/F,i,n)	Find P Given A (P/A,i,n)	Find A Given P (A/P,i,n)
1	1.1000	0.9091	1.0000	1.0000	0.9091	1.1000
2	1.2100	0.8264	2.1000	0.4762	1.7355	0.5762
3	1.3310	0.7513	3.3100	0.3021	2.4869	0.4021
4	1.4641	0.6830	4.6410	0.2155	3.1699	0.3155
5	1.6105	0.6209	6.1051	0.1638	3.7908	0.2638
6	1.7716	0.5645	7.7156	0.1296	4.3553	0.2296
7	1.9487	0.5132	9.4872	0.1054	4.8684	0.2054
8	2.1436	0.4665	11.4359	0.0874	5.3349	0.1874
9	2.3579	0.4241	13.5795	0.0736	5.7590	0.1736
10	2.5937	0.3855	15.9374	0.0627	6.1446	0.1627
11	2.8531	0.3505	18.5312	0.0540	6.4951	0.1540
12	3.1384	0.3186	21.3843	0.0468	6.8137	0.1468
13	3.4523	0.2897	24.5227	0.0408	7.1034	0.1408
14	3.7975	0.2633	27.9750	0.0357	7.3667	0.1357
15	4.1772	0.2394	31.7725	0.0315	7.6061	0.1315
16	4.5950	0.2176	35.9497	0.0278	7.8237	0.1278
17	5.0545	0.1978	40.5447	0.0247	8.0216	0.1247
18	5.5599	0.1799	45.5992	0.0219	8.2014	0.1219
19	6.1159	0.1635	51.1591	0.0195	8.3649	0.1195
20	6.7275	0.1486	57.2750	0.0175	8.5136	0.1175
21	7.4002	0.1351	64.0025	0.0156	8.6487	0.1156
22	8.1403	0.1228	71.4027	0.0140	8.7715	0.1140
23	8.9543	0.1117	79.5430	0.0126	8.8832	0.1126
24	9.8497	0.1015	88.4973	0.0113	8.9847	0.1113
25	10.8347	0.0923	98.3471	0.0102	9.0770	0.1102
26	11.9182	0.0839	109.1818	0.0092	9.1609	0.1092
27	13.1100	0.0763	121.0999	0.0083	9.2372	0.1083
28	14.4210	0.0693	134.2099	0.0075	9.3066	0.1075
29	15.8631	0.0630	148.6309	0.0067	9.3696	0.1067
30	17.4494	0.0573	164.4940	0.0061	9.4269	0.1061
31	19.1943	0.0521	181.9434	0.0055	9.4790	0.1055
32	21.1138	0.0474	201.1378	0.0050	9.5264	0.1050
33	23.2252	0.0431	222.2515	0.0045	9.5694	0.1045
34	25.5477	0.0391	245.4767	0.0041	9.6086	0.1041
35	28.1024	0.0356	271.0244	0.0037	9.6442	0.1037
36	30.9127	0.0323	299.1268	0.0033	9.6765	0.1033
37	34.0039	0.0294	330.0395	0.0030	9.7059	0.1030
38	37.4043	0.0267	364.0434	0.0027	9.7327	0.1027
39	41.1448	0.0243	401.4478	0.0025	9.7570	0.1025
40	45.2593	0.0221	442.5926	0.0023	9.7791	0.1023
45	72.8905	0.0137	718.9048	0.0014	9.8628	0.1014
50	117.3909	0.0085	1163.9085	0.0009	9.9148	0.1009
60	304.4816	0.0033	3034.8164	0.0003	9.9672	0.1003
75	1271.8954	0.0008	12708.9537	0.0001	9.9921	0.1001
100	13780.6123	0.0001	137796.1234	0.0000	9.9993	0.1000

TABLE B.15 11% Interest Factors for Discrete Compounding

	Single-Payment		Equal-Payment-Series			
	Compound- Amount	Present- Worth	Compound- Amount	Sinking- Fund	Present- Worth	Capital- Recovery
n	*Find F Given P* *(F/P,i,n)*	*Find P Given F* *(P/F,i,n)*	*Find F Given A* *(F/A,i,n)*	*Find A Given F* *(A/F,i,n)*	*Find P Given A* *(P/A,i,n)*	*Find A Given P* *(A/P,i,n)*
1	1.1100	0.9009	1.0000	1.0000	0.9009	1.1100
2	1.2321	0.8116	2.1100	0.4739	1.7125	0.5839
3	1.3676	0.7312	3.3421	0.2992	2.4437	0.4092
4	1.5181	0.6587	4.7097	0.2123	3.1024	0.3223
5	1.6851	0.5935	6.2278	0.1606	3.6959	0.2706
6	1.8704	0.5346	7.9129	0.1264	4.2305	0.2364
7	2.0762	0.4817	9.7833	0.1022	4.7122	0.2122
8	2.3045	0.4339	11.8594	0.0843	5.1461	0.1943
9	2.5580	0.3909	14.1640	0.0706	5.5370	0.1806
10	2.8394	0.3522	16.7220	0.0598	5.8892	0.1698
11	3.1518	0.3173	19.5614	0.0511	6.2065	0.1611
12	3.4985	0.2858	22.7132	0.0440	6.4924	0.1540
13	3.8833	0.2575	26.2116	0.0382	6.7499	0.1482
14	4.3104	0.2320	30.0949	0.0332	6.9819	0.1432
15	4.7846	0.2090	34.4054	0.0291	7.1909	0.1391
16	5.3109	0.1883	39.1899	0.0255	7.3792	0.1355
17	5.8951	0.1696	44.5008	0.0225	7.5488	0.1325
18	6.5436	0.1528	50.3959	0.0198	7.7016	0.1298
19	7.2633	0.1377	56.9395	0.0176	7.8393	0.1276
20	8.0623	0.1240	64.2028	0.0156	7.9633	0.1256
21	8.9492	0.1117	72.2651	0.0138	8.0751	0.1238
22	9.9336	0.1007	81.2143	0.0123	8.1757	0.1223
23	11.0263	0.0907	91.1479	0.0110	8.2664	0.1210
24	12.2392	0.0817	102.1742	0.0098	8.3481	0.1198
25	13.5855	0.0736	114.4133	0.0087	8.4217	0.1187
26	15.0799	0.0663	127.9988	0.0078	8.4881	0.1178
27	16.7386	0.0597	143.0786	0.0070	8.5478	0.1170
28	18.5799	0.0538	159.8173	0.0063	8.6016	0.1163
29	20.6237	0.0485	178.3972	0.0056	8.6501	0.1156
30	22.8923	0.0437	199.0209	0.0050	8.6938	0.1150
31	25.4104	0.0394	221.9132	0.0045	8.7331	0.1145
32	28.2056	0.0355	247.3236	0.0040	8.7686	0.1140
33	31.3082	0.0319	275.5292	0.0036	8.8005	0.1136
34	34.7521	0.0288	306.8374	0.0033	8.8293	0.1133
35	38.5749	0.0259	341.5896	0.0029	8.8552	0.1129
36	42.8181	0.0234	380.1644	0.0026	8.8786	0.1126
37	47.5281	0.0210	422.9825	0.0024	8.8996	0.1124
38	52.7562	0.0190	470.5106	0.0021	8.9186	0.1121
39	58.5593	0.0171	523.2667	0.0019	8.9357	0.1119
40	65.0009	0.0154	581.8261	0.0017	8.9511	0.1117
45	109.5302	0.0091	986.6386	0.0010	9.0079	0.1110
50	184.5648	0.0054	1668.7712	0.0006	9.0417	0.1106
60	524.0572	0.0019	4755.0658	0.0002	9.0736	0.1102
75	2507.3988	0.0004	22785.4434	0.0000	9.0873	0.1100
100	34064.1753	0.0000	309665.2297	0.0000	9.0906	0.1100

TABLE B.16 12% Interest Factors for Discrete Compounding

	Single-Payment		Equal-Payment-Series			
	Compound-Amount	Present-Worth	Compound-Amount	Sinking-Fund	Present-Worth	Capital-Recovery
n	Find F Given P (F/P,i,n)	Find P Given F (P/F,i,n)	Find F Given A (F/A,i,n)	Find A Given F (A/F,i,n)	Find P Given A (P/A,i,n)	Find A Given P (A/P,i,n)
1	1.1200	0.8929	1.0000	1.0000	0.8929	1.1200
2	1.2544	0.7972	2.1200	0.4717	1.6901	0.5917
3	1.4049	0.7118	3.3744	0.2963	2.4018	0.4163
4	1.5735	0.6355	4.7793	0.2092	3.0373	0.3292
5	1.7623	0.5674	6.3528	0.1574	3.6048	0.2774
6	1.9738	0.5066	8.1152	0.1232	4.1114	0.2432
7	2.2107	0.4523	10.0890	0.0991	4.5638	0.2191
8	2.4760	0.4039	12.2997	0.0813	4.9676	0.2013
9	2.7731	0.3606	14.7757	0.0677	5.3282	0.1877
10	3.1058	0.3220	17.5487	0.0570	5.6502	0.1770
11	3.4785	0.2875	20.6546	0.0484	5.9377	0.1684
12	3.8960	0.2567	24.1331	0.0414	6.1944	0.1614
13	4.3635	0.2292	28.0291	0.0357	6.4235	0.1557
14	4.8871	0.2046	32.3926	0.0309	6.6282	0.1509
15	5.4736	0.1827	37.2797	0.0268	6.8109	0.1468
16	6.1304	0.1631	42.7533	0.0234	6.9740	0.1434
17	6.8660	0.1456	48.8837	0.0205	7.1196	0.1405
18	7.6900	0.1300	55.7497	0.0179	7.2497	0.1379
19	8.6128	0.1161	63.4397	0.0158	7.3658	0.1358
20	9.6463	0.1037	72.0524	0.0139	7.4694	0.1339
21	10.8038	0.0926	81.6987	0.0122	7.5620	0.1322
22	12.1003	0.0826	92.5026	0.0108	7.6446	0.1308
23	13.5523	0.0738	104.6029	0.0096	7.7184	0.1296
24	15.1786	0.0659	118.1552	0.0085	7.7843	0.1285
25	17.0001	0.0588	133.3339	0.0075	7.8431	0.1275
26	19.0401	0.0525	150.3339	0.0067	7.8957	0.1267
27	21.3249	0.0469	169.3740	0.0059	7.9426	0.1259
28	23.8839	0.0419	190.6989	0.0052	7.9844	0.1252
29	26.7499	0.0374	214.5828	0.0047	8.0218	0.1247
30	29.9599	0.0334	241.3327	0.0041	8.0552	0.1241
31	33.5551	0.0298	271.2926	0.0037	8.0850	0.1237
32	37.5817	0.0266	304.8477	0.0033	8.1116	0.1233
33	42.0915	0.0238	342.4294	0.0029	8.1354	0.1229
34	47.1425	0.0212	384.5210	0.0026	8.1566	0.1226
35	52.7996	0.0189	431.6635	0.0023	8.1755	0.1223
36	59.1356	0.0169	484.4631	0.0021	8.1924	0.1221
37	66.2318	0.0151	543.5987	0.0018	8.2075	0.1218
38	74.1797	0.0135	609.8305	0.0016	8.2210	0.1216
39	83.0812	0.0120	684.0102	0.0015	8.2330	0.1215
40	93.0510	0.0107	767.0914	0.0013	8.2438	0.1213
45	163.9876	0.0061	1358.2300	0.0007	8.2825	0.1207
50	289.0022	0.0035	2400.0182	0.0004	8.3045	0.1204
60	897.5969	0.0011	7471.6411	0.0001	8.3240	0.1201
75	4913.0558	0.0002	40933.7987	0.0000	8.3316	0.1200
100	83522.2657	0.0000	696010.5477	0.0000	8.3332	0.1200

TABLE B.17   13% Interest Factors for Discrete Compounding

	Single-Payment		Equal-Payment-Series			
	Compound- Amount	Present- Worth	Compound- Amount	Sinking- Fund	Present- Worth	Capital- Recovery
n	Find F Given P (F/P,i,n)	Find P Given F (P/F,i,n)	Find F Given A (F/A,i,n)	Find A Given F (A/F,i,n)	Find P Given A (P/A,i,n)	Find A Given P (A/P,i,n)
1	1.1300	0.8850	1.0000	1.0000	0.8850	1.1300
2	1.2769	0.7831	2.1300	0.4695	1.6681	0.5995
3	1.4429	0.6931	3.4069	0.2935	2.3612	0.4235
4	1.6305	0.6133	4.8498	0.2062	2.9745	0.3362
5	1.8424	0.5428	6.4803	0.1543	3.5172	0.2843
6	2.0820	0.4803	8.3227	0.1202	3.9975	0.2502
7	2.3526	0.4251	10.4047	0.0961	4.4226	0.2261
8	2.6584	0.3762	12.7573	0.0784	4.7988	0.2084
9	3.0040	0.3329	15.4157	0.0649	5.1317	0.1949
10	3.3946	0.2946	18.4197	0.0543	5.4262	0.1843
11	3.8359	0.2607	21.8143	0.0458	5.6869	0.1758
12	4.3345	0.2307	25.6502	0.0390	5.9176	0.1690
13	4.8980	0.2042	29.9847	0.0334	6.1218	0.1634
14	5.5348	0.1807	34.8827	0.0287	6.3025	0.1587
15	6.2543	0.1599	40.4175	0.0247	6.4624	0.1547
16	7.0673	0.1415	46.6717	0.0214	6.6039	0.1514
17	7.9861	0.1252	53.7391	0.0186	6.7291	0.1486
18	9.0243	0.1108	61.7251	0.0162	6.8399	0.1462
19	10.1974	0.0981	70.7494	0.0141	6.9380	0.1441
20	11.5231	0.0868	80.9468	0.0124	7.0248	0.1424
21	13.0211	0.0768	92.4699	0.0108	7.1016	0.1408
22	14.7138	0.0680	105.4910	0.0095	7.1695	0.1395
23	16.6266	0.0601	120.2048	0.0083	7.2297	0.1383
24	18.7881	0.0532	136.8315	0.0073	7.2829	0.1373
25	21.2305	0.0471	155.6196	0.0064	7.3300	0.1364
26	23.9905	0.0417	176.8501	0.0057	7.3717	0.1357
27	27.1093	0.0369	200.8406	0.0050	7.4086	0.1350
28	30.6335	0.0326	227.9499	0.0044	7.4412	0.1344
29	34.6158	0.0289	258.5834	0.0039	7.4701	0.1339
30	39.1159	0.0256	293.1992	0.0034	7.4957	0.1334
31	44.2010	0.0226	332.3151	0.0030	7.5183	0.1330
32	49.9471	0.0200	376.5161	0.0027	7.5383	0.1327
33	56.4402	0.0177	426.4632	0.0023	7.5560	0.1323
34	63.7774	0.0157	482.9034	0.0021	7.5717	0.1321
35	72.0685	0.0139	546.6808	0.0018	7.5856	0.1318
36	81.4374	0.0123	618.7493	0.0016	7.5979	0.1316
37	92.0243	0.0109	700.1867	0.0014	7.6087	0.1314
38	103.9874	0.0096	792.2110	0.0013	7.6183	0.1313
39	117.5058	0.0085	896.1984	0.0011	7.6268	0.1311
40	132.7816	0.0075	1013.7042	0.0010	7.6344	0.1310
45	244.6414	0.0041	1874.1646	0.0005	7.6609	0.1305
50	450.7359	0.0022	3459.5071	0.0003	7.6752	0.1303
60	1530.0535	0.0007	11761.9498	0.0001	7.6873	0.1301
75	9569.3681	0.0001	73602.8316	0.0000	7.6915	0.1300
100	203162.8742	0.0000	###########	0.0000	7.6923	0.1300

TABLE B.18 14% Interest Factors for Discrete Compounding

	Single-Payment		Equal-Payment-Series			
	Compound-Amount	Present-Worth	Compound-Amount	Sinking-Fund	Present-Worth	Capital-Recovery
n	*Find F Given P* (F/P,i,n)	*Find P Given F* (P/F,i,n)	*Find F Given A* (F/A,i,n)	*Find A Given F* (A/F,i,n)	*Find P Given A* (P/A,i,n)	*Find A Given P* (A/P,i,n)
1	1.1400	0.8772	1.0000	1.0000	0.8772	1.1400
2	1.2996	0.7695	2.1400	0.4673	1.6467	0.6073
3	1.4815	0.6750	3.4396	0.2907	2.3216	0.4307
4	1.6890	0.5921	4.9211	0.2032	2.9137	0.3432
5	1.9254	0.5194	6.6101	0.1513	3.4331	0.2913
6	2.1950	0.4556	8.5355	0.1172	3.8887	0.2572
7	2.5023	0.3996	10.7305	0.0932	4.2883	0.2332
8	2.8526	0.3506	13.2328	0.0756	4.6389	0.2156
9	3.2519	0.3075	16.0853	0.0622	4.9464	0.2022
10	3.7072	0.2697	19.3373	0.0517	5.2161	0.1917
11	4.2262	0.2366	23.0445	0.0434	5.4527	0.1834
12	4.8179	0.2076	27.2707	0.0367	5.6603	0.1767
13	5.4924	0.1821	32.0887	0.0312	5.8424	0.1712
14	6.2613	0.1597	37.5811	0.0266	6.0021	0.1666
15	7.1379	0.1401	43.8424	0.0228	6.1422	0.1628
16	8.1372	0.1229	50.9804	0.0196	6.2651	0.1596
17	9.2765	0.1078	59.1176	0.0169	6.3729	0.1569
18	10.5752	0.0946	68.3941	0.0146	6.4674	0.1546
19	12.0557	0.0829	78.9692	0.0127	6.5504	0.1527
20	13.7435	0.0728	91.0249	0.0110	6.6231	0.1510
21	15.6676	0.0638	104.7684	0.0095	6.6870	0.1495
22	17.8610	0.0560	120.4360	0.0083	6.7429	0.1483
23	20.3616	0.0491	138.2970	0.0072	6.7921	0.1472
24	23.2122	0.0431	158.6586	0.0063	6.8351	0.1463
25	26.4619	0.0378	181.8708	0.0055	6.8729	0.1455
26	30.1666	0.0331	208.3327	0.0048	6.9061	0.1448
27	34.3899	0.0291	238.4993	0.0042	6.9352	0.1442
28	39.2045	0.0255	272.8892	0.0037	6.9607	0.1437
29	44.6931	0.0224	312.0937	0.0032	6.9830	0.1432
30	50.9502	0.0196	356.7868	0.0028	7.0027	0.1428
31	58.0832	0.0172	407.7370	0.0025	7.0199	0.1425
32	66.2148	0.0151	465.8202	0.0021	7.0350	0.1421
33	75.4849	0.0132	532.0350	0.0019	7.0482	0.1419
34	86.0528	0.0116	607.5199	0.0016	7.0599	0.1416
35	98.1002	0.0102	693.5727	0.0014	7.0700	0.1414
36	111.8342	0.0089	791.6729	0.0013	7.0790	0.1413
37	127.4910	0.0078	903.5071	0.0011	7.0868	0.1411
38	145.3397	0.0069	1030.9981	0.0010	7.0937	0.1410
39	165.6873	0.0060	1176.3378	0.0009	7.0997	0.1409
40	188.8835	0.0053	1342.0251	0.0007	7.1050	0.1407
45	363.6791	0.0027	2590.5648	0.0004	7.1232	0.1404
50	700.2330	0.0014	4994.5213	0.0002	7.1327	0.1402
60	2595.9187	0.0004	18535.1333	0.0001	7.1401	0.1401
75	18529.5064	0.0001	132346.4742	0.0000	7.1425	0.1400
100	490326.2381	0.0000	###########	0.0000	7.1428	0.1400

TABLE B.19   15% Interest Factors for Discrete Compounding

	Single-Payment		Equal-Payment-Series			
	Compound-Amount	Present-Worth	Compound-Amount	Sinking-Fund	Present-Worth	Capital-Recovery
n	Find F Given P (F/P,i,n)	Find P Given F (P/F,i,n)	Find F Given A (F/A,i,n)	Find A Given F (A/F,i,n)	Find P Given A (P/A,i,n)	Find A Given P (A/P,i,n)
1	1.1500	0.8696	1.0000	1.0000	0.8696	1.1500
2	1.3225	0.7561	2.1500	0.4651	1.6257	0.6151
3	1.5209	0.6575	3.4725	0.2880	2.2832	0.4380
4	1.7490	0.5718	4.9934	0.2003	2.8550	0.3503
5	2.0114	0.4972	6.7424	0.1483	3.3522	0.2983
6	2.3131	0.4323	8.7537	0.1142	3.7845	0.2642
7	2.6600	0.3759	11.0668	0.0904	4.1604	0.2404
8	3.0590	0.3269	13.7268	0.0729	4.4873	0.2229
9	3.5179	0.2843	16.7858	0.0596	4.7716	0.2096
10	4.0456	0.2472	20.3037	0.0493	5.0188	0.1993
11	4.6524	0.2149	24.3493	0.0411	5.2337	0.1911
12	5.3503	0.1869	29.0017	0.0345	5.4206	0.1845
13	6.1528	0.1625	34.3519	0.0291	5.5831	0.1791
14	7.0757	0.1413	40.5047	0.0247	5.7245	0.1747
15	8.1371	0.1229	47.5804	0.0210	5.8474	0.1710
16	9.3576	0.1069	55.7175	0.0179	5.9542	0.1679
17	10.7613	0.0929	65.0751	0.0154	6.0472	0.1654
18	12.3755	0.0808	75.8364	0.0132	6.1280	0.1632
19	14.2318	0.0703	88.2118	0.0113	6.1982	0.1613
20	16.3665	0.0611	102.4436	0.0098	6.2593	0.1598
21	18.8215	0.0531	118.8101	0.0084	6.3125	0.1584
22	21.6447	0.0462	137.6316	0.0073	6.3587	0.1573
23	24.8915	0.0402	159.2764	0.0063	6.3988	0.1563
24	28.6252	0.0349	184.1678	0.0054	6.4338	0.1554
25	32.9190	0.0304	212.7930	0.0047	6.4641	0.1547
26	37.8568	0.0264	245.7120	0.0041	6.4906	0.1541
27	43.5353	0.0230	283.5688	0.0035	6.5135	0.1535
28	50.0656	0.0200	327.1041	0.0031	6.5335	0.1531
29	57.5755	0.0174	377.1697	0.0027	6.5509	0.1527
30	66.2118	0.0151	434.7451	0.0023	6.5660	0.1523
31	76.1435	0.0131	500.9569	0.0020	6.5791	0.1520
32	87.5651	0.0114	577.1005	0.0017	6.5905	0.1517
33	100.6998	0.0099	664.6655	0.0015	6.6005	0.1515
34	115.8048	0.0086	765.3654	0.0013	6.6091	0.1513
35	133.1755	0.0075	881.1702	0.0011	6.6166	0.1511
36	153.1519	0.0065	1014.3457	0.0010	6.6231	0.1510
37	176.1246	0.0057	1167.4975	0.0009	6.6288	0.1509
38	202.5433	0.0049	1343.6222	0.0007	6.6338	0.1507
39	232.9248	0.0043	1546.1655	0.0006	6.6380	0.1506
40	267.8635	0.0037	1779.0903	0.0006	6.6418	0.1506
45	538.7693	0.0019	3585.1285	0.0003	6.6543	0.1503
50	1083.6574	0.0009	7217.7163	0.0001	6.6605	0.1501
60	4383.9987	0.0002	29219.9916	0.0000	6.6651	0.1500
75	35672.8680	0.0000	237812.4532	0.0000	6.6665	0.1500
100	1174313.4507	0.0000	###########	0.0000	6.6667	0.1500

TABLE B.20   16% Interest Factors for Discrete Compounding

	Single-Payment		Equal-Payment-Series			
	Compound-Amount	Present-Worth	Compound-Amount	Sinking-Fund	Present-Worth	Capital-Recovery
n	Find F Given P (F/P,i,n)	Find P Given F (P/F,i,n)	Find F Given A (F/A,i,n)	Find A Given F (A/F,i,n)	Find P Given A (P/A,i,n)	Find A Given P (A/P,i,n)
1	1.1600	0.8621	1.0000	1.0000	0.8621	1.1600
2	1.3456	0.7432	2.1600	0.4630	1.6052	0.6230
3	1.5609	0.6407	3.5056	0.2853	2.2459	0.4453
4	1.8106	0.5523	5.0665	0.1974	2.7982	0.3574
5	2.1003	0.4761	6.8771	0.1454	3.2743	0.3054
6	2.4364	0.4104	8.9775	0.1114	3.6847	0.2714
7	2.8262	0.3538	11.4139	0.0876	4.0386	0.2476
8	3.2784	0.3050	14.2401	0.0702	4.3436	0.2302
9	3.8030	0.2630	17.5185	0.0571	4.6065	0.2171
10	4.4114	0.2267	21.3215	0.0469	4.8332	0.2069
11	5.1173	0.1954	25.7329	0.0389	5.0286	0.1989
12	5.9360	0.1685	30.8502	0.0324	5.1971	0.1924
13	6.8858	0.1452	36.7862	0.0272	5.3423	0.1872
14	7.9875	0.1252	43.6720	0.0229	5.4675	0.1829
15	9.2655	0.1079	51.6595	0.0194	5.5755	0.1794
16	10.7480	0.0930	60.9250	0.0164	5.6685	0.1764
17	12.4677	0.0802	71.6730	0.0140	5.7487	0.1740
18	14.4625	0.0691	84.1407	0.0119	5.8178	0.1719
19	16.7765	0.0596	98.6032	0.0101	5.8775	0.1701
20	19.4608	0.0514	115.3797	0.0087	5.9288	0.1687
21	22.5745	0.0443	134.8405	0.0074	5.9731	0.1674
22	26.1864	0.0382	157.4150	0.0064	6.0113	0.1664
23	30.3762	0.0329	183.6014	0.0054	6.0442	0.1654
24	35.2364	0.0284	213.9776	0.0047	6.0726	0.1647
25	40.8742	0.0245	249.2140	0.0040	6.0971	0.1640
26	47.4141	0.0211	290.0883	0.0034	6.1182	0.1634
27	55.0004	0.0182	337.5024	0.0030	6.1364	0.1630
28	63.8004	0.0157	392.5028	0.0025	6.1520	0.1625
29	74.0085	0.0135	456.3032	0.0022	6.1656	0.1622
30	85.8499	0.0116	530.3117	0.0019	6.1772	0.1619
31	99.5859	0.0100	616.1616	0.0016	6.1872	0.1616
32	115.5196	0.0087	715.7475	0.0014	6.1959	0.1614
33	134.0027	0.0075	831.2671	0.0012	6.2034	0.1612
34	155.4432	0.0064	965.2698	0.0010	6.2098	0.1610
35	180.3141	0.0055	1120.7130	0.0009	6.2153	0.1609
36	209.1643	0.0048	1301.0270	0.0008	6.2201	0.1608
37	242.6306	0.0041	1510.1914	0.0007	6.2242	0.1607
38	281.4515	0.0036	1752.8220	0.0006	6.2278	0.1606
39	326.4838	0.0031	2034.2735	0.0005	6.2309	0.1605
40	378.7212	0.0026	2360.7572	0.0004	6.2335	0.1604
45	795.4438	0.0013	4965.2739	0.0002	6.2421	0.1602
50	1670.7038	0.0006	10435.6488	0.0001	6.2463	0.1601
60	7370.2014	0.0001	46057.5085	0.0000	6.2492	0.1600
75	68288.7545	0.0000	426798.4658	0.0000	6.2499	0.1600
100	2791251.1994	0.0000	###########	0.0000	6.2500	0.1600

TABLE B.21   17% Interest Factors for Discrete Compounding

	Single-Payment		Equal-Payment-Series			
	Compound-Amount	Present-Worth	Compound-Amount	Sinking-Fund	Present-Worth	Capital-Recovery
n	Find F Given P (F/P,i,n)	Find P Given F (P/F,i,n)	Find F Given A (F/A,i,n)	Find A Given F (A/F,i,n)	Find P Given A (P/A,i,n)	Find A Given P (A/P,i,n)
1	1.1700	0.8547	1.0000	1.0000	0.8547	1.1700
2	1.3689	0.7305	2.1700	0.4608	1.5852	0.6308
3	1.6016	0.6244	3.5389	0.2826	2.2096	0.4526
4	1.8739	0.5337	5.1405	0.1945	2.7432	0.3645
5	2.1924	0.4561	7.0144	0.1426	3.1993	0.3126
6	2.5652	0.3898	9.2068	0.1086	3.5892	0.2786
7	3.0012	0.3332	11.7720	0.0849	3.9224	0.2549
8	3.5115	0.2848	14.7733	0.0677	4.2072	0.2377
9	4.1084	0.2434	18.2847	0.0547	4.4506	0.2247
10	4.8068	0.2080	22.3931	0.0447	4.6586	0.2147
11	5.6240	0.1778	27.1999	0.0368	4.8364	0.2068
12	6.5801	0.1520	32.8239	0.0305	4.9884	0.2005
13	7.6987	0.1299	39.4040	0.0254	5.1183	0.1954
14	9.0075	0.1110	47.1027	0.0212	5.2293	0.1912
15	10.5387	0.0949	56.1101	0.0178	5.3242	0.1878
16	12.3303	0.0811	66.6488	0.0150	5.4053	0.1850
17	14.4265	0.0693	78.9792	0.0127	5.4746	0.1827
18	16.8790	0.0592	93.4056	0.0107	5.5339	0.1807
19	19.7484	0.0506	110.2846	0.0091	5.5845	0.1791
20	23.1056	0.0433	130.0329	0.0077	5.6278	0.1777
21	27.0336	0.0370	153.1385	0.0065	5.6648	0.1765
22	31.6293	0.0316	180.1721	0.0056	5.6964	0.1756
23	37.0062	0.0270	211.8013	0.0047	5.7234	0.1747
24	43.2973	0.0231	248.8076	0.0040	5.7465	0.1740
25	50.6578	0.0197	292.1049	0.0034	5.7662	0.1734
26	59.2697	0.0169	342.7627	0.0029	5.7831	0.1729
27	69.3455	0.0144	402.0323	0.0025	5.7975	0.1725
28	81.1342	0.0123	471.3778	0.0021	5.8099	0.1721
29	94.9271	0.0105	552.5121	0.0018	5.8204	0.1718
30	111.0647	0.0090	647.4391	0.0015	5.8294	0.1715
31	129.9456	0.0077	758.5038	0.0013	5.8371	0.1713
32	152.0364	0.0066	888.4494	0.0011	5.8437	0.1711
33	177.8826	0.0056	1040.4858	0.0010	5.8493	0.1710
34	208.1226	0.0048	1218.3684	0.0008	5.8541	0.1708
35	243.5035	0.0041	1426.4910	0.0007	5.8582	0.1707
36	284.8991	0.0035	1669.9945	0.0006	5.8617	0.1706
37	333.3319	0.0030	1954.8936	0.0005	5.8647	0.1705
38	389.9983	0.0026	2288.2255	0.0004	5.8673	0.1704
39	456.2980	0.0022	2678.2238	0.0004	5.8695	0.1704
40	533.8687	0.0019	3134.5218	0.0003	5.8713	0.1703
45	1170.4794	0.0009	6879.2907	0.0001	5.8773	0.1701
50	2566.2153	0.0004	15089.5017	0.0001	5.8801	0.1701
60	12335.3565	0.0001	72555.0381	0.0000	5.8819	0.1700
75	129998.8861	0.0000	764693.4475	0.0000	5.8823	0.1700
100	6585460.8858	0.0000	##########	0.0000	5.8824	0.1700

TABLE B.22   18% Interest Factors for Discrete Compounding

	Single-Payment		Equal-Payment-Series			
	Compound-Amount	Present-Worth	Compound-Amount	Sinking-Fund	Present-Worth	Capital-Recovery
n	Find F Given P (F/P,i,n)	Find P Given F (P/F,i,n)	Find F Given A (F/A,i,n)	Find A Given F (A/F,i,n)	Find P Given A (P/A,i,n)	Find A Given P (A/P,i,n)
1	1.1800	0.8475	1.0000	1.0000	0.8475	1.1800
2	1.3924	0.7182	2.1800	0.4587	1.5656	0.6387
3	1.6430	0.6086	3.5724	0.2799	2.1743	0.4599
4	1.9388	0.5158	5.2154	0.1917	2.6901	0.3717
5	2.2878	0.4371	7.1542	0.1398	3.1272	0.3198
6	2.6996	0.3704	9.4420	0.1059	3.4976	0.2859
7	3.1855	0.3139	12.1415	0.0824	3.8115	0.2624
8	3.7589	0.2660	15.3270	0.0652	4.0776	0.2452
9	4.4355	0.2255	19.0859	0.0524	4.3030	0.2324
10	5.2338	0.1911	23.5213	0.0425	4.4941	0.2225
11	6.1759	0.1619	28.7551	0.0348	4.6560	0.2148
12	7.2876	0.1372	34.9311	0.0286	4.7932	0.2086
13	8.5994	0.1163	42.2187	0.0237	4.9095	0.2037
14	10.1472	0.0985	50.8180	0.0197	5.0081	0.1997
15	11.9737	0.0835	60.9653	0.0164	5.0916	0.1964
16	14.1290	0.0708	72.9390	0.0137	5.1624	0.1937
17	16.6722	0.0600	87.0680	0.0115	5.2223	0.1915
18	19.6733	0.0508	103.7403	0.0096	5.2732	0.1896
19	23.2144	0.0431	123.4135	0.0081	5.3162	0.1881
20	27.3930	0.0365	146.6280	0.0068	5.3527	0.1868
21	32.3238	0.0309	174.0210	0.0057	5.3837	0.1857
22	38.1421	0.0262	206.3448	0.0048	5.4099	0.1848
23	45.0076	0.0222	244.4868	0.0041	5.4321	0.1841
24	53.1090	0.0188	289.4945	0.0035	5.4509	0.1835
25	62.6686	0.0160	342.6035	0.0029	5.4669	0.1829
26	73.9490	0.0135	405.2721	0.0025	5.4804	0.1825
27	87.2598	0.0115	479.2211	0.0021	5.4919	0.1821
28	102.9666	0.0097	566.4809	0.0018	5.5016	0.1818
29	121.5005	0.0082	669.4475	0.0015	5.5098	0.1815
30	143.3706	0.0070	790.9480	0.0013	5.5168	0.1813
31	169.1774	0.0059	934.3186	0.0011	5.5227	0.1811
32	199.6293	0.0050	1103.4960	0.0009	5.5277	0.1809
33	235.5625	0.0042	1303.1253	0.0008	5.5320	0.1808
34	277.9638	0.0036	1538.6878	0.0006	5.5356	0.1806
35	327.9973	0.0030	1816.6516	0.0006	5.5386	0.1806
36	387.0368	0.0026	2144.6489	0.0005	5.5412	0.1805
37	456.7034	0.0022	2531.6857	0.0004	5.5434	0.1804
38	538.9100	0.0019	2988.3891	0.0003	5.5452	0.1803
39	635.9139	0.0016	3527.2992	0.0003	5.5468	0.1803
40	750.3783	0.0013	4163.2130	0.0002	5.5482	0.1802
45	1716.6839	0.0006	9531.5771	0.0001	5.5523	0.1801
50	3927.3569	0.0003	21813.0937	0.0000	5.5541	0.1800
60	20555.1400	0.0000	114189.6665	0.0000	5.5553	0.1800
75	246122.0637	0.0000	###########	0.0000	5.5555	0.1800
100	###########	0.0000	###########	0.0000	5.5556	0.1800

TABLE B.23 19% Interest Factors for Discrete Compounding

	Single-Payment		Equal-Payment-Series			
	Compound-Amount	Present-Worth	Compound-Amount	Sinking-Fund	Present-Worth	Capital-Recovery
n	Find F Given P (F/P,i,n)	Find P Given F (P/F,i,n)	Find F Given A (F/A,i,n)	Find A Given F (A/F,i,n)	Find P Given A (P/A,i,n)	Find A Given P (A/P,i,n)
1	1.1900	0.8403	1.0000	1.0000	0.8403	1.1900
2	1.4161	0.7062	2.1900	0.4566	1.5465	0.6466
3	1.6852	0.5934	3.6061	0.2773	2.1399	0.4673
4	2.0053	0.4987	5.2913	0.1890	2.6386	0.3790
5	2.3864	0.4190	7.2966	0.1371	3.0576	0.3271
6	2.8398	0.3521	9.6830	0.1033	3.4098	0.2933
7	3.3793	0.2959	12.5227	0.0799	3.7057	0.2699
8	4.0214	0.2487	15.9020	0.0629	3.9544	0.2529
9	4.7854	0.2090	19.9234	0.0502	4.1633	0.2402
10	5.6947	0.1756	24.7089	0.0405	4.3389	0.2305
11	6.7767	0.1476	30.4035	0.0329	4.4865	0.2229
12	8.0642	0.1240	37.1802	0.0269	4.6105	0.2169
13	9.5964	0.1042	45.2445	0.0221	4.7147	0.2121
14	11.4198	0.0876	54.8409	0.0182	4.8023	0.2082
15	13.5895	0.0736	66.2607	0.0151	4.8759	0.2051
16	16.1715	0.0618	79.8502	0.0125	4.9377	0.2025
17	19.2441	0.0520	96.0218	0.0104	4.9897	0.2004
18	22.9005	0.0437	115.2659	0.0087	5.0333	0.1987
19	27.2516	0.0367	138.1664	0.0072	5.0700	0.1972
20	32.4294	0.0308	165.4180	0.0060	5.1009	0.1960
21	38.5910	0.0259	197.8474	0.0051	5.1268	0.1951
22	45.9233	0.0218	236.4385	0.0042	5.1486	0.1942
23	54.6487	0.0183	282.3618	0.0035	5.1668	0.1935
24	65.0320	0.0154	337.0105	0.0030	5.1822	0.1930
25	77.3881	0.0129	402.0425	0.0025	5.1951	0.1925
26	92.0918	0.0109	479.4306	0.0021	5.2060	0.1921
27	109.5893	0.0091	571.5224	0.0017	5.2151	0.1917
28	130.4112	0.0077	681.1116	0.0015	5.2228	0.1915
29	155.1893	0.0064	811.5228	0.0012	5.2292	0.1912
30	184.6753	0.0054	966.7122	0.0010	5.2347	0.1910
31	219.7636	0.0046	1151.3875	0.0009	5.2392	0.1909
32	261.5187	0.0038	1371.1511	0.0007	5.2430	0.1907
33	311.2073	0.0032	1632.6698	0.0006	5.2462	0.1906
34	370.3366	0.0027	1943.8771	0.0005	5.2489	0.1905
35	440.7006	0.0023	2314.2137	0.0004	5.2512	0.1904
36	524.4337	0.0019	2754.9143	0.0004	5.2531	0.1904
37	624.0761	0.0016	3279.3481	0.0003	5.2547	0.1903
38	742.6506	0.0013	3903.4242	0.0003	5.2561	0.1903
39	883.7542	0.0011	4646.0748	0.0002	5.2572	0.1902
40	1051.6675	0.0010	5529.8290	0.0002	5.2582	0.1902
45	2509.6506	0.0004	13203.4242	0.0001	5.2611	0.1901
50	5988.9139	0.0002	31515.3363	0.0000	5.2623	0.1900
60	34104.9709	0.0000	179494.5838	0.0000	5.2630	0.1900
75	463470.5086	0.0000	##########	0.0000	5.2631	0.1900
100	##########	0.0000	##########	0.0000	5.2632	0.1900

TABLE B.24 20% Interest Factors for Discrete Compounding

	Single-Payment		Equal-Payment-Series			
	Compound-Amount	Present-Worth	Compound-Amount	Sinking-Fund	Present-Worth	Capital-Recovery
n	Find F Given P (F/P,i,n)	Find P Given F (P/F,i,n)	Find F Given A (F/A,i,n)	Find A Given F (A/F,i,n)	Find P Given A (P/A,i,n)	Find A Given P (A/P,i,n)
1	1.2000	0.8333	1.0000	1.0000	0.8333	1.2000
2	1.4400	0.6944	2.2000	0.4545	1.5278	0.6545
3	1.7280	0.5787	3.6400	0.2747	2.1065	0.4747
4	2.0736	0.4823	5.3680	0.1863	2.5887	0.3863
5	2.4883	0.4019	7.4416	0.1344	2.9906	0.3344
6	2.9860	0.3349	9.9299	0.1007	3.3255	0.3007
7	3.5832	0.2791	12.9159	0.0774	3.6046	0.2774
8	4.2998	0.2326	16.4991	0.0606	3.8372	0.2606
9	5.1598	0.1938	20.7989	0.0481	4.0310	0.2481
10	6.1917	0.1615	25.9587	0.0385	4.1925	0.2385
11	7.4301	0.1346	32.1504	0.0311	4.3271	0.2311
12	8.9161	0.1122	39.5805	0.0253	4.4392	0.2253
13	10.6993	0.0935	48.4966	0.0206	4.5327	0.2206
14	12.8392	0.0779	59.1959	0.0169	4.6106	0.2169
15	15.4070	0.0649	72.0351	0.0139	4.6755	0.2139
16	18.4884	0.0541	87.4421	0.0114	4.7296	0.2114
17	22.1861	0.0451	105.9306	0.0094	4.7746	0.2094
18	26.6233	0.0376	128.1167	0.0078	4.8122	0.2078
19	31.9480	0.0313	154.7400	0.0065	4.8435	0.2065
20	38.3376	0.0261	186.6880	0.0054	4.8696	0.2054
21	46.0051	0.0217	225.0256	0.0044	4.8913	0.2044
22	55.2061	0.0181	271.0307	0.0037	4.9094	0.2037
23	66.2474	0.0151	326.2369	0.0031	4.9245	0.2031
24	79.4968	0.0126	392.4842	0.0025	4.9371	0.2025
25	95.3962	0.0105	471.9811	0.0021	4.9476	0.2021
26	114.4755	0.0087	567.3773	0.0018	4.9563	0.2018
27	137.3706	0.0073	681.8528	0.0015	4.9636	0.2015
28	164.8447	0.0061	819.2233	0.0012	4.9697	0.2012
29	197.8136	0.0051	984.0680	0.0010	4.9747	0.2010
30	237.3763	0.0042	1181.8816	0.0008	4.9789	0.2008
31	284.8516	0.0035	1419.2579	0.0007	4.9824	0.2007
32	341.8219	0.0029	1704.1095	0.0006	4.9854	0.2006
33	410.1863	0.0024	2045.9314	0.0005	4.9878	0.2005
34	492.2235	0.0020	2456.1176	0.0004	4.9898	0.2004
35	590.6682	0.0017	2948.3411	0.0003	4.9915	0.2003
36	708.8019	0.0014	3539.0094	0.0003	4.9929	0.2003
37	850.5622	0.0012	4247.8112	0.0002	4.9941	0.2002
38	1020.6747	0.0010	5098.3735	0.0002	4.9951	0.2002
39	1224.8096	0.0008	6119.0482	0.0002	4.9959	0.2002
40	1469.7716	0.0007	7343.8578	0.0001	4.9966	0.2001
45	3657.2620	0.0003	18281.3099	0.0001	4.9986	0.2001
50	9100.4382	0.0001	45497.1908	0.0000	4.9995	0.2000
60	56347.5144	0.0000	281732.5718	0.0000	4.9999	0.2000
75	868147.3693	0.0000	##########	0.0000	5.0000	0.2000
100	##########	0.0000	##########	0.0000	5.0000	0.2000

TABLE B.25 25% Interest Factors for Discrete Compounding

	Single-Payment		Equal-Payment-Series			
	Compound- Amount	Present- Worth	Compound- Amount	Sinking- Fund	Present- Worth	Capital- Recovery
n	Find F Given P (F/P,i,n)	Find P Given F (P/F,i,n)	Find F Given A (F/A,i,n)	Find A Given F (A/F,i,n)	Find P Given A (P/A,i,n)	Find A Given P (A/P,i,n)
1	1.2500	0.8000	1.0000	1.0000	0.8000	1.2500
2	1.5625	0.6400	2.2500	0.4444	1.4400	0.6944
3	1.9531	0.5120	3.8125	0.2623	1.9520	0.5123
4	2.4414	0.4096	5.7656	0.1734	2.3616	0.4234
5	3.0518	0.3277	8.2070	0.1218	2.6893	0.3718
6	3.8147	0.2621	11.2588	0.0888	2.9514	0.3388
7	4.7684	0.2097	15.0735	0.0663	3.1611	0.3163
8	5.9605	0.1678	19.8419	0.0504	3.3289	0.3004
9	7.4506	0.1342	25.8023	0.0388	3.4631	0.2888
10	9.3132	0.1074	33.2529	0.0301	3.5705	0.2801
11	11.6415	0.0859	42.5661	0.0235	3.6564	0.2735
12	14.5519	0.0687	54.2077	0.0184	3.7251	0.2684
13	18.1899	0.0550	68.7596	0.0145	3.7801	0.2645
14	22.7374	0.0440	86.9495	0.0115	3.8241	0.2615
15	28.4217	0.0352	109.6868	0.0091	3.8593	0.2591
16	35.5271	0.0281	138.1085	0.0072	3.8874	0.2572
17	44.4089	0.0225	173.6357	0.0058	3.9099	0.2558
18	55.5112	0.0180	218.0446	0.0046	3.9279	0.2546
19	69.3889	0.0144	273.5558	0.0037	3.9424	0.2537
20	86.7362	0.0115	342.9447	0.0029	3.9539	0.2529
21	108.4202	0.0092	429.6809	0.0023	3.9631	0.2523
22	135.5253	0.0074	538.1011	0.0019	3.9705	0.2519
23	169.4066	0.0059	673.6264	0.0015	3.9764	0.2515
24	211.7582	0.0047	843.0329	0.0012	3.9811	0.2512
25	264.6978	0.0038	1054.7912	0.0009	3.9849	0.2509
26	330.8722	0.0030	1319.4890	0.0008	3.9879	0.2508
27	413.5903	0.0024	1650.3612	0.0006	3.9903	0.2506
28	516.9879	0.0019	2063.9515	0.0005	3.9923	0.2505
29	646.2349	0.0015	2580.9394	0.0004	3.9938	0.2504
30	807.7936	0.0012	3227.1743	0.0003	3.9950	0.2503
31	1009.7420	0.0010	4034.9678	0.0002	3.9960	0.2502
32	1262.1774	0.0008	5044.7098	0.0002	3.9968	0.2502
33	1577.7218	0.0006	6306.8872	0.0002	3.9975	0.2502
34	1972.1523	0.0005	7884.6091	0.0001	3.9980	0.2501
35	2465.1903	0.0004	9856.7613	0.0001	3.9984	0.2501
36	3081.4879	0.0003	12321.9516	0.0001	3.9987	0.2501
37	3851.8599	0.0003	15403.4396	0.0001	3.9990	0.2501
38	4814.8249	0.0002	19255.2994	0.0001	3.9992	0.2501
39	6018.5311	0.0002	24070.1243	0.0000	3.9993	0.2500
40	7523.1638	0.0001	30088.6554	0.0000	3.9995	0.2500
45	22958.8740	0.0000	91831.4962	0.0000	3.9998	0.2500
50	70064.9232	0.0000	280255.6929	0.0000	3.9999	0.2500
60	652530.4468	0.0000	###########	0.0000	4.0000	0.2500
75	###########	0.0000	###########	0.0000	4.0000	0.2500
100	###########	0.0000	###########	0.0000	4.0000	0.2500

TABLE B.26   30% Interest Factors for Discrete Compounding

	Single-Payment		Equal-Payment-Series			
	Compound- Amount	Present- Worth	Compound- Amount	Sinking- Fund	Present- Worth	Capital- Recovery
n	Find F Given P (F/P,i,n)	Find P Given F (P/F,i,n)	Find F Given A (F/A,i,n)	Find A Given F (A/F,i,n)	Find P Given A (P/A,i,n)	Find A Given P (A/P,i,n)
1	1.3000	0.7692	1.0000	1.0000	0.7692	1.3000
2	1.6900	0.5917	2.3000	0.4348	1.3609	0.7348
3	2.1970	0.4552	3.9900	0.2506	1.8161	0.5506
4	2.8561	0.3501	6.1870	0.1616	2.1662	0.4616
5	3.7129	0.2693	9.0431	0.1106	2.4356	0.4106
6	4.8268	0.2072	12.7560	0.0784	2.6427	0.3784
7	6.2749	0.1594	17.5828	0.0569	2.8021	0.3569
8	8.1573	0.1226	23.8577	0.0419	2.9247	0.3419
9	10.6045	0.0943	32.0150	0.0312	3.0190	0.3312
10	13.7858	0.0725	42.6195	0.0235	3.0915	0.3235
11	17.9216	0.0558	56.4053	0.0177	3.1473	0.3177
12	23.2981	0.0429	74.3270	0.0135	3.1903	0.3135
13	30.2875	0.0330	97.6250	0.0102	3.2233	0.3102
14	39.3738	0.0254	127.9125	0.0078	3.2487	0.3078
15	51.1859	0.0195	167.2863	0.0060	3.2682	0.3060
16	66.5417	0.0150	218.4722	0.0046	3.2832	0.3046
17	86.5042	0.0116	285.0139	0.0035	3.2948	0.3035
18	112.4554	0.0089	371.5180	0.0027	3.3037	0.3027
19	146.1920	0.0068	483.9734	0.0021	3.3105	0.3021
20	190.0496	0.0053	630.1655	0.0016	3.3158	0.3016
21	247.0645	0.0040	820.2151	0.0012	3.3198	0.3012
22	321.1839	0.0031	1067.2796	0.0009	3.3230	0.3009
23	417.5391	0.0024	1388.4635	0.0007	3.3254	0.3007
24	542.8008	0.0018	1806.0026	0.0006	3.3272	0.3006
25	705.6410	0.0014	2348.8033	0.0004	3.3286	0.3004
26	917.3333	0.0011	3054.4443	0.0003	3.3297	0.3003
27	1192.5333	0.0008	3971.7776	0.0003	3.3305	0.3003
28	1550.2933	0.0006	5164.3109	0.0002	3.3312	0.3002
29	2015.3813	0.0005	6714.6042	0.0001	3.3317	0.3001
30	2619.9956	0.0004	8729.9855	0.0001	3.3321	0.3001
31	3405.9943	0.0003	11349.9811	0.0001	3.3324	0.3001
32	4427.7926	0.0002	14755.9755	0.0001	3.3326	0.3001
33	5756.1304	0.0002	19183.7681	0.0001	3.3328	0.3001
34	7482.9696	0.0001	24939.8985	0.0000	3.3329	0.3000
35	9727.8604	0.0001	32422.8681	0.0000	3.3330	0.3000
36	12646.2186	0.0001	42150.7285	0.0000	3.3331	0.3000
37	16440.0841	0.0001	54796.9471	0.0000	3.3331	0.3000
38	21372.1094	0.0000	71237.0312	0.0000	3.3332	0.3000
39	27783.7422	0.0000	92609.1405	0.0000	3.3332	0.3000
40	36118.8648	0.0000	120392.8827	0.0000	3.3332	0.3000
45	134106.8167	0.0000	447019.3890	0.0000	3.3333	0.3000
50	497929.2230	0.0000	##########	0.0000	3.3333	0.3000
60	6864377.1727	0.0000	##########	0.0000	3.3333	0.3000
75	##########	0.0000	##########	0.0000	3.3333	0.3000
100	##########	0.0000	##########	0.0000	3.3333	0.3000

TABLE B.27 35% Interest Factors for Discrete Compounding

	Single-Payment		Equal-Payment-Series			
	Compound-Amount	Present-Worth	Compound-Amount	Sinking-Fund	Present-Worth	Capital-Recovery
n	Find F Given P (F/P,i,n)	Find P Given F (P/F,i,n)	Find F Given A (F/A,i,n)	Find A Given F (A/F,i,n)	Find P Given A (P/A,i,n)	Find A Given P (A/P,i,n)
1	1.3500	0.7407	1.0000	1.0000	0.7407	1.3500
2	1.8225	0.5487	2.3500	0.4255	1.2894	0.7755
3	2.4604	0.4064	4.1725	0.2397	1.6959	0.5897
4	3.3215	0.3011	6.6329	0.1508	1.9969	0.5008
5	4.4840	0.2230	9.9544	0.1005	2.2200	0.4505
6	6.0534	0.1652	14.4384	0.0693	2.3852	0.4193
7	8.1722	0.1224	20.4919	0.0488	2.5075	0.3988
8	11.0324	0.0906	28.6640	0.0349	2.5982	0.3849
9	14.8937	0.0671	39.6964	0.0252	2.6653	0.3752
10	20.1066	0.0497	54.5902	0.0183	2.7150	0.3683
11	27.1439	0.0368	74.6967	0.0134	2.7519	0.3634
12	36.6442	0.0273	101.8406	0.0098	2.7792	0.3598
13	49.4697	0.0202	138.4848	0.0072	2.7994	0.3572
14	66.7841	0.0150	187.9544	0.0053	2.8144	0.3553
15	90.1585	0.0111	254.7385	0.0039	2.8255	0.3539
16	121.7139	0.0082	344.8970	0.0029	2.8337	0.3529
17	164.3138	0.0061	466.6109	0.0021	2.8398	0.3521
18	221.8236	0.0045	630.9247	0.0016	2.8443	0.3516
19	299.4619	0.0033	852.7483	0.0012	2.8476	0.3512
20	404.2736	0.0025	1152.2103	0.0009	2.8501	0.3509
21	545.7693	0.0018	1556.4838	0.0006	2.8519	0.3506
22	736.7886	0.0014	2102.2532	0.0005	2.8533	0.3505
23	994.6646	0.0010	2839.0418	0.0004	2.8543	0.3504
24	1342.7973	0.0007	3833.7064	0.0003	2.8550	0.3503
25	1812.7763	0.0006	5176.5037	0.0002	2.8556	0.3502
26	2447.2480	0.0004	6989.2800	0.0001	2.8560	0.3501
27	3303.7848	0.0003	9436.5280	0.0001	2.8563	0.3501
28	4460.1095	0.0002	12740.3128	0.0001	2.8565	0.3501
29	6021.1478	0.0002	17200.4222	0.0001	2.8567	0.3501
30	8128.5495	0.0001	23221.5700	0.0000	2.8568	0.3500
31	10973.5418	0.0001	31350.1195	0.0000	2.8569	0.3500
32	14814.2815	0.0001	42323.6613	0.0000	2.8569	0.3500
33	19999.2800	0.0001	57137.9428	0.0000	2.8570	0.3500
34	26999.0280	0.0000	77137.2228	0.0000	2.8570	0.3500
35	36448.6878	0.0000	104136.2508	0.0000	2.8571	0.3500
36	49205.7285	0.0000	140584.9385	0.0000	2.8571	0.3500
37	66427.7334	0.0000	189790.6670	0.0000	2.8571	0.3500
38	89677.4402	0.0000	256218.4004	0.0000	2.8571	0.3500
39	121064.5442	0.0000	345895.8406	0.0000	2.8571	0.3500
40	163437.1347	0.0000	466960.3848	0.0000	2.8571	0.3500
45	732857.5768	0.0000	##########	0.0000	2.8571	0.3500
50	3286157.8795	0.0000	##########	0.0000	2.8571	0.3500
60	##########	0.0000	##########	0.0000	2.8571	0.3500
75	##########	0.0000	##########	0.0000	2.8571	0.3500
100	##########	0.0000	##########	0.0000	2.8571	0.3500

TABLE B.28 40% Interest Factors for Discrete Compounding

	Single-Payment		Equal-Payment-Series			
	Compound-Amount	Present-Worth	Compound-Amount	Sinking-Fund	Present-Worth	Capital-Recovery
n	*Find F Given P* $(F/P,i,n)$	*Find P Given F* $(P/F,i,n)$	*Find F Given A* $(F/A,i,n)$	*Find A Given F* $(A/F,i,n)$	*Find P Given A* $(P/A,i,n)$	*Find A Given P* $(A/P,i,n)$
1	1.4000	0.7143	1.0000	1.0000	0.7143	1.4000
2	1.9600	0.5102	2.4000	0.4167	1.2245	0.8167
3	2.7440	0.3644	4.3600	0.2294	1.5889	0.6294
4	3.8416	0.2603	7.1040	0.1408	1.8492	0.5408
5	5.3782	0.1859	10.9456	0.0914	2.0352	0.4914
6	7.5295	0.1328	16.3238	0.0613	2.1680	0.4613
7	10.5414	0.0949	23.8534	0.0419	2.2628	0.4419
8	14.7579	0.0678	34.3947	0.0291	2.3306	0.4291
9	20.6610	0.0484	49.1526	0.0203	2.3790	0.4203
10	28.9255	0.0346	69.8137	0.0143	2.4136	0.4143
11	40.4957	0.0247	98.7391	0.0101	2.4383	0.4101
12	56.6939	0.0176	139.2348	0.0072	2.4559	0.4072
13	79.3715	0.0126	195.9287	0.0051	2.4685	0.4051
14	111.1201	0.0090	275.3002	0.0036	2.4775	0.4036
15	155.5681	0.0064	386.4202	0.0026	2.4839	0.4026
16	217.7953	0.0046	541.9883	0.0018	2.4885	0.4018
17	304.9135	0.0033	759.7837	0.0013	2.4918	0.4013
18	426.8789	0.0023	1064.6971	0.0009	2.4941	0.4009
19	597.6304	0.0017	1491.5760	0.0007	2.4958	0.4007
20	836.6826	0.0012	2089.2064	0.0005	2.4970	0.4005
21	1171.3556	0.0009	2925.8889	0.0003	2.4979	0.4003
22	1639.8978	0.0006	4097.2445	0.0002	2.4985	0.4002
23	2295.8569	0.0004	5737.1423	0.0002	2.4989	0.4002
24	3214.1997	0.0003	8032.9993	0.0001	2.4992	0.4001
25	4499.8796	0.0002	11247.1990	0.0001	2.4994	0.4001
26	6299.8314	0.0002	15747.0785	0.0001	2.4996	0.4001
27	8819.7640	0.0001	22046.9099	0.0000	2.4997	0.4000
28	12347.6696	0.0001	30866.6739	0.0000	2.4998	0.4000
29	17286.7374	0.0001	43214.3435	0.0000	2.4999	0.4000
30	24201.4324	0.0000	60501.0809	0.0000	2.4999	0.4000
31	33882.0053	0.0000	84702.5132	0.0000	2.4999	0.4000
32	47434.8074	0.0000	118584.5185	0.0000	2.4999	0.4000
33	66408.7304	0.0000	166019.3260	0.0000	2.5000	0.4000
34	92972.2225	0.0000	232428.0563	0.0000	2.5000	0.4000
35	130161.1116	0.0000	325400.2789	0.0000	2.5000	0.4000
36	182225.5562	0.0000	455561.3904	0.0000	2.5000	0.4000
37	255115.7786	0.0000	637786.9466	0.0000	2.5000	0.4000
38	357162.0901	0.0000	892902.7252	0.0000	2.5000	0.4000
39	500026.9261	0.0000	###########	0.0000	2.5000	0.4000
40	700037.6966	0.0000	###########	0.0000	2.5000	0.4000
45	3764970.7413	0.0000	###########	0.0000	2.5000	0.4000
50	###########	0.0000	###########	0.0000	2.5000	0.4000
60	###########	0.0000	###########	0.0000	2.5000	0.4000
75	###########	0.0000	###########	0.0000	2.5000	0.4000
100	###########	0.0000	###########	0.0000	2.5000	0.4000

TABLE B.29 50% Interest Factors for Discrete Compounding

	Single-Payment		Equal-Payment-Series			
	Compound- Amount	Present- Worth	Compound- Amount	Sinking- Fund	Present- Worth	Capital- Recovery
n	Find F Given P (F/P,i,n)	Find P Given F (P/F,i,n)	Find F Given A (F/A,i,n)	Find A Given F (A/F,i,n)	Find P Given A (P/A,i,n)	Find A Given P (A/P,i,n)
1	1.5000	0.6667	1.0000	1.0000	0.6667	1.5000
2	2.2500	0.4444	2.5000	0.4000	1.1111	0.9000
3	3.3750	0.2963	4.7500	0.2105	1.4074	0.7105
4	5.0625	0.1975	8.1250	0.1231	1.6049	0.6231
5	7.5938	0.1317	13.1875	0.0758	1.7366	0.5758
6	11.3906	0.0878	20.7813	0.0481	1.8244	0.5481
7	17.0859	0.0585	32.1719	0.0311	1.8829	0.5311
8	25.6289	0.0390	49.2578	0.0203	1.9220	0.5203
9	38.4434	0.0260	74.8867	0.0134	1.9480	0.5134
10	57.6650	0.0173	113.3301	0.0088	1.9653	0.5088
11	86.4976	0.0116	170.9951	0.0058	1.9769	0.5058
12	129.7463	0.0077	257.4927	0.0039	1.9846	0.5039
13	194.6195	0.0051	387.2390	0.0026	1.9897	0.5026
14	291.9293	0.0034	581.8585	0.0017	1.9931	0.5017
15	437.8939	0.0023	873.7878	0.0011	1.9954	0.5011
16	656.8408	0.0015	1311.6817	0.0008	1.9970	0.5008
17	985.2613	0.0010	1968.5225	0.0005	1.9980	0.5005
18	1477.8919	0.0007	2953.7838	0.0003	1.9986	0.5003
19	2216.8378	0.0005	4431.6756	0.0002	1.9991	0.5002
20	3325.2567	0.0003	6648.5135	0.0002	1.9994	0.5002
21	4987.8851	0.0002	9973.7702	0.0001	1.9996	0.5001
22	7481.8276	0.0001	14961.6553	0.0001	1.9997	0.5001
23	11222.7415	0.0001	22443.4829	0.0000	1.9998	0.5000
24	16834.1122	0.0001	33666.2244	0.0000	1.9999	0.5000
25	25251.1683	0.0000	50500.3366	0.0000	1.9999	0.5000
26	37876.7524	0.0000	75751.5049	0.0000	1.9999	0.5000
27	56815.1287	0.0000	113628.2573	0.0000	2.0000	0.5000
28	85222.6930	0.0000	170443.3860	0.0000	2.0000	0.5000
29	127834.0395	0.0000	255666.0790	0.0000	2.0000	0.5000
30	191751.0592	0.0000	383500.1185	0.0000	2.0000	0.5000
31	287626.5888	0.0000	575251.1777	0.0000	2.0000	0.5000
32	431439.8833	0.0000	862877.7665	0.0000	2.0000	0.5000
33	647159.8249	0.0000	##########	0.0000	2.0000	0.5000
34	970739.7374	0.0000	##########	0.0000	2.0000	0.5000
35	1456109.6060	0.0000	##########	0.0000	2.0000	0.5000
36	2184164.4091	0.0000	##########	0.0000	2.0000	0.5000
37	3276246.6136	0.0000	##########	0.0000	2.0000	0.5000
38	4914369.9204	0.0000	##########	0.0000	2.0000	0.5000
39	7371554.8806	0.0000	##########	0.0000	2.0000	0.5000
40	##########	0.0000	##########	0.0000	2.0000	0.5000
45	##########	0.0000	##########	0.0000	2.0000	0.5000
50	##########	0.0000	##########	0.0000	2.0000	0.5000
60	##########	0.0000	##########	0.0000	2.0000	0.5000
75	##########	0.0000	##########	0.0000	2.0000	0.5000
100	##########	0.0000	##########	0.0000	2.0000	0.5000

TABLE B.30   60% Interest Factors for Discrete Compounding

	Single-Payment		Equal-Payment-Series			
	Compound- Amount	Present- Worth	Compound- Amount	Sinking- Fund	Present- Worth	Capital- Recovery
n	Find F Given P (F/P,i,n)	Find P Given F (P/F,i,n)	Find F Given A (F/A,i,n)	Find A Given F (A/F,i,n)	Find P Given A (P/A,i,n)	Find A Given P (A/P,i,n)
1	1.6000	0.6250	1.0000	1.0000	0.6250	1.6000
2	2.5600	0.3906	2.6000	0.3846	1.0156	0.9846
3	4.0960	0.2441	5.1600	0.1938	1.2598	0.7938
4	6.5536	0.1526	9.2560	0.1080	1.4124	0.7080
5	10.4858	0.0954	15.8096	0.0633	1.5077	0.6633
6	16.7772	0.0596	26.2954	0.0380	1.5673	0.6380
7	26.8435	0.0373	43.0726	0.0232	1.6046	0.6232
8	42.9497	0.0233	69.9161	0.0143	1.6279	0.6143
9	68.7195	0.0146	112.8658	0.0089	1.6424	0.6089
10	109.9512	0.0091	181.5853	0.0055	1.6515	0.6055
11	175.9219	0.0057	291.5364	0.0034	1.6572	0.6034
12	281.4750	0.0036	467.4583	0.0021	1.6607	0.6021
13	450.3600	0.0022	748.9333	0.0013	1.6630	0.6013
14	720.5759	0.0014	1199.2932	0.0008	1.6644	0.6008
15	1152.9215	0.0009	1919.8692	0.0005	1.6652	0.6005
16	1844.6744	0.0005	3072.7907	0.0003	1.6658	0.6003
17	2951.4791	0.0003	4917.4651	0.0002	1.6661	0.6002
18	4722.3665	0.0002	7868.9441	0.0001	1.6663	0.6001
19	7555.7864	0.0001	12591.3106	0.0001	1.6664	0.6001
20	12089.2582	0.0001	20147.0970	0.0000	1.6665	0.6000
21	19342.8131	0.0001	32236.3552	0.0000	1.6666	0.6000
22	30948.5010	0.0000	51579.1683	0.0000	1.6666	0.6000
23	49517.6016	0.0000	82527.6693	0.0000	1.6666	0.6000
24	79228.1625	0.0000	132045.2709	0.0000	1.6666	0.6000
25	126765.0600	0.0000	211273.4334	0.0000	1.6667	0.6000
26	202824.0960	0.0000	338038.4934	0.0000	1.6667	0.6000
27	324518.5537	0.0000	540862.5894	0.0000	1.6667	0.6000
28	519229.6859	0.0000	865381.1431	0.0000	1.6667	0.6000
29	830767.4974	0.0000	##########	0.0000	1.6667	0.6000
30	1329227.9958	0.0000	##########	0.0000	1.6667	0.6000
31	2126764.7933	0.0000	##########	0.0000	1.6667	0.6000
32	3402823.6692	0.0000	##########	0.0000	1.6667	0.6000
33	5444517.8707	0.0000	##########	0.0000	1.6667	0.6000
34	8711228.5932	0.0000	##########	0.0000	1.6667	0.6000
35	##########	0.0000	##########	0.0000	1.6667	0.6000
36	##########	0.0000	##########	0.0000	1.6667	0.6000
37	##########	0.0000	##########	0.0000	1.6667	0.6000
38	##########	0.0000	##########	0.0000	1.6667	0.6000
39	##########	0.0000	##########	0.0000	1.6667	0.6000
40	##########	0.0000	##########	0.0000	1.6667	0.6000
45	##########	0.0000	##########	0.0000	1.6667	0.6000
50	##########	0.0000	##########	0.0000	1.6667	0.6000
60	##########	0.0000	##########	0.0000	1.6667	0.6000
75	##########	0.0000	##########	0.0000	1.6667	0.6000
100	##########	0.0000	##########	0.0000	1.6667	0.6000

TABLE B.31   70% Interest Factors for Discrete Compounding

	Single-Payment		Equal-Payment-Series			
	Compound- Amount	Present- Worth	Compound- Amount	Sinking- Fund	Present- Worth	Capital- Recovery
n	*Find F Given P* *(F/P,i,n)*	*Find P Given F* *(P/F,i,n)*	*Find F Given A* *(F/A,i,n)*	*Find A Given F* *(A/F,i,n)*	*Find P Given A* *(P/A,i,n)*	*Find A Given P* *(A/P,i,n)*
1	1.7000	0.5882	1.0000	1.0000	0.5882	1.7000
2	2.8900	0.3460	2.7000	0.3704	0.9343	1.0704
3	4.9130	0.2035	5.5900	0.1789	1.1378	0.8789
4	8.3521	0.1197	10.5030	0.0952	1.2575	0.7952
5	14.1986	0.0704	18.8551	0.0530	1.3280	0.7530
6	24.1376	0.0414	33.0537	0.0303	1.3694	0.7303
7	41.0339	0.0244	57.1912	0.0175	1.3938	0.7175
8	69.7576	0.0143	98.2251	0.0102	1.4081	0.7102
9	118.5879	0.0084	167.9827	0.0060	1.4165	0.7060
10	201.5994	0.0050	286.5706	0.0035	1.4215	0.7035
11	342.7190	0.0029	488.1699	0.0020	1.4244	0.7020
12	582.6222	0.0017	830.8889	0.0012	1.4261	0.7012
13	990.4578	0.0010	1413.5111	0.0007	1.4271	0.7007
14	1683.7783	0.0006	2403.9690	0.0004	1.4277	0.7004
15	2862.4231	0.0003	4087.7472	0.0002	1.4281	0.7002
16	4866.1192	0.0002	6950.1703	0.0001	1.4283	0.7001
17	8272.4026	0.0001	11816.2895	0.0001	1.4284	0.7001
18	14063.0845	0.0001	20088.6921	0.0000	1.4285	0.7000
19	23907.2436	0.0000	34151.7765	0.0000	1.4285	0.7000
20	40642.3141	0.0000	58059.0201	0.0000	1.4285	0.7000
21	69091.9339	0.0000	98701.3342	0.0000	1.4286	0.7000
22	117456.2877	0.0000	167793.2681	0.0000	1.4286	0.7000
23	199675.6890	0.0000	285249.5557	0.0000	1.4286	0.7000
24	339448.6713	0.0000	484925.2447	0.0000	1.4286	0.7000
25	577062.7412	0.0000	824373.9160	0.0000	1.4286	0.7000
26	981006.6601	0.0000	##########	0.0000	1.4286	0.7000
27	1667711.3222	0.0000	##########	0.0000	1.4286	0.7000
28	2835109.2477	0.0000	##########	0.0000	1.4286	0.7000
29	4819685.7211	0.0000	##########	0.0000	1.4286	0.7000
30	8193465.7258	0.0000	##########	0.0000	1.4286	0.7000
31	##########	0.0000	##########	0.0000	1.4286	0.7000
32	##########	0.0000	##########	0.0000	1.4286	0.7000
33	##########	0.0000	##########	0.0000	1.4286	0.7000
34	##########	0.0000	##########	0.0000	1.4286	0.7000
35	##########	0.0000	##########	0.0000	1.4286	0.7000
36	##########	0.0000	##########	0.0000	1.4286	0.7000
37	##########	0.0000	##########	0.0000	1.4286	0.7000
38	##########	0.0000	##########	0.0000	1.4286	0.7000
39	##########	0.0000	##########	0.0000	1.4286	0.7000
40	##########	0.0000	##########	0.0000	1.4286	0.7000
45	##########	0.0000	##########	0.0000	1.4286	0.7000
50	##########	0.0000	##########	0.0000	1.4286	0.7000
60	##########	0.0000	##########	0.0000	1.4286	0.7000
75	##########	0.0000	##########	0.0000	1.4286	0.7000
100	##########	0.0000	##########	0.0000	1.4286	0.7000

TABLE B.32 80% Interest Factors for Discrete Compounding

	Single-Payment		Equal-Payment-Series			
	Compound- Amount	Present- Worth	Compound- Amount	Sinking- Fund	Present- Worth	Capital- Recovery
n	*Find F Given P* *(F/P,i,n)*	*Find P Given F* *(P/F,i,n)*	*Find F Given A* *(F/A,i,n)*	*Find A Given F* *(A/F,i,n)*	*Find P Given A* *(P/A,i,n)*	*Find A Given P* *(A/P,i,n)*
1	1.8000	0.5556	1.0000	1.0000	0.5556	1.8000
2	3.2400	0.3086	2.8000	0.3571	0.8642	1.1571
3	5.8320	0.1715	6.0400	0.1656	1.0357	0.9656
4	10.4976	0.0953	11.8720	0.0842	1.1309	0.8842
5	18.8957	0.0529	22.3696	0.0447	1.1838	0.8447
6	34.0122	0.0294	41.2653	0.0242	1.2132	0.8242
7	61.2220	0.0163	75.2775	0.0133	1.2296	0.8133
8	110.1996	0.0091	136.4995	0.0073	1.2387	0.8073
9	198.3593	0.0050	246.6991	0.0041	1.2437	0.8041
10	357.0467	0.0028	445.0584	0.0022	1.2465	0.8022
11	642.6841	0.0016	802.1051	0.0012	1.2481	0.8012
12	1156.8314	0.0009	1444.7892	0.0007	1.2489	0.8007
13	2082.2965	0.0005	2601.6206	0.0004	1.2494	0.8004
14	3748.1337	0.0003	4683.9171	0.0002	1.2497	0.8002
15	6746.6406	0.0001	8432.0508	0.0001	1.2498	0.8001
16	12143.9531	0.0001	15178.6914	0.0001	1.2499	0.8001
17	21859.1156	0.0000	27322.6445	0.0000	1.2499	0.8000
18	39346.4081	0.0000	49181.7601	0.0000	1.2500	0.8000
19	70823.5345	0.0000	88528.1682	0.0000	1.2500	0.8000
20	127482.3622	0.0000	159351.7027	0.0000	1.2500	0.8000
21	229468.2519	0.0000	286834.0649	0.0000	1.2500	0.8000
22	413042.8534	0.0000	516302.3168	0.0000	1.2500	0.8000
23	743477.1361	0.0000	929345.1702	0.0000	1.2500	0.8000
24	1338258.8451	0.0000	###########	0.0000	1.2500	0.8000
25	2408865.9211	0.0000	###########	0.0000	1.2500	0.8000
26	4335958.6580	0.0000	###########	0.0000	1.2500	0.8000
27	7804725.5843	0.0000	###########	0.0000	1.2500	0.8000
28	###########	0.0000	###########	0.0000	1.2500	0.8000
29	###########	0.0000	###########	0.0000	1.2500	0.8000
30	###########	0.0000	###########	0.0000	1.2500	0.8000
31	###########	0.0000	###########	0.0000	1.2500	0.8000
32	###########	0.0000	###########	0.0000	1.2500	0.8000
33	###########	0.0000	###########	0.0000	1.2500	0.8000
34	###########	0.0000	###########	0.0000	1.2500	0.8000
35	###########	0.0000	###########	0.0000	1.2500	0.8000
36	###########	0.0000	###########	0.0000	1.2500	0.8000
37	###########	0.0000	###########	0.0000	1.2500	0.8000
38	###########	0.0000	###########	0.0000	1.2500	0.8000
39	###########	0.0000	###########	0.0000	1.2500	0.8000
40	###########	0.0000	###########	0.0000	1.2500	0.8000
45	###########	0.0000	###########	0.0000	1.2500	0.8000
50	###########	0.0000	###########	0.0000	1.2500	0.8000
60	###########	0.0000	###########	0.0000	1.2500	0.8000
75	###########	0.0000	###########	0.0000	1.2500	0.8000
100	###########	0.0000	###########	0.0000	1.2500	0.8000

TABLE B.33   90% Interest Factors for Discrete Compounding

	Single-Payment		Equal-Payment-Series			
	Compound-Amount	Present-Worth	Compound-Amount	Sinking-Fund	Present-Worth	Capital-Recovery
n	*Find F Given P* (F/P,i,n)	*Find P Given F* (P/F,i,n)	*Find F Given A* (F/A,i,n)	*Find A Given F* (A/F,i,n)	*Find P Given A* (P/A,i,n)	*Find A Given P* (A/P,i,n)
1	1.9000	0.5263	1.0000	1.0000	0.5263	1.9000
2	3.6100	0.2770	2.9000	0.3448	0.8033	1.2448
3	6.8590	0.1458	6.5100	0.1536	0.9491	1.0536
4	13.0321	0.0767	13.3690	0.0748	1.0259	0.9748
5	24.7610	0.0404	26.4011	0.0379	1.0662	0.9379
6	47.0459	0.0213	51.1621	0.0195	1.0875	0.9195
7	89.3872	0.0112	98.2080	0.0102	1.0987	0.9102
8	169.8356	0.0059	187.5951	0.0053	1.1046	0.9053
9	322.6877	0.0031	357.4308	0.0028	1.1077	0.9028
10	613.1066	0.0016	680.1185	0.0015	1.1093	0.9015
11	1164.9026	0.0009	1293.2251	0.0008	1.1102	0.9008
12	2213.3149	0.0005	2458.1277	0.0004	1.1106	0.9004
13	4205.2983	0.0002	4671.4426	0.0002	1.1108	0.9002
14	7990.0669	0.0001	8876.7410	0.0001	1.1110	0.9001
15	15181.1270	0.0001	16866.8078	0.0001	1.1110	0.9001
16	28844.1414	0.0000	32047.9348	0.0000	1.1111	0.9000
17	54803.8686	0.0000	60892.0762	0.0000	1.1111	0.9000
18	104127.3503	0.0000	115695.9448	0.0000	1.1111	0.9000
19	197841.9656	0.0000	219823.2951	0.0000	1.1111	0.9000
20	375899.7346	0.0000	417665.2606	0.0000	1.1111	0.9000
21	714209.4957	0.0000	793564.9952	0.0000	1.1111	0.9000
22	1356998.0418	0.0000	##########	0.0000	1.1111	0.9000
23	2578296.2795	0.0000	##########	0.0000	1.1111	0.9000
24	4898762.9310	0.0000	##########	0.0000	1.1111	0.9000
25	9307649.5688	0.0000	##########	0.0000	1.1111	0.9000
26	##########	0.0000	##########	0.0000	1.1111	0.9000
27	##########	0.0000	##########	0.0000	1.1111	0.9000
28	##########	0.0000	##########	0.0000	1.1111	0.9000
29	##########	0.0000	##########	0.0000	1.1111	0.9000
30	##########	0.0000	##########	0.0000	1.1111	0.9000
31	##########	0.0000	##########	0.0000	1.1111	0.9000
32	##########	0.0000	##########	0.0000	1.1111	0.9000
33	##########	0.0000	##########	0.0000	1.1111	0.9000
34	##########	0.0000	##########	0.0000	1.1111	0.9000
35	##########	0.0000	##########	0.0000	1.1111	0.9000
36	##########	0.0000	##########	0.0000	1.1111	0.9000
37	##########	0.0000	##########	0.0000	1.1111	0.9000
38	##########	0.0000	##########	0.0000	1.1111	0.9000
39	##########	0.0000	##########	0.0000	1.1111	0.9000
40	##########	0.0000	##########	0.0000	1.1111	0.9000
45	##########	0.0000	##########	0.0000	1.1111	0.9000
50	##########	0.0000	##########	0.0000	1.1111	0.9000
60	##########	0.0000	##########	0.0000	1.1111	0.9000
75	##########	0.0000	##########	0.0000	1.1111	0.9000
100	##########	0.0000	##########	0.0000	1.1111	0.9000

TABLE B.34 100% Interest Factors for Discrete Compounding

	Single-Payment		Equal-Payment-Series			
	Compound-Amount	Present-Worth	Compound-Amount	Sinking-Fund	Present-Worth	Capital-Recovery
n	Find F Given P (F/P,i,n)	Find P Given F (P/F,i,n)	Find F Given A (F/A,i,n)	Find A Given F (A/F,i,n)	Find P Given A (P/A,i,n)	Find A Given P (A/P,i,n)
1	2.0000	0.5000	1.0000	1.0000	0.5000	2.0000
2	4.0000	0.2500	3.0000	0.3333	0.7500	1.3333
3	8.0000	0.1250	7.0000	0.1429	0.8750	1.1429
4	16.0000	0.0625	15.0000	0.0667	0.9375	1.0667
5	32.0000	0.0313	31.0000	0.0323	0.9688	1.0323
6	64.0000	0.0156	63.0000	0.0159	0.9844	1.0159
7	128.0000	0.0078	127.0000	0.0079	0.9922	1.0079
8	256.0000	0.0039	255.0000	0.0039	0.9961	1.0039
9	512.0000	0.0020	511.0000	0.0020	0.9980	1.0020
10	1024.0000	0.0010	1023.0000	0.0010	0.9990	1.0010
11	2048.0000	0.0005	2047.0000	0.0005	0.9995	1.0005
12	4096.0000	0.0002	4095.0000	0.0002	0.9998	1.0002
13	8192.0000	0.0001	8191.0000	0.0001	0.9999	1.0001
14	16384.0000	0.0001	16383.0000	0.0001	0.9999	1.0001
15	32768.0000	0.0000	32767.0000	0.0000	1.0000	1.0000
16	65536.0000	0.0000	65535.0000	0.0000	1.0000	1.0000
17	131072.0000	0.0000	131071.0000	0.0000	1.0000	1.0000
18	262144.0000	0.0000	262143.0000	0.0000	1.0000	1.0000
19	524288.0000	0.0000	524287.0000	0.0000	1.0000	1.0000
20	1048576.0000	0.0000	##########	0.0000	1.0000	1.0000
21	2097152.0000	0.0000	##########	0.0000	1.0000	1.0000
22	4194304.0000	0.0000	##########	0.0000	1.0000	1.0000
23	8388608.0000	0.0000	##########	0.0000	1.0000	1.0000
24	##########	0.0000	##########	0.0000	1.0000	1.0000
25	##########	0.0000	##########	0.0000	1.0000	1.0000
26	##########	0.0000	##########	0.0000	1.0000	1.0000
27	##########	0.0000	##########	0.0000	1.0000	1.0000
28	##########	0.0000	##########	0.0000	1.0000	1.0000
29	##########	0.0000	##########	0.0000	1.0000	1.0000
30	##########	0.0000	##########	0.0000	1.0000	1.0000
31	##########	0.0000	##########	0.0000	1.0000	1.0000
32	##########	0.0000	##########	0.0000	1.0000	1.0000
33	##########	0.0000	##########	0.0000	1.0000	1.0000
34	##########	0.0000	##########	0.0000	1.0000	1.0000
35	##########	0.0000	##########	0.0000	1.0000	1.0000
36	##########	0.0000	##########	0.0000	1.0000	1.0000
37	##########	0.0000	##########	0.0000	1.0000	1.0000
38	##########	0.0000	##########	0.0000	1.0000	1.0000
39	##########	0.0000	##########	0.0000	1.0000	1.0000
40	##########	0.0000	##########	0.0000	1.0000	1.0000
45	##########	0.0000	##########	0.0000	1.0000	1.0000
50	##########	0.0000	##########	0.0000	1.0000	1.0000
60	##########	0.0000	##########	0.0000	1.0000	1.0000
75	##########	0.0000	##########	0.0000	1.0000	1.0000
100	##########	0.0000	##########	0.0000	1.0000	1.0000

Appendix C

Linear Interpolation

Linear interpolation is a way to approximate the value of a function at an arbitrary point based on a straight-line interpolation between two known points. The approach is shown graphically in Figure C.1. The graph demonstrates how to find the unknown value of Y_U at the given X_G when two known points, (X_0, Y_0) and (X_1, Y_1), are given.

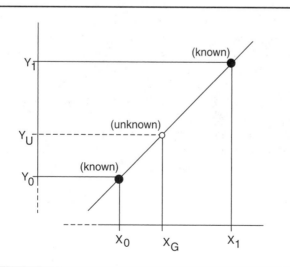

FIGURE C.1 A graphical description of linear interpolation

The calculation starts with the general equation for a straight line:

$$Y = m * X + b$$

The slope of the line, m, can be found using the following:

$$m = \frac{Y_1 - Y_0}{X_1 - X_0}$$

The Y-intercept of the line, b, can be found using either

$$b = Y_0 - m * X_0 \quad \text{or} \quad b = Y_1 - m * X_1$$

Now that m, b, and X_G are known, the unknown Y_U can be calculated using the following:

$$Y_U = m * X_G + b$$

As an example, suppose that the interest rate, i, for (F/A,i,8) = 3.852 is needed. The interest tables in Appendix B show that (F/A,18%,8) = 3.759 and (F/A,19%,8) = 4.021, so the unknown interest rate is somewhere between 18% and 19%.

The slope, m, of the linear interpolation equation can be found using the following:

$$m = \frac{Y_1 - Y_0}{X_1 - X_0} = \frac{19 - 18}{4.021 - 3.759} = 3.817$$

The Y-intercept, b, of the interpolation equation can be found using the following:

$$b = Y_0 - m * X_0 = 18 - 3.817 * 3.759 = 3.652$$

Y_U, the unknown interest rate, can now be found using m, b, and the given X_G:

$$Y_U = m * X_G + b = 3.817 * 3.852 + 3.652 = 18.355\%$$

The interpolated result, 18.335%, is only an approximation—the interest function is actually nonlinear (curved), not linear, but you'll usually end up with a more accurate result than if you just took the nearest answer from the tables. The actual interest rate in this case is 18.362%; the linear interpolation is off by 0.027%.

EXTRAPOLATION

When the point being approximated is not in between the two known points, the process is known as extrapolation. The mathematics of extrapolation are identical to interpolation; the difference is how accurate the approximated value may turn out to be. Using linear extrapolation, the difference between the approximated value and the actual value tends to increase the farther from the known points you are extrapolating. If you are forced to extrapolate, be sure that you understand the shape of the function well enough to have confidence that the extrapolated value is accurate enough for your intended use.

Appendix D

Derivatives

This appendix is a refresher on derivatives. The derivative of a function $f(x)$ is another function $f'(x)$ that describes the slope of the line tangent to $f(x)$ at corresponding values of x. Figure D.1 shows an example function $f(x)$ and its derivative function $f'(x)$. Notice that $f(x)$ has a negative (downward) but decreasingly so slope at smaller values of x and that the derivative function $f'(x)$ has correspondingly negative but closer-to-0 values over that same range. For larger values of x, $f(x)$ has a positive (upward) and increasingly so slope and that the derivative function $f'(x)$ has increasingly positive values.

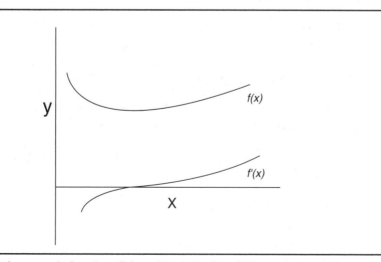

FIGURE D.1 An example function, $f(x)$, and its derivative, $f'(x)$

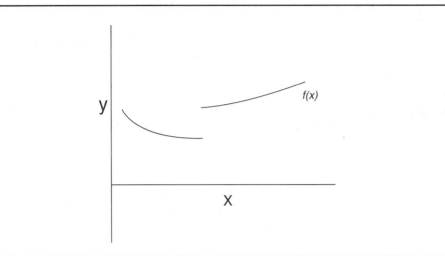

FIGURE D.2 An example of a noncontinuous function

In Figure D.1, there is a value of x where the slope of $f(x)$ is 0. The slope of a function will only be 0 when there is a local minimum or maximum value (an inflection point). At that same value of x, the derivative function, $f'(x)$ will always equal 0. This is one of the properties of derivatives that make them useful. If $f(x)$ has a derivative function $f'(x)$, then $f'(x)$ can be used analytically to solve for points where $f(x)$ is at a local minimum or maximum. This happens whenever $f'(x) = 0$, so setting the derivative function equal to 0 and solving yields the x values where the original equation has minimums or maximums. The other way to find the maximum or minimum points is by brute force: solving $f(x)$ for a large number of x's while recording and interpreting the results. The brute-force approach almost always requires a lot more number crunching than using the derivative function.

Derivatives are particularly useful in decisions involving optimization. The optimization problem will often be described in terms of a function, $c(x)$. By calculating where $c'(x) = 0$, we can analytically find maximum and minimum points of the original function.

Not every function has a derivative. The original function needs to be continuous—there can't be any gaps or breaks. Figure D.2 shows an example of a function that isn't continuous.

Formally, function $f(x)$ is continuous at a when the following conditions hold:

- $f(a)$ exists
- $\lim[x \longrightarrow a] f(x)$ exists
- $\lim[x \longrightarrow a] f(x) = f(a)$

If any of these conditions don't hold, the function is discontinuous at a and doesn't have a derivative. In optimization analysis, the function will almost always be simple polynomial, and simple polynomials always have a derivative.

The simplest case in derivatives is the constant function, $f(x) = k$, where k is a constant:

$$\frac{d}{dx}(f(x)) = 0$$

Simply put, the derivative of a constant function is always 0.

The next simplest case is a simple linear function, $f(x) = x$:

$$\frac{d}{dx}(f(x)) = 1$$

The next simplest case is a constant linear function, $f(x) = kx$:

$$\frac{d}{dx}(f(x)) = k$$

Adding some complexity, a polynomial term, $f(x) = kx^n$:

$$\frac{d}{dx}(f(x)) = (nk)x^{n-1}$$

A general case polynomial equation has the following form:

$$y = k_n x^n + k_{n-1}x^{n-1} + \ldots + k_2 x^2 + k_1 x + k_0$$

Its derivative is found by multiplying each constant, k_i, by the corresponding exponent, i, followed by subtracting 1 from the exponent:

$$\frac{dy}{dx} = nk_n x^{n-1} + (n-1)k_{n-1}x^{n-2} + \ldots 2k_2 x + k_1$$

For example, the derivative of

$$y = -3x^2 + 30x + 12$$

is

$$\frac{dy}{dx} = -6x + 30$$

Setting the first derivative to 0 to find the minimums and/or maximums

$$-6x + 30 = 0$$

$$x = 5$$

The original function has a local minimum or maximum point at 5. If the original function were a cost function for an alternative, $x = 5$ would be a local maximum or minimum point.

Table D.1 shows derivatives of some of the more common mathematical functions.

TABLE D.1 Derivatives of Some Common Mathematical Functions

$$\frac{d}{dx}(k * f(x)) = k * f'(x)$$

$$\frac{d}{dx}(f(x) + g(x)) = f'(x) + g'(x)$$

$$\frac{d}{dx}(f(x) * g(x)) = f(x) * g'(x) + f'(x) * g(x)$$

$$\frac{d}{dx}\left(\frac{f(x)}{g(x)}\right) = \frac{g(x) * f'(x) - f(x) * g'(x)}{g(x)^2}$$

$$\frac{d}{dx}(f(x)^c) = cf(x)^{c-1} * f'(x)$$

$$\frac{d}{dx}(|f(x)|) = \frac{f(x)}{|f(x)|} * f'(x), \text{ as long as } f(x) \neq 0$$

$$\frac{d}{dx}(\ln(f(x))) = \frac{f'(x)}{f(x)}$$

$$\frac{d}{dx}(e^{f(x)}) = e^{f(x)} * f'(x)$$

$$\frac{d}{dx}(\sin(f(x))) = \cos(f(x)) * f'(x)$$

$$\frac{d}{dx}(\cos(f(x))) = -\sin(f(x)) * f'(x)$$

$$\frac{d}{dx}(\tan(f(x))) = \sec(f(x))^2 * f'(x)$$

Continues

TABLE D-1 (*Continued*)

$$\frac{d}{dx}(\cot(f(x))) = -\csc(f(x))^2 * f'(x)$$

$$\frac{d}{dx}(\sec(f(x))) = (\sec(f(x) * \tan(f(x)))) * f'(x)$$

$$\frac{d}{dx}(\csc(f(x))) = -(\csc(f(x) * \cot(f(x)))) * f'(x)$$

$$\frac{d}{dx}(\arcsin(f(x))) = \frac{f'(x)}{\sqrt{1-f(x)^2}}$$

$$\frac{d}{dx}(\arccos(f(x))) = \frac{-f'(x)}{\sqrt{1-f(x)^2}}$$

$$\frac{d}{dx}(\arctan(f(x))) = \frac{-f'(x)}{1+f(x)^2}$$

$$\frac{d}{dx}(arc\cot(f(x))) = \frac{-f'(x)}{1+f(x)^2}$$

$$\frac{d}{dx}(arc\sec(f(x))) = \frac{f'(x)}{|f(x)| * \sqrt{f(x)^2-1}}$$

$$\frac{d}{dx}(arc\csc(f(x))) = \frac{-f'(x)}{|f(x)| * \sqrt{f(x)^2-1}}$$

Appendix E

Introduction to Probability and Statistics

Some of the concepts and techniques in this book are based on probability and statistics. In particular, the chapters on estimation, risk, and uncertainty in Part VI. If you are not already familiar with the subject, or it's been a long time since you've used it and could use a refresher, this appendix provides an overview. This appendix explains the basic concepts of probability, presents a set of probability axioms, and explains probability functions.

Basic Probability Concepts

The most fundamental concept of probability theory is that the future can't be known for certain. What *will* happen can't be known in advance, but the future can still be dealt with in terms of what *could* happen. Take rolling a die like the one shown in Figure E-1. It can never be known for certain which side will come up on the next roll; but we do know that there are exactly six possibilities.

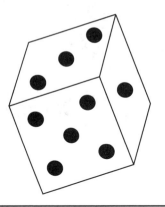

FIGURE E.1 A Common Die

Probability assumes that the likelihood of each possible outcome can be expressed as a number. The likelihood numbers can sometimes be derived analytically. Our sense of rolling a die, assuming it's a fair die, is that each side is equally likely to come up. Knowing that there are six possible outcomes, we can calculate that the likelihood of each separate outcome is one in six—which can also be expressed as 1/6 or 16.7%.

Another way to find the likelihood numbers is to derive them from past experience, statistics. A baseball player's batting average expresses the likelihood that he will get a hit any given time at bat based on his actual performance in past games. A batting average of .318 means that the player has gotten a hit 31.8% of the time. All other things being equal, the next time that player is at bat he should stand about that same chance of getting a hit. Similarly, we could have rolled a die 1,000 times and counted the number of times that the side with two dots came up. Maybe it came up 167 times. If we were to roll that same die 1,000 more times, the side with two dots would probably come up about 167 more times. From this we can say that the probability of the side with two dots coming up on any given roll is about 167/1000 or 16.7%.

Finally, the likelihood numbers can be estimated using expert judgment, analogy, or the other techniques discussed in Chapter 22.

Probability Axioms

Probability and statistics are based on a handful of fundamental axioms:

FOR ANY OUTCOME *A*, THE PROBABILITY OF *A* OCCURRING IS $0 \le P(A) \le 1$

In the language of probability and statistics, $P(X)$ means "the probability of X occurring." X can either be a single outcome, such as the toss of a coin coming up heads, or it could be a set of possible outcomes, such as rolling a die and coming up with any even number. For any given outcome, A, if that outcome is impossible then $P(A) = 0$; its probability is 0. When rolling a standard die, which has sides labeled 1 through 6, the probability of rolling 7 is 0 because 7 isn't in the set of possible outcomes. If the outcome is at least possible, its probability has to be greater than 0. A fair coin, for instance, has $P(\text{Heads}) = 0.5$ and $P(\text{Tails}) = 0.5$. The greater the probability, the proportionally greater the number will be; if $P(\text{XYZ}) = 0.54$ and $P(\text{ABC}) = 0.27$, then outcome XYZ is exactly twice as likely as outcome ABC.

WHEN *S* IS THE SET OF ALL POSSIBLE OUTCOMES, $P(S) = 1$

When the set S includes all possible outcomes, one of those outcomes is bound to happen. You won't know which one, but one of them will. When a die is rolled, a number between one and six will come up. When a coin is tossed, either heads or tails will come up. The term $P(S)=1$ means certainty—S (or one of the outcomes in S if it is a set) is bound to happen.

FOR TWO MUTUALLY EXCLUSIVE OUTCOMES, *A* AND *B*, THE PROBABILITY OF EITHER A OR B HAPPENING, $P(A + B)$, IS EQUAL TO $P(A) + P(B)$

When outcomes are mutually exclusive, it means that one or the other of them could happen, but not both. On rolling a single die, coming up with a two *and* a three is impossible. Only one number can come up on each roll, so the outcomes two and three are mutually exclusive. The probability of coming up with a two *or* a three on a single roll is equal to the probability of rolling a two plus the probability of rolling a three. If the probability of each one separately is 0.1666 . . . (1 in 6), the probability of coming up with either one in a single roll is 0.3333 . . . (2 in 6).

WHEN *A* AND *B* ARE NOT MUTUALLY EXCLUSIVE, THEY WILL EITHER BE INDEPENDENT OR CONDITIONAL

When outcomes are not mutually exclusive, it means that both of them can happen. Rolling an even number on a die and coming up heads on the toss of a coin are not mutually exclusive because one occurring does not prevent the other from occurring. Given that two outcomes are not mutually exclusive, they can be independent or conditional.

When _A_ and _B_ Are Independent Outcomes, _P_(_AB_) = _P_(_A_) * _P_(_B_) Independent outcomes have no connection between them—one outcome does not affect the probability of the other. Rolling an even number on a die and coming up heads on the toss of a coin are independent outcomes. Similarly, rolling an even number on one roll and rolling an odd number on a different roll are independent because the outcome of one roll has no effect on the outcome of any other. The probability of two independent outcomes both occurring equals the product of their individual probabilities. _P_(Rolling an even number on a die) = 0.5 (3 in 6) and _P_(Fair coin comes up heads) = 0.5 (1 in 2) so _P_(Rolling an even number on a die together with a fair coin coming up heads) = 0.5 * 0.5 = 0.25.

When _A_ Is Conditional on _B_, _P_(_AB_) = _P_(_A_) * _P_(_B_ | _A_) In contrast with independent outcomes, conditional outcomes are correlated; one does affect the probability of the other. Suppose we know that 11% of all commercial airplane flights depart late. (Late is defined as leaving more than 10 minutes after the scheduled departure time.) Suppose we also know that 14% of all commercial airplane flights arrive late. (Again, defined as later than 10 minutes after the scheduled arrival time.) Arriving late and departing late are correlated: Departing late is likely to lead to arriving late.

The term $P(B \mid A)$ represents the probability that outcome B will happen given that outcome A is known to have happened. For instance the term

$$P(ArriveLate \mid DepartLate)$$

Represents "the probability of arriving late given that the departure is known to be late." Note that

$$P(B \mid A) \neq P(B)$$

is the essence of conditional probability. If $P(B \mid A) = P(B)$, then A and B must be independent. The probability of having a bumpy flight, P(Bumpy flight), is the same as the probability of having a bumpy flight given a late departure, P(Bumpy flight | Depart late)—bumpiness of the flight and lateness of the departure are independent. The probability of a late arrival is not the same as the probability of a late arrival given a late departure—the late arrival is usually (although not exclusively) caused by the late departure. Arriving late is conditional on departing late.

The conditional probability formula is as follows:

$$P(AB) = P(A) * P(B \mid A)$$

Which can also be written as follows:

$$P(B \mid A) = \frac{P(AB)}{P(A)}$$

Suppose we are told that 66% of the time, given that a flight departs late it also arrives late. In statistical form

$$P(ArriveLate \mid DepartLate) = .66$$

Using the conditional probability formula, we can calculate the probability that a flight will depart late *and* arrive late:

$$P(DepartLate \& ArriveLate) = P(DepartLate) * P(ArriveLate \mid DepartLate)$$
$$= .11 * .66 = .07$$

A randomly selected flight has a 7% chance of both departing late and arriving late.

$P(A \mid B)$ IS NOT NECESSARILY EQUAL TO $P(B \mid A)$

Conditional probabilities are not necessarily symmetrical. Just because P(ArriveLate | DepartLate) = 66% [given that a flight departed late, it arrived late 66% of the time] does not mean that P(DepartLate | ArriveLate) = 66% [given that the flight arrived late, it departed late 66% of the time]. For that you need Bayes' rule.

Bayes' rule is based on a different symmetry:

$$P(AB) = P(A) * P(B \mid A)$$

And

$$P(AB) = P(B) * P(A \mid B)$$

So

$$P(A) * P(B \mid A) = P(B) * P(A \mid B)$$

Therefore

$$P(B \mid A) = \frac{P(B) * P(A \mid B)}{P(A)}$$

Using the departure and arrival probabilities

$$P(DepartLate \mid ArriveLate) = \frac{P(DepartLate) * P(ArriveLate \mid DepartLate)}{P(ArriveLate)}$$

$$= \frac{.11 * .66}{.14} = .52$$

The probability that a flight departed late given that we know it arrived late is 52%.

Another application of Bayes' rule can be found in Baysian spam filters (see, for example, http://spambayes.sourceforge.net/). Some estimates are that about 50% of all Internet e-mail traffic is spam (unwanted junk e-mail), and Baysian spam filters are useful tools for battling it. One reason Baysian spam filters are so useful is that they are adaptive—they learn over time.

Spam filters are often based on a set of cues, such as the message

- Has more than 25% of its text in uppercase.
- Contains HTML text in red.
- Contains the word *free*.
- Contains the phrase *limited offer*.
- Contains the word *click*.
- Contains the word *spam*.

Incoming e-mail is evaluated against these cues and a score is assigned based on how many of the cues are present and how effective each cue is at identifying spam. Whenever the score is over a specified threshold, that e-mail is marked as being spam. For this explanation we'll focus on just one cue, spam e-mail often contains the word *spam*.

To assign a score based on this cue, we need to know the probability that a given e-mail message containing the word *spam* is, in fact, spam. Bayes' rule is used as follows:

$$P(IsSpam \mid Has\text{'}spam\text{'}) = \frac{P(IsSpam) * P(Has\text{'}spam\text{'} \mid IsSpam)}{P(Has\text{'}spam\text{'})}$$

The term P(IsSpam) is the probability that any random incoming e-mail message is spam. This is derived from experience; the filter just adds up the number of times

- A message was marked as spam and the user didn't override that decision.
- A message wasn't automatically marked as spam but was later overridden by the user.

That sum is divided by the total number of messages received. Suppose that the spam rate for this user is 47%.

The term P(Has'spam' | IsSpam) is the conditional probability that a message contains the word *spam* given that it is known to be spam e-mail. The filter calculates this by searching for the word *spam* in e-mail that is known to be spam. Suppose *spam* is found in 29% of all mail that is known to be spam.

The term P(Has 'spam') is the probability that the word *spam* appears in any randomly selected e-mail message. The filter simply monitors incoming e-mail and counts the percentage in which the word *spam* appears. Let's say that it happens 32% of the time.

Then, using Bayes' rule

$$P(IsSpam \mid Has'spam') = \frac{.47 * .29}{.32} = .43$$

Based on observed data for this user, a message containing the word *spam* has a 43% chance of being spam. The filter will combine the scores for its entire set of cues to derive an overall score for the e-mail message being checked. The Baysian probabilities can be updated at regular intervals, say every 100 messages, or when the user marks a specific message as having been misidentified by the filter. (It missed identifying something that was really spam or it called something spam that really wasn't.)

Probability Functions

A **probability function** is a mathematical function that describes, for each outcome being considered, the probability of that outcome. A probability function is sometimes called a random variable. Figure E.2 shows the graph of the probability function for rolling a fair die.

As a probability function, Figure E.2 is an example of a **uniform distribution**; each outcome has the same probability as the others. A uniform distribution represents our notion of fairness—each outcome is equally likely. When a distribution is not uniform, by definition some outcomes are more likely than others. An unfair die, for instance, may be weighted so that it is more likely to come up a six rather than a one. The height of adult human males is also not uniform; many people have the average height of about 5' 11", whereas only a few are very short (say, under 4' 10") or very tall (over 6' 10").

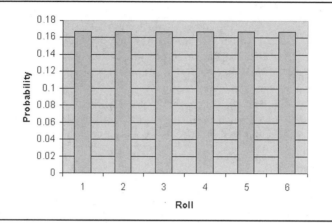

FIGURE E.2   The probability function for a fair die

MEAN AND VARIANCE

Two parameters are commonly used to describe the shape of a probability function, **mean** and **variance**. The mean describes the "central tendency" of the probability function. That central tendency represents the value that actual outcomes are equally likely to be greater than as less than. If the mean height of adult human males is 5′ 10.5″, any randomly selected adult human male is equally likely to be taller than 5′ 10.5″ as he is to be shorter than that. The terms *mean* and *average* are typically considered to be equivalent; statisticians use the term *mean*, whereas the general public uses the term *average*. Another term used by statisticians is *expected value*. This term is based on the idea that half the time a randomly selected occurrence would be greater than the mean and half the time it would be less. Over the long run, "the value you can expect" to observe is that mean value.

Variance measures the "spread" of the probability function; how far away from the mean are the values in that function? A probability function with low variance has values that tend to be close to the mean, whereas a function with high variance has values that tend to be further away from the mean. The vast majority of adult human males are between 4′ 10″ and 6′ 10″ tall. Six-foot electrical extension cords, on the other hand, might vary between 5′ 11″ and 6′ 1″; the variation in the length of extension cords is significantly less than the variation in height of adult human males. Variance is essentially the mean of the differences between the values in the probability function and that function's mean.

Figure E.3 shows graphs of two different probability functions; say scores on two different tests in a particular class. The lighter shaded curve has a higher mean than the darker curve, the typical score on this test was higher than the typical score on the other test. The lighter shaded curve also has a lower variance; the scores tend to be much closer to the mean value than on the darker curve.

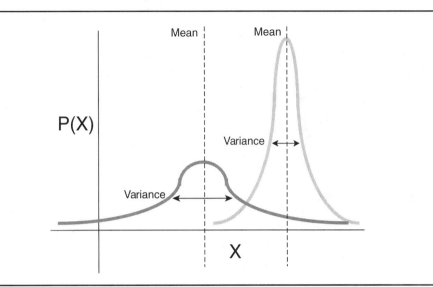

FIGURE E.3   Mean and variance

TABLE E.1   MIDTERM EXAM SCORES FROM A SOFTWARE ENGINEERING COURSE

Student #	Score	Student #	Score
1	79	11	66
2	90	12	77
3	85	13	76
4	64	14	74
5	98	15	76
6	82	16	63
7	71	17	93
8	76	18	60
9	75	19	83
10	77	20	69

MEAN AND VARIANCE OF DISCRETE PROBABILITY FUNCTIONS

Probability functions fall into two major categories: discrete and continuous. A discrete probability function represents a finite set of outcomes, those possible outcomes could be written as a list. The outcomes on the roll of a die can be written as a list (1, 2, 3, 4, 5, 6), so it's an example of a discrete probability function. Students' scores on a test is another example; there are a limited number of scores that students can get. Table E.1 shows sample scores for a midterm exam in a software engineering course.

For discrete probability functions, the mean is calculated using the following formula:

$$E(x) = \sum_{i=1}^{n} x_i \times P(x_i)$$

Where each x_i *is one of the possible outcomes, and* $P(x_i)$ is the probability of that outcome occurring. The mean of the midterm exam scores in Table E.1 is 76.7.

The variance for a discrete probability function is calculated using the following formula:

$$E(x^2) = \sum_{i=1}^{n} (x_i - E(x))^2 \times P(x_i)$$

The variance of the midterm exam scores in Table E.1 is 94.2.

Another useful concept in probability and statistics, standard deviation, is the square root of the variance:

$$\sigma = \sqrt{E(x^2)} = \sqrt{\sum_{i=1}^{n} (x_i - E(x))^2 \times P(x_i)}$$

The standard deviation of the midterm exam scores in Table E.1 is 9.7.

MEAN AND VARIANCE OF CONTINUOUS PROBABILITY FUNCTIONS

A continuous probability function has an infinite set of possible outcomes: It would be impossible to list them. You might think that heights of adult human males is a discrete probability function because heights could be listed as 4′10, 4′ 11″, 5′ 0″, 5′ 1″, and so on. But just the same, heights could be listed as 4′ 10.0″, 4′ 10.1″, 4′ 10.2″, etc. There's a limit to how precisely we can *measure* height, but in reality the number of possible heights is infinite.

The infinite number of possible outcomes means it's not logical to speak of the probability of any single one of them. We can say that the mean height of adult human males is 5′ 10.5″, but we can't talk about the probability of an adult human male being exactly that tall because that probability is essentially 0. In a continuous probability distribution, single outcomes don't have probabilities. All we can meaningfully talk about is the probability of an outcome being within some specified range—for instance, the probability of an adult human male being between 5′ 10″ and 5′ 11″ or the probability that he is taller than 6′ 3″.

Continuous probability functions are described using a **probability density function**. The probability density function doesn't describe the probability at a single point; it describes the probability over ranges. Probability density functions have the following properties:

- $f(x) \geq 0$ for all values of x
- $\int_{-\infty}^{\infty} f(x)dx = 1$
- $P(a < x < b) = \int_{a}^{b} f(x)dx$

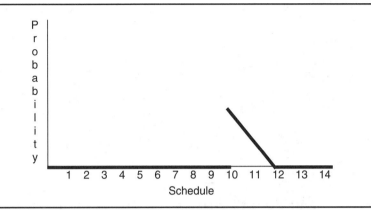

FIGURE E.4   Graph of the probability density function for the Discus project's schedule

Consider the Discus project at TropicalFishTanks.com. Due to factors beyond the proj-ect team's control, the project is known to have a minimum possible schedule of 10 months. It's also known to have a maximum possible schedule of 12 months. Assume that the probability is highest that the project will take 10 months, 0 that it will take more than 12 months, and that it drops linearly as the schedule ranges from 10 to 12 months. The probability density function for $10 \leq x \leq 12$ would be

$$P(x) = 1 - \frac{(x-10)}{2}$$

Figure E.4 shows a graph of the probability density function.

The third property of a probability density function is that the probability of an out-come being in the range a → b is equal to the integral of the probability function over that same range. A description of how to find the integral of a polynomial function can be found in any calculus textbook. The integral of the probability function for the Dis-cus project is as follows:

$$\int_{a \geq 10}^{b \leq 12} P(x) = 6x - \frac{x^2}{4}$$

The probability of the Discus project finishing in less than 11 months is as follows:

$$6x - \frac{x^2}{4} \Big]_{10}^{11} = 0.75 = 75\%$$

The probability of the project finishing between 11.5 and 12 months is as follows:

$$6x - \frac{x^2}{4} \Big]_{11.5}^{12} = 0.0625 = 6.25\%$$

For continuous probability functions, the mean is calculated using the following formula:

$$E(x) = \int_{-\infty}^{\infty} xP(x)dx$$

For the Discus project

$$E(x) = 3x^2 - \frac{x^3}{6}$$

So the mean schedule is this:

$$3x^2 - \frac{x^3}{6}\bigg]_{10}^{12} = 10.6667$$

The variance of a continuous probability function is calculated using the following formula:

$$E(x^2) = \int_{-\infty}^{\infty} (x - E(x))^2 \, P(x)dx$$

For the Discus project

$$E(x^2) = \int_{10}^{12} \frac{2048x}{3} - \frac{832x^2}{9} + \frac{50x^3}{9} - \frac{x^4}{8}$$

So the schedule variance is as follows:

$$\frac{2048x}{3} - \frac{832x^2}{9} + \frac{50x^3}{9} - \frac{x^4}{8}\bigg]_{10}^{12} = \frac{2}{9} = 0.2222$$

Summary

This appendix provided an overview of the basic concepts of probability, presented a set of probability axioms, and explained probability functions. This appendix is included to give readers who are unfamiliar with probability and statistics, or haven't used it in a long time, the background necessary to understand the probability and statistics used in the rest of the book.

Suggested Resources

Anderson, David, Dennis Sweeney, and Thomas Williams. *Statistics for Business and Economics, Eighth Edition*. South-Western College Publications, 2001.

Larsen, Richard, and Morris Marx. *An Introduction to Mathematical Statistics and Its Applications, Third Edition*. Prentice Hall, 2001.

McClave, James, P. George Benson, and Terry Sincich, *Statistics for Business and Economics, Eighth Edition*. Prentice Hall, 2000.

Appendix F

Answers to Selected
Self-Study Questions

Chapter 1 Self-Study Questions

1. $850k * 1.45 = $1,232,500, 10 months * 1.63 = 16.3 months

Chapter 2 Self-Study Questions

1. Actual profit = $1,669,800, Profit margin = $1,669,800 / 12,500,000 = 0.1336 = 13.36%

9. Assuming an FTE rate of $200,000 per year, a six-person-year project would cost $1,200,000.

13. Choosing between buying a house vs. renting, investing in the stock market or other long-term investment, choosing between a zero interest loan vs. cash back when buying a car

Chapter 3 Self-Study Questions

1.
   - Initial investment: Buy sufficient GPS hardware, train the developers in GPS navigation, and so on.
   - Operating and maintenance: Costs to operate and maintain the development environment. Salary costs of the project staff and so on.
   - Sales income: Income from selling the software to customers, income from customization services that a given customer might want, and so on.
   - Cost avoidance: Using the product internally for other purposes; for instance, in helping the sales staff find customer offices when they make sales calls and so forth.
   - Salvage value: The remaining value in the development environment and other project-related hardware and software.

3.

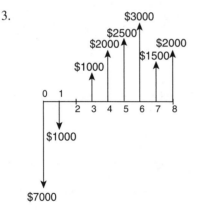

8. Monthly personal finances
    Income
        Employment income
        Investment income
        Gift income
        Scholarships
        Grants

Expenses
    Housing expenses
    Utilities
        Electricity
        Water
        Garbage
        Telephone
    Food
    Transportation
    Insurance
    Taxes
        Income taxes
        Property taxes
        Other taxes
    Entertainment
        Cable TV
        Movies
        Other

Chapter 4 Self-Study Questions

1. Do a certain project or not, which feature(s) to include in the product, buy vs. build, algorithm or data structure selection, upgrade developer's computing environment, move to different office space, hire more people

2. Buy vs. build, for example, should be based on criteria such as price, delivery date, quality, vendor reputation, vendor history (such as how long they have been in business), the likelihood for, and severity of, loss of key intellectual property, and so on.

4. Vendor reputation and history would probably be irreducible. Quality might be irreducible depending on how you choose to represent it. Price and delivery date would not be irreducible.

6. "The system shall be fast"—maybe it means 100 transactions per second, maybe it means 10 transactions per second.

Chapter 5 Self-Study Questions

1. Depends on the situation. Assuming that the savings account interest rate is 6% and the loan interest rate is 10%, the company borrowing $10,000 would pay $1000 in interest to the financial institution, whereas the financial institution would pay $600 in interest to the depositor. The financial institution would net $1000 – $600 = $400.

2. I = $2500 * 7 years * 0.09 = $1575, F = P + I = $2500 + $1575 = $4075

3a.

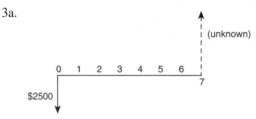

3b. Single-payment compound-amount

3c. F = $2500 (F/P,9%,7) = $2500 * 1.8280 = $4570

3d. It's $495 more than the simple interest amount because of the effect of the compounding of interest owed in the earlier interest periods.

3e.

Year	Amount Owed Queue Co. at The Start of That Year	Amount of Interest Queue Co. Earns That Year	Compound Amount Owed Queue Co. at End of That Year
1	$2500	$2500 * 0.09 = $225	$2500 + $225 = $2725
2	$2725	$2725 * 0.09 = $245	$2725 + $245 = $2970
3	$2970 ·	$2970 * 0.09 = $267	$2970 + $267 = $3238
4	$3238	$3237 * 0.09 = $291	$3237 + $291 = $3529
5	$3529	$3528 * 0.09 = $318	$3528 + $318 = $3847
6	$3847	$3846 * 0.09 = $346	$3846 + $346 = $4193
7	$4193	$4192 * 0.09 = $377	$4192 + $377 = $4570

5a.

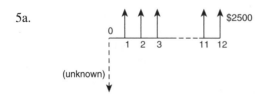

5b. Equal-payment-series present-worth

5c. P = $2500 (P/A,11%,12) = $2500 (6.4924) = $16,231

8a.

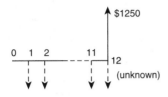

8b. Equal-payment-series sinking-fund

8c. A = $1250 (A/F,0.75%,12) = $1250 (0.0800) = $100

Chapter 6 Self-Study Questions

1. i = (1 + 0.07 / 12) ^12 – 1 = 0.723 = 7.23%

3. r = 12 (12th root (1 + 0.07) – 1) = 0.0678 = 6.78%

5. i = (1 + 0.05 / 26) ^ 4 – 1 = 0.0077 = 0.77%

7. r = 13 (4th root (1 + 0.0254) – 1) = 0.0818 = 8.18%

9. i = (1 + 0.078 / 12) ^ 1 – 1 = 0.0065 = 0.65%

$$A/P,0.65,60$$
$$A = \$25,000\ (0.0202) = \$505$$

11. Their actual interest rate is i = 6.6% / 52 = 0.127% per week.

$$\underset{F/P,.127,20}{^{19}} \qquad \underset{F/P,.127,12}{^{11}} \qquad \underset{F/P,.127,8}{^{7}}$$
$$\$5000\ (1.0257) - 2325\ (1.0153) + 1788\ (1.0102) - 457 = \$4117.17$$

13. Their actual interest rate is i = 7.6% / 4 = 1.9% per quarter.

    The first quarter cash-flow instance is $5000.

    The second quarter cash-flow instance is –$537.

    The third quarter cash-flow instance is –$457.

    $$\overset{F/P,1.9,2}{\$5000\ (1.0384)} - \overset{F/P,1.9,1}{537\ (1.0190)} - 457 = \$4187.80$$

15. i = 12th root (64,000 / 16,000) – 1 = 0.1225 = 12.25%

17.

    $$P = \overset{P/A,0.65,60-25+1}{\$505\ (32.0060)} = \$16,163$$

18.

    $$I(t) = \overset{P/A,0.65,60-2+1}{\$505\ (48.8741)}\ 0.0065 = \$160.43 \text{ for their second payment}$$

    $$I(t) = \overset{P/A,0.65,60-60+1}{\$505\ (0.9935)}\ 0.0065 = \$3.26 \text{ for their last payment}$$

19. (P/A,0.65,j) = $25,000 / ($505 + $100) = 41.3223. This is between (P/A,0.65,48) = 41.1199 and (P/A,0.65,49) = 41.8478, so it would take them 49 months to pay off the loan. This is 11 months earlier.

20. The present value of the equal series of full (A + E) payments (using the smaller j) is

    $$Pj = (\$505 + \$100) * \overset{P/A,0.65,48}{(41.1199)} = \$24,877.53$$

    So their final payment would be

    $$Pl = (\$25,000.00 - 24,877.53) * \overset{F/P,0.65,1}{(1.0065)} = \$123.27$$

Chapter 7 Self-Study Questions

1.

$P/F,6,1$ $P/A,6,4$ $P/F,6,3$ $P/F,6,8$ $P/F,6,9$

-\$100 + -\$20 (0.9434) + \$50 (3.4651)(0.8396) + \$80 (0.6274) + \$100 (0.5919)

−\$100 − \$19 + \$145 + \$50 + \$59 = \$135

2. Equivalence the flows in years 0 through 2 back to the end of year 0 at 6%:

$P/F,6,1$
−\$100 + −\$20 (0.9434) = −\$100 − \$19 = −\$119

Next, equivalence the flows in years 3 through 9 back to the end of year 2 at 8%:

$P/A,8,4$ $P/F,8,1$ $P/F,8,6$ $P/F,8,7$
\$50 (3.3121)(0.9259) + \$80 (0.6302) + \$100 (0.5835) = \$153 + \$50 + \$58 = \$261

Then equivalence the \$261 at the end of year 2 back to the end of year 0 at 6%:

$P/F,6,2$
\$261 (0.8900) = \$232

Finally, add this to the −\$119 originally obtained for years 0 through 2:

−\$119 + \$232 = \$113

6.

$A/P,8,20$
Principal = \$1,000,000 (0.1019) = \$101,900

8. Their monthly payments would be (\$20,000 − \$1,000) / 60 = \$19,000 / 60 = \$316.67.

9. SaylorSoft's business interest rate in monthly terms is 3% / 12 = 0.0025 = 0.25% per month. The 0% option is equivalent to −\$316.67 (P/A,0.0025,60) = −\$316.67 * 55.6524 = −\$17,263.45 today.

Chapter 8 Self-Study Questions

1. $287.14

4. $48.10

6. PW(0%) = $4000, PW(2%) = $2750.68, PW(4%) = $1664.08, PW(6%) = $715.85, PW(8%) = –$114.29, PW(10%) = –$843.27

   Because PW(6%) > 0 and PW(8%) < 0, the IRR is between 6% and 8%. Note that because PW(8%) is closer to zero than PW(6%), the IRR is closer to 8% than 6%.

9. 7.8 years

15. CE(12%) = 300,000/0.12 = $2,500,000

Chapter 9 Self-Study Questions

1.

Alternative	P1	P2	P3	Meaning
A0	0	0	0	Do nothing
A1	1	0	0	P1 only
A2	0	1	0	P2 only
A3	1	1	0	P1 and P2
A4	0	0	1	P3 only
A5	1	0	1	P1 and P3
A6	0	1	1	P2 and P3
A7	1	1	1	All

2. Alternatives A2 and A6 are infeasible because they contain proposal P2 without its contingent proposal, P1. Alternatives A6 and A7 are infeasible because they contain mutually exclusive proposals (P2 and P3). Alternative A7 is also infeasible because of budget constraints.

Alternative	P1	P2	P3	Meaning	
A0	0	0	0	Do nothing	
A1	1	0	0	P1 only	
A2	0	1	0	P2 only	No P1
A3	1	1	0	P1 and P2	Budget
A4	0	0	1	P3 only	
A5	1	0	1	P1 and P3	
A6	0	1	1	P2 and P3	No P1, exclusive
A7	1	1	1	All	Exclusive, budget

The feasible alternatives are A0, A1, A4, and A5.

3.

	A0	A1	A4	A5
Investment	$0	$800,000	$400,000	$1,200,000
Annual revenue	$0	$450,000	$300,000	$750,000
Annual cost	$0	$200,000	$150,000	$350,000
Salvage value	$0	$100,000	$60,000	$160,000

Chapter 10 Self-Study Questions

1. After-tax MARR $\approx (0.15)(1 - 0.22) = 0.117$ or 11.7%

3. Before-tax MARR $\approx 0.20 / (1 - 0.35) = 0.308$ or 30.8%

5. They should be compared in the following order: A0, A2, A1, A6.

6.
   1. Start with alternative A0 as the current best because it has the smallest initial investment.

   2. Choose A2 as the first candidate.

3. Compute the differential cash-flow stream, A2 – A0. Because A0 is the do nothing alternative, the differential cash-flow stream is the same as the cash-flow stream for A.

	A2 – A0
Initial investment	$600,000
Annual income	$400,000
Annual expenses	$180,000
Salvage value	$80,000

4. Compute the PW(MARR) for the differential cash-flow stream

PW(MARR) = –$600k + $220k(P/A,15,8) + $80k (P/F,15,8)

= –$600k + ($220k*4.4873) + ($80k*0.3269)

= –$600k + $987.2k + $26.2k = $413.4k

5. Since the PW(MARR) of the differential cash-flow stream is greater than $0, A2 becomes the current best.

6. Choose A1 as the next candidate.

7. Compute the differential cash-flow stream, A1 – A2.

	A1 – A2
Initial investment	$200,000
Annual income	$50,000
Annual expenses	$20,000
Salvage value	$20,000

8. Compute the PW(MARR) for the differential cash-flow stream.

   PW(MARR) = –$200k + $30k(P/A,15,8) + $20k (P/F,15,8)

   = –$200k + ($30k*4.4873) + ($20k*0.3269)

   = –$200k + $134.6k + $6.5k = –$58.9k

9. Because the PW(MARR) of the differential cash-flow stream is less than $0, A2 remains the current best.

10. Choose A6 as the candidate.

11. Compute the differential cash-flow stream, A6 – A2.

	A6 – A2
Initial investment	$400,000
Annual income	$300,000
Annual expenses	$150,000
Salvage value	$60,000

12. Compute the PW(MARR) for the differential cash-flow stream.

    PW(MARR) = –$400k + $150k(P/A,15,8) + $60k (P/F,15,8)

    = –$400k + ($150k * 4.4873) + ($60k * 0.3269)

    = –$400k + $673.0k + $19.6k = $292.6k

13. Because the PW(MARR) of the differential cash-flow stream is greater than 0, A6 becomes the current best.

14. There are no more alternatives. Alternative A6 is the current best at the end so it's selected as the best alternative.

Chapter 11 Self-Study Questions

1.

End of Year	(1) Salvage Value if Retired at Year n	(2) AE(i) Cost if Retired in Year n [CR(i)]	(3) Operating and Maintenance Costs for Year n	(4) PW(i) of O&M for Year n in Year 0	(5) Sum of Year 0 O&Ms through Year n	(6) AE(i) Cost of Operating for n Years	(7) Total AE(i) if Retired at Year n
1	$1000	$344	$100	$89	$89	$100	$444
2	$850	$309	$125	$100	$189	$112	$421
3	$700	$292	$150	$107	$296	$123	$415
4	$550	$280	$175	$111	$407	$134	$414
5	$400	$270	$200	$113	$520	$144	$414
6	$250	$261	$225	$114	$634	$154	$415
7	$100	$253	$250	$113	$747	$164	$417

2. The economic life of the laser printer is either 4 years or 5 years, and the total AE(i) of retiring it then is $414.

3. If the economic life was chosen to be 4 years, then

$$\underset{P/A,12,2}{\$280\ (1.6901)} + \underset{P/F,12,2}{\$550\ (0.7972)} = \$473 + \$438 = \$911$$

If the economic life was chosen to be 5 years, then

$$\underset{P/A,12,3}{\$270\ (2.4018)} + \underset{P/F,12,3}{\$400\ (0.7118)} = \$648 + \$285 = \$933$$

7. First compute CR(14%).

$$CR(14\%) = (\$600{,}000 - \$30{,}000)\ (A/P,14,10) + \$30{,}000 * 0.14$$

$$= \$570{,}000 * 0.1917 + \$30{,}000 * 0.14$$

$$= \$109{,}269 + \$4200 = \$113{,}469$$

Now compute Fn*.

Fn* = \$113,469 (P/A,14%,10 − 7) + \$15,000 * (P/F,14%,10 − 7)

= \$113,469 * 2.3216 + \$15,000 * 0.6750

= \$263,430 + \$10,125 = \$273,555

Chapter 12 Self-Study Questions

1. Salvage value of the existing accelerator today = 30% of \$175k = \$52.5k.

   Processing per year today = 12 months/year * 21 days/mo * 12 hrs/day * \$250/hr = \$756k/year

   PW(15) of keeping the current system = −\$52.5K + \$756k (2.8550) $\overset{P/A,15,4}{}$ + $\overset{P/F,15,4}{}$ \$30k (0.5718) = \$2123.1k

   Counting trade-in, installation cost of new accelerator = \$250k − \$52.5k = \$197.5k

   Processing per year = \$756k/year * 1.22 = \$922.3k/year

   PW(15) of replacing the accelerator = −\$197.5K + \$922.3k (2.8550) $\overset{P/A,15,4}{}$ + $\overset{P/F,15,4}{}$ \$45k (0.5718) = \$2461.4k

   Replacing the accelerator has a PW(15) of \$2461.4k − \$2123.1k = \$338.3k over not replacing so it is better to do the replacement.

4. The PW(16) of immediate retirement is \$3040.

   The PW(16) of retiring at the end of year 1 is

   \$2640 (0.8621) $\overset{P/F,16,1}{}$ + \$5080 (0.8621) $\overset{P/F,16,1}{}$ − \$2040 (0.8621) $\overset{P/F,16,1}{}$ = \$4897

The PW(16) of retiring at the end of year 2 is

$$\overset{P/F,16,2}{\$1840\ (0.7432)} + \overset{P/A,16,2}{\$5080\ (1.6052)} - [\overset{P/F,16,1}{\$2040\ (0.8621)} + \overset{P/F,16,2}{\$3840\ (0.7432)}] = \$4910$$

The PW(16) of retiring at the end of year 3 is

$$\overset{P/F,16,3}{\$1600\ (0.6407)} + \overset{P/A,16,3}{\$5080\ (2.2459)}$$

$$- [\overset{P/F,16,1}{\$2040\ (0.8621)} + \overset{P/F,16,2}{\$3840\ (0.7432)} + \overset{P/F,16,3}{\$3640\ (0.6407)}] = \$5490$$

The PW(16) of retiring at the end of year 4 is

$$\overset{P/F,16,4}{\$0000\ (0.5523)} + \overset{P/A,16,4}{\$5080\ (2.7982)}$$

$$- [\overset{P/F,16,1}{\$2040\ (0.8621)} + \overset{P/F,16,2}{\$3840\ (0.7432)} + \overset{P/F,16,3}{\$3640\ (0.6407)} + \overset{P/F,16,4}{\$4440\ (0.5523)}] = \$4818$$

The PW(16) of retiring at the end of year 5 is

$$\overset{P/F,16,5}{\$0000\ (0.4761)} + \overset{P/A,16,5}{\$5080\ (3.2743)}$$

$$- [\overset{P/F,16,1}{\$2040\ (0.8621)} + \overset{P/F,16,2}{\$3840\ (0.7432)} + \overset{P/F,16,3}{\$3640\ (0.6407)} + \overset{P/F,16,4}{\$4440\ (0.5523)} +$$

$$\overset{P/F,16,5}{\$5240\ (0.4761)}] = \$4742$$

The best alternative is to retire at the end of year 3.

Chapter 13 Self-Study Questions

2. Price Index = ($1.50 / $1.00) * 100 = 150

3. $60 * 150 / 100 = $90

6. Annual inflation rate = (106.6 − 105.8) / 105.8 = 0.076 = 0.76%

8. Average annual inflation rate = 10th root of (105.8 / 88.0) − 1 = 0.0186 = 1.86%

10. k-bar = 1 − 10th root (13.0 / 23.8) = 5.9%. To show how the loss of purchasing power and inflation are related, 1/(1 − 0.059) = 1 − 0.062.

12a. F = P (F/P,9,15) = $7,500 (3.642) = $27,315.00

12b. i' = [(1 + 0.090) / (1 + 0.048)] − 1 = 4.0%

12c. F' = P (F/P,4,15) = $7,500 (1.801) = $13,507.50

12d. Actual dollars = (1 + 0.048) ^ 15 * $13,507.50 = $27,289.41 (which is close enough to $27,315)

14.

Year	Actual Dollar Cash Flow	Present-Worth Factor	Constant dollar Cash Flow
0	−$10,000	P/F,4,0 (1.000)	−$10,000
1	−$850	P/F,4,1 (0.9615)	−$817
2	$650	P/F,4,2 (0.9246)	$601
3	$2900	P/F,4,3 (0.8890)	$2578
4	$8150	P/F,4,4 (0.8548)	$6967
5	$5900	P/F,4,5 (0.8219)	$4849
6	$3650	P/F,4,6 (0.7903)	$2885
7	$1400	P/F,4,7 (0.7599)	$1064

15. PW(9%) = $2136. The PW(9%) of the actual dollar cash-flow stream is $4557, it's less than half.

18.

$$A = \$156,710 * \overset{A/F,4.7,39}{(0.0094)} = \$1473$$

This is slightly more than half of what she would have to deposit annually if she starts at age 34 ($2648).

20. Mr. Johnson's inflation-free interest rate is i' = (1.095 / 1.032) – 1 = 6.1%.

The amount he needs in his account at retirement is P = $33,000 (P/A,6.1,20) = $33,000 * 11.3774 = $375,454.

To have that amount, he needs to deposit A = $375,454 (A/F,6.1,36) = $375,454 * 0.0082 = $3079.

Chapter 14 Self-Study Questions

1. The depreciation amount is ($22,500 – $500) / 5 years = $4400/year.

End of Year	Depreciation Amount in Year	Book Value at End of Year
0	—	$22,500
1	$4400	$18,100
2	$4400	$13,700
3	$4400	$9300
4	$4400	$4900
5	$4400	$500

2. The depreciation factor is $\alpha = 2.00 / 5 = 0$.

End of Year	Depreciation Amount in Year	Book Value at End of Year
0	—	$22,500
1	$9000	$13,500
2	$5400	$8100
3	$3240	$4860
4	$1944	$2916
5	$1166	$1750

3. The depreciation factor is $\alpha = 1.50 / 5 = 0.3$

End of Year	Depreciation Amount in Year	Book Value at End of Year
0	—	$22,500
1	$6750	$15,750
2	$4725	$11,025
3	$3308	$7717
4	$2351	$5366
5	$1610	$3756

4. The 150% declining balance depreciation factor is $\alpha = 1.50 / 5 = 0.3$

   The straight-line depreciation amount is $22,500 / 5 = $4500. (Salvage value is ignored.)

End of Year	Depreciation Amount in Year	Book Value at End of Year
0	—	$22,500
1	$6750	$15,750
2	$4725	$11,025
3	$4500	$6525
4	$4500	$2025
5	$2025	$0

Note the switch from declining balance to straight-line in Year 3.

5. The following table shows the depreciation factors.

Year	Year in Reverse Order	Depreciation Factor	Multiplier
1	5	5/15	0.33
2	4	4/15	0.27
3	3	3/15	0.20
4	2	2/15	0.13
5	1	1/15	0.07
Sum	K = 15		

End of Year	Depreciation Amount in Year	Book Value at End of Year
0	—	$22,500
1	$7260	$15,240
2	$5940	$9300
3	$4400	$4900
4	$2860	$2040
5	$1540	$500

6.

End of Year	Depreciation Amount in Year	Book Value at End of Year
0	—	$22,500
1	$3375	$19,125
2	$4950	$14,175
3	$4725	$9450
4	$4725	$4725
5	$4725	$0

7.

End of Year	Depreciation Amount in Year	Book Value at End of Year
0	—	$22,500
1	$4500	$18,000
2	$7200	$10,800
3	$4320	$6480
4	$2592	$3888
5	$2592	$1296
6	$1296	$0

15. Per-page depreciation = $2000 / 1,000,000 copies = $0.002

End of Year	Pages Printed During Year	Depreciation Amount in Year	Book Value at End of Year
0	—	—	$2000
1	140,000	$280	$1720
2	60,000	$120	$1600
3	120,000	$240	$1360
4	192,000	$384	$976
5	200,000	$400	$576

Chapter 15 Self-Study Questions

2. $3,655,712 = $2,721,066 + owners' equity

   $3,655,712 – $2,721,066 = Owners' equity = $934,646

4. Profit and loss statement

Operating income	
Sales and operating income	0
Cost of goods sold	0
Net operating income (loss)	0

Operating expenses

Selling expenses	0
General and administrative expenses	0
Research and development	0
Investment-related expenses	
Interest expense	0
Investment expense	0
Depreciation	0
Net earnings before income taxes (loss)	0

Income taxes

Federal, state, and local income taxes	0
Net earnings after taxes (loss)	0

Cash-flow statement

Cash from operating activities

Net earnings	0
Depreciation	0
Changes in accounts receivable	0
Changes in accounts payable	0
Changes in inventory	0
Net cash from operating activities	0

Cash from investing activities

Capital expenditures	(24)
Acquisitions	0
Proceeds from dispositions	0
Net cash from investing activities (loss)	(24)

Cash from financing activities

New borrowing	0
Debt repayment	0
Net stock	0
Dividends paid	0
Net cash from financing activities (loss)	0

Net change in cash	(24)
Cash at beginning	90
Cash at end	66

Balance sheet

Assets

Cash and cash equivalents	66
Accounts receivable	175
Plant and equipment	240
Total assets	481

Liabilities

Accounts payable	198
Debt	122
Declared dividends	87
Total liabilities	407

Owners' equity

Stock	58
Retained earnings	16
Total owners' equity	74

Total liabilities and owners' equity	481

7.

Direct material		
In process Jan. 1, 20x3	40	
Applied during the year	468	
Total	508	
In process Dec. 31, 20x3	37	471
Direct labor		
In process Jan. 1, 20x3	43	
Applied during the year	624	
Total	667	
In process Dec. 31, 20x3	57	610
Manufacturing overhead		
In process Jan. 1, 20x3	58	
Applied during the year	721	
Total	779	
In process Dec. 31, 20x3	71	708
Cost of goods made		1789
Finished goods Jan. 1, 20x3		162
Total		1627
Finished goods Dec. 31, 20x3		213
Cost of goods sold		1414

8. Total direct-material dollars = 18,000 * $5.67 + 14,000 * $10.47 = $102,060 + $146,580 = $248,640

Direct materials cost rate = $360,800 / $248,640 = 1.451 per direct material dollar

The unit cost for goldfish bowls using the direct-material-cost method would be as follows.

Direct material	$5.67
Direct labor	4.39
Overhead, 1.451 * $5.67	8.23
	$18.29

The unit cost for deluxe aquariums would be as follows.

Direct material	$10.47
Direct labor	9.19
Overhead, 1.451 * $10.47	15.19
	$34.85

11.

Activity	Average
Maintain bowl inventory	$5.94
Maintain aquarium glass inventory	$0.89
Maintain aquarium frame inventory	$0.38
Maintain air pump inventory	$2.78
Maintain sand inventory	$0.35
Maintain owner's manual inventory	$1.02
Maintain fish food inventory	$0.35
Maintain packing material inventory	$0.81
Assemble aquarium	$3.31
Pack bowl	$3.27
Pack aquarium	$6.22
Sales, marketing, and administration	$36.00

12a.

Activity	Average Cost	Quantity per Bowl	Cost per Bowl
Maintain bowl inventory	$5.94	1.00	$5.94
Maintain aquarium glass inventory	$0.89	0.00	
Maintain aquarium frame inventory	$0.38	0.00	
Maintain air pump inventory	$2.78	1.00	$2.78
Maintain sand inventory	$0.35	1.00	$0.35
Maintain owner's manual inventory	$1.02	1.00	$1.02
Maintain fish food inventory	$0.35	2.00	$0.70
Maintain packing material inventory	$0.81	1.00	$0.81
Assemble aquarium	$3.31	0.00	
Pack bowl	$3.27	1.00	$3.27
Pack aquarium	$6.22	0.00	
Sales, marketing, and administration	$36.00	0.11	$3.96
Total			$18.83

13. Using a profit margin of 25%, the minimum sales price for each product under each overhead allocation method would be as follows.

	Direct-Material-Cost Method	Direct-Labor-Hour Method	Direct-Labor-Cost Method
Widget	$828	$928	$908
Fubar	$1593	$1546	$1555

	Direct-Material-Cost Method	Direct-Labor-Hour Method	Direct-Labor-Cost Method
Widget	Stay in	Get out	Stay in
Fubar	Get out	Stay in	Stay in

Gizmo Corporation would probably consider getting out of the widget market if they used the direct-labor-hour method and would probably consider getting out of the fubar market if they used the direct-material-cost method.

15a. 6,000 * $115 = $690,000

15b. 12,000 * $115 = $1,380,000

15c. 18,000 * $115 = $2,070,000

Chapter 16 Self-Study Questions

1. Their taxable income is less than $50,000, so the entire amount is taxed at 15%. They owe $5625.

3. The first $50,000 is taxed at 15% for a liability of $7500. The next $25,000 is taxed at 25% for a liability of $6250. The last $7000 is taxed at 34% for a liability of $2380. The total liability is $16,130.

6. The tax at $85,000 is $17,150. The tax at $105,000 is $24,200.

   $$T = (24,200 - 17,150) / (105,000 - 85,000) = 7050 / 20,000 = 35.25\%$$

7. $T = (35.25\%)(1 - 8\%) + 8\% = (0.3525)(0.92) + 0.08 = 0.3243 + 0.08 = 0.4043$ or 40.43%

10.

(A) End of Year	(B) Before-Tax Cash-Flow Stream	(C) Loan Principal	(D) Loan Interest	(E) Depreciable Investment	(F) Depreciation Expense	(G) Taxable Income (B + D + F)	(H) IncomeTax Cash-Flow Stream (– Rate * G)	(I) After-Tax Cash-Flow Stream (B + C + D + E + H)
0	–$75,000					–$75,000	$33,000	–$42,000
1	$28,000					$28,000	–$12,320	$15,680
2	$34,000					–$2340	–$14,960	$19,040
3	$36,000					$970	–$15,840	$20,160
4	$34,000					$6937	–$14,960	$19,040
5	$32,000					$4882	–$14,080	$17,920
6	$30,000					$3246	–$13,200	$16,800
7	$28,000					$1400	–$12,320	$15,680

PW(15%) of the after-tax cash-flow stream = $32,241

IRR of the after-tax cash-flow stream = 37.9%

Chapter 17 Self-Study Questions

1. Effective after-tax interest rate = (1 − Effective income tax rate) * Loan interest rate
   = (1 − .30) * .07 = 0.049 = 4.9%

3. The IRR on the municipal bond is 7%. The corporate bond's annual income of $900 is reduced by $216 in income taxes to $684. The after-tax IRR on the municipal bond is 6.84%. She's better off with the municipal bond.

6. The depreciation schedule will be as follows:

$$\alpha = \frac{2}{5} = 0.40$$

End of Year	Depreciation Amount in Year	Book Value at End of Year
0	—	$60,000
1	0.40 * 60,000 = $24,000	$36,000
2	0.40 * 36,000 = $14,400	$21,600
3	0.40 * 21,600 = $8640	$12,960
4	0.40 * 12,960 = $5184	$7776
5	0.40 * 7776 = $3110	$4666

So the after-tax cash-flow stream will be this:

(A) End of Year	(B) Before-Tax Cash-Flow Stream	(C) Loan Principal	(D) Loan Interest	(E) Depreciable Investment	(F) Depreciation Expense	(G) Taxable Income (B + D + F)	(H) IncomeTax Cash-Flow Stream (− Rate * G)	(I) After-Tax Cash-Flow Stream (B + C + D + E + H)
0	$0		N/A	−$60,000	N/A	$0	$0	−$60,000
1	$20,000				−$24,000	−$4,000	$1600	$21,600
2	$20,000				−$14,400	$5600	−$2240	$17,760
3	$20,000				−$8640	$11,360	−$4544	$15,456
4	$20,000				−$5184	$14,816	−$5926	$14,073
5	$20,000				−$3110	$16,890	−$6756	$13,244

The PW(12%) of the after-tax cash-flow stream is $904.

9.

(A) End of Year	(B) Before- Tax Cash- Flow Stream	(C) Loan Principal	(D) Loan Interest	(E) Depreciable Investment	(F) Depreciation Expense	(G) Taxable Income (B + D + F)	(H) IncomeTax Cash-Flow Stream (– Rate * G)	(I) After-Tax Cash-Flow Stream (B + C + D + E + H)
0	$0		N/A	-$25,000	N/A	$0	$0	-$25,000
1	$10,000				-$8333	$1667	-$733	$9267
2	$10,000				-$11,113	-$1113	$490	$10,490
3	$10,000				-$3703	$6297	-$2771	$7229
4	$10,000				-$1853	$8147	-$3585	$6415
5	$10,000					$10,000	-$4400	$5600

The PW(16%) of the after-tax cash-flow stream is $1625.

Chapter 18 Self-Study Questions

1. Customers get faster access to their bills and other relevant information.

3. The local electric utility company would pay. The costs would be for development along with ongoing operation and maintenance costs. Utility reduces help staff, cutting operating costs.

4. The present-worth of the net savings is $34,500 (P/A,13,5) = $34,500 (3.5172) = $121,343. The cost is $115,000 so the benefit-cost ratio is 1.055.

9. Start by calculating the PW(12%) for each system using Initial cost – (P/A,12,10) * Savings.

(P/A,12,10) is 5.6502

A: 1200 – (100 * 5.6502) = 635
B: 2000 – (140 * 5.6502) = 1209
C: 2600 – (230 * 5.6502) = 1300
D: 4000 – (340 * 5.6502) = 2079
E: 5100 – (500 * 5.6502) = 2275

System	PW(i) of Net Investment in Millions of $	Effectiveness in Millions of Letters Processed per Day	Effectiveness (in Millions of Letters per Day) per Million Dollars
A	$635	5	7.87E-3
B	$1209	8	6.61E-3
C	$1300	12	9.22E-3
D	$2079	13	6.25E-3
E	$2275	14	6.15E-3

Chapter 19 Self-Study Questions

1. Plan one: Cost = $0.75 * Copies

   Plan two: Cost = $600 + $0.25 * Copies

2. $0.75 * Copies = $600 + $0.25 * Copies

   $0.50 * Copies = $600

   Copies = 1,200

3. Plan two: Cost = $600 + 0.25 * 2,500 = $1225

4. Plan one: Plan three

   $0.75 * Copies = $1000 + $0.15 * Copies

   $0.60 * Copies = $1000

   Copies = 1,667

   Plan Two: Plan Three

   $600 + $0.25 * Copies = $1000 + $0.15 * Copies

   $0.10 * Copies = $400

   Copies = 4,000

5. Stay with plan two, it's cheaper than plan three at 2,500 copies. Plan three is only the best at more than 4,000 copies.

6. The plan one-plan three break-even point is 1,667 copies (from Question 4). At 1,667 copies, the price under plan one and plan three is $1250.25. At 1,667 copies, the price under plan two is $1016.75. Plan two is cheaper than either plan one or plan three at that point, so the break-even point is irrelevant.

Chapter 20 Self-Study Questions

1. $dt/ds = 15\ s - 5625$

     Setting this equal to 0 to find the optimum point:

          $0 = dt/ds = 15\ s - 5625$

               $15\ s = 5625$

               $s = 5625 / 15 = 375$

3. Routine 1) $dt/ds = 4\ s - 148$, $s = 148 / 4 = 37$

    Routine 2) $dt/ds = 3\ s - 126$, $s = 126 / 3 = 42$

    When $s = 37$, Routine 1 yields $t = 8566$. When $s = 42$, Routine 2 yields $t = 8462$. Select routine 2 and hold the input stream at 42.

Chapter 21 Self-Study Questions

1.

Milestone	A	B	C	D	E	F
Project scope defined	1.09	1.33	0.50	0.60	1.80	1.60
Requirements complete	1.41	1.07	0.90	0.71	1.29	1.60
Design complete	1.33	1.33	0.78	1.09	1.20	1.33
Code complete	1.20	1.00	0.95	1.00	1.29	1.33
Testing complete	1.04	1.00	0.95	0.96	1.09	1.14
Actual schedule	1.00	1.00	1.00	1.00	1.00	1.00

2. If you used min, mean, and max . . .   ✓

Milestone	Lower Relative Value	Mean Relative Value	Upper Relative Value
Project scope defined	0.50	1.15	1.80
Requirements complete	0.71	1.16	1.60
Design complete	0.78	1.18	1.33
Code complete	0.95	1.13	1.33
Testing complete	0.95	1.03	1.14
Project complete	1.00	1.00	1.0

If you used plus and minus two standard deviations . . .

Milestone	Lower Relative Value	Mean Relative Value	Upper Relative Value
Project scope defined	0.10	1.15	2.21
Requirements complete	0.50	1.16	1.83
Design complete	0.74	1.18	1.61
Code complete	0.80	1.13	1.46
Testing complete	0.88	1.03	1.18
Project complete	1.00	1.00	1.00

3.

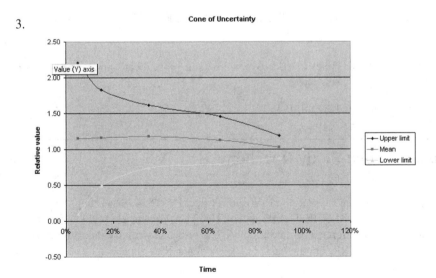

Cone of Uncertainty

4. If you used min, mean, and max . . .

    Minimum = 11 months * 0.71 = 7.8 months

    Mean = 11 months * 1.16 = 12.8 months

    Maximum = 11 months * 1.60 = 17.6 months

    f you used plus and minus two standard deviations . . .

    Minimum = 11 months * 0.50 = 5.5 months

    Mean = 11 months * 1.16 = 12.8 months

    Maximum = 11 months * 1.83 = 20.1 months

11. Yes, it's a good estimate because the actual schedule of 12 months is within the uncertainty limits of 8 to 13 months at the point the estimate was made.

13. We should be confident that features F6, F3, F5, F1, and F8 will make the release because the sum of their worst-case estimates is 2 + 4 + 3 + 3 + 6 = 18. We should be confident that features F9 and F7 won't make the release because the sum of the best-case estimates for the higher-priority features is 1 + 2 + 1 + 2 + 4 + 4 + 2 + 2 = 18.

Chapter 22 Self-Study Questions

1a. Approximate hardware cost = $84,000 + (6 * $92,000) = $636,000

2. Analogy

5. A total of 335,000 lines of code over 75 person years means an average of 4,467 lines of code per person year.

7. Statistical (parametric) estimation

Chapter 23 Self-Study Questions

1. Using the risk-free MARR, the PW(8) of Project P1 is $14,963. Using the risk-free MARR, the PW(8) of Project P2 is $14,911. The projects are within $52 of each other; that's a difference of about 0.3%. They have essentially the same PW(i) at the risk-free MARR. On the basis of PW(8) alone, they appear to be about equally desirable.

5. Least favorable = –$274,804, Fair = $26,373, Most favorable = $208,760

6.

Equipment Cost	% Change in Equipment Cost	PW(8)	% Change in PW(8)
$7000	–30%	29,373	11%
$8000	–20%	28,373	8%
$9000	–10%	27,373	4%
$10,000	0%	26,373	0%
$11,000	10%	25,373	–4%
$12,000	20%	24,373	–8%
$13,000	30%	23,373	–11%

Chapter 24 Self-Study Questions

1. $(0.20 * -\$2166) + (0.55 * \$2008) + (0.25 * \$6124) = -\$433 + \$1104 + \$1531 = \$2202$

3. The PW(14) of the project given the law is repealed in any year Y is as follows:

$$\text{PW}(14) = -\$50,000 + \$20,000 * \left(\overset{P/A,14,Y}{} \right)$$

Number of Years Until Law Is Repealed	Probability of Repeal That Year	PW(i) if Repealed That Year	PW(i) * Probability
1	0.1	–$32,556	–$3256
2	0.2	–$17,066	–$3413
3	0.2	–$3568	–$714
4	0.3	$8274	$2482
5	0.1	$18,662	$1866
6	0.1	$27,774	$2777
		Total	–$258

The expected value of the project is –$258; the company should not invest in the project.

6. Slightly more than 12 calendar months

8. 19.3 calendar months

9. About 40 staff months

13.

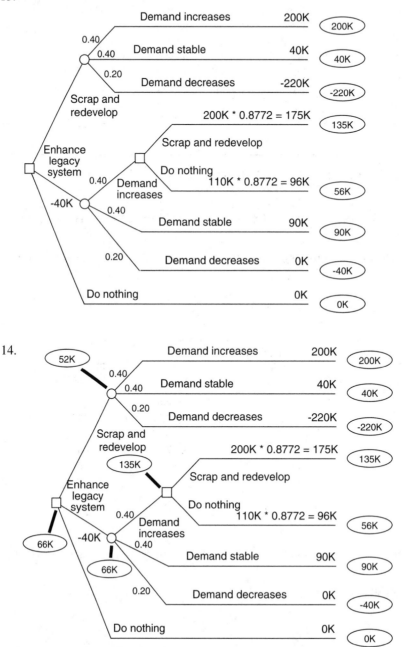

14.

The expected value of the root node is $66k; this corresponds to an initial decision to enhance the legacy system.

15. Knowing that demand will increase, the best path would be to scrap and redevelop the system. Knowing that demand stays stable, the best path would be to enhance the existing system. Knowing that demand decreases, the best path is to do nothing. The expected value of having perfect information is (0.40 * $200k) + (0.40 * $50k) + (0.20 * $0k) = $100k. The expected value given current information is $66k, so the expected value of perfect information is $44k.

Chapter 25 Self-Study Questions

1. C3 is dominated by C1. The reduced payoff matrix is as follows.

Equipment	P1	P2	P3
C1	100	90	60
C2	30	30	140
C4	70	80	90
C5	100	20	120

2.

Equipment	P1	P2	P3	Average Payoff
C1	100	90	60	83
C2	30	30	140	67
C4	70	80	90	80
C5	100	20	120	80

Equipment C1 would be chosen.

3.

Equipment	P1	P2	P3	Worst Payoff
C1	100	90	60	60
C2	30	30	140	30
C4	70	80	90	70
C5	100	20	120	20

Equipment C4 would be chosen.

4.

Equipment	P1	P2	P3	Best Payoff
C1	100	90	60	100
C2	30	30	140	140
C4	70	80	90	90
C5	100	20	120	120

Equipment C2 would be chosen.

5.

	Best Payoff	Worst Payoff	$\alpha = 0.3$	Blended Payoff
A2	100	60	0.3 * 100 + 0.7 * 60	72
A3	140	30	0.3 * 140 + 0.7 * 30	63
A4	90	70	0.3 * 90 + 0.7 * 70	76
A5	120	20	0.3 * 120 + 0.7 * 20	50

Equipment C4 would be chosen.

6. The regret matrix is as follows.

Equipment	P1	P2	P3
C1	0	0	80
C2	70	60	0
C4	30	10	50
C5	0	70	20

Equipment	Maximum Regret
C1	80
C2	70
C4	50
C5	70

Equipment C4 would be chosen.

Chapter 26 Self-Study Questions

1. Cost to build, size/square footage of building, number of offices and amount of common area, utility costs, taxes

3a. Ordinal

3b. Ratio

3c. Ordinal

5. No, none of her choices are dominated.

7. Because of the competitors' price-match offer, the prices should be considered identical, so they are not a differentiator. Consider the next highest-priority feature, RAM. Stores A and C have equal RAM, but Store B has lower RAM than A and C, so throw out Store B. Consider the next highest-priority feature, disk capacity. It is identical between A and C, so consider DVD next. Both A and C have DVD, so go on to monitor screen size. Screen size on C is best, so select that one.

10. In preparation for using compensatory decision techniques, calculate the common scale values for the cost attribute. Use a range of 0 to 100 with 100 being the best.

    (Answer)

    Modify = 100 * ($360k – $90k) / ($360 – $90) = 100

    Redevelop = 100 * ($360k – $360k) / ($360 – $90) = 0

    Package A = 100 * ($360k – $200k) / ($360 – $90) = 59

    Package B = 100 * ($360k – $180k) / ($360 – $90) = 67

13. The relative weights would be as follows:

Attribute	Points	Weight
Cost	20	0.67
Availability	10	0.33

The additive weighting results would be as follows:

Alternative	Cost (0.67)	Availability (0.33)	Weighted Score
Modify	100	0	67
Redevelop	0	100	33
Package A	59	91	70
Package B	67	100	78

The Package B alternative would be chosen in this situation.

15.

$$CM = \begin{vmatrix} 1 & 3 & 5 \\ 1/3 & 1 & 3 \\ 1/5 & 1/3 & 1 \end{vmatrix} = \begin{vmatrix} 1.000 & 3.000 & 5.000 \\ 0.333 & 1.000 & 3.000 \\ 0.200 & 0.333 & 1.000 \end{vmatrix}$$

Sum(1) = 1.533, Sum(2) = 4.333, Sum(3) = 9.0000

$$CM' = \begin{vmatrix} 0.652 & 0.692 & 0.556 \\ 0.217 & 0.231 & 0.333 \\ 0.130 & 0.077 & 0.111 \end{vmatrix}$$

High = (0.652 + 0.692 + 0.556) / 3 = 0.633

Medium = (0.217 + 0.231 + 0.333) / 3 = 0.260

Low = (0.130 + 0.077 + 0.111) / 3 = 0.106

Value	Common Scale Score
High	(0.106 – 0.633) / (0.106 – 0.633) * 100 = 100
Medium	(0.106 – 0.260) / (0.106 – 0.633) * 100 = 24
Low	(0.106 – 0.106) / (0.106 – 0.633) * 100 = 0

19. The eigenvalue of the comparison matrix is 3.039, so the inconsistency ratio is (3.039 − 3) / (3 − 1) = 0.039/2 = 0.0195 = 1.95%.

Chapter 27 Self-Study Questions

No answers given.

Appendix G

Glossary

50/50 estimate The estimated outcome that is (thought to be) as likely to be exceeded as not. It's an informal name for the more formal concept of expected value. See also *expected value*.

A

Accelerated cost recovery system The depreciation system in place in the United States between 1981 and 1986.

Accounting The process of recording the financial history of a company. Informally, keeping track of the money coming into, moving around in, and going out of a company.

Accuracy Closeness to the truth. In estimation, how close is an estimate to its eventual actual outcome? Contrast with *precision*.

Acquisition cost The entire cost to acquire an asset, also known as its cost basis. This includes the purchase price, delivery, installation, and any other costs to put the asset into service.

ACRS See *accelerated cost recovery system*.

Activity-based costing (ABC) A cost accounting method that allocates overhead costs based on specific production activities rather than allocating from a single overhead pool. Contrast with *direct-material-cost*, *direct-labor-cost*, and *direct-labor-hour* cost accounting.

Actual depreciation   The true loss in value of an asset; it can't be determined without actually selling that asset. Contrast with *depreciation accounting*.

Actual dollar analysis   In addressing inflation/deflation, using cash-flow amounts that represent actual amounts of money at the time of the cash flow. Contrast with *constant dollar analysis*.

Actual interest rate   The actual rate of interest that applies over a stated compounding period. Contrast with *effective interest rate*.

Additive weighting   A member of the compensatory decision techniques that uses weighting factors to give some decision attributes more importance in the analysis than others. Contrast with *nondimensional scaling* and *analytic hierarchy process*.

After-tax cash-flow stream   The cash-flow stream for a proposal or alternative that has the effects of income tax accounted for. Contrast with *before-tax cash-flow stream*.

After-tax MARR   A minimum attractive rate of return (MARR) that is stated in after-tax terms. This MARR should be used on after-tax cash-flow streams. Contrast with *before-tax MARR*.

Alternative   A mutually exclusive course of action made up of zero or more proposals.

Analogy   An estimation technique that bases the estimate of the new thing on the actual results from a known thing plus adjustments for known differences. Contrast with *expert judgment*, *bottom-up*, and *statistical* methods.

Analytic hierarchy process (AHP)   A member of the compensatory decision techniques that uses matrices to manage pair-wise relationships. Contrast with *nondimensional scaling* and *additive weighting*.

Annual equivalent, AE(i)   The basis for comparison that represents the value of a cash-flow stream in terms of a series of equal annual payments (at the stated interest rate, *i*) over the planning horizon. See also *present worth*, *future worth*, etc.

Annual percentage rate (APR)   A nominal annual interest rate.

Annuity   Referred to as *A* in many of the interest formulas, this represents the amount of a series of equal payments at regular intervals over a planning horizon.

Asset   Informally, any thing of value that the company owns or is owed by others. Cash, accounts receivable, and equipment are examples of common assets. More formally, the term often refers to an item of value that is subject to depreciation accounting. See also *depreciation* and *depreciation accounting*.

Attribute   In business decision making, an attribute is one of the criteria that a decision is being based on.

Average annual inflation rate An inflation rate over one or more years expressed as an annual average rate over that same time period. Using average annual inflation rates avoids the need to apply a separate annual inflation rate for each year in the planning horizon.

B

Balance sheet One of the main financial statements, it shows the financial position of a company at a particular moment in time. It's a "snapshot" or "freeze-frame" view of the financial strength of the company. It answers the question, "How much is the company worth at this point in time?"

Basis for comparison One of a collection of "bases of comparison" that allow cash-flow streams to be compared in a consistent manner. See also *present worth*, *future worth*, *internal rate of return*, etc.

Bayes' rule The statistical formula that relates the conditional probability P(A | B) to the inverse conditional probability P(B | A).

Before-tax cash-flow stream The cash-flow stream for a proposal or alternative that has not had the effects of income tax accounted for. Contrast with *after-tax cash-flow stream*.

Before-tax MARR A minimum attractive rate of return (MARR) that is stated in before-tax terms. This MARR should be used on before-tax cash-flow streams. Contrast with *after-tax MARR*.

Benefit A positive financial impact on a population; part of a benefit-cost analysis. See also *dis-benefit*.

Benefit-cost analysis In not-for-profit decision analysis, this method bases the desirability of an alternative on the ratio of the net benefits to the population (measurable benefits minus dis-benefits) to the net costs to the sponsor (measurable costs minus measurable cost savings).

Bond A form of investment that behaves like an interest-only loan. The investor buys the bond for some amount, receives interest-only payments over time, and then receives the initial investment plus the final interest installment at the end of the term. Bonds are a typical means for government units to raise needed capital. Revenue bonds are secured by future revenue generated from the activity being funded, whereas general obligation bonds are secured by the issuing entity's ability to tax.

Book value The estimated value, based on depreciation accounting, of an asset. It's the tax authorities' best estimate of that asset's actual value. This is equal to the acquisition cost minus the sum of the annual depreciation amounts charged off so far. See also *depreciation accounting*.

Bottom-up A means of estimating based on dividing the overall item into smaller pieces, estimating the smaller pieces, and rolling up the overall estimate from the sum of the smaller estimates. Contrast with *expert judgment, analogy,* and *statistical methods*.

Break-even analysis An analysis technique that analyzes two or more objective functions to find where, if at all, they have the same value.

Business decision Basing a decision on business criteria (e.g., in terms of desirability of the net present value of the alternatives).

C

Capital Money that is, or can be, used for the purpose of making more money.

Capital gains and losses "Passive" increases (gains) or decreases (losses) in the value of a capital asset. The term *passive* means that the change in value is not due to active involvement of the owner, the value changed for other external reasons. For instance, if a person buys a plot of land and the value increases, say, because of development in that area, the difference between the current value and the original basis cost (what it cost the owner to acquire the asset) is considered a capital gain.

Capital recovery with return, CR(i) Describes the cost of ownership of an asset in terms of an equal-payment-series over a given timespan of ownership. CR(i) is a major component in economic-life calculations.

Capitalized equivalent amount, CE(i) A dollar amount now which, at a given interest rate, is equivalent to the net difference of the income and payments if the cash-flow pattern were repeated indefinitely. Informally, CE(i) is the amount that would need to be invested at interest rate *i* to produce an equivalent cash-flow stream on interest alone.

Cash-flow diagram A graph describing the cash-flow stream for a proposal or alternative. See also *cash-flow stream* and *cash-flow instance*.

Cash-flow instance A separate (usually net) flow of money for an associated proposal or alternative at a specified point in time (i.e., a component of a cash-flow stream).

Cash-flow statement One of the main financial statements, it shows how the company is paying for its current operations and future growth by detailing the actual flow of cash between the company and the outside. It answers the question, "How much more or less cash does the company have now than it did before?"

Cash-flow stream The representation of the (estimated) financial perspective of a proposal or alternative. A collection of cash-flow instances associated with a proposal or alternative. Often pictured as a cash-flow diagram.

Codependent proposals   Two or more proposals that depend on each other to be carried out. Carrying out less than that full set of proposals does not make sense for one reason or another. Contrast with *dependent proposals*, *independent proposals*, and *contingent proposals*.

Compensatory decision techniques   The family of multiple attribute decision techniques that allow lower performance in some of the attributes to be compensated for (traded off against) better performance in one or more other attributes. Contrast with *noncompensatory decision techniques*. See also *additive weighting, analytic hierarchy process*, and *nondimensional scaling*.

Compound interest   The form of interest calculation that adds unpaid interest to the loan principal. Contrast with *simple interest*.

Computer science   A department of systematized knowledge about computing as an object of study; a system of knowledge covering general truths or the operation of general laws of computing, especially as obtained and tested through scientific method. See also *science*. Contrast with *software engineering*.

Conditional probability   A probabilistic outcome whose probabilities are affected by prior probabilistic outcomes. The lateness of a software project can be thought of as a conditional probability if the chance of finishing late is affected by the chances that the project started late.

Cone of uncertainty   A description of how the uncertainties inherent in software projects decrease over the duration of those projects.

Constant dollar analysis   In addressing inflation/deflation, using cash-flow amounts that represent money values that have been referenced to a fixed time in the planning horizon (typically the beginning). Contrast with *actual dollar analysis*.

Consumer Price Index (CPI)   In the United States, a measure of inflation from year to year from the perspective of the typical household (i.e., retail) consumer. See also *Producer Price Index (PPI)* and *price index*.

Contingent proposal   One or more proposals that depend on another proposal before this proposal makes sense. Contingency is a one-way dependency (contrast with codependent proposal); if Proposal B depends on Proposal A, but Proposal A does not depend on Proposal B, then Proposal B is a contingent proposal. Contrast with *dependent proposals, codependent proposals*, and *mutually exclusive proposals*.

Continuous compounding of interest   The form of interest calculation that computes interest due continuously (i.e., the compounding period approaches zero). Contrast with *discrete compounding*. See also *compound interest*.

Cost accounting The branch of general accounting that gives the company a basis to manage the cost of production. See also *cost of goods sold* and *unit cost*.

Cost avoidance A form of revenue (positive cash flow) that comes as a result not of increasing income but rather by decreasing expenses.

Cost-effectiveness analysis A form of not-for-profit analysis, derived from benefit-cost analysis, which seeks to maximize the effectiveness for a minimum cost. See also *fixed-cost analysis* and *fixed-effectiveness analysis*.

Cost function In a break-even or optimization analysis, this is an objective function that characterizes the cost associated with different values of the decision variable. Contrast with *income function*.

Cost of goods sold The total cost to produce the goods and services sold by a company over some period of time. Covers production costs only, not research and development nor cost of sales. See also *direct material cost*, *direct labor cost*, *indirect material cost*, and *indirect labor cost* (manufacturing overhead).

Cumulative probability function The mathematical function that describes the probability of achieving an actual outcome less than or equal to the estimated value. Formally, it's the integral of the probability function. See also *probability function*.

D

Decision tree A form of decision under risk that maps out a sequential series of possible decisions together with externally determined (i.e., random) outcomes.

Decision variable In a break-even or optimization analysis, a decision variable represents different decision values that the decision maker can choose. For example, in an economic-life calculation, the decision variable is how long to keep the asset.

Declining-balance depreciation A value-time function that expresses the decline in value as a percentage decrease in the book value from one year to the next. Contrast with *straight-line depreciation*.

Declining-balance switching to straight-line depreciation A value-time function that expresses the decline in value as the larger of the straight-line amount and the declining-balance amount. See also *declining-balance depreciation* and *straight-line depreciation*.

Deduction A reduction in income, or an increase in allowed expenses, that reduces the net taxable income for an organization. Contrast with *tax credit*.

Deflation The opposite of inflation (i.e., the price of the market basket of goods is going down not up).

Dependent proposals Two or more proposals for which there is some dependency between them. See also *contingent proposals* and *codependent proposals*.

Depletion   A cousin of depreciation accounting that is based on piecemeal removal of a natural resource such as a mine.

Depreciation   The word *depreciation* has two different meanings in business decisions. First, it refers to how an asset loses value over time due to effects like wear and tear. This can be called *actual depreciation*. Second, it refers to how the organization accounts for that loss in value. This can be called *depreciation accounting*.

Depreciation accounting   How the loss in value of one or more assets is accounted for by an organization.

Depreciation recapture   In income taxes, this refers to recovering taxes when an asset is sold for more than its book value (i.e., it was overdepreciated and the taxing authority needs to recapture the taxes on that overdepreciation). An asset that has a book value of $1000 but was sold for $1500 would be subject to $500 of depreciation recapture.

Derivative   The derivative of a function $f(x)$ is another function $f'(x)$ that describes the slope of the line tangent to $f(x)$ at corresponding values of x. Derivatives can be used to analytically identify inflection points (local minima and maxima) in the original function, $f(x)$. See also *optimization analysis*.

Deterioration   Literally, the process of wearing out.

Differential cash-flow stream   A cash-flow stream that represents the difference between the cash-flow streams of two proposals or alternatives. Certain forms of for-profit decision analysis (specifically, using IRR as the basis for comparison) need to be done using differential cash-flow streams. See also *incremental analysis*.

Direct labor   Personnel costs that are charged directly to the units of production. Direct-labor costs often include wages and benefits. Contrast with *indirect labor* and *direct material*.

Direct-labor-cost   A unit cost allocation method that allocates overhead costs to product types based on the ratio of the cost of direct labor used in making those products.

Direct-labor-hour   A unit cost allocation method that allocates overhead costs to product types based on the ratio of the hours of direct labor used in making those products.

Direct material   The cost of raw material and purchased components that are charged directly to the units of production. Direct material costs tend to include items that are easily measurable, used in the same quantity on identical products, and used in financially significant amounts. Contrast with *direct labor* and *indirect material*.

Direct-material-cost   A unit cost allocation method that allocates overhead costs to product types based on the ratio of the cost of direct materials used in making those products.

Dis-benefit   A negative financial impact on a population; part of a benefit-cost analysis. See also *benefit*.

Discount rate   Another name for the interest rate. Called that because the value of money is discounted the further out in the future it is.

Discounted payback period   The basis for comparison that represents the value of a cash-flow stream in terms of the time it will take (including interest) to recover the proposal's initial investment. Discounted payback period is an indicator of exposure to risk: If the proposal is cancelled before it reaches its payback period, the organization will, by definition, have lost money. Contrast with *payback period*. See also *present worth*, *future worth*, *annual equivalent*, etc.

Discrete compounding of interest   The form of interest calculation that computes interest at regular intervals. Contrast with *continuous compounding*. See also *compound interest*.

Dividend   Typically, money paid out of the net income after taxes to the owners of that company. This is one way the owners of a company make money from their investment; the other is from an increase in the stock value.

Do nothing alternative   The alternative that represents not investing in any of the other proposed alternatives in a decision analysis. This doesn't really mean doing nothing at all. Instead, it means the money is put into investments that give a predetermined rate of return (bonds, interest bearing accounts, put into a more profitable part of the corporation, etc.).

Dominance   A member of the noncompensatory decision techniques that looks for one alternative to be at least as good in every attribute and better in at least one. Contrast with *lexicography* and *satisficing*.

E

Economic life   A kind of optimization analysis that optimizes the costs of ownership based on the length of time the asset is kept. Also called *minimum cost life* or *economic replacement interval*.

Economics   The science of choice. See also *engineering economy*.

EDGAR   The Electronic Data Gathering, Analysis, and Retrieval system. Run by the U.S. Securities and Exchange Commission, it makes corporate financial statements available on the World Wide Web.

Effective annual interest rate   An annual interest rate that has been adjusted for more frequent, or less frequent, compounding. Contrast with *nominal annual interest rate*.

Effective income tax rate   An average income tax rate over a particular range of taxable income. Effective income tax rates simplify calculation of after-tax cash-flow streams because the actual tax rate for each specific income need not be computed.

Effective interest rate   An interest rate that has been adjusted for more or less frequent compounding. Contrast with *actual interest rate*.

Eigenvalue   Used in the analytic hierarchy process (AHP) to calculate the inconsistency ratio. See also *inconsistency ratio* and *analytic hierarchy process*.

End of period convention   A convention in business decision analysis that shows cash-flow instances at the end of the period in which they occur (in contrast to showing them at the beginning). The initial investment is shown at the end of period zero.

Engineering   "The profession in which a knowledge of the mathematical and natural sciences gained by study, experience, and practice is applied with judgment to develop ways to utilize, economically, the materials and forces of nature for the benefit of mankind" [ABET00]. Contrast with *science*. See also *software engineering*.

Engineering economy   The subject of this book; engineering economy is applied microeconomics where the fundamental question is this: Is it better to use the organization's resources in this particular way, or could a better return be obtained by doing something else?

Equal-payment-series capital-recovery (A/P)   The compound interest formula that computes the equivalent sequence of periodic payments, A, of a known present amount, P, at a given interest rate, i, over a stated time period, n. This is the standard formula for calculating loan payments.

Equal-payment-series compound-amount (F/A)   The compound interest formula that computes the future value, F, of a known sequence of periodic payments, A, at a given interest rate, i, over a stated time period, n.

Equal-payment-series present-worth (P/A)   The compound interest formula that computes the present value, P, of a known sequence of periodic payments, A, at a given interest rate, i, over a stated time period, n.

Equal-payment-series sinking-fund (A/F)   The compound interest formula that computes the equivalent sequence of periodic payments, A, of a known future amount, F, at a given interest rate, i, over a stated time period, n.

Equity   A company's net worth, the difference between the company's assets and liabilities.

Equivalence   The property, due to the effect of interest, where a given amount of money at one point in time has the same value as another amount of money at some other point in time. The interest formulas in Chapter 5 are actually statements of equivalence. Equivalence gives the decision maker a rational basis for comparing one proposal's cash-flow stream to another: If they are not equivalent, the one that has higher value is preferred.

Estimate   "An assessment of the likely quantitative result. Usually applied to project costs and durations and should always include some indication of accuracy (e.g.,+/– *x* percent)" [PMI00].

Estimation   The process(es) of producing an estimate. See also *estimate*.

Expectation variance   The amount of variation that can be expected in an estimated value. In decisions under risk, the decision maker may choose an alternative with a lower expected value than another because the expectation variance of this alternative leads to more certain desirability of the eventual outcome.

Expected value   The estimated outcome that is as likely to be exceeded as not. Statistically, this is the mean of the probability distribution. It's the point where the cumulative probability function equals 0.5. See also *50/50 estimate*.

Expected value of perfect information   Part of decision-tree analysis, the expected value of perfect information is the difference between the expected value of the decision tree and the value of the decision tree if all random outcomes were known in advance. Helps the decision maker determine whether it is justifiable to invest in activities that would reduce uncertainties.

Expert judgment   An estimation technique that's based on the best professional judgment of the individual(s) making the estimate. Contrast with *analogy*, *bottom-up*, and *statistical methods*.

Extrapolation   Approximates the value of a function at a point by projecting beyond two or more known points. Contrast with *interpolation*.

F

First cost   See *initial investment*.

Fixed cost   Any cost, such as facilities cost or loan interest, that is not dependent on the rate of production. Even when the rate of production decreases, fixed costs will tend to stay the same. Contrast with *variable cost*.

Fixed-cost analysis   A form of cost-effectiveness analysis that seeks to maximize the effectiveness that can be attained from a fixed, maximum investment. See also *fixed-effectiveness analysis*.

Fixed-effectiveness analysis   A form of cost-effectiveness analysis that seeks to minimize the investment needed to attain a fixed, minimum degree of effectiveness. See also *fixed-cost analysis*.

FTE   See *full-time equivalent*.

Full-time equivalent   The total annual cost of an employee that includes salary, benefits, along with all other overhead costs for that employee.

Future worth   The basis for comparison that translates a cash-flow stream into an equivalent single cash-flow instance at the end of the planning horizon. See also *present worth, annual equivalent*, etc.

G

General accounting   The process of recording the financial history of an organization. Sometimes referred to as "the language of business," general accounting tracks the money coming into, moving around in, and going out of a company so that management decisions can be made wisely and monitored.

General and administrative expenses   In general accounting, a category of expenses (such as rent and property taxes) that are over and above the cost of goods sold.

General obligation bond   A government bond that is secured by the ability of the issuing authority to raise taxes. Contrast with *revenue bond*.

Gross revenue   The total amount of money brought into the company. See also *operating income*.

H

Half-year convention   In depreciation accounting, a convention that assumes all assets are placed in service and retired from service in the middle of the tax year. Assets are assumed to go into service on July 1 and be retired on June 30 regardless of the actual dates.

Hurwicz rule   In decision making under uncertainty, this rule allows the decision maker to blend optimism and pessimism. Contrast with *Maximin rule* and *Maximax rule*.

I

Implied salvage value   An estimate of the residual (salvage) value of an asset at some point before its economic life.

Impossible zone   The region in an estimate's range that is impossible under any circumstances to achieve. It is impossible to drive a car 500 miles in less than one hour, so the one-hour outcome for a 500-mile car trip is in the impossible zone for the estimate of how long it will take to drive 500 miles.

Income function   In a break-even or optimization analysis, this is an objective function that characterizes the income generated by different values of the decision variable. Contrast with *cost function*.

Income statement   See *profit and loss statement*.

Income tax   A tax on the net profit (gross revenue minus expenses) of a company or individual.

Inconsistency ratio   In analytic hierarchy process (AHP), this is a function, based on eigenvalues, that measures how consistently the decision analyst assigned the values to the pair-wise comparisons.

Incremental analysis   An analysis technique based on looking at the differences between alternatives. If the incremental benefit of the second alternative over the first is more than the incremental investment between them, the second alternative is a better investment than the first. Both IRR and benefit-cost analysis must be done using incremental analysis.

Incremental benefit   The additional income from one alternative over another. If Alternative A generates $10,000 and Alternative B generates $12,000, the incremental benefit between A and B is $2000.

Incremental investment   The avoidable additional investment between one alternative and another. If Alternative A costs $10,000 and Alternative B costs $12,000, the incremental investment between A and B is $2000.

Independent proposals   A set of proposals that have no dependencies between them. Contrast with *dependent proposals*, *codependent proposals*, and *contingent proposals*.

Indirect labor   Personnel costs that are not charged directly to the units of production. Contrast with *direct labor* and *indirect material*.

Indirect material   The cost of raw material and purchased components that are not charged directly to the units of production. Indirect material costs are not easily measurable, not used in the same quantity on identical products, or are not used in financially significant amounts. Contrast with *direct material* and *indirect labor*.

Inflation   A general increase in prices over time. Contrast with *deflation*.

Inflation-free interest rate   An interest rate that has been adjusted for the effects of inflation. See also *interest rate*.

Inflation rate   A measure of the rate of increase in prices (for a fixed set of goods) over time as a percentage of the increase over the original price. Contrast with *purchasing power*.

Initial investment   The investment required just to start an activity (proposal).

Interest   Literally, the rental fee for money. Someone who borrows money from another is usually obligated to return the original amount borrowed plus some additional money. The additional money is the interest.

Interest rate   A measure of the rental fee for money in terms of a percentage over some period of time. At 10% interest for a year, someone who borrows $100 is obligated to pay $110 back at the end of one year. See also *simple interest* and *compound interest*.

Internal rate of return (IRR)   The basis for comparison that represents the value of a cash-flow stream in terms of a compound interest rate over the planning horizon. Contrast with *present worth, future worth, annual equivalent*, etc.

Interpolation   Approximates the value of a function at a point that is between two or more known points. Contrast with *extrapolation*. See also *linear interpolation*.

Interval scale   In measurement theory, a scale that has constant differences between consecutive measurement values. Temperatures in degrees Fahrenheit and Centigrade are examples of interval scales. Contrast with *nominal scale, ordinal scale*, and *ratio scale*.

Investment   Money put into a venture on the assumption that it will lead to even more money at some point later in time.

Investment expense   Expenses related to owning investments. Typically includes interest expense on loans and depreciation as well as expenses related to buying, selling, and maintaining other investments such as stocks and bonds.

Irreducible   A decision attribute (criterion) that cannot be expressed in terms of money.

L

Labor costs   The costs of labor used in producing the goods and services of the company. Contrast with *material costs*.

Laplace rule   A form of decision making under uncertainty that assumes all states of nature are equally likely.

Lease   Typically, a fixed-term rental agreement where the renter pays a periodic amount to the owner in exchange for being able to use some asset. For instance, a company can lease a building to use as office space.

Lexicography   A member of the noncompensatory decision techniques that prioritizes the decision attributes. See also *dominance* and *satisficing*.

Liability   The opposite of assets; liabilities represent money the company owes to others. Loans and accounts payable are typical liabilities.

Linear interpolation   Approximates the value of a function at an arbitrary point based on a straight-line interpolation between two known points. Contrast with *extrapolation*.

Liquidity   An expression of the ease that an investment in an asset can be converted into cash. Liquid assets are easily convertible, whereas frozen assets are hard to convert.

Loan   A financial arrangement between a lender and a borrower where the borrower uses some amount of the lender's money over a period of time and repays the lender the amount borrowed plus interest. See also *interest*.

M

MACRS   See *modified accelerated cost recovery system.*

Manufacturing overhead   The total of the indirect costs in a manufacturing corporation. See also *indirect labor* and *indirect material.*

Marginal tax rate   In income taxes, a tax rate that applies over a specified range of taxable income.

Market basket   In calculating a price index, the set of goods and services that represent the average spending habits of the typical buyer. See also *price index*, *Consumer Price Index (CPI)*, and *Producer Price Index (PPI).*

MARR   See *minimum attractive rate of return.*

Material costs   The costs for the raw material and components used in producing the goods and services of the company. Contrast with *labor costs.*

Maximax rule   In decision making under uncertainty, this rule assumes that the best state of nature will happen, so you should pick the alternative that has the best payoff from all of the best payoffs. The Maximax rule is the most optimistic of the uncertainty techniques.

Maximin rule   In decision making under uncertainty, this rule assumes that the worst state of nature will happen, so you should pick the alternative that has the best payoff from all of the worst payoffs. The Maximin rule is the most pessimistic of the uncertainty techniques.

Mean   In statistics, the "central tendency" of a probability function. More precisely, it's the expected value of the probability function. See also *expected value.*

Minimax regret rule   In decision making under uncertainty, this rule bases the decision on minimizing the regret that you would have if you chose the wrong alternative under each state of nature. Choose the alternative that has the smallest maximum regret.

Minimum attractive rate of return   The rate of return that the organization considers to be the minimum before it will be interested in any investment. It's an expression of the rate of return that the organization is confident it can achieve through typical activities. The MARR represents the organization's opportunity cost and is the interest rate used in business decision analysis. See also *before-tax MARR* and *after-tax MARR.*

Modified accelerated cost recovery system   The depreciation system in place in the United States since 1987.

Monte Carlo analysis   Related to sensitivity analysis, Monte Carlo analysis uses randomly generated combinations of the input variables (estimated factors) and runs them through the cost function to calculate the result under those conditions (much like "rolling the dice" at the casinos in Monte Carlo). This is repeated a large number of times, then the statistical distribution of the outcomes is analyzed.

Multi-attribute decision (multiple-attribute decision) A decision that considers more than just one attribute (criterion). For example, a decision might be based on price, delivery date, and quality all at the same time.

Mutually exclusive (proposals) Two or more proposals that do not make sense to do together. Either you do one, the other, or neither. Decisions are much easier when the choices are presented in mutually exclusive terms.

N

Net cash-flow diagram A cash-flow diagram that shows net cash flow per time period. See also *cash-flow diagram.*

Net cash-flow instance A cash-flow instance that represents the net cash flow into or out of an organization at (the end of) a given time period. See also *net cash-flow diagram* and *cash-flow instance.*

Net earnings See *net income before taxes.*

Net income after taxes The result after subtracting income taxes from net income before taxes. This is the actual after-tax profit earned by the company.

Net income before taxes The result after subtracting the cost of goods sold, operating expenses, and investment expenses from operating income. Represents the amount of money the company made before it paid income taxes (i.e., the amount of income that it has to pay taxes on).

Net profit ratio The ratio of net income after taxes to operating income. A company that ends up with $100,000 net income after taxes from an operating income of $1,000,000 has a net profit ratio of 10%.

Nominal interest rate An annual interest rate that has not been adjusted for more-frequent or less-frequent compounding. A nominal interest rate is calculated by multiplying an actual interest rate per compounding period by the number of compounding periods in one year. Contrast with *effective annual interest rate.*

Nominal scale In measurement theory, a nominal scale used for classification only. Examples of nominal scales include house types (A-frame, Craftsman, ranch, colonial, bungalow, Cape Cod, contemporary, and so on) and climate types (desert, tropical, alpine, polar). Contrast with *ordinal scale, interval scale,* and *ratio scale.*

Noncompensatory decision techniques The family of multi-attribute decision techniques that do not allow lower performance in one attribute to be traded off (compensated for) by better performance in another. Contrast with *compensatory decision techniques.*

Nondimensional scaling A member of the compensatory decision techniques that converts the attribute values into a common scale where they can be added together to make a composite score for each alternative. Contrast with *additive weighting* and *analytic hierarchy process.*

Nonprofit organization An organization that exists to serve a particular population and not make a profit from that service. Government units and professional societies such as the Institute of Electrical and Electronics Engineers (IEEE) and the Object Management Group (OMG) are examples of nonprofit organizations.

O

Objective function A mathematical formula that relates a decision variable to either the cost or the revenue of an alternative. See also *cost function* and *income function*.

Obsolescence Changes in the environment of an asset that make it worth less than before. Either more-capable assets are available now or the demand on the asset has changed significantly.

Operating expenses Money a company is spending, beyond the cost of goods sold. This includes research and development costs, cost of sales, facilities rent, etc.

Operating income Money the company brings in by selling its products and services. Sometimes called gross income.

Operation and maintenance costs Costs associated with using an asset as well as costs of keeping it in a usable condition.

Opportunity cost The implicit cost associated with investing money in a certain activity. Making that investment means that the same money cannot be invested elsewhere, where it could be earning the MARR. See also *minimum attractive rate of return (MARR)*.

Optimization analysis A form of decision analysis that balances competing components to achieve the best performance under the situation. Software's classic space-time trade-off is an example of optimization; an algorithm that runs faster will typically use more memory. Optimization balances the value of the faster run time against the cost of the additional memory.

Ordinal scale In measurement theory, an ordinal scale orders (ranks) the measurement values. The Software Engineering Institute's Capability Maturity Model (SEI-CMM) is an ordinal scale, being rated as Level 2 is more desirable than being rated as Level 1. Contrast with *nominal scale*, *interval scale*, and *ratio scale*.

Outsider's viewpoint An assumption that the decision analyst is someone who needs the service provided by either the existing asset or a proposed replacement(s) but doesn't own either. As an outsider, they have the choice of either buying the existing asset at its salvage value or buying (any one of) the replacement candidate(s). This viewpoint allows sunk cost and salvage values to be properly accounted for in a replacement decision. See also *sunk cost*.

Owner's equity   See *equity*.

P

Parametric estimation   See *statistical methods*.

Payback period   The basis for comparison that represents the value of a cash-flow stream in terms of the time it will take (ignoring interest) to recover the proposal's initial investment. Payback period is an indicator of exposure to risk; if the proposal is cancelled before it reaches its payback period, the organization will, by definition, have lost money. Contrast with *discounted payback period*. See also *present worth, future worth, annual equivalent*, etc.

Payoff matrix   In decisions under uncertainty, it is a matrix that relates the desirability of a set of alternatives to a set of future "states of nature."

Peer review   A set of techniques that have people who are qualified to do certain work examine the same kind of work done by others. The intent is to increase quality of the work done as well as reduce cost by finding and fixing mistakes as soon as possible after those mistakes are made.

Planning horizon   A consistent timespan that will be used to compare two or more proposals. Sometimes called the *study period*.

Precision   In estimation, how finely the estimate is being expressed. Saying that the 500-mile drive would take "about 11 hours" is a lot less precise than saying it would take "11 hours, 13 minutes, and 42.7693 seconds," regardless of how long the trip actually takes. Contrast with *accuracy*.

Present economy   The decision-analysis techniques, including break-even and optimization, that do not normally need to include the effects of interest. Contrast with *future economy*.

Present worth   The basis for comparison that translates a cash-flow stream into an equivalent single cash-flow instance at the beginning of the planning horizon. See also *future worth, annual equivalent*, etc.

Price index   A measure of annual inflation in terms of the relative increase in price of a representative "market basket" of goods from one point in time to another point in time. See also *Consumer Price Index (CPI)* and *Producer Price Index (PPI)*.

Principal   The (remaining unpaid) balance of a loan. Each loan payment goes partially to paying interest and partially to paying principal (unless it's an interest-only loan).

Probability   The branch of mathematics that deals with predictions of random future events. Probability theory underlies both estimation and decision under risk techniques.

Probability function A mathematical function that describes the probability of the various candidate outcomes.

Producer Price Index (PPI) In the United States, a family of measures of year-to-year inflation from the perspective of a company in a given industry sector. See also *Consumer Price Index (CPI)* and *price index*.

Profit The money that a company has after subtracting all of its expenses from all of its income.

Profit and loss statement One of the main financial statements, sometimes called an income statement, it summarizes the income and expenses that happened during the reporting period: between one balance sheet and the next. It answers the question, "How quickly is the company gaining or losing value?"

Profit margin See *net profit ratio*.

Project balance The representation, as a series of cash amounts at regular intervals, of the cumulative to-date value of an alternative.

Proposal A single, separate option that is being considered, such as carrying out a particular software development project or not. Proposals represent a unit of choice; you can either choose to carry out that proposal or you can choose not to.

Purchasing power Measures how much can be bought for a constant amount of money. Contrast with *inflation rate*.

R

Rank on rate of return A for-profit decision-analysis technique that sorts proposals in order of decreasing IRR and then selects as many from the top of the list as can be afforded. A fairly well-known approach, it suffers two fundamental weaknesses.

Ratio scale In measurement theory, a scale with constant differences between consecutive measurement values as well as a meaningful zero point. Temperatures in degrees Kelvin is a ratio scale. Money is also a ratio scale. Contrast with *nominal scale*, *ordinal scale*, and *interval scale*.

Replacement decision A business decision that considers replacing some existing asset with a different asset.

Retained earnings Money that the company has retained after earning it some time in the past as net after-tax profit. Retained earnings are part of the owner's equity in the company; the other part is the company's stock.

Retirement decision (asset) A business decision that considers ending some activity altogether.

Return on investment As a general concept, it refers to getting more value out of a financial venture than was put in. Unfortunately the term sometimes refers to internal rate of return, sometimes to a benefit/cost ratio, and sometimes to other not generally recognized formula.

Revenue   Positive cash flow (i.e., cash flow into the organization). Sometimes called income.

Revenue alternative   An alternative that is described in terms of its complete cash-flow stream; the cash-flow stream has both expense and income cash flows. Contrast with *service alternative*.

Revenue bond   A government bond that is secured by the (future) income from the activity being financed (e.g., a toll bridge or state park). Contrast with *general obligation bond*.

Risk   In business decision making, risk refers to quantified variation. The known probabilities for the variations are used in the decision analysis. Contrast with *uncertainty*.

Risk-adjusted MARR   A MARR that has been adjusted to account for the risk in an alternative.

Risk-free MARR   A MARR that has not been adjusted to address the risk in an alternative. The term *risk free* is somewhat misleading in that it doesn't really mean zero risk. It just means that the risk is not so significant that it needs to be explicitly addressed in the decision analysis. The risk in this case comes from inaccuracy in the estimate(s); the actual outcome may turn out less favorably than anticipated.

Rolling-wave planning   A project planning best-practice recommended by the Project Management Institute (PMI): "A progressive detailing of the project plan by providing the details of the work to be done in the current project phase but also providing some preliminary description of work to be done in later project phases" [PMI00].

S

Sales income   Income that is directly resulting from sales of an organization's products and services.

Salvage value   The remaining value of an asset at some point in time.

Satisficing   A member of the noncompensatory decision techniques that discards any alternative with an attribute value outside of a defined, acceptable range. Contrast with *dominance* and *lexicography*.

Science   "A department of systematized knowledge as an object of study; knowledge or a system of knowledge covering general truths or the operation of general laws esp. as obtained and tested through scientific method" [Webster94]. See also *computer science*. Contrast with *engineering*.

Sensitivity analysis   A risk-analysis technique that studies how changes in the values of estimated parameters affect the desirability of an alternative. Parameters where small changes in estimated values cause larger changes in desirability are said to be more sensitive. Sensitivity analysis guides the decision maker in identifying the estimated parameters (the sensitive ones) that deserve more careful study to make sure that estimate is accurate.

Service alternative   An alternative that is assumed to provide equivalent service to another alternative over their lives; all the revenue cash flows are being ignored to simplify the comparison. Only the expense cash flows are shown for a service alternative. Contrast with *revenue alternative*.

Service life   See *economic life*.

Simple interest   The form of interest, not usually available in practice, which computes interest due as the product of the amount borrowed times the interest rate times the duration of the loan. Contrast with *compound interest*.

Single-payment compound-amount (F/P)   The compound interest formula that computes the future value, F, of a known present value, P, at a given interest rate, i, over a stated time period, n.

Single-payment present-worth (P/F)   The compound interest formula that computes the present value, P, of a known future value, F, at a given interest rate, i, over a stated time period, n.

Software engineering   The profession in which a knowledge of the mathematical and computing sciences gained by study, experience, and practice is applied with judgment to develop ways to utilize, economically, computing systems for the benefit of mankind. See also *engineering*. Contrast with *computer science*.

State of nature   A possible future outcome that can affect one or more proposals. This is a component in decision under uncertainty techniques.

Statistical methods   A family of estimation methods that are based on mathematical formulas that convert something that is measurable at estimation time into the thing(s) that a decision is being based on. Cocomo II is an example of a statistical estimation method that converts lines of code into project cost and schedule. Sometimes called parametric estimation. Contrast with *expert judgment*, *analogy*, and *bottom-up* estimation.

Statistics   The branch of mathematics that deals with analysis of the outcomes of past random events. Statistics theory underlies both estimation and decision under risk techniques.

Stock   The representation of a unit of ownership in a for-profit organization. "Publicly traded" stocks are bought and sold on public stock exchanges such as NYSE and NASDAQ in the United States. "Privately held" stocks are not available to the general public.

Stockholder   Someone who holds stock in a company; an owner.

Straight-line depreciation   A value-time function that assumes the asset loses value at a constant rate (i.e., as a fixed percentage of the asset's original value) over its lifetime. Contrast with *declining balance depreciation.*

Sum-of-the-year's-digits depreciation   A value-time function that assumes the asset loses value at a rate determined by a fraction derived from the current year and the number of years of depreciable service.

Sunk cost   Any cost that is irrecoverable by future actions. Psychologically people tend to pay attention to sunk costs even though they are irrelevant in business decisions. See also *outsider's viewpoint.*

T

Tax   "A charge, usually of money, imposed by authority on persons or property for public purposes, or a sum levied on members of an organization to defray expenses." [Websters86]

Tax bracket   A range of taxable income over which the marginal tax rate is the same.

Tax credit   Money from a taxing authority that is a direct reimbursement of taxes paid. Contrast with *deduction.*

Time value   A concept that addresses how the value of a thing, such as money, changes over time.

Two-phase acquisition   A means to deal with inherent uncertainty in projects by delaying the final decision. The project is broken into an early phase that focuses on gathering requirements, addressing major risks, and project planning and a later phase that completes the project if the outcome of the first phase is favorable. The final decision on whether to do the full project is deferred from the point when the uncertainties are the greatest (the beginning) to a point where the uncertainties are significantly reduced.

U

Uncertainty   The degree to which something (such as an estimate) is unknown. Saying a project will finish in 12 months +/– 6 months is a lot more uncertain than saying the project will finish in 12 months +/– 6 days. In business decision making, uncertainty refers to unquantified variation; the probabilities of the variations cannot be used in the decision analysis. Contrast with *risk.*

Unit cost The average marginal cost to produce one more unit of production, given the current rate of production. Unit cost provides a rational basis for establishing a minimum sales price for goods and services.

Units of production depreciation A method of depreciation based on the amount of actual use the asset is subject to. All other depreciation methods are based on time, regardless of actual use.

V

Value (use value/esteem value) A measure of the desirability that a person puts in a certain thing.

Value-time function A mathematical function that models how an asset loses value over time. The simplest value-time function is known as straight-line, which assumes that the asset loses value at a constant rate (i.e., as a fixed percentage of the asset's original value) over its lifetime.

Variable cost Any cost, such as raw materials cost, which is directly dependent on the rate of production. As the rate of production decreases, variable costs will tend to decrease at a proportional rate. Contrast with *fixed cost*.

Variance See *uncertainty*.
Variation See *uncertainty*.

W

Work breakdown structure (WBS) A decomposition of all of the work associated with a proposal (e.g., a candidate software project) being studied. A tool that helps you better understand the size and scope of the proposal; it can be a useful planning and management tool if the proposal is given the go-ahead.

References

[ABET00] *Criteria for Accrediting Programs in Engineering in the United States.* Accreditation Board of Engineering and Technology, Baltimore, Maryland, 2000. See http://www.abet.org.

[Beck00] Kent Beck. *eXtreme Programming Explained.* Addison-Wesley, 2000.

[BLS2001] *Relative Importance of Components in the Consumer Price Indexes.* Bureau of Labor Statistics, December, 2001. See http://www.bls.gov/cpi/cpiri_2001.pdf.

[Boehm81] Barry W. Boehm. *Software Engineering Economics.* Prentice Hall, 1981.

[Boehm00] Barry Boehm, et al. *Software Cost Estimation with Cocomo II.* Prentice Hall, 2000.

[Cockburn02] Alistair Cockburn. *Agile Software Development.* Addison-Wesley, 2002.

[Cooper88a] Robin Cooper. "The Rise of Activity-Based Costing - Part One: What Is an Activity-Based Cost System?" *Journal of Cost Management*, Vol.2, No.2, Summer 1988.

[Cooper88b] Robin Cooper. "The Rise of Activity-Based Costing - Part Two: What Is an Activity-Based Cost System?" *Journal of Cost Management*, Vol.2, No.3, Fall 1988.

[Copeland01] Lee Copeland. "More for the Money." *Computerworld*, September 3, 2001. Available at http://www.computerworld.com/careertopics/careers/recruiting/story/0,10801,63423,00.html.

[DeBono92] Edward De Bono. *Serious Creativity: Using the Power of Lateral Thinking to Create New Ideas.* Harper Collins, 1992.

[DeGarmo93] E. DeGarmo, W. Sullivan, and J. Bontadelli. *Engineering Economy, Ninth Edition.* Prentice Hall, 1993.

[DeMarco99] Tom DeMarco and Tim Lister. *Peopleware, Tenth Anniversary Edition.* Dorset House, 1999.

[DoD98] *Handbook: Work Breakdown Structure.* MIL-HDBK-881B, U.S. Department of Defense, 2 January 1998. Available at http://www.acq.osd.mil/pm/newpolicy/wbs/mil_hdbk_881/mil_hdbk_881.htm.

[Eschenbach03] Ted G. Eschenbach, *Engineering Economy: Applying Theory to Practice, Second Edition.* Oxford University Press, 2003.

[Fleming00] Quentin Fleming and Joel Koppelman. *Earned Value Project Management, Second Edition.* Project Management Institute, 2000.

[Ford91] Gary Ford. *1991 SEI Report on Graduate Software Engineering Education.* Technical Report CMU/SEI-91-TR-2, Software Engineering Institute, Carnegie Mellon University, Pittsburgh, Pennsylvania, April, 1991 http://www.sei.cmu.edu/pub/documents/91.reports/pdf/tr02.91.pdf.

[Fowler03] Martin Fowler with Kendall Scott. *UML Distilled: Applying the Standard Object Modeling Language, Third Edition.* Addison-Wesley, 2003.

[Freedman90] Daniel Freedman and Gerald Weinberg. *Handbook of Walkthroughs, Inspections, and Technical Reviews: Evaluating Programs, Projects, and Products, Third Edition.* Dorset House, 1990.

[Galorath] See http://www.galorath.com/home.shtm.

[Garmus00] David Garmus and David Herron. *Function Point Analysis.* Addison-Wesley, 2000. See also the International Function Point User's Group Web site, http://www.ifpug.org.

[Gause89] Donald C. Gause and Gerald M. Weinberg. *Exploring Requirements: Quality Before Design.* Dorset House, 1989.

[Gilb93] Tom Gilb and Dorothy Graham. *Software Inspection.* Addison-Wesley, 1993.

[Grant90] Grant; Eugene L., Ireson, Grant W., and Leavenworth, Richard S. *Principles of Engineering Economy, Eighth Edition.* Wiley, 1990.

[Grosso01] William Grosso. *Java RMI.* O'Reilly & Associates, 2001.

[Hooten90] Karen Hooten. "An Engineer by Any Other Name." In the EOF column, *Computer Language*, January, 1990.

[IEEEACM99] IEEE-CS/ACM Joint Task Force on Software Engineering Ethics and Professional Practices, *Software Engineering Code of Ethics and Professional Practice.* IEEE & ACM, 1999. Available at http://www.computer.org/tab/seprof/code.htm.

[IRS95] *Depreciating Property Placed in Service Before 1987.* Publication 534, Internal Revenue Service, Revised November, 1995. Available at www.irs.gov.

[IRS01] *Your Federal Income Tax (2001): Tax Guide For Individuals.* Internal Revenue Service Publication 17, Department of the Treasury, 2001.

[IRS02] *How to Depreciate Property.* Publication 946, Internal Revenue Service, 2002. Available at www.irs.gov.

[Jeffries01] Ron Jeffries, Ann Anderson, and Chet Hendrickson. *eXxtreme Programming Installed.* Addison-Wesley, 2001.

[Kaner93] Cem Kaner, Jack Faulk, and Hung Quoc Nguyen. *Testing Computer Software, Second Edition.* International Thompson Computer Press, 1993.

[Kidder81] Tracy Kidder. *The Soul of a New Machine.* Little, Brown & Co., 1981.

[Kruchten00] Philippe Kruchten. *The Rational Unified Process: An Introduction, Second Edition.* Addison-Wesley, 2000.

[Larman01] Craig Larman. *Applying UML and Patterns: An Introduction to Object-Oriented Analysis and Design and the Unified Process, Second Edition.* Prentice Hall, 2001.

[Lawlis95] Dr. Patricia Lawlis, Capt. Robert Flowe, and Capt. James Thordahl. "A Correlational Study of the CMM and Software Development Performance." *Crosstalk*, September 1995.

[Levy87] Leon Levy. *Taming the Tiger - Software Engineering and Software Economics.* Springer-Verlag, 1987.

[Mellor02] Stephen Mellor and Marc Balcer. *Executable UML: A Foundation for Model Driven Architecture.* Addison-Wesley, 2002.

[McConnell96] Steve McConnell. *Rapid Development.* Microsoft Press, 1996.

[McConnell98] Steve McConnell. *Software Project Survival Guide.* Microsoft Press, 1998.

[McConnell03] Steve McConnell. *Professional Software Development*. Addison-Wesley, 2003.

[McConnell04] Steve McConnell. *Code Complete, Second Edition*. Microsoft Press, 2004.

[Moore65] Gordon E. Moore. "Cramming More Components onto Integrated Circuits." *Electronics*, Volume 38, Number 8, April 19, 1965.

[Musa98] John Musa. *Software Reliability Engineering*. McGraw-Hill, 1998.

[OMG02] *Common Object Request Broker Architecture: Core Specification, Version 3.0*. Object Management Group, Document number formal/02-12-06, December, 2002. Available at http://www.omg.org/technology/documents/spec_catalog.htm.

[OMG03] *The Unified Modeling Language*. Object Management Group, 2003. The latest version can be found at the OMG Web site http://www.omg.org.

[OMG04] "OMG Background Information." Available at http://www.omg.org/news/about/.

[Ortiz92] Edgar Ortiz, "Predicting Software Quality: The Generalized Goel-Okumoto Model." *Proceedings of the Second International Conference on Software Quality*, October 5–7, 1992. (Published by the American Society of Quality Control, Milwaukee, Wisconsin).

[PMI00] PMI Standards Committee. *Guide to the Project Management Body of Knowledge*. Project Management Institute, 2000.

[PMI02] Project Management Institute, *Practice Standard for Work Breakdown Structures*. Project Management Institute, 2002.

[Price] See http://www.pricesystems.com.

[Putnam92] Lawrence Putnam and Ware Myers. *Measures for Excellence*. Prentice Hall, 1992.

[QSM] See http://www.qsm.com.

[Robertson99] Suzanne Robertson and James Robertson. *Mastering the Requirements Process*. Addison-Wesley, 1999.

[Saaty80] Thomas Saaty. *The Analytic Hierarchy Process*. McGraw Hill, 1980.

[Saaty94] Thomas Saaty. *Fundamentals of Decision Making and Priority Theory with the Analytic Hierarchy Process*. RWS Publications, 1994. See also: Ernest H. Forman, Decision by Objectives, http://mdm.gwu.edu/forman/dbo.pdf.

[Schwaber02] Ken Schwaber and Mike Beedle. *Agile Software Development with Scrum*. Prentice Hall, 2002.

[SEI01] CMMI Product Team. *Capability Maturity Model Integration, Version 1.1*. Software Engineering Institute, Carnegie Mellon University, CMU/SEI-TR-002, December, 2001. Available at http://www.sei.cmu.edu.

[Shaw90] Mary Shaw, "Prospects for an Engineering Discipline of Software." *IEEE Software*, November, 1990.

[Shlaer84] Sally Shlaer, Stephen J Mellor, and Diana Grand. "The Project Matrix: A Model for Software Engineering Project Management." *Proceedings of the Third Software Engineering Standards Application Workshop* (SESAW III), IEEE, October, 1984.

[Simons91] Charles Simons, *Software Sizing and Estimating: Mk II*. John Wiley & Sons, 1991.

[Standish01a] *EXTREME CHAOS*. The Standish Group, West Yarmouth, MA, 2001.

[Standish01b] *CHAOS Chronicles*. The Standish Group, West Yarmouth, MA, 2001.

[SWEBOK01] *Guide to the Software Engineering Body of Knowledge*. IEEE, 2001. Available at www.swebok.org.

[TBPE98] "Board Establishes Software Engineering Discipline." Texas Board of Professional Engineers, 1998. Available at http://www.tbpe.state.tx.us/sofupdt.htm.

[Thuesen50] H. G. Thuesen. *Engineering Economy*. First Edition, Prentice Hall, 1950.

[Thuesen93] G. J. Thuesen and W. J. Fabrycky. *Engineering Economy, Eighth Edition*. Prentice Hall, 1993.

[vonOesch98] Roger von Oesch. *A Whack on the Side of the Head, Revised Edition*. Warner Business, 1998.

[Websters86] *Webster's Ninth New Collegiate Dictionary*. Merriam-Webster, 1986.

[Webster94] *The Merriam-Webster Dictionary*. New Edition, Merriam-Webster, 1994.

[Wellington1887] A. Wellington, *The Economic Theory of the Location of Railways, Second Edition*. John Wiley & Sons, 1887.

[Wheeler96] David Wheeler, Bill Brykczynski, and Reginald Meeson. *Software Inspection - An Industry Best Practice*. IEEE Computer Society Press, 1996.

[Wiegers02] Karl Wiegers. *Peer Reviews in Software*. Addison-Wesley, 2002.

[Wiegers03] Karl E. Wiegers. *Software Requirements, Second Edition*. Microsoft Press, 2003.

Index

Register
Your Book

at www.awprofessional.com/register

You may be eligible to receive:
- Advance notice of forthcoming editions of the book
- Related book recommendations
- Chapter excerpts and supplements of forthcoming titles
- Information about special contests and promotions throughout the year
- Notices and reminders about author appearances, tradeshows, and online chats with special guests

Contact us

If you are interested in writing a book or reviewing manuscripts prior to publication, please write to us at:

Editorial Department
Addison-Wesley Professional
75 Arlington Street, Suite 300
Boston, MA 02116 USA
Email: AWPro@aw.com

Visit us on the Web: http://www.awprofessional.com

informIT

Quick Reference Guide

Converting Interest Rates Between Arbitrary Time Periods

$$i = (1 + \frac{r}{m})^c - 1$$

r = nominal interest rate
m = number of compounding periods in r's interest period
c = number of r's compounding periods in i's compounding period
i = actual interest rate over i's compounding period

Present Worth

$$PW(i) = \sum_{t=0}^{n} F_t(1 + i)^{-t}$$

F_t = net cash flow instance in period t

Future Worth

$$FW(i) = \sum_{t=0}^{n} F_t(1 + i)^{n-t}$$

F_t = net cash flow instance in period t

Annual Equivalent

$$AE\,(i) = \left[\sum_{t=0}^{n} F_t(1 + i)^{-t}\right] \times \left[\frac{i(1 + 1)^n}{(1 + i)^n - 1}\right]$$

F_t = net cash flow instance in period t

Internal Rate of Return

$$0 = PW(i^*) = \sum_{t=0}^{n} F_t(1 + i)^{-t}$$

F_t = net cash flow instance in period t

Discounted Payback Period

The smallest n where

$$\sum_{t=0}^{n} F_t(1 + i)^{-t} \geq 0$$

F_t is the net cash flow instance in period t

Capital Recovery with Return

$$CR(i) = (\,P - F\,)\,(\overset{A/P,i,n}{\quad\quad})+ Fi$$

P = acquisition cost
F = estimated salvage value
n = length of time asset is kept
i = interest rate (e.g., MARR)